BEGINNING
SHAREPOINT® DESIGNER 2010

BEGINNING

SharePoint® Designer 2010

BEGINNING

SharePoint® Designer 2010

Woodrow Windischman

Bryan Phillips

Asif Rehmani

Marcy Kellar

WILEY

Wiley Publishing, Inc.

Beginning Sharepoint® Designer 2010

Published by
Wiley Publishing, Inc.
10475 Crosspoint Boulevard
Indianapolis, IN 46256
www.wiley.com

Copyright © 2011 by Wiley Publishing, Inc., Indianapolis, Indiana

Published simultaneously in Canada

ISBN: 978-0-470-64316-7
ISBN: 978-1-118-01389-2 (ebk)
ISBN: 978-1-118-01390-8 (ebk)
ISBN: 978-1-118-01493-6 (ebk)

Manufactured in the United States of America

10 9 8 7 6 5 4 3 2 1

For general information on our other products and services please contact our Customer Care Department within the United States at (877) 762-2974, outside the United States at (317) 572-3993 or fax (317) 572-4002.

Wiley also publishes its books in a variety of electronic formats. Some content that appears in print may not be available in electronic books.

Library of Congress Control Number: 2010932453

For my new family Brenda, Justine, and Drew.
Everything I do from here on out is all for you.

—WOODY WINDISCHMAN

To my wife Anisa for always supporting me and being
my own personal idea generator.

—ASIF REHMANI

This book is dedicated to the memory of Larry Page
who lived every day as if it were his last and showed
everyone that you are never too old to learn something
new.

—BRYAN PHILLIPS

To my son, Austin, for believing in me. To my mom
and dad for their patience.

—MARCY KELLAR

ABOUT THE AUTHORS

WOODY WINDISCHMAN is a technology trainer and consultant with more than 20 years' experience in a variety of roles, allowing him to see problems holistically and come up with appropriate solutions. His experience in SharePoint-related technologies started even before SharePoint became a product, with predecessors such as Site Server, the Digital Dashboard Resource Kit, and the earliest versions of Microsoft FrontPage. Since then, Woody's been deeply involved in the SharePoint community — first having been awarded Microsoft SharePoint MVP from October 2005 through September 2007, and again in 2009. He spent a year working directly for the SharePoint product team. He's active on Twitter (as WoodyWindy) as well as several other online SharePoint communities, including the TechNet and MSDN forums. His SharePoint blog, www.thesanitypoint.com, has been based on SharePoint for almost its entire existence.

BRYAN PHILLIPS is a senior partner at Composable Systems, LLC (www.composablesystems .net) and a Microsoft Most Valuable Professional in SharePoint Services. He is a co-author of Professional Microsoft Office SharePoint Designer 2007 and maintains a SharePoint-related blog at http://bphillips76.spaces.live.com. Bryan has worked with Microsoft technologies since 1997 and holds the Microsoft Certified Trainer (MCT), Microsoft Certified Solution Developer (MCSD), Microsoft Certified Database Administrator (MCDBA), and Microsoft Certified Systems Engineer (MCSE) certifications.

ASIF REHMANI has been training and consulting on primarily SharePoint technologies since 2004. He is a SharePoint Server MVP and MCT. Asif runs a SharePoint Videos website (www .sharepoint-videos.com), which provides no-code video tutorials on SharePoint, SharePoint Designer, and InfoPath. Some of his videos have also been published and appear at Microsoft's TechNet site. Asif also provides in-person and online SharePoint training publicly and in private workshops through Critical Path Training (www.criticalpathtraining.com). Over the years, Asif has been a speaker on SharePoint topics at several conferences, including Microsoft's TechEd, SharePoint Conference, SharePoint Connections, and Advisor Live. He is also the co-author of the books *Professional SharePoint Designer 2007* and *Real World SharePoint 2010* by Wrox publications. Asif was the co-founder and is currently one of the active leaders of the Chicago SharePoint User Group (www.cspug.org).

MARCY KELLAR is SharePoint User Experience Architect and co-founder of SharePoint Soapbox. She is a strong advocate for user-centered implementation of SharePoint. She has an extensive background in visual design, web content management, relational data modeling, and life sciences. Marcy is an active member in the SharePoint community and frequent presenter. She has a bachelor's degree in Life Sciences from Indiana University. She pursues hobbies passionately and is award-winning photographer and fine artist.

ABOUT THE TECHNICAL EDITORS

REZA ALIREZAEI MVP, MCP, MCPD, MCIPT, and MCTS for SharePoint 2010, is a solution architect focused on designing custom applications with SharePoint, Office, and Microsoft Business Intelligence products and technologies. As a technical leader with over 10 years of experience in software, he has helped many development teams design and build large-scale, mission-critical applications. In addition to consulting, Reza is an instructor and speaker. He speaks in many local and international conferences. Reza achieved the status of Microsoft Most Valuable Professional (MVP) for SharePoint in 2006, which he still is today. He has also co-authored *Professional SharePoint 2010 Development* and *SharePoint 2007 Reporting with SQL Server 2008 Reporting Services*. His blog can be found at `http://blogs.devhorizon.com/reza` and he tweets on Twitter under the alias @RezaAlirezay.

COSKUN CAVUSOGLU has been designing and implementing technology solutions for more than 10 years in both large, enterprise organizations and fast-growth midmarket firms, and is currently a Senior Architect in the Customer Solutions practice at West Monroe Partners. Coskun has completed SharePoint projects for over 100 clients, one of them being Microsoft, where he was a part of the team that wrote the questions for the SharePoint 2007 Developer Certification exams. Coskun has authored two books on SharePoint: *Professional Microsoft® SharePoint® 2007 Design* and *Professional Microsoft SharePoint 2007 Reporting with SQL Server 2008 Reporting Services* published by Wrox Publishing. He is currently working on a new book, *SharePoint 2010 Developer Certification Study Guide*. In addition, Coskun also is a speaker who attends various community events both local and international, where he talks about various SharePoint topics, and his past and future engagements can be found at his blog, `www.sharepointcoskun.com`. Coskun is a Microsoft Certified Professional and is also a MCTS for SharePoint technologies.

RYAN KELLER has been working with SharePoint technologies since 2007 and has worked as a consultant with SharePoint911 since 2009. Prior to joining the SharePoint911 team, he worked for Boulder Valley School District, where he had his first introduction to SharePoint. He has since worked with many companies and organizations troubleshooting issues and helping them plan successful SharePoint deployments. In addition, Ryan helped author and edit material related to SharePoint 2010 for Microsoft. He was a contributing author on *Professional SharePoint 2010 Administration*, and a technical editor for *Professional SharePoint 2010 Branding*. Ryan lives in Firestone, Colorado with his wife Brittany, their two dogs, and a cat. He and his wife are expecting their first child in April 2011.

SUNDAR NARASIMAN works as Technical Architect with Microsoft Solutions Center of Excellence at Cognizant Technology Solutions, Chennai. He has been a Microsoft Most Valuable Professional in SharePoint since 2008. He has more than 10 years of industry experience. He is primarily into the Architecture & Technology Consulting on Microsoft space. He has passion for programming and is excited about SharePoint 2010. He blogs at `http://msmvps.com/blogs/sundar_narasiman/` and can be reached at sundar.architect@gmail.com.

CREDITS

Acquisitions Editor
Paul Reese

Project Editor
Christopher J. Rivera

Technical Editors
Reza Alirezaei
Coskun Cavusoglu
Ryan Keller
Sundar Narasiman

Production Editor
Daniel Scribner

Copy Editor
Paula Lowell

Editorial Director
Robyn B. Siesky

Editorial Manager
Mary Beth Wakefield

Associate Director of Marketing
David Mayhew

Production Manager
Tim Tate

Vice President and Executive Group Publisher
Richard Swadley

Vice President and Executive Publisher
Barry Pruett

Associate Publisher
Jim Minatel

Project Coordinator, Cover
Lynsey Stanford

Proofreader
Word One

Indexer
Robert Swanson

Cover Designer
Michael E. Trent

Cover Image
© Lisa Davis/istockphoto

ACKNOWLEDGMENTS

WELL, HERE IT IS — another book! I thought things would be easier the second time around, but it was not to be. Although writer's block wasn't the same issue it was the first time around, my life itself has been a whole lot more complicated. The biggest thing, of course, was getting married. I met my lovely new wife, Brenda, after I had started working on the book. She has been absolutely marvelous in her support and encouragement, even though this project took away time that could (should?) have been for us. My deepest thanks must belong to her.

Of course, I can't forget to thank everyone else who made this possible: Asif Rehmani and Bryan Phillips, my cohorts from the first book, reprised their roles, now joined by first-timer Marcy Kellar; Our Wrox editorial team — Paul Reese, Christopher Rivera, and Jim Minatel — along with our technical editors, and everyone at Wrox and Wiley who make the production of a book like this flow smoothly.

Finally, I thank you, our readers. Without your interest in the subject, there wouldn't be a reason for the patience, encouragement, and hard work.

—Woody Windischman

FIRST, I THANK GOD for the opportunity to contribute to this book and all the other opportunities that have come my way. Writing a book is never an easy feat. It requires hard work and support from friends and family. I want to thank my very awesome wife, Anisa, for supporting me throughout this process and letting me skip out on things as needed so I could hit my deadlines. I'm also very thankful to my boys, Armaan and Ayaan, for the comic relief they provide every time I start stressing out about little things.

There is a lot of material in this book, and I'm thankful to my co-authors (Woody, Bryan, and Marcy) for joining forces to provide a thorough breakdown of all the awesome bells and whistles that ship with SharePoint Designer 2010. Also, thanks to Paul Reese and Jim Minatel at Wiley Publishing for giving us all the opportunity to write this book.

—Asif Rehmani

THIS BOOK IS DEDICATED to the memory of Larry Page, who lived every day as if it were his last and showed everyone that you are never too old to learn something new.

—Bryan Phillips

I WOULD LIKE TO THANK co-authors, Bryan Phillips and Woody Windischman, for pitching in and giving up so much of their time to help make sense of my writing. Woody, you are a saint. Bryan, you have a true gift for teaching. I was blessed to have you both on the team in the 11th hour. Thank you to Christopher Rivera, Project Editor, for always being positive and responsive. Your email replies and candid advice helped more than you know. Thanks to Lisa Atarian, talented SharePoint architect and friend. You dove right in without complaint to research SharePoint 2010 with me. Your subsequent empathy will not be forgotten. Thanks to Jeremy Thake and Mark Miller for working with me as my time on your project shrank so I could focus on the book. Thank you to David Shadle, my UX mentor at Microsoft. Your stories and advice inspired and influenced me right out of the nest. Thank you to the team at PointBridge for making it so easy to transition into the next chapter of my life. Finally, thank you to T. William. I can't overlook how often you were there for me with your technical genius and fascinating recollection of how to diagram a sentence. You are a brilliant man.

—Marcy Kellar

CONTENTS

INTRODUCTION

Microsoft SharePoint is taking the world by storm. More and more, web designers are being blown along with it — whether they want to be or not. SharePoint is a large, complicated web application. There is a lot of conflicting, confusing (and sometimes just plain bad) advice floating around with regard to how to go about customizing SharePoint for a particular customer. *Beginning SharePoint Designer 2010* can be your eye of calm at the heart of this maelstrom.

WHO THIS BOOK IS FOR

Maybe you are an experienced web designer who has been asked to brand a SharePoint site. Perhaps you're a business analyst who needs a workflow to manage a QA process, or a power user of SharePoint who wants to mash-up data from a line of business systems (or several) into an online map. Or, maybe you're new to both SharePoint and web design, and just want to see what it's all about.

Beginning SharePoint Designer 2010 offers something for all of you. Although it is not an HTML primer, it does contain some valuable pointers that someone new to web design can use. Yet, because SharePoint Designer is about far more than page editing, even if you never have (and probably never will) gaze upon raw HTML code, this book has plenty to offer you.

WHAT THIS BOOK COVERS

This book provides a broad overview of Microsoft SharePoint Designer 2010. It covers everything from basic page editing to workflow design. You'll be taken from master pages to Silverlight and points beyond. Even the companion technologies of Microsoft InfoPath and Visio find their way between these covers.

This book does far more than scratch the surface in many areas. You will find detailed information on integrating data from other sources into SharePoint, and some of the most comprehensive documentation on the internals of SharePoint's master pages and CSS anywhere.

Since you're reading a Wrox book, you would expect to find programming examples, and those are here as well. There are two chapters dedicated to using the SharePoint client-side object model to take your applications above and beyond. Beyond what? Well, that's going to depend on your own imagination!

HOW THIS BOOK IS STRUCTURED

This book starts at the beginning, with an overview of the SharePoint Designer 2010 user interface elements that are common to most of its functions. Since many readers are going to be creating visual elements for SharePoint, the next several chapters deal with editing and styling pages (aka *branding*).

Following the chapters relating to "form" are chapters that deal with using SharePoint designer to introduce "function" into your sites. This function ranges from designing lists and libraries for storing data, to putting that data into action with workflows, custom forms, and Web Part connections.

Finally, there are two chapters dedicated to expanding the capabilities of SharePoint itself through programming.

You will also find three appendixes designed to give you the SharePoint background and reference material you need to understand and implement many of the concepts introduced throughout the rest of this book.

WHAT YOU NEED TO USE THIS BOOK

With such an array of material to cover, this book has to make some assumptions about both you as a reader, and the environment in which you work.

First, a bit about you. This book assumes you have a solid understanding of Windows and using Windows-based applications. That means you already know how to move your mouse around, click on items, drag to select text, and drag-and-drop to move things. Copying, cutting, and pasting should be second nature, and you should know the difference between a menu and a font — just to name a few.

Although you can use much of the book without any programming experience, Chapters 12 and 13 assume you know how to program in (or at least read) the JavaScript programming language. Chapter 2 assumes you know something about HTML markup. Although several of the chapters deal with XSLT-based web parts, most of these cover the use of visual design tools, and therefore, a deep understanding of XSL is not required.

Now, on to your environment. The biggest assumption made is that you have access to both a copy of Microsoft SharePoint Designer 2010, and at least some access to a site based on either: Microsoft SharePoint Server 2010, Microsoft SharePoint Foundation 2010, or Microsoft Search Server 2010. SharePoint Designer 2010, SharePoint Foundation 2010, and the Express edition of Search Server 2010 are available for download without charge.

Some exercises may require SharePoint Server 2010, as it has many features that are not built into SharePoint Foundation or Search Server. Others will also require Microsoft InfoPath 2010 or Microsoft Visio 2010. To use these products in production requires paid licenses; however, they are all available for free download in time-limited trial form.

Finally, Chapter 13 requires certain development tools:

➤ Microsoft Visual Studio 2010

➤ Silverlight 4 Tools for Visual Studio 2010

➤ Silverlight Toolkit

➤ Microsoft Expression Blend 4 (optional, but recommended)

All of these tools are also available for download either free, as part of an MSDN subscription, or as trial copies.

CONVENTIONS

To help you get the most from the text and keep track of what's happening, we've used a number of conventions throughout the book.

TRY IT OUT

The *Try It Out* is an exercise you should work through, following the text in the book.

1. It usually consists of a set of steps.

2. Each step has a number.

3. Follow the steps through with your copy of the database.

How It Works

After each *Try It Out*, the code you've typed will be explained in detail.

WARNING *Boxes with a warning icon like this one hold important, not-to-be-forgotten information that is directly relevant to the surrounding text.*

NOTE *The pencil icon indicates notes, tips, hints, tricks, or asides to the current discussion.*

As for styles in the text:

➤ We *highlight* new terms and important words when we introduce them.

➤ We show keyboard strokes like this: Ctrl+A.

➤ We show file names, URLs, and code within the text like so: `persistence.properties`.

➤ We present code in two different ways:

```
We use a monofont type with no highlighting for most code examples.
```

```
We use bold to emphasize code that is particularly important in the present context
or to show changes from a previous code snippet.
```

SOURCE CODE

As you work through the examples in this book, you may choose either to type in all the code manually, or to use the source code files that accompany the book. All the source code used in this book is available for download at www.wrox.com. When at the site, simply locate the book's title (use the Search box or one of the title lists) and click the Download Code link on the book's detail page to obtain all the source code for the book. Code that is included on the Web site is highlighted by the following icon:

Available for download on Wrox.com

Listings include the filename in the title. If it is just a code snippet, you'll find the filename in a code note such as this:

Code snippet filename

> **NOTE** *Because many books have similar titles, you may find it easiest to search by ISBN; this book's ISBN is 978-0-470-64316-7.*

Once you download the code, just decompress it with your favorite compression tool. Alternately, you can go to the main Wrox code download page at www.wrox.com/dynamic/books/download.aspx to see the code available for this book and all other Wrox books.

ERRATA

We make every effort to ensure that there are no errors in the text or in the code. However, no one is perfect, and mistakes do occur. If you find an error in one of our books, like a spelling mistake or faulty piece of code, we would be very grateful for your feedback. By sending in errata, you may save another reader hours of frustration, and at the same time, you will be helping us provide even higher-quality information.

To find the errata page for this book, go to www.wrox.com and locate the title using the Search box or one of the title lists. Then, on the book details page, click the Book Errata link. On this page, you can view all errata that have been submitted for this book and posted by Wrox editors. A complete book list, including links to each book's errata, is also available at www.wrox.com/misc-pages/booklist.shtml.

If you don't spot "your" error on the Book Errata page, go to www.wrox.com/contact/techsupport.shtml and complete the form there to send us the error you have found. We'll check the information and, if appropriate, post a message to the book's errata page and fix the problem in subsequent editions of the book.

P2PWROX.COM

For author and peer discussion, join the P2P forums at p2p.wrox.com. The forums are a Web-based system for you to post messages relating to Wrox books and related technologies and interact with other readers and technology users. The forums offer a subscription feature to e-mail you topics of interest of your choosing when new posts are made to the forums. Wrox authors, editors, other industry experts, and your fellow readers are present on these forums.

At http://p2p.wrox.com, you will find a number of different forums that will help you, not only as you read this book, but also as you develop your own applications. To join the forums, just follow these steps:

1. Go to p2p.wrox.com and click the Register link.

2. Read the terms of use and click Agree.

3. Complete the required information to join, as well as any optional information you wish to provide, and click Submit.

4. You will receive an e-mail with information describing how to verify your account and complete the joining process.

> **NOTE** *You can read messages in the forums without joining P2P, but in order to post your own messages, you must join.*

Once you join, you can post new messages and respond to messages other users post. You can read messages at any time on the Web. If you would like to have new messages from a particular forum e-mailed to you, click the Subscribe to this Forum icon by the forum name in the forum listing.

For more information about how to use the Wrox P2P, be sure to read the P2P FAQs for answers to questions about how the forum software works, as well as many common questions specific to P2P and Wrox books. To read the FAQs, click the FAQ link on any P2P page.

PART I
The Lay of the Land

▶ **CHAPTER 1:** Exploring SharePoint Designer

1

Exploring SharePoint Designer

WHAT YOU WILL LEARN IN THIS CHAPTER

- ➤ How SharePoint Designer fits into Microsoft's toolset
- ➤ SharePoint Designer's basic features
- ➤ How to create a SharePoint site
- ➤ How to open an existing SharePoint site
- ➤ How a SharePoint site is represented in SharePoint Designer
- ➤ How to change site-wide SharePoint properties
- ➤ Restricting what SharePoint Designer users can do

WHAT IS SHAREPOINT DESIGNER 2010?

Microsoft SharePoint 2010 is a large and sophisticated web application. It should come as no surprise, therefore, that the tool meant to customize it — Microsoft SharePoint Designer 2010 — is a large, sophisticated desktop application. Microsoft SharePoint Designer 2010 is the premier tool for customizing sites based on Microsoft SharePoint 2010. It provides features for:

- ➤ Creating and editing master pages and page layouts
- ➤ Creating and editing cascading style sheets (CSS)
- ➤ Designing and editing workflows
- ➤ Connecting SharePoint to various external data sources
- ➤ Creating and modifying lists, libraries, and views of data
- ➤ Managing virtually all other aspects of a user's experience in SharePoint 2010

One very important thing is *not* on this list: editing SharePoint content. Although SharePoint Designer 2010 does contain powerful page editing tools, these are primarily used in the service of editing the other elements described previously. SharePoint itself is a powerful web-based content management system. Site owners and users use these web-based tools to create and modify the content of their sites.

Your role as a user of SharePoint Designer is to customize the consistent *presentation* of that content (master pages and CSS), or rules by which it is gathered and manipulated (external data connections and workflow).

ALL IN THE FAMILY

In the 2007 Microsoft Office System, Microsoft replaced many of the traditional user interface elements in several client applications, such as Microsoft Word, with what it calls the Fluent user interface, the most noticeable feature of which is a tabbed mega-toolbar called the *ribbon*. For 2010, this user interface has been expanded to include virtually all Microsoft client applications, including SharePoint Designer 2010. In addition, even SharePoint itself has been endowed with this very popular element (see Appendix B). Figure 1-1 shows an example of the ribbon in SharePoint Designer.

FIGURE 1-1

Many tabs on the ribbon are dynamic, or context sensitive, meaning that different tabs are available depending on what you are doing at the time. In Figure 1-1, for example, the tabs in the Code View Tools and List View Tools sections would only be visible simultaneously because the user is editing the design of a list view while the code view portion of SharePoint Designer's split was active. List views and the code view are described in detail later in this book.

A BACKSTAGE PASS

In the 2010 client products, Microsoft has taken the Fluent UI a step further. The Office 2007 applications had a *Jewel* menu that replaced the traditional File menu. For 2010, the name *File* has been restored, but the functions under that label have expanded even further. Rather than summoning a menu, clicking on the File tab brings forth a new element that Microsoft calls *Backstage*. Backstage is essentially a full-screen configuration page.

Most *ribbon tabs* affect a specific piece of a document, such as the font of a word, or the style of a table. Backstage allows you to work with items that affect either the application itself, or the document you are working on as a whole. Different Office applications expose different levels of functionality through Backstage as appropriate. Figure 1-2 shows the SharePoint Designer Backstage.

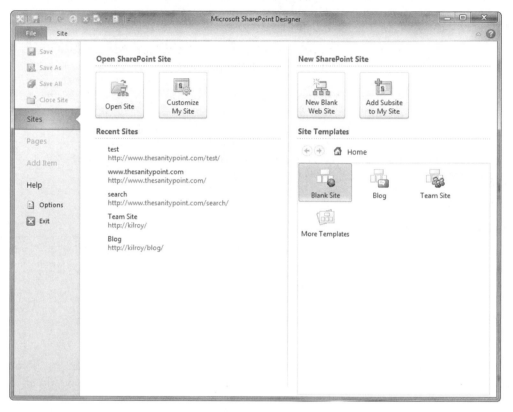

FIGURE 1-2

TRY IT OUT Open a SharePoint Site

1. From the Start menu, select Microsoft Office, Microsoft SharePoint Designer 2010. (The File tab will be selected by default.) Observe that very little functionality is available, and many options are "grayed out."

2. Click the large Open Site button.

3. In the Site Name box in the Open Site dialog, type the URL of your test SharePoint 2010 site, and click Open.

4. Observe the stages of the site opening process as displayed in the status box. When the opening process is complete, the Site tab is given focus, and you will see an overview of the site you have opened.

5. Click File to return to Backstage. Observe the different elements that are now "lit up" and available for selection.

> **NOTE** *SharePoint Designer can be configured to open the most recently used site automatically. If this is the case on your installation, and a site has previously been opened, it will appear as if you have already completed up to Step 3 in the preceding Try It Out. You learn how to change this setting later in this chapter.*
>
> *Most Try It Out exercises in this book require you to have a SharePoint 2010 site open in SharePoint Designer in order to follow along. Such a site is not provided with this book. Unless otherwise specified, you may use any edition of SharePoint 2010 and any site template as the basis for your exercises. Microsoft SharePoint Foundation 2010 and Microsoft Search Server Express 2010 are available — without licensing costs — directly from Microsoft. Many other editions and licensing options are also available. Please see Microsoft's website (http://sharepoint.microsoft.com) for details on editions, system requirements, downloads, and installation instructions.*

How It Works

Most Office applications open in a "ready" state, with a default blank document available for content creation and editing. This was also true of the previous version of SharePoint Designer, and most versions of FrontPage before it. SharePoint Designer 2010, on the other hand, does not allow you to perform any meaningful action without a site open.

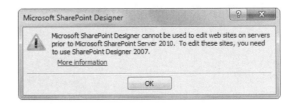

FIGURE 1-3

More specifically, the site in question must also be a SharePoint 2010 site. If you had attempted to open anything other than a SharePoint 2010 site, after SharePoint Designer detected that, you would have been faced with the alert shown in Figure 1-3.

Until you have a site open, SharePoint Designer's Backstage will only allow you to open an existing site, create a new site, or modify some program settings. After you have a site open, however, Backstage also provides options for adding new elements, or *artifacts*, to your site. These may include pages of various types, new *lists* and *libraries*, or even *workflows*.

Backstage Sections

Within Backstage, a shaded area at the left of the page contains commands and command sections. The contents of this area are shown in Figure 1-4.

Being able to tell the commands from the command sections at a glance can be difficult. One way to determine this is to observe the shape of the highlight when you hover over an option with the mouse pointer. A command, as shown in Figure 1-5, has a highlight that encircles only the text of the command. A command section, shown in Figure 1-6, is highlighted with a band that extends the entire width of the shaded area.

FIGURE 1-4

The first four items — Save, Save As, Save All, and Close Site — are individual commands that allow you to save a specific file being edited, all currently open files, or completely close the currently open site.

FIGURE 1-5

The Sites Section

The Sites section is shown by default when you open SharePoint Designer, and was shown earlier in Figure 1-2. The four primary regions in the Sites section are:

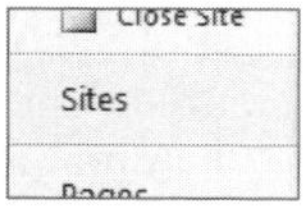

FIGURE 1-6

➤   Open Site

➤   New Site

➤   Recent Sites

➤   Site Templates

Open Site and New Site each have two large buttons. "Open Site" and "New Blank Web Site" are for opening or creating a general purpose SharePoint site. The "Customize My Site" and "Add Subsite to My Site" buttons are dedicated to working with the My Site feature of SharePoint.

> **NOTE** *A My Site is a special site within SharePoint Server (but not SharePoint Foundation) that contains information by, about, and for a particular user and his social network. Microsoft Office, and by extension SharePoint Designer, recognizes each user's My Site the first time it is accessed through SharePoint. After the site is recognized, the various Office applications will provide easy and direct access to this site.*

If you have opened other SharePoint sites in the past, they appear in the Recent Sites region of the Sites dialog. You may click the name to select it. Double-clicking a site name in the Open Site dialog drills you into that site and allows you to choose a child site to open (if any). After you have selected a site to open by any of these methods, click the Open button to open the site in SharePoint Designer. You may be prompted to enter credentials for the website, either upon drilling down, or after clicking the Open button.

Until you close all instances of SharePoint Designer, any other site you open in the same URL domain will attempt to use the same credentials. You are prompted again if the account used does not have sufficient permission to open the new site. You may determine the current ID you are using for the open site, or log in as a different user, by clicking the small "person" icon at the far left of the status bar.

> **NOTE** *Successfully opening a site in SharePoint Designer does not guarantee you can perform all editing functions on that site. See the section "Governing SharePoint Designer" later in this chapter for details on how the usage of SharePoint Designer may be limited by site administrators.*

SharePoint Designer can only have one site open within an application window. If you attempt to open another site while one is currently open, the new site opens in a new instance of SharePoint Designer.

All SharePoint sites are created based upon a site definition, or template. A template defines the features available by default in that particular type of site. These typically include pre-defined lists and libraries, special pages, and default content. The Site Templates area shows certain common SharePoint templates that you may use to create a new site. Other templates may be available depending upon a server's configuration. Clicking the More Templates icon allows you to browse to a SharePoint server and retrieve the list of templates available in that installation.

The Pages Section

The Pages section of the SharePoint Designer Backstage (File tab) enables you to retrieve recently opened files, or browse for other files to open or import. For the purposes of this section, the word "pages" is very loosely defined, and may also include layouts, style sheets, or other file types.

Figure 1-7 shows the Pages section.

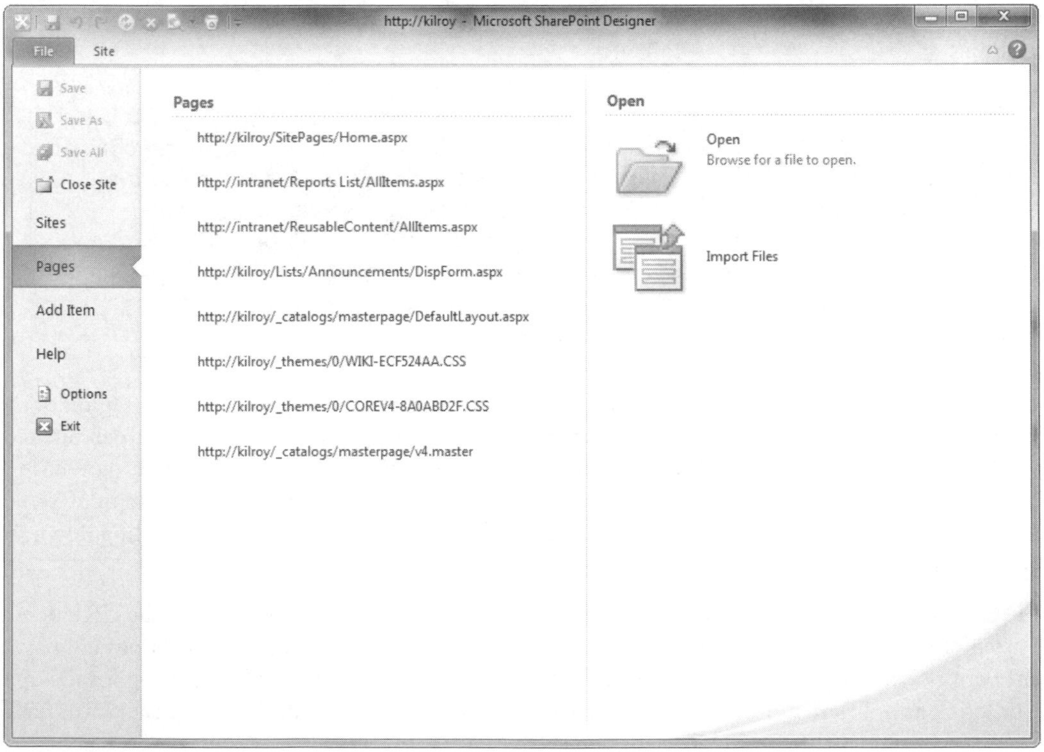

FIGURE 1-7

When you have a SharePoint 2010 site open, you have the ability to open and edit files, not only within the current site, but from other locations as well — even those that are not SharePoint 2010 sites.

> **NOTE** *Even though you can open files from older versions of SharePoint, SharePoint Designer 2010 only recognizes the final rendered content of the pages. You cannot manipulate the source material, such as the XSLT of a data view, as you can with SharePoint 2010 artifacts.*

The Add Item Section

The Add Item section of Backstage gives you a convenient place to create pages and various other SharePoint artifacts without first drilling into the section dedicated to a particular type. The types of items available may vary depending upon the site you have open. Figure 1-8 shows a typical array of choices for Add Item.

You can find brief introductions to these artifacts throughout this chapter. Later chapters describe in detail how SharePoint Designer allows you to manipulate most of them.

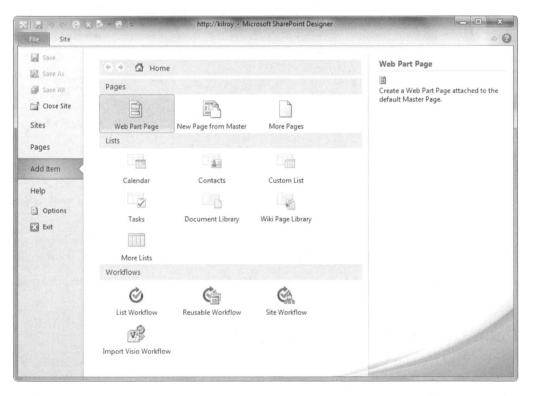

FIGURE 1-8

The Help Section

The Help section of Backstage, shown in Figure 1-9, provides tools and information relating to SharePoint Designer itself.

FIGURE 1-9

The right half of the page is taken up by the "about" information. This tells you the precise version and patch level of SharePoint Designer. It also includes copyright information, as well as what licensing mode the product is in (such as Trial, or Activated).

The Support zone gives links to different kinds of help, from classic-style pop-up window help to online support resources. Certain aspects of this help are only available if you are connected to the Internet.

The Tools zone allows you to check for newer versions of SharePoint Designer, or change various program settings. These settings are described in more detail in the next section.

SharePoint Designer Application Options

When you click the Options link in the Tools zone, or the options button in the Help section, instead of a new section page, the SharePoint Designer Options dialog appears. From here, you can control many aspects of your SharePoint Designer experience.

In addition, some items in the Options dialog are shared across all the Microsoft Office 2010 applications you have installed. Where an (otherwise shared) option is not relevant to your current SharePoint Designer configuration, that section of the Options dialog appears grayed out.

Like many aspects of SharePoint Designer 2010, this dialog is made up of pages selected from a list along the left-hand side. The following sections describe each of these pages in detail.

The General Page

The General page of the SharePoint Designer Options dialog is shown in Figure 1-10.

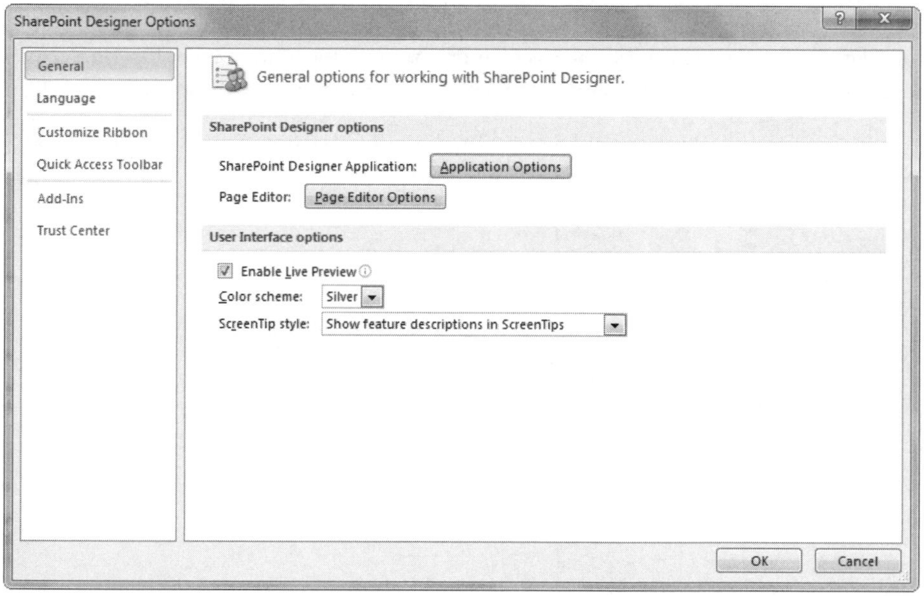

FIGURE 1-10

One option on this page is the Color Scheme. Your choice of Silver, Black, or Blue for the tabs and trim in SharePoint Designer also impacts Word, Excel, and PowerPoint.

The General page also contains two buttons: Application Options and Page Editor Options. Chapter 2 covers the Page Editor Options. Clicking Application Options summons the dialog shown in Figure 1-11.

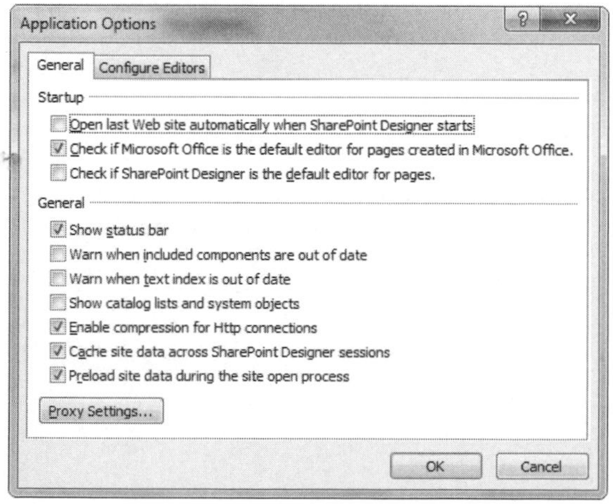

FIGURE 1-11

This dialog has two tabs: the General tab (shown — and yes, many tabs are called *General* in SharePoint Designer) and the Configure Editors tab. Most of the items in the General tab are SharePoint Designer settings such as whether to open the most recent site automatically; they are simple checkboxes and should be self-explanatory.

The Proxy Settings button allows you to quickly access your PC's settings for connecting to files on the Internet. These settings are actually controlled by Internet Explorer and shared across most applications on the PC.

The Configure Editors tab, shown in Figure 1-12, allows you to determine which application(s) you want used to edit files of various types.

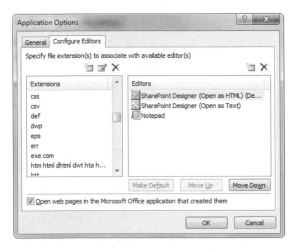

FIGURE 1-12

Most file types you will encounter when editing SharePoint sites are already defined. Many are set by default to be edited within SharePoint Designer. Files created by Microsoft Office applications default to using the application that created them. If you want, however, you may add new types or reassign existing file types for editing by any application installed on your PC.

The Language Page

Figure 1-13 shows the Language page of the SharePoint Designer Options dialog.

Here, you can install new proofing tools and select the user-interface languages for SharePoint Designer. The languages available depend upon the working languages installed on both your client PC and with SharePoint Designer.

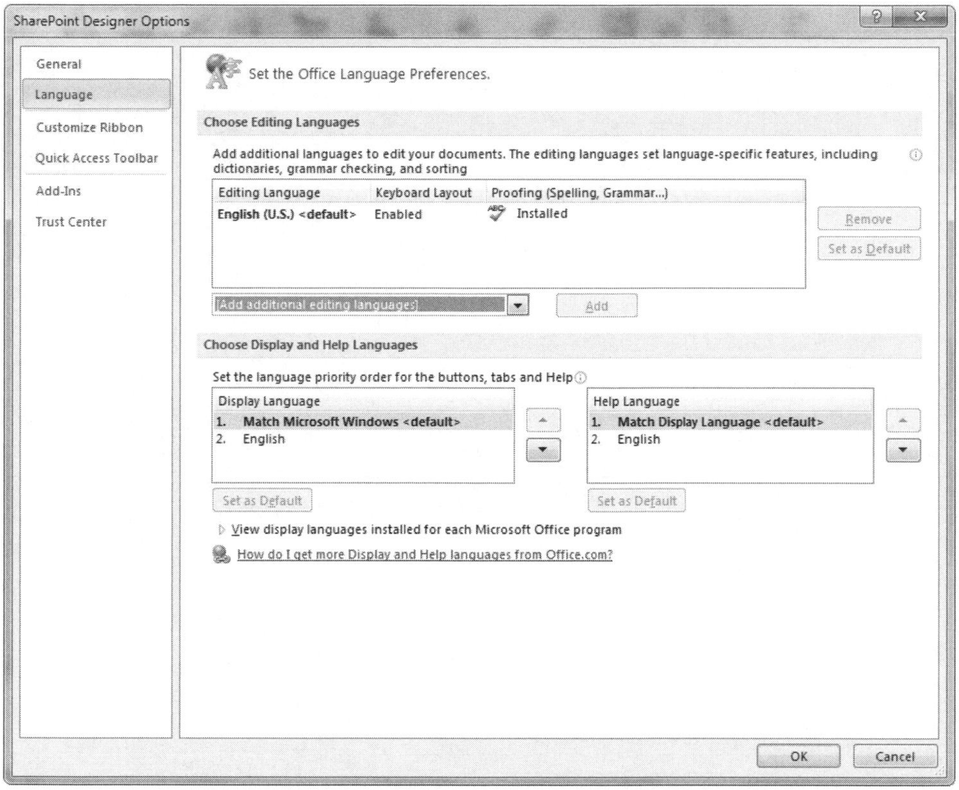

FIGURE 1-13

The Customize Ribbon Page

Figure 1-14 shows the Customize Ribbon page of the SharePoint Designer Options dialog.

Like the Quick Access Toolbar, the ribbon in SharePoint Designer 2010 is highly customizable. You use steps similar to those used in the Quick Access Toolbar (QAT) Try It Out later in this chapter.

One major difference between customizing the QAT and customizing the ribbon is the fact that the QAT is a single, linear array of icons. The ribbon, on the other hand, is a hierarchical structure. In other words, the ribbon is made up of containers, which contain other containers, and so on, until you ultimately find the icons for the commands.

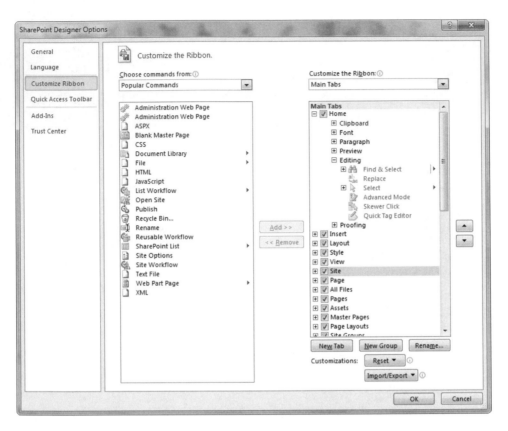

FIGURE 1-14

The two main levels of the ribbon container are Tab and Group. Tabs are shown across the top of the SharePoint Designer window, just below the title bar. Within a tab are one or more groups of command icons.

TRY IT OUT   Create and Delete a Custom Ribbon Tab

1. Open a site with SharePoint Designer 2010.

2. Click the File tab.

3. Click the Help section heading.

4. Click the Options link in the Tools zone.

5. Click Customize Ribbon.

6. Click New Tab. Observe that a section is automatically created along with your tab, and that section is highlighted. Observe that both are indicated as (Custom) elements.

7. Click the Publish command (in the left column).

8. Click the Add button (between the columns).

9. Click the Rename command.

10. Click the Add button.

11. Click the New Tab (Custom) element that you created in Step 6.

12. Click the Rename button. A Rename dialog appears.

13. Edit the name to read Beginning SPD and click OK.

14. Click OK in the main SharePoint Designer Options dialog.

15. Observe that a new tab entitled "**Beginning SPD**" appears in the ribbon.

16. Click the Beginning SPD tab. Observe that the commands you added in Steps 7–10 appear in it.

17. Click the File tab.

18. Click Options. The SharePoint Designer Options dialog appears.

19. Click Customize Ribbon.

20. Click the Beginning SPD (Custom) tab (in the right column).

21. Click the Remove button (between the columns).

22. Click OK. Observe that the custom tab has been deleted.

How It Works

With so many possible commands at your disposal, it would have been quite unwieldy to put all of them in the ribbon. By allowing you to customize the ribbon and the QAT, you can finely tune SharePoint Designer 2010 to your own way of working. You can even save that fine tuning and take it with you by using the Import/Export option that appears under the Ribbon list.

The Quick Access Toolbar Page

The Quick Access Toolbar (QAT) is a constantly visible toolbar containing a customizable set of icons. The same Quick Access Toolbar Options page lets you choose the position of the QAT. By default, it appears "above the ribbon" within the title bar of your application, as shown in Figure 1-15.

You can also set the QAT to appear below the ribbon, where it displays in the full width of your SharePoint Designer window, as shown in Figure 1-16.

FIGURE 1-15   **FIGURE 1-16**

TRY IT OUT Add an Icon to the Quick Access Toolbar

1. Open a site with SharePoint Designer 2010.

2. Click the File tab.

3. Click the Help section heading.

4. Click the Options link in the Tools zone.

5. Click the Quick Access Toolbar link.

6. Select All Commands from the "Choose commands from:" dropdown.

7. Find and highlight the Options command from the commands list.

8. Click the Add button.

9. Click OK.

10. Note that the icon for Options has appeared in the upper-left corner of the application window.

11. Click the newly present icon.

12. Click Cancel.

How It Works

The Quick Access Toolbar page allows you to select the commands available on the QAT. Depending upon your work style, or even the particular project, you may wish to change these to suit the task at hand.

The Add-Ins Page

SharePoint Designer allows you to install *add-ins* to enhance its functionality. You manage any add-ins you may have on the Add-Ins page of the SharePoint Designer Options dialog; however, no add-ins are included with SharePoint Designer or installed by default. If you acquire an add-in, its author should include documentation relating to its installation and use.

The Trust Center Page

The Trust Center page of the SharePoint Designer Options dialog, shown in Figure 1-17, displays a "splash" screen that provides links to various Microsoft-hosted websites.

The sites listed detail the latest privacy and security policies and information related to Microsoft products, including SharePoint Designer. If you look carefully, however, you will notice the Trust Center Settings button. Clicking this button summons the dialog shown in Figure 1-18.

This is the actual Trust Center configuration dialog. Here, you can configure what potentially unsafe actions and content are allowed in SharePoint Designer. Most of the options in this dialog are self-explanatory, but use caution before changing them. The defaults are set to minimize the risk of untrustworthy code (for example, viruses, worms, or even just badly written code) damaging or infecting SharePoint Designer, or using SharePoint Designer as a vector for damage or infection of other systems.

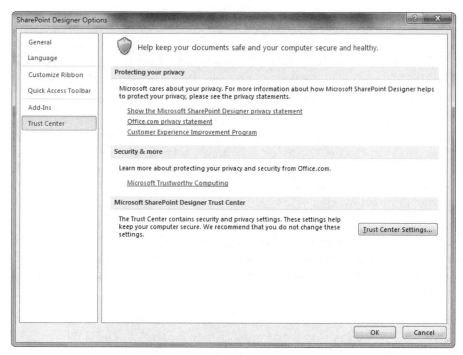

FIGURE 1-17

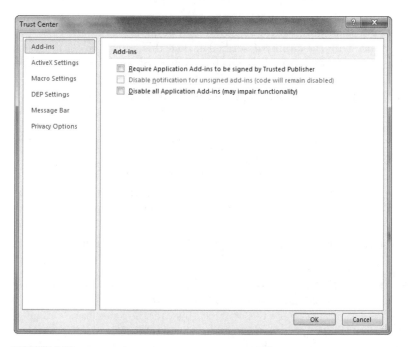

FIGURE 1-18

DIGGING FOR ARTIFACTS

In some respects, working with SharePoint Designer is like working in an integrated development environment (IDE) such as Visual Studio, web design and development tools like Adobe Dreamweaver (formerly of Macromedia), or even earlier versions of SharePoint Designer and FrontPage. Although the underlying concepts are similar, the overall presentation of site components is very different.

If you are new to the IDE experience, you want to be aware of the need for development and design tools to manage projects consisting of many interrelated files. These files are sometimes called *artifacts*. Some SharePoint Designer functions operate on the individual files, whereas others work on a project as a whole. This dichotomy will surface in a number of different ways. For example, in the earlier discussion of Backstage, you saw that the options for opening and creating sites were literally on a different page from those for working with files.

The collection of artifacts that is treated as a project unit in SharePoint Designer is called a *site*. SharePoint sites have a similar naming structure, but also include an element called a *web*. Although both terms are used interchangeably when discussing user interface elements throughout most of this book, the SharePoint development API makes a significant distinction. See Appendix B for a more thorough discussion of SharePoint's architecture.

> **NOTE** *Remember: you cannot open an individual file in SharePoint Designer 2010 without first opening a SharePoint 2010 site.*

With SharePoint Designer, you are usually working against a live (though not necessarily production) environment. When combined with the duality described earlier, this has the result that certain changes have immediate effect, whereas others aren't visible unless or until you save the component you are working on. In general, changes to overall site structure (such as renaming, deleting, or moving a file) are immediate, but you need to save changes made within a page or graphic file to see them on the site.

> **NOTE** *Many SharePoint environments are source-controlled or content-managed. This means your file(s) may need to go through a check-in and approval process before certain changes become visible.*

Figure 1-19 shows SharePoint Designer with a typical site open. Please refer to this image in the following discussion:

1. Most IDEs display a hierarchical tree that shows where the various files are physically or logically located in the project. Although SharePoint Designer 2010 offers such a view, it is not your primary way of discovering your site's artifacts. Instead, the SharePoint Designer navigation pane organizes them into *object views* of the related items. The next section gives quick descriptions of these views. You can show and hide the navigation pane by clicking the button containing "<" in the title. This icon rotates when the pane is in the hidden position.

2. You can have multiple objects open at once. Each open object is represented as a tab across the top of the page. Many tabs include a breadcrumb that allows you to navigate through the hierarchy that leads to the current view.

3. The main content area shows you either relevant information about the item in the currently highlighted tab or provides a design surface for that type of item. Most of what you will learn about throughout the remainder of the book is based on what you see and do in this area.

4. The ribbon, which you saw earlier, is context sensitive. The tabs and icons available on it vary depending on what is highlighted in the content area.

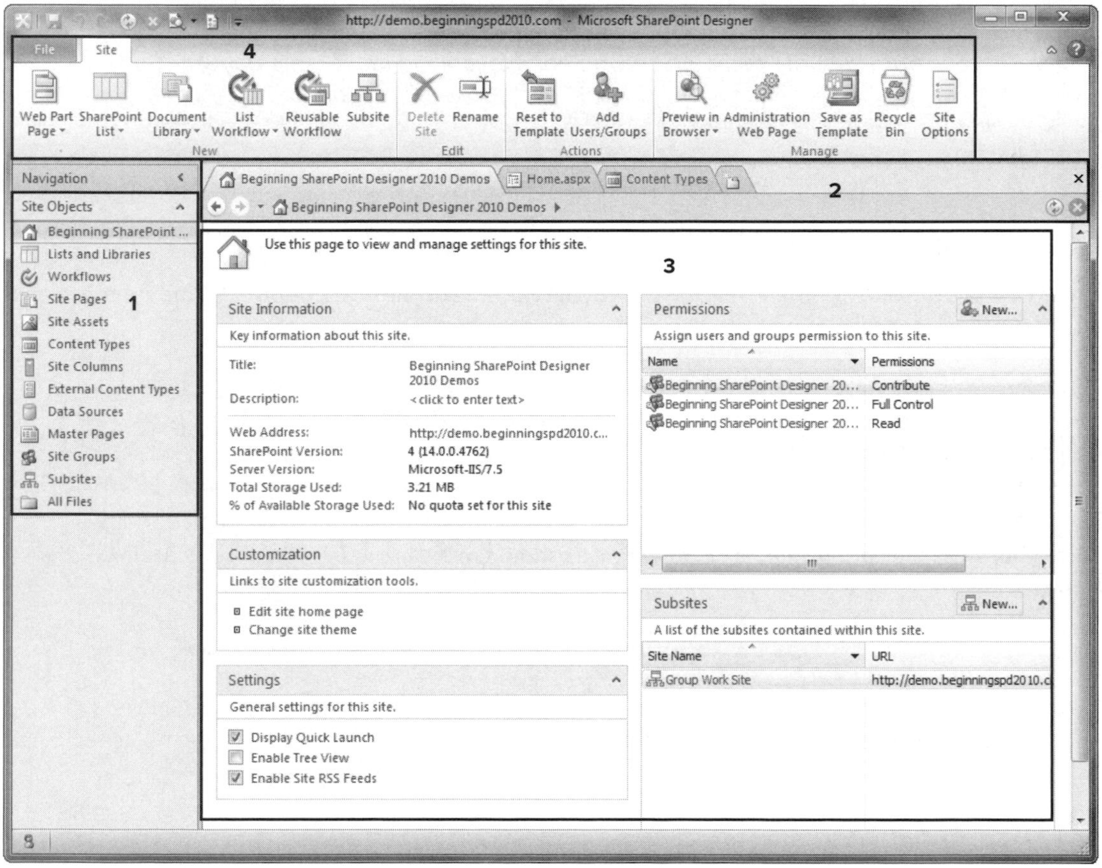

FIGURE 1-19

The Site Summary Page

The Site Summary page is shown when you click the title of your site in the Navigation pane. It gives you the basic information about your SharePoint site, provides quick access to create many site artifacts, and allows you to change many site-wide settings. Unlike the other views listed in the next section, the label in the navigation pane for this section changes. It reflects the actual name of your site.

Many of the functions available through Site Summary are also available through the SharePoint web user interface, or elsewhere in SharePoint Designer. However, they are distributed across many different pages and program sections. In addition, you may have customized SharePoint to remove direct end-user links to these functions, therefore making this page the only convenient place to perform them.

> **NOTE** Total removal of access to "administrative" functions is often a request handed down from management. Although you are able to do so through the customization tools provided by SharePoint Designer, keep in mind that such functions are security trimmed, and are not available to most users anyway. See Appendix B, as well as the "Site Groups" and "Governing SharePoint Designer" sections later in this chapter.

Site Ribbon Tab

When viewing the Site Summary page, you will have access to the Site ribbon tab, and its functions will be available for selection.

> **NOTE** The Site ribbon tab is also visible when you don't have a site open; however, the icons will be grayed out and non-functional.

Four groups of icons are in the Site ribbon tab, as shown in Figure 1-20: *New*, *Edit*, *Actions*, and *Manage*.

FIGURE 1-20

The icons in the New group allow you to create a new item of the specified type. Most of these (for example, lists, libraries, and workflows) are discussed in detail later in the book in the relevant chapters. Clicking the Subsite icon in this group summons the dialog shown in Figure 1-21.

The actual list of site types available is based upon a number of factors, and will be queried from the SharePoint server. Therefore, it may vary slightly from the items shown in Figure 1-21.

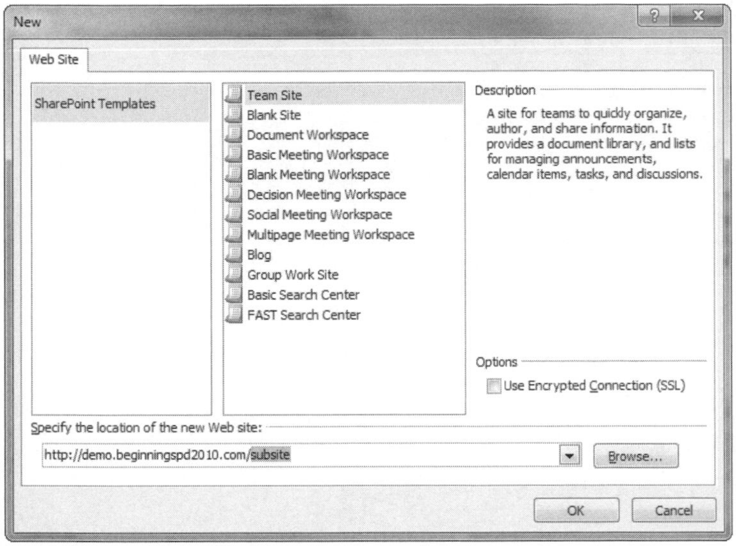

FIGURE 1-21

The Edit section of the Site ribbon tab contains two icons: *Delete Site* and *Rename*. Delete Site is only available if the current SharePoint site is a subsite of another site. If it is available, clicking this icon will summon an alert warning you that deleting the site is permanent, and will impact all the content contained therein. Click Yes if you really want to delete the site.

Clicking the Rename icon directs focus to the Title field shown in the Site Information block (described later).

The icons in the Actions group of the Site ribbon tab are Reset to Template and Add Users/Groups. The Reset to Template icon allows you to revert individual pages, or the entire site, to the site definition files upon which they are based. When you click it, you are prompted with a confirmation alert. If you click the Yes button, a browser window opens that shows the Reset to Site Definition management page in SharePoint. To understand this function better, see the discussions of "ghosted" or "customized" files in Appendix A and Chapter 3.

> **NOTE** *Many of the management functions that are accessed through SharePoint Designer will ultimately redirect you to the SharePoint web UI to perform the actual task.*

Clicking the Add Users/Groups icon summons the Add Permissions dialog shown in Figure 1-22.

This dialog allows you to select individual users, as well as already-existing groups, and assign them permission to resources. In this instance, you are working with an entire SharePoint site, but the same dialog (or portions thereof) is used wherever SharePoint Designer needs you to assign permissions to a resource.

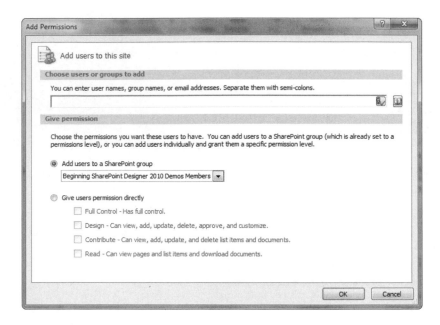

FIGURE 1-22

As indicated in the dialog's descriptive text, you can enter a user or group ID in the text field provided. Clicking the small icon containing the checkmark validates your entries against the SharePoint membership provider. If an exact match is not found, you may be able to select from a list of similar members (if any).

You also have the option of clicking the address book icon beside the text box. This summons the SharePoint Contacts dialog shown in Figure 1-23.

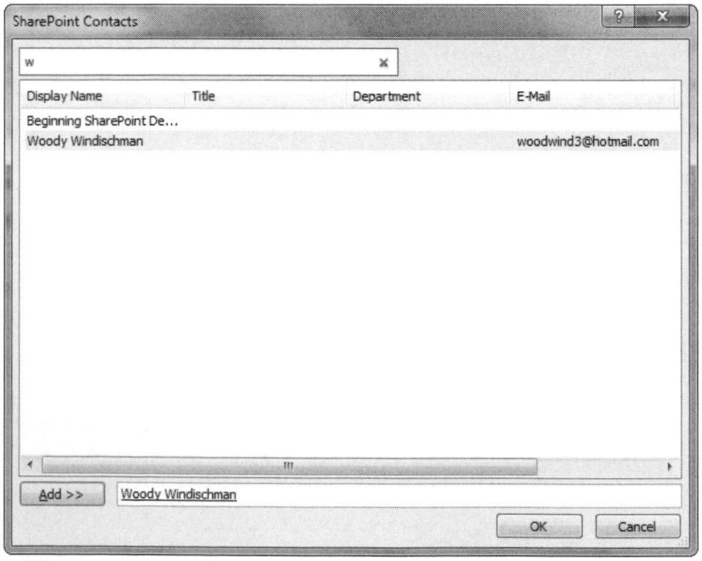

FIGURE 1-23

In the SharePoint Contacts dialog, you can enter part of the name you want to find in the text field at the top of the form, and press the Enter key. Any matching results appear in the list. You can then highlight individual entries and click the Add button. You can repeat this process as often as needed before clicking the OK button, which then moves your selections into the Add Permissions dialog.

> **NOTE** *Some places in SharePoint that require permission assignment will only accept a single entry.*

The Manage section of the Site ribbon tab contains five icons. Of these, three of them — Administration Web Page, Save as Template, and Recycle Bin — redirect you to the appropriate SharePoint web UI for that element.

The Preview in Browser button allows you to view your site in one of the web browsers installed on your PC. As Figure 1-24 shows, you can also force the browser window to a particular size.

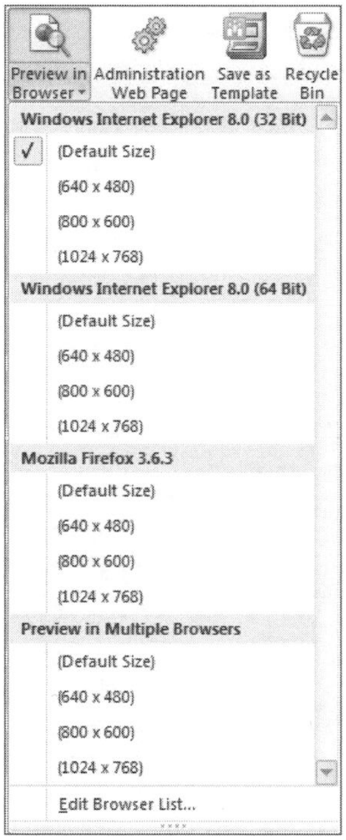

FIGURE 1-24

TRY IT OUT   **Modify the Browser Preview List**

1. Open a site in SharePoint Designer.

2. Click the label of the Preview in Browser icon in the ribbon.

3. From the dropdown menu, select Edit Browser List.

4. Observe that the list of available browsers includes any common browsers you may have had installed at the time you installed SharePoint Designer 2010.

5. Observe that all browsers and sizes are selected by default, and will appear in the Preview in Browser menu. (This may not be the current state if you have already visited this dialog.)

6. Click the checkboxes to deselect 640 × 408 and 1024 × 768.

7. Click OK.

8. Click the label of the Preview in Browser icon in the ribbon.

9. Observe that the list is now shortened to reflect your selections in Step 6.

10. (optional) From the dropdown menu, select Edit Browser List.

11. (optional) Change the settings to reflect browsers and sizes appropriate to your target audience, and click OK.

How It Works

One of the most frustrating things about designing for the web is the wide array of browsers and screen formats in which your site may be displayed. SharePoint Designer itself cannot perfectly reproduce the environment of a web browser.

Not only can a page be rendered differently in a browser from within SharePoint Designer, but different browsers and even different versions of the same browser have their own ways of rendering pages. To resolve this, SharePoint Designer provides the option to preview your page directly in web browsers. Other design aids are discussed in Chapter 2.

> **NOTE** *A page must be saved before it can be previewed in a web browser.*

The final icon in the Site ribbon tab is Site Options. Most of the settings here relate to general web management and are beyond the scope of this book. However, two areas merit your attention.

The first item is that, when you initially click the icon and summon the Site Settings dialog, you see the Parameters tab as shown in Figure 1-25.

Two of the parameters listed — vti_siteusage-totalvisits and vti_siteusagetotalbandwidth — are actually "reports." They tell you the total number of visits to your site, and the total amount of data that has been transferred. Although not comprehensive, observing the changes in these values over time can help you get a quick feel for the popularity of your site.

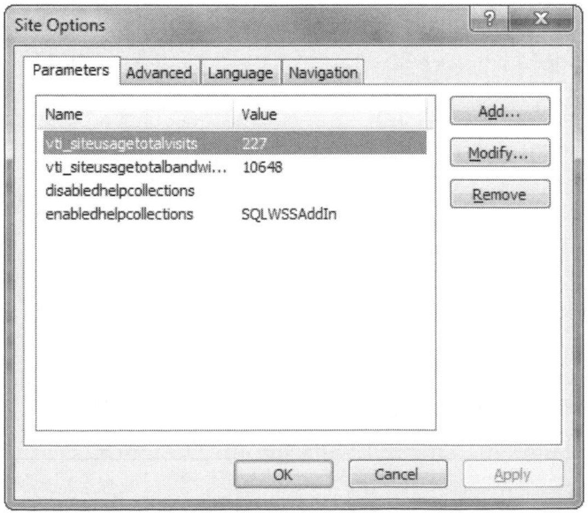

FIGURE 1-25

The second relevant area is the Advanced tab, where two settings are called out in Figure 1-26.

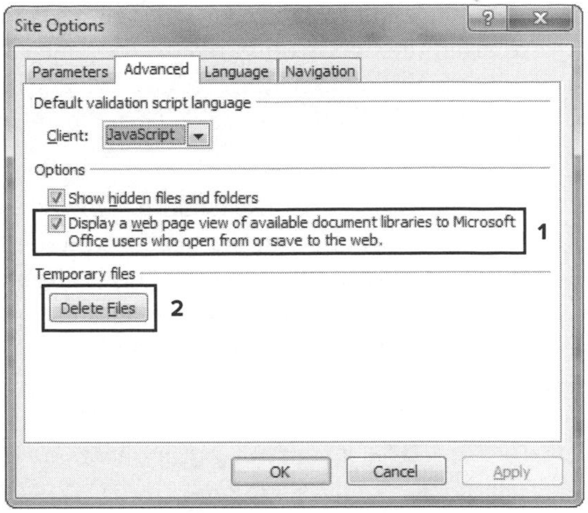

Callout 1 is an option for showing a "web page view" in the file dialog for Microsoft Office applications. This view provides easy and direct navigation to the document libraries on your site. Deselecting this option forces Office applications to use a standard "file and folder" style dialog to navigate your site, which may expose elements you would rather leave hidden.

Callout 2 highlights the Delete Files button in the Temporary files section. As you work in SharePoint Designer, it will keep temporary copies of many files in a cache on your hard disk for quicker access. If this cache becomes too full or corrupt, performance of SharePoint Designer can

FIGURE 1-26

deteriorate. Clicking this button clears the cache and gives SharePoint Designer a fresh start.

Site Summary Page Blocks

The content area of the Site Summary page contains several blocks of information. The exact content of these blocks, of course, varies depending on various aspects of the open SharePoint Site.

The first block in the left column is labeled *Site Information*. The Site Information block tells you the following:

➤ Your site's title, and allows you to edit it

➤ Your site's description, and allows you to edit it

➤ The name of the folder your site resides in, and allows you to edit it (if in a child site within a site collection)

➤ The URL/path of your site

➤ The version and build of SharePoint being run

➤ The version of the underlying web server

➤ The amount of storage used in your site collection (if on the root site of a collection)

➤ Remaining quota if set (if on the root site of a collection)

Figures 1-27 and 1-28 show the Site Information blocks from the root site of a collection, and a subsite, respectively.

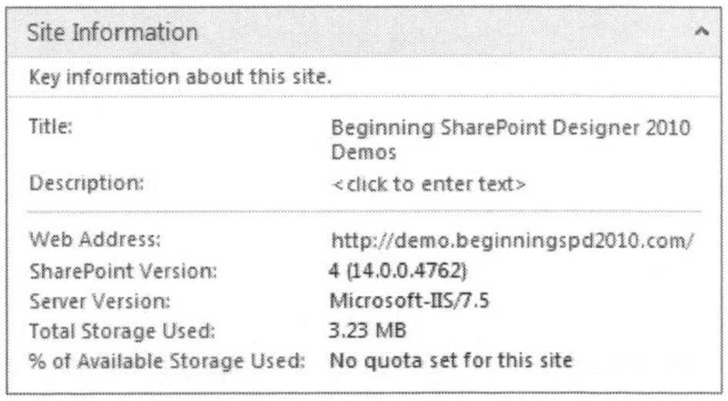

Below the Site Information block is the Customization block. This block contains two links. On non-publishing sites, the Edit Site Home Page opens the home page in the SharePoint Designer Page Editor, which is described in the next chapter. On publishing sites, this link produces a warning that publishing page content

FIGURE 1-27

cannot be edited in SharePoint Designer, and you are given the opportunity to edit the page layout upon which the home page is based. The Change Site Theme link opens the Site Theme page in the web user interface.

The final block in the left column is the Settings block. The three options here allow you to determine whether to show the Quick Launch or tree view on the site, and whether to allow RSS feeds of list and library information.

Site Information	
Key information about this site.	
Title:	Group Work Site
Description:	< click to enter text>
Folder:	groupie
Web Address:	http://demo.beginningspd2010.com/groupie/
SharePoint Version:	4 (14.0.0.4762)
Server Version:	Microsoft-IIS/7.5

FIGURE 1-28

> **NOTE** *If your master page design does not include the left navigation area, the Quick Launch and tree view settings will have no visible effect.*

The top block in the right column lists the Permission groups currently active in your site. This block may have a New button in the title bar. If so, clicking it will summon the same dialog you get when clicking the Add Users/Groups icon in the ribbon.

If you are on a subsite, the button may say Stop Inheriting instead of New. In this case, permissions are inherited from the site's immediate parent, and normally managed from there. Clicking Stop Inheriting breaks this inheritance and allows you to manage permissions for the current subsite alone.

> **WARNING** *SharePoint Designer does not have a way to restore permission inheritance after it is broken. Breaking inheritance can only be "undone" from the web user interface.*

Within the Permissions list, clicking one of the groups summons the dialog shown in Figure 1-29.

Edit Permissions

Change the permissions for Beginning SharePoint Designer 2010 Demos Owners

Choose the permissions you want for this group

☑ Full Control - Has full control.

☐ Design - Can view, add, update, delete, approve, and customize.

☐ Contribute - Can view, add, update, and delete list items and documents.

☐ Read - Can view pages and list items and download documents.

OK   Cancel

FIGURE 1-29

This dialog allows you to determine which permission levels are applied to members of that group. A group may be assigned multiple permission levels. See the description of the Site Groups view in the next section, as well as Appendix B, for more information about managing permissions in SharePoint and SharePoint Designer.

The Subsites block also contains a New button in the title bar. Clicking the New button summons the same dialog you get when clicking the corresponding button in the ribbon, as described earlier in this chapter.

In the Subsites block, clicking on a subsite summons the "Subsites" ribbon tab (described later in this chapter). Double-clicking a subsite in this list opens the site in a new SharePoint Designer window.

Other Site Object Views

You will typically find many other site object (artifact) views while working on a SharePoint site. Some of these may not be visible due to the site's configuration (see the "Governing SharePoint Designer" section later in this chapter) or enabled features. As you work through this book, you will learn about the contents of these other sections in detail. Each of the following views is summoned by selecting the corresponding link in the Site Objects navigation pane.

Lists and Libraries

Lists and libraries are the fundamental units of storage in SharePoint. Figure 1-30 shows the lists and libraries that make up a basic Team Site in SharePoint 2010.

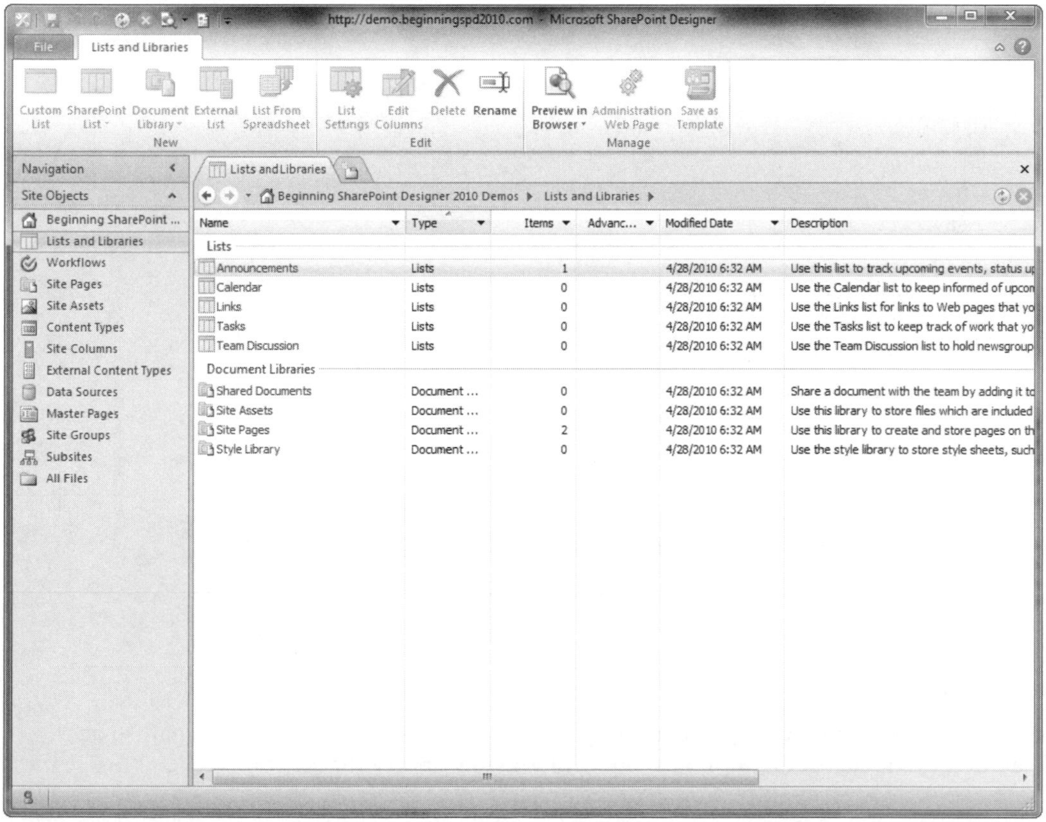

FIGURE 1-30

Workflows

Workflows in SharePoint allow you to automate processes such as document approval and feed-back collection. SharePoint Designer allows you to supplement the stock workflows with custom workflows.

Site Pages

The Site Pages library on most SharePoint sites is a *Wiki* library that shows you each page in your site as a separate document. This library is different from the Pages library on a SharePoint publishing site. Although they perform similar functions, fundamental distinctions exist between these libraries and the pages they contain. You'll learn how to tell the difference, as well as how to edit these pages, in Chapter 3. Figure 1-31 shows the Site Pages library on a Team Site.

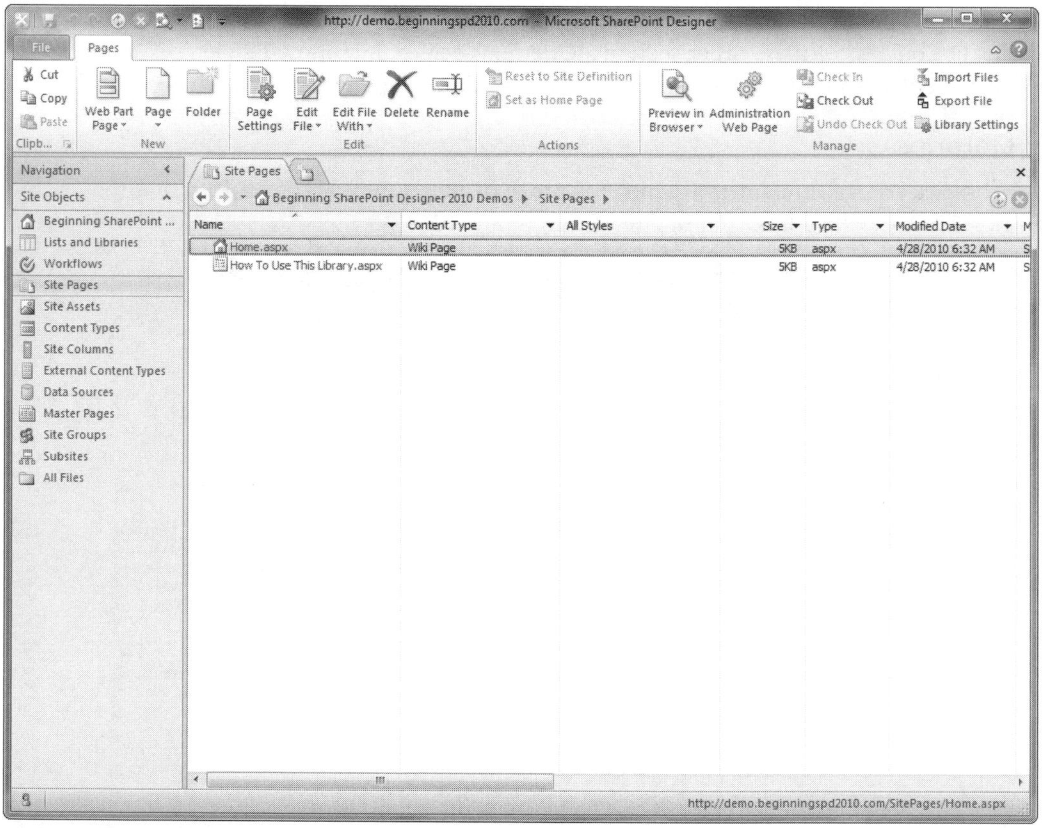

FIGURE 1-31

Site Assets

Site assets are files that can be used in multiple places within the site. Assets may include images, style sheet files, even videos. Figure 1-32 shows a Site Assets library that contains several image files.

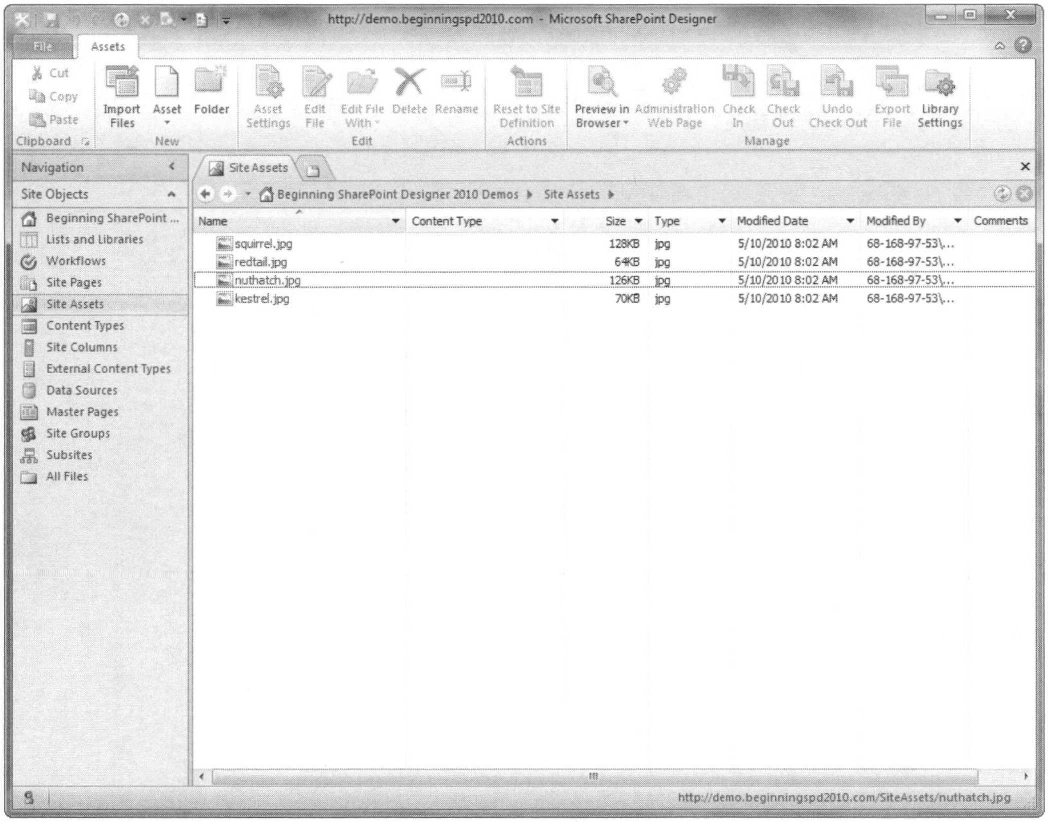

FIGURE 1-32

Content Types

A content type defines the default set of fields that a particular list or library item contains. The Content Types page allows you to manage (add, edit, or remove) the content types defined in the site. As shown in Figure 1-33, the content types are grouped into broad categories such as documents, folders, or list items.

You learn more about using SharePoint Designer to modify content types in Chapter 6.

Site Columns

Site columns define a particular field type that can be used in lists or libraries throughout your site. You can create your own reusable columns, such as a common calculated field (for example, assembling a label address from separate street, city, state, and zip columns) or a pre-defined choice field. Figure 1-34 shows some of the many site columns already defined in SharePoint 2010.

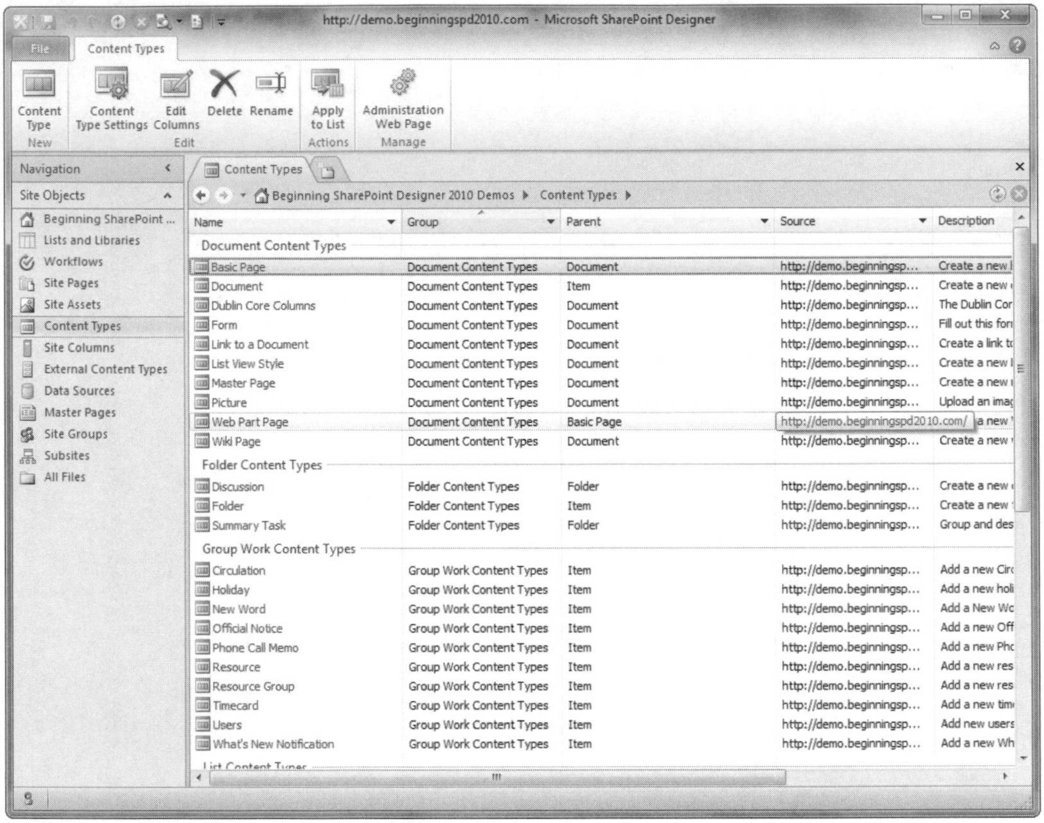

FIGURE 1-33

External Content Types

External content types are a function of Business Connectivity Services (BCS) that allows you to treat information hosted outside of SharePoint as if it were a native SharePoint list. Several chapters in this book deal with accessing external data.

Data Sources

The Data Sources page allows you to manage both SharePoint and non-SharePoint data sources, making them available for use in data views. Data sources can be managed by BCS or individually.

> **NOTE** *Although you can use any data source defined here to create a data view, only information you define in BCS can be used in external content types.*

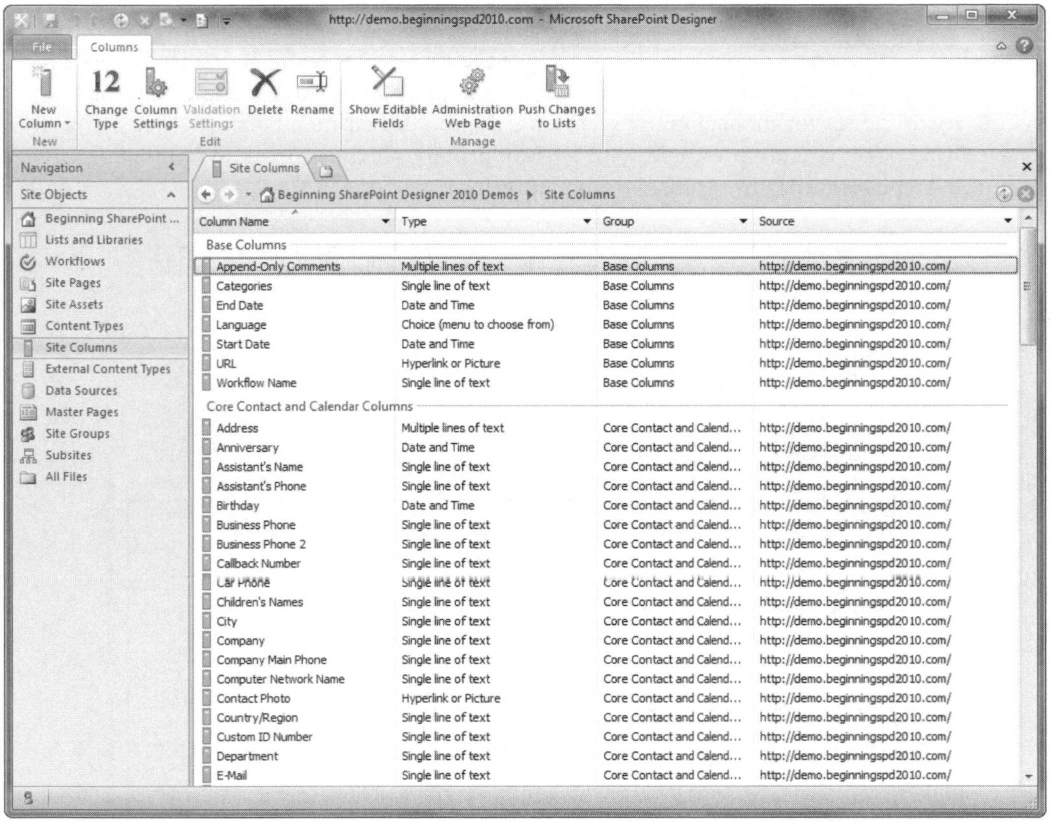

FIGURE 1-34

Master Pages, and Page Layouts

The Master Pages and Page Layouts pages allow you to view and edit the master pages and page layouts in your site. The page layouts view is only available in SharePoint sites that have the Publishing feature activated.

Master pages control the overall look and feel of your SharePoint site. You can significantly change the style of your site without impacting its function or content simply by swapping to a different master page. Page layouts work within the master pages to control the presentation of content on different page types within a SharePoint publishing site.

Chapter 4 provides details about using SharePoint Designer 2010 for the creation of master pages and layouts.

Site Groups

SharePoint allows site owners to manage user access to their sites. Appendix B describes how this is performed through the web interface. The Site Groups page of SharePoint Designer provides an enhanced user experience for managing site security groups and their memberships. When you initially click on this page, you are presented with a list of groups. Clicking on an individual group shows a summary page similar to that shown in Figure 1-35.

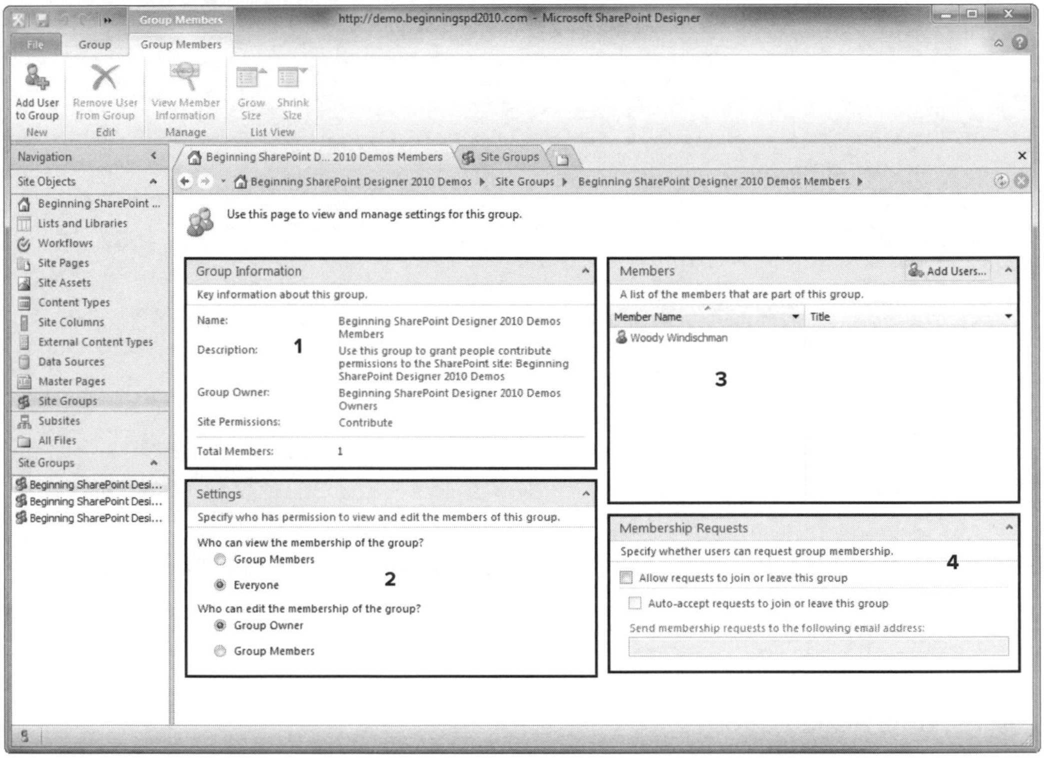

FIGURE 1-35

From this screen, you can edit all the key information about the group in one place. The following descriptions refer to the callouts in Figure 1-35.

> **NOTE** Site groups are defined at the Site Collection level. Even if you are editing a subsite with broken inheritance, any groups you create here will be available for use throughout the site collection.

The first block in the left column (Callout 1) is an informational block. As with the Site information block described in the previous section, the Name and Description blocks are directly editable. Clicking the Group Owners link provides a user selector dialog as described earlier in this chapter. Clicking the Permissions link summons a dialog that lets you choose which permission levels you want to assign to the group.

The second block in the left column (Callout 2) allows you to set who can view or modify the membership of the group.

The first block in the right column (Callout 3) shows you the current membership of the group. Clicking in this block summons the Group Members contextual ribbon tab, shown in Figure 1-36.

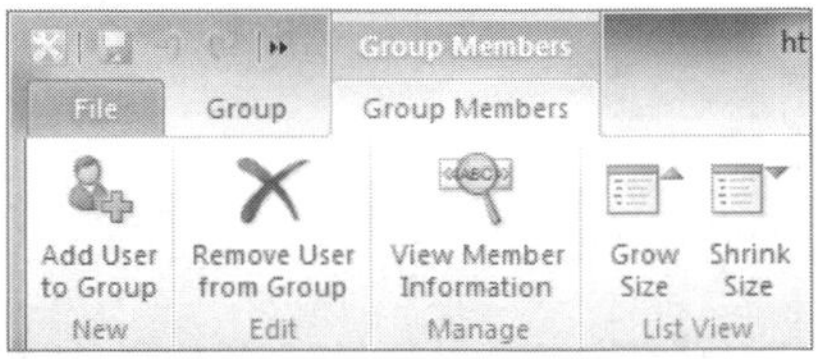

FIGURE 1-36

Adding, removing, and viewing member information are self-explanatory commands, and are available both from the ribbon and in the block itself. You add a user through the Add Users button and use the same user selector described earlier in this chapter. You can see a user's details by clicking on his name, or right-clicking anywhere on the row and selecting View Member Information from the context menu. You can also delete a member from the group from the right-click context menu.

The final block (Callout 4) lets you control whether a user can request or withdraw his membership in the group. You may also allow requests for addition or deletion to be automatically approved by SharePoint. The final field allows you to enter an e-mail address to which SharePoint will forward membership requests. Unlike most user entry forms, this does not include access to the user selector dialog. You may enter any freeform e-mail address in this box.

Subsites

A site or web in SharePoint can contain other sites. When the site on which you are working has such children, they will be listed in the Subsites page. Clicking on one of these subsites opens it in a new instance of SharePoint Designer.

All Files

The All Files page gives you a traditional file and folder view of the contents of your site. You can also find most of the artifacts found in the other Site Object view pages in the All Files page. The main difference is that this view reflects the URL path the user would see when accessing your site through a web browser. Figure 1-37 shows the all-files view with the Site Pages folder open, and the Site Objects list group closed.

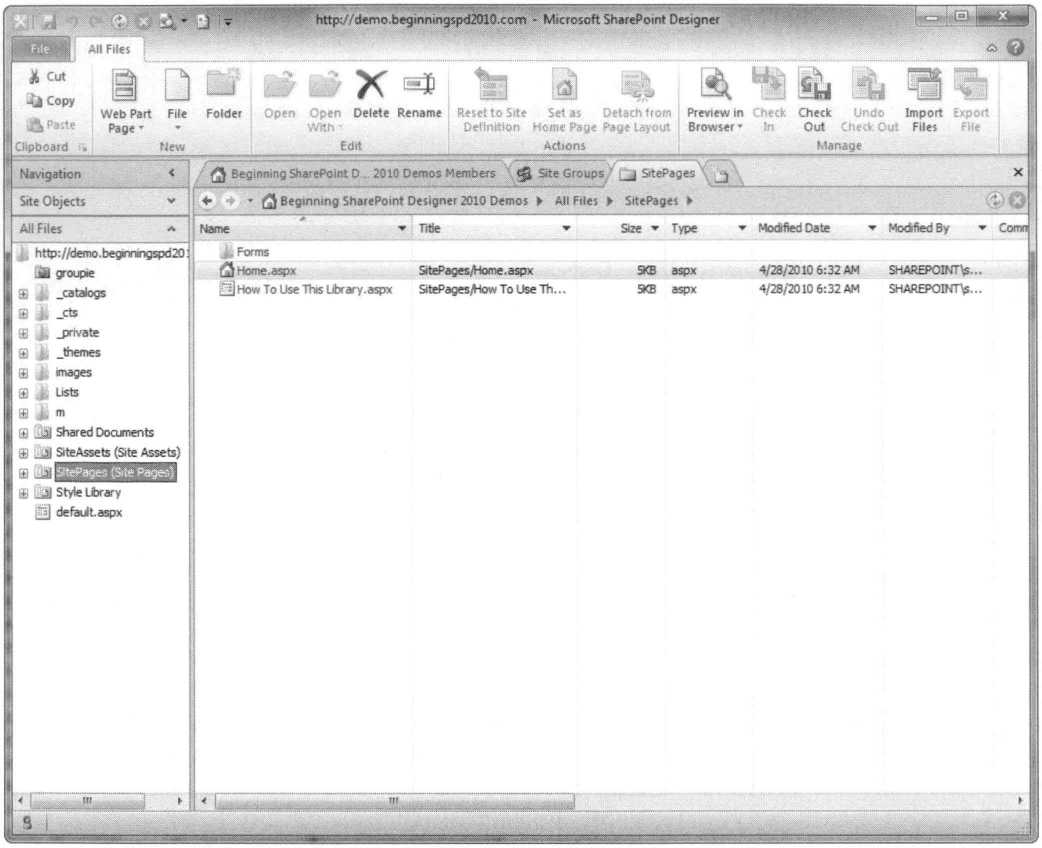

FIGURE 1-37

GOVERNING SHAREPOINT DESIGNER

SharePoint Designer provides a great deal of customizing power to its users. In some environments, particularly in an enterprise, giving all users access to this level of power may not be appropriate. To address this, SharePoint allows system administrators and site owners to configure different levels of access for users of SharePoint Designer.

First and foremost in the governance of SharePoint Designer is the proper application of regular security roles to a SharePoint site. Quite simply, even if a user downloads and installs SharePoint Designer, he cannot use it to make any changes to a site he would not otherwise be permitted to make. For example, a typical user in the Member role cannot change themes or master pages, or modify the schema of a list or library. SharePoint Designer would not suddenly enable him to do so. A user would need to be in (for example) the Web Designer or Administrator role on the site in order to make such changes, regardless of any tool he has installed.

In SharePoint 2010, you also have the settings for directly managing the use of SharePoint Designer, irrespective of the regular security of a site. These settings allow or prevent access to certain features by users of SharePoint Designer.

Figure 1-38 shows the SharePoint Designer controls screen.

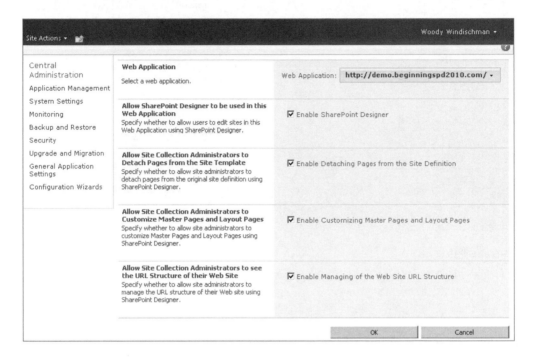

FIGURE 1-38

This page is accessible at different levels within SharePoint, depending upon the scope over which control is to be exerted. You can set these options at the web application or site collection level. If SharePoint Designer or one of its features is blocked at the web application level, it cannot be overridden by a site collection owner. Nevertheless, a site collection owner can invoke tighter restrictions than are set at the web application.

> **NOTE** *Restrictions implemented at the site collection level impact most users, but do not apply to the site collection administrators themselves.*

Regardless of which method or methods you use to restrict SharePoint Designer, your choices will be reflected in the experience presented to the users. The user interface of SharePoint Designer is *security trimmed*. This means that users are only shown the functions that they have the right to see or control. Figure 1-39 shows a Site Objects list with all the SharePoint Designer options of Figure 1-38 disabled.

Compare this figure to Figure 1-40, which is the same site with the options enabled.

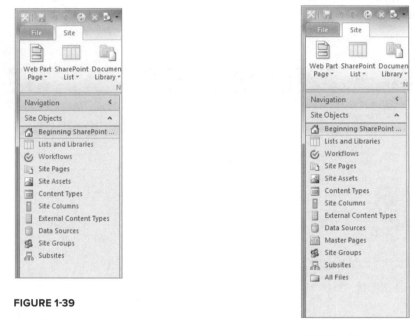

FIGURE 1-39

FIGURE 1-40

Observe that access to the Master Pages gallery and direct access to the site files are not visible in the restricted site. Other elements throughout the user interface, such as context menus, are similarly trimmed.

SUMMARY

This chapter gave you an overview of Microsoft Office SharePoint Designer 2010. You learned how to get around its various views. You discovered:

➤ SharePoint Designer 2010 is dedicated to SharePoint 2010.

➤ SharePoint Designer's user interface is consistent with many other Microsoft applications.

➤ It is consistent and can be adapted to almost anyone's needs through customizing the ribbon and Quick Access Toolbar, as well as managing security.

The next chapter takes you deep into the page editor of SharePoint Designer. You will see how it is used, not only for editing web pages, but as a design surface for many of the other feature editors in SharePoint Designer 2010.

PART II
Let's Get Visual

2

Editing Pages

WHAT YOU WILL LEARN IN THIS CHAPTER

➤ How to show and hide task panes and ribbon tabs

➤ About page editing modes

➤ About Code view features like IntelliSense and snippets

➤ How to incorporate SharePoint and other elements on a page

As Chapter 1 discusses, SharePoint Designer 2010 is about far more than editing pages. However, page layout and design is still an important part of the product. Indeed, many of the functions you will learn about in later chapters also rely on the page editor.

WHAT'S IN A "PAGE"?

Chapter 1 briefly introduced you to the broad array of artifacts you can work with in SharePoint Designer 2010. Some of them, such as site pages and master pages, are truly pages and labeled as such. Other files, such as layouts and Cascading Style Sheets (CSS), are not; however, you will still use the "page" editor to create and make changes to these files. Some SharePoint elements, such as data view web parts, can only be effectively modified in SharePoint Designer while they are placed on a page.

Although this chapter touches on some of these items, it is more about the tools available for working on all file types rather than working with particular artifacts. Such artifacts are covered in detail in their respective chapters. For example, this chapter discusses the table editing tools. Chapters 6–8 assume you know how to work with these tools in the discussion of how to use them to modify data views.

The Page Editor in SharePoint Designer is the workspace where you compose the elements of your page. The major elements of the SharePoint Designer editing workspace include the ribbon (discussed in Chapter 1), the design surface itself, the status bar, and a wide array of task panes. The workspace is quite customizable. Virtually every task pane can be resized, shown, hidden, set to float, or docked.

The design surface offers three primary modes, or views, of the page that is currently open — *Design*, *Code*, and *Split*. You can select these modes via icons in the View ribbon tab, or with the Page Mode toolbar, which is always visible at the left along the lower window margin.

> **NOTE** All three views are available for web page file types (.htm, .aspx, and .master, for example). Files such as .css, .js, and .txt that do not have a direct visual component only have Code view and do not display the Page Mode toolbar.

Figure 2-1 shows the Page Editor in Design view, with the maximum possible design surface shown. All the task panes are hidden, and the ribbon and navigation pane are minimized.

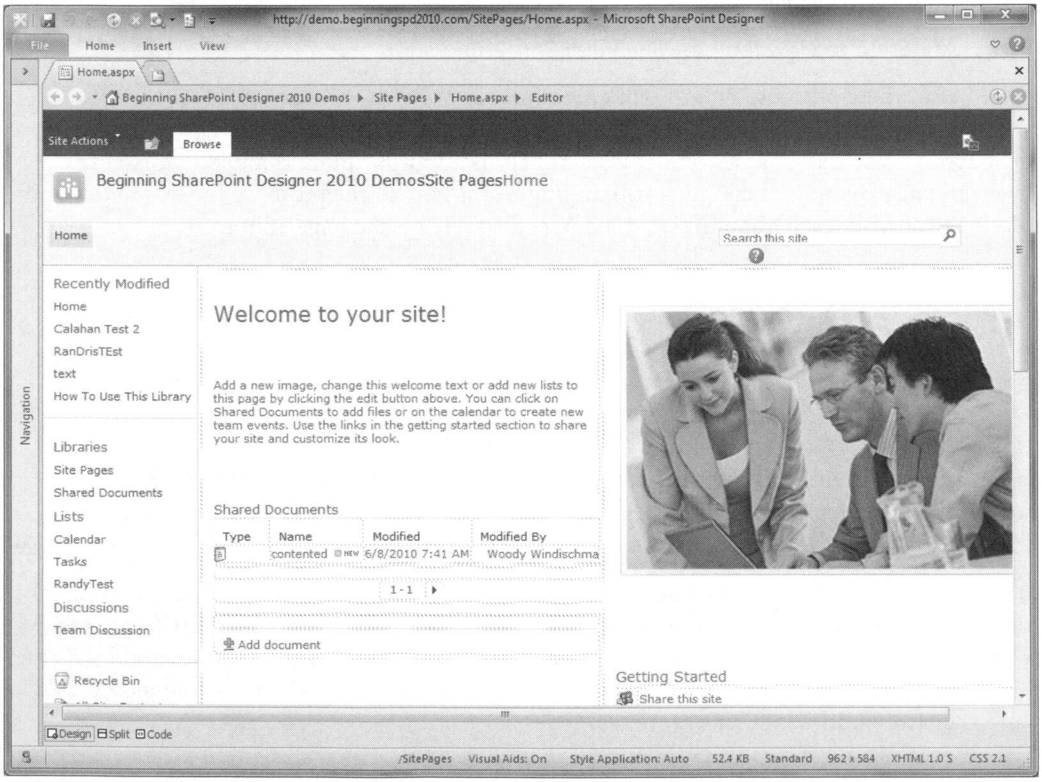

FIGURE 2-1

You can minimize the ribbon by double-clicking the active tab. You can display a tab when needed by clicking on its name. It overlays the design surface menu-style until you click an element, and then re-hides. You can restore the ribbon to normal operation by double-clicking any tab title. Task panes and their positioning are discussed later in this chapter.

In addition to the design surface itself, the Page Editor has the following elements (see Figure 2-2):

➤ **Tab bar** — Across the top of the Page Editor is a tab bar, which gives access to each file or summary view that is currently open in SharePoint Designer. Files that have been modified since being opened or last saved are indicated with an asterisk (*).

➤ **Page Mode toolbar** — Below the design surface and to the left is the Page Mode toolbar. This selects which of the three editing modes to display.

➤ **Quick Tag Selector** — To the right of the Page Mode toolbar is the Quick Tag Selector. Although, on the surface, it appears to be a simple HTML breadcrumb, displaying the hierarchy of tags nesting down to the currently selected element, it is much more than that. Clicking a tag in the Selector immediately selects that element in the current view (hence the name). In addition, each tag in the Selector provides a context menu (as shown in Figure 2-2), allowing you quickly to adjust the parameters of the tag, create a containing tag, or even to remove the tag without removing any child controls.

➤ **Status bar** — The status bar tells you all about your page design experience, but like the Quick Tag Selector, the status bar is also your active partner in the editing process. In addition to being context-sensitive (the set of elements displayed on the status bar is dependent upon the current selection), many status segments also provide the option to edit the setting they are reporting.

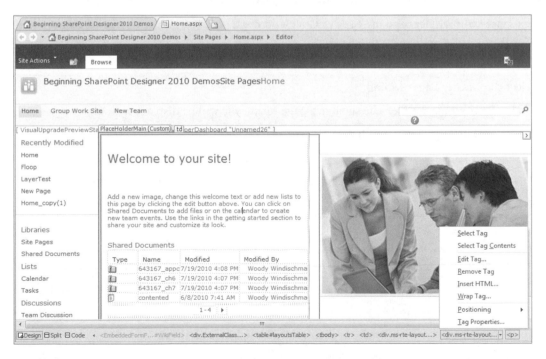

FIGURE 2-2

Design View

The Design view offers a what-you-see-is-what-you-get (WYSIWYG) editing experience. It supports many traditional GUI document-editing functions:

➤ Fonts, styles, and item placements correspond very closely to the final page rendering.

➤ You can copy, cut, and paste, both within SharePoint Designer and between SharePoint Designer and other applications.

➤ You can drag elements from one place and drop them elsewhere.

> **NOTE** *This book assumes you already know these and other basics of using Microsoft Windows to edit documents. Unless otherwise specified, all "normal" Windows functions apply within SharePoint Designer, and will not be separately described.*

Design view also supports the use of the ruler and grid options (with and without snap-to) typically found in graphics and page layout programs. In addition, a wide array of specialty tools is provided to improve your design experience. Some of them, such as Visual Aids and Table Tools, are described in this chapter, whereas others are covered later in the book.

The following sections discuss some of the features of the Design view.

TRY IT OUT **Skewer Click and Quick Tag Editor**

In this exercise, you will learn to use Skewer Click and the Quick Tag Editor — two features that make working with complex web pages much easier.

1. Open a site in SharePoint Designer.

2. Select the Master Pages section.

3. Click on the v4.master file. The summary page for the file will be displayed.

4. Click Edit File (either in the ribbon or the summary page).

> **NOTE** *You will not be saving any changes in this exercise, so if prompted to check out the page, do not do so.*

5. Click Design in the View Selector toolbar. (It may already be selected by default in your environment.)

6. Click the Home ribbon tab icon labeled Skewer Click.

7. Click the title of your site.

8. Hover your mouse pointer briefly over several of the objects on the list.

9. Observe that as you hover over each list item, the relevant object in the page is highlighted.

10. Find the item that begins "asp:ContentPlace" and click it.

11. Click the ribbon icon labeled Quick Tag Editor.

12. Observe that the contents of the pop-up editor consist only of information for the selected tag.

13. Close the pop-up editor with the red X (cancel) icon in the upper-right corner.

How It Works

All web pages are made up of a series of nested and overlapped objects. SharePoint pages are more complicated than most in this regard, which can make it difficult to ensure that you are changing the correct object.

The Skewer Click function simplifies page editing by letting you select from a menu of all the objects that may be relevant at a particular page position. After you select the object you want to edit, the Quick Tag Editor allows you to make your changes without the distraction of the entire page's contents in the window. Most of the features of Code view (described later in this chapter) are functional in the Quick Tag Editor window.

Visual Aids and Page Sizes

To assist you with your page designs, SharePoint Designer provides a number of visual aids. Visual aids provide a way for you to see and access page elements that may not normally be visible, such as ActiveX controls, content placeholders, or items with a hidden attribute. Figure 2-3 shows a page with all visual aids enabled.

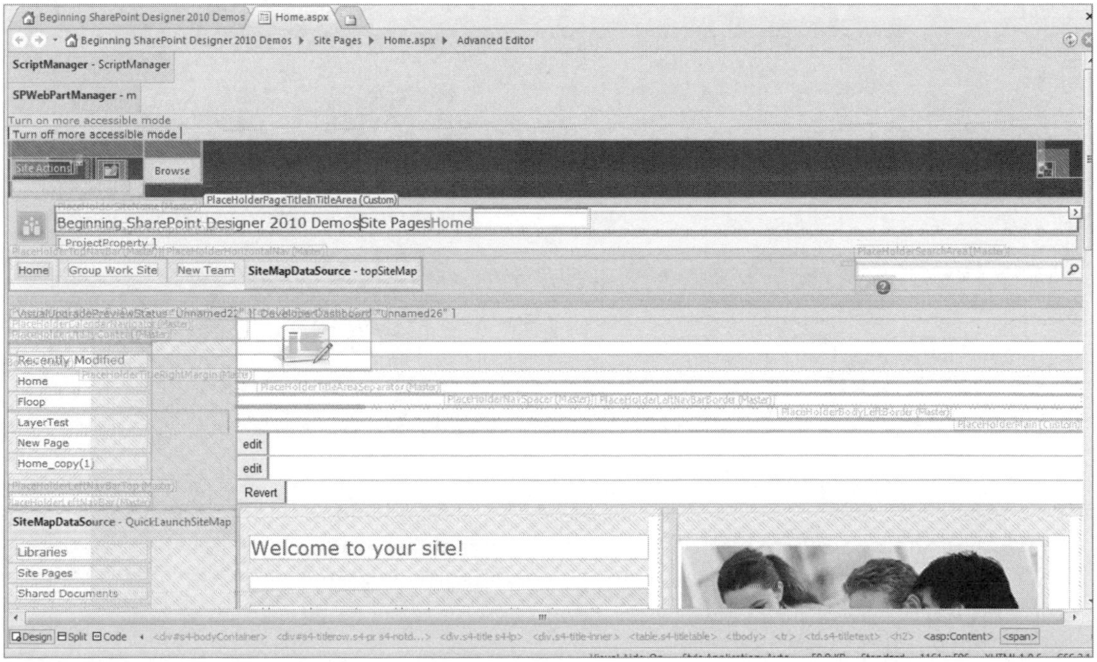

FIGURE 2-3

To keep your workspace uncluttered, you can enable or disable specific types of visual aids, either by using the drop-down menu on the Visual Aids icon in the View tab (see Figure 2-4) or by clicking the Visual Aids segment in the status bar. You can turn all enabled visual aids off or on at once by clicking the ribbon icon directly or by clicking the Show link at the top of the menu.

Visual aids only appear in the Design and Split views, although the setting displays in the status bar and is configurable in Code view.

Although visual aids can make the design of a page much easier, they also can significantly affect the layout as seen in Design view. Turn off visual aids occasionally to verify precise positioning. Figure 2-5 shows the same page shown in Figure 2-3, with the visual aids turned off.

FIGURE 2-4

You can further improve the accuracy of your layout experience by setting the Design view to a specific set of dimensions. In the status bar, you can see the current dimensions of the window that the Design view represents. Click the dimensions entry to see the menu shown in Figure 2-6, which allows you to choose from several page sizes.

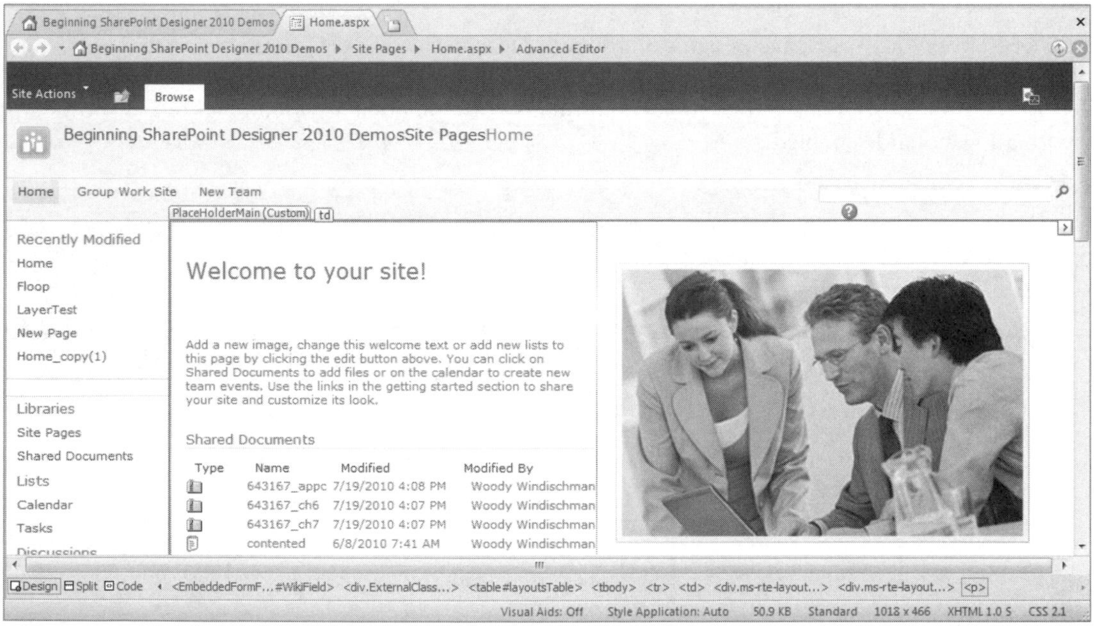

FIGURE 2-5

If the selected dimensions are smaller than the current design window, the width of the working area is reduced to the horizontal dimension selected. If the selected dimensions are larger than the current design window, the workspace is expanded horizontally, and the scroll bar at the bottom of the window is activated.

Several common page sizes are provided by default. You can add your own dimensions.

FIGURE 2-6

When you select a fixed page size, the dimension status shows a hash symbol. The Page Size menu is also available under the View menu.

> **NOTE** *Even though fixing sizes and turning off visual aids give you a more accurate view of your page, they can't compensate for differences in rendering between browsers. Remember to use the Preview in Browser function periodically (discussed in Chapter 1) to give your pages a "real" test.*

Safe and Advanced Editing Modes

As noted earlier, SharePoint pages are very complicated beasts. As such, accidentally changing "the wrong thing" and rendering a page unusable is possible. Visual aids and Skewer Click are two ways SharePoint Designer 2010 helps you select the right thing. SharePoint Designer can also help prevent selecting the wrong thing by offering two different modes for editing pages — *Safe mode* and *Advanced mode*.

Safe Mode

SharePoint opens most *site pages* (non-publishing web part pages, list and library form pages, and Wiki pages) and *layout pages* in safe mode by default. In this mode, many page elements are considered "off limits" for editing. The number of editing tools available is also reduced. For example, the main Layout and Style ribbon tabs are not shown in Safe mode. The Table Layout contextual tab is available, however.

The only things you can change in Safe mode are the contents of Wiki fields and web part zones — essentially the same elements that can be edited through the Web. You do, however, have much finer control over the contents of those areas in SharePoint Designer.

When editing in Safe mode, the mouse pointer turns into a null symbol when you move it over areas you are not permitted to change. In Code view, uneditable areas appear with highlighting, as shown in Figure 2-7.

Advanced Mode

Advanced mode brings the full power of SharePoint Designer's editing tools to bear. For example, in a site page, you are no longer limited to modifying the contents of a content zone. In particular, you can now override the contents of many of the default components (the `<asp:ContentPlaceholder>` tags) specified in your master page.

> **WARNING** *Overriding master page elements for specific pages via SharePoint Designer can result in significant inconsistencies in the look or operation of your site. This is why these operations are not considered "safe."*

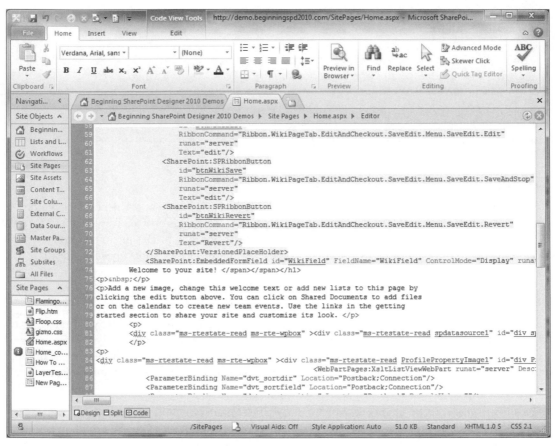

FIGURE 2-7

Master pages themselves are a special case. SharePoint Designer always opens master pages in Advanced mode because you use them to actually define the look and feel of your site. By definition, you need the functions available in Advanced mode to control the layout and style of these pages. See Chapter 3 for details about creating master pages and including content placeholders.

Code View

Although the SharePoint Designer Design view provides an easy and powerful way to create, lay out, and edit the pages of your site, at the end of the day, these pages remain what they have always been — plaintext HTML and script. Fortunately, SharePoint Designer is just as adept at helping you work with code as it is with page design. Figure 2-8 shows the same page you have seen in the prior shots in SharePoint Designer's Code view.

Although it may be difficult to see on a book page, Code view uses color coding to help you recognize tags, delimiters, parameters, inline text, comments, and many other code elements. In fact, Code view offers all the assistance typical of any modern development environment, and then some, as discussed in the following sections.

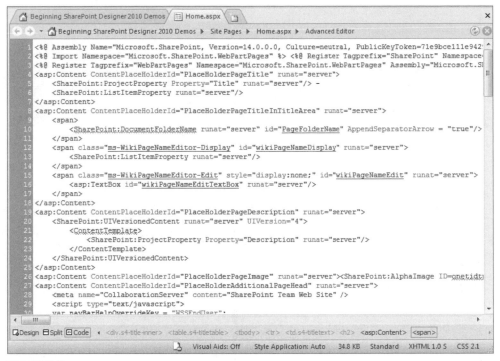

FIGURE 2-8

IntelliSense

IntelliSense has been a part of Microsoft development tools for more than a decade. Usually manifesting as a pop-up, it detects what you are typing and offers suggestions for completing your task. Though originally limited to program code, in SharePoint Designer Code view, IntelliSense has been expanded far beyond that. It now includes such features as:

➤ Automatic tag and brace closure

➤ Parameter selection (as shown in Figure 2-9)

➤ CSS statement completion

➤ Automatic code hyperlinks

➤ Programming code completion

Not everyone wants or needs this level of automatic assistance. You can therefore enable or disable IntelliSense for each of the available elements. The IntelliSense tab (see Figure 2-10) of the Page Editor Options dialog provides a complete list of IntelliSense settings available.

IntelliSense in Code view further helps you by being sensitive to your settings for browsers, HTML, and CSS version. For example, the primary IntelliSense options shown in Figure 2-10 are the Authoring options that are available in a tab on the Page Editor Options dialog. You can access this dialog either by clicking one of the authoring mode indicators on the right side of the status bar (Standard, XHTML 1.0 S, and CSS 2.1 are the indicators, shown earlier in Figure 2-8), or by selecting File ➪ Options and clicking the Page Editor Options button.

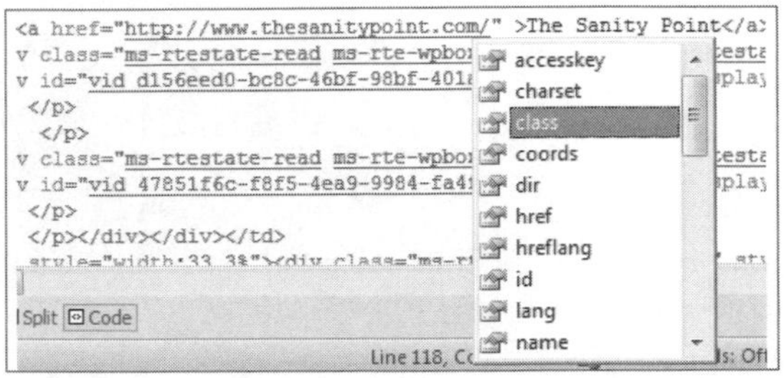

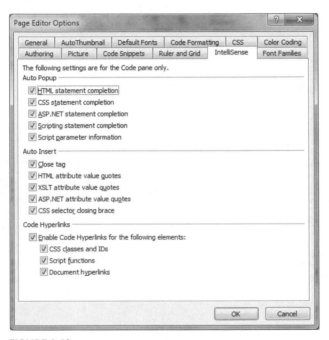

FIGURE 2-9

FIGURE 2-10

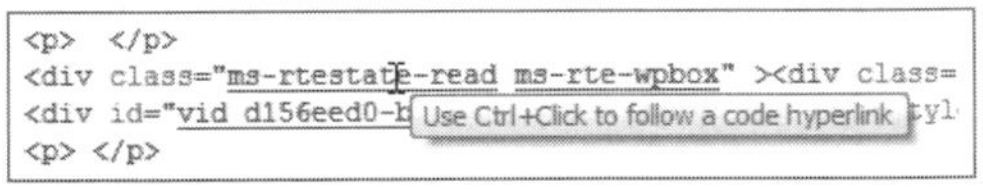

Notice that the bottom section of the IntelliSense tab shows options for Code Hyperlinks. These are not hyperlinks you create for your users. Rather, they are links created by SharePoint Designer to help you navigate within your code. When you hover over such a link, SharePoint Designer displays the tooltip shown in Figure 2-11, indicating that you can press the Ctrl key when you click in to open the target.

```
<p> </p>
<div class="ms-rtestate-read ms-rte-wpbox" ><div class=
<div id="vid d156eed0-b [ Use Ctrl+Click to follow a code hyperlink ] yl
<p> </p>
```

FIGURE 2-11

Code Snippets

Another handy shortcut offered by Code view is *code snippets*. SharePoint Designer includes pre-defined snippets for such things as HTML document types, script blocks, and style sheet links. You can insert a snippet by pressing Ctrl+Enter and typing the snippet name/keyword, or by selecting the one you want from a list just like an IntelliSense parameter.

TRY IT OUT   Watch IntelliSense in Action as You Create a Code Snippet

1. Open a site in SharePoint Designer.

2. Click the All Files section in the Site Objects list. Observe that the ribbon changes to the All Files tab.

3. In the New section of the All Files tab, click File, and select HTML.

4. Name the new file **Snippet.html**.

5. Click the filename to open the file.

6. Click Code in the Page Mode toolbar.

7. Click between the `<body>` and `</body>` tags.

8. Begin to type the following line of code:

```
<div class="|"><div>
```

While typing, observe the operation of IntelliSense as it offers to complete the tag for you.

9. As soon as the class parameter is highlighted by IntelliSense, press the Tab key. Observe that the cursor is placed between the "quotes." Also observe that SharePoint Designer creates red squiggled underlines to indicate that the code following the inserted text doesn't (yet) match the expected syntax for HTML.

10. Type the vertical bar/pipe symbol (|).

11. Use your right-arrow key to move the cursor outside of the quotes, and type the **>** character. Notice that IntelliSense automatically adds the closing `</div>` tag and SharePoint Designer now recognizes the remaining page syntax as correct.

12. Copy the typed text to the Clipboard.

13. Press Ctrl+Enter. Select the first item on the pop-up list (Customize List), which opens the Code Snippets tab (see Figure 2-12) of the Page Editor Options dialog.

14. Click Add to summon the Add Code Snippet dialog (see Figure 2-13).

15. Type **DIV** into the Keyword field.

16. Type **A fully built DIV tag** into the Description field.

17. Paste your code into the Text box. (Alternatively, you can manually enter any desired text, but using copy and paste from a known-good source is more reliable.)

18. Click OK to save and close each currently open dialog.

19. Place your cursor on a blank line.

20. Press Ctrl+Enter. Notice that the snippet you created is now available on the list.

21. Select the DIV snippet and hit enter.

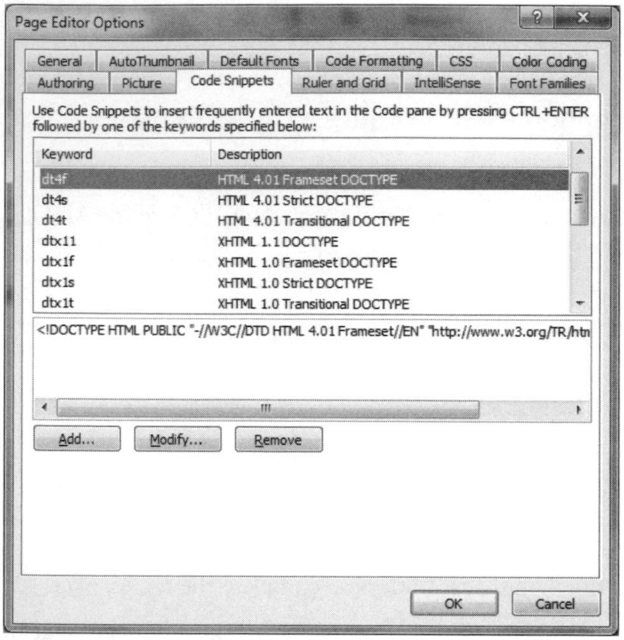

FIGURE 2-12

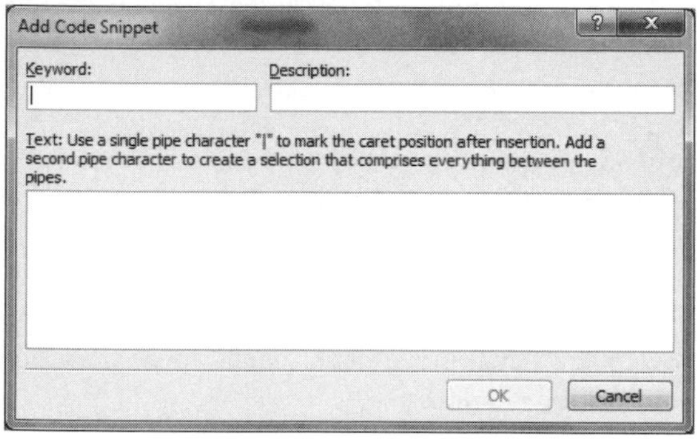

FIGURE 2-13

How It Works

If you find yourself frequently typing the same thing, maybe with minor variations, you can define your own code snippets to help you. You can define a text entry point with a pipe symbol, as shown in the exercise. If you surround some text with two pipe symbols, you define a range to be selected upon insertion of the snippet.

In addition to using the copy/paste/Ctrl+Enter method to create a snippet described in the exercise, you can directly add and edit snippets through the Code Snippets tab of the Page Editor Options dialog.

Visual Coding

In the past, you might have gone back and forth between an application's Design and Code views, depending on what you needed to change. For example, after editing a piece of script in Code view, you would return to Design view to set some text formatting. Otherwise, you would need to enter or edit the formatting tags in code manually. In SharePoint Designer, that kind of toggling is much less necessary. SharePoint Designer allows you to use many of the same techniques for formatting text in Code view as in Design view.

Figure 2-14 shows that formatting options (bold, italic, and underline) are available while you are editing in Code view. In fact, they are fully active and interactive with your HTML.

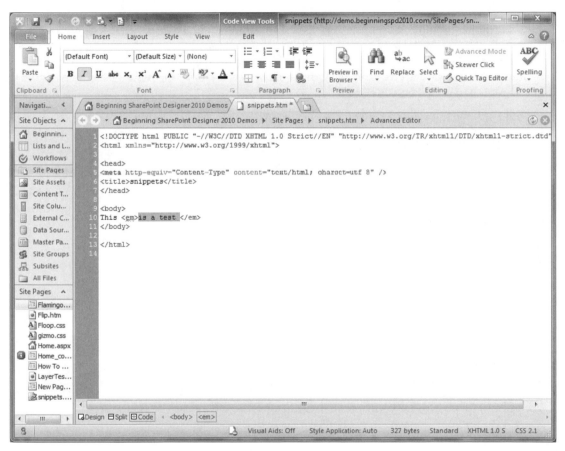

FIGURE 2-14

Just as in Design view, selecting a formatting command from the toolbar applies that format to (or removes it from) your selection. Unlike Design view, Code view does not show you the item in its formatted state. Instead, you see the HTML tags that are applied to make that format happen.

In addition, the state of the toolbar icons follows the current HTML. In Figure 2-14, the highlighted text is inside an <em> (emphasis) tag, which is rendered in *italic* on a web page. Also, notice that the Quick Tag Selector for the emphasis tag is active.

The same holds true when adding elements to a page. You can easily drag an item from the Toolbox task pane into the Code view editing window. SharePoint Designer automatically creates and inserts the appropriate HTML, just as if you had dropped the item into position in Design view.

> **WARNING** *One quirk of SharePoint Designer is that immediately after you insert a snippet, some formatting options (for example, text alignment) are disabled. You must switch to Design view or Split view (see the following section) and then back to Code view to restore full visual coding functionality.*

Split View

The Split view of the Page Editor provides all the advantages of both Design and Code view. Each half of the view behaves exactly like its dedicated view. Code view, for example, gives you IntelliSense, whereas Design view maintains rulers and any page sizes you have set. In Figure 2-15, a table row has been selected from the Quick Tag Selector. Notice the highlighting in both the Code and Design panes of the Split view.

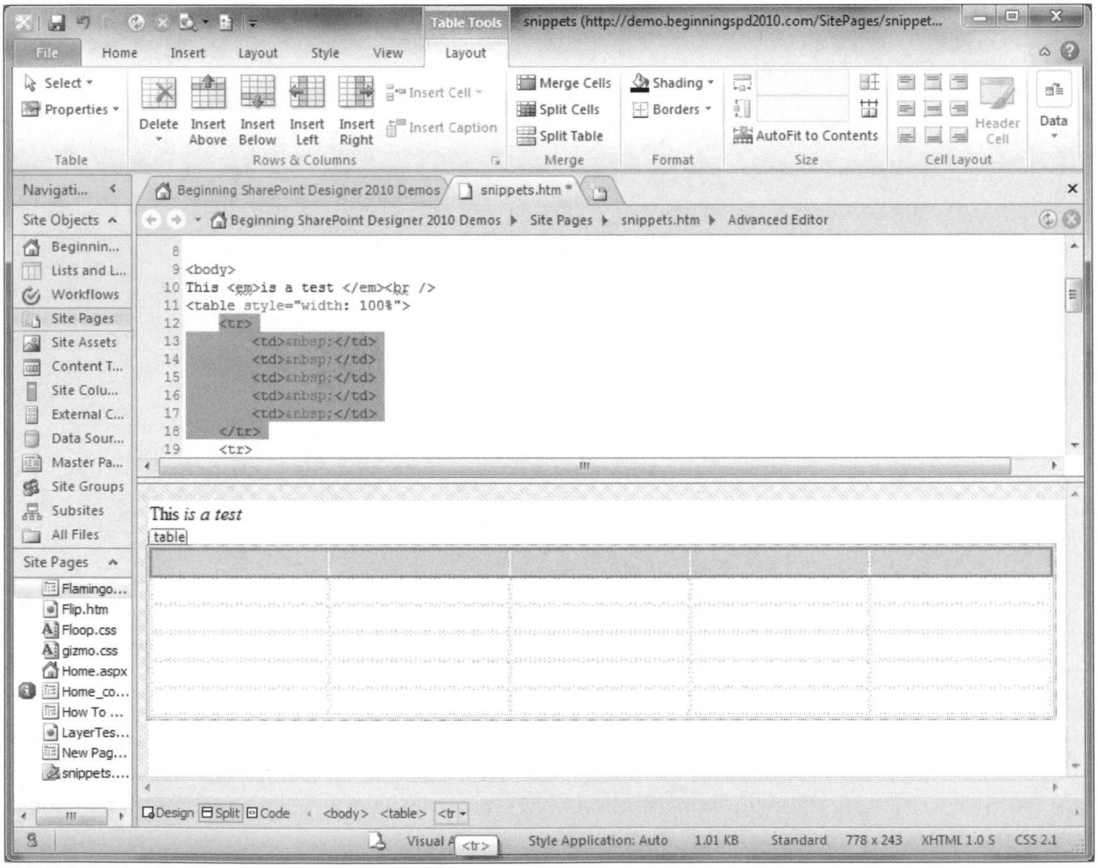

FIGURE 2-15

As you make changes in the Design pane, you can immediately see the effect on your code. The reverse is not true. Changes you make as you are editing code are not visible in the Design pane right away. You must act to indicate to SharePoint Designer that you are done with your edits, such as by clicking in the Design pane or saving your file, before the edits are reflected. This is because while you are editing in the Code pane, much of the time your markup may be in a transitional state that does not have a valid rendering. By waiting until you explicitly select the Design view, SharePoint Designer helps avoid the confusion that can result from page elements jumping all over the place as the rendering engine tries to make sense of the invalid markup.

> **NOTE** Any styles you select are applied following the rules defined in the CSS tab of the Page Editor Options dialog, regardless of whether you use Design, Code, or Split view. See Chapter 6 for more information about using CSS styles in SharePoint Designer.

USING TASK PANES AND RIBBON TABS TO GET WORK DONE

SharePoint Designer is a versatile, powerful application. Helping you control that power and versatility is the province of the ribbon tabs and task panes. Each ribbon tab and task pane controls a related set of functions. The following sections briefly discuss the common ribbon tabs and task panes, and how to manage them.

Managing Task Panes

SharePoint Designer 2010 offers 17 task panes. With that many possible control elements in the application, showing them all at once is totally impractical. Assuming they fit at all, you would have no room left on the screen for the Page Editor to perform any work. Fortunately, SharePoint Designer provides a great deal of flexibility in their display.

Task panes can be individually shown, hidden, docked, or floating. The possible docking positions are the four edges of the SharePoint Designer window — above, below, right, and left of the design surface (which is always visible). You can move a visible task pane to any of these positions by dragging its title. Floated task panes may be within or outside of the SharePoint Designer application workspace. Figure 2-16 shows task panes in many of their possible visible states and positions.

You can place multiple task panes along the same edge by either "stacking" them, "paging" them, or both. Stacked task panes are arrayed along the docked edge. Paged task panes all occupy the same space, and are selectable via tabs in that space's title area, as shown by the Toolbox and Data Source Details task panes in Figure 2-16. If there is not enough room to display all the tabs, scroll icons will appear in the title area of the pane.

You can float task panes by dragging the pane's group either into the design surface, or completely off of the SharePoint Designer application window. You may also right-click the title bar and choose Float. When you first float docked, paged task panes, the entire block of pane pages will float as a unit. You can then float an individual pane.

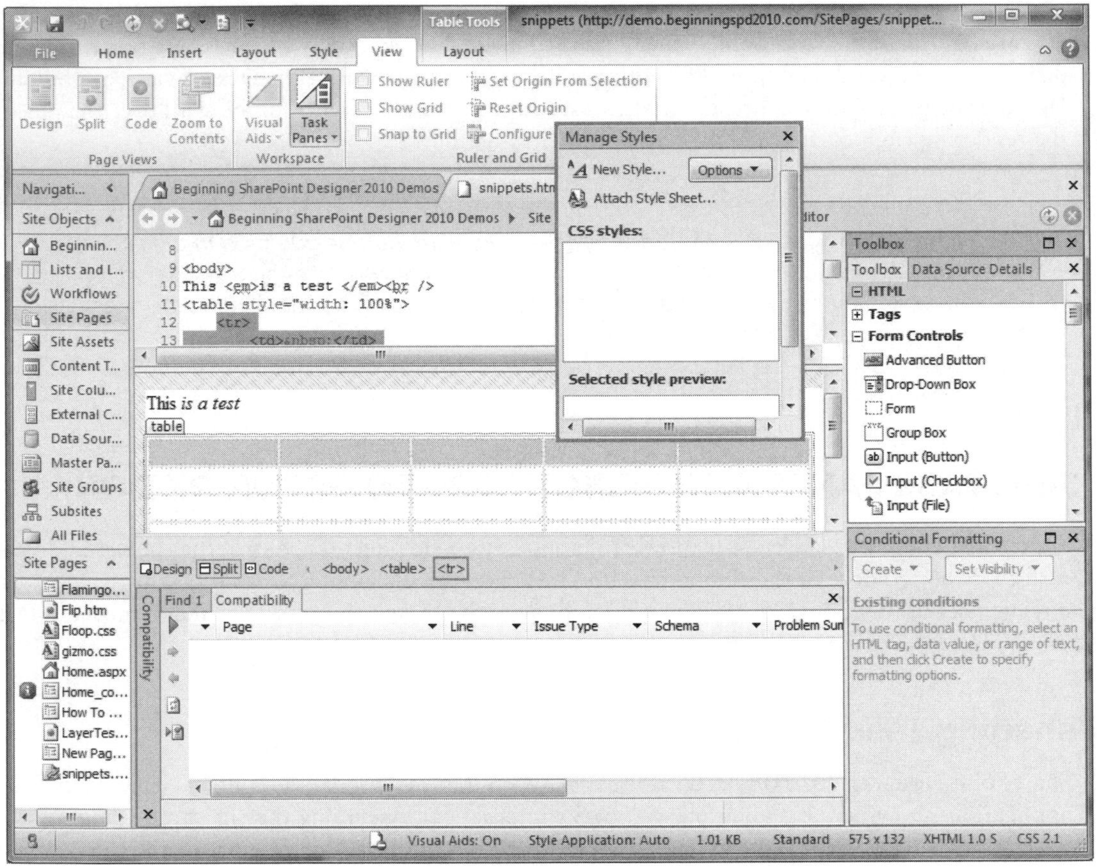

FIGURE 2-16

You can resize a task pane by dragging its edge. If the pane is docked, the combination of panes at the docked edge will always take up the entire side of the window; however, you can adjust the proportions of two stacked task panes by dragging their shared edge. You can maximize a task pane to take up its entire docking zone, and restore it to its former size. You can show and hide individual task panes by selecting them from the Task Panes icon menu of the View ribbon tab. You can also hide a currently shown task pane by clicking the X icon in its title bar or right-clicking its tab and selecting Close.

> **NOTE** *Some task panes are displayed automatically when you access features or functions that depend on them. However, any task pane may be displayed at will by selecting it from the Task Panes icon menu of the View ribbon tab.*

After showing, hiding, and moving task panes around extensively, you may have a difficult time locating a particular item. SharePoint Designer offers a quick way to reset the task panes to a known state. If you select Reset Workspace Layout from the Task Panes icon menu of the View ribbon tab, the task panes are hidden, and when redisplayed, will appear in their default positions.

Task Pane Function Overview

Although many task panes are in SharePoint Designer, they fall into a few functional categories. When you reset the workspace layout, each of the groups is set to appear in a separate block; the panes within each group are set to appear paged within that block. The following sections describe each category and list the task panes therein, along with (at least) a brief description of each. The detailed functions contained within the panes themselves are described where appropriate throughout this book.

Properties Panes

The Tag and CSS Properties panes show a grid of their respective type of properties and allow you to edit them. Properties that are changed from their default values are shown in bold font. The properties available vary depending upon the particular object currently selected on the design surface. Figure 2-17 shows the Tag Properties and CSS Properties panes.

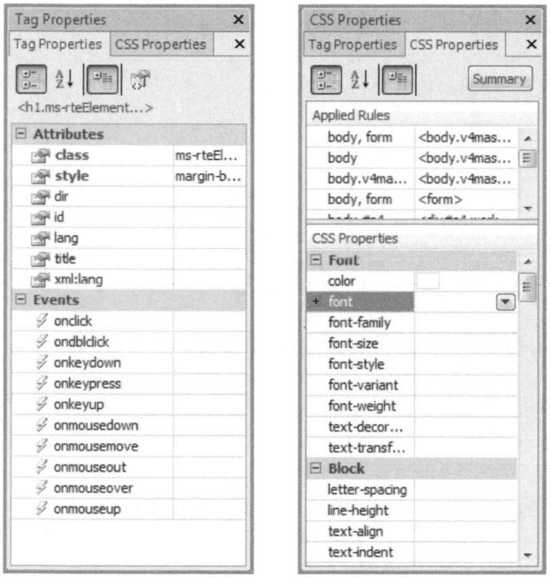

FIGURE 2-17

CSS properties may come from a number of different sources. The CSS Properties pane therefore lists the sources that contribute to the current object.

CSS Management Panes

Four task panes deal with the management of styles on your page. They are the Manage Styles, Apply Styles, Behaviors, and Layers task panes. Unlike the CSS Properties task pane, which modifies the specific properties of a single object, the task panes in this group deal with items that can apply to multiple objects.

Figure 2-18 shows the Manage Styles and Apply Styles task panes.

FIGURE 2-18

The Manage Styles task pane helps you manage the classes (style attribute groupings) that you can apply to various objects. The Apply Styles task pane enables you to apply specific style classes to the currently selected object.

The Behaviors task pane enables you to assign one or more *behaviors* to the currently selected object. Behaviors are small script or CSS attribute segments that perform specific actions when certain events take place, such as rolling the mouse pointer over the object.

> **NOTE** *CSS behaviors were originally tied to Internet Explorer and implemented through a special "behavior" tag. That method was never adopted as an official standard by the W3C. The behaviors generated by this task pane, therefore, are browser-independent and implemented through standard CSS and JavaScript calls.*

The Layers task pane manages `<div>` tags in your page, but not just any `<div>` tags. To be considered a layer in this task pane, the `<div>` must have a defined position type other than "none." Such layers are frequently used to lay out content and placeholders for content (see Chapter 3 for more details on placeholders).

TRY IT OUT   Create a Hierarchy of Layers (tags), and Compare the Layers Task Pane to the Layout Ribbon Tab

1. Open a site in SharePoint Designer.

2. On the File tab, select the Add Item page, then More Pages to advance to the next page (there are two "pages" of page items to choose from!).

3. Click the HTML icon button.

4. Click the Create button. The New HTML Page dialog opens.

5. Type **LayerTest** into the field provided. Leave the location to save to unchanged. (This is typically the SitePages library.)

6. Click the OK button. The page opens in Advanced mode because no SharePoint functions exist to protect on a plain HTML page.

7. Click the View ribbon tab.

8. Click the Design icon.

9. Select Reset Workspace Layout from the Task Panes icon menu.

10. Ensure that Visual Aids is on and that the Visible Borders aid is active. This will allow you to see the layers you are about to create.

11. Click the Layout ribbon tab, shown in Figure 2-19.

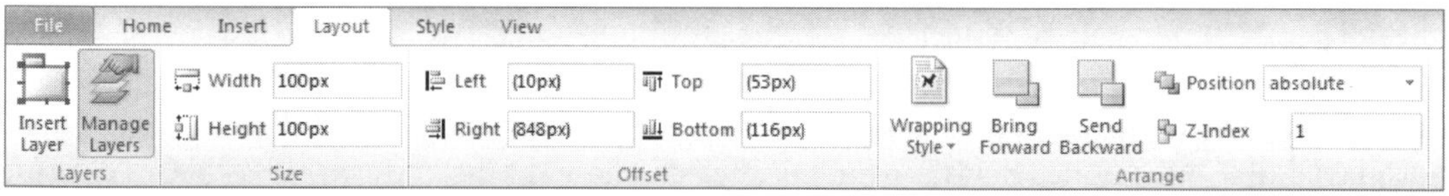

FIGURE 2-19

12. Click the Manage Layers icon. The Layers task pane appears. Observe that the pane is currently empty. Also notice that an Insert Layer icon is present in both the Layout ribbon tab and Layers task pane.

13. Click either Insert Layer button five times. This results in a display similar to that shown in Figure 2-20.

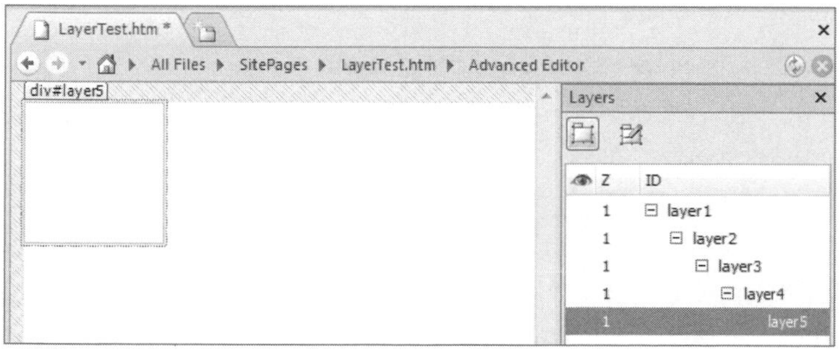

FIGURE 2-20

Observe that although the Layers task pane shows five layers, you can only see one box outline.

14. Using the Page Mode toolbar, switch to Code view briefly to observe in the HTML that, indeed, five nested `<div>` tags are present, then return to Design view.
Observe that the Quick Tag Selector also indicates the hierarchy of `<div>` tags.

15. In the Layers task pane, double-click "layer1." Observe that you can now edit the name.

16. Type **pageheading** and press Enter.

17. In the Layout ribbon tab, select relative from the Position selector, and Left from the Wrapping Style selector.

18. Using the technique described in Steps 15 through 17, rename and reposition the remaining layers as shown in the following table.

OLD LAYER NAME	NEW LAYER NAME
layer2	**body**
layer3	**menu**
layer4	**leftnav**
layer5	**maincontent**

19. In the Layers task pane, drag the body layer below all the other layers listed. (Release the mouse button when the cursor changes to an arrow with a shadow box beneath it.)
Observe that two separate layers are now visible on the design surface, and that the body layer is displayed first. Also notice that the listing of the "children" of the body layer has been "collapsed."

20. Click the + icon to re-expand the children of the body layer.

21. Drag the maincontent layer onto the body layer. The body layer becomes highlighted and the cursor changes to a shadow box with a + when the mouse is in the correct position.

22. Drag the leftnav layer into the body layer, above the maincontent layer. A fine line appears between the body layer and maincontent layer when the cursor is in the correct position.

23. Drag the menu layer into the pageheading layer.

24. Switch to Code view. Observe the changes that have taken place in the code.

25. Click the pageheading layer in the Layers task pane. Observe that the entire pageheading `<div>` and its contents are selected in the design surface.

26. In the design surface, drag the selected text and drop it above the first shown `<div>` tag (the "body" layer).

27. Switch to Split view. Your screen should resemble that shown in Figure 2-21. Observe that only now is the visible position of the body layer shown after the pageheading layer.

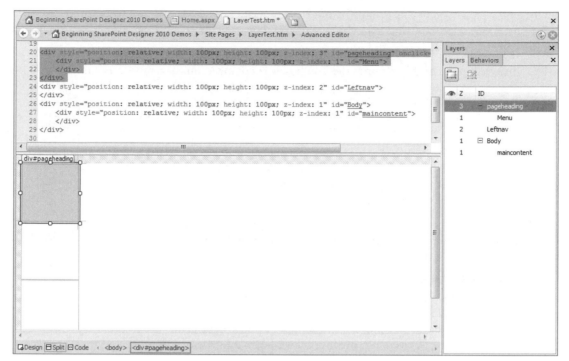

FIGURE 2-21

How It Works

The Layout ribbon tab and the Layers task pane both control `<div>` tags that you can use to help you lay out a page, but each works with a different aspect. The Layout tab provides direct access to key attributes of an individual tag, whereas the Layers task pane is used mainly to configure the relationships between layers. Most of the functions provided by the Layout tab are also available through the Layers task pane by right-clicking the layer.

Why, you might ask, is the Layers task pane in the CSS Management group? The key lies in some of the names you gave the layers in the exercise. `Div`-based layers, along with CSS styles, form the foundation of modern website visual design. The default layers you inserted in this exercise have certain attributes *hard-coded* (declared inline, directly on the tag, shown in the Layout tab). Chapter 6 covers how you can use *Cascading Style Sheets* (CSS) instead of hard-coded values to provide central management of these attributes, and how SharePoint Designer can help you manage these styles. This can help you implement a more consistent look and feel to your sites.

Internal Insertable Elements Panes

The "internal" insertable elements are those items that are sourced from within the SharePoint Designer application. From a content perspective, these may still represent items that come from an external source (such as a database or web service). However, SharePoint Designer is the primary control mechanism for the objects themselves.

Three task panes are in this group. Two of them — Data Source Details and Conditional Formatting — relate to using data view web parts. Both task panes and their functions are described in more detail in Chapters 7 and 8.

The third task pane in this group is the Toolbox — a compendium of almost every individual element that can be added to a page. The primary exceptions to this are tables and SharePoint "web parts," which you add through the Insert ribbon tab (described later in this chapter).

The Toolbox task pane is organized into three collapsible sections, as shown in Figure 2-22.

Each section represents a different class of objects that can be added to a page and is further broken down into related groups of individual controls. The sections are as follows:

➤ **HTML Controls,** including client-side form elements. HTML controls are passive — they do not directly control functionality on the server.

➤ **ASP.NET Controls,** which are client-side representations of server-side functionality. This may include database access or access to other components that reside on the server without "direct" access from the Web. Many of these controls resemble those in the HTML block, but maintain an active connection to the server.

➤ **SharePoint Controls,** which are also ASP.NET controls, so they access server-side functionality. However, these are specific to accessing SharePoint functions, such as list fields or user profile information from SharePoint Server.

FIGURE 2-22

The tools in the Toolbox task pane can be displayed in three different modes:

➤ Icons Only

➤ Icons and Names

➤ Names Only

You choose one of these modes by right-clicking the Title tab and selecting the desired mode from the context menu. You can also choose to expand or collapse all the Toolbox control groups from this menu. Figure 2-23 shows the same section of tools in each of the three views.

You can add a control to your page from the Toolbox in several ways:

➤ Drag and drop

➤ Double-click

➤ Right-click

When you use the drag-and-drop method, you can drop the control in any valid place in your open document. Double-clicking a control in the Toolbox inserts the control at the current document text cursor position.

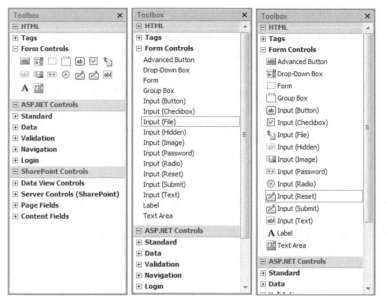

FIGURE 2-23

Right-clicking a control in the Toolbox displays two choices. The Insert option inserts the control at the current text cursor, just as double-clicking would. Certain controls, however, such as `<div>` or `<span>` tags, also activate the Wrap option. If you have a block of text highlighted when choosing this option, an opening tag will be inserted at the beginning of the block, and the corresponding closing tag will be inserted after the block.

> **NOTE** *Not every control can be added in every context. When you attempt to drag a control into an invalid region, or in the wrong page mode, the mouse pointer will appear as a "null" symbol. Certain SharePoint controls are only listed if you are on appropriate page types (for example, publishing "layout pages" — see Chapter 5).*

Reporting Panes

The task panes in the reporting group share a few unique characteristics (besides "reporting," that is). For example, they are the only task panes whose default position is docked to the bottom of the window. In addition, they are not limited in scope to a single document.

Each reporting pane has a toolbar along its left edge. Figure 2-24 shows the toolbar from the Accessibility task pane, which contains tools found across many of the reporting task panes. See the callouts for descriptions of the shared icons. Icons specific to a particular report type are described later in its respective section.

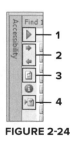

FIGURE 2-24

The icons shown in the figure are as follow:

1. **Execute the report** — Clicking this icon typically summons a dialog where you can select the desired scope and other options appropriate to the report type. This icon does not appear on the Hyperlinks report task pane.

2. **Next and previous result** — This icon advances your cursor to the next or previous result in the list. If the page containing that result is open, the text cursor advances to its position. If it is not, the corresponding page opens automatically. You may also open the page containing any given result by double-clicking the result line.

3. **Refresh the results** — Re-runs the report with the same options as the previous execution, updating the result set as needed.

4. **Generate HTML report** — This produces a web page containing the detailed results of the report. You may find this to be an easier-to-read presentation than the small task pane view. It also serves as a convenient checklist for addressing any issues discovered.

The Find 1 and Find 2 task panes are identical in function. As you might expect, they allow you to find or replace text. By having two of them, however, you can perform two independent searches and have them available to re-execute at your leisure.

When you click the Execute icon in a Find task pane, or press Ctrl+F, you summon the Find and Replace dialog, shown in Figure 2-25.

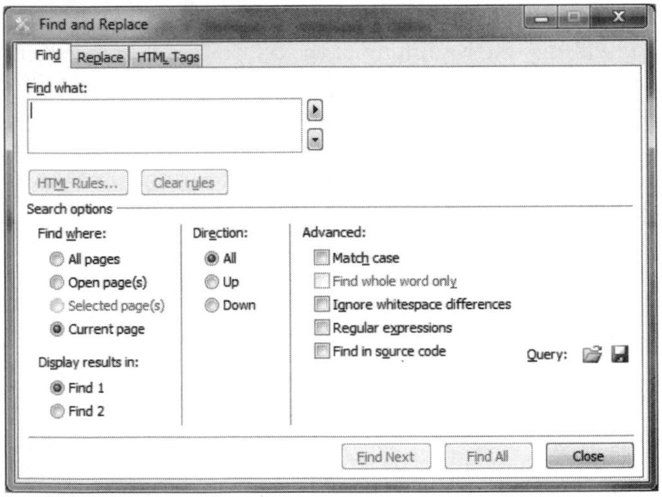

FIGURE 2-25

Notice that in the lower-left corner of this dialog, you can select which of the Find task panes will receive your results. The Find and Replace tabs of this dialog are very similar, except that in Replace, you have an extra block for the replacement text, as well as buttons to invoke the actual replacement.

Because of the complex nature of page code, you can perform searches based on more than just static text. In the Find and Replace panes, you can enter *regular expressions* for the search text. Figure 2-26 shows the list of regular expression elements available.

Finally, you can find and replace individual HTML elements without needing to define them with regular expression syntax using the HTML tab of the Find dialog, shown in Figure 2-27.

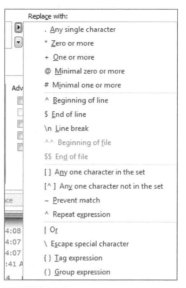

FIGURE 2-26

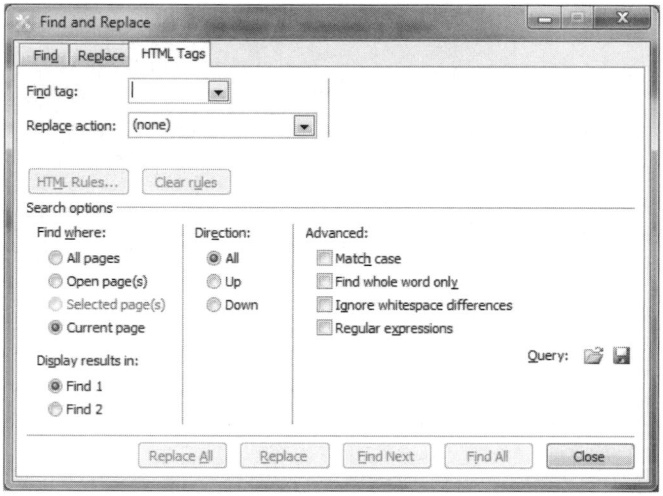

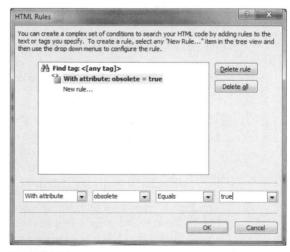

FIGURE 2-27

One of the most powerful elements of HTML Find is the HTML Rules builder. This allows you to select tags based on attributes, value strings, or virtually any other aspect of a tag. Figure 2-28 shows the HTML Rules builder with a simple attribute rule defined.

The Accessibility task pane report examines your file(s) for compliance with various standards. It then reports on design issues that may cause problems for people with limited vision. Figure 2-29 shows the options and standards you can include when running the Accessibility report.

FIGURE 2-28

The Accessibility report includes one icon not described at the beginning of this section. The circle containing the letter *i* will display a pop-up containing the details of the currently highlighted result item.

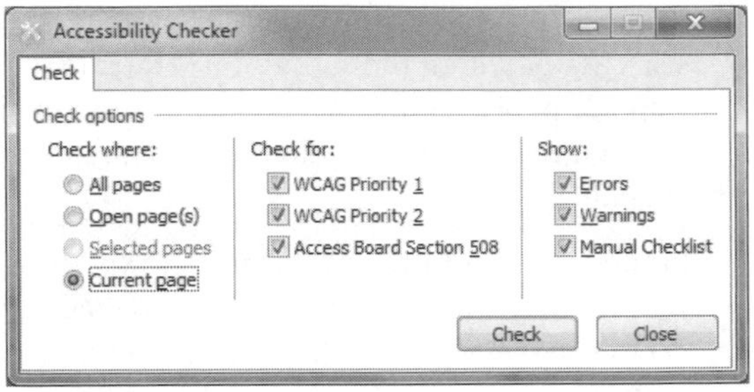

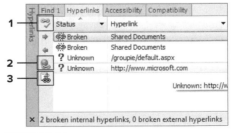

FIGURE 2-29

The Compatibility task pane produces reports on design issues that may cause problems with particular browser and CSS standards. As Figure 2-30 shows, the options available in this report are selected via dropdowns rather than with checkboxes (as were the Accessibility Checker report options).

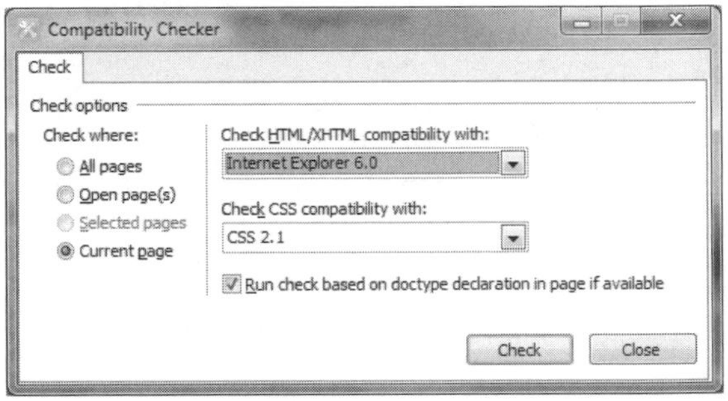

Because so many possible HTML and CSS standards exist, some of which are mutually exclusive, you can only explicitly check against one of each per report. In addition, you can tell the report to validate each individual page against its embedded type declaration, if any.

FIGURE 2-30

The Hyperlinks task pane reports on the status of hyperlinks used on the site. This report has several unique characteristics:

➤ It always reports across the current web, not just the open page.

➤ You have the opportunity to modify one or more hyperlinks without opening the individual pages in the editor (similar to the Find/Replace function).

➤ A "preliminary" report is automatically executed upon the summoning of the task pane, so there is no "run" icon.

➤ Several toolbar icons are unique to this task pane.

The unique toolbar icons are shown and called out in Figure 2-31, and described thereafter.

1. The Verify Hyperlinks icon crawls the links displayed and determines whether they are broken or valid. The options for this, shown in Figure 2-32, allow you to select whether to recheck hyperlinks that are already tested.

2. The Edit Hyperlink icon summons the dialog in Figure 2-33, which allows you to modify the currently selected link. You may edit only the current instance, or any or all other pages where it occurs throughout the current web.

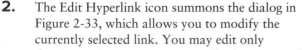

FIGURE 2-31

3. The Show Internal icon toggles the display to include or exclude links to intrinsic SharePoint resources, such as those in the _layouts folder.

FIGURE 2-32

The CSS Reports task pane shows styles in use, style sheet files, and references to styles that do not exist. Unlike the Compatibility reports, the CSS reports do not validate against any particular standard. See Chapter 6 for more information about using CSS in SharePoint and SharePoint Designer.

External Insertable Elements Panes

Unlike the internal insertable elements block, these task panes allow you to work with specific objects that were created outside of SharePoint Designer and bring them into the application. These are typically individual elements like images or blocks of text.

FIGURE 2-33

The Clip Art and Clipboard task panes form a special group and behave differently from the other task panes you have encountered so far. They always occupy the same space. Only one of them can be displayed at a time, and you can toggle between them via a drop-down menu in the task pane's title bar. They can be floated and docked like other task panes, but will not join any other pane in the same zone. Rather than docking within the design surface, they dock at the actual edge of the window; therefore, any elements other than the ribbon itself will be "inside" relative to this pane.

The Clip Art task pane allows you to search for and select images and other media from various sources. The results of your query are shown as a gallery of tiles within the task pane. Figure 2-34 shows an example result set from the Clip Art task pane.

The Clipboard task pane shows a history of items copied or cut from various Office applications. You can then specify which (if any) you want to paste into your document.

Regardless of whether you are using the Clipboard or Clip Art task panes, selecting one of the items therein will insert it at the current position of your text cursor.

Ribbon Tabs and Their Functions

As you learned in Chapter 1, the ribbon plays a very important role in modern Microsoft products. Each SharePoint artifact

FIGURE 2-34

type will generally have its own ribbon tab. The items on these ribbon tabs are discussed as appropriate throughout the book.

Within this chapter, you have also already been using several ribbon tabs. In particular, the Home and View ribbon tabs have provided access to most of the tasks you have performed to this point. Many of the tools provided on these tabs are either self-explanatory, or are common across multiple Microsoft applications.

The Layout ribbon tab was also touched upon when controlling layers in conjunction with the Layers task pane. You can use the controls on this tab to adjust the size or positioning of virtually any element on your page.

The Styles ribbon tab and its various tools will be discussed in detail in Chapter 6.

The remainder of this chapter will be devoted to the many types of items you can add to your pages via the Insert ribbon tab. The Insert ribbon tab, shown in Figure 2-35, allows you to insert virtually any appropriate object onto your page.

FIGURE 2-35

The Insert ribbon tab is like the Home, Layout, Style, and View ribbon tabs in that it is considered to have global, rather than contextual scope. That means that it is visible at all times when a document is open, rather than when a specific object is selected within the document. The Insert ribbon tab is broken into several blocks:

➤ **Tables** — Inserts an HTML table of the specified size.

➤ **Pictures** — Inserts pictures either by browsing to a file on your computer, or via the Clip Art task pane.

➤ **Links** — Inserts hyperlinks to another location, or target bookmarks on the current page.

➤ **Data Views and Forms** — Chapters 6 through 8 are dedicated to these objects, so they are not discussed further in this chapter.

➤ **Controls** — Inserts essentially the same objects available through the Toolbox task pane, but grouped in a more flexible fashion.

➤ **Web Parts** — Inserts SharePoint or ASP.NET components that represent some self-contained functionality.

➤ **Symbols** — Provides easy access to special characters that may not be available directly from your keyboard.

Some of the objects you can insert, such as tables and pictures, have contextual ribbon tabs associated with them. These are described as appropriate in the sections that follow.

Tables

SharePoint Designer Design view supports creating traditional HTML tables either visually or through the entry of parameters. You can insert standard tables three ways:

➤ **Select Table ➪ Insert Table** to summon the Insert Table dialog, shown in Figure 2-36, which allows you to set all the core properties of the table prior to its insertion.

➤ **Click the Table** icon and click within the displayed grid to visually select the initial number of rows and columns. While you do this, a "preview" insertion of the table shows you what your table will look like.

➤ **Highlight a block of text and select Table ➪ Convert Text to Table** to summon a dialog that allows you to determine how the selected text will be interpreted during the conversion. You can select breaks at paragraphs, tabs, commas, or an arbitrary character of your choice. You may also choose to have the selected text occupy a single table cell.

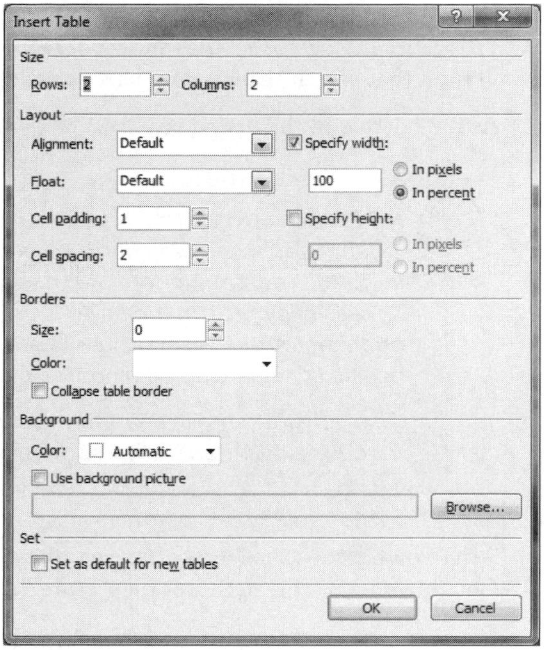

FIGURE 2-36

As long as your text cursor is within a table object on your page, the Table Tools Layout contextual ribbon tab will be visible. This tab is specific to working with tables, and other than its name, has nothing in common with the global Layout ribbon tab. Figure 2-37 shows the Table Tools Layout tab.

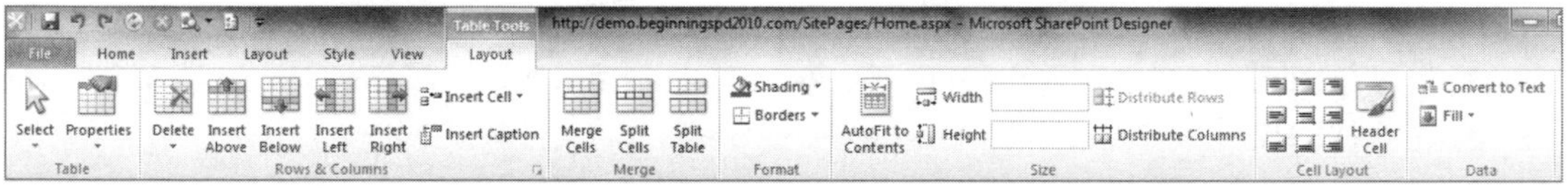

FIGURE 2-37

Pictures

You can insert pictures in your page two ways. If you click the Picture icon in the Insert Ribbon tab, you get a standard Windows file browser dialog (entitled Picture). You can then browse your file system and network for any image files you may have available.

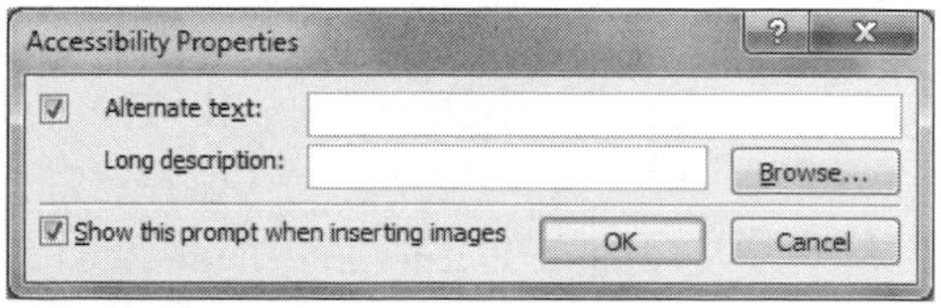

You can also use the Clip Art icon to summon the Clip Art task pane, which was described earlier in this chapter.

FIGURE 2-38

In either case, after you have selected the image you want to insert, by default, an Accessibility Properties dialog appears, as shown in Figure 2-38. This allows you to enter extra descriptive information that screen readers can detect and read.

At the bottom of the dialog is a checkbox you can activate to keep it from popping up every time.

> **NOTE** *As you might gather from this dialog and the Accessibility reports, ensuring that your sites are usable by people of varying levels of physical ability is an important part of modern web design. Although you have the ability to avoid the Accessibility prompt, doing so is not recommended. Instead, take into consideration the purpose the picture is serving, and whether that purpose justifies the possibility of excluding a portion of your audience.*
>
> *Also consider that in some jurisdictions and for some types of sites, designing for accessibility isn't just a good idea, it is the law.*

After you have inserted a picture, regardless of its source, you have a great deal of control over it. Clicking on a picture activates the Picture Tools' Format contextual ribbon tab, shown in Figure 2-39.

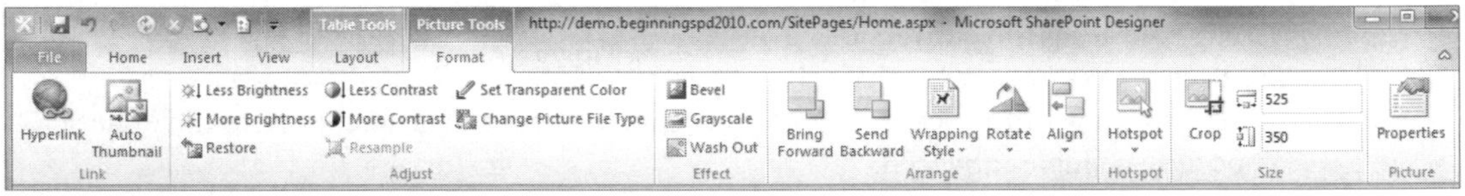

FIGURE 2-39

Most of the elements on this tab are similar to functions you would find in any image manipulation tool, and therefore not described here. However, a few of these tools are specific to the use of an image on a web page:

- ➤ **Hyperlink** — This uses the entire image as a link to another location. Creation of hyperlinks is described in more detail later in this chapter.

- ➤ **Auto Thumbnail** — Images can be very large files. Click this icon to reduce the picture's size for display, but store and link to the original image for viewing upon user request.

- ➤ **Restore** — Undoes all changes you have made to the picture since your last save.

- ➤ **Set Transparent Color** — This only operates on images in GIF format. By setting a color (typically the background color of the picture), you allow elements that may be behind the picture to show through. This can be useful for creating the effect of an irregularly shaped object "floating" on the screen.

- ➤ **Change Picture File Type** — Clicking this icon summons the Picture File Type dialog shown in Figure 2-40 and enables you to change the image to any of the types supported by SharePoint Designer and typical web browsers.

- ➤ **Wrapping Style** — The wrapping style determines how the image flows in relation to the surrounding text. A selection of None means that the image is placed inline, with text stopping immediately before it, and resuming after it. Selecting Right or Left aligns the image to the indicated side of the page (or container), and text will flow along the opposite side of the picture.

➤ **Align** — The Align option determines the *vertical* position of an image with respect to the text on its current line. Defining a Wrapping Style will supersede the value defined here for alignment.

➤ **Hotspot** — A *hotspot* is a hyperlink that overlays a fragment of an image. A group of hotspots over the same image can resemble a geographical map, so such a collection is often referred to as an *image map*. You can draw oval, rectangular, or irregular polygonal hotspots at any position over an image. Each hotspot may be linked to a different location. If the image itself has a hyperlink defined, clicking any part of the image not contained within a hotspot will link to that default location. Hyperlinks for hotspots are defined in the same manner as other hyperlinks (see the next section).

FIGURE 2-40

Links

Two icons are in the links section of the Insert ribbon tab. Both insert what, in HTML lingo, are called *anchor tags* (`<a></a>`). The parameters within the anchor determine whether it forms what is commonly called a *hyperlink* (an anchor that goes someplace), or a *bookmark* (an anchor that serves as a destination inside a page).

Bookmarks are the simpler of the two. Clicking the Bookmark button in the Insert ribbon summons the Bookmark dialog shown in Figure 2-41.

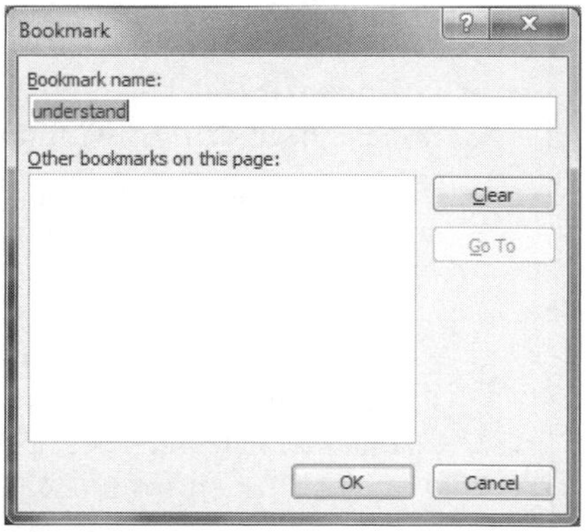

All a bookmark requires is a name. If you have text highlighted when you click the Bookmark button, that text will be used as the basis for the default name. The dialog will also show any other bookmarks already defined in the current page. Although no "content" is mandatory for a bookmark anchor, making the anchor tags surround the text of a page section heading is good practice.

To refer to a bookmark, you append a hash or pound sign (#), plus the name of the bookmark, to the name of the page when entering a URL. When such a link is clicked, the

FIGURE 2-41

browser opens the indicated page and scrolls immediately to the position of the bookmark.

Inserting a hyperlink is a little more complicated. When you click the hyperlink button, you summon the Insert Hyperlink dialog, shown in Figure 2-42. This dialog is also used when you're defining image hyperlinks and hotspots as described earlier in this chapter.

FIGURE 2-42

Just as with a bookmark, if you have text highlighted when you click the Hyperlink button, that text will be wrapped in the anchor tag. Unlike the bookmark, that anchor becomes the active hyperlink you can click on. This text is typically shown and editable in the Text to display field of the Insert Hyperlink dialog. If you are inserting a hyperlink on an image or for a hotspot, the Text to display field is grayed out and contains code representing the hotspot or image.

The bulk of the Insert Hyperlink dialog is dedicated to a file browser for the destination of your link. This operates much like the File Open and Save As dialogs, with icons to select different areas to browse, and a list of files and folders through which you may drill. The address of any file selected appears in the Address field of the dialog.

The buttons to the right of the file browser allow you to choose various options for your hyperlink:

➤ **Screen Tip** — You may click the Screen Tip button to add some descriptive text that can show up on screen as a tooltip and is available for screen readers.

➤ **Bookmark** — The Bookmark button allows you to browse any bookmark anchors that may have been defined within your selected target page.

➤ **Target Frame** — A web page may be made up of several frames. Clicking the Target Frame button summons a dialog that lets you select among any frames that may be defined, or several special frame designations. These names are case-sensitive.

➤ **Parameters** — You can add extra GET parameters to the URL of your hyperlink. These take the form of a set of name/value pairs that is appended to the URL. This is also referred to as the *query string*. These parameters are appended to the URL following a question mark (?), and separated from one another by ampersands (&).

Controls

The Controls section of the Insert ribbon tab includes icons for HTML, ASP.NET, and SharePoint controls, as well as Data Sources (described in later chapters). These are the same controls you found in the Toolbox task pane described earlier in this chapter; however, in the ribbon context, they are presented in the form of individual drop-down galleries. The HTML gallery is shown in Figure 2-43.

The galleries have sections that can be displayed individually, or all at once. To select a section, you click on the small triangle in the gallery's title bar (next to All HTML Controls in the figure). If you right-click a displayed gallery, the context menu allows you to add a link to that gallery directly to the Quick Access Toolbar. This allows you to keep your ribbon minimized and insert objects from that gallery while other ribbon tabs are displayed.

Web Parts

The Web Parts section of the Insert ribbon tab contains two icons. The Web Parts icon displays a gallery that allows you to insert many of the web parts available on the currently open site. Unlike the Controls galleries, this gallery does not allow you to collapse to an individual class of web parts. In addition, the web parts displayed can vary considerably from site to site. Several types of web parts and how to manipulate them in SharePoint Designer are described in other chapters throughout this book.

FIGURE 2-43

A web part zone is a container on your page for web parts. SharePoint contains tools that allow your users to easily add web parts to a zone, delete them, or even move them from zone to zone — all within the web interface. Within SharePoint Designer, you have the option of limiting some or all of this functionality.

When you click the Web Part Zone button, if you have an ASPX page open, SharePoint Designer will also add any other supporting components the page may need to support its functionality. When you highlight a web part zone on the page, the Web Part Zone Tools ➪ Format contextual ribbon tab becomes available. This tab contains:

> ➤ **Zone Title** — A field for you to edit the title of the zone.

> ➤ **Zone Layout** — A button that lets you determine whether the web parts added to the zone are arranged horizontally or vertically.

> ➤ **Properties** — Summons the Web Part Zone Properties dialog, shown in Figure 2-44.

The Web Part Zone Properties dialog provides the same Title and Layout control that the ribbon tab contains, plus:

> ➤ **Frame style** — Allows you to determine the default presentation of web parts added to the zone, such as whether to show a border, the web part's title, both, or neither. This can be overridden for individual web parts within the zone.

FIGURE 2-44

> ➤ **Browser Settings** — Checkboxes that let you determine whether users can customize the contents of the zone — either for all users, or on a personalized basis — via the web interface.

Symbols

The Symbols section simply contains the option to insert a character onto your page that may not appear on your keyboard. Clicking this icon displays a limited gallery for quick insertion, as well as a More Symbols menu item. The More Symbols item summons the Symbol dialog, shown in Figure 2-45.

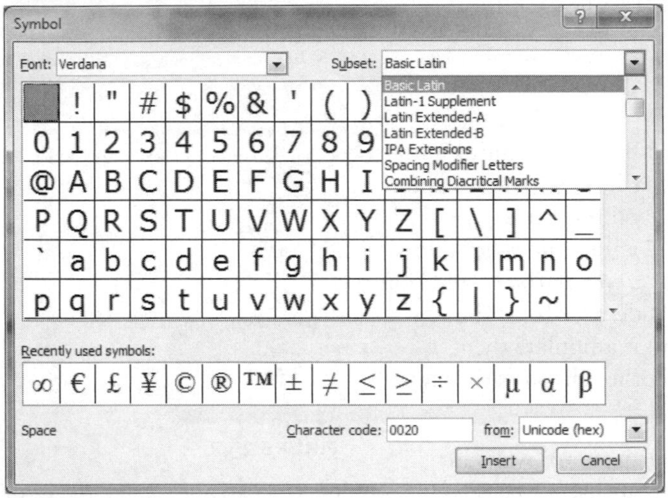

FIGURE 2-45

The Symbol dialog allows you to insert virtually any character, from any language, supported by your computer.

SUMMARY

This chapter showed you how to use the page-editing tools of SharePoint Designer 2010. You learned about the Page Editor, and how to get around its various views. You discovered:

➤ SharePoint Designer's user interface is very flexible and can be adapted to almost anyone's work style.

➤ How to leverage IntelliSense and code snippets.

➤ How to insert various objects onto a page.

In Chapter 3, you will learn how to apply these tools to customizing SharePoint master pages.

3

The Anatomy of a SharePoint Page

WHAT YOU WILL LEARN IN THIS CHAPTER

➤ The primary types of pages in SharePoint

➤ How SharePoint assembles pages

➤ How to edit a master page

➤ Major content placeholders in a SharePoint Master Page

SharePoint 2010 comes in two flavors, SharePoint Foundation and SharePoint Server. This chapter covers the pages found in SharePoint Foundation. The goal of this chapter is to give you the conceptual and technical fundamentals required to customize your SharePoint site. The assumption is that you have a basic understanding of HTML, CSS, and web development concepts.

HOW SHAREPOINT PAGES WORK

A basic understanding of SharePoint site architecture will help you understand the nuts and bolts of SharePoint pages. The entry point to a SharePoint site is a *web application*, which is the highest level "container" for sites and has common services and features available to all sites within it. Within a web application is at least one site collection. A site collection is a group of sites that share properties for managing content and user permissions. The top-level or root site within a site collection is where you manage many administrative functions and store common files used in all sub sites.

Figure 3-1 illustrates the site hierarchy in SharePoint and highlights the libraries discussed in this chapter. SharePoint pages can be stored in any document library.

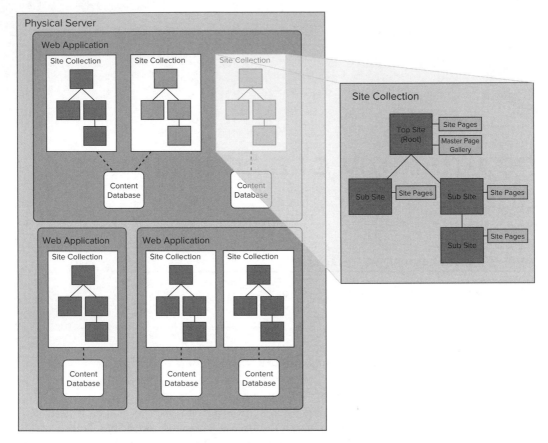

FIGURE 3-1

If you have a background in web design and development, you are familiar with physical web pages that you can edit directly using page editing software or Notepad. This type of site is fine for very small sites. Larger sites with more than a few pages are inefficient and cumbersome to maintain because of the redundant structural and behavioral instructions repeated in each page.

In contrast, SharePoint manages web content efficiently by storing content separately from structural and behavioral instructions. That way, only one physical copy of the page file is required.

The physical pages that live in the SharePoint file system serve as the master blueprint for any page inheriting from it. You should think of these as the "sacred originals that should never be touched." These "sacred originals," along with other information that helps define your site, form a master template called a *site definition*. This site definition lives on the hard disk of each file server (or *web front end*), and is used to build each actual SharePoint site that a user creates.

Most pages on a SharePoint site are assembled from a combination of these "sacred original" physical pages, and *instance data* for the page that lives in the *content database*. Content such as page content, HTML, and most scripts and styles live in this database and not on the file system.

Construction of the page takes place when the browser requests it. That means that when you look at a SharePoint page in your browser, a physical version of that web page does not exist. It blows your mind, doesn't it?

Figure 3-2 shows the process by which a page is assembled by a SharePoint server.

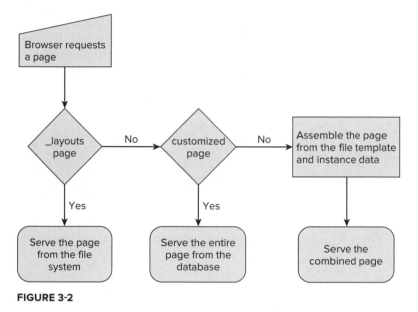

FIGURE 3-2

> *NOTE For more details about how SharePoint is physically structured, see Appendix B.*

PAGE TYPES

Two core types of pages are in SharePoint 2010: *application pages* and *site pages*. Understanding the differences between the two types of pages can save you a few headaches. This chapter focuses on site pages as used in SharePoint Foundation 2010. SharePoint Server 2010 also includes special site pages, called *publishing pages*, with extra features specifically for managing large amounts of web content. These will covered in detail in Chapter 4, but keep in mind that everything covered in this chapter also applies to publishing pages.

Application pages are more like traditional web pages, in that they are stored directly on the file system of the web front-end, and are complete in themselves. While they will reflect the styles you apply to your site (see Chapter 5), you do not otherwise have any ability to edit these pages through SharePoint Designer.

Site pages are pages that users edit, add web parts to, and can create and customize through the browser or with tools such as SharePoint Designer. Site pages are stored in the site collection's content database.

SharePoint Content Pages

Most SharePoint pages have the following key characteristics:

➤ They are .ASPX (ASP.NET) form pages.

➤ They use an ASP.NET master page that contains SharePoint-related *placeholders* that provide the majority of the page's look and feel.

➤ One of these placeholders, PlaceHolderMain, contains the actual instance information for the page. Within that placeholder is the magic that makes each page type unique.

Web Part Pages

The Web Part Page is the primary page for presenting web parts, libraries, and lists. If you have a need for unstructured content such as text and images, you should plan to use a wiki page, which you will learn about later in this chapter.

Web part pages organize content through *web part zones*. A web part zone is a predefined area for adding web parts. You can create web part pages using the browser or with SharePoint Designer.

As you can see in Figure 3-3, web parts sit in web part zones that are part of a page template known in SharePoint as the master page. You will learn more about Master Pages in detail later in this chapter.

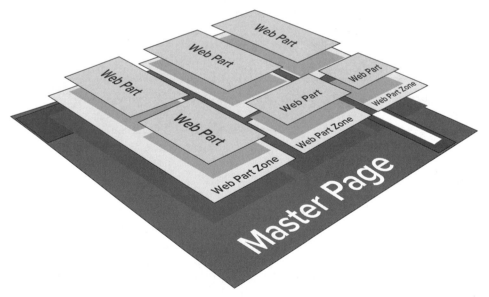

FIGURE 3-3

Users with appropriate permissions can create new pages and add, configure, or remove web parts through the web interface. You may ask why you would need to create a new Web Part Page in SharePoint Designer instead of the browser. With SharePoint Designer, you can do much more than you can through the browser. You can customize the content areas or create custom web parts called *Data View Web Parts,* which are covered in Chapter 8, "XSLT Data Views and Forms."

Wiki Pages

Wiki pages are a specialized version of the standard Web Part page and incorporate the wiki concept, which is collaborative and "living" because it continually changes through input from multiple users. Like Web Part pages, wiki pages have several pre-defined layouts, with different zone patterns. Unlike Web Part pages, these wiki content zones allow both rich text and web parts to be freely intermingled. Figure 3-4 illustrates the freeform layout of a wiki page. You can add web parts, images, and text directly to the rich content area or wiki field.

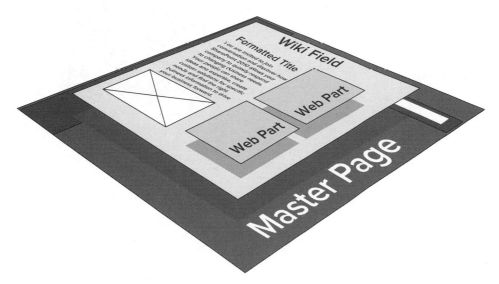

FIGURE 3-4

If you have worked with previous versions of SharePoint, you may be pleasantly surprised when you create your first *collaboration site* in SharePoint 2010. Instead of the boxy, data-driven presentation that was standard in team sites, you will be working with a new type of page, the *Wiki Page*. MOSS 2007 and WSS 3.0 had a separate site type called a *wiki*. SharePoint 2010 removes Wiki as a site type but incorporates much-enhanced wiki functionality directly in the standard team site template.

Seen below in Figure 3-5 is the Welcome Page, a wiki page used as the home page of a team site.

Because Microsoft understood that there was a need for unstructured collaboration, you can make the Welcome Page the home page of any site template in SharePoint. You can activate this feature in the Site Features section of the Site Settings page.

Although you can create additional Wiki libraries with any name, by default, SharePoint 2010 team sites create one called Site Pages. (Yes, it can easily be confused with the generic idea of "site pages" described earlier in the chapter. The builders of SharePoint have a penchant for using general terms to name specific objects....) You can find *these* site pages in SharePoint Designer under the Site Objects menu, as shown in Figure 3-6.

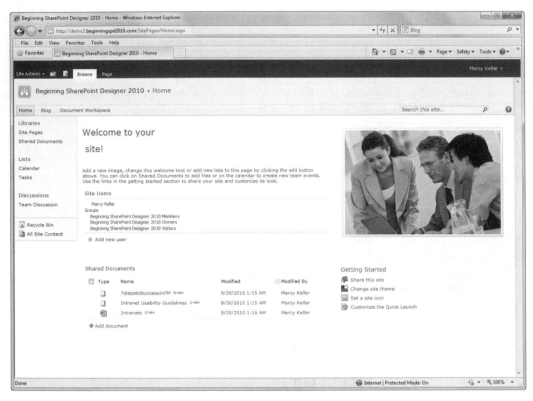

FIGURE 3-5

FIGURE 3-6

View Pages

In the root of each list and library is the Forms folder. In this folder is a collection of pages used for entering and displaying the information in that list. These pages are called *view pages*, yet they are also web part pages.

End users can create view pages through the web interface, but unlike the generic web part pages mentioned earlier, view pages are both edited and created in SharePoint Designer.

Figure 3-7 shows a list view page for a Shared Documents Library as seen in the browser.

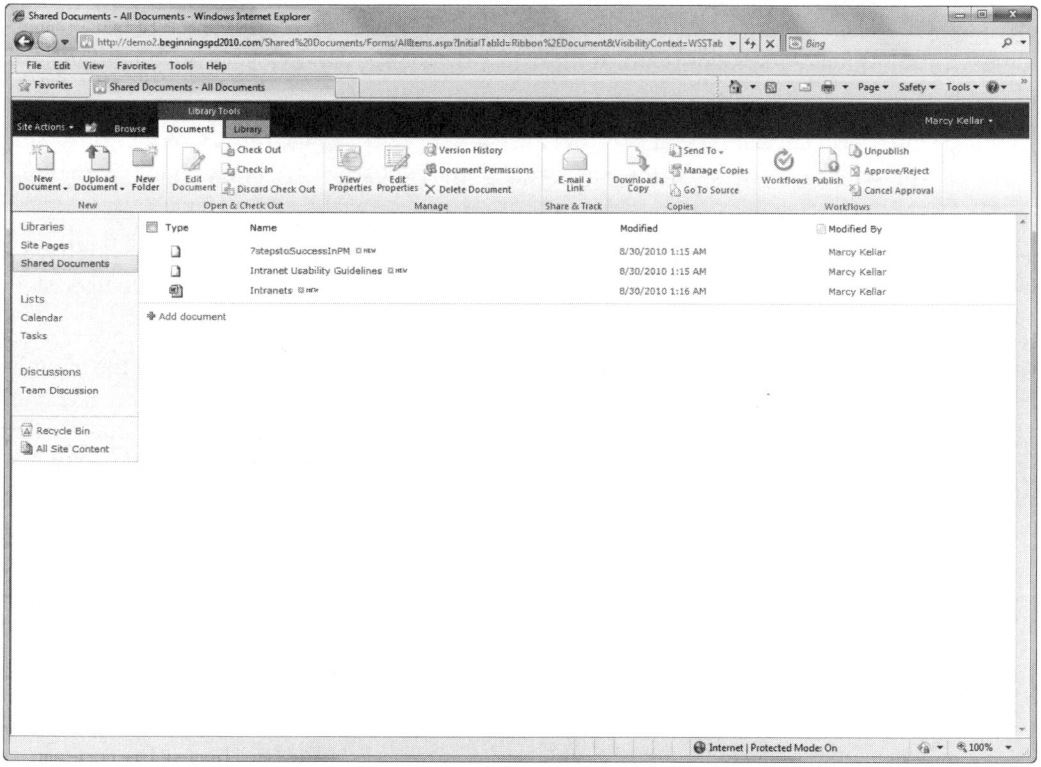

FIGURE 3-7

View pages typically contain HTML controls to display or edit a list item. For more information about creating a view page, see Chapter 8, "XSLT Data Views and Forms."

A Note about Page Customization

By default, most SharePoint content pages, regardless of type, are based upon the "sacred original" site definition file plus instance information pulled from the content database. When you edit such a page in SharePoint Designer and save it, the link to its site definition file is broken. A copy of the site definition file is merged with its instance information and the result is then stored in the content database. Such a page is called a *customized* page.

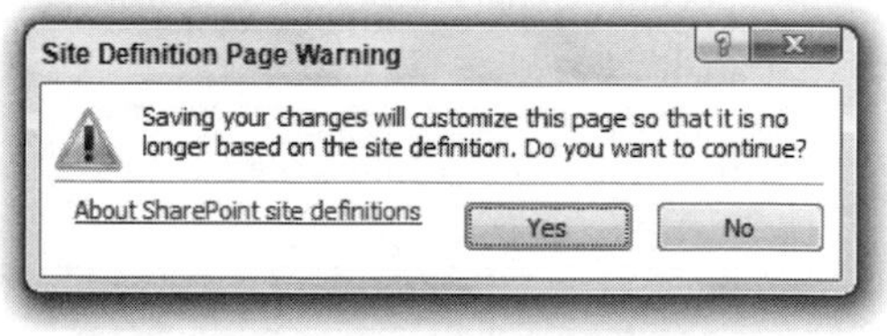

FIGURE 3-8

When this happens, SharePoint gives you the warning shown in Figure 3-8 before breaking the link.

You can restore the link to the site definition file by right-clicking the page in SharePoint Designer and selecting "Reset to Site Definition" from the context menu. This will re-establish the link, but it will also leave any content you have added to web part or content zones within the page intact. Additionally, the customized file is renamed and stored in the same folder for backup reasons.

MASTER PAGES

Master pages are responsible for the consistent structural elements of a SharePoint page. The headings, navigation, footers, and logos that are consistent throughout many pages are contained in the master page.

Master pages provide a special type of control called a `ContentPlaceHolder`. *Content placeholders* are areas of replaceable content on the master page. In the code, they are book-ended by the following: `<asp:ContentPlaceHolder>`.

Although a master page may define many `ContentPlaceHolder` controls, a page does not have to implement a corresponding content control. You can think of these controls as little television screens: the content may change, but it is always delivered through the same little box.

The most common `ContentPlaceHolder` control is `PlaceHolderMain`, which displays the main body of the page. Other `ContentPlaceHolder` controls include `PlaceHolderLeftNavBar`, which contains the Quick Launch bar on the left side of the page, `PlaceHolderTopNavBar`, which contains the Top Navigation tabs at the top of the page, and `PlaceHolderSearchArea`, which contains the page's search controls. Depending on whether you are using SharePoint Foundation 2010 versus SharePoint Server 2010, your master pages may have many more additional `ContentPlaceHolder` controls.

When you create a new page in your site, the page will automatically inherit its basic layout and structure from the site's master page. Optionally, a page can contain one or more `Content` controls to specify the content to display in the corresponding `ContentPlaceHolder` controls provided by the master page. For instance, if you want to display the text "Hello, World!" in your page, you add the following code to your page:

```
<asp:Content ContentPlaceHolderId="PlaceHolderMain" runat="server">
    Hello, World!
</asp:Content>
```

When the page is requested from the server, the master page is loaded, which provides the `ContentPlaceHolder` controls for the page, and the page provides the `Content` controls to specify the content. In the previous code snippet, "Hello, World!" would appear in the main body of the page because the `Content` control's `ContentPlaceHolderId` attribute was set to `PlaceHolderMain`. The value of the `ContentPlaceHolderId` attribute must match the `ID` attribute of one of the master page's `ContentPlaceHolder` controls or the page will not load, leaving the user with a friendly, but uninformative error message.

> **WARNING** *Do not delete any* `ContentPlaceHolder` *controls from your master pages. You will get an error if a page that references a missing* `ContentPlaceHolder` *control is requested from the server. If you want to hide a single* `ContentPlaceHolder` *control, simply set its* `Visible` *attribute to* `False`.

You can use `Content` controls for more than just content; you can use them to hide content as well. If you want to hide the search controls from a particular page in your site, add an empty `Content` control to the page and set its `ContentPlaceHolderId` attribute to `PlaceHolderSearchArea`. When the page loads, the "blank" content of the empty Content control replaces the default search controls that appear on the page.

Master Page Locations

Master pages are stored in a special Master Page Gallery library located within each site collection in the /_catalogs/masterpage directory. This library is accessible from the Site Collection Settings page as well as in SharePoint Designer, as shown in Figure 3-9.

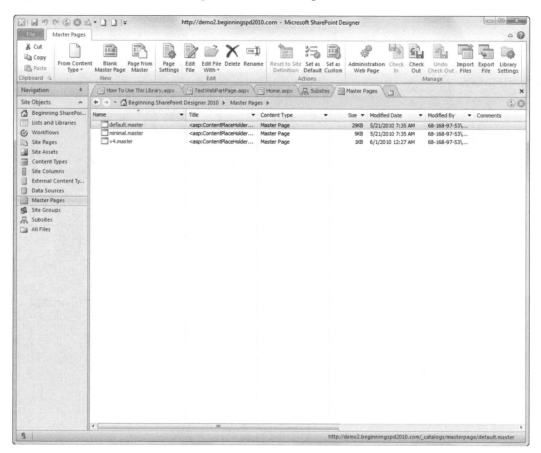

FIGURE 3-9

Only one gallery exists per site collection and it is automatically populated when a new site collection is provisioned. Master pages cannot be shared across site collections, but a root site can share its master pages with the other sites in its site collection.

Default Master Pages

There are many master pages available in SharePoint Foundation Server. SharePoint provides a variety of master pages: *v4.master, default.master, minimal.master, simple.master*, and

MWSDefaultv4.master. Another master page, *nightandday.master* is available in SharePoint Server 2010. It has slightly different content placeholders specializing in managing web content and is discussed in detail in Chapter 4.

v4.master

`v4.master`, shown in Figure 3-10, is the default master page for most non-publishing sites in SharePoint 2010. It is also the default system master page in both SharePoint Foundation and SharePoint Server.

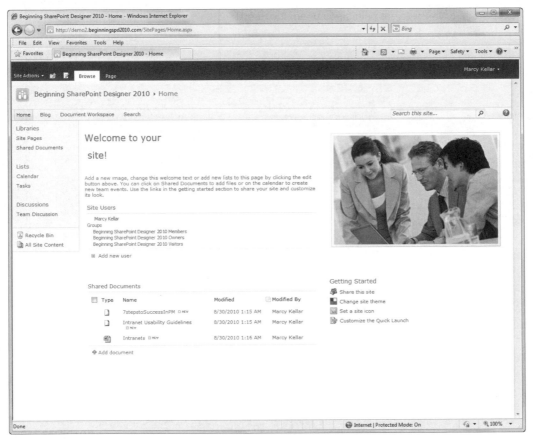

FIGURE 3-10

default.master

The `default.master` page in SharePoint 2010 should look familiar to you if you worked with SharePoint 2007. Both visually and in the code, this master page looks like the `default.master` page seen in collaboration sites in SharePoint 2007, the previous version of SharePoint. Use this master page if you are using or require a legacy (2007) interface for your site and you will not be using the ribbon.

The inclusion of this master page in SharePoint Foundation and SharePoint Server ensures that upgrading from SharePoint 2007 to SharePoint 2010 is an easy process. It is automatically used when you upgrade a SharePoint 2007 site to SharePoint 2010. Although it does not include the ribbon, you could add the ribbon and other SharePoint 2010 user interface content placeholders.

As shown in Figure 3-11, when `default.master` is applied to a SharePoint 2010 team site, the look and feel transforms to the familiar "baby blue" branding of SharePoint 2007.

FIGURE 3-11

minimal.master

The `minimal.master` page is best suited for pages with minimal branding and navigation. The `minimal.master` is used with search pages and Office web applications. Because this master page does not include the ribbon or navigation, you should use it for pages that require a lot of real estate.

Figure 3-12 shows a search page with `minimal.master` applied.

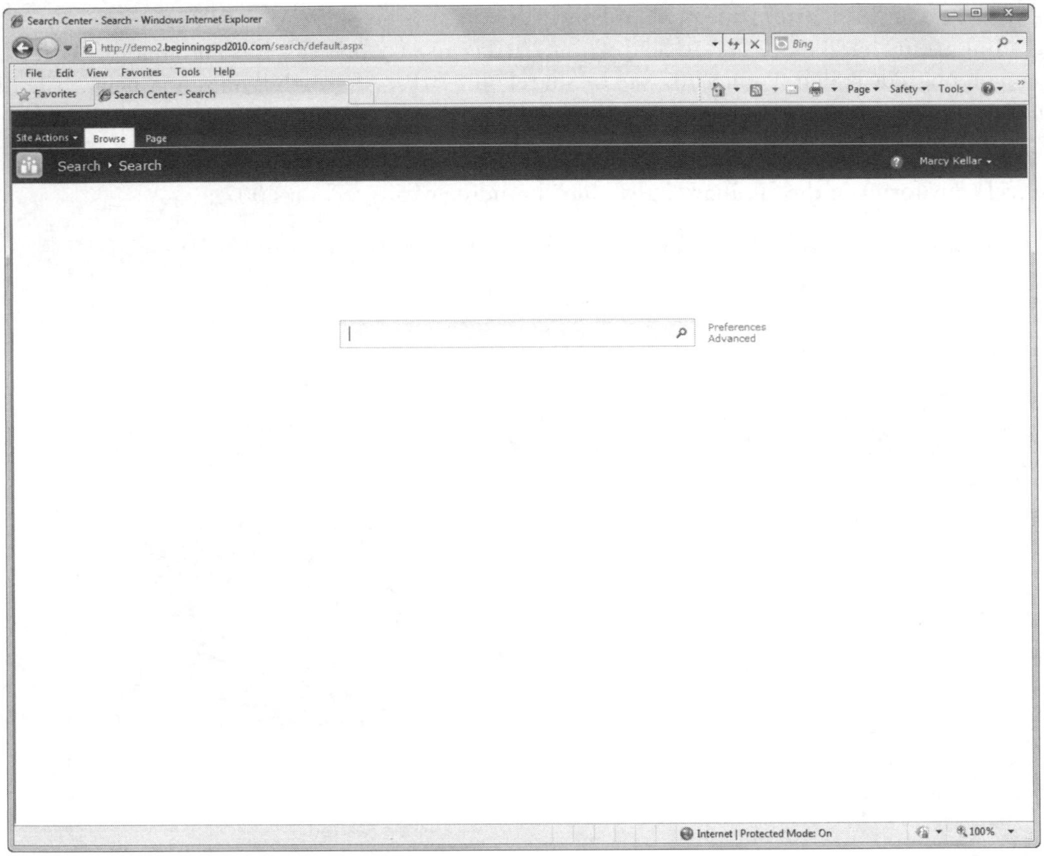

FIGURE 3-12

> **NOTE** *The search pages use different master pages from the rest of your site. If you customize your site, you will need to create a new master page based on the minimal master page. This way, you can add a reference to your custom styling in the* minimal.master, *which is the master page that search pages use.*

simple.master

simple.master is the master page used for error and login pages. It lives in the file system and is not available in the master page gallery. If you are creating a custom login or error page, you will want to use the simple.master page. Figure 3-13 shows an error page with simple.master applied.

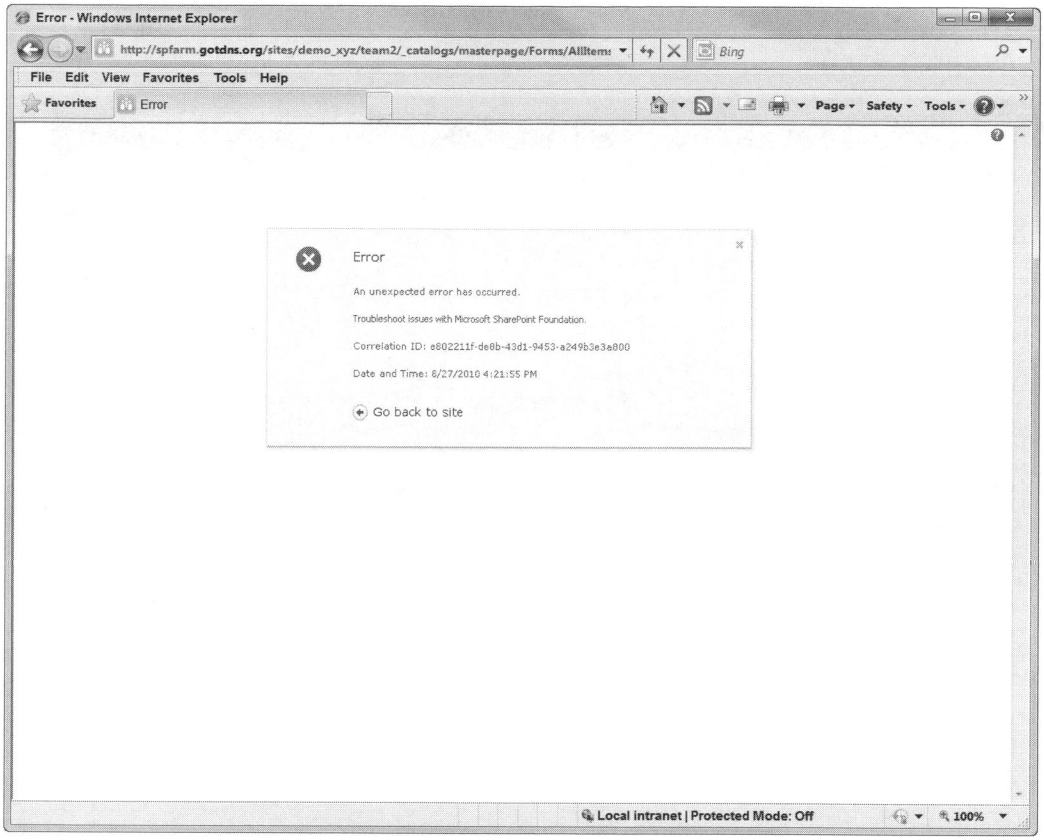

FIGURE 3-13

MWSDefaultv4.master

The *MWSDefaultv4.master* is found in the master page gallery of meeting workspace sites. It is almost identical to the v4.master with the exception of a couple of content placeholders such as the MeetingNavigator, shown in the left navigation area in Figure 3-14.

nightandday.master

The `nightandday.master` page, seen below in Figure 3-15, is only available in SharePoint Server 2010. It contains controls specialized for publishing web content management. You learn more about this master page in Chapter 4.

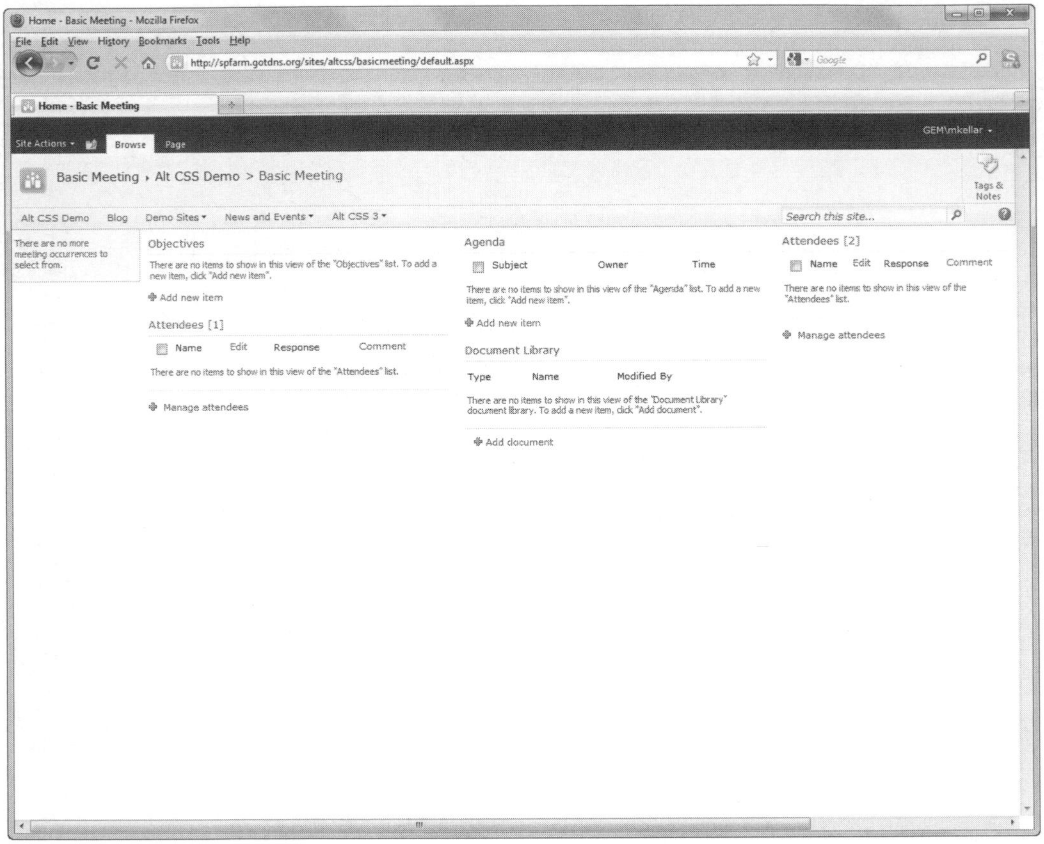

FIGURE 3-14

Other Master Pages

There are more master pages included in SharePoint Foundation Server and SharePoint Server 2010, such as legacy (SharePoint 2007) master pages for managing application pages for non-UI upgraded sites. Master pages such as applicationV4.master and mysite.master are for specific types of scenarios or sites, live in the file system, and are customized using development tools and techniques.

Modifying the Default Master Page

The v4.master page is included in every site in both SharePoint Foundation and SharePoint Server 2010. It can be used with publishing sites and non-publishing sites. You learned earlier that master pages contain HTML, CSS, SharePoint controls, and ContentPlaceholder controls.

It is a best practice to make a copy of a default master page and make changes in the copy rather than directly in the original file, v4.master. This protects your work from being overwritten by software patches.

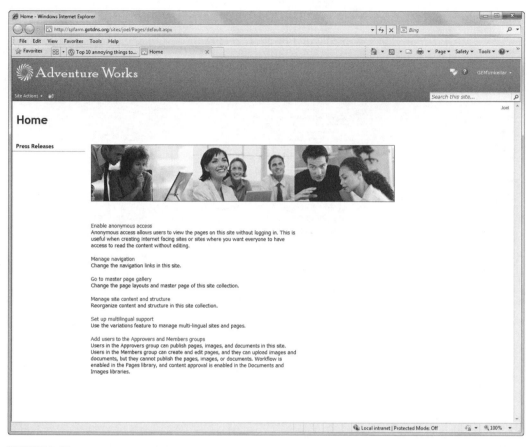

FIGURE 3-15

You can create a copy of v4.master with either the browser or SharePoint Designer. If you use SharePoint Designer, don't copy the file and paste it back into the gallery. You should create a completely new master page in order to break all ties from the original file. In SharePoint Designer 2010, a new function is available that allows you to import and export files.

TRY IT OUT Importing and Exporting Master Pages

In this exercise, you will use SharePoint Designer to export v4.master to your desktop, rename it, and then import it as a copy into your SharePoint site.

1. Open SharePoint Designer.

2. Click the Open Site button.

3. When the Open Site dialog appears, enter the URL to your site in the Site name textbox and click the OK button.

4. If prompted, enter password for the SharePoint site and click the OK button.

5. Select Master Pages from the Navigation bar on the left.

6. Select the `v4.master` so that it is highlighted by clicking once on its name, as shown in Figure 3-16.

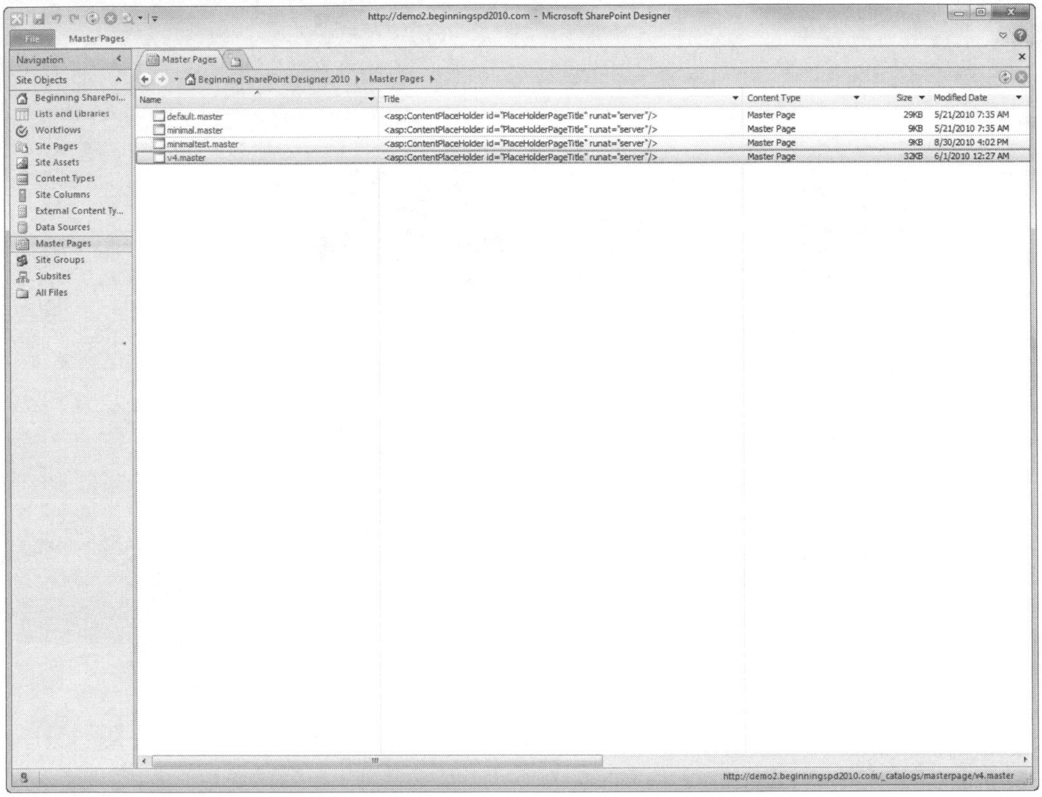

FIGURE 3-16

7. Click the Export button on the right, as shown in Figure 3-17.

8. A Save dialog box appears.

9. Save the file as **v4Demo.master**.

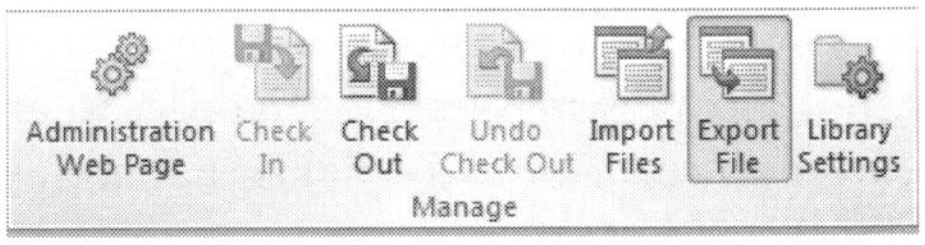

FIGURE 3-17

10. Select the Import Files button from the Master Pages ribbon.

11. When the Import dialog appears, click Add File.

12. In the Add File to Import List dialog, browse to v4Demo.master and select the file.

13. Click OK.

How It Works

When you exported the `v4.master` page out of SharePoint, it became a copy of the original master page. The original still exists in the master page gallery. By importing it back in as a renamed file, you have created a new master page that has all of the same code as the original `v4.master`.

If you make changes directly to v4.master and try to save the file, you will receive the warning message seen earlier in the chapter in Figure 3-8. Although editing a default master page should not be part of a permanent solution, it can be a fast way to help you troubleshoot or test a change.

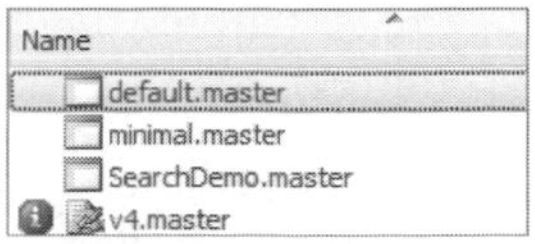

FIGURE 3-18

When you change a default file from the site definition, SharePoint Designer provides an indicator that the file is changed from the original site definition with a blue icon to the left of the file, shown in Figure 3-18.

You can always revert to the original file by right-clicking the customized file and selecting "Reset to Site Definition" from the context menu. The Site Definition Page Warning dialog box will appear, as shown in Figure 3-19.

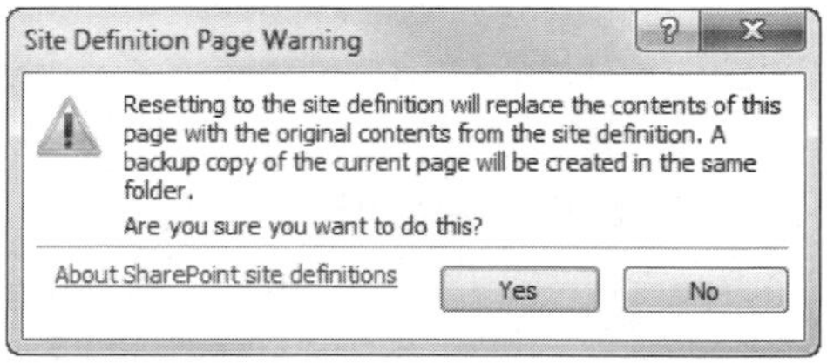

FIGURE 3-19

Click Yes and SharePoint will re-link the file to its site definition file. For backup reasons, a copy of the customized file is renamed and stored in the same folder.

Applying a New Master Page

In order for your site to reflect any changes made to your master page, you will need to apply the master page to your site. You can do this through the browser or by using SharePoint Designer.

TRY IT OUT   Applying a New Master Page

1. Open SharePoint Designer.

2. Click the Open Site button.

3. When the Open Site dialog appears, enter the URL to your site in the Site name textbox and click the OK button.

4. If prompted, enter the password for the SharePoint site and click the OK button.

5. Click Master Pages in Site Objects.

6. Locate the Master Page you want to use (in this case, v4Demo.master).

7. Right-click the Master Page and select Set as Default Master Page on the context menu.

How It Works

After you set the v4Demo.master file as the default master page, all existing pages and any new pages will be attached to it. This means any changes you make to this file will be reflected in all pages inheriting from it.

CREATING CUSTOM MASTER PAGES

You may find that modifying the default master pages is too constraining for your needs. If this is the case, you can create a custom master page for more flexibility. A custom master page is created from your own HTML and then required code and content placeholders are added in appropriate areas. Before you decide to implement a custom master page in your site, consider the following points:

➤ **Testing Time** — Microsoft already tested the functionality and user experience of default SharePoint master pages. If you create your own master page, you will need to identify key areas of functionality (i.e., adding web parts, adding new calendar entries, etc…).

➤ **Loss of Default Functionality** — Your custom markup may change the way default components of SharePoint work (i.e., the ribbon scroll or the page editing experience). Identifying these areas early and communicating the risk of losing functionality to decision makers is critical to your project's success.

Required Placeholders

As previously mentioned, a master page must have all of the required content placeholders in the code, even if you are not going to use them. The following table lists the required placeholders, their placement in the document flow, and their descriptions:

PLACEMENT	PLACEHOLDER NAME	DEFAULT CONTENT/FUNCTION
\<head\>	PlaceHolderPageTitle	Title of the site. Found in head of master page.
\<head\>	PlaceHolderAdditionalPageHead	Placeholder in the head section of the page used to add extra components such as JavaScript and CSS.
\<head\>	PlaceHolderTitleAreaClass	The CSS for the title area (now in the head tag). ***Changed since 2007. Make sure to move to \<head\> when upgrading***
Anywhere	PlaceHolderBodyAreaClass	A content placeholder for adding additional CSS style to the page.
Ribbon	SPNavigation	Control used for additional page editing controls. (Was used as a Publishing console control in 2007.)
Ribbon	PlaceHolderGlobalNavigation	Breadcrumb control in the Ribbon.
Ribbon	PlaceHolderGlobalNavigationSiteMap	Placeholder to show the Global Site Map (displayed as the Popout menu in the ribbon).
TitleRow	PlaceHolderSiteName	Name of the site where the current page resides.

PLACEMENT	PLACEHOLDER NAME	DEFAULT CONTENT/FUNCTION
TitleRow	PlaceHolderPageTitleInTitleArea	Title of the page, which appears in the title area on the page.
TitleRow	PlaceHolderPageDescription	Description text from the page's definition.
TitleRow	PlaceHolderSearchArea	Location of search controls.
Top Nav	PlaceHolderTopNavBar	Container used to hold the top navigation bar.
Top Nav	PlaceHolderHorizontalNav	The navigation menu that is inside the top navigation bar.
Left Nav	PlaceHolderQuickLaunchTop	Top of the Quick Launch menu that contains backwards compatible HTML for legacy (2007) sites.
Left Nav	PlaceHolderQuickLaunchBottom	Bottom of the Quick Launch menu that contains backwards compatible HTML for legacy (2007) sites.
Left Nav	PlaceHolderLeftNavBarDataSource	Location of the data source used to populate left navigation.
Left Nav	PlaceHolderCalendarNavigator	Date picker used when a calendar is visible on the page.
Left Nav	PlaceHolderLeftNavBarTop	Top section of the left navigation bar.
Left Nav	PlaceHolderLeftNavBar	Container for Quick Launch (current navigation).
Left Nav	PlaceHolderLeftActions	Additional objects above the Quick Launch bar, "Recent Items" in Wiki pages.
Main Body	PlaceHolderMain	Main content of the page.
Main Body	PlaceHolderTitleBreadcrumb	Breadcrumb text for the breadcrumb control.
Bottom (Not Visible)	PlaceHolderFormDigest	Container where the page form digest control is stored.

continues

(continued)

PLACEMENT	PLACEHOLDER NAME	DEFAULT CONTENT/FUNCTION
Bottom (Not Visible)	PlaceHolderUtilityContent	Additional content at the bottom of the page. This placeholder should be placed outside of the form tag.
Legacy	PlaceHolderPageImage	Not present in SharePoint 2010 user interface, but required for legacy master pages.
Legacy	PlaceHolderTitleLeftBorder	
Legacy	PlaceHolderMiniConsole	
Legacy	PlaceHolderTitleRightMargin	
Legacy	PlaceHolderTitleAreaSeparator	
Legacy	PlaceHolderNavSpacer	
Legacy	PlaceHolderLeftNavBarBorder	
Legacy	PlaceHolderBodyLeftBorder	
Legacy	PlaceHolderBodyRightMargin	

Unused Placeholders

Some of the required placeholders may not be necessary for your design, so what do you do with them? Hide them! Include them inside an `<asp:Panel>` control you add to the page and set the control's `Visible` attribute to `False` as shown in the following code snippet. Since the `<asp:Panel>` control is not visible, the `ContentPlaceHolder` controls within it and their corresponding `Content` controls will not be rendered to the browser.

```
<!--Hidden Placeholders -->
<asp:Panel visible="false" runat="server">
<!-- Top Nav -->
<asp:ContentPlaceHolder id="PlaceHolderHorizontalNav" runat="server"/>
<asp:ContentPlaceHolder id="PlaceHolderTopNavBar" runat="server"/>
<!-- Left Nav -->
<asp:ContentPlaceHolder id="PlaceHolderQuickLaunchTop" runat="server"/>
<asp:ContentPlaceHolder id="PlaceHolderQuickLaunchBottom" runat="server"/>
<asp:ContentPlaceHolder id="PlaceHolderLeftNavBarDataSource" runat="server" />
<asp:ContentPlaceHolder id="PlaceHolderCalendarNavigator" runat ="server" />
<asp:ContentPlaceHolder id="PlaceHolderLeftNavBarTop" runat="server" />
<!-- For adding CSS to child pages -->
<asp:ContentPlaceHolder id="PlaceHolderBodyAreaClass" runat ="server"/>
<asp:ContentPlaceHolder id="PlaceHolderTitleAreaClass" runat ="server"/>
```

```
<!-- Required for Legacy UI -->
<asp:ContentPlaceHolder id="PlaceHolderSiteName" runat="server"/>
<asp:ContentPlaceHolder ID="PlaceHolderPageImage" runat="server"/>
<asp:ContentPlaceHolder ID="PlaceHolderTitleLeftBorder" runat="server"/>
<asp:ContentPlaceHolder id="PlaceHolderMiniConsole" runat="server"/>
<asp:ContentPlaceHolder id="PlaceHolderTitleRightMargin" runat="server"/>
<asp:ContentPlaceHolder ID="PlaceHolderTitleAreaSeparator" runat="server"/>
<asp:ContentPlaceHolder ID="PlaceHolderNavSpacer" runat="server"/>
<asp:ContentPlaceHolder id="PlaceHolderLeftNavBarBorder" runat="server"/>
<asp:ContentPlaceHolder ID="PlaceHolderBodyLeftBorder" runat="server"/>
<asp:ContentPlaceHolder id="PlaceHolderBodyRightMargin" runat="server" />

</asp:Panel>
```

Required Controls

There are several required controls for a SharePoint master page to function. When you create a custom master page or are troubleshooting any errors with a modified master page, make sure that these controls are in place.

PLACEMENT	CONTROL	DESCRIPTION
<head>	SPPageManager	Controls routing commands to page components such as the ribbon and toolbars.
<head>	ScriptLink	Creates a reference to the SharePoint ECMAScript libraries.
<body>	ScriptManager	Manages all of the ECMAScript functions on the page and their ability to communicate back to the server without refreshing the page in the browser.

NOTE ECMAScript *is the name of the official standard from which Microsoft Jscript and JavaScript are derived.*

Broken Master Pages

It is inevitable, as you are learning the ins and outs of customizing with SharePoint Designer, that you will break a master page. Broken master pages are not actually broken; rather, they cannot be rendered in the browser. Use the following list of the most common problems to help you troubleshoot broken master pages.

➤ **Required Content Placeholders** — You must have all required content placeholders in the code of the master page even if you are not using them.

➤ **Typos** — Be sure to copy and paste code from an existing, working master page instead of typing the code manually. This ensures you do not introduce a typo. If you are copying and pasting code from a browser, such as example code you find on the Internet, paste the code into Notepad first to remove any error-causing formatting. Then, copy and paste the code from Notepad into the destination master page. Notepad is usually available from the Accessories folder on your Start menu.

➤ **Duplicate Content Placeholders** — Duplicate content placeholders are easy to spot in SharePoint Designer, as well as the browser, since an error will be generated when the page is loaded in either application.

> **NOTE** *Opening master pages outside of a SharePoint environment can change the contents of the master page. When this happens, you will receive an error. Often the error is due to a typo in the first few lines of code in the master page. In Figure 3-20, the references to content template pages are incorrect because they are missing the leading tilde and forward slash* (~/).

```
<%@ Import Namespace="Microsoft.SharePoint.ApplicationPages" %>
<%@ Register Tagprefix="WebPartPages" Namespace="Microsoft.SharePoint.WebParti
Culture=neutral, PublicKeyToken=71e9bce111e9429c" %>
<%@ Register TagPrefix="wssuc" TagName="Welcome" src=" controltemplates/Welcon
<%@ Register TagPrefix="wssuc" TagName="MUISelector" src=" controltemplates/MI
<%@ Register TagPrefix="wssuc" TagName="DesignModeConsole" src=" controltemple
<!DOCTYPE html PUBLIC "-//W3C//DTD XHTML 1.0 Strict//EN"
"http://www.w3.org/TR/xhtml1/DTD/xhtml1-strict.dtd">
```

FIGURE 3-20

> *Adding* ~/ *after the quotation mark to make* src="_ *look like* src="~/_ *will fix this error and allow you to open your pages without error. The corrected code is shown in Figure 3-21.*

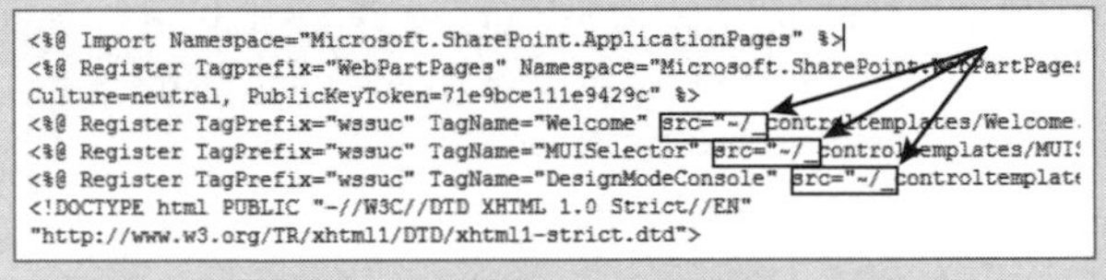

```
<%@ Import Namespace="Microsoft.SharePoint.ApplicationPages" %>
<%@ Register Tagprefix="WebPartPages" Namespace="Microsoft.SharePoint.WebPartPages
Culture=neutral, PublicKeyToken=71e9bce111e9429c" %>
<%@ Register TagPrefix="wssuc" TagName="Welcome" src="~/ controltemplates/Welcome.
<%@ Register TagPrefix="wssuc" TagName="MUISelector" src="~/ controltemplates/MUI!
<%@ Register TagPrefix="wssuc" TagName="DesignModeConsole" src="~/ controltemplate
<!DOCTYPE html PUBLIC "-//W3C//DTD XHTML 1.0 Strict//EN"
"http://www.w3.org/TR/xhtml1/DTD/xhtml1-strict.dtd">
```

FIGURE 3-21

EXAMPLE SCENARIOS

Regardless of your role, as you work with SharePoint, you will encounter requests to change the look and feel of your site. It takes time and practice to understand whether user interface requests are a big effort or a minor change.

The following scenarios and exercises are meant to give you experience in three different types of user interface requests. Each solution has its own set of issues depending on browser and content requirements.

Scenario 1: Fixed Width Layout

In Figure 3-22, the out-of-the-box layout of the v4.master is represented by Layout A. A common user interface change request is to optimize a site for a target screen resolution (usually 1024 pixels by 768 pixels, the most common screen resolution). This changes the layout of a site so that pages are fixed and centered as shown in Layout B.

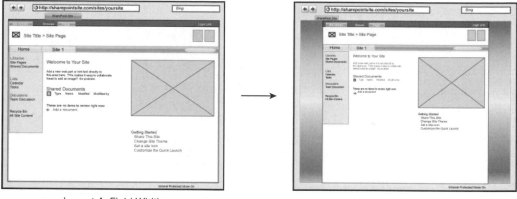

Layout A: Fluid Width   Layout B: Fixed Width

FIGURE 3-22

NOTE *A fixed-width design is a layout optimized for a target screen resolution. It is generally used to control the presentation of content regardless of the size of a user's window. There are several benefits to using this type of layout:*

➤ ***Readability*** *— A fixed width shortens lines of text and makes reading easier.*

➤ ***Consistency*** *— Content placement is predictable regardless of browser size. A controlled space allows for the communication of content relationships.*

➤ ***Aesthetics*** *— It simply looks good.*

A fixed-width design can be beneficial with managed content but can be troublesome when applied to collaboration sites because it can impact the intended functionality.

➤ ***User Adoption*** *— Users will be responsible for choosing appropriate sizes for content. If users are not comfortable making design decisions, they may choose to collaborate through e-mail or by phone instead of through the SharePoint site.*

➤ ***Design strength*** *— Any solution that fixes the width of the page impacts the out-of-the-box SharePoint functionality, including the scrolling of the ribbon, browser compatibility, and the behavior of large content.*

TRY IT OUT **Fix the Width of a Master Page**

In this activity, you will add an embedded style sheet that will fix the width of pages inheriting from this master page.

1. Open a team site in SharePoint Designer.

2. Select the Master Pages section of Site Objects.

3. Create a new master page by following the steps you used to create v4Demo.master.

4. Instead of naming the file `v4Demo.master`, name it `FixedWidthv4.master`.

5. Right-click on the file and select "Set as Default Master Page."

6. Right click on the file and select "Edit File in Advanced Mode." Add the following embedded style sheet into the master page just before the closing `</head>` tag:

```
<style type="text/css">
/*fixed width */
#s4-workspace > div,#s4-bodyContainer > div,body #s4-titlerow > div{
 width:1000px;
 margin:0 auto;
 float:none;
 padding:0;
}

body #s4-mainarea{
    /*make main area have background of white and add a border */
 background:#fff;
    border:1px solid #ddd;
    border-top:0px;
    min-height:580px;
    /*contain content in all browsers but IE7 */
 display:table;
}

/*add padding back to title table*/
.s4-title-inner{
    padding:0 0 0 5px;
}
/*background color of site*/
#s4-workspace {
    background:#efefef /*none*/;
}

/*body container */
#s4-bodyContainer{
    position:relative;
    width:100%;
}
/*fix overhanging tables*/
.ms-v4propertysheetspacing
{margin:0;}

</style>
```

7. Save and check in your changes.

8. Navigate to your browser and preview your changes in the browser to see your site is fixed-width, as shown in Figure 3-23.

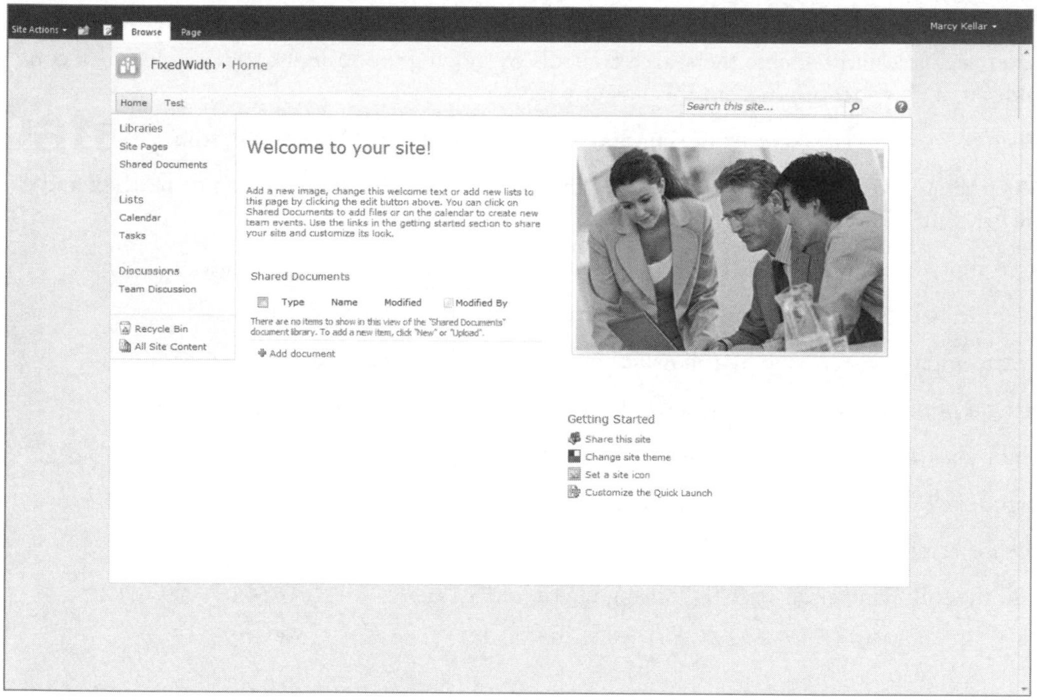

FIGURE 3-23

How It Works

This exercise illustrates how quickly you can implement significant changes to all pages in your site with only a few steps in SharePoint Designer. When you apply this master page as the default master page to your site, all content pages are displayed with a fixed width. If you also want the system or application pages to have a fixed width, you can right-click and select, "set as custom master page."

This particular scenario will be encountered often by those asked to redesign a SharePoint site. You should note that this solution works differently in different browsers and can be affected by the content in your site, such as list views with multiple columns. One of the attributes used to contain content that extends outside of the defined width, "display:table" is not recognized by Internet Explorer 7.

> **NOTE** FixedWidth.master *is available for download from the Wrox site and includes additional styling with CSS comments.*

Scenario 2: Changing the Location of the Search Box

In this scenario, the search control needs to be moved to a new location within the master page.

TRY IT OUT   Move the Search Box to a New Location

In this exercise, you will relocate the search controls by moving the `PlaceHolderSearchArea` content placeholder to a new location within the master page.

1. Open SharePoint Designer from your Start menu and click the Open Site button.

2. When the Open Site dialog appears, enter the URL to your site in the Site name textbox and click the OK button.

3. If prompted, enter the password for the SharePoint site and click the OK button.

4. Select Master Pages from the Navigation bar on the left.

5. Create a new master page by following the steps you used to create `v4Demo.master`.

6. Instead of naming the master page `V4Demo.master`, name it `SearchDemo.master`.

7. Right-click the file and select Set as Default Master Page.

8. Right-click the file and select Edit File in Advanced Mode.

9. Locate `<td class="s4-titletext">`.

10. Add the following code after the closing tag of `<td class="s4-titletext">`:

    ```
    <td class="customSearch" valign="middle" style="padding:0 5px;">
    </td>
    ```

    Next, you will grab the search control. Although you can see the search box in the Design View of SharePoint Designer, you will want to verify that you have the right control and HTML before moving it. The next steps walk you through a common activity when editing master pages, finding the correct content. Using the Find and Replace dialog is a common yet invaluable method to find elements and styles in SharePoint Designer.

11. If you are not already in Split View, select Split from the View tab of the ribbon and place your cursor inside the code window.

12. Use the shortcut key Ctrl+F to open the Find and Replace dialog.

13. To find the search content control, type the word "search" in the "Find What" field, as shown in Figure 3-24.

14. Click the Find All button.

15. The results of your search are displayed below the page editor in the Find1 window.

16. Double-click on the `ContentPlaceHolder` control whose `ID` attribute is set to `PlaceholderSearchArea` in the Find1 box and your cursor will jump to the location of the search control in the code window, as shown in Figure 3-25.

17. Select the following code and copy with Ctrl+C:

```
<asp:ContentPlaceHolder id="PlaceHolderSearchArea" runat="server">
<SharePoint:DelegateControl runat="server" ControlId="SmallSearchInputBox"
Version="4"/>
</asp:ContentPlaceHolder>
```

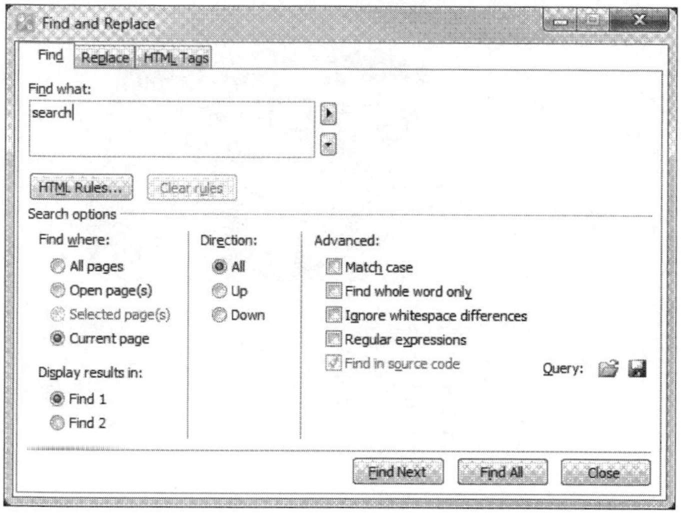

FIGURE 3-24

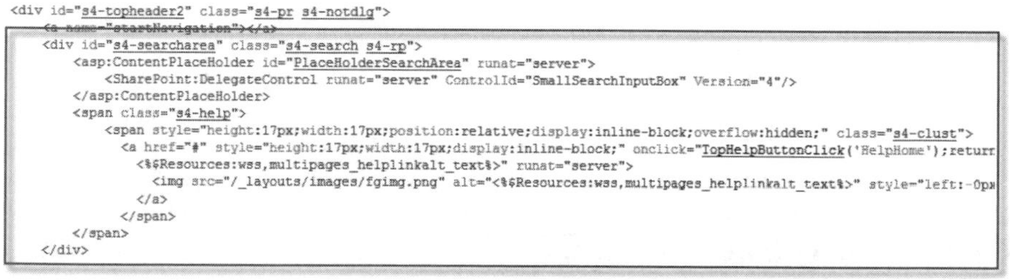

```
<div id="s4-topheader2" class="s4-pr s4-notdlg">
    <a name="startNavigation"></a>
    <div id="s4-searcharea" class="s4-search s4-rp">
        <asp:ContentPlaceHolder id="PlaceHolderSearchArea" runat="server">
            <SharePoint:DelegateControl runat="server" ControlId="SmallSearchInputBox" Version="4"/>
        </asp:ContentPlaceHolder>
        <span class="s4-help">
            <span style="height:17px;width:17px;position:relative;display:inline-block;overflow:hidden;" class="s4-clust">
              <a href="#" style="height:17px;width:17px;display:inline-block;" onclick="TopHelpButtonClick('HelpHome');returr
                <%$Resources:wss,multipages_helplinkalt_text%>" runat="server">
                  <img src="/_layouts/images/fgimg.png" alt="<%$Resources:wss,multipages_helplinkalt_text%>" style="left:-0px
                </a>
              </span>
        </span>
    </div>
```

FIGURE 3-25

18. Paste the copied code inside the `<td class="customSearch">` tag.
19. Save and Check in the file.
20. Navigate to the site's URL and preview your changes in the browser.
21. Notice the search controls have moved from the top navigation bar to the header, as shown in Figure 3-26.

How It Works

You can move placeholders around a master page. In this example, you moved the default search box to a new location. With minimal styling and structure changes, you were able to move the search box.

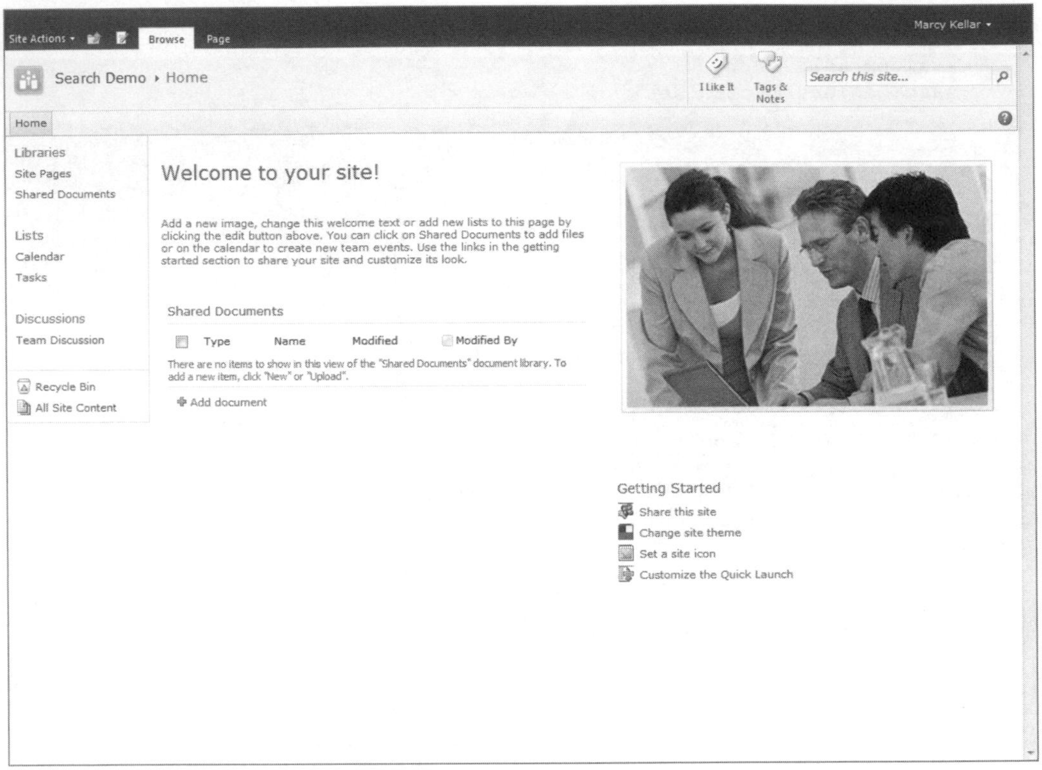

FIGURE 3-26

Scenario 3: Registering External CSS

The following example fulfills another common design request. Although you will learn more about CSS styles in Chapter 5, you may be asked to update your master page to reference external CSS files. For this example, an external style sheet and images are provided at the Wrox download site. A reference to the style sheet simply needs to be added to the master page so that the top navigation's tabs are styled with rounded top corners.

TRY IT OUT Add CSS Registration to a Master Page

In this exercise, you will create the external style sheet with the styling for the rounded navigation.

> **NOTE** This example requires two images. You can download the source code and images from the Wrox Download page at http://www.wrox.com.

1. Open SharePoint Designer from your Start menu.

2. Click the Open Site button.

3. When the Open Site dialog appears, enter the URL to your site in the Site name textbox and click the OK button.

4. If a Windows Security dialog appears, enter your username and password for the SharePoint site and click the OK button.

5. Select Master Pages from the Navigation bar on the left.

6. Create a new master page by following the steps you used to create v4Demo.master earlier in this chapter.

7. Name the new master page `NavDemo.master`.

8. Right-click the file and select Edit File in Advanced Mode.

9. Add the following to the end of the `<head>` tag:

```
<SharePoint:CssRegistration name="<% $SPUrl:~sitecollection/Style
Library/SPDDemo/css/roundednav.css %>" After="corev4.css" runat="server"/>
```

10. Check in `NavDemo.master`.

11. Right-click `NavDemo.master` and select "Set as Default Master."

12. Open a browser window and navigate to the site.

13. Select All Files from the Navigation bar on the left.

14. Double-click on the Style Library folder.

15. Place your mouse in the library and right-click.

16. Right-click Add ➪ New Item.

17. Select New ➪ Folder.

18. Name the folder `SPDDemo`.

19. In the `SPDDemo` folder, place your mouse in the library and right-click.

20. Select New ➪ Folder.

21. Name the folder **CSS**.

22. Double-click the folder and right-click.

23. Select New ➪ CSS.

24. Rename the new **Untitled_1.css** file to **roundednav.css**.

25. Add the following code into the roundednav.css file:

```
/*----Top Nav--------------- */
.s4-tn {min-height:34px;}
/*allow nav item to be taller than 15px*/
.s4-tn LI.static > .menu-item{height:auto;}

/*Transform top nav links to uppercase
and give top links bg color */
```

```
body #s4-topheader2{
background:#fff repeat-x left 0px;
border-bottom:transparent;border-top:transparent;
}

/*bottom border of nav bar*/
.s4-tn {border-bottom: 5px solid #016c9b;}
.s4-tn > .horizontal {
/*move horizontal nav to the right by 20 px*/
margin-left:20px;
}
/*keep nav from wrapping */
.menu-horizontal{min-width:790px;}

/*If you define nav styles and don't define them
in dynamic children selectors,
dynamic will inherit the style */
.s4-tn li.static > .menu-item{
border:0;
border:none;
color:#efefef;
display:inline-block;
min-width:70px;
height:36px;
padding:0px;
margin:0px;
vertical-align:middle;
white-space:nowrap;
text-align:center;
font-size:19px;
white-space:nowrap;
padding-top:12px;
}
.s4-toplinks .s4-tn > .menu-item.text {
padding:6px 24px 0 24px;}

/*nav link hover and nav header hover*/
.s4-tn li.static > a:hover,
.s4-tn li.static > .dynamic-children:hover{
display:block;
background:transparent none;
color:#fff;
text-decoration:none;
}
/*rounded nav*/
.s4-toplinks .s4-tn .static > li {
background:url("../images/tl.png")
no-repeat scroll 0 0 #79BBEC;
color:#efefef
}
.s4-toplinks .s4-tn .static > li > .menu-item{
background:url("../images/tr.png")
no-repeat scroll top right ;
}
```

```css
/*Rounded nav selected (left) background color goes here*/
.s4-toplinks .s4-tn .static > li.selected {
background:url("../images/tl.png")
no-repeat scroll 0 0 #efefef;
color:#5893CF
}
/*Rounded nav selected (right)*/
.s4-toplinks .s4-tn .static > li.selected > .menu-item{
background:url("../images/tr.png")
no-repeat scroll top right ;
color:#5893CF
}
.s4-toplinks .s4-tn .static > li.selected > a:hover {
color:#fff;
}
.s4-toplinks .s4-tn ul.static >
li.dynamic-children .menu-item-text ,
.s4-toplinks .s4-tn ul.static >
li.static .menu-item-text{
padding: 0 33px;
}

/*arrows in tabs with dynamic children*/
.menu-horizontal span.dynamic-children
SPAN.additional-background {
background-position:90% ;
}
.menu-horizontal a.dynamic-children
SPAN.additional-background {
background-position:90%;
}

/*flyout navigation */
.s4-tn ul.dynamic{
background:#A2CFEC;
margin:5px 0 0 10px;
background-color:#A2CFEC;
border:1px solid #44A0E5;
}
.s4-tn li.dynamic a{padding:5px;color:#1987DC;}
.s4-toplinks .s4-tn ul.dynamic .menu-item .menu-item-text {
padding: 5px 8px!important;
}
.s4-tn li.dynamic > .menu-item{
padding:3px 12px;
font-size:12px;
white-space:nowrap;
border-bottom:none;
font-weight:normal;
color:#003B55;
font-family:Verdana;
min-width:150px;
}
```

```
.s4-tn li.dynamic {border-bottom:1px #88C7F0 solid;}
.s4-tn li.dynamic > a:hover{
font-weight:400;
display:block;
background-color:#C7E2F3;
color:#1E6592;
}
```

26. Save and Check in your CSS file.

27. Using the browser, navigate to the site you customized.

28. Press F5 to refresh the browser and your site should like Figure 3-27.

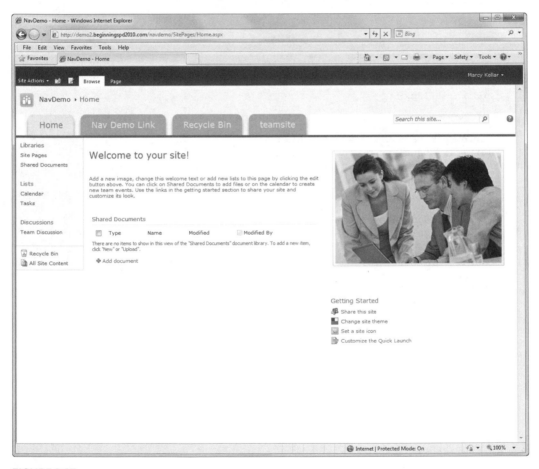

FIGURE 3-27

How It Works

When you added the `<SharePoint:CSSRegistration>` control to the master page, SharePoint created a reference link to the external CSS file, `navdemo.css`. Because you changed the `After` property to corev4.css, navdemo.css will load after corev4.css, which contains default SharePoint styling, and override any conflicting styles in corev4.css.

SUMMARY

This chapter explained how a typical SharePoint Page is constructed. You saw the power of Master Pages to change the look and feel of your site. You also found out:

➤ How to edit and apply master pages.

➤ You can change the way SharePoint looks from the out-of-the-box style.

➤ Points to consider when creating a custom master page.

This is only the first step in understanding how to customize the look and feel of your SharePoint 2010 site with SharePoint Designer. In the next chapter, you will learn about Web Content Management and the Publishing pages of SharePoint 2010.

4

Publishing Pages

WHAT YOU WILL LEARN IN THIS CHAPTER

➤ Web Content Management in SharePoint

➤ The features enabled by the SharePoint publishing infrastructure

➤ The components of SharePoint publishing pages

➤ More about master pages

➤ How to build page layouts and their underlying content types

In Chapter 3, you learned the basics of how pages were assembled in SharePoint, and how to customize the overall layout of a site by editing master pages. This chapter builds upon that knowledge by introducing the publishing infrastructure and web content management (WCM) features of SharePoint Server 2010 and SharePoint Designer 2010.

WEB CONTENT MANAGEMENT OVERVIEW

Early in this book, it was pointed out that SharePoint Designer 2010 is not a tool for creating web content (pages). Rather, it is primarily a tool for controlling the presentation of that content. SharePoint Server 2010 itself is the tool by which that content is created and managed. In other words, SharePoint Server 2010 acts as a *web content management* (WCM) system.

Web content management is a set of processes that lets you manage the *life cycle* of the information stored and presented by your website — wherein you create, customize, deploy, and dispose of web content. The content life cycle starts when content is created, whether manually through human effort, or as the output of an automated system or application. It completes when that content reaches its final disposition, which may be anything from simple deletion, through relocation into a permanent archival storage system. In between may be any number of stages of review, editing, scheduling, and approval.

By automating many (if not all) of these stages, a web content management system enables non-technical authors to create and maintain large volumes of content in a consistent and timely manner.

Web content management typically includes:

➤   Electronic forms or other means of input.

➤   An approval process or *workflow*.

➤   Scheduling workflows to ensure that the content is displayed, reviewed, *and removed from view* on a timely basis. (Using SharePoint Designer to create and customize workflows is discussed in detail in later chapters.)

➤   Templates to ensure visual consistency.

In many respects, these processes resemble those by which traditional printed publications, such as newspapers or magazines, are produced or published. In fact, within SharePoint Server 2010, the functions that enable WCM are called the *publishing features*. Using these features, you can develop, customize, and publish many different kinds of websites.

> **NOTE** *This chapter deals with features and functionality provided with SharePoint Server 2010, but not with SharePoint Foundation 2010 or Search Server 2010. You will need access to a site collection based upon SharePoint Server 2010 in order to perform the exercises in this chapter.*

Creating a Web Content Management Strategy

Web content management may sound easy, and it does simplify the nuts and bolts of putting together a website. However, significant planning is still needed before you start building or customizing. Without the answers to several key questions, you could end up with very pretty, very easy to update, and yet very *wrong* information on your website.

Here are a few things to think about as you start building a WCM strategy...

Who Owns The Content?

Where does "the buck stop" when it comes to determining whether information is accurate and appropriate? Chances are, different areas of your site will have different content owners. Except for true IT content, that owner will not be someone in the IT department!

Who Will Review And Approve The Content?

Is it the owner, or a trusted delegate? Must the content be approved by one person, or a group of people, before it becomes live on the site? While, in some cases, the owner will be directly creating the content and no approval will be needed, this is usually an exception, not the rule.

Does Content Already Exist?

If so, who will be responsible for migrating it? How much of it will need to be migrated, and who decides what to keep? If new content is to be created, who will be the authors of the content? Managing the content of a website, even with state-of-the-art WCM tools, is a big job. In fact, it could be a full-time job. Yet, as important as this job is, many companies expect people whose "real" job is something else to also create content for their web sites. It should come as no surprise that in these cases, this "extra" work tends to fall to the bottom of their priority list.

Do You Want To Apply The Company Brand To The Site?

If so, how customized will you make it? How aggressively will you restrict the look and feel and the layout of the pages that can be created on the site? SharePoint Designer 2010 gives you the power to make this happen, but be careful: if you customize too heavily, you can lose some of the benefits that make SharePoint such a great WCM tool. While many companies strive for some level of consistency, being too restrictive can discourage creativity and the desire to contribute content.

> **NOTE** Throughout this list, very little is said about technology. Almost all of it is about policy. While SharePoint and SharePoint Designer offer a wide array of tools to help IT professionals implement these policies, the policies themselves usually need to originate elsewhere in the organization. Any WCM project needs input from the content owners and end users, testing by the content creators, and the unwavering support of executive management in order to succeed.
>
> Many other communication and policy factors need to be taken into account before beginning any web design project. While some will be pointed out where task-critical, exploring them in detail is beyond the scope of this book. For a more thorough discussion of these matters, please consider Professional SharePoint 2010 Branding and User Interface Design, by Randy Drisgill et al.

GETTING STARTED WITH PUBLISHING

You've already learned about some non–publishing site collection templates from among the standard site templates that come with SharePoint Foundation. When you use SharePoint Server 2010, several additional site collection templates become available. Two of these templates are most relevant to web content management — the Publishing Portal site collection template and the Enterprise Wiki site collection template.

Creating a site collection via one of these two site collection templates enables publishing features automatically. These templates are specifically designed for web content management and, by default, limit the available site templates, lists, and libraries to those types relevant to publishing. That doesn't mean the classic "team" functions are gone forever.

Mixing Publishing and Collaboration Features

Generally speaking, collaboration site templates activate one set of features, while publishing site templates activate a different set. SharePoint is nothing if not flexible! What if, for example, you want to use the calendar list template in your publishing site? To gain access to this list (and many others), you simply activate the collaboration lists feature. If you want to create subsites with non–publishing site templates, you enable their use through the Page Layout and Site Template Settings page, accessed through Site Actions ➪ Site Settings.

You can also use publishing features in non-publishing sites, such as the Team Site and Blog Site templates. To use publishing features within a non-publishing site requires two features to be activated. First, activate the *Publishing Infrastructure* at the site collection level. This enables several functions that are used site-collection–wide, but the most obvious change is in the objects used for managing SharePoint's navigation. Rather than manipulating the top Tab Bar and side Quick Launch separately, these become facets of a single hierarchy.

Once you have the Publishing Infrastructure activated, you need to activate the *Publishing Features* within each lower-level site in which you intend to use them. In addition to default lists and libraries typical of the non-publishing site template, you will then be able to take advantage of all the functionality normally included in the publishing site collection templates.

TRY IT OUT   **Activate Publishing in a Team Site from the Web User Interface**

1. From the web interface of your team site, click Site Actions ➪ Site Settings. This will bring you to the settings page.

2. If you see a link under Site Collection Administration entitled "Go to top level site settings," click it to change to the appropriate context.

3. Under the Site Collection Administration heading, click the Site Collection Features link. This will summon the feature list. Observe that a number of features are available.

4. Scroll down to SharePoint Server Publishing Infrastructure, and click the Activate button. Observe that an "Active" icon appears next to the feature.

5. Return to the Site Settings page. You may notice that some of the options on this page have changed. These changes will be described in detail later.

6. Under the Site Actions heading, select Manage Site Features. A different Feature list from that shown by Step 3 will be displayed.

7. Scroll to the SharePoint Server Publishing feature.

8. Click the Activate button. The Active icon will appear next to the feature.

How It Works

SharePoint is very modular. While there are many different types of functionality within SharePoint, most of them are grouped and deployed via *Features*. Different site types have different combinations of features activated by default. Features can be activated at different levels, or *scopes*, within SharePoint. These include not only the Site and Site Collection scopes you saw in this exercise, but

Web Application and Farm-wide scopes as well. Features can depend upon other features. In this exercise, the Site scoped Publishing features rely upon the Site Collection scoped Publishing Infrastructure in order to function.

The SharePoint Server Publishing Infrastructure feature creates a number of objects, and modifies many other areas of your team site. The following table describes the key changes made when you activate the Publishing Infrastructure.

AREA	ACTIONS
Permissions and Groups	Adds these groups and permission levels: Approvers (Approve permission level) Designers (Design, Limited Access permission levels) Hierarchy Managers (Manage Hierarchy permission level) Restricted Readers (Restricted Read permission level) Style Resource Readers (Limited Access permission level)
Site Templates	Adds the following site templates to the Site Templates gallery: Publishing Site Publishing Site with Workflow Enterprise Wiki
Site Settings Page	Adds many new links to the Site Settings page (described following this table).
Navigation	Replaces the top link bar with the global navigation menu. Global and Current navigation are set to show subsites by default.
Lists and Libraries	Creates a Pages library to house publishing pages; for example, `http://yoursitename.com/Pages`.
Lists and Libraries	Creates an Images library for managing publishing images; for example, `http://yoursitename.com/PublishingImages`.
Lists and Libraries	Creates the Content and Structure Reports List, which allows Collaborative Application Markup Language (CAML) query customization for the View list area of the Site Content and Structure tool.
Lists and Libraries	The Reusable Content List contains HTML, images, or text that is inserted into and reused across web pages. Edit the content of this list instead of updating multiple pages.
Lists and Libraries	The Site Collection Documents Library is storage for documents that are used throughout the site collection.

continues

(continued)

AREA	ACTIONS
Lists and Libraries	The Site Collection Images Library stores images that are used throughout the site collection.
Master Page Gallery	Adds the NightandDay.master publishing master page.
	Adds default page layouts to the Master Page Gallery (found in the Page Layouts folder in SharePoint Designer).
	Creates a Preview Images folder containing the Page Layout thumbnail image. The folder is named using the language that was used for installation.
	Adds an Editing Menu folder that contains XSL styling files for the Page Editing menu.
Site Columns	Many site columns are added to the Site Columns gallery that assist with managing content and workflows:
	Page Layout: Byline and Page Content
	Publishing: Article Date, Scheduling Start Date, and Scheduling End Date
	Custom: Wiki Categories
Content Types	Adds Publishing and Page Layout content types. These content type groups contain content types such as Publishing Master Page, Page Layout, Article Page, Project Page, and so on.
Web Parts	Enables the following web parts for all sites in the site collection:
	Content Query Web Part
	Media Web Part
	Summary Links Web Part
	Table Of Contents Web Part
Page Editing Menu	Adds additional page-editing functionality for managing text, images, and media files.
Host Server	Enables timer jobs for scheduling publishing content and managing variation hierarchies.
Site Themes	Adds Inherit Theme and Apply Theme sections to the Site Themes page.

Although the SharePoint Server Publishing Infrastructure feature enables these functions, to use most of them, you also need to enable the Site scoped SharePoint Server Publishing feature. The Publishing Features feature enables links that allow additional customization of the user interface, such as the use of page layouts and the direct selection of master pages. Figure 4-1 shows the Site Settings page of a site after the Publishing Infrastructure and Publishing Features have been activated. Several links that were added or changed after the publishing functions were activated have been highlighted.

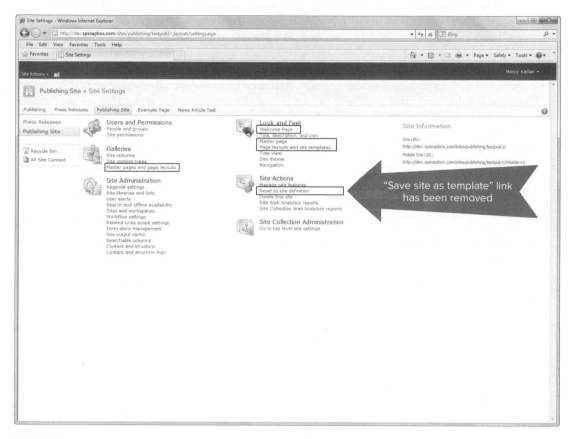

FIGURE 4-1

"Reset to site definition" is highlighted in the figure to show where the "Save site as template" option would have been prior to activation of the publishing features. This option is removed because customizations in publishing sites tend to have dependencies on information in other sites — particularly the root site of their original site collection. These cannot be guaranteed to be available in whatever arbitrary context a new site may be instantiated.

> **NOTE** *While you cannot save publishing sites as templates, you do have many options for reusing your work. You can export the individual master pages, layouts, and style sheets you create within SharePoint Designer, as described elsewhere in this chapter. You can also use site backups, database migrations, or the content deployment model to copy and move entire sites from one environment to another. These methods rely on SharePoint administrative techniques that are beyond the scope of this book.*

A Question Of Understanding

Web content management and SharePoint's publishing infrastructure can be confusing — even to the most SharePoint-savvy users — because the relevant concepts are often framed within an internal business environment. Many businesses have cultures wherein certain words or phrases have acquired meanings different from those commonly used in the SharePoint or WCM worlds. For example, if the word *intranet* is synonymous with *fileshare* or *collaboration* in your organization, imagining your intranet as having pages with news stories instead of document links might be hard. The following table matches some common objectives with functionality in the publishing infrastructure:

OBJECTIVE	PUBLISHING FEATURE/AREA
You want each department site in your intranet to roll-up content from other areas of your intranet.	Content Query Web Part and Article Page Layout
You want to publish your content in multiple languages.	Variations
You need extensive structural user interface changes and customizations.	Page Layouts, Master Pages
You have a group of authors who are assigned topics about which to write. Their articles are managed using a publishing paradigm.	Approval workflow
You want to have precise stylistic control over values displayed in a web part.	Content Query Web Part
You want to roll-up related information from more than one site, or multiple content types.	Search Results Web Part
You want broad control over colors and fonts used in your site, and the way they are inherited.	Themes, Alternate CSS
You want all of your department sites to have exactly the same structure, but you want any non-technical department administrator to be able to create new content pages.	Page Layouts
You have a large amount of slowly changing, highly organized content that is applicable to a large audience.	Page Layouts

PUBLISHING PAGES

Whether you are creating an intranet or a large public-facing news site, SharePoint can present your web content through the use of publishing pages. In Chapter 3, you learned that two types of pages are standard in SharePoint: *site pages* and *application pages*. When you activate the SharePoint

Publishing Infrastructure feature, you can work with one more type of page, the *publishing page,* which is also referred to as a *content page.*

For the Publishing pages to be available, you must have SharePoint Server 2010 and activate the publishing functionality as described earlier in this chapter. When these features are activated, they create the underlying structure required for publishing pages and managing content, such as the Pages library and approval workflow.

Although you can create sites with any type of page in SharePoint, the publishing page should be your system page of choice for managing web content. Web content is not just the copy that's on the page. It's the *chrome* (visual elements that surround content, but aren't critical to the specific content being displayed), reusable content, fixed text, bullets, images, graphic design, interactive media...the list goes on. Analogous to a newspaper, magazine, or book, web content often targets a broad audience and has a smaller group of authors. It's traditionally a unilateral communication of information, although recently, the explosion of the social web blurs that line a little bit.

Publishing pages are the most structured of SharePoint content pages. They provide a very controlled layout of text, graphics, and dynamic content.

The operational difference between publishing pages and non-publishing content pages is that publishing pages are composed of three parts, rather than two: the content itself, a master page, and a third element called a page layout. Master pages were covered initially in Chapter 3, where you learned about pages, content placeholders, and content controls. Publishing master pages have some special considerations, which are described later in this chapter.

A *page layout* is an ASP.NET (ASPX) page that defines the layout for content. In some respects, it is like a master page within a master page. It contains components that are substituted at run-time for the actual page content. The biggest difference is that it resides in just a portion of the page. Essentially, the master page defines the overall look of your site, while page layouts control the presentation of an individual type of information, such as a news article, or a product description page. Figure 4-2 shows the typical relationship between a master page and a page layout.

FIGURE 4-2

Master pages and page layouts together form a powerful user interface (UI) toolset. Because your overall look and feel is managed in one place, it is easy to ensure consistency and ease of UI design administration. If you need to update your design, changes are made to one or two files, which are then propagated to all pages inheriting from that master page and page layout combination.

> **TIP** *The publishing feature makes managing your site's user interface design and enforcing a consistent company branding easy. However, allowing just anyone to edit these pages introduces risks to the design and management of the site. Only a small number of trained users should be able to edit master pages and page layouts in SharePoint Designer.*
>
> *Out of the box, SharePoint comes with preconfigured permission levels that help you control the ability to customize the user interface with SharePoint Designer. The permission levels that allow, by default, the use of SharePoint Designer include Full Control, Design, and Manage Hierarchy. By ensuring that your "average" user is not a member of these groups, you can minimize the risk of inadvertent design changes.*

Publishing Master Pages

A publishing master page serves the same basic function as a non-publishing master page. It supplies the outer portion of the page with the global layout of the site, controlling objects like the logo, navigation, and general structures such as the header and footer, search box, sign-in link, and the Site Actions menu.

While superficially similar, publishing pages are not quite the same type of pages as the others discussed so far in this book. Technically speaking, to implement publishing features, they inherit from the `Microsoft.SharePoint.Publishing` class, which is in an entirely different class hierarchy from the previously discussed site pages, which inherit solely from the `Microsoft.SharePoint.WebPartPages.WebPartPage` class.

> **NOTE** *It is possible for a page to inherit from both hierarchies. Such a page is still considered a publishing page for purposes of site design.*

As you saw in Chapter 3, editing a master page can give you a great deal of control over your site's look and feel. This capability is even more critical when you are working in a publishing/WCM environment. These sites usually not only are heavily branded, but also experience a heavy volume of read traffic. This often requires special considerations when designing your pages.

For example, Internet sites rarely use the collaboration capability of SharePoint. Including them (by inheriting from the WebPartPage object noted earlier in this section, and making use of those features) introduces unnecessary overhead, and can reduce performance for your users. In particular, v4.master, though functional and flexible, is a very complicated and "heavy" page (lots of code and subsidiary components), and is therefore rarely a suitable basis for a high-volume website.

The next subsection describes the Master Page gallery, which will hold any master pages you create. The subsections following it describe some of the options available for creating and editing publishing master pages.

The Master Page Gallery

Master pages and page layout templates are both located in the Master Page gallery. Because it is a document library, it behaves just as does a traditional document library. Files in this library have the following attributes:

➤ Versioning is turned on by default and major and minor versions are tracked. Draft item security is enabled so only users who can edit items can see and work with the draft (minor versions) of the items.

➤ Content approval is required for newly created or changed items in the library. *Note: During site customization, turning content approval off until you have completed the final build is safe (and much more efficient).*

➤ Documents are required to be checked out before they can be edited.

➤ Permissions to this library are limited to those who can create and add files. In SharePoint 2010, this is limited to Designers, Site Owners, and Site Collection Administrators, so make sure you give your designer appropriate rights!

The Master Page gallery exists in the root site of a site collection. It's accessible through the site collection's Site Settings page, or through SharePoint Designer. Master Pages and Page Layouts are stored in a single library. Recall from Chapter 1 that SharePoint Designer 2010 organizes site artifacts by their object type, rather than their storage location. This results in Page layouts being listed in one section of SharePoint Designer, and master pages themselves listed in another. Figure 4-3 shows the Master Pages section.

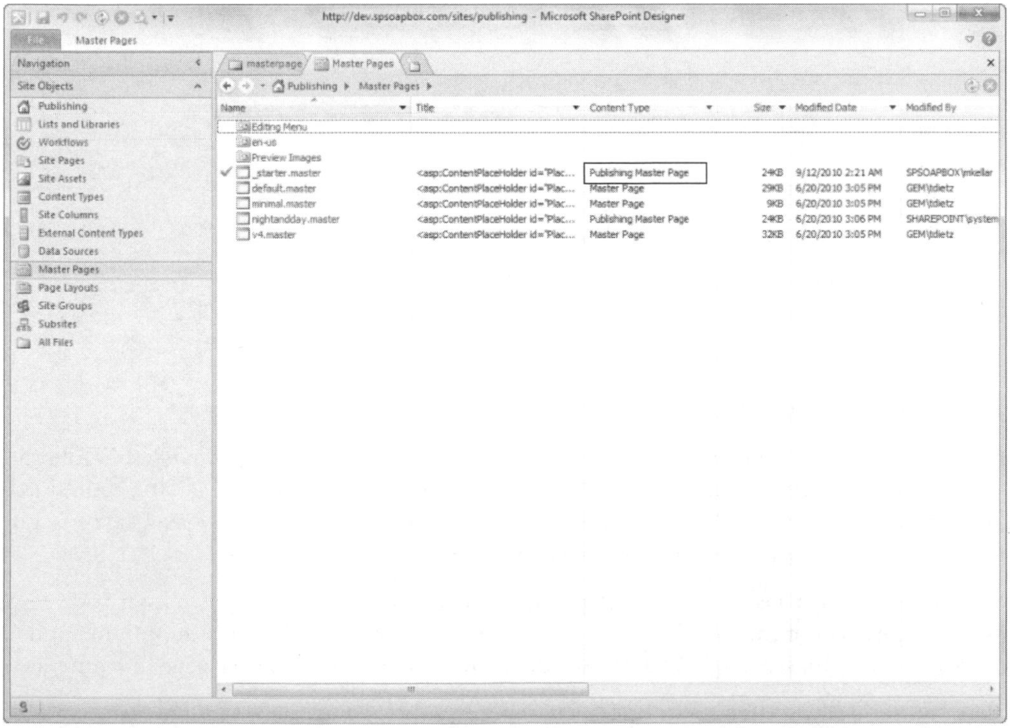

FIGURE 4-3

Any page with a Page Layout content type will be displayed in the Page Layouts section. Any page with a Master Page content type displays in the Master Pages section. If you select All Files and drill down through the `_catalogs/masterpage` folder, you can see the full contents of the Master Pages library, similar to how it was displayed in SharePoint Designer 2007. Figure 4-4 shows the contents of a typical master page folder.

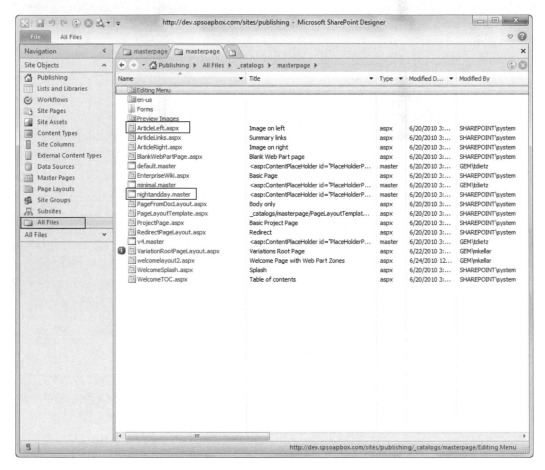

FIGURE 4-4

Editing the Example Publishing Master Page

The default publishing master page in SharePoint 2010 is called nightandday.master. While the page is reasonably attractive, it is assumed that you will not use the page "as-is" for your sites (most companies aren't named "Adventure Works"). However, it can be useful as a starting point, as it illustrates several key publishing master page concepts.

Like the v4.master you learned about in Chapter 3, or any other master page, this master page controls the general look and feel of the site. The header, navigation, search, social icons, sign-in link, and CSS references reside in the master page. You can see the nightandday.master master page in Figure 4-5.

Notice that nightandday.master does not display top, or global, navigation. On many sites, global navigation helps guide users to key areas within the site. However, this can come at the expense of making the content of any particular area as easy as possible to find. The lack of global navigation, on the other hand, could impede content creation or administrative functions.

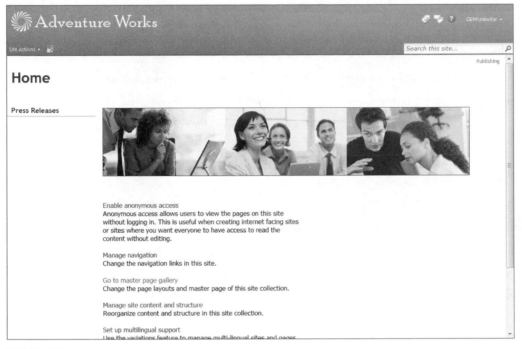

FIGURE 4-5

SharePoint helps with this dichotomy by providing the option to use different master pages for content pages (the *site master page*), and system-related pages (the *system master page*). By default, when you create a new publishing site, nightandday.master is assigned to be the site master and v4.master is used as the system master, as shown in Figure 4-6.

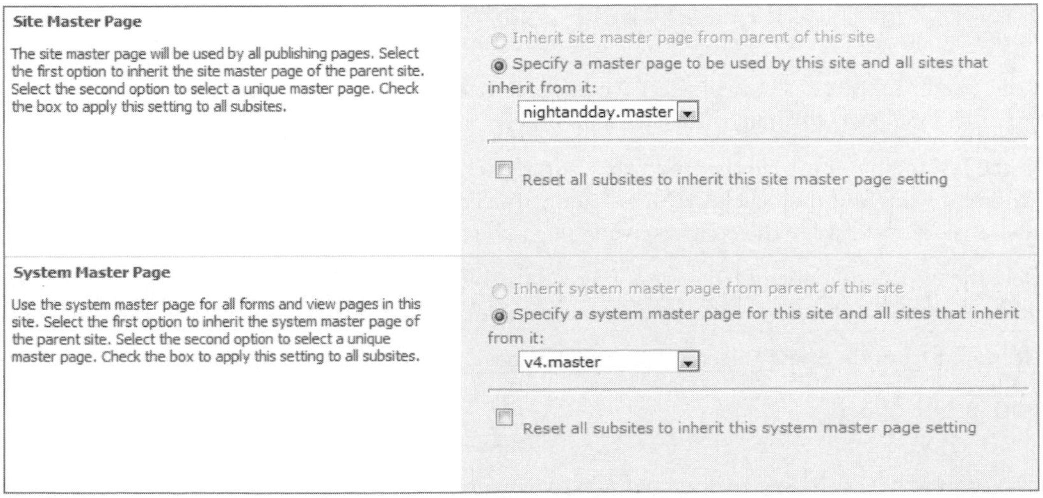

FIGURE 4-6

TRY IT OUT   Add Top Navigation to nightandday.master

1. Before you begin, make sure you have a new site with publishing features enabled.

2. Open the site in SharePoint Designer.

3. Click the Master Pages section of the Site Objects list. All master pages available for use in this site are displayed.

4. Double-click the Master Page tab to expose the ribbon, if you have it minimized.

5. Click the line in the Master Pages list for nightandday.master. (Do not click the filename itself.)

6. In the Clipboard section of the ribbon tab, click the Copy icon. Observe that the Paste icon becomes enabled.

7. In the Clipboard section of the ribbon tab, click the Paste icon. Observe that a new file, entitled nightandday_copy(1).master, is created.

8. Click the line in the Master Pages list for nightandday_copy(1).master.

9. In the Edit section of the ribbon, click the Rename icon. The filename becomes editable.

10. Edit the filename to read nightandday_globanav.master and hit Enter.

11. In the Edit section of the ribbon, click Edit File. The page will open in the design surface. (If prompted to check out the file, do so.)

12. If not already in Design view, click Design in the View Selector Toolbar.

13. In the Editing section of the Home ribbon tab, click the Skewer Click icon.

14. Click the breadcrumb just below the blue banner, and select the `<tr>` tag. The row containing the breadcrumb will be highlighted.

15. On the Table Tools ⇨ Layout contextual ribbon tab, in the Rows & Columns section, click the Insert Above icon. A new row will be added.

16. Click into the newly created row.

17. On the Quick Selector Toolbar, click the td.breadcrumb object.

18. In the Tag Properties task pane, select the menu-horizontal class. (You may need to display the Tag Properties task pane through the View ribbon tab.)

19. On the Insert ribbon tab, in the Controls section, click the SharePoint icon. (You may need to click a different icon, and then click the SharePoint icon again in order to allow SharePoint Designer time to correctly display the controls available in your site.)

20. Select the AspMenu control from the Server Controls (SharePoint) section. A data source selector will appear briefly, but you will probably not be able to select the data source before it disappears.

21. Select Split from the View Selector Toolbar. The newly inserted SharePoint:AspMenu tag should be visible.

22. Click the SharePoint:AspMenu tag.

23. In the Tag Properties task pane, set the Data Source to SiteMapDS, and the Orientation to Horizontal.

24. Save the file. (If necessary in your environment, also check in and approve a major version.)

25. Select Site Actions ⇨ Site Settings ⇨ Look and Feel ⇨ Master Page.

26. Select nightandday_globalnav.master for the System Master Page.

27. Click OK. Observe that the page now has the Night and Day style, but also includes a global navigation menu.

How It Works

There are many pages within SharePoint that use the system master page, some of which, though hidden from readers, are seen regularly by your content producers. It can be jarring for your users to suddenly be switched from one look and feel to another, so many companies require that all pages in the site at least resemble one another.

Creating Custom Master Pages

You aren't limited to modifying existing master pages. For a highly customized site, such as an Internet presence, or a large corporate intranet, you can also create master pages from scratch. This will give you the complete control needed to implement any wire frames (or other prototypes) that have been defined.

> **NOTE** Someone familiar with SharePoint structure and functionality should be involved in creating or approving prototypes. This helps to ensure that any desired SharePoint features are reflected in the design, and that any desired functionality that doesn't map to stock SharePoint features can be more easily accommodated.

When you create a blank master page, you need to add a number of placeholders in order to keep SharePoint from "breaking," even if you never intend to have those components displayed on the page. This is because, while you don't need to use every placeholder you put on a master page, the master page must contain every placeholder referenced by the content page.

Typically, you need to add a panel object to your master page, with its Visible property set to False in order to hold these required placeholders. The placeholders required in a SharePoint master page can vary depending upon the type of page you are creating.

For this reason, starting from a truly "blank" canvas can be counterproductive. There is a middle ground, however: starter master pages.

Importing a Starter Master Page

Given the minimum placeholder requirements, not to mention support for the ribbon, and other good stylistic practices, it can be helpful to start with a master page that already includes the minimum necessary placeholders to ensure the page will work in SharePoint.

While SharePoint itself does not include such a master page, various members of the SharePoint community do provide them, under the name "starter master pages."

Starter master pages are simplified, commented master pages. If you use one of these pages, you will have an easier customization experience. You can create a design, slice it up, and implement it with one of these community goodies.

Thank you to Randy Drisgill, Kyle Schaeffer, and MSDN for making these possible. You can download a selection of starter master pages from the Microsoft CodePlex site: `http://startermasterpages.codeplex.com/releases/view/41533`.

> **WARNING** *Starter master pages are the equivalent to the minimal master pages in SharePoint 2007. However, this should not be confused with the "minimal.master" that is provided with SharePoint 2010. This master page does not include all of the necessary placeholders to support all page types. It is designed specifically for supporting simplified search sites and the Office Web Applications.*

> **NOTE** *By default, all files imported into the master page gallery via SharePoint Designer are assigned the page layout content type. Since page layouts and master pages are filtered into different views in SharePoint Designer 2010 based on their content type, this can make it difficult to find an imported master page. Look for it in the Page Layouts directory.*
>
> *You can correct the content type to Publishing Master Page through the web UI. However, it is a better practice to import a master page through the web UI in the first place, and then make any desired changes in SharePoint Designer. This is because SharePoint Designer expects files to be "pre-processed" by SharePoint when it opens them. It automatically compensates for that processing before working with its local copy, so that it can properly show you the original file. Unfortunately, SharePoint Designer will still try to perform this compensation even if the file isn't pre-processed.*
>
> *The net effect is that pages (like master pages and page layouts) that use certain internal references, called* tokens, *can become unusable if SharePoint Designer opens them directly from the file system. This is also a key reason you should not edit pages from the _layouts folder in SharePoint Designer, as almost all of the pages here contain such tokens.*

Page Layouts

Content is what drives users to a website, whether internally or externally. The nature of your site's content should drive its presentation, so that all pages that show a certain kind of information are visually consistent. The mechanism SharePoint uses to help you provide that consistency is called a *page layout*.

Foreshadowing Content Types

Page layouts allow you to control the positioning of content on a publishing page by placing controls that display specific pieces of information from a *content type*. Although content types are described briefly here to assist your understanding of page layouts, see Chapter 6 for a thorough discussion. The content type designated for a particular page layout determines the elements that are available for display on any pages that inherit from that page layout.

> **NOTE** *Virtually every object in SharePoint has a content type. Some, like calendar events, are implied by the list or library they are a member of. Others can be reassigned at will. Still others, like the page layout, can contain references to other content types. It is this last relationship that is being described here.*

Content types contain columns that define particular aspects of a piece of content. A content type defining an inventory item, for example, might include a name, description, wholesale and retail prices, as well as the quantity on hand. Each field control you see on a page layout is a column from its associated content type. You do not need to use every column in your page layout. Even if a column is not included as content displayed, the content it contains is still associated with the page as metadata.

The columns used in your content types define the kind of content in them, as well as default control associated with the column. Column types may be defined as a single line of text, a block of rich text, a date, a hyperlink, a picture, or many other things, but each column only has one data type.

Content types used as the basis for publishing pages must be *site content types*. This means they can only be created in the top-level site of a site collection. After a site content type is created, however, it is available to all subsites.

An individual Page layout can only be associated with one content type, but multiple page layouts per content type can exist. Figure 4-7 displays

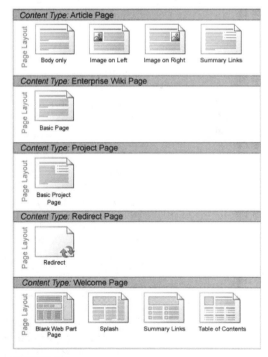

FIGURE 4-7

the default page layout content types. You can see that both the Article Page content type and the Welcome Page content type have multiple page layouts associated with them.

> **TIP**
>
> ➤ Do not rename your content types. Instead, delete the content type after reassociating all items that inherit from it. Even in the rapid prototyping and proof of concept phase, diagramming your content metadata prior to configuring is better.
>
> ➤ Users creating new items in a library that manages multiple content types will see the content type description when they are choosing to create a new item through the UI (see Figure 4-8). Create a description that will make sense to a user creating a new item in a library that manages multiple content types.

FIGURE 4-8

> ➤ Name your content types in the singular. "News Article Page Layout" is correct. "News Article Pages" is not. A user can only create one item based on the content type at a time. When you name a content type, think of it in the context of "I want to create a new [Content Type Name]; for example, News Article Page."
>
> ➤ If you want to add a custom site column, such as Article Abstract, to a page layout such as an Article Page, begin by creating a custom content type that inherits from the Article Page layout. Add your site column to the child content type. This leaves the default content type untouched and gives you greater flexibility for growth and scalability of your content type architecture. Leaving the objects that Microsoft ships with SharePoint in their original state and either inheriting from or making copies of these objects is always the best practice.

Page Layouts for Micro-design

While page layouts are primarily used to control the layout of objects on a publishing page, they can also facilitate creating controlled exceptions to your corporate branding. For example, promotional microsites or seasonal branding can be managed easily by adding references to CSS files that override the ones defined in your master page. This can make one type of page layout radically different from the rest of the site, without impacting your mainline content.

PUTTING IT ALL TOGETHER

Throughout this chapter, you have learned about the components of the SharePoint Publishing web content management model, and how you can use SharePoint Designer to build each piece individually. This section will help you understand how they all work together by walking you through the creation of a simple publishing site from start to finish.

> **NOTE** *Each "Try It Out" exercise in this section will use the one before it as the starting point.*

You are part of a SharePoint intranet team. You have been given the following requirements and supplemental information and asked to create an appropriate solution:

Requirements

➤ Our news content should be reviewed by designated Corporate Communications team members to validate that submitted news content meets corporate brand and style guidelines.

➤ All intranet users should be able to rate news content.

Content Definition

➤ **News Content** — Timely information that is company-relevant and requires archiving. News content captures the following information:

> ➤ **Byline** — Text
>
> ➤ **Article Abstract** — Multiple Lines of Text
>
> ➤ **Body Content** — Multiple Lines of Text
>
> ➤ **Summary** — Multiple Lines of Text
>
> ➤ **Publication Date** — Date/Time
>
> ➤ **Archive Date** — Date/Time
>
> ➤ **Source** — URL
>
> ➤ **Key Contact** — Text
>
> ➤ **Owner** — Text
>
> ➤ **RollupImage** — Image

> ➤ **Page Image1** — Image
> ➤ **Page Image 2** — Image
> ➤ **Ratings** — Ratings

Solution and Design

First of all, congratulations for being a member of an organization that states requirements that do not include the solution! Bravo! Although it has some unanswered questions that would require clarification if this were a real example, you could use this information as a starting point. You determine that your solution includes the following:

> ➤ Publishing site with approval workflow
> ➤ Custom page layout
> ➤ Custom content type
> ➤ Custom site columns
> ➤ Field controls

First, you must create the custom page layout content type. Page layouts should be defined by content pattern and content purpose. Do not be surprised if you have to give it a few tries before getting the architecture correct. You will learn a lot as you go.

Based on the required content, the content type you choose as a parent would be the Article Page layout. This content type closely matches your requirements and is a good starting point.

TRY IT OUT   Create a Publishing Page Layout Content Type

1. Using SharePoint Designer, open a site that has publishing enabled.
2. Click Content Types.
3. Click the Content Types tab to expose the ribbon if it is minimized/hidden. If you have not hidden your ribbon, you can ignore this step in this and future exercises.
4. Navigate to the New section of the ribbon and click Content Type.
5. Name your content type **Custom Article Page**.
6. Fill out the Description field. Remember, this description will be displayed whenever the user creates a new page based on this content type.
7. Click OK.

How It Works

SharePoint creates a new content type based on the parent content type you select, in this case, the Article Page content type. All the site columns associated with the Article Page content type will initially be inherited by your custom content type. SharePoint categorizes the new content type based on the group you select, the Page Layout Content Types group.

Creating Custom Site Columns

Next, you add site columns to your new content type. For the purpose of this example, you will only add the Article Abstract site column. It uses the column template or field type called "Multiple Lines of Text."

Start this exercise in the same site in which you created the Custom Article content type in the preceding Try It Out.

TRY IT OUT   Create Custom Site Columns

1. Using SharePoint Designer, open a site that has publishing enabled.

2. Click Site Columns.

3. Click the Site Columns tab to expose the ribbon.

4. Navigate to the New section of the ribbon and click New Column.

5. Select the data type for the column. The Create a Site Column dialog appears.

6. Name your content type **Article Abstract**.

7. Fill out the Description field. When you are finished, the Create a Site Column dialog should resemble Figure 4-9.

8. Click OK.

9. Click the Save button to commit the changes.

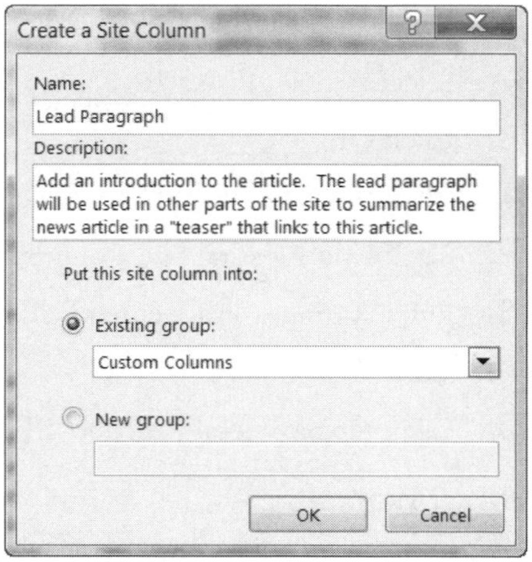

Create a Site Column

Name:

Lead Paragraph

Description:

Add an introduction to the article. The lead paragraph will be used in other parts of the site to summarize the news article in a "teaser" that links to this article.

Put this site column into:

◉ Existing group:

Custom Columns

◯ New group:

OK   Cancel

FIGURE 4-9

How It Works

When you click "New Site Column," SharePoint opens a form to collect the appropriate attributes of the site column, such as Name, Description, and Group. Depending upon the data type you select, you are asked to provide other input, such as a list of choices. Clicking OK creates a new site column called Article Abstract. Clicking the Save button commits your changes to the content database. The site column now is available to be added to all content types in any subsites. If you update any properties of the site column, you can push your changes to all children of the site column.

TRY IT OUT   Add Site Columns to a Custom Content Type

In this exercise, you will add the Ratings and Article Abstract site columns to your custom content type. To do this in SharePoint Designer, follow these steps:

1. Using SharePoint Designer, open a site that has publishing enabled.

2. Click Content Types.

3. Scroll down to the Page Layout Content Types section.

4. Right-click Custom Article Page to go to the Content Type Settings Page.

5. In the Customization Section, click the "Edit Content Type Columns" link.

6. Click the Columns tab.

7. Click Add Existing Site Column. The dialog shown in Figure 4-10 will appear. (The column you are looking for is called out in the figure.)

8. Start typing **Article Abstract** in the form's search field. Notice how the list is quickly filtered to show only the desired column.

9. Select Article Abstract.

10. Click OK.

11. Click the Columns tab.

12. Click Add Existing Site Column.

13. Enter **Ratings** in the search field and **Select Ratings**.

14. Click OK.

15. Click the Save icon (or choose File ⇨ Save) to commit your work.

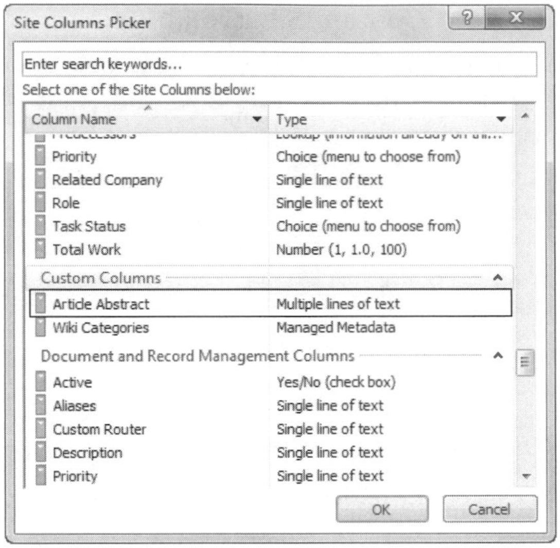

FIGURE 4-10

How It Works

When you added the Article Abstract and Ratings site columns to the content type Custom Article Page, these columns became part of the page properties or metadata. You will be able to filter pages based on the ratings field or present content summaries using the Article Abstract column. All pages inheriting from this content type now have these fields associated with them and they can be added to a custom page layout.

Creating a Custom Page Layout

Now that you have created a custom content type with the appropriate site columns, you can create your custom page layout. Make sure to set up a content type field for each field that you want to appear on the publishing page.

TRY IT OUT   **Create a Custom Publishing Page Layout**

In this exercise, you create a custom page layout based on the content type Custom Article Page. Do this exercise in the same site where you created the Custom Article content type in the earlier Try It Out.

1. Click Page Layouts.

2. Navigate to the New section of the ribbon and click New Page Layout.

3. Choose the Page Layout content type group.

4. Select Custom Article Page.

5. Give the page layout a meaningful URL name without spaces, such as NewsArticlePagewithRatings.

6. Make the title **News Article Page with Ratings**.

7. Click OK. The new page layout opens in the Advanced Editor mode.

How It Works

Inheriting from a custom content type rather than a default SharePoint content type allows flexibility in management of web content architecture. When you create a page layout from a custom page layout content type, the site columns associated with the content type are also available to the page layout.

Field Controls

Content on a page is stored as metadata for items in the Pages document library. When users view or edit the page, content is pulled from the SharePoint Pages library and displayed in field controls.

Field controls are simple controls that correspond to site columns defined in the underlying content type of the page layout. Field controls are great for placing content in a fixed location on the page to create a consistent look and feel. An added benefit is that the content in the field control is also versioned when the page is versioned. Figure 4-11 shows several field controls on a page.

TRY IT OUT Add a Field Control to Your Page Layout

In this exercise, you will add the `Ratings` and `Article Abstract` controls to your page layout. Do this exercise in the same site where you created the Custom Article content type in the earlier Try It Out. If you are proceeding directly to this exercise from the previous one, you may skip Steps 1 and 2.

1. Using SharePoint Designer, open the default `ArticleLeft` page layout.

2. A dialog box appears, asking if you would like to check out the file.

3. Click No. You will not be editing the file.

Another dialog box appears and asks whether you would like the edit the file in advanced mode.

4. Click No.

5. Copy the contents of the page to your clipboard. If the `NewsArticlePagewithRatings` page layout is open, skip to Step 8.

6. Select Page Layouts from Site Objects.

7. Right-click the `NewsArticlePagewithRatings` page layout and select "Edit File in Advanced Mode."

8. Select all the content in code view editor using Ctrl+A.

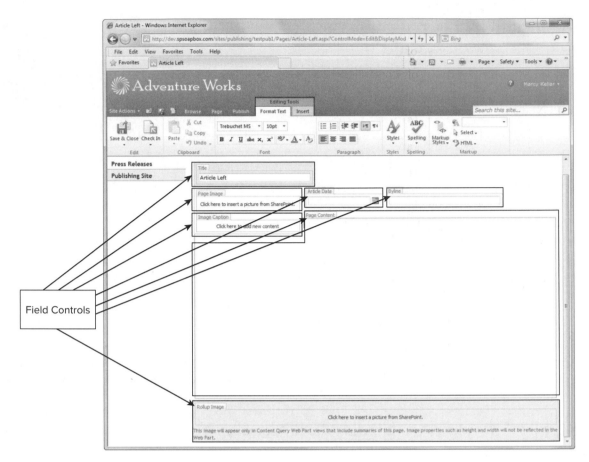

FIGURE 4-11

9. Paste your clipboard content into NewsArticlePagewithRatings using Ctrl+V.

10. Save your file.

Next, you will add the Article Abstract control to the end of the publishing page content.

11. Place your cursor just before the closing <PublishingWebControls:EditModePanel> tag.

12. Click the Insert tab.

13. In the Controls section of the ribbon, select SharePoint.

14. In the SharePoint Controls menu, scroll down to the Custom Fields section and select "Article Abstract," as shown in Figure 4-12.

Next, you will add the Ratings control to the Title area of your page.

```
□ 🗀 Style Library
  □ 🗀 assets
    ⊞ 🗀 css
    ⊞ 🗀 fonts
    ⊞ 🗀 images
    ⊞ 🗀 js
```

FIGURE 4-12

15. Place your cursor in the code view just after <SharePointWebControls:FieldValue FieldName="Title" runat="server"/>.

16. Click the Insert tab.

17. In the Controls section of the ribbon, select SharePoint.

18. In the SharePoint Controls menu, scroll down to the Page Fields section and select `Ratings (0-5)`.

Your code will look like the following snippet:

```
<SharePointWebControls:UIVersionedContent UIVersion="4" runat="server">
<ContentTemplate>
<SharePointWebControls:FieldValue FieldName="Title" runat="server"/>

<CustomTag_0:AverageRatingFieldControl
FieldName="5a14d1ab-1513-48c7-97b3-657a5ba6c742"
runat="server">
</CustomTag_0:AverageRatingFieldControl>

</ContentTemplate>
</SharePointWebControls:UIVersionedContent>
```

19. Wrap the Ratings control in a block level element, `<div class="ratings">` so that the ratings can be styled to appear in a specific location.

21. Locate the SharePoint Web Control `<SharePointWebControls:FieldValue id="PageStylesField" FieldName="HeaderStyleDefinitions" runat="server"/>`.

22. Add a closing tag `</SharePointWebControls:FieldValue>`.

23. Remove the slash from after `runat="server"`.

24. Add the following CSS style sheet before the closing tag of the `HeaderStylesDefinitions` field:

```
<style type="text/css">
    .ratings { display:inline;float:right;
}
</style>
```

The control should now resemble the following:

```
<SharePointWebControls:FieldValue id="PageStylesField"
FieldName="HeaderStyleDefinitions" runat="server">
<style type="text/css">
  .ratings { display:inline;float:right;
}
</style>
</SharePointWebControls:FieldValue>
```

How It Works

Adding field controls to a site allows for filtering of pages just as you would documents. The content of the field control is the metadata or page properties. The Article Abstract field was placed in an edit panel so that it is only seen by authors when they are editing. An embedded style sheet was added to the page to style the ratings control.

TRY IT OUT Create a Page from a Page Layout

In this exercise, you will create a page from the custom page layout NewsArticlewithRatings. Do this exercise in the same site where you created the Custom Article Page content type in the earlier Try It Out. If you are proceeding directly to this exercise from the previous one, you may skip Steps 1 and 2.

1. Navigate to the site where you created the Custom Article Page content type.

2. Select Site Actions ⇨ Site Settings ⇨ Page layouts and Site Templates.

3. In the Page Layouts section, locate Custom Article Page in the field on the left.

4. Select CustomArticlePage, and click the Add button to move it into the field on the right.

5. A warning dialog appears to warn that the subsites will all reset to inherit only the available page layouts in the Available Page Layouts field on the right.

6. Check the box "Reset all subsites to inherit these preferred page layout settings."

7. In the "New Page Default Settings" section, select the News Article with Ratings page layout.

8. Check the box "Reset all subsites to inherit these preferred page layout settings," as seen in Figure 4-13.

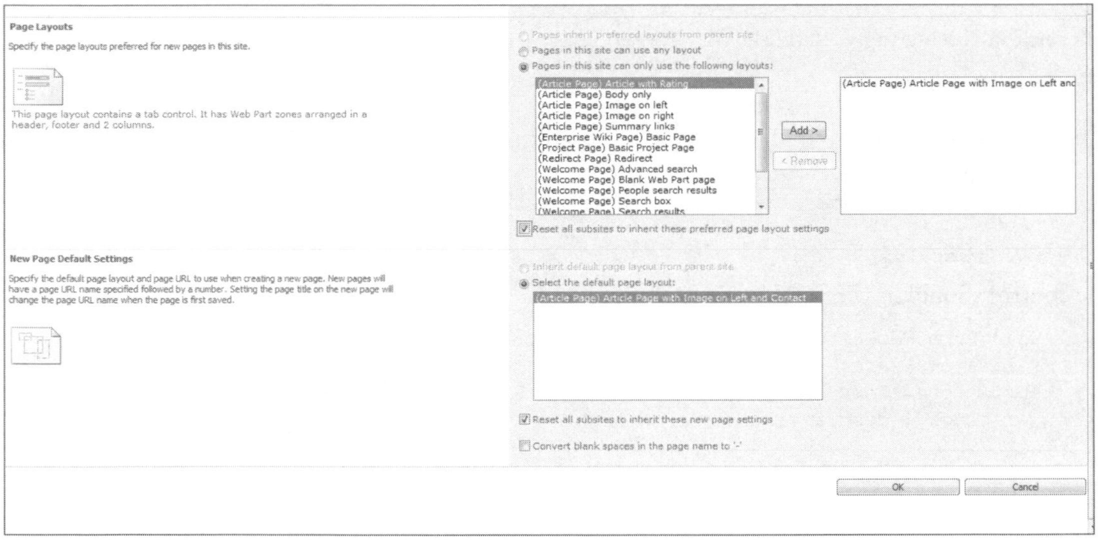

FIGURE 4-13

9. Click OK.

10. Select Site Actions ⇨ New Page.

11. The New Page dialog box appears, as shown in Figure 4-14.

FIGURE 4-14

12. Enter the name of your page, **Your Very First Publishing Page.**

13. The page opens in edit mode.

14. Add images and text.

15. Select Page tab and Publish.

16. Publish the page and preview in the browser.

Now, you have built a publishing page, one of the key building blocks of a web publishing portal. The page layout still needs additional site columns added to the content types, and field controls added to the page layout.

> *✎ **NOTE** The page layout used in this chapter is available for download from the Wrox site. See if you can add the rest of the site columns mentioned in this chapter as field controls.*

How It Works

You have limited the page layouts that are available in the site to only the New Article with Ratings page layout; see Figure 4-15. You have also set the default page layout of the site to use this page layout. All new pages are created using this page layout.

FIGURE 4-15

SUMMARY

This chapter focused on using SharePoint's web content management facilities to build publishing pages. The combination of master page and page layout is used to build the layout of the final publishing page, which a content author uses to create and present content. You experienced a taste of the publishing power of SharePoint Designer 2010 and the ability to complete a majority of your publishing tasks without ever leaving the client tool.

Major points to remember from this chapter are:

➤ Publishing sites provide web content management features in SharePoint.

➤ SharePoint Designer 2010 is very powerful and permissions should only be granted to trained team members.

➤ Master pages can be created using SharePoint Designer.

➤ Page layouts, also created using SharePoint Designer, display the body elements of a page, such as field controls and web parts.

➤ Publishing pages are created by content authors and are always based on an existing page layout.

5

Styles and Themes

WHAT YOU WILL LEARN IN THIS CHAPTER

➤ What cascading style sheets (CSS) are

➤ The components of a style sheet

➤ How to manage CSS with SharePoint Designer tools and features

➤ Key CSS classes used by SharePoint 2010

➤ Using SharePoint Designer to apply CSS styles to your site

In the previous chapters, you learned how to use the page-editing tools of SharePoint Designer to control the content layout and structure of your SharePoint pages. This chapter builds on this foundation and shows you how to use SharePoint Designer's *cascading style sheet* (CSS) tools to apply fonts, colors, and other finishing touches to your sites.

STYLE DEFINED

The original intention of the HTML specification was to define the content of a web page and not how the content on the page should appear. Yet, over time, stylistic elements such as the <FONT> tag crept into the specification. Embedding these elements in pages throughout a website proved to be a nightmare. Web developers hard-coded font names and colors in each and every web page, and, as you can imagine, deciding to change what font should be used was a very time-consuming and error-prone activity.

The *Cascading Style Sheets (CSS)* specification was created to solve this problem. CSS is a language that solely focuses on describing how web pages should look. Because CSS is independent of the actual HTML, web pages can easily share common display characteristics. Not only can colors, fonts, and positioning be defined in a single location, web pages can be formatted for devices such as printers and mobile phones without your having to create separate HTML.

The Anatomy of CSS Rule Sets

A style sheet contains at least one *rule set*. A CSS rule set comprises a selector and a declaration block. Think of a rule set as a term and a definition. When you combine multiple defined terms, you get a glossary. Combine multiple glossaries and you get a dictionary. Collectively, the rule sets are your style sheets and these style sheets define your site's visual language. The following code snippet shows three examples of CSS rule sets:

```
body {
color: black;
padding: 10px;
}

.ms-quickLaunch{
padding-top:5px;
}

#navcontainer{
font-family: Tahoma;
}
```

Everything up to (but not including) the first left curly brace ({) in each of the preceding statements is the *selectors*. A selector "selects" the HTML elements on the page that are affected by the rule set. The selector in a CSS statement can represent all HTML elements of a type by specifying no prefix, a *class* specified for the element with a "dot" (.) prefix, or the ID of a specifically named element with the hash, or pound, (#) prefix. In the code snippet, the selectors in the three examples are the `<body>` HTML element, the CSS class `.ms-quickLaunch`, and the HTML element with an ID attribute set to `navcontainer`, respectively.

When a rule set targets an HTML element without a class or name, every instance of that element will be affected. This type of selector is also called an element selector because it refers to structural HTML elements such as paragraphs (`<p>`) or headings (`<h1>`). The following code snippet shows more examples of element selectors:

```
<html>
    <head>
        <style type="text/css">
            h1 {
                color: black;
            }
            p {
                font-family: Tahoma
            }
        </style>
    </head>
<body>
    <h1>This text will appear in black.</h1>
    <p>This text will appear in the font Tahoma.</p>
    <p>This text will appear in the font Tahoma, too.</p>
    <span> This text will NOT appear in the font Tahoma.</span>
</body>
</html>
```

In the code snippet, the header (<h1>) element displays its contents in black with the default font of the browser. Both of the paragraph (<p>) elements will display their text with the Tahoma font. The <span> element will not appear in black or use the Tahoma font (unless the user sets the Tahoma font as the default font for their browser) because none of the CSS rule sets apply to it.

You can group and apply selectors more specifically. Consider the following:

```
ul li a {
font-color:red
}
```

If this is the only style applied to a document, only links that are found in an unordered list will appear red. All other links will be displayed in blue, the browser default.

Another type of selector is the <input> element is a special element in that it represents several different types of controls based on the value of its type attribute. Although not often seen in default SharePoint, the following list outlines the values you use for the type attribute and the control that appears in the browser:

INPUT TYPE VALUE	CONTROL SHOWN
button	button
checkbox	checkbox
file	textbox and button for uploading files
hidden	(nothing appears)
image	image
password	textbox whose characters are masked so they cannot be read by passersby
radio	radiobutton
reset	button that resets the <input> elements inside the <form> element to their original values
submit	button that submits the page to the server
text	textbox

It is difficult to style an <input> element using only type selectors because a type selector would target all the <input> elements on the page that did not have a class or name. To address this issue, *attribute selectors* were created. Attribute selectors allow you to target HTML elements using one of their attributes in addition to their element type. In the following code snippet, attribute selectors are used to style textboxes (<input type="text">) and radio buttons (<input type="radio">):

```
<style type="text/css">
  input[type="button"] {
    width: 100px;
  }
```

```
   input[value="red"] {
     background: red;
   }

   input[value="green"] {
     background: green;
   }

   input[value="blue"] {
     background: blue;
   }
}
</style>

<input name="color" type="radio" value="red">Red</input>
<input name="color" type="radio" value="green">Green</input>
<input name="color" type="radio" value="blue">Blue</input>
<input type="text" value="red"/>
<br/>

<input name="okButton" type="button" value="OK" />
<input name="cancelButton" type="button" value="Cancel" />
```

In the code snippet, the attribute selectors are the square braces and their contents, and appear to the right of the `input` type selector. To create an attribute selector, you add opening and closing square braces to the right of the type selector and place an equality expression between them that compares an attribute with the value you are targeting. In the code snippet, the selector `input[type="button"]` targets only the `<input>` elements whose `type` attribute is set to `button`. The `type` attribute is the most commonly used attribute, but you can target other attributes as well. In the code snippet, the last three CSS rule sets target `<input>` elements based on the value of their `value` attribute. When the HTML is loaded in the browser, the background color of the radio buttons (`<input type="radio">`) will be styled with the CSS rule set whose attribute selector matches the value specified for their `value` attribute. Additionally, the background of the textbox (`<input type="text">`) will also be red since its value attribute is set to `red`.

> **NOTE** *Attribute selectors are case-sensitive for all attributes except* `type`. *If the value of the target attribute does not match the value in the attribute selector in both characters and casing, the match will not be made. For example, the attribute selector* `input[value="red"]` *will not match* `<input value="Red">` *because the attribute value in the* `<input>` *element is in proper case whereas the attribute selector value is in lower case.*

If you want to target multiple types of HTML elements, you use class selectors. Class selectors will style any HTML element with that class assigned. Class selectors always start with a period (.). You can apply many class selectors to one HTML element. In the following example, the paragraph (`<p>`) element is styled with two different rule sets:

```
<html>
<head>
<style type="text/css">
```

```
.heavy {
font-weight: bold;
}
.quote {
font-style:italic;
}
</style>
</head>
<body>
<p class="heavy quote">This paragraph will appear bold and italic.</p>
</body>
</html>
```

In the code snippet, both the .heavy class and the .quote class are applied to the paragraph <p> element. One additional way to define a selector is to target a specific type of HTML element and a specific class. In the following code snippet, both type and class selectors are used:

```
<html>
<head>
<style type="text/css">
p.title {
color: blue;
font: Arial;
}
</style>
</head>
<body>
<p>This text will NOT be blue or in font Arial.</p>
<p class="title">This text will be blue and in font Arial.</p>
<span class="title">This text will NOT be blue or in font Arial.</span>
</body>
</html>
```

Note that only the second paragraph (<p>) will appear in blue in the font Arial. This is because the rule set targets only the HTML elements that are paragraphs (<p>) and have the .title class.

> **WARNING** *Do not create class names that begin with a number. They will not work in some browsers, including FireFox, Opera, and Chrome.*

Sometimes, you will want to style a specific element on the page. ID selectors, such as #navcontainer, match the element with the attribute id="navigation". ID selectors should be unique and must be prefixed with a hash symbol (#). The major difference between ID and class selectors is that an ID selector normally only applies to one element on the page, whereas a class selector could apply to several elements. The following code snippet shows how to use an ID selector:

```
<html>
<head>
<style type="text/css">
     #navcontainer{
     font-weight: bold;
     font-family: Tahoma;
     font-style: italic;
     }
```

```
</style>
</head>
<body>
<div id="navcontainer">
  This text will appear bold and italic in the Tahoma font.
</div>
<div id="footer">
  This text will appear with the browser default color and font.
</div>
</body>
</html>
```

In the code snippet, only the first <div> element is affected by the #navcontainer ID selector because the <div> element's id attribute is set to navcontainer.

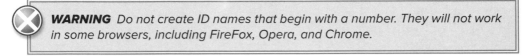 **WARNING** *Do not create ID names that begin with a number. They will not work in some browsers, including FireFox, Opera, and Chrome.*

The declaration block of a CSS rule set is represented by the curly braces ({}) and their contents. The contents of the declaration blocks are the declarations. A declaration block will contain one or more declarations.

The declarations themselves are in the form of *property: value,* where *property* represents the property of the HTML element to be modified and *value* represents the value of the modification. Each declaration ends in a semicolon (;) because some declarations can have values that contain spaces, as in the following code snippet:

```
td {
border: 1px solid black;
}
```

In the code snippet, a black, solid border one pixel in size is applied to every table cell (<td>) on the page.

WARNING *When specifying a unit of measure in a CSS property declaration, do not place a space between the number and the unit of measure. Otherwise, the property declaration will not work in some browsers. See the following code snippet for proper usage:*

```
td {
border: 1px solid black; /* This will work. */
}

td {
border: 1 px solid black; /* This will not work. */
}
```

Applying CSS to Your HTML

In the previous code examples, the CSS rule sets were embedded in the HTML page itself. You can embed a style sheet by using the `<style>` element within the `<head>` tag. The `type` attribute is required and used to specify a media type. Placing the following example within a master page would enable you to manage all paragraph (`<p>`) and web part body styles through the master page.

```
<style type="text/css">
p {
margin-bottom:5px;
}
.ms-WPBody {
font-size:1em;
background:#fff;
}
</style>
```

Another way to apply styles is to use inline styles. Inline styles are styles set within one tag. They affect only the current tag; every other similar tag on the page will have the default styles. In the following code snippet, you see a comparison of using embedded versus inline styles:

```
<html>
<head>
<style type="text/css">
            .warning {
            font-weight: bold;
            color: red;
            }
</style>
</head>
<body>
<p>This text has no styling applied.</p>
<p style="font-weight: bold; font-style:italic;">This text has an inline style
and is bold and italic.</p>
<p class="warning">This text uses a CSS rule set embedded in the page and is
bold and red. </p>
</body>
</html>
```

In the code snippet, the first paragraph (`<p>`) has no styles and is shown using the browser default color and font. The second paragraph (`<p>`) uses an inline style, which sets the text to be bold and italic. The third paragraph (`<p>`) uses a CSS rule set embedded in the page, and its text is displayed in bold and red.

To create an inline style, you simply add a `style` attribute to the target HTML element. Afterwards, you set the value of the attribute to the CSS declarations that define the style you want. To convert the third paragraph (`<p>`) to use inline styles instead, remove the `class` attribute and add the `style` attribute. Then, set the `style` attribute to the declarations inside the declaration block of the `.warning` class CSS rule set. The result should look like this:

```
<p style="font-weight: bold; color: red;">This text uses a CSS rule set embedded
in the page and is bold and red. </p>
```

One interesting feature of CSS styles is that you can combine inline and embedded styles. When you combine both kinds of styles, the target HTML element will have a `class` attribute that applies the embedded style, and a `style` attribute that applies the inline style. Here is an example of using both kinds of styles:

```
<html>
<head>
<style type="text/css">
          .warning {
          font-weight: bold;
          color: red;
          }
</style>
</head>
<body>
<p class="warning" style="font-style: italic">This text uses a CSS rule set
embedded in the page and is bold and red.
It also happens to be in italics.</p>
</body>
</html>
```

In the code snippet, the paragraph (`<p>`) is bold, red, and in italics. The bold font weight and the red color are applied using the `.warning` class CSS rule set embedded in the page. The italic font style is applied using the inline style via the `style` attribute.

External styles are the last way to apply styles to your HTML. They are the same as embedded styles in every respect except that they are stored separately from the HTML page. An external style sheet is a `.css` file that contains style declarations. To use an external style sheet, you create a `.css` file that contains your CSS rule sets, and then add a `<link>` element inside the `<head>` tag on your page. The following code snippet shows an example referring to an external style sheet:

```
<html>
<head>
<link rel="stylesheet" type="text/css" href="styles.css" />
</head>
<body>
<p class="warning" style="font-style: italic">This text uses a CSS rule set
embedded in the page and is bold and red. It also happens to be in italics.</p>
</body>
</html>
```

In the code snippet, the previous example was updated by moving the `.warning` class CSS rule set to a file named `styles.css` and replacing the `<style>` tag with a `<link>` tag referring to the new `.css` file. All of the styles in the `.css` file will still be applied to the HTML elements on the page. When adding a `<link>` tag to your page, you only need to set the value of the `href` attribute to an absolute or relative URL to the location of the `.css` file.

> ⊗ **WARNING** *Do not remove or modify the values of the rel or type attributes or the link tag will not work.*

The best practice for managing the styles in your site is to use an external style sheet. External style sheets will allow you to use the same styles on every page of your site, lending it a consistent look and feel. SharePoint 2010 has its own external style sheet named `corev4.css`, which is located at `http://yoursiteurl/_layouts/locale/styles/Themable/corev4.css`, where *yoursiteurl* is the URL of your site and *locale* is the locale for your site. If you are using the locale for United States English (en-us), the value for *locale* is 1033. If you are styling a non-English site, the locale will become important since the layout, size, and position of elements could change if the target language is right-to-left or if the language needs extra space to display things like the Site Actions menu button. Regardless of the language of your site, SharePoint 2010 has thousands of CSS rule sets that you can override to apply your own brand to your site.

TRY IT OUT   Apply CSS Styles

In this activity, you apply styles to a simple HTML page.

1. Open SharePoint Designer from your Start menu.

2. Click the Open Site button.

3. When the Open Site dialog appears, enter the URL to your site in the Site name textbox and click the OK button.

4. If a Windows Security dialog appears, enter your username and password for the SharePoint site and click the OK button.

5. After the site opens, select Site Pages from the Navigation bar on the left.

6. Select Page ⇨ ASPX from the ribbon.

7. Rename the newly created file in the Site Pages list to **CSSExample.aspx**. To rename a file in SharePoint Designer, right-click the file and select Rename from the context menu.

8. Double-click the newly renamed CSSExample.aspx file to open it.

9. If a dialog asks you to open the page in advanced mode, click Yes.

10. Type the following HTML between the <form> element's opening and closing tags:

    ```
    <label>Name:</label>
    <input name="nameTextBox" type="text" value="John Q. Public" />
    <br/>

    <label>Credit Score:</label>
    <input name="creditScoreTextBox" type="text" class="readOnlyBox"
    readonly="readonly" value="750"/>
    <br/>

    <input name="color" type="radio" value="red">Red</input>
    ```

```
<input name="color" type="radio" value="green">Green</input>
<input name="color" type="radio" value="blue">Blue</input>
<br/>

<input name="okButton" type="button" value="OK" />
<input name="cancelButton" type="button" value="Cancel" />
```

11. Add the following `<script>` block just before the ending `<head>` tag at the top of the page:

```
<style type="text/css">
    label {
        color: green;
        font-family: Arial, Helvetica, sans-serif;
        font-size: 12pt;
    }

    .readOnlyBox {
        background: #CCCCCC;
    }

    input {
        font-family: "Courier New", Courier, monospace;
    }

    input[type="button"] {
        width: 100px;
    }

    input[value="red"] {
        background: red;
    }

    input[value="green"] {
        background: green;
    }

    input[value="blue"] {
        background: blue;
    }
}
</style>
```

12. Save the page by clicking the Save button in the Quick Access Toolbar at the top of the SharePoint Designer window.

13. Run the page in the browser by selecting Preview in Browser from the Home tab on the ribbon.

How It Works

The first CSS rule set styles the font, color, and size of the two `<label>` elements by targeting their element type. The second CSS rule set targets the `creditScoreTextBox<input>` element using a class selector matching its configured class name `readOnlyBox`. The CSS rule set with the `input` type selector sets the font of the textboxes, the radio buttons, and the buttons. The rest of the CSS rule sets target `<input>` elements based on the values of their `type` and `value` attributes.

Inheritance and Priority

One of the most useful features of CSS is the ability to apply a rule set to an HTML element high in the page's hierarchy that will apply the rule set's style declarations to that element and its descendants. If you were to create the following rule set, every element on the page would use the Arial font since every element is ultimately a child element of the `<body>` tag.

```
body {
font-family: Arial;
}
```

The ability to "cascade" a style from the target element to its lowest descendants is useful since you will not have to write many redundant rule sets for each type of HTML element that you use in your pages. You can also override an inherited style by defining a style that targets an HTML element lower in the page's hierarchy. When that occurs, the CSS rule set with the most specific selector is used to style the target HTML element. For example, you may want every page in your site to use the Arial font, except that links in your site use the Verdana font. To apply that rule, you could write the following code snippet:

```
<html>
<head>
<style type="text/css">
body {
font-family: Arial;
}
a {
font-family: Verdana;
}
</style>
</head>
<body>
    This text is in Arial font.
<p>This text is in Arial font, too</p>
<a href="help.html">This text is in Verdana font.</a>
</body>
</html>
```

In the code snippet, CSS rule sets are defined for the `<body>` tag and the anchor (`<a>`) tags. All of the text on the page is displayed using the Arial font except for the anchor (`<a>`) tag, which is displayed using the Verdana font. The CSS rule set with the most specific selector is used to style the target HTML element. Think of each selector like an adjective. The more adjectives you assign to a noun, the more descriptive you are and the easier you can communicate. This conversation illustrates the concept:

> Nice man: "*I would like to buy a piece of jewelry for my lady.*"

> Jewelry store clerk: "*We have lots of jewelry here.*"

> Nice man: "*I would like to buy a necklace. A diamond necklace. A diamond necklace with rubies. A diamond necklace with rubies and a matching bracelet.*"

> Jewelry store clerk: "*I know just the piece. Let me go find it!*"

The jewelry store clerk knows exactly which piece of jewelry to go get because of the very specific description given by the nice man.

To further illustrate the point, examine the following code snippet:

```html
<html>
<head>
<style type="text/css">
            .comp {
            background: gray;
            color: red;
            }
            p.comp {
            background: black;
            color: blue;
            }
            #main p.comp {
            background: black;
            color: white;
            }
</style>
</head>
<body>
<p>This text is in the browser's default color and background.</p>
<span class="comp">This text is in red with a gray background.</span>
<p class="comp">This text is in blue with a black background.</p>
<div id="main" class="comp">
    This text is in red with a gray background.
<p class="comp">This text is in white with a black background.</p>
<span class="comp">This text is in red with a gray background</span>
<p>This text is in red with a gray background.</p>
</div>
</body>
</html>
```

In the code snippet, three CSS rule sets are defined: one for the .comp class, one for paragraphs (<p>) that use the .comp class, and one for paragraphs (<p>) that use the .comp class and are also descendant from any element whose ID attribute is main. In the code snippet, the first paragraph (<p>) is displayed using the browser's default color and background because it is not styled using the .comp class. The first <span> element is displayed in red with a gray background because it does implement the .comp class but it is not a paragraph (<p>). The second paragraph (<p>) is displayed in blue with a black background because it matches the selector for the p.comp rule set by being a paragraph (<p>) and having its class attribute set to comp.

The tricky part of the code snippet is the <div> element. Its ID attribute is set to main and the class attribute is set to comp. But the #main p.comp rule set does not affect it directly because it does not meet every condition of the selector, as it is not a paragraph (<p>). However, the #main p.comp rule set does affect the <div> element's children if they are paragraphs (<p>) that also have their class attribute set to comp. That is why the first paragraph (<p>) inside the <div> element is displayed in white with a black background and the second paragraph <p> is not. Like the previous example with the <body> element and the anchor (<a>) elements, the second paragraph <p> is displayed in red with a gray background because an ancestor element, the<div> element, is styled using the .comp class.

Up to now, you have learned three different places to place CSS rule sets, inline, embedded, and external, and three different ways to create selectors, type of element, CSS class, and by element

ID. Inevitably, the same selector will be defined in more than one place but with different property declarations. When that happens, the browser applies rules to determine which declaration will be applied. The following rules are applied in order of least to most importance:

1. The browser's default settings.

2. A local CSS file configured by the end user in browser settings. (This is common with users who are visually impaired.)

3. External style sheets referenced with a `<link>` element and embedded styles contained within a `<style>` element on the page itself. (When there are multiple `<link>` or `<style>` elements on the page, the importance is determined by their position on the page. The first element is the least important and the last element is the most important.)

4. Inline styles contained within the `style` attribute of the target HTML element.

5. Declarations that have `!important` right before the semicolon (`;`).

The following code snippet shows how the rules in the previous list work:

```
<html>
<head>
<style type="text/css">
body {
font-family: Arial;
color: red;
}
a {
font-family: Verdana;
color: blue;
}
a {
color: green;
}
</style>
</head>
<body>
   This text is in red using the Arial font.
<p>This text is in red using the Arial font, too</p>
<a href="help.html">This text is in green using the Verdana font.</a>
</body>
</html>
```

In the code snippet, the anchor (`<a>`) element is displayed in green using the Verdana font. The two CSS rule sets targeting anchor (`<a>`) elements are applied in the order in which they appear on the page. When the second CSS rule set is encountered by the browser, its property declaration for setting the text to green is used because the second CSS rule set is lower on the page than the first one and is treated as being more important. Note that the font declaration in the first CSS rule set targeting anchor (`<a>`) elements is still applied because no other CSS rule set with higher importance has a declaration for font. The thing to remember is that it is the declarations that conflict, not the selectors themselves.

In the previous list, item 5 has not been previously mentioned because it is best to save it for last, especially since CSS declarations marked with `!important` will override all other conflicting CSS declarations for the target HTML element. The following code snippet shows how order and importance works:

```html
<html>
<head>
<style type="text/css">
body {
font-family: Arial;
color: red;
}
a {
color: blue !important;
}
a {
font-family: Verdana;
color: green;
}
</style>
</head>
<body>
  This text is in red using the Arial font.
<p>This text is in red using the Arial font, too</p>
<a href="help.html" style="color: orange;">
This text is in blue using the Verdana font.
</a>
</body>
</html>
```

In the code snippet, there are two CSS rule sets that target anchor (<a>) elements. The first CSS rule set styles the text inside anchor (<a>) elements to be blue, whereas the second styles the text to be green instead and use the Verdana font. Additionally, the anchor (<a>) element has an inline style to set the text color to be orange. However, the color declaration in the first CSS rule set is applied because it is marked with !important. The inline style, which would have been more important than the embedded style, is now less important because declarations marked with !important are treated as most important of all.

SharePoint 2010 has become more sophisticated in the way that the cascade of styles is architected. Because of this and the use of more advanced CSS design patterns in play, understanding the fundamentals of CSS is important. You can find more in-depth explanations of these concepts and many more at http://w3schools.com/css.

CSS Best Practices

Before you start designing your award-winning website, take time to read and apply the following best practices to ensure your success with CSS:

➤ **Validation** — Validating your CSS is always important. This is to make sure that your CSS is error-free and is interpreted the right way in all browsers. You can submit your CSS for validation via a URL, file upload, or direct input using the free CSS Validation Service located at the following URL:

   http://jigsaw.w3.org/css-validator/

➤ **Comments** — Just as in any other language, commenting your code is a sign of good crafts-manship. It helps you troubleshoot what you are building and helps others maintain it long after your site is in production. For example:

```
/*this is appropriate commenting syntax*/
```

➤ **Naming** — Naming classes according to their function rather than what they will look like is a best practice. No matter how tempted you are to name a class "bigredbox" because doing so makes sense at the time, don't do it. If "bigredbox" were changed later to have a blue background instead of red, the class name would become meaningless.

➤ **Compression** — In this chapter, the CSS code snippets were formatted for reading by humans by adding spaces and carriage returns, which increase the size of .css files. Computers do not need this unnecessary white space to read .css files properly. Therefore, it is a best practice to remove the white space from your .css files before you put the files in production. Smaller .css files will make your site load faster in the browser. You can use a CSS compressor like the one at the following URL to automati-cally remove the white space for you: http://cleancss.com. A similar tool for HTML is located at http://www.mycoolform.com.

SHAREPOINT DESIGNER'S CSS TOOLS

SharePoint Designer offers an abundance of tools to delight the web designer and serve to identify, create, modify, delete, and manage styles. The web designer's tool belt in SharePoint Designer 2010 is available primarily through a series of task panes.

To explore the functionality in these task panes, you should create a safe environment that you can alter without recourse. The following activity will guide you through the initial steps to start man-aging styles in SharePoint by creating a copy of a site's master page and linking it to the custom.css file created in a previous activity.

TRY IT OUT Setup for Branding a SharePoint Site

In this activity, you create a custom master page and a custom CSS file and apply them to your SharePoint site.

1. Open SharePoint Designer from your Start menu.

2. Click the Open Site button.

3. When the Open Site dialog appears, enter the URL to your site in the Site name textbox and click the OK button.

4. If a Windows Security dialog appears, enter your username and password for the SharePoint site and click the OK button.

5. After the site opens, select Master Pages from the Navigation bar on the left.

6. In the list of master pages, right-click v4.master and select Copy from the context menu.

7. Select Paste from the ribbon.

8. Rename the newly created `.master` file to `custom.master`. To rename a file in SharePoint Designer, right-click the file and select Rename from the context menu.

9. Right-click the newly renamed `custom.master` file and select Set as Default Master Page from the context menu.

10. When the Set as Default Master Page dialog appears, click the Yes button.

11. Double-click the `custom.master` file to open it.

12. If a dialog stating "The file is under source control" appears, click the Yes button to check out the `custom.master` file.

13. Select All Files from the Navigation bar on the left.

14. When the list of files and folders is displayed, double-click the Style Library folder to open it.

15. Select File ➪ CSS from the ribbon.

16. Rename the newly created `.css` file to `custom.css`. To rename a file in SharePoint Designer, right-click the file and select Rename from the context menu.

17. Switch back to the `custom.master` file.

18. Select Attach Style Sheet from the Style tab on the ribbon.

19. In the Attach Style Sheet dialog, type **/Style Library/custom.css** in the URL textbox and click the OK button.

20. Select Split from the View tab on the ribbon.

21. Locate the ending tag for the `<head>` element.

22. Ensure the newly added `<link>` element pointing to the `custom.css` file is the last element before the ending tag for the `<head>` element.

23. Save the `custom.master` file by clicking the Save button in the Quick Access Toolbar at the top of the SharePoint Designer window.

24. In the Site Definition Page Warning dialog, click the Yes button to confirm that you are customizing the master page.

How It Works

Making a copy of `v4.master` and editing that copy ensures you can make your customizations while maintaining the ability to rollback to another page if your customizations were to cause a problem with the site. Setting the `custom.master` file as the default master page configures the site to use your master page instead of `v4.master` for the site pages in your site. Any modifications you make to `custom.master` will appear on any site page in the site. Creating and attaching the `custom.css` file to the `custom.master` file gives you a place to store the CSS rules sets you write to style the site. Since the `<link>` element appears last inside the `<head>` element, any CSS rule sets you write should have priority over those in `corev4.css`. Note that any inline styles, embedded styles that appear inside the `<body>` element, and styles marked as `!important` will not be overridden in your `custom.css` file unless you mark your conflicting styles as `!important`, too. Do not mark your styles as `!important` if they do not conflict with a style whose priority is higher than yours.

> ✖ **WARNING** *Do not modify the built-in forms and files in SharePoint. If you break one of these forms or files, you can irreparably break your SharePoint installation. If you need to modify a built-in form, such as a master page, always make a copy of the file and edit the copy. That way, you will always be able to "rollback" to a file that works.*

View and Style Tabs

In the previous activity, you created a copy of the `v4.master` master page. When you open the master page, you will see a screen similar to the one in Figure 5-1. In the center of the screen, the master page is displayed in split mode. You can view your pages in design view, code view, or split view, which shows the code view on top and the design view on the bottom. To switch between the different views, click the Design, Split, or Code buttons at the bottom of the screen. Alternately, you can select the Design, Split, or Code buttons from the View tab on the ribbon. Normally, you will use the Split view so you can work with the HTML code and the Design view at the same time.

The Workspace section of the View tab has two useful drop-down buttons: Visual Aids and Task Panes. The Visual Aids button will allow you to display HTML elements in the Design view that normally would be invisible in the browser. Elements that are not visible in the browser include empty `<div>` elements and elements styled with `display:none` or `visibility:hidden`. The Task Panes button toggles the display of various task panes you will use later in the chapter. You can click the top half of the Visual Aids and Task Panes buttons to hide or show the currently enabled visual aids and task panes.

One interesting feature of the Code view and Split view is that you can hold down the Control (Ctrl) key and click any of the CSS class names, and SharePoint Designer will automatically open the `.css` file where the class name is defined. The CSS functionality in SharePoint is provided by the `corev4.css` file. This file is located on the SharePoint web server's file system and if you modify this file, you affect every site in your farm. If you break the file, you just broke every site in the farm, so it is best to only look and not touch the file.

The `corev4.css` file contains thousands of CSS rule sets used by the many elements of SharePoint pages. They affect everything from the color and font to display for text and links to even the border surrounding web parts. The main CSS rule sets used in SharePoint are covered later in the chapter.

If you want to "brand" or "skin" your SharePoint site, you have many options. Usually, web designers will either tweak the look and feel of a SharePoint site by adding an additional CSS file to their master page whose CSS rule sets override the default SharePoint rule sets, or they will completely start from scratch. When web designers create a master page from scratch, they start with a completely blank master page and update its HTML content with the output from a professional design tool, such as Adobe Photoshop or Microsoft Expression Design. Once the master page has the initial look and feel, they add the various SharePoint elements using one of the existing built-in master pages. Though it is worth mentioning, styling a SharePoint site in this way is very difficult and is out of scope for this book.

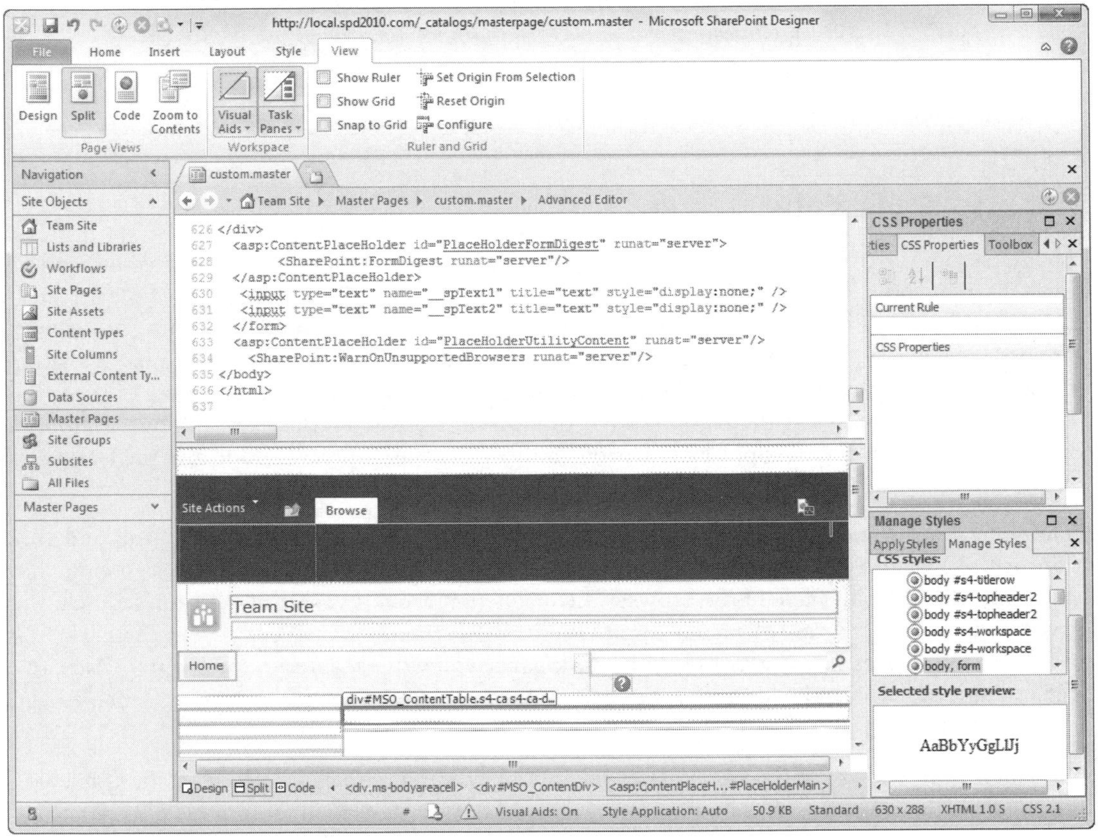

FIGURE 5-1

> **NOTE** If you must create a master page from scratch, be sure to include ALL of the `<asp:ContentPlaceHolder>` and `<SharePoint:DelegateControl>` elements from `v4.master` in your master page. If you leave out an element, your site will probably not work. If you want to hide one of the elements, set its `Visible` attribute to `False`.

Clicking the Style tab exposes the features of SharePoint Designer that are important for managing your styles (see Figure 5-2). You can create a new style, attach a style sheet, and open key task panes from this part of the ribbon.

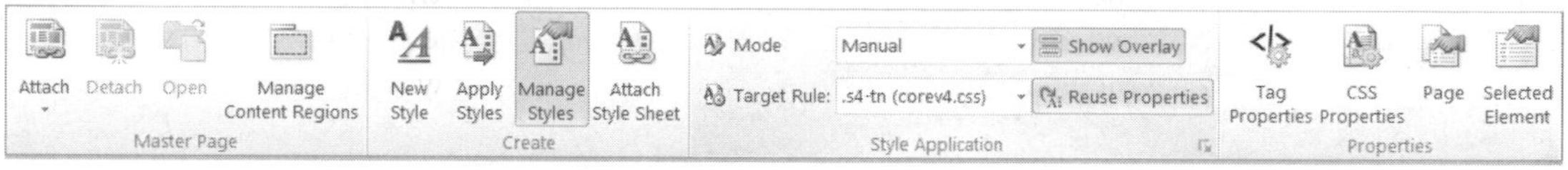

FIGURE 5-2

When you click the Attach Style Sheet button, the dialog in Figure 5-3 appears. The Attach Style Sheet dialog allows you to browse to a .css file in your site and attach it to the current page. If you select the option to attach as a link, a <link> element pointing to the .css file is added just before the ending tag of the <head> element. The option to attach as an import adds a <style> element instead. Inside the <style> element, SharePoint Designer adds a CSS

FIGURE 5-3

instruction to include the .css file. The best practice, though, is to link your .css file using a <link> element. If you want to include additional .css files, you can add more <link> elements or add the CSS import instruction to your .css file. The latter minimizes the changes you have to make to your HTML pages when you want to add or remove multiple .css files.

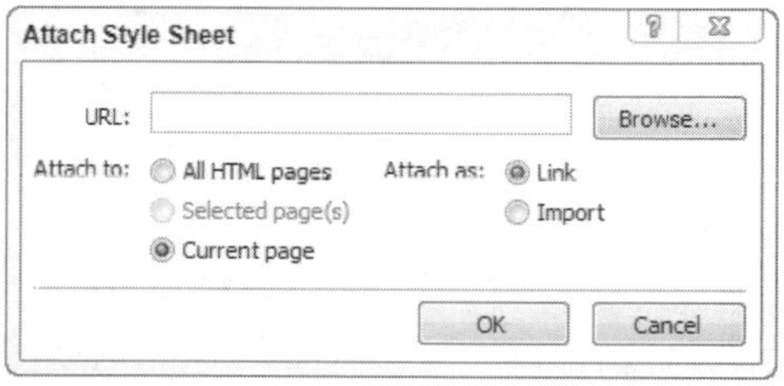

Clicking the New Style button will display the New Style dialog in Figure 5-4. The New Style dialog allows you to create a new CSS rule set without writing it by hand. First, you select an option from or type directly into the Selector drop-down list. Then, you select an option from the Define in drop-down list to indicate where the new rule set should be saved. The best practice is to select "Existing style sheet" and then select the .css file you attached to the page from the URL drop-down list. If you selected an element on the page before clicking the New Style button, you can also select the "Apply new style to document selection" checkbox to automatically apply the style to the element you selected.

The Category list box contains the categories of CSS declarations you can use. When you select a category, the declarations to the right of the list box change to the declarations in that category. While you are configuring the declarations for your rule set, the Preview box at the bottom of the dialog will update itself with a preview of how your rule set will look in your page. The Description box displays the actual CSS declarations that will be saved to your rule set once you click the OK or Apply buttons.

In the Style Application section of the Style tab, the Mode drop-down list is used to indicate if SharePoint Designer should automatically determine where to apply your CSS changes. If you select Auto from the Mode drop-down list, SharePoint Designer will use the preferences on the CSS tab of the Page Editor Options dialog in Figure 5-6 when applying your styles. To display the Page Editor Options dialog, select the File tab from the ribbon. Then, click Options to display the SharePoint Designer Options dialog in Figure 5-5. Finally, click the Page Editor Options button to display the Page Editor Options dialog.

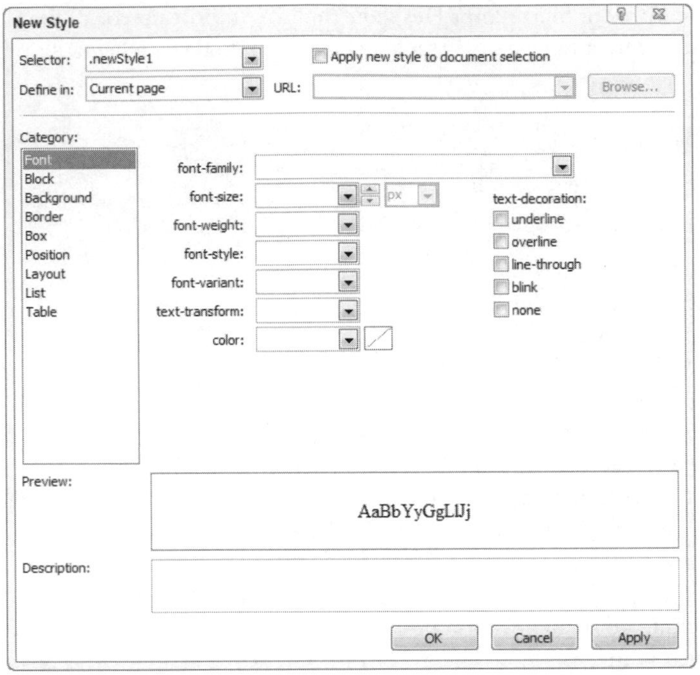

FIGURE 5-4

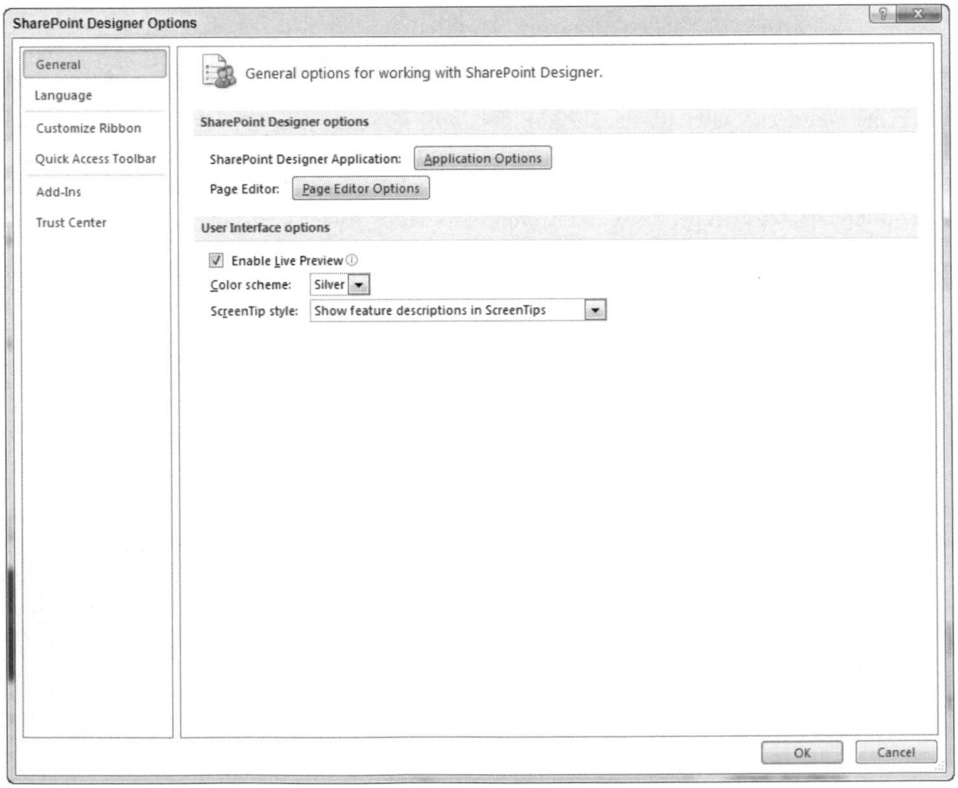

FIGURE 5-5

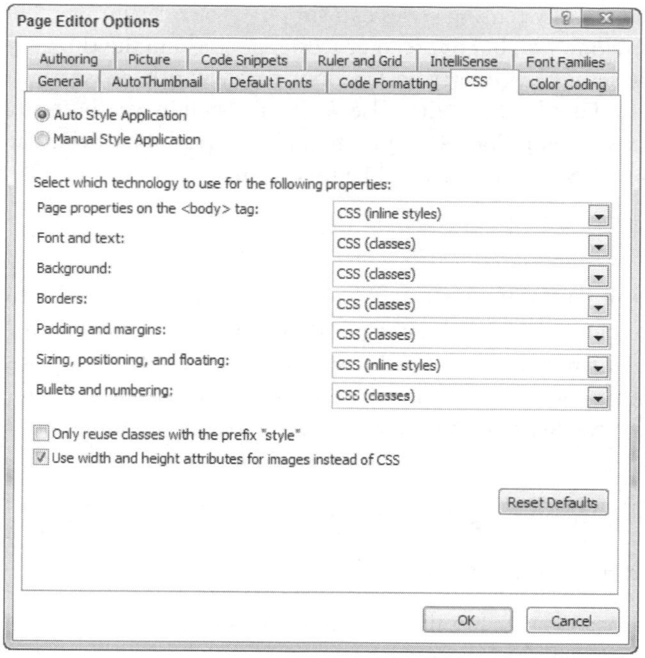

FIGURE 5-6

In the CSS tab of the Page Editor Options dialog, the radio button list at the top of the dialog is used to set the default value for the Mode drop-down list on the Style tab in the ribbon. The drop-down lists in the center of the dialog are used to indicate whether SharePoint Designer should use CSS classes or inline styles for the various categories of CSS declarations when updating your CSS styles. The following table lists those CSS categories and the properties they affect:

CATEGORY	PROPERTIES AFFECTED
`<body>` tag	Body properties such as background images and background colors
Font and Text	Font and font formatting such as bold, italics, and color
Background	Background properties such as background images and colors
Borders	Border properties such as patterns and colors
Padding and Margins	Properties for paddings and margins for borders, cells, and other structural elements
Sizing Positioning and Floating	Applied to alignment, position, and layers
Bullets and Numbering	Applied to bullets and numbering properties

If you decide to allow SharePoint to automatically manage your styles, you can select the "Only reuse classes with the prefix 'style' " checkbox to control which styles will be automatically reused when you make your CSS changes. Automatically reusing styles can simplify your design by reducing the overall number of CSS rule sets in your site, but SharePoint Designer could make things worse by junking up an existing CSS rule set with property declarations that you otherwise would not have done if you were to do it by hand. Finally, select the "Use width and height attributes for images instead of CSS" checkbox if you want SharePoint Designer to add the width and height attributes directly on your images. Otherwise, CSS declarations will be used instead.

Task Panes

As previously stated, the Task Panes button on the View tab in the ribbon is used to toggle the display of the various task panes you use to manage CSS styles in SharePoint Designer. Clicking the bottom half of the Task Panes button will display the list of task panes you can enable. The following table lists a brief description of the most commonly used task panes for managing styles and pages. You can access these panes through the Style or the View tabs in the ribbon in SharePoint Designer.

TASK PANE	DESCRIPTION
Tag Properties	Shows the attributes for the selected element.
CSS Properties	Shows all styles associated with the current document. Can give a more granular view of styles applied to current element.
Apply Styles	Allows you to apply, remove, modify, rename, and delete styles, attach or detach external cascading style sheets (CSS), select all instances of a style, and go to the code that contains a style's rule set.
Manage Styles	Lists all styles defined in the external and internal style sheets of the current document and displays a preview of the style.
Layers	Lists all the layers that are positioned, either absolutely or relatively. Displays the stacking order of the layers.
Accessibility	Provides accessibility reports based on the DocType declared in your page.
Compatibility	Allows you to run a compatibility check based on HTML and XHTML standards and browsers.
CSS Reports	Check for undefined and orphaned files using the CSS reports feature.

The Tag Properties task pane displays the attributes of the selected HTML element, whether it was selected in the Design view, Code view, or Split view. In Figure 5-7, the Top Navigation bar is selected, which updates the Tag Properties task pane to display the attributes of the Top Navigation bar. In Figure 5-7, the AccessKey, SkipLinkText and CssClassattribute names are displayed in bold, dark blue text, which indicates that those attributes have been configured on the HTML element. Attributes that are not configured appear in normal, black text and the default value for the attribute is displayed to the right of the attribute name.

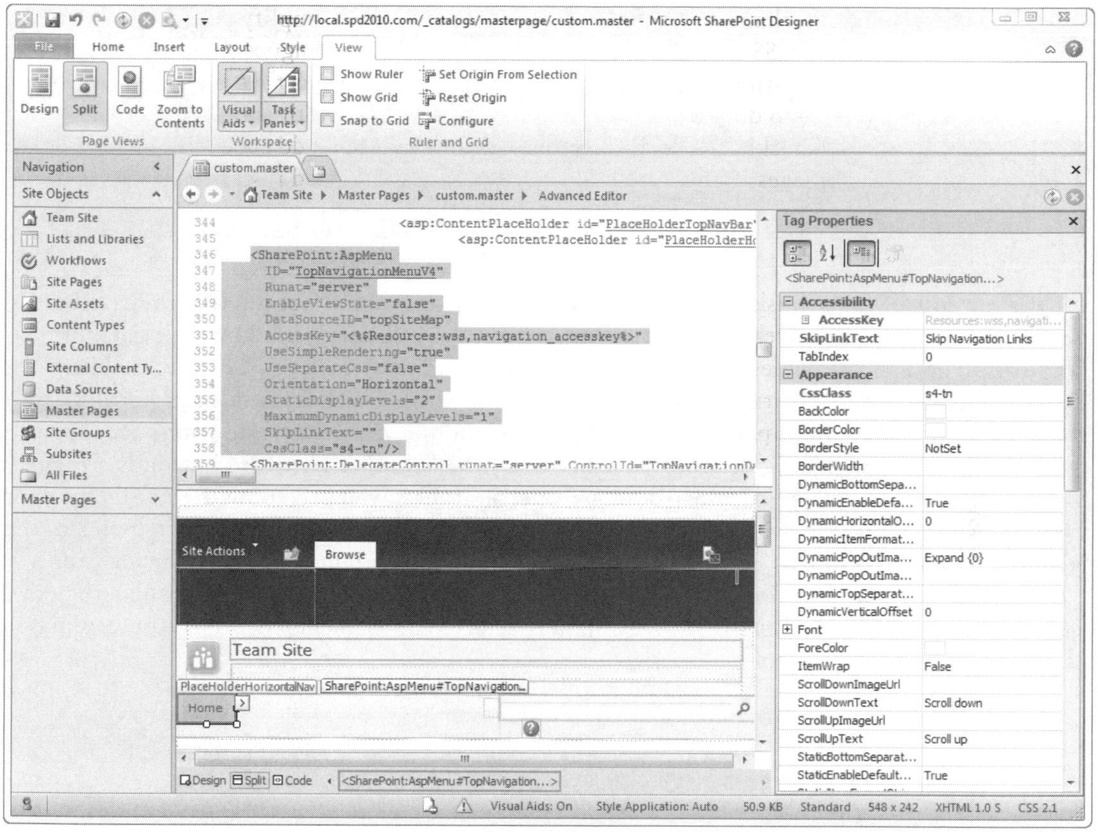

FIGURE 5-7

> **NOTE** Applying a CSS class to ASP.Net and SharePoint elements is a little different than applying them to HTML elements. Use the CssClass attribute to configure the CSS classes for ASP.Net and SharePoint elements. For HTML elements, use the class attribute instead. The easiest way to tell if an element is HTML versus ASP.Net or SharePoint is that ASP.Net or SharePoint elements have a colon (:) in their tag name, whereas HTML elements do not. The following code snippet shows these differences:
>
> ```
> <!-- Example HTML elements and their CSS classes. -->
>
> <span class="s4-help"></span>
> <div class="s4-rp s4-app"></div>
>
> <!-- Example ASP.Net elements and their CSS classes. -->
>
> <asp:Label runat="server" CssClass="s4-breadcrumb-header" />
> <asp:TextBox runat="server" CssClass="ReadOnlyText" />
> ```

```
<!-- Example SharePoint elements and their CSS classes. -->

<SharePoint:AspMenu ID="TopNavigationMenuV4" Runat="server"
CssClass="s4-tn" />
<Sharepoint:SPNavigationManager id="QuickLaunchNavigationManager"
runat="server"
CssClass="ms-quicklaunch-navmgr" />
```

At the top of the Tag Properties task pane are four buttons that affect the way the attributes are displayed. If you click the first button, the attributes will be grouped by their category and sorted alphabetically as shown. In Figure 5-7, you can see the categories Accessibility and Appearance and their properties listed underneath them. If you click the second button, the attributes are sorted alphabetically but not grouped. While you are styling your pages, you will find yourself switching between both buttons, which is OK. The third button is a toggle button. When the button is depressed, any properties that have been configured will appear at the top of the list. If the attributes are being grouped, they appear as the first attributes in the group. Clicking the fourth button will select the immediate parent element of the location where your cursor is located, which in turn updates the Tag Properties task pane to display the newly selected element's attributes. If you have already selected an element, the fourth button may be disabled.

NOTE *You have learned that CSS keeps content separate from its presentation and is a best practice for managing styles in SharePoint. Many controls have HTML formatting attributes available for styling. When using the Tag Properties task pane, you will see many styling attributes, including "*backcolor*." If you must add an inline style to an HTML element, be sure to document it, as it may cause annoying issues during troubleshooting later on.*

The CSS Properties task pane in Figure 5-8 is similar to the Tag Properties task pane, except that it only shows the rule sets and CSS property declarations for the selected element. The CSS Properties task pane also has buttons at the top to control whether the properties are grouped or simply sorted and whether configured CSS properties appear at the top of the list. It also displays a configured property's name in bold, dark blue text. The Summary button at the top of the task pane is very useful in that when depressed, only the configured CSS properties will appear in the task pane. Click the button again to display all the CSS properties again.

In the center of the task pane is the Applied Rules list. The Applied Rules list contains all the rule sets that apply to the selected element, including its ancestors up to the <html> element itself. In the right-hand column of the list, the HTML element that is configured for the rule set is shown.

Whenever you click a rule set in the Applied Rules list, the CSS Properties list below it will change to reflect only the CSS property declarations for the selected rule set. As previously stated, configured properties appear in a bold, dark blue font. However, if the configured property has been overridden by another rule set, the property name will appear with a red strikethrough line, as shown in Figure 5-9 for the `min-height` CSS property.

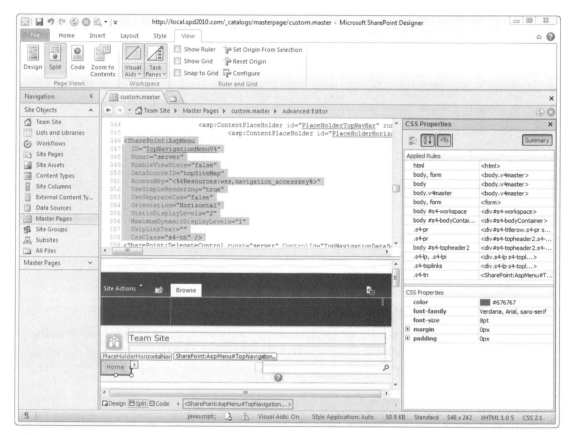

FIGURE 5-8

Another feature of the Applied Rules list is that the name of the `.css` file where the selected rule set is stored is displayed as a blue hyperlink just under the Summary button. Clicking the `.css` file hyperlink will open it in a new tab in SharePoint Designer. Since a `.css` file can have thousands of rule sets defined in it, you can double-click any of the rule sets in the Applied Rules list and its `.css` file will open in a new tab. Additionally, the text cursor will be automatically positioned at the location of the CSS rule set so you do not have to search or scroll to find it. Right-clicking inside the Applied Rules list will display a context menu giving you options for creating a new style, copying an existing style, renaming or removing a style, and creating a new inline style. In the following activity, you will use what you have learned so far to style a few elements in your `custom.master` master page.

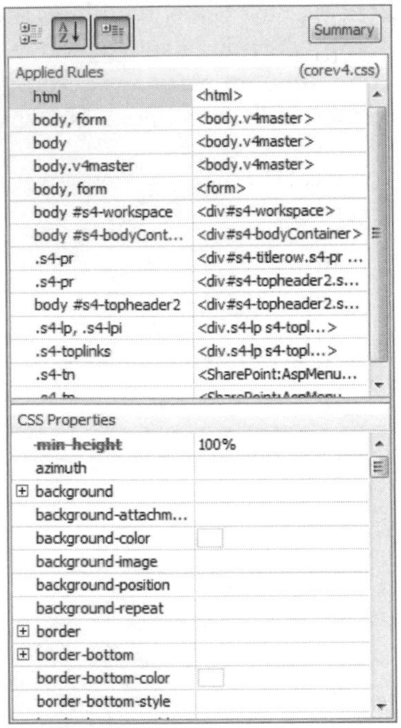

FIGURE 5-9

TRY IT OUT Create a New Style Using the CSS Properties Task Pane

In this exercise, you create a new style for an element. You must complete the "Setup for Branding a SharePoint Site" activity earlier in the chapter before starting this activity.

1. Open SharePoint Designer from your Start menu.

2. Click the Open Site button.

3. When the Open Site dialog appears, enter the URL to your site in the Site name textbox and click the OK button.

4. If a Windows Security dialog appears, enter your username and password for the SharePoint site and click the OK button.

5. After the site opens, select Master Pages from the Navigation bar on the left.

6. In the list of master pages, double-click `custom.master` to open it.

7. Display the CSS Properties task pane by selecting Task Panes ⇨ CSS Properties from the View tab on the ribbon.

8. Place the `.master` page in Design mode by selecting the Design from the View tab on the ribbon.

9. Click the site's title, located to the right of the site's logo.

10. Note that the CSS Properties task pane has changed to reflect the styles applied to the site's title.

11. Right-click inside the Applied Rules list of the CSS Properties task pane and select New Inline Style from the context menu. Ensure that <inline style> is selected in the Applied Rules list.

12. In the CSS Properties task pane, click the second button at the top of the pane to store the CSS properties alphabetically.

13. In the CSS Properties task pane, locate the font property and click the plus sign to the left of the font property to expand it.

14. Click inside the value box for (font-family) to display the drop-down list controls for picking the font.

15. Click the drop-down list and select Comic Sans MS as the value for font.

16. Enter **20pt** as the value for (font-size).

17. Save the `custom.master` file by clicking the Save button in the Quick Access Toolbar at the top of the SharePoint Designer window.

18. Select Team Site from the Navigation bar on the left.

19. Select Preview in Browser from the Home tab on the ribbon.

20. Notice that the site's title font and size have changed.

21. Click any of the links to navigate around the site. Notice that the change to the site's title appears there, too.

How It Works

The CSS Properties list inside the CSS Properties pane is driven by two things: the selected element in the master page and the selected CSS rule set in the Applied Rules list. When you created the new inline style, the property changes you made were applied to that inline style. Since the element styled was in the site's master page, your changes appeared on every site page in the site.

The Apply Styles task pane (Figure 5-10) displays the styles defined in all style sheets related to the page. At the top of the task pane, there are buttons to create a new style and to attach a style sheet. Clicking these buttons will display the same dialogs found in Figure 5-3 and Figure 5-4. There is also an Options button that you can use to categorize the styles by their order in their respective .css files or their type. The Options button can also be used to filter the styles to display all styles, only the styles used in the current page, only the styles used in the current element, or only the styles used in the current selection.

The Select CSS style to apply list box contains the list of the styles you can apply to the selected element. If you want to remove all styles from the element, select Clear Styles at the top of the list. Each of the styles listed is displayed in the font, color, and background of the style. That allows you to preview the style before applying it to the selected element. To apply a style to the selected element, simply select it from the list. That will replace the current style, if any, with the style you selected. If you want to apply multiple styles, hold down the Control (Ctrl) key and click each style you want to apply.

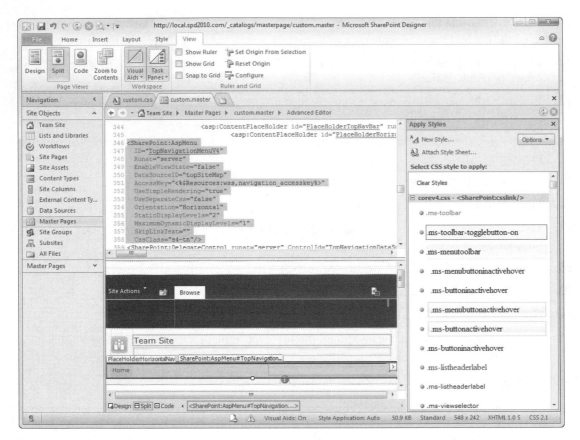

FIGURE 5-10

The CSS is grouped by the source of the style, whether external, embedded, or inline. Class-based and ID-based styles appear under either the name of the external `.css` file that contains the style, or Current Page if the style is in an internal CSS. Element-based styles are organized the same way but appear under a separate heading named Contextual Selectors below the list of class-based and ID-based styles.

In Figure 5-11, the Manage Styles task pane is shown. This task pane appears the same as the Apply Styles task pane, but it has a few unique features. One feature is the additional option, Separate Grouped Selectors, which toggles via the Options button. In CSS, if you have two rule sets with the same declarations, you can combine the selectors for the two rule sets so they share a common declaration block, as shown in the following code snippet:

```
/* Ungrouped selectors */
th {
  color:green;
  font-size: 12pt;
  font-family: arial, verdana;
}
```

```
td {
  color:green;
  font-size: 12pt;
  font-family: arial, verdana;
}

/* Grouped selectors */

th,td {
  color:green;
  font-size: 12pt;
  font-family: arial, verdana;
}
```

In the code snippet, the first two rule sets have type selectors for table headings (`<th>`) and table cells (`<td>`), respectively, and they have the same CSS declarations. The third rule set combines the first two by placing both selectors before the declaration block and separating them with a comma. The third rule set is applied as an HTML element that matches either of the two type selectors.

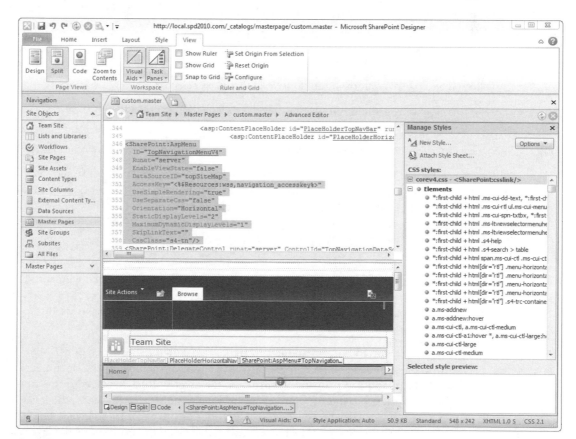

FIGURE 5-11

By default, the Manage Styles task pane would display only one item in the CSS styles list box (`th`, `td`). If the Separate Grouped Selectors option is enabled, two items are displayed as if they were truly separate rule sets. This would be handy if you wanted to move the `td` rule set from the code snippet of one `.css` file to another. That leads to the next unique feature of the Manage Styles task pane, the ability to move styles by dragging them to another `.css` file in the CSS styles list box. You can also reorder the styles in the `.css` file simply by dragging them to the desired location.

> **NOTE** *Reordering styles only works if you enabled the Categorize By Order option via the Options button.*

You may have noticed the icons to the left of the styles on the Apply Styles and Manage Styles task pages. These icons serve as a visual aid to indicate the style's selector type, whether or not the style is used on the current page, and other valuable information. The following list outlines the various icons and their meanings:

- ➤ A blue icon is displayed for a style with a type selector.
- ➤ A red icon is displayed for a style with an ID selector.
- ➤ A green icon is displayed for a style with a class selector.
- ➤ A yellow icon is displayed for an inline style with a class selector.
- ➤ An icon with a circle around it indicates that the style is used on the current page.

There are two more icons that may be displayed for your `.css` files. If the style sheet is missing or the URL is incorrect, an error icon is displayed to the left of the style sheet name, as shown in Figure 5-12.

If the style sheet is attached to the current page using the CSS `@import` directive, an @ sign will appear next to the style sheet name. The following code snippet shows how to use `@import` to attach a style sheet to the current page instead of using a `<link>` element:

```
<style type="text/css">
  @import url('../../Style%20Library/custom.css');
</style>
```

The Layers task pane lists the CSS layers in the current page. A CSS layer is a `<div>` element that uses the `position` property of CSS. The `position` property is set to `absolute` or `relative` and the `left` property is used to position the layer on the horizontal axis. The `top` property is used to position the layer on the vertical axis.

Normally, a page is rendered top to bottom and left to right, also called a "flow" layout. If the layer's `position` property is set to `absolute`, the layer is taken out of the flow of the document. If the layer also has the `left` and `top` properties set to `0px`, the layer will be displayed in the top-left corner of the page regardless of where it appears in the page's HTML. In this case, the layer is always rendered at a position calculated from the top-left corner of the page. If the layer's `position` property is set to `relative`, the position of the layer is calculated from the position of the layer as if the `position` property had not been set. In other words, setting a layer's `position` property to `relative` and its `top` property to `5px` will move the layer down five pixels from its original location.

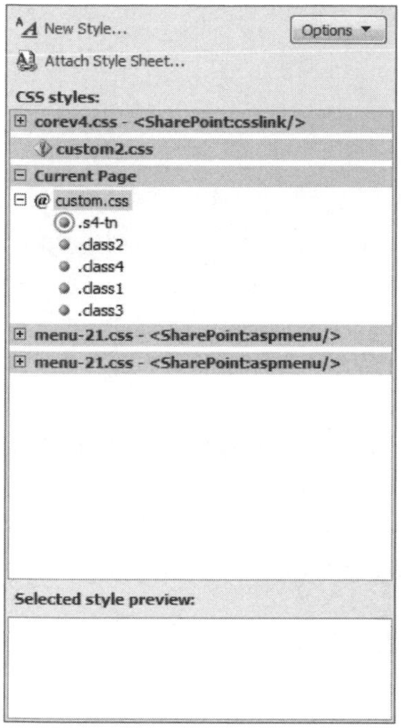

FIGURE 5-12

In Figure 5-13, the Layers task pane is displayed with two buttons at the top of the task pane. The first button is the New Layer button, which creates a new layer as a child of the selected layer in the list. If no layer has been selected and the page is in Design view, the new layer is added as the first child of the <body> element. Otherwise, the new layer is added at the location of the text cursor in the code window. The second button is the Draw Layer button, which allows you to draw a rectangle on the Design view surface. Once the rectangle has been drawn, the layer is created and assigned the next available z-index value. z-index is a CSS property that determines how these layers should appear when they visually overlap.

The layer with the highest z-index value is displayed in front of all other layers. The layer with the lowest z-index value is displayed behind all other layers. If you were to imagine these layers as a deck of cards, the card on the top would have the highest value and the card on the bottom would have the lowest value. It is completely possible that a layer could be completely obscured by a layer with a higher z-index value. Of course, if none of the layers overlap, the z-index value really does not come into play when the page is rendered in the browser.

Underneath the buttons is the list of layers in the current page. The list has three columns. The first column has an "eye" in its column header. This column is used to indicate whether the CSS visibility property is set to visible, hidden, or not set at all. If the visibility property is set to visible, an open eye is displayed in the column. If it is set to hidden, a closed eye appears. If the property is not set at all, the column is left blank. Clicking in the column will cycle the visibility value from default (blank) to visible to hidden and back to default again.

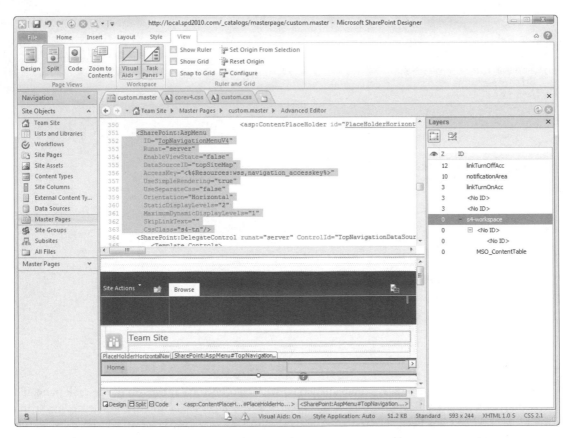

FIGURE 5-13

The second column displays the z-index value of the layer. You may have noticed that the layers are sorted in descending z-index order. That puts the topmost layer at the top of the list and the bottommost at the bottom. If you want to change a z-index value, double-click it to put the value in edit mode.

The third column displays the layer's ID attribute. It is also used to indicate if a layer has any child layers, meaning that the <div> element has other <div> elements nested between its tags. If a layer has child layers, an expand/collapse icon will appear to the left of the layer's ID value. In Figure 5-13, the s4-workspace layer has an unnamed layer as a child, which in turn has another unnamed layer as a child. Unnamed layers are <div> elements whose ID attribute has not been set. <No ID> is displayed in the ID column for those layers. If you want to change the ID value, double-click it to put the value in edit mode.

If you need to reposition the layers, simply drag the layer in the task pane to the place you want to move it. The layer's z-index value will be adjusted automatically to an appropriate value for the layer's new position. You can also nest a layer by moving it on top of another layer.

CSS layers, which enable advanced scripting and layouts, are a complex topic. You can find specifications at www.w3.org/TR/CSS2/visuren.html#layers.

To improve usability of your site for people with visual or auditory impairments, you should check your site for accessibility issues. Figure 5-14 shows the Accessibility task pane, which appears by default at the bottom of the screen. The first thing you will notice is the green arrow in the task pane toolbar. Clicking the green arrow displays the Accessibility Checker dialog in Figure 5-15.

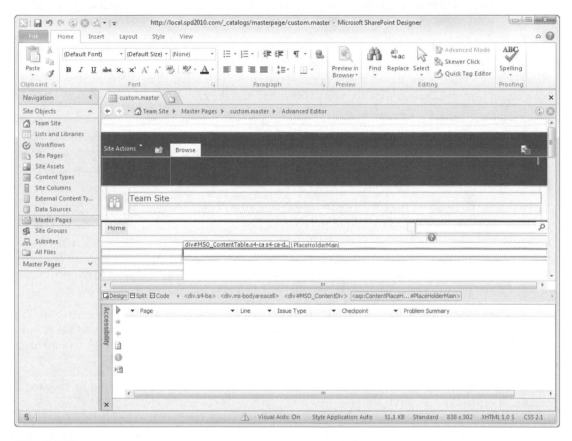

FIGURE 5-14

Use the radio buttons on the left side of the dialog to indicate which pages you want to check. The checkboxes in the middle of the dialog are the standards that the Accessibility Checker can use to check your pages. The first two options are the Web Content Accessibility Guidelines (WCAG) and were created by the World Wide Web Consortium (W3C). Priority 1 guidelines *must* be satisfied or at least one group of users will not be able to use your site at all. Priority 2 guidelines *should* be satisfied or at least one group of users will have significant difficulty in using your site. You can read more about meeting WCAG guidelines at `http://www.w3.org/TR/WCAG10/#Guidelines`.

FIGURE 5-15

The last option is for the accessibility guidelines from Section 508 of the United States Rehabilitation Act. If you work or are affiliated with the United States Federal government, you will need to meet these standards, especially if your site is public-facing or will be considered an "enterprise-level" application used by many federal employees and contractors. The Section 508 standards are similar to the WCAG guidelines, but they are not prioritized in the amount of impact they have on accessibility.

The checkboxes on the right side of the dialog are used to indicate whether errors or warnings should be shown in the Accessibility Checker results. You can also select the Manual Checklist checkbox to include a list of stock issues that you would check manually against your site. Once you have configured the dialog, click the Check button to run the report.

Once the report is complete, a list of issues will be displayed in the Accessibility task pane. Except for the Manual Checklist issues, each issue will indicate the page and line where the issue occurs. The Problem Summary column displays the gist of the issue. If you want more information about the problem, including possible tips to address the problem, right-click the issue and select Problem Details from the context menu.

You can also navigate to the issue on the affected page by double-clicking the issue or right-clicking the issue and selecting Go to Page from the context menu. One convenient feature of this task pane is that you can navigate straight to the guideline on the Internet by right-clicking the issue and selecting Learn More. Unfortunately, Learn More only works for WCAG guidelines. If you need to share your results with others, click the bottom button on the task pane toolbar to export the results to an HTML report. The generated report will open in a new tab in SharePoint Designer.

The Compatibility task pane (Figure 5-16) is used to check your pages against XHTML and CSS standards. When you display the Compatibility task pane, it appears at the bottom of the screen. As with the Accessibility task pane, there is a green arrow you can click to show the Compatibility Checker dialog in Figure 5-17.

The left side of the dialog has radio buttons you use to indicate which pages should be checked. The right side of the dialog has two drop-down lists that you use to select which HTML/XHTML and CSS guidelines you want to use during the compatibility checks. Select the checkbox if you want to include the page's DOCTYPE declaration in the checks. Once you are ready to run the report, click the Check button.

The results of the checks are displayed in the Compatibility task pane. Just as with the Accessibility task pane, you can double-click an issue to navigate to the problem and generate an HTML report by clicking the bottom button in the task pane toolbar.

> **NOTE** You may get false positives for incompatibility or code errors for content controls since they are not populated until the page is accessed via the browser.

The CSS Reports task pane in Figure 5-18 allows you to check your CSS for errors. Clicking the green arrow button displays the CSS Reports dialog in Figure 5-19. In the dialog, the Errors tab is shown. Like the dialogs in the previous figures, you can use the radio buttons on the left side of the dialog to indicate which pages should be checked. The right side of the dialog contains the options for the types of problems that can be checked. Once you have made your selection, click the Check button to run the report.

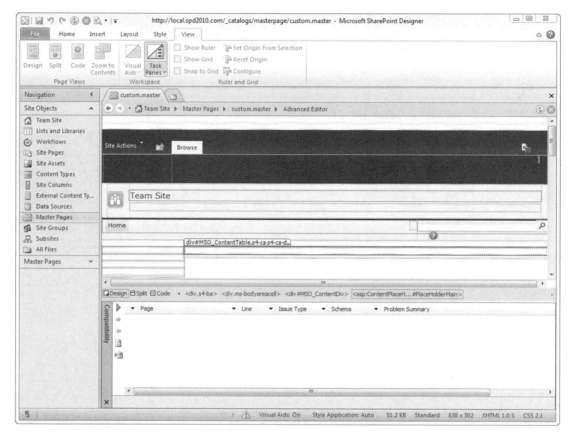

FIGURE 5-16

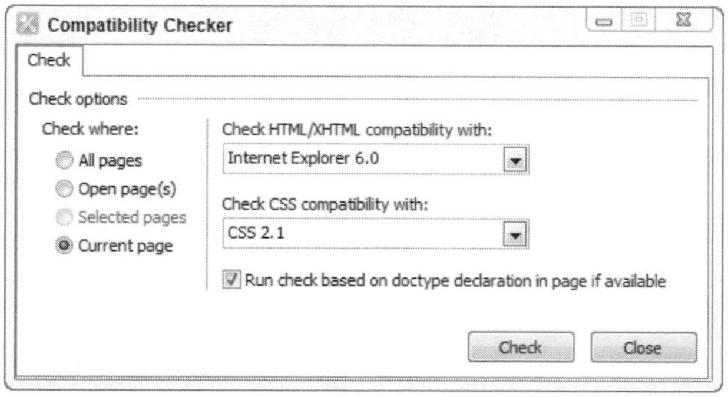

FIGURE 5-17

The results of the CSS checks are displayed in the task pane. The task pane has columns for the page, line, and style where the issues are encountered. The Error Summary column indicates the nature of the issue. To navigate to the spot where an issue has been encountered, double-click the issue or right-click the issue and select Go to Page from the context menu.

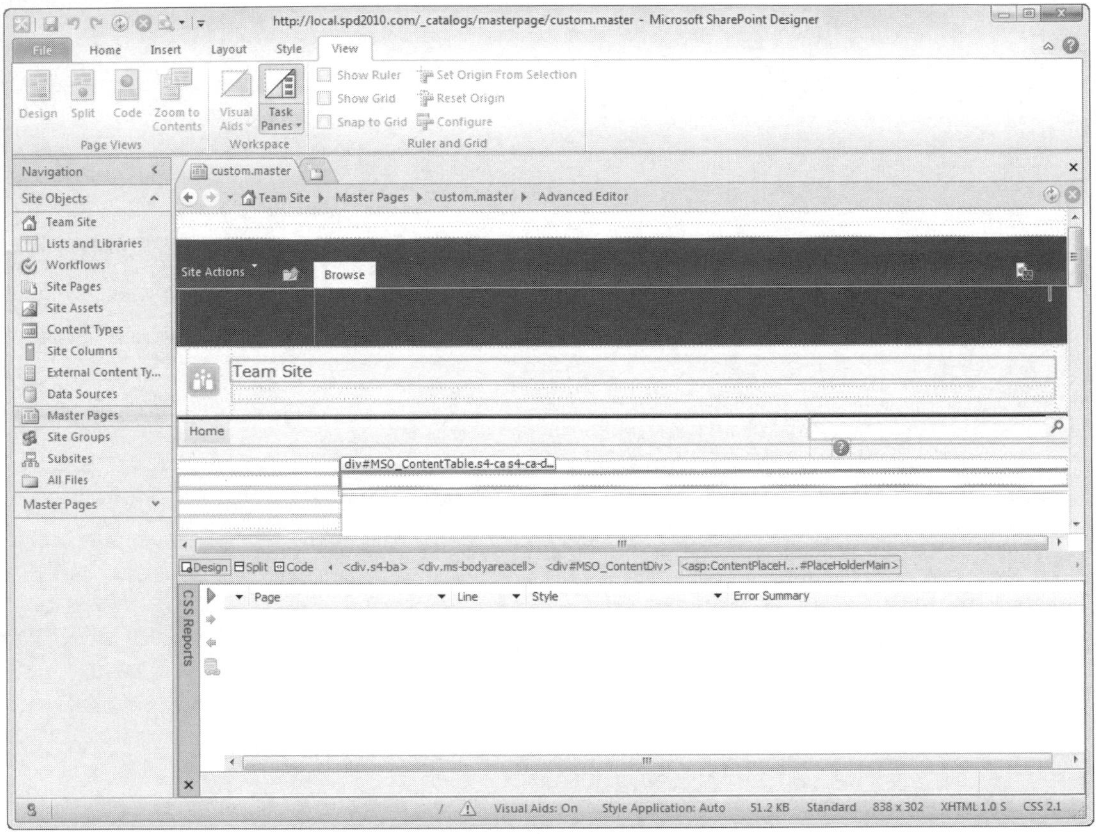

FIGURE 5-18

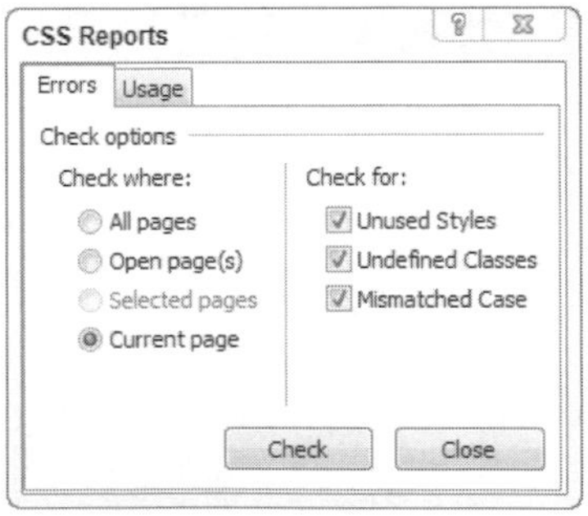

FIGURE 5-19

Having efficient and clean CSS is important. No matter much you plan in advance, the iterative and dynamic nature of business will lead to changes in markup and styling. Sometimes, these changes happen quickly and code is left in a messy state with undefined and orphaned selectors.

Leaving your pages in a messy state will greatly increase the costs of future maintenance and cause an undue burden for anyone who inherits the responsibility for maintaining such a site. You should remove unused code from your final product prior to launch. The smaller your files are, the faster your site will perform.

The CSS Reports task pane also gives you the ability to audit the usage of CSS styles in your site. Instead of filling out the Errors tab of the CSS Reports dialog, you fill out the Usage tag as shown in Figure 5-20. The main difference between the two tabs of the CSS Reports dialog is the set of options on the right side of the Usage tab. The checkboxes allow you to choose which types of CSS rule sets will appear in the usage report. Once you have made your selection, click the Check button to run the report.

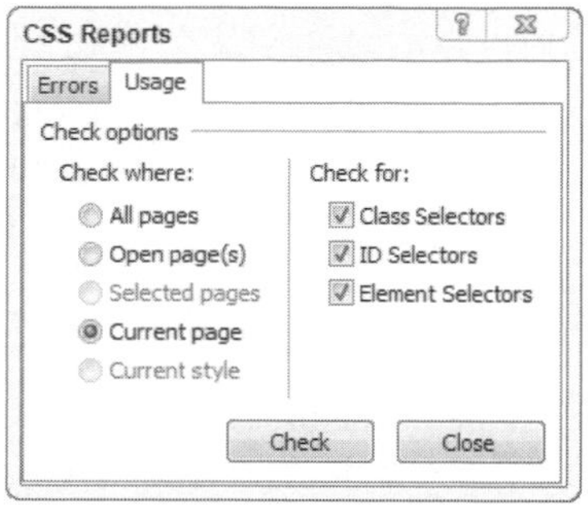

FIGURE 5-20

In Figure 5-21, the usage report is displayed. The columns shown are different from those for the CSS errors report. The report lists the styles used, the pages that use them, the lines where they are used, and where the style is defined. If you click the name of the .css file in the Definition Location column, the .css file will open in a new tab and the text cursor will be positioned at the place where the style is located in the file. As with the CSS errors report, double-clicking a style in the report will navigate to where that style is used in the page listed in the Usage Location column.

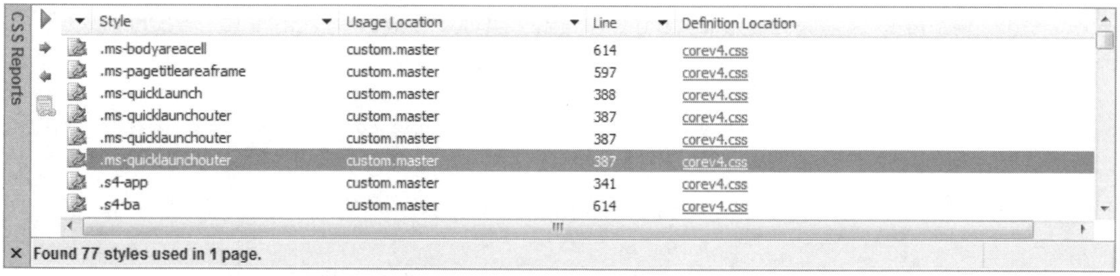

FIGURE 5-21

STYLING YOUR SITE

SharePoint provides the Style Library document library in the root of every site collection, and you use it to store your branding files, including CSS, ECMA Script (also known as JavaScript or JScript), and image files. By default, the Style Library is empty, but if your site was created using the Publishing site template or you activate the SharePoint Server Publishing Infrastructure feature, the Style Library will be populated with the images and XSL files used by the Content Query Web Part and other publishing web parts.

> **NOTE** *The SharePoint Server Publishing Infrastructure feature is only available in the Standard and Enterprise editions of SharePoint 2010.*

Although different schools of thought exist as to how much you should rely on the Style Library for all of your branding artifacts (especially when working on very large projects), getting in the habit of using the library for these types of files is a good idea. Having a central location that is easily managed through SharePoint Designer enables you to customize a site efficiently, especially if you are working as part of a team.

The best way to learn about SharePoint styles is to get your hands dirty and play with the styles. Later in the chapter, you will see the CSS related to the key user interface elements of SharePoint pages. Customarily, a designer will override the CSS styles for these key UI elements and store those overriding styles in a custom `.css` file.

Key UI Elements in SharePoint

One of the first things users want is for you to make SharePoint look like something other than SharePoint. Their requests can range from simple tweaks, including custom color schemes, to complete overhauls that make the site look so different that nobody would guess that it is based on SharePoint. Currently, there are several hundreds of public-facing websites based on SharePoint 2007 and SharePoint 2010. To get an idea of what is possible when branding a SharePoint site, visit the following URL to see a list of example websites:

```
http://www.wssdemo.com/SitePages/SitesByIndustry.aspx
```

The most common UI elements you would modify are in this section of the chapter, including the ribbon, menus, headings, links, and toolbars. The good thing is that all of the CSS styles you need to override are in the `corev4.css` file and only a few styles for each control will likely need to be overridden. However, the final number of styles you need to override will depend on the number of changes you wish to make to these controls. When you read about the controls in the next paragraphs, remember that these styles and figures are from a Team Site using the `v4.master` and the `corev4.css` file.

The ribbon, shown in Figure 5-22, is a new feature in SharePoint 2010.

FIGURE 5-22

The new ribbon control has 520 styles associated with it. These styles rely heavily on the `!important` attribute to enforce their property declarations. If you override the styles in the ribbon control, you will have to add the `!important` attribute to your property declarations, too. The following styles are most commonly overridden when this control is customized:

CSS SELECTOR	WHERE USED
.ms-cui-tts	The ribbon's tab headers
.ms-cui-tt	A ribbon tab header
.ms-cui-tt-s	A selected ribbon tab header
.ms-cui-tt-a	The anchor (<a>) element in a ribbon tab header
.ms-cui-tt-span	The tab header text
.ms-cui-tabBody	The ribbon tab's body containing the sections and buttons
.ms-cui-groupContainer	A ribbon section
.ms-cui-groupSeparator	The vertical line separating ribbon sections
.ms-cui-groupBody	A ribbon section's body, where the buttons are located
.ms-cui-groupTitle	A ribbon section's title
.ms-cui-ctl-large	A ribbon button displayed with a large image
.ms-cui-ctl-largelabel	A ribbon button's text when displayed with a large image
.ms-cui-ctl-medium	A ribbon button displayed with a medium image
.ms-cui-ctl-mediumlabel	A ribbon button's text when displayed with a medium image
.ms-cui-ctl	A ribbon button displayed with a small image
.ms-cui-hidden	A ribbon button hidden from the UI

The site's title appears directly under the ribbon. The site title displays as a link, and the page and path are displayed as breadcrumbs, as shown in Figure 5-23.

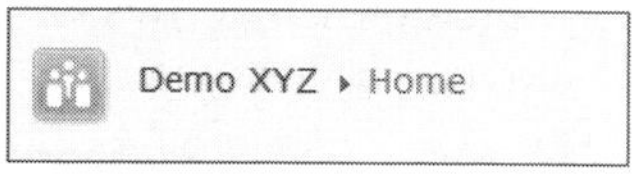

FIGURE 5-23

The following styles are most commonly overridden when this control is customized:

CSS SELECTOR	WHERE USED
.s4-titlelogo	The site logo
.s4-titletext	The site title

continues

(continued)

CSS SELECTOR	WHERE USED
`.s4-title h1, .s4-title h2`	The site title font and size
`.s4-title h1 a, .s4-title h2 a`	The site title link color
`.s4-titlesep`	The separator between breadcrumbs in the site title area
`.s4-pagedescription`	The site description

> **NOTE** *SharePoint 2010 uses a technique called CSS sprites to compile multiple graphics into one image. Using the* `background-position` *attribute in CSS, SharePoint displays one specific graphic from the larger CSS sprite image. By using CSS sprites, SharePoint reduces the number of files requested and downloaded, resulting in noticeable decreases in page-load time and bandwidth.*
>
> *One example of a CSS sprite image used in SharePoint styles is the* `bgximg.png` *image found in the* `layouts` *directory:* `http://yoursitename.com/_layouts/images/bgximg.png`.
>
> *This one-pixel-wide image is used to apply a gradient to the background of various elements on the page. If you were to open this URL in your browser, the page would look blank since the image is so thin, but when it is repeated many times in a horizontal direction, it looks like a larger, elaborate image. The best part is that the file is extremely small, which makes it download almost instantly.*

The search controls appear on the top right of the page, inside the navigation bar, as shown in Figure 5-24.

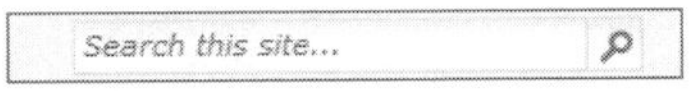

FIGURE 5-24

The following styles are most commonly overridden when this control is customized:

CSS SELECTOR	WHERE USED
`.s4-search`	The search control container
`.ms-sbplain`	The search textbox's font and border
`.s4-search input.ms-sbplain`	The search textbox's text color
`.srch-gosearchimg`	The search button

The sign-in link is at the top right of the screen, as shown in Figure 5-25.

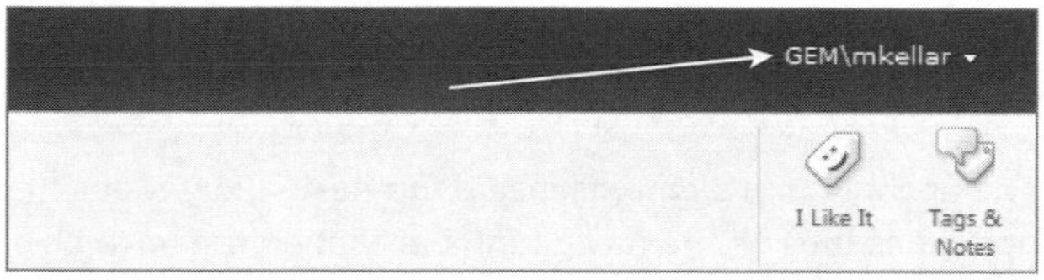

FIGURE 5-25

Override the `.s4-signInLink` style to restyle the link. You have to add the `!important` attribute to override the link's text color.

The social media notification buttons on the right-side of the ribbon in SharePoint 2010 are shown in Figure 5-26.

FIGURE 5-26

The following styles are most commonly overridden when this control is customized:

CSS SELECTOR	WHERE USED
`.ms-socialNotif-Container`	The `<div>` element containing the buttons
`.ms-socialNotif-groupSeparator`	The vertical separator to the left of the I Like It button
`.ms-socialNotif`	The buttons themselves
`.ms-socialNotif:hover`	The buttons when the mouse is hovering over them
`.ms-socialNotif-text`	The text on the buttons

The top navigation bar of the site (see Figure 5-27) is located at the top of the site's pages, just under the ribbon.

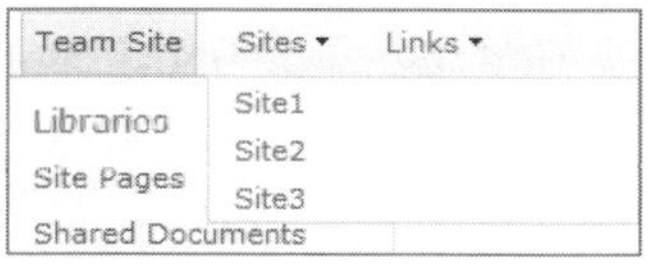

FIGURE 5-27

The clickable HTML elements in the top navigation bar are called navigation nodes. Navigation nodes with children have a down arrow that appears to the right, and when the arrow is clicked, a fly-out menu appears displaying the navigation node's children. The following styles are most commonly overridden when this control is customized:

CSS SELECTOR	WHERE USED
`.s4-tn`	The `<div>` element that spans the width of the page and contains the top navigation bar.
`.s4-tn ul.static`	The unordered list (`<ul>`) elements containing the navigation nodes that appear as tabs on the navigation bar.
`.s4-tn li.static> .menu-item`	The navigation nodes that appear as tabs on the navigation bar that do not have children.

continues

(continued)

CSS SELECTOR	WHERE USED
`.s4-tn li.static> a:hover`	The anchor (`<a>`) elements inside the navigation nodes that appear as tabs on the navigation bar that do not have children when the mouse is hovering over them.
`.s4-tn li.dynamic> .menu-item`	The navigation nodes that appear as tabs on the navigation bar that have children.
`.s4-tn ul.dynamic`	The flyout menu containing the children of a navigation node.
`.s4-tn li.dynamic> a:hover`	The anchor (`<a>`) elements inside the navigation nodes that appear as tabs on the navigation bar that have children when the mouse is hovering over them.
`.s4-toplinks .s4-tn a.selected`	Styles the navigation node currently selected. A navigation node is considered to be selected when the browser has navigated to that navigation node's destination URL. In Figure 5-29, the Team Site navigation node is currently selected because the browser had navigated to the site's home page.
`.s4-toplinks .s4-tn a.selected:hover`	Styles the navigation node currently selected when the mouse is hovering over it.

In a site with Publishing features enabled, a yellow status bar (Figure 5-28), called the Page Status Bar, will appear just under the ribbon on each site page. The Page Status Bar indicates the current page's checkout and publishing status.

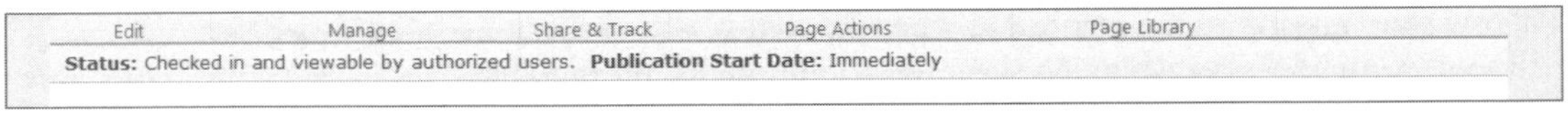

Edit	Manage	Share & Track	Page Actions	Page Library

Status: Checked in and viewable by authorized users. **Publication Start Date:** Immediately

FIGURE 5-28

The following styles are most commonly overridden when this control is customized:

CSS SELECTOR	WHERE USED
`body #s4-statusbarcontainer`	The `<div>` element containing the page status bar
`body #pageStatusBar`	The page status bar itself
`.s4-status-s1`	The page status bar and its descendants
`body #pageStatusBar a:link,body #pageStatusBar a:visited`	Any anchor (`<a>`) elements inside the page status bar

The Site Actions menu (see Figure 5-29) appears just above the ribbon in the upper left-hand corner of the page. Of all of the component parts of the Site Actions menu, the actual Site Actions button you click to display the menu is the most commonly styled element. Since many of the menu items have icons next to them in the menu, you will need to take care if you style the background behind the images to avoid making them difficult to see. The button to the right of the Site Actions menu is the Navigate Up button, which displays the breadcrumb trail for the current page. Figure 5-30 shows the breadcrumb trail that appears when the Navigate Up button is clicked.

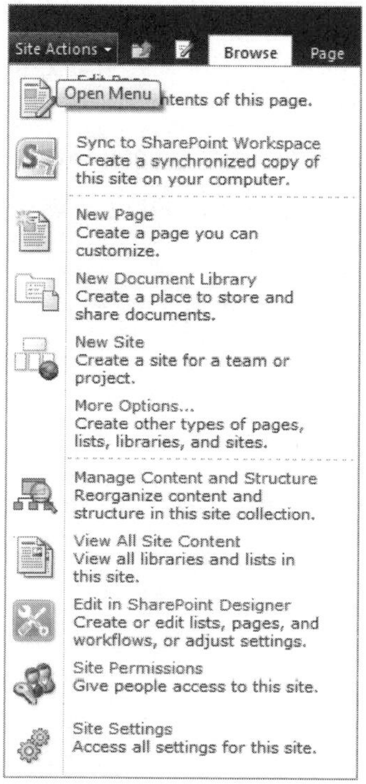

FIGURE 5-29

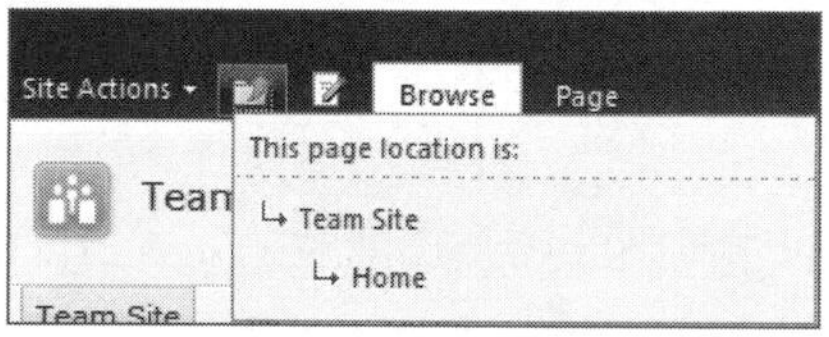

FIGURE 5-30

The following styles are most commonly overridden when this control is customized:

CSS SELECTOR	WHERE USED
.ms-siteactionscontainer	The `<div>` element containing the Site Actions menu, Navigate Up, and Edit Page buttons
.ms-siteactionsmenu	The Site Actions menu itself
.s4-breadcrumb-anchor	The Navigate Up button to the right of the Site Actions menu button
.s4-breadcrumb-anchor-open	The Navigate Up button to the right of the Site Actions menu button when the Navigate Up button is clicked and the Navigation popup menu is open

continues

(continued)

CSS SELECTOR	WHERE USED
.s4-breadcrumb-menu	The Navigation popup menu
.s4-breadcrumb-top	The top of the Navigation popup menu
.s4-breadcrumb-header	The text "This page location is:" that appears at the top of the Navigation popup menu
.s4-breadcrumb	The bottom of the Navigation popup menu where the breadcrumb trail is shown
.s4-breadcrumbRootNode	The root node of the Navigation popup menu
.s4-breadcrumbCurrentNode	The currently selected node in the Navigation popup menu
.s4-breadcrumbNode	The nodes in the Navigation popup menu that are not selected

The Quick Launch bar in Figure 5-31 is located on the left side of site pages. The quick launch navigation has two different areas: the left navigation links and the special navigation links for Recycle Bin and All Site Content. All of these areas are *security trimmed*. Security trimmed elements do not appear on the page when the user does not have permission to see the element or navigate to the element's destination URL when clicked.

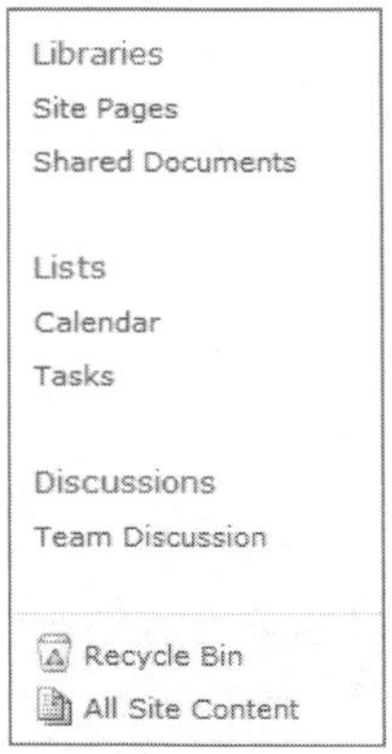

FIGURE 5-31

The following styles are most commonly overridden when this control is customized:

CSS SELECTOR	WHERE USED
.ms-quicklaunchouter	The <div> element containing the Quick Launch bar.
.ms-quickLaunch	The Quick Launch bar.

CSS SELECTOR	WHERE USED
.ms-quicklaunch-navmgr	The top area of the Quick Launch bar above the Recycle Bin.
.menu-item	The items in the top area of the Quick Launch bar.
.menu-item-text	The text of the items in the top area of the Quick Launch bar.
.s4-ql ul.root > li > .menu-item	The headings in the top area of the Quick Launch bar. In Figure 5-31, the headings are Libraries, Lists, and Discussions.
.s4-ql ul.root ul > li > a	The items under the headings in the Quick Launch bar.
.s4-specialNavLinkList	The bottom area of the Quick Launch bar containing the Recycle Bin and All Site Content links.
.s4-rcycl	The Recycle Bin.
.s4-specialNavIcon	All Site Content link.
.ms-splinkbutton-text	The anchor (<a>) elements for the Recycle Bin and All Site Content links.

Web parts have many HTML elements that can be styled. Web parts have a title bar, a web part menu, the divider between the title bar and the web part's content, the web part's content area, and the "chrome" border around the web part. In Figure 5-32, the HTML Form Web Part is displayed along with its web part menu on the right.

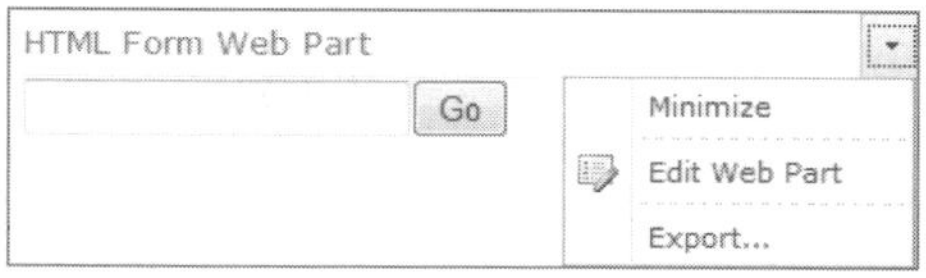

FIGURE 5-32

The following styles are most commonly overridden when this control is customized:

CSS SELECTOR	WHERE USED
.ms-WPHeader	The title bar at the top of the web part
.ms-wpTdSpace	The empty space to the left of the web part title
.ms-WPTitle	The web part title
.ms-WPHeaderTd	The area to the left of the web part menu arrow that contains the web part's title
.ms-WPHeaderTdMenu	The down arrow that displays the web part menu when clicked
.ms-SrvMenuUI	The web part menu

continues

(continued)

CSS SELECTOR	WHERE USED
`.ms-WPBorder`	The border around the web part body
`.ms-WPBody`	The web part body

Themes

SharePoint themes are a collection of CSS and images applied at runtime to control the look and feel of your site. Themes have been tailored for use by non-technical people. In fact, themes can be completely managed through the user interface without the user having any knowledge of CSS.

In SharePoint 2007, you created a theme by creating a subfolder under the `C:\Program Files\ Common Files\Microsoft Shared\Web Server Extensions\12\TEMPLATE\THEMES` folder where the out-of-the-box themes were stored. Usually, you named the subfolder to match the name of the theme. Inside the subfolder, you would places the images and CSS files comprising your theme.

In SharePoint 2010, themes have changed dramatically as you now design your themes using Microsoft PowerPoint 2010 the same way you design a custom Microsoft Office theme. A Microsoft Office 2010 theme includes a set of theme colors, fonts, and visual effects that are stored in a special `.thmx` file. In SharePoint 2010, these `.thmx` files can be uploaded to SharePoint, which allows site owners to choose one of those new themes for their site. SharePoint 2010 comes with 20 themes out of the box, but you can easily create your own.

To create a new theme, open Microsoft PowerPoint 2010. Once the program has opened, click the Design tab as shown in Figure 5-33. To choose your theme's colors, select the Colors drop-down from the ribbon and click Create New Theme Colors to display the Create New Theme Colors dialog in Figure 5-34.

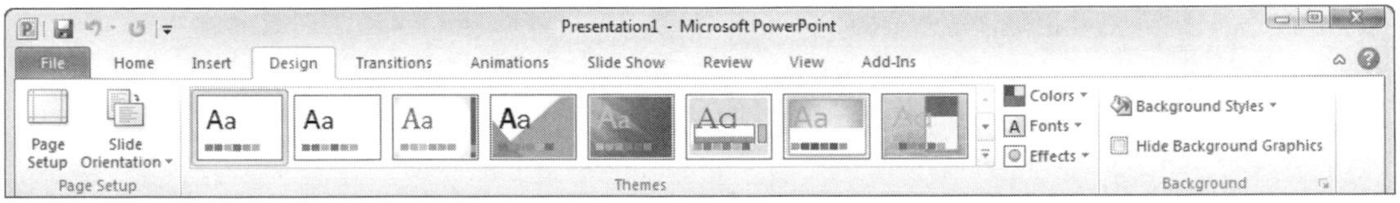

FIGURE 5-33

In the dialog, choose the colors for your theme, enter your theme name in the Name textbox, and click the Save button. You can use the Sample images on the right side of the dialog to preview your color scheme.

Once you have made your color selection, select the Fonts drop-down from the ribbon and click Create New Theme Fonts to display the Create New Theme Fonts dialog in Figure 5-35. Select a font for Headings from the Heading font drop-down list and a font for body text from the Body font drop-down list, enter your theme name in the Name textbox, and click the Save button. The Sample textbox shows a preview of your font selection.

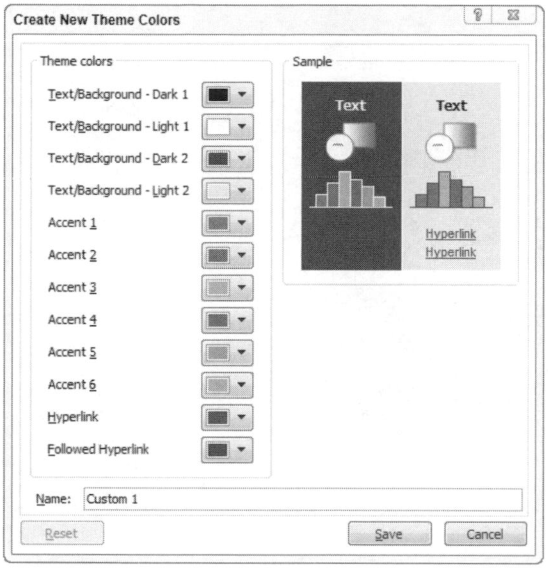

FIGURE 5-34

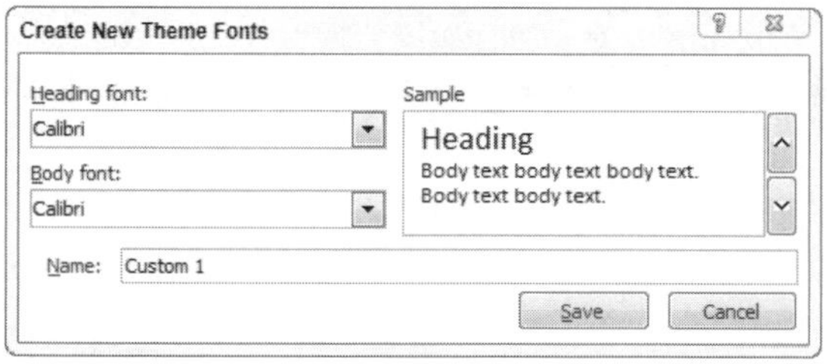

FIGURE 5-35

Now that you have selected your colors and fonts, click the down arrow just to the right of the Effects drop-down list and click Save current theme (Figure 5-36) to save your theme to a `.thmx` file. In the Save Current Theme dialog, select a convenient folder for your `.thmx` file, such as My Documents or Desktop, enter the name of your theme, and click the Save button.

When you are ready to deploy your theme to SharePoint, you may be tempted to deploy the files to `C:\Program Files\Common Files\Microsoft Shared\Web Server Extensions\14\TEMPLATE\THEMES`, but that folder is for backwards compatibility purposes. Now, you can upload your themes in the browser or SharePoint Designer. In SharePoint 2010, the new Theme Gallery (Figure 5-37) is provided for you to store your themes. To open the Theme Gallery using your browser, select Site Settings from the Site Actions menu. Then, click the Theme Gallery link under the Galleries section of the Site Settings page. Alternately, you can use SharePoint Designer to access the Theme Gallery by clicking All Files in the Navigation bar on the left side of the screen and navigating the site's folder structure to `/_catalogs/theme` as shown in Figure 5-38.

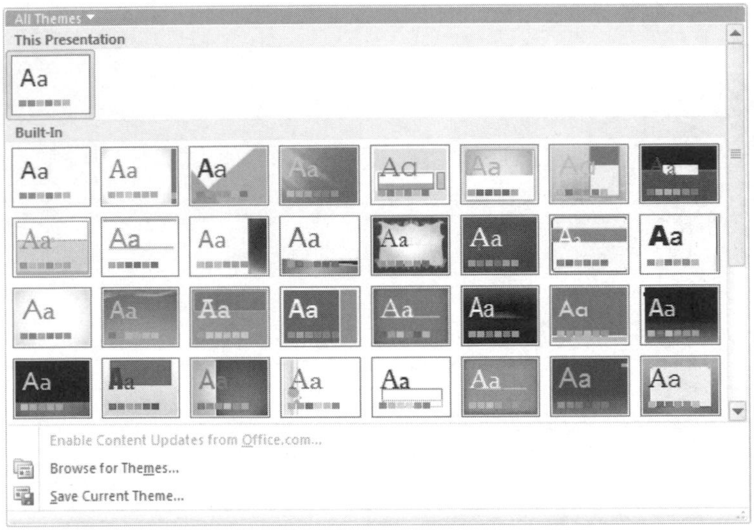

FIGURE 5-36

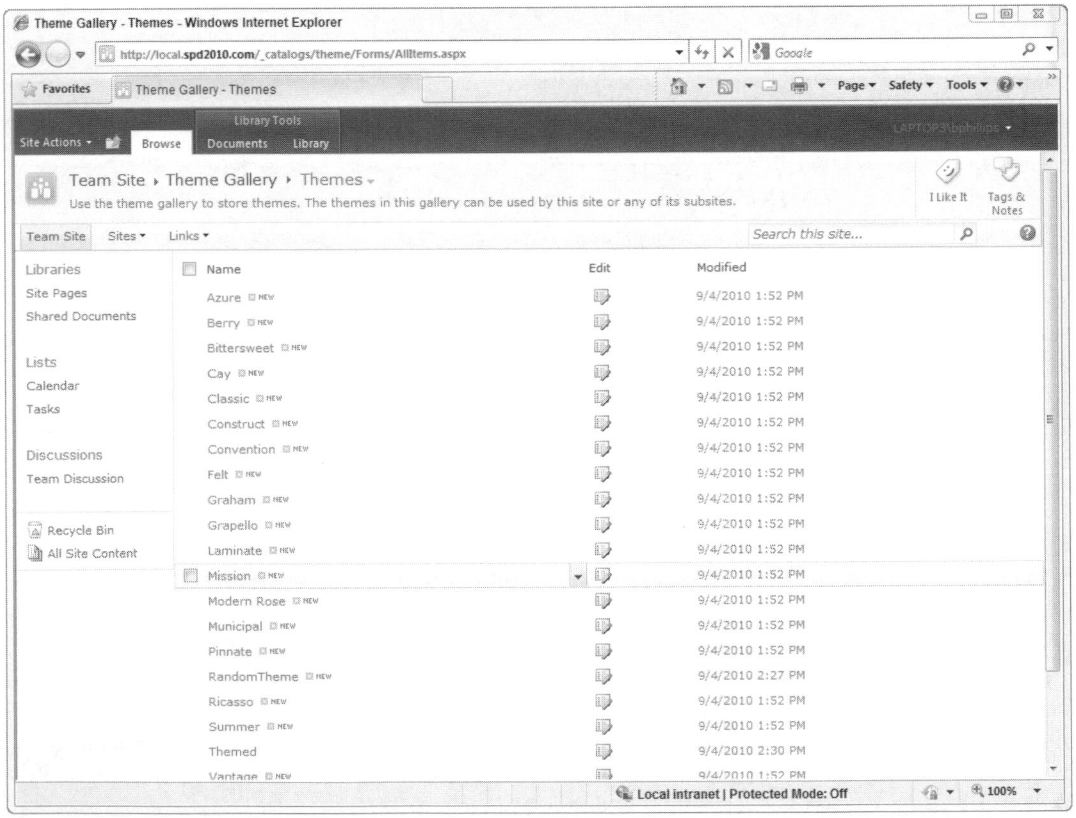

FIGURE 5-37

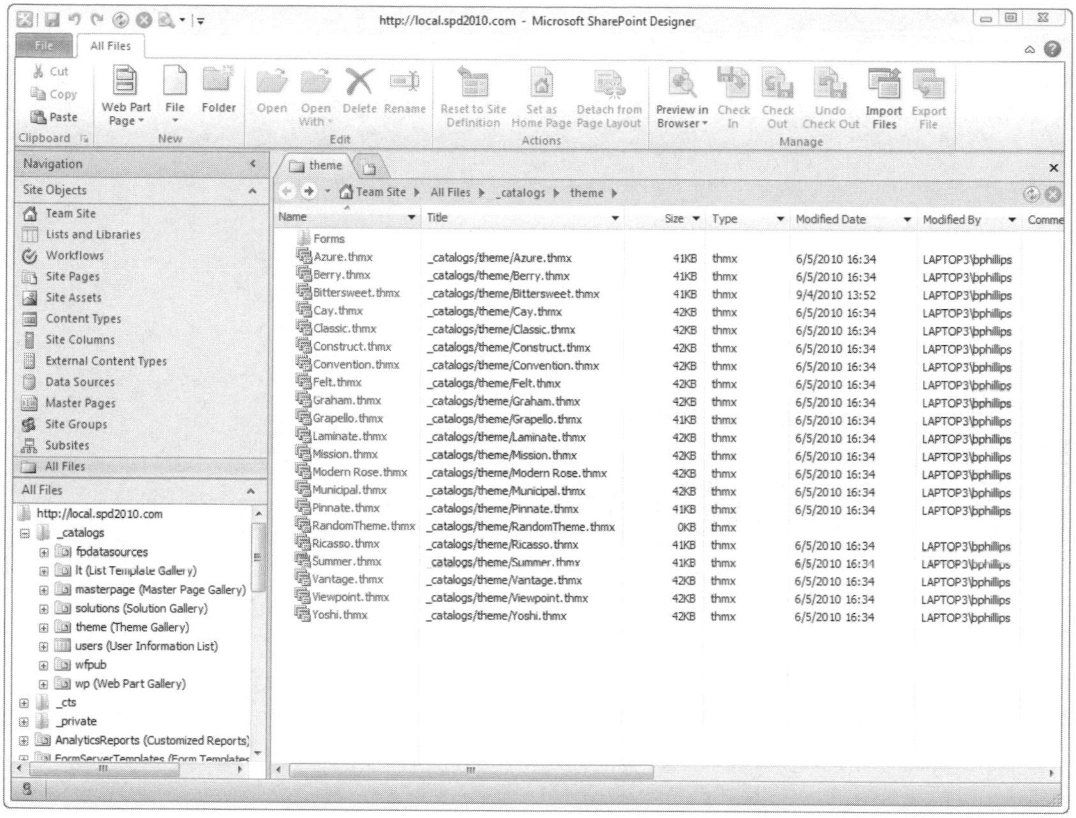

FIGURE 5-38

> **NOTE** Unlike the Master Page Gallery, the Theme Gallery only exists at the site collection level. Once you upload your theme, it will be available to all sites in the site collection.

Once your theme is uploaded to SharePoint, use the Site Theme page to apply it to your site. You access the Site Theme page by selecting Site Settings from the Site Actions menu and clicking Site theme under the Look and Feel section of the Site Settings page.

The Site Theme page in Figure 5-39 is very powerful. You can select a theme for your site from the Select a Theme list box and apply the theme to all subsites using the Inherit Theme and Apply Theme radio button lists. To customize your selected theme, make your changes in the Customize Theme section of the page. Clicking Select a color next to one of the colors will display the Colors dialog in Figure 5-40. In the Colors dialog, you can manually enter the RGB value in the textbox or select a color from the color wheel. You can also preview the site using your selected theme by clicking the Preview button to display the Preview dialog in Figure 5-41. Once you are satisfied with your changes, click the Apply button to apply them to your site.

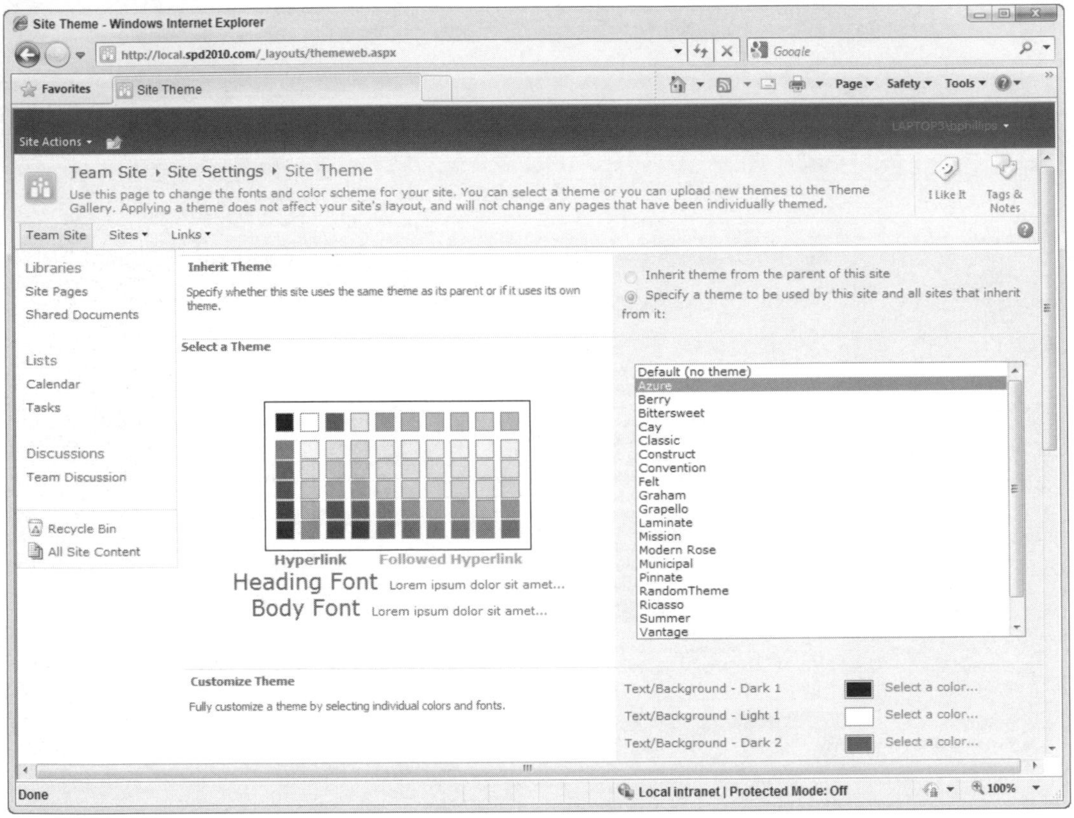

FIGURE 5-39

NOTE *The Preview dialog previews the theme using your site's home page, but you will not be able to navigate to any other page to preview it. Clicking a link in the Preview dialog will open a new browser window, which will not have the previewed theme applied to it. However, you can use the* ThemeOverride *query string variable to preview your theme on any page. The* ThemeOverride *query string variable needs to be set to the relative URL of the theme's* .thmx *file in the Theme Gallery. For example, to preview the Vantage theme with the Site Settings page, use* http://**siteurl**/_layouts/settings .aspx?ThemeOverride=/_catalogs/theme/Vantage.thmx, *where* **siteurl** *is the URL of your site. If your URL already contains query string variables, modify your URL like so:* http://**siteurl**/_layouts/people.aspx?Membership GroupId=5&ThemeOverride=/_catalogs/theme/Vantage.thmx.

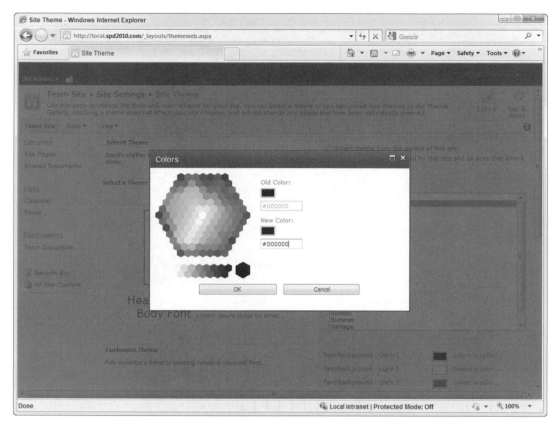

FIGURE 5-40

If you have a theme you created for SharePoint 2007 and want to upgrade it to work in SharePoint 2010, you have two options: recreate the theme by hand in PowerPoint 2010 or deploy the theme's files to the Style Library and use the techniques you learned in this chapter to style your master page with them. Specifically, you must attach the .css file from the old theme to your master page. Keep in mind that many of the CSS class names have changed between SharePoint 2007 and SharePoint 2010, so you will have to substitute the new class names for the old ones.

TRY IT OUT Create and Use a Custom Theme

In this activity, you will use Microsoft PowerPoint 2010 to create a custom theme and apply it to your site.

1. Open Microsoft PowerPoint 2010.

2. Select Colors ⇨ Create New Theme Colors from the Design tab on the ribbon.

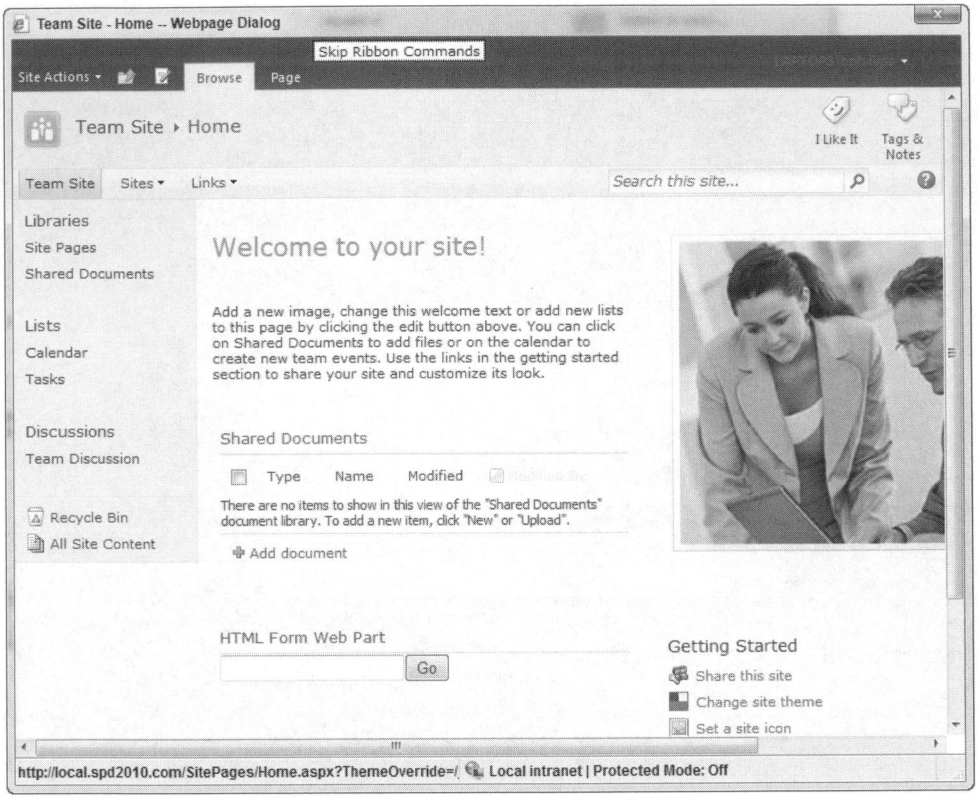

FIGURE 5-41

3. In the Create New Theme Colors dialog, select a different color for each of the Theme Colors drop-down lists.

4. Enter **RandomTheme** in the Name textbox.

5. Click the Save button to close the dialog.

6. Select Fonts ⇨ Create New Theme Fonts from the Design tab on the ribbon.

7. In the Create New Theme Fonts dialog, select a different font for each of the font drop-down lists.

8. Enter **RandomTheme** in the Name textbox.

9. Click the Save button to close the dialog.

10. Click the down arrow to the left of Effects in the Design tab on the ribbon.

11. Select Save Current Theme at the bottom on the Themes drop-down menu.

12. In the Save Current Theme dialog, navigate to your desktop and enter **RandomTheme** in the File name textbox.

13. Click the Save button to save your theme.

14. Close Microsoft PowerPoint 2010. If prompted, do not save the new presentation that was created when you first opened Microsoft PowerPoint 2010.

15. Open your browser and navigate to your SharePoint site.

16. Select Site Settings from the Site Actions menu.

17. Click Themes under the Galleries section of the Site Settings page.

18. Select Upload Document from the Documents tab on the ribbon.

19. In the Upload Document dialog, click the Browse button and navigate to the .thmx file on your desktop.

20. Select the .thmx file and click Open to close the dialog.

21. In the Upload Document dialog, click OK to upload your theme to your SharePoint site.

22. When the Theme Gallery - RandomTheme.thmx dialog appears, click the Save button.

23. Notice that your theme is now available in the list.

24. Select Site Settings from the Site Actions menu.

25. Click Site Theme under the Look and Feel section of the Site Settings page.

26. Select RandomTheme from the Select a Theme list box.

27. Notice that a preview of the selected theme now appears to the left of the Select a Theme list box.

28. Click the Preview button at the bottom of the page.

29. After the preview dialog opens and navigates to your site's home page, notice how the site has changed.

30. Close the preview dialog.

31. Click the Apply button at the bottom of the page to set RandomTheme as the site's theme.

32. Click the site's title to return to the site's home page.

33. To revert back to the site's default theme, follow Steps 24–32, selecting Default (no theme) in Step 26.

How It Works

The theme colors and fonts you selected in Microsoft PowerPoint 2010 were saved in a .thmx file. The .thmx file is actually a .zip archive and is structured according to the Office Open XML File Formats. Other examples of Office Open XML files are Microsoft Word (.docx), Microsoft Excel (.xlsx), and Microsoft PowerPoint (.pptx) files. When you uploaded the .thmx file to the Theme gallery, SharePoint read the theme colors and fonts from the file and allowed you to select the theme on the Site Theme page. When you applied the theme to the site and viewed the site's home page, SharePoint replaced the default values of the theme-able styles in corev4.css on-the-fly with the ones you chose in Microsoft PowerPoint 2010. This modified version of corev4.css was sent to the browser instead of the real one.

Other Things to Consider

A SharePoint site's look and feel is much more than just colors and a logo. Understanding the different areas of visual design and user experience can guide your customizations. The extent of your intended customizations determines whether you use master pages, page layouts, themes, or custom CSS to implement your designs.

The layout of your website is controlled by your master pages, page layouts, and web part pages. If you want to hide or move UI elements that appear on every page, including the Quick Launch and Top Navigation Bars and the Site Actions menu, you need to create a custom master page. If you only want to change the size, location, or orientation of where web parts should go, you only need to change the page layouts and web part pages in your site.

If you decide to create a custom master page, you can customize the existing master page v4.master or start from a *minimal master page*. A minimal master page has only the bare minimum controls and styling needed to run SharePoint. Out-of-the-box, SharePoint provides minimal.master located in the Master Page Gallery. The minimal.master file is very small and mainly contains the ribbon and the ContentPlaceHolder controls required by SharePoint site pages. At the very bottom of the file are the ContentPlaceHolder controls PlaceHolderMain, where the main content appears on the page, and an invisible <div> tag containing the ContentPlaceHolder controls that most designers would want to hide, as shown in the following code snippet:

```
<div id="maincontent" class="s4-pr">
<asp:ContentPlaceHolder id="PlaceHolderMain" runat="server" />
</div>
<div style="display:none;">
<asp:ContentPlaceHolder id="PlaceHolderLeftNavBar" runat="server" />
<asp:ContentPlaceHolder id="PlaceHolderNavSpacer" runat="server" />
<asp:ContentPlaceHolder id="PlaceHolderBodyLeftBorder" runat="server" />
<asp:ContentPlaceHolder id="PlaceHolderPageImage" runat="server" />
<asp:ContentPlaceHolder id="PlaceHolderTitleLeftBorder" runat="server" />
<asp:ContentPlaceHolder id="PlaceHolderSearchArea" runat="server" />
<asp:ContentPlaceHolder id="PlaceHolderTitleAreaClass" runat="server" />
<asp:ContentPlaceHolder id="PlaceHolderTitleAreaSeparator" runat="server" />
</div>
```

You can use minimal.master as a starting point by creating a copy of it and making your changes in the copy.

If you need to create new or modify the existing Page Layout pages, they are located the Master Page Gallery. As with other built-in files, you should not modify the existing files directly; rather, you should make a copy for editing. Page Layout pages are actually templates that define where content should appear. The pages that are derived from Page Layout pages are called Publishing Pages and get their content from the columns of the document library where they are stored. When you activate the Publishing features of SharePoint, a Pages document library is created where these Publishing Pages are stored.

> **NOTE** *Page layouts are only available in the Standard and Enterprise editions of SharePoint Server 2010. They are not available in SharePoint Foundation 2010.*

Modifying web part pages is much simpler. Because they effectively fill in the holes left open by their master page, you are limited in how you can change them. For example, you will not be able to change where the Quick Launch bar appears, but you could hide it by adding a blank `<asp:Content>` tag whose `ContentPlaceHolderId` attribute is set to `PlaceHolderLeftNavBar`. The other most common change to a web part page is simply resizing or repositioning the web part zones. The web part zones are actually `<WebPartPages:WebPartZone>` controls. These controls have two main attributes: `ID`, which uniquely identifies the control and doubles as the name of the zone it represents, and `Orientation`, which determines whether web parts will appear in a horizontal or vertical line. A web part zone's `Orientation` is `Vertical` by default.

> **NOTE** *You must edit a web part page in Advanced Mode to change web part zones. Normal Mode only allows you to change web parts, just as in the browser.*

Branding is more than just the look and feel of the website. It is the core of the website's identity. The colors, fonts, images, and other embellishments are the elements that make a website visually unique. Web designers call this type of styling "branding" because it is the brand of your website. Whether you are branding your intranet or a public-facing website, you have a range of options.

The easiest option to brand your site is to simply choose one of the out-of-the-box themes and click Apply on the Site Theme page. If your organization already has a list of fonts and colors mandated by the marketing department, you could create a custom theme using Microsoft PowerPoint 2010 and apply that.

Another option would be to create a custom `.css` file and attach it to your master page. In your custom `.css` file, you would create CSS rule sets whose CSS selectors match those of the controls in SharePoint that you want to style. Then, you add new property declarations that append or override the properties of the controls. Since your custom `.css` files must appear after all other `.css` files in order to have any effect on the page, use the `<SharePoint:CssRegistration>` control to register your `.css` files with SharePoint at runtime. You modified a master page in Chapter 3 by adding this control to a style sheet that rounded the corners of top navigation. The following code snippet shows the `<SharePoint:CssRegistration>` control in action:

```
<SharePoint:CssRegistration runat="server" After="corev4.css"
Name="/Style Library/custom.css" />
```

In the code snippet, the `Name` attribute is used to specify the URL of the `.css` file, and the `After` attribute is used to specify the name of the `.css` file that it should load after. If you have multiple `.css` files to load and their load order is important, you need to register them in reverse order, as shown in the following code snippet:

```
<SharePoint:CssRegistration runat="server" After="corev4.css"
  Name="/Style Library/third.css" />
<SharePoint:CssRegistration runat="server" After="corev4.css"
  Name="/Style Library/second.css" />
<SharePoint:CssRegistration runat="server" After="corev4.css"
  Name="/Style Library/first.css" />
```

In the code snippet, the three `.css` files are registered in reverse order so that the `first.css`, `second.css`, and `third.css` are loaded in that order, respectively.

> **NOTE** *If you are using SharePoint Server 2010 and Publishing features are activated for your site, you can skip using the* `<SharePoint:CssRegistration>` *control and configure the site using the browser instead. Your* `.css` *file can be specified in the Alternate CSS Url section of the Site Master Page Settings page. You open the page by selecting Site Settings from the Site Actions menu and clicking Master Page under the Look and Feel section.*

SUMMARY

This chapter explained how SharePoint Designer 2010 helps you build, design, and style your SharePoint sites, provided a brief overview of CSS basics, and walked you through the styling tools in SharePoint Designer.

The main points to remember from this chapter are:

- ➤ CSS is a major part of branding SharePoint sites.
- ➤ The `corev4.css` file contains most of the CSS rule sets that you need to override when styling your site.
- ➤ SharePoint Designer provides you with a variety of task panes and toolbars that allow you to easily discover existing styles and create new ones.
- ➤ The key UI elements in SharePoint pages to style and their main CSS rule sets to override.
- ➤ Users who are not confident in their CSS abilities can still brand their sites using an out-of-the-box theme or a theme created with Microsoft PowerPoint.

PART III
Data Galore

6

Lists, Libraries, & Internal Content Types

WHAT YOU WILL LEARN IN THIS CHAPTER

➤ How SharePoint stores and organizes your data

➤ How to create lists and document libraries

➤ How to use views to filter, sort and group the content of lists and libraries

➤ How to create content types to apply a well-defined structure to your data and documents

SHARING YOUR DOCUMENTS AND DATA

SharePoint stores its information in lists. A *list* is a like a database table with columns and rows. When you create a list in SharePoint, you have the option to create a list with predefined columns or a completely custom list. There are two main types of lists. The first is the generic list. The rows in a generic list are called *items*. The other type of list is the *document library*. The rows in a document library represent *files*.

The focus of a list item is its fields whereas the focus of an item in a document library is the file itself. Most list items can have attachments but they are optional. A document library on the other hand must have files in order to have items. The files in a document library can also have fields but they are considered properties or metadata for those files.

BUILT-IN LISTS AND LIBRARIES

Depending on the template or site definition used to create a SharePoint site, certain lists are automatically created. Additional lists can be created by anyone with sufficient permissions. The list types available depend mainly on the edition of SharePoint installed (SharePoint Foundation versus SharePoint Server) and the features activated. You can also add additional list types by installing extensions to SharePoint created by yourself or third-parties.

To see the lists and libraries in your site, click Lists and Libraries in the Navigation bar on the left. In Figure 6-1, you can see the lists automatically created for the Team Site template. You can create additional lists by clicking the buttons in the New section of the ribbon. To create a list based on a template from your site, select the SharePoint List button from the ribbon and a dropdown list containing the list templates in your site will appear as shown in Figure 6-2. You can also select Custom List from the ribbon to create a brand new list with only the columns you want. This is recommended if one of the existing templates does not meet your needs. If you want to create a document library, select Document Library from the ribbon instead. The following table describes several of the common list and library templates.

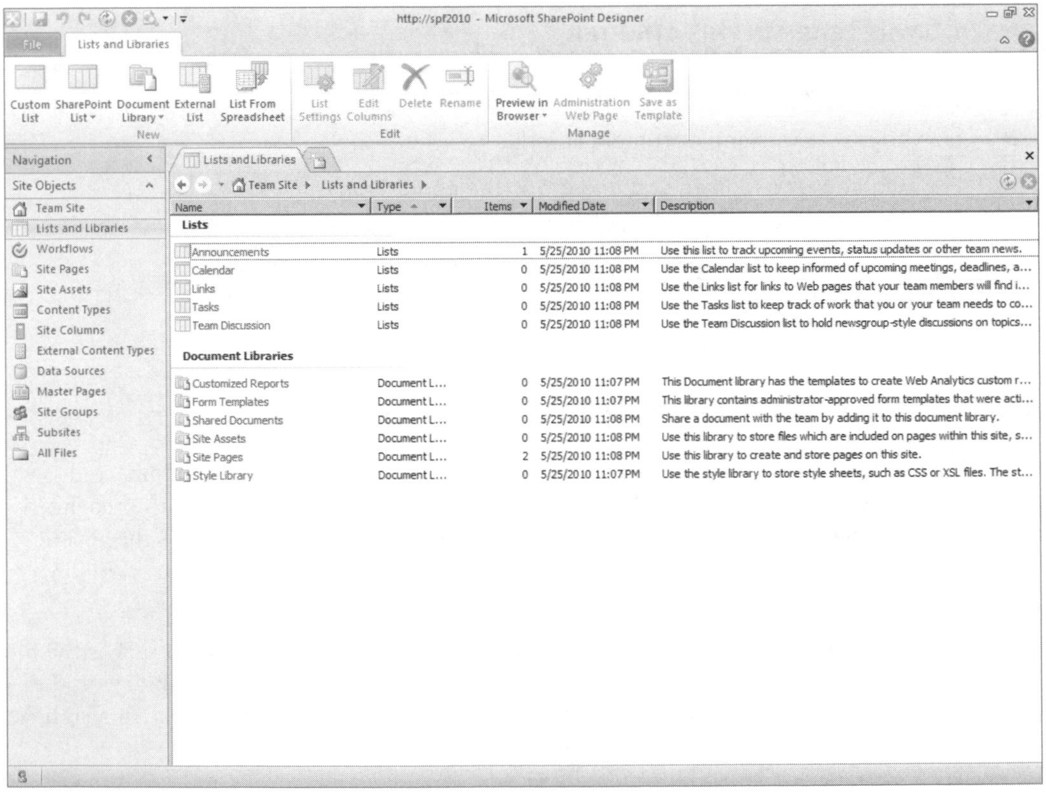

FIGURE 6-1

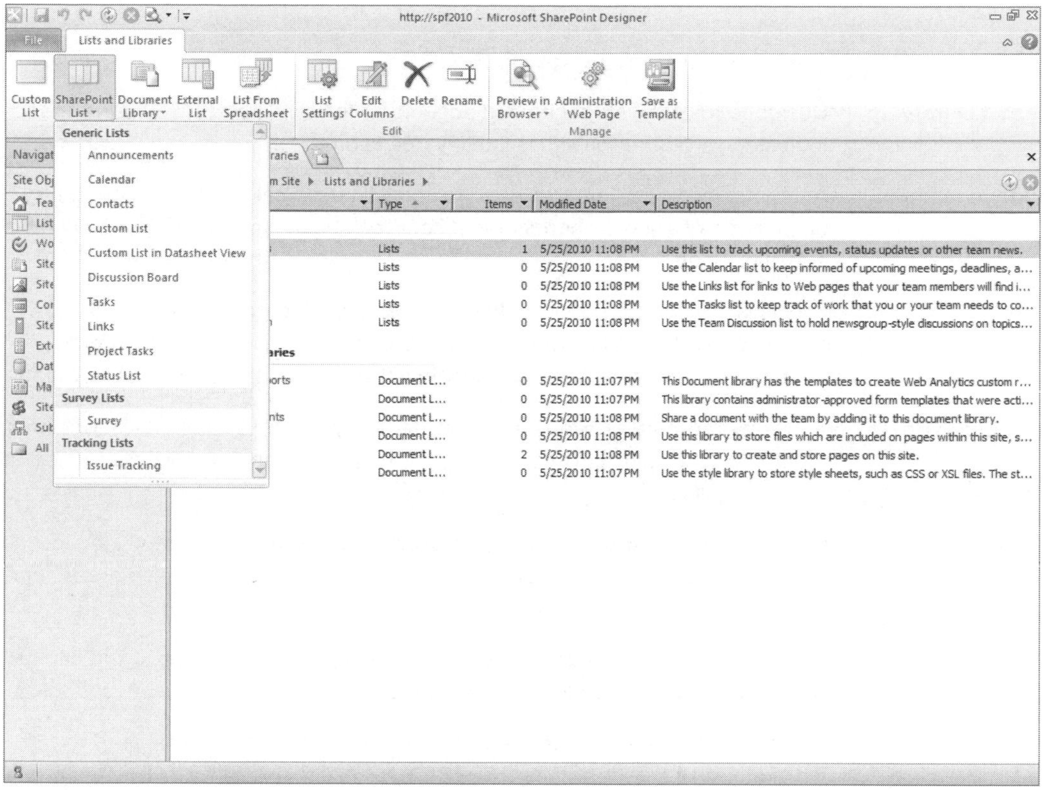

FIGURE 6-2

TYPE	PRINCIPAL CHARACTERISTICS
Document Library	Contains files such as Word documents. It provides easy access to version control, folders, and check out/in. This library can be e-mail-enabled. Fields in this library can be derived from and written to embedded-file metadata in supported formats.
Form Library	Designed to hold XML files, each file representing the data in a single instance of a form, such as InfoPath.
Wiki Page Library	Wiki libraries form the basis of SharePoint's Wiki functionality. They support pages, images, and automatic generation of new pages from Wiki links.
Picture Library	Picture libraries contain picture files and contain predefined views, which include thumbnail images, slideshows, and bulk download options.
Slide Library	Slide libraries are unique to SharePoint Server, and therefore not available in SharePoint Foundation. They are used in conjunction with Microsoft PowerPoint to store individual slides for reuse.
Asset Library	Asset libraries are designed to store and manage rich media files, including images, audio clips, and videos.

continues

(continued)

TYPE	PRINCIPAL CHARACTERISTICS
Report Library	Designed to hold web pages and documents to track metrics, key performance indicators, and other business intelligence information.
Announcements	Announcements lists are designed to show time-critical information on the home page of a site. Announcement items can be set to expire. This list can be e-mail-enabled.
Contacts	Contacts lists have predefined fields that are suitable for holding information about people. In addition, functions are provided for synchronizing contact information with SharePoint-compatible applications such as Microsoft Outlook.
Discussion Board	A discussion board provides the ability to host persistent communications on a SharePoint site. It includes facilities for thread management, post approval, and e-mail enabling.
Links	Links lists automatically display their items as hyperlinks to the specified locations, rather than list items. Although you can sort most lists, you can also order items in links lists explicitly.
Calendar	Calendar lists have features convenient for maintaining schedules, and can be synchronized with SharePoint-aware applications such as Microsoft Outlook.
Tasks	Tasks lists include fields for due dates and status and can be assigned to individual site users.
Project Tasks	Project tasks lists include all Tasks functions listed in the preceding, plus Gantt chart views and the ability to be opened in SharePoint-aware applications.
Issue Tracking	Issue tracking lists are similar to Tasks lists, but also maintain a revision history to track changes to the issue's status.
Survey	Survey lists are designed for streamlined handling of large sets of response data.
External List	Allows the user to interact with external content types (covered in Chapter 6, Data Sources & External Content Types).
Status List	Specifically designed to contain goals, which are also known as *key performance indicators*. Items in the Status list are configured to perform calculations on data from any combination of SharePoint sites, Excel files (via Excel Services), and SQL Server Analysis Server cubes. The calculations are compared against the item's thresholds and the item will display a green, yellow, or red icon whenever the calculation crosses a threshold.
Custom Lists	You can define Custom lists to contain arbitrary information and present it in various ways. They can be displayed as a static text table, or as an editable datasheet, by default. You can also import the contents of simple Excel worksheets into a custom list and have the fields defined automatically from the columns present in the workbook.

Other list and library types may be available in your particular installation of SharePoint.

> **NOTE** *You are not stuck with the lists and libraries created by default in a site. New lists and libraries can be created, and those existing deleted, at any time. In addition, you can display information from diverse sources both inside and outside of your enterprise with such features as data views and Business Data Services (you'll see more about these in Chapters 6, Data Sources & External Content Types and 7, XSLT Data Views & Forms). When creating a new list or library, you can choose from several standard and custom types.*

When you select Custom List from the ribbon, the dialog in Figure 6-3 appears. In this dialog, you can enter a name and description for your list. The same dialog appears when you select SharePoint List or Document Library from the ribbon and choose a list template from the dropdown list as shown in Figure 6-2. Once you have entered at least the name of the list, click OK and the list will be created and be visible in the list in Figure 6-1.

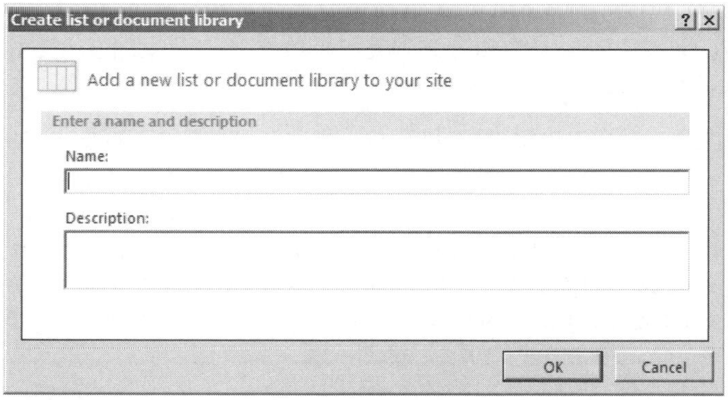

FIGURE 6-3

TRY IT OUT **Create a List Using the Browser**

In this exercise, you create a list using the browser.

1. Navigate your browser to your SharePoint site.

2. Click Site Actions ➪ More Options.

3. When the Create dialog loads, choose the Tasks list type.

4. In the Name textbox, enter **MyTasks** and click the Create button.

After the list has been created, your browser automatically redirects to the newly created list.

How It Works

When the list is created, SharePoint reads the list template you chose and creates the default columns, forms and views for the list. If the list is a document library, it may also create a document template that would be used when creating a new document in the library. Finally, the virtual file system of the site is updated to reflect the new list's root folder and built-in forms.

TRY IT OUT   Create a List Using SharePoint Designer

In this exercise, you create a list using SharePoint Designer.

1. Open SharePoint Designer from your Start menu.

2. Click the Open Site button.

3. When the Open Site dialog appears, enter the URL to your site in the Site name textbox and click the OK button.

4. If a Windows Security dialog appears, enter your username and password for the SharePoint site and click the OK button.

5. When the site opens, choose Custom List from the ribbon. The Create list or document library dialog appears.

6. Enter **Projects** in the Name textbox and click the OK button. After the list is created, a new tab with the name of the newly created list appears.

7. If the new tab in step 6 does not appear, click your list and select List Settings from the ribbon.

How It Works

When you selected Custom List from the ribbon, SharePoint Designer displayed the dialog in Figure 6-3 to prompt you for the name and description of the list. After you clicked OK, SharePoint created the list and a new tab was opened to display the settings of the new list.

CUSTOMIZING LISTS AND LIBRARIES

To modify your list's settings, select your list and choose List Settings from the ribbon. A tab with your list's settings will be appear as shown in Figure 6-4. On this tab, you can change the list's settings and manage the list's content types, views, forms, workflows, and custom actions. More about these will be covered later in the book.

When you want to change the settings of your list, select or unselect the appropriate checkboxes and click the Save button on the Quick Access toolbar at the top of the screen. The following table lists the settings and their effects on your list.

SETTING	EFFECT
Display this list on the Quick Launch	Adds the list to the Quick Launch bar on the left side of the screen in the browser.
Hide from browser	Removes any links to the list from the Quick Launch bar and View All Site Content page.

SETTING	EFFECT
Allow attachments	Allows users to attach files to list items. This applies only to lists, not document libraries.
Display New Folder command on the New menu	Allows the user to create subfolders in the list or library to organize its contents.
Require content approval for submitted items	Prevents new and changed items and documents from being accessed by users until approved.
Create a version each time you edit an item	Saves previous versions of items and documents when they are changed.
Allow management of content types	Allows users to add and remove content types from the list by using the browser.

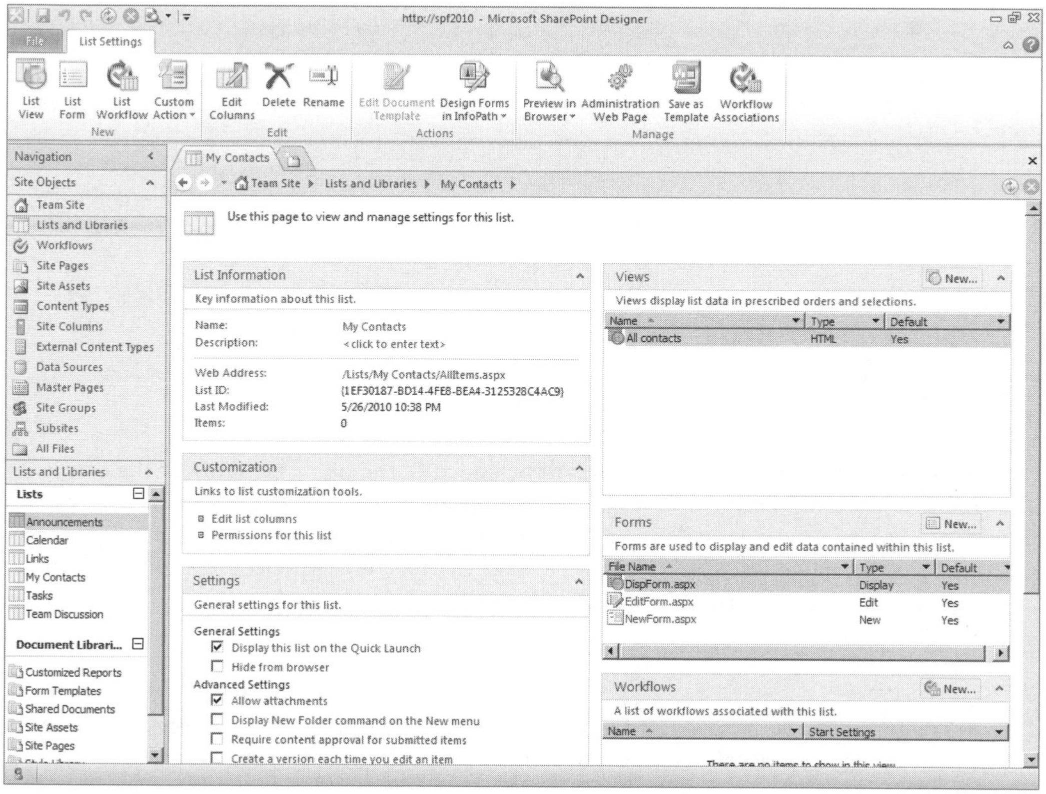

FIGURE 6-4

Adding Fields

To view your list's columns, select Edit Columns from the ribbon. The tab in Figure 6-5 will appear. The tab shows the list's columns along with their data type, description and if they are required. You can add a column by selecting Add New Column or Add Existing Site Column from the ribbon.

When you select Add New Column, the dropdown list containing data types will appear as shown in Figure 6-6.

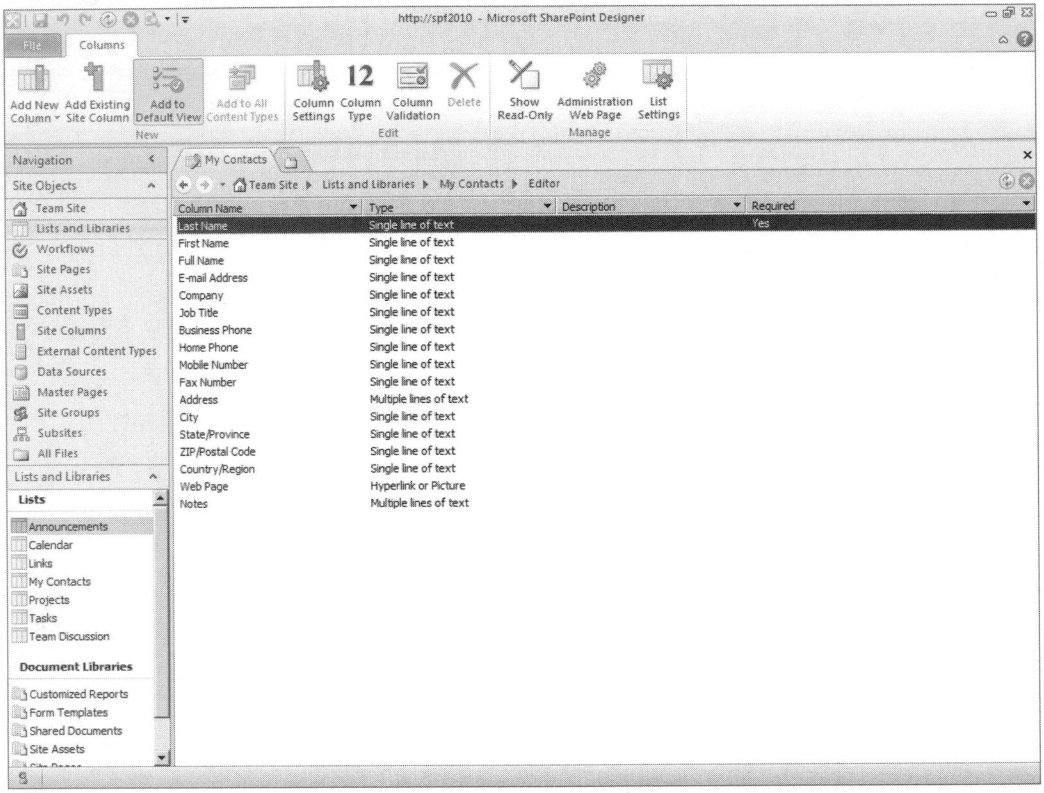

FIGURE 6-5

After you select a data type, a new column will be added to the list. The name of the column will be similar to "NewColumn1." But you can change it by pressing F2. If you selected Choice, Lookup or Calculated, a dialog will appear allowing you to configure the column before it is added to the list. When you need to change the settings of a column, select the column in the list and choose Column Settings from the ribbon. To remove a column, select Delete from the ribbon instead.

> **NOTE** *You cannot remove key identity columns, such as ID and Title (Name in some lists), and administrative columns, such as Modified By, from a list or library.*

The Calculated column type allows you to create a column whose value is the result of a formula based on Excel-like functions and the other columns in the list. If you have trouble figuring out how to use the built-in functions, you can test your formula in a Microsoft Excel spreadsheet.

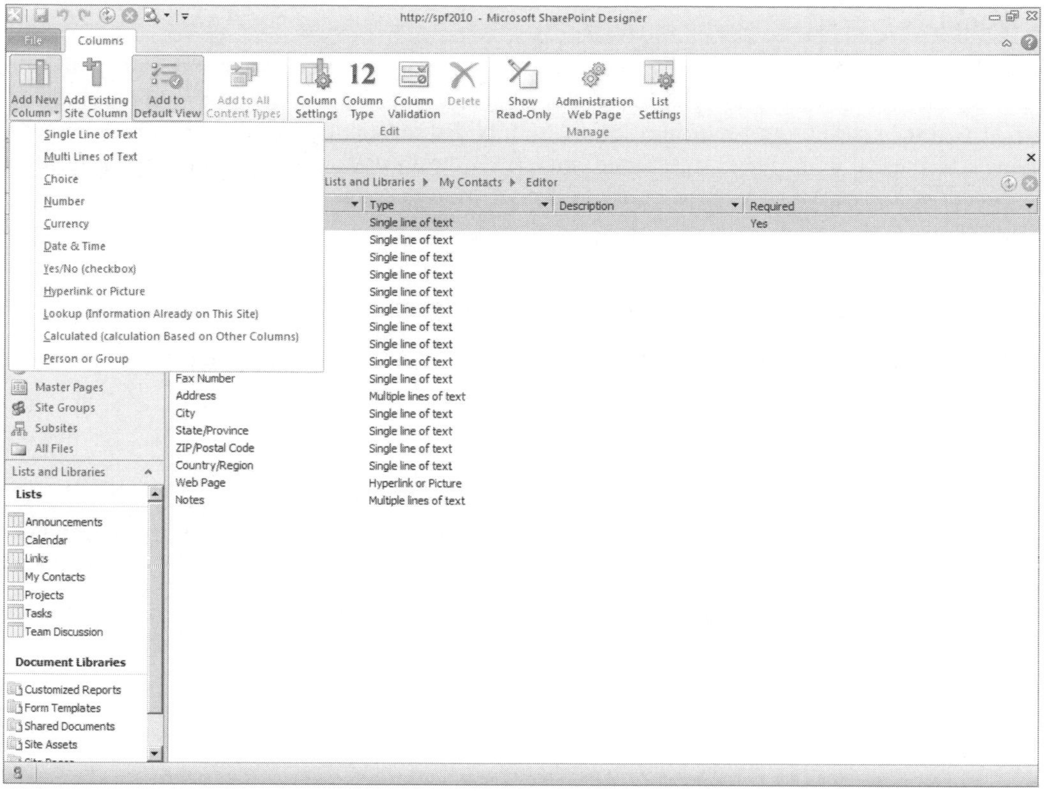

FIGURE 6-6

TRY IT OUT | **Add a Field Using the Browser**

In this exercise, you use the browser to add a field to the Projects list you created in the preceding Try It Out.

1. Navigate your browser to your SharePoint site.

2. Click the Projects list in the Quick Launch bar on the left side of the screen.

3. On the ribbon, click the List tab and choose Create Column.

4. When the Create Column dialog loads, enter **Project Type** in the Column name textbox and choose Choice as the column type.

5. Type each item in the following list on a separate line in the Type each choice on a separate line textbox:

   a. Billable

   b. Non-billable

6. Click the OK button. When the column is created, the browser is redirected back to the list.

How It Works

When you chose Create Column, SharePoint displayed the list of available data types and various settings. The settings changed depending on the data type you chose. Once you made your selection and configured the rest of the columns' settings, SharePoint added the column to the list and redirected your browser back to the All Items view page. Since you left the Add to Default View checkbox selected, the column was added to the All Items view and you can see it on the page.

TRY IT OUT   **Add a Field Using SharePoint Designer**

In this exercise, you use SharePoint Designer to add a field to the MyTasks list you created in an earlier Try It Out in this chapter.

1. Open SharePoint Designer from your start menu.

2. Click the Open Site button.

3. When the Open Site dialog appears, enter the URL to your site in the Site name textbox and click the OK button.

4. If a Windows Security dialog appears, enter your username and password for the SharePoint site and click the OK button.

5. After the site opens, click Lists and Libraries in the Navigation bar on the left.

6. Click the MyTasks list in the Lists and Libraries tab.

7. From the ribbon, select Edit Columns.

8. From the ribbon, select Add New Column ⇨ Lookup.

9. Choose Projects from the List or document library drop-down list.

10. Choose Title from the Field drop-down list.

11. Ensure the following checkboxes are unselected:

   a. Allow blank values?

   b. Allow multiple values?

12. Click the OK button.

13. After the column is added to the list, it will have a name like NewColumn1. Rename this column to "Project" by right-clicking the column, entering **Project**, and pressing Enter.

14. To save the list, click the Save button in the Quick Access Toolbar at the top of the screen.

How It Works

After you chose to add a new lookup column to the list, a dialog appeared for you to configure the list to pull values from and the column to display when the user made their selection. When a user adds an item to the list, they will be presented with a dropdown list for the Project column containing a list of projects from the Projects list. Clicking Save committed your changes to SharePoint.

You should know about a few other column features, too. One is that you can enforce unique values. Choose Yes for the Enforce unique values radio button on the column's new or edit page to ensure that users only enter unique values for the column. This feature can only be configured in the browser. If you are working in SharePoint Designer, click your column and select Administration Web Page from the ribbon. If you make any changes in the browser at this point, be sure to press F5 to refresh your list of columns before you continue making modifications.

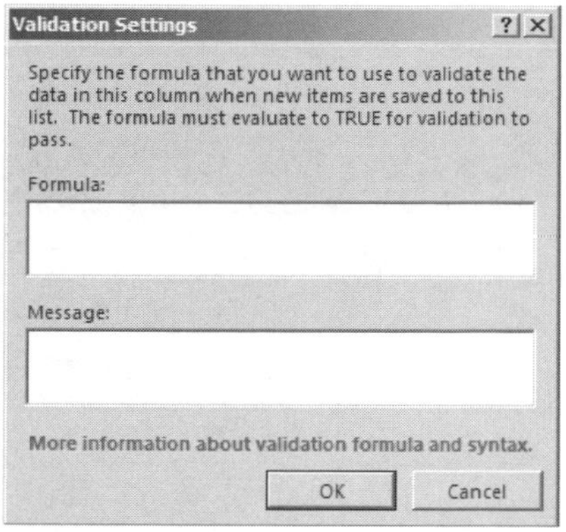

You can also add validation for the values entered for the column. To add validation to a column, click the column and select Column Validation from the ribbon. The Figure

FIGURE 6-7

in 6-7 will appear and you can enter a formula to validate the column's value in the Formula text-box. You can also enter a message for users should the value they enter be deemed invalid by your formula.

Is It Data or Metadata?

Metadata is data about data. If a Microsoft Word document is considered data, the properties of the document, including Author, Comments, and Title, would be considered metadata because they are data about the document (data). This distinction only applies to documents because the document is the central focus and its metadata is stored separately from it.

Normal versus Promoted Fields

Normal fields are fields that you can add to any list or document library. *Promoted fields* can only be added to document libraries because their values are "promoted" or read from the document itself. Examples of built-in promoted fields are Author, Comments, and Date Picture Taken. Whenever a document is saved to a library, SharePoint examines the document and pulls out the values for any promoted fields in the library. This functionality is very useful because it allows users to sort, filter, group, and search for documents based on those promoted fields. Additionally, because the values of those fields are "cached" inside SharePoint, any operation involving those promoted fields run much faster than if the document had to be opened every time someone ran a search. Chapter 9, InfoPath Integration, shows you how to promote your own fields from InfoPath forms saved to a SharePoint library.

Changing Permissions

By default, lists and document libraries "inherit" their permissions from the site in which they are located. In general, if a user has Read access to a site, he would in turn have Read access to all the lists and document libraries inside that site. Permissions can only be set in the browser so click the Permissions for this list hyperlink on the list settings page to open the browser and display the screen in Figure 6-8. This screen shows the permissions page for a document library, which looks the same as the one for a list.

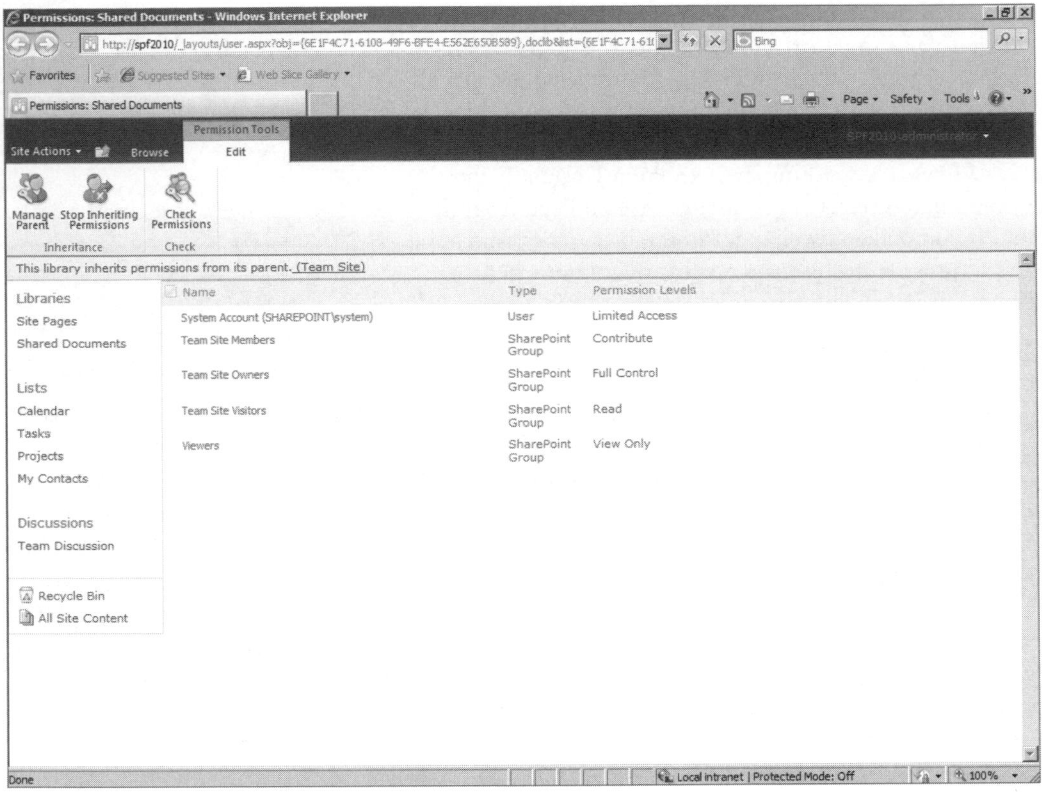

FIGURE 6-8

Whenever you want to assign different permissions for a list or library from the permissions it inherits from its parent site, you must click the Edit tab on the ribbon and choose Stop Inheriting Permissions, as shown in Figure 6-8. If you want to change the list back to inheriting its permission from the site, select Inherit Permissions from the ribbon and any custom permissions that you previously configured will be removed.

> **WARNING** *Do not take changing permissions lightly. Whenever you choose to stop inheriting permissions, any changes to the parent site will not affect the list or library. Additionally, the more places you change permissions, the more difficult managing the site effectively will be for you and your SharePoint administrators.*

Out of the box, SharePoint comes with the following permission levels:

PERMISSION LEVEL	DESCRIPTION
Full Control	Can do anything to the list/library and its contents, including modify permissions
Design	Can modify the configuration of the list/library and includes Contribute rights
Contribute	Can read, modify, and delete items and documents
Read	Can read items and documents
Limited Access	Can read items and documents only when given specific permissions; is only assigned at the site level
Approve	Can approve items and documents; only applies to lists and libraries configured to require approval of new and updated items and documents
Manage Hierarchy	For lists and libraries; is the same as the Contribute permission level
Restricted Read	Can read items and documents, but cannot view previous versions of items and documents or view user permissions
View Only	Can read items, but can only read documents when the document is configured to be rendered as HTML in the browser

Depending on your edition of SharePoint and the template used to create your site, you may have fewer permission levels.

Do not assign multiple users the same permissions for a list individually. Creating a SharePoint group that contains those users and then assigning the permission to the new SharePoint group is better. This best practice helps reduce the time required to manage your site.

Versioning

SharePoint lists and libraries support the retention of previous versions. When *versioning* is enabled, any changes to items and documents will cause SharePoint to keep the old version in history. To enable versioning for a list or document library, select Create a version each time you edit an item on the list settings screen in Figure 6-4 and major versioning will be enabled. If you need to enable minor versioning or want to limit the number of versions kept, select Administration Web Page from the ribbon and the browser will open the screen in Figure 6-9. Next, click Versioning settings under the General Settings section.

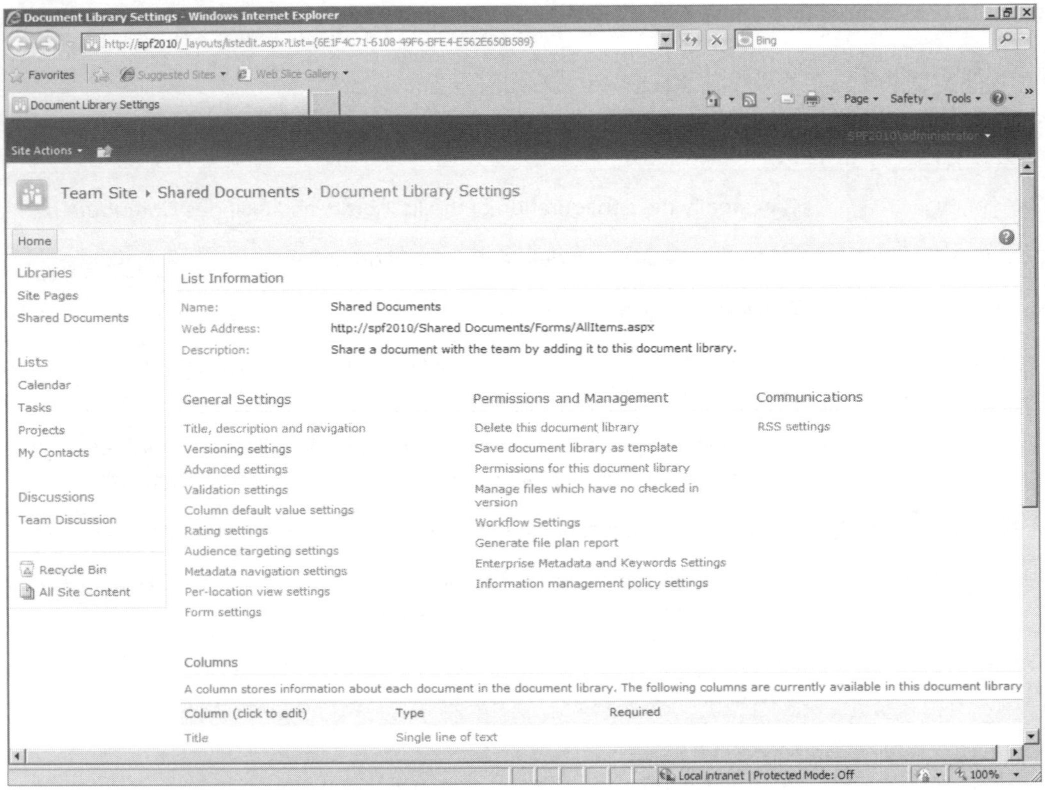

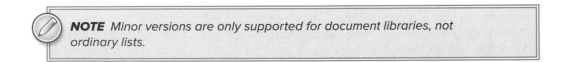

FIGURE 6-9

On the Versioning Settings screen (see Figure 6-10), you can enable content approval, enable and configure versioning, and require checkout of items and documents before they can be edited. The two levels of versioning are *major* and *minor*. With major versions, only published/approved copies of items and documents are kept in history. With minor versions, even draft versions are kept. Minor versioning is useful when many changes will be made over time or by several people.

> **NOTE** *Minor versions are only supported for document libraries, not ordinary lists.*

Limiting the number of versions you retain is a good idea. SharePoint stores full copies of your items and documents in version history. If you have documents with many images, the size of those documents and their versions can take up a great deal of space over time.

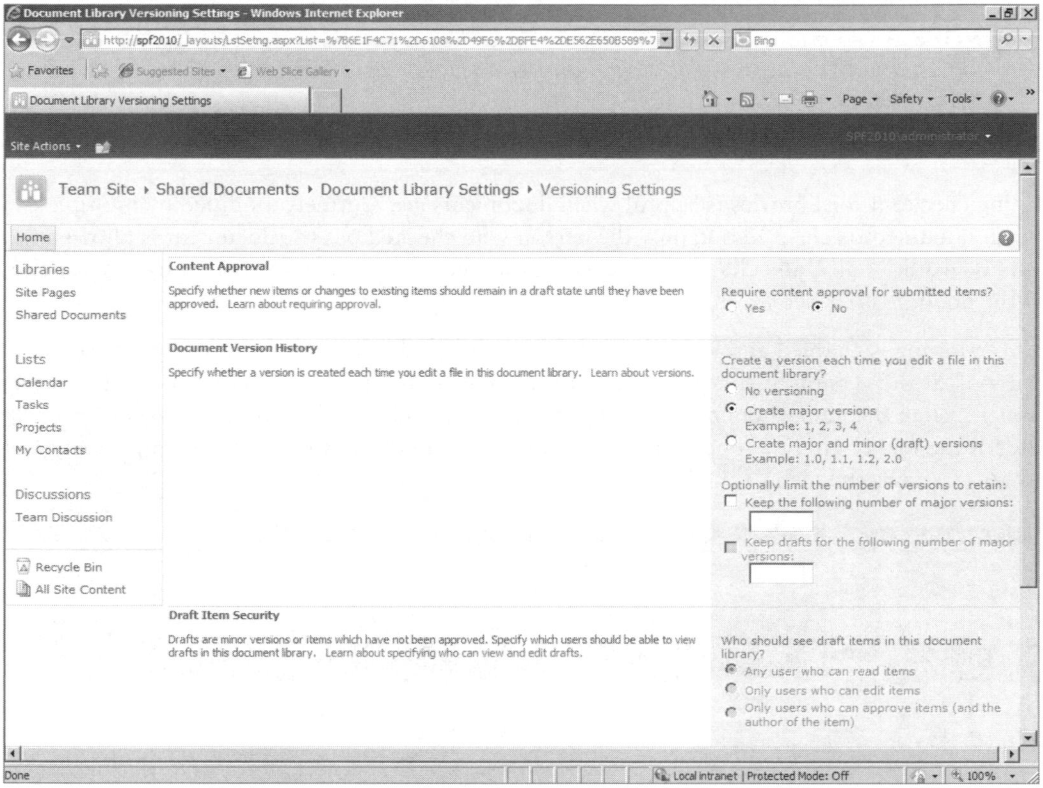

FIGURE 6-10

In addition to versioning, you can enable content approval for the list or library. When content approval is enabled, changes to an item or document in the list or library is saved in Draft mode that only the author and users with the Approval permission can view and edit. Users with Approval permission can reject or approve the change. An additional field named Approval Status is also added to the list or library to show the status of the item or document. Changes to items or documents start with "Pending" as their approval status.

> **NOTE** *You can configure which users can view drafts by selecting a different option in the Draft Item Security section on the Versioning Settings screen (refer to Figure 6-10).*

After the changes are approved, the status of the item or document becomes "Approved." Otherwise, the status will be "Rejected." Optionally, the approver can enter comments when she approves or rejects the status of the item or document.

NOTE *Be sure to write helpful comments whenever you decide to reject a pending change. This saves a lot of time and e-mail when communicating with the item's author.*

Enabling checkout for libraries is helpful when documents are routinely modified by multiple people. Once an document is checked out, only the person who checked out the document is allowed to modify it. Additionally, any changes to a checked-out document are not viewable by anyone else until the document is checked in.

After versioning is enabled and you have added and modified some items or documents, you can take a look at the version history for an item or document. To view the older versions of an item or document, click the item or document's drop-down menu and click Version History. The drop-down arrow for the menu will not appear unless you hover the cursor over top of the item or document. Figure 6-11 shows the menu in action.

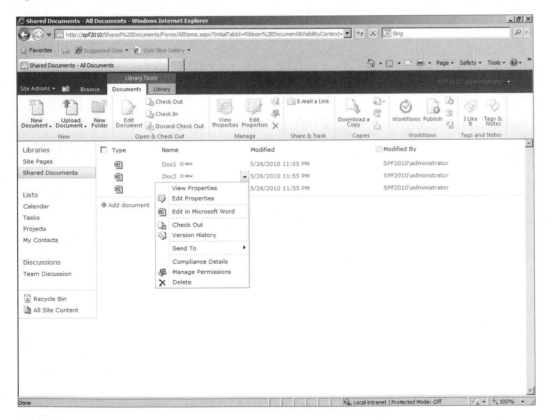

FIGURE 6-11

After you click the Version History option, a screen similar to Figure 6-12 appears. The previous versions of the document are listed in descending order. For each version of the document, the version number, the date and time of the modification, the person who modified the document, the size of the document, and any comments entered during the approval process are listed. Additionally, if any fields were changed, each field's name and its new value are displayed. Clicking the link under the Modified column opens that version of the item or document.

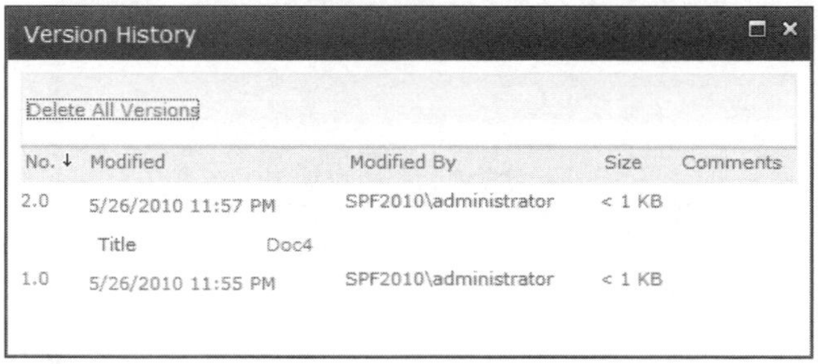

FIGURE 6-12

Reusing Your Lists and Libraries

After your lists and libraries are created, you can save them as list templates. A *list template* is a file containing the columns for a list or library and other configuration elements to create another copy of the list. When you create a list template, you can optionally include the data in the list as a part of the template so that when the template is used, the data in the template will be automatically applied to the list or library.

List templates are stored in the List Template Gallery located at Site Actions ⇨ Site Settings ⇨ List templates. When you add templates to the List Template Gallery, they will be available in the Create dialog screen shown in Figure 6-13. This dialog is displayed when you select More Options from the Site Actions menu. Because the template is actually a file in a SharePoint library, you can download the file to your computer and upload it to the List Template Gallery in another site.

> **NOTE** *Only one List Template Gallery exists per site collection. When you want to use a list template you have created, you only need to upload it to the new site if the site is in a different site collection. All the sites in the same site collection can use the list template automatically.*

TRY IT OUT **Create and Use List Templates**

In this exercise, you create a list template for the Projects list you created earlier and use it in the same site and another site in a different site collection.

Populating the Projects List

1. Navigate your browser to your SharePoint site.

2. Click the Projects list in the Quick Launch bar on the left side of the screen.

3. When the Projects list screen loads, click Add new item.

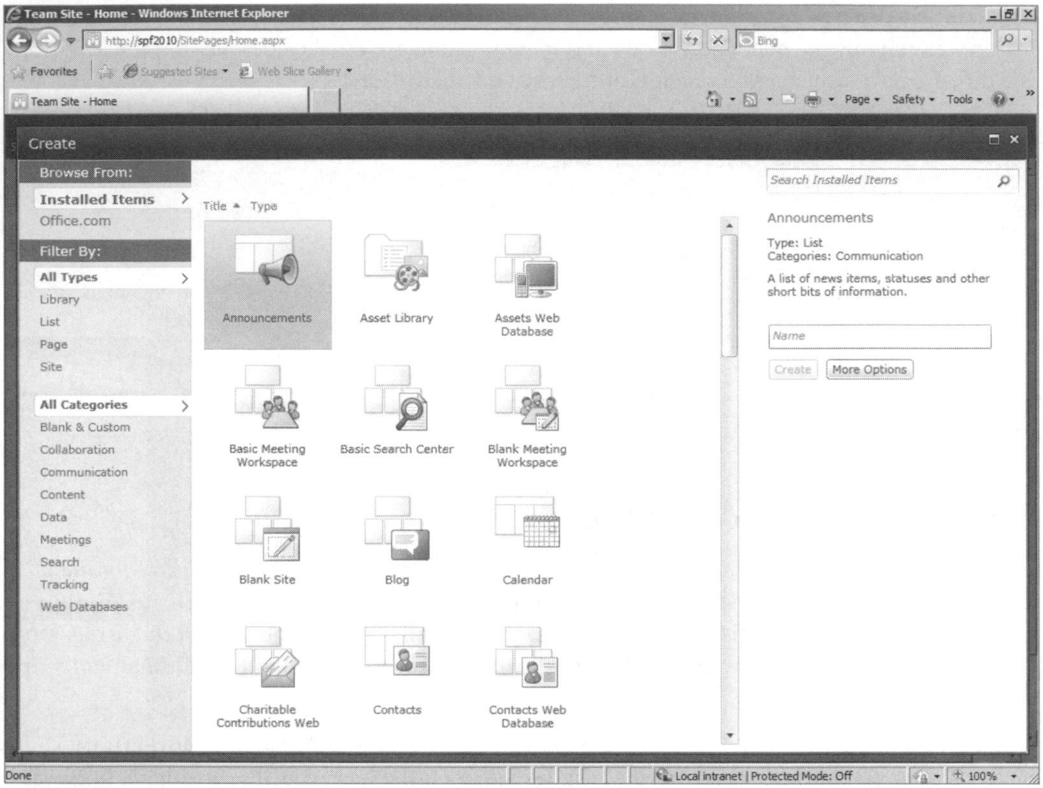

FIGURE 6-13

4. In the Projects – New Item dialog, enter these values and click the Save button:

NAME	VALUE
Title	SharePoint Implementation
Project Type	Billable

5. Add these other items by repeating step 4:

TITLE	PROJECT TYPE
Internal SharePoint Upgrade to 2010	Non-billable
End-user training	Non-billable

Creating the Template

1. From the ribbon, click the List tab and choose List Settings.

2. Under the Permissions and Management section, click Save list as template.

3. Enter the following values and click the OK button:

NAME	VALUE
File name	Projects
Template name	Projects
Include Content	Checked

4. After the template has been created, the Operation Completed Successfully dialog should appear. Click the link to navigate to the List Templates Gallery.

5. Notice that the new template is now present in the list.

Reusing the Template in a Site in the Same Site Collection

1. To reuse the list template you just created, choose Site Actions ⇨ More Options.

2. In the Create dialog, choose the Projects list type and enter **Projects2** in the Name textbox.

3. Click the Create button to create the list and navigate the browser to the newly created list.

4. Notice the new list has the three items you entered in step 3 and the additional Project Type column. Also, notice the Projects2 link in the Quick Launch bar on the left.

Reusing the Template in a Site in a Different Site Collection

1. To reuse the list template in a site in a different site collection, you must save the list template locally and then upload it to the other site. Navigate to the List Templates Gallery again by choosing Site Actions ⇨ Site Settings.

2. Click the List Templates link under the Galleries section on the Site Settings page.

3. Click the name of the list template and when prompted, save it to your desktop.

4. Navigate your browser to the other site.

5. Navigate to the List Templates Gallery again by choosing Site Actions ⇨ Site Settings.

6. Click the List Templates link under the Galleries section on the Site Settings page.

7. Click the Documents tab on the ribbon and click the Upload Document button.

8. Click the Browse button to select the template file you saved earlier and click the Open button to return to the Upload Template dialog.

9. Click the OK button to upload the template.

10. When the Edit Item dialog appears, click the Save button.

11. Now that the template has been uploaded you can use it to create a list.

12. Choose Site Actions ⇨ More Options to display the Create dialog.

13. In the Create dialog, choose the Projects list type and enter **Projects** in the Name textbox.

14. Click the Create button to create the list and navigate the browser to the newly created list.

15. Notice the new list has the three items you entered in step 3 and the additional Project Type column. Also, notice the Projects link in the Quick Launch bar on the left.

How It Works

When you save a list as a template, SharePoint makes a copy of the list and optionally its content. This copy is compressed into a template file and stored in the List Templates gallery. You can download this file and upload it for use in other site collections. Once the template has been added to the List Templates gallery, the template can be used to create a new list that is a duplicate of the original list. If you selected the option to include content, the new list will contain the same items or files as the original list.

SORTING, FILTERING, AND GROUPING

Creating Views

To display the existing views for a list, open the list's settings tab in SharePoint Designer. The list of views will appear in the top right-hand corner of the screen as shown in Figure 6-4. Every list and library has at least one view and you can create new ones by clicking the New button just above the list of views. When you click the New button, the dialog in Figure 6-14 appears. This dialog allows you to enter the name for the view and make it the default view for the list or library. Making a view the default view will cause that view to be displayed first whenever you access the list or library in the browser. You can still select a different view afterwards.

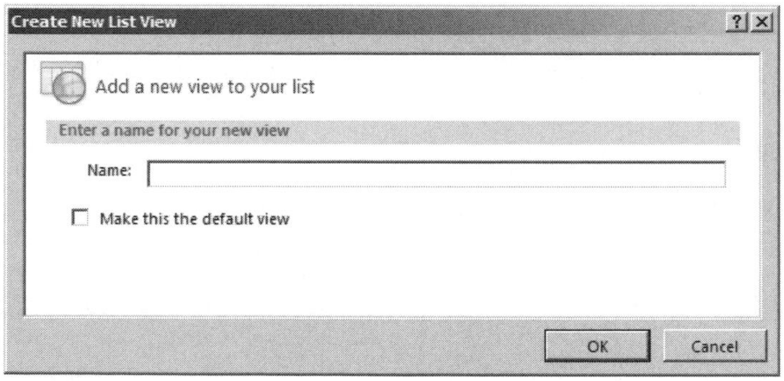

FIGURE 6-14

Once you click OK, the view is added to the list of views. You can edit the columns displayed in the view by clicking the view and selecting Open from the ribbon. Opening a view will display a screen similar to that in Figure 6-15. If you do not see the same tabs as shown in Figure 6-15, click the view in the page and the tabs should appear.

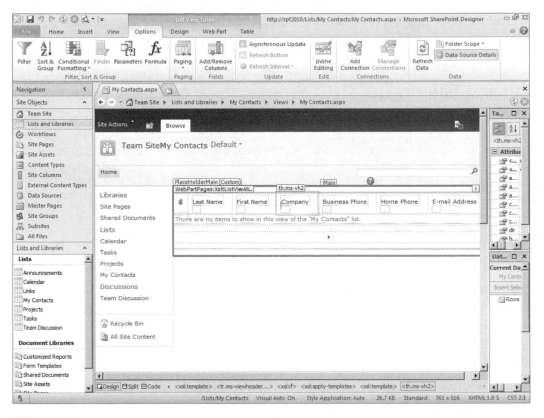

FIGURE 6-15

By selecting Add/Remove Columns from the ribbon, you can change the columns displayed in the view and their order by configuring the dialog in Figure 6-16. Once you click OK, the view will be updated to reflect your changes. You can also change the number of rows displayed in the view. This is helpful when you have a large number of items or documents and do not want the user to scroll down in their browser to see them all. You can change the paging of the view by selecting Paging from the ribbon and selecting one of the available options. By default, views will show 30 items or documents on each page.

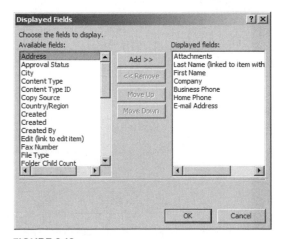

FIGURE 6-16

> **NOTE** *Some columns such as Title are listed more than once. They all contain the same data but display that data differently, such as a clickable value that allows you to navigate to the item, or a drop-down menu when you hover the mouse cursor over the data.*

Sorting and Filtering

To sort the data in your view, select Sort & Group from the ribbon and the dialog in Figure 6-17 will appear. From the available fields, you can select the fields to sort and group by. After you select the fields and add them to the Sort order listbox, clicking each field will give you the option to sort it in ascending or descending order and to use it to group the data together by that column's value. Figure 6-18 shows a view that is grouping its data by state and then by city.

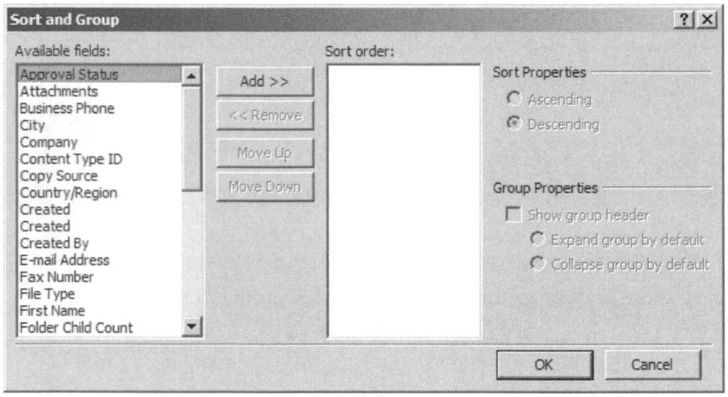

FIGURE 6-17

To filter the values displayed in a view, select Filter from the ribbon. The dialog in Figure 6-19 will appear and allow you to build the criteria that will be applied to the data in the list or library to determine which items or documents will be shown. If you need to change the order in which the criteria will be evaluated due to having both And and Or in the filter, highlight two or more rows by holding the shift key down and clicking with the mouse. Finally, click the Group button.

> **NOTE** *If you want to compare the value of a Date column to today's date, select* [Current Date] *from the Value column. If you want to compare the value of a Person column to the current user, select* [Current User] *from the Value column.*

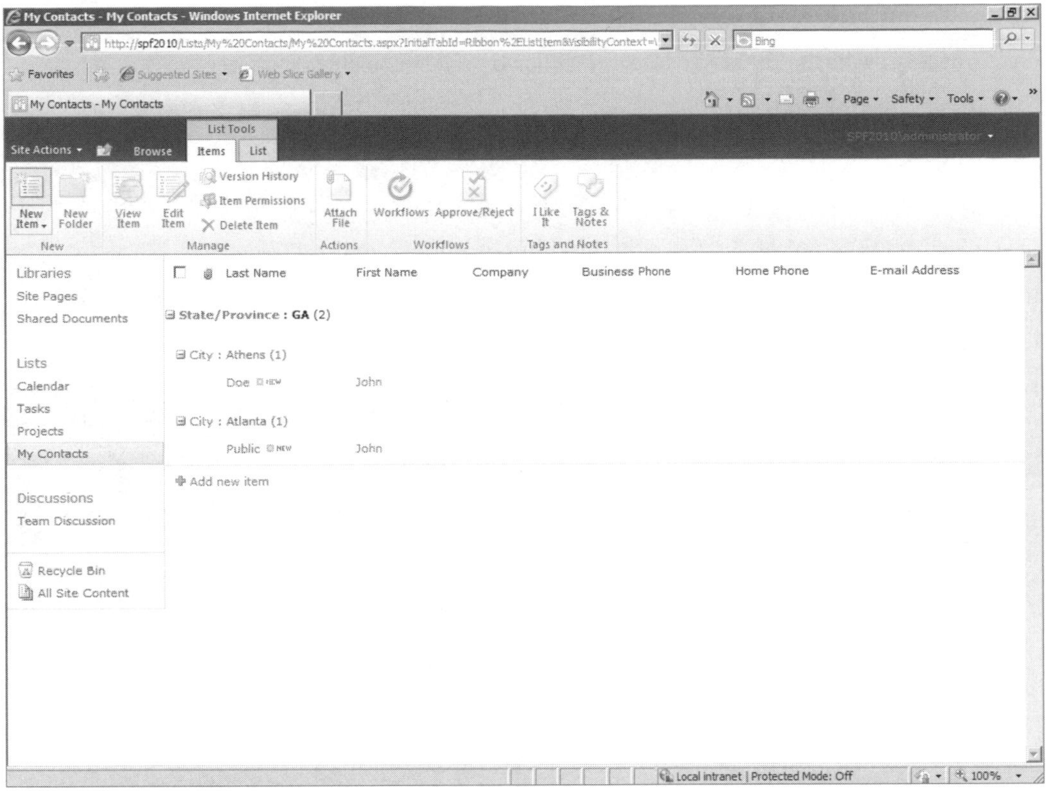

FIGURE 6-18

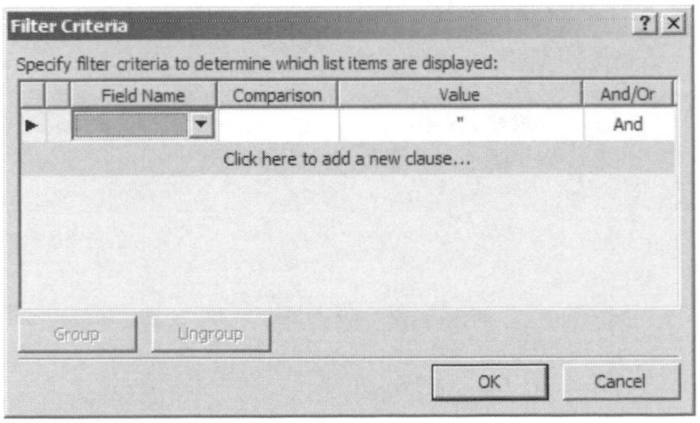

FIGURE 6-19

TRY IT OUT   Create a View with a Custom Sort and Filter Using the Browser

In this exercise, you create a new view for the MyTasks list created in the Try It Out "Create a List using the Browser" previous in the chapter.

1. Navigate your browser to your SharePoint site.

2. Click the MyTasks list in the Quick Launch bar on the left side of the screen.

3. Choose the List tab and click the Create View button in the ribbon.

4. Click the My Tasks link under Start from an existing view.

5. When the Create View page loads, enter **My SharePoint Project Tasks** in the View Name textbox.

6. In the Sort section, set the First sort by the column drop-down list to Due Date.

7. In the Filter section, click the Show More Columns link.

8. In the Filter section, enter the values as listed here:

NAME	VALUE
Show items only when the following is true	Selected
Show the items when column	Assigned To
	is equal to
	[Me]
And	Selected
When column	Project
	is equal to
	SharePoint
And	Selected
When column	Status
	is not equal to
	Completed

9. Click the OK button at the bottom of the screen.

How It Works

When you click OK to create the view, SharePoint creates a web page in the list's root folder with the name of the view. The web page contains a XsltListViewWebPart control that is configured with the Sort and Filter settings you specified for the view. Whenever you change the active view for the list, the browser navigates to the view's web page which shows the data in the list as filtered and sorted by the view.

TRY IT OUT Create a View with a Custom Sort and Filter Using SharePoint Designer

In this exercise, you create the same view you created in the preceding Try It Out using the browser but using SharePoint Designer instead.

1. Open SharePoint Designer from your Start menu.

2. Click the Open Site button.

3. When the Open Site dialog appears, enter the URL to your site in the Site name textbox and click the OK button.

4. If a Windows Security dialog appears, enter your username and password for the SharePoint site and click the OK button.

5. After the site opens, click Lists and Libraries in the Navigation bar on the left.

6. Click the MyTasks list in the Lists and Libraries tab.

7. If the list settings screen does not appear, click the List Settings button in the ribbon.

8. In the Views section, click the New button in the upper right-hand corner of the list settings screen as shown in Figure 6-4.

9. In the Create New List View dialog, enter **My SharePoint Tasks2** in the Name textbox and click the OK button.

10. Click the name of the newly created My SharePoint Tasks2 view in the Views section.

11. When the view's aspx page loads, ensure "List View Tools" is displayed in the title bar of SharePoint Designer. If it is not displayed, follow these steps:

a. Click the Design tab at the bottom of the page.

b. Click the paperclip icon in the table on the page.

12. Click the Filter button in the ribbon.

13. When the Filter Criteria dialog loads, enter the following filters, clicking the Click here to add a new clause link as needed:

FIELD NAME	COMPARISON	VALUE	AND/OR
Assigned To	Equals	[Current User]	And
Project	Equals	SharePoint	And
Status	Not Equal	Completed	

14. Click the OK button.

15. If the data view is refreshing, wait until it is complete.

16. Click the Sort & Group button from the ribbon.

17. Add Due Date and Priority to the Sort order list box.

18. Click the OK button.

20. Click the Save button in the Quick Access Toolbar at the top of the screen.

How It Works

When you click the New button, a new web page for the view is added to the list's root folder. By default, the view will be configured with the same columns as the default view of the list. The control on the page is the XsltListViewWebPart control and when you make changes to the view, you are actually setting properties on control itself. Configuring a filter and sort for the view will filter and sort the data in the list when the web page for view is loaded in the browser.

Grouping and Aggregations

Views also allow you to group the items in a list together. This feature is helpful when you want to add totals at the bottom of your columns. To configure grouping for your view, select Sort & Group from the ribbon and the dialog in Figure 6-17 will appear. Select the columns you want to group by and add them to the Sort order list box. Next, click each column and select the Show group header checkbox. Finally, you can choose to show the group expanded or collapsed by selecting the appropriate radio button. Once you have made your changes, click the OK button to return to the view.

> **NOTE** *You can only group by two columns using the Sort and Group dialog. If you want to group by more than two columns, you must change the view to use an XSL data view instead. XSL data views are covered in the next chapter.*

You can also configure aggregations for your view. For instance, if you are creating a view for a list that stores the amount of time that employees spend on projects, you could add aggregation to sum the hours of the list items that appear in the view which would display at the top of the list. If you group by the project column, running totals of the hours for each project would also be displayed. The data type of the column determines which aggregation functions are available. The following table lists the available functions and when they can be used:

FUNCTION	DESCRIPTION	WHEN AVAILABLE
Count	Returns a count of the rows	Available for every column type
Average	Returns an average of the column	Available for currency, number, and date and time columns
Maximum	Returns the maximum value of the column	Available for currency, number, and date and time columns

FUNCTION	DESCRIPTION	WHEN AVAILABLE
Minimum	Returns the minimum value of the column	Available for currency, number, and date and time columns
Sum	Returns the sum of the values in the column	Available for currency and number columns
Std Deviation	Returns the standard deviation of the values in the column	Available for currency and number columns
Variance	Returns the variance of the values in the column	Available for currency and number columns

To add an aggregation for your view, click somewhere inside your view and the Formula button should become available on the ribbon. Clicking the Formula button will display the dialog in Figure 6-20. In this dialog, you select the aggregation by double-clicking one of the functions in the Select a function to insert list box which will add it to the XPath textbox. Immediately after the function is added to the textbox, a dropdown list will appear with a variety of functions and XPath variables. You can select an option from the list or double-click one of the list columns in the left-hand list box. Afterwards, your column will be added to the XPath textbox.

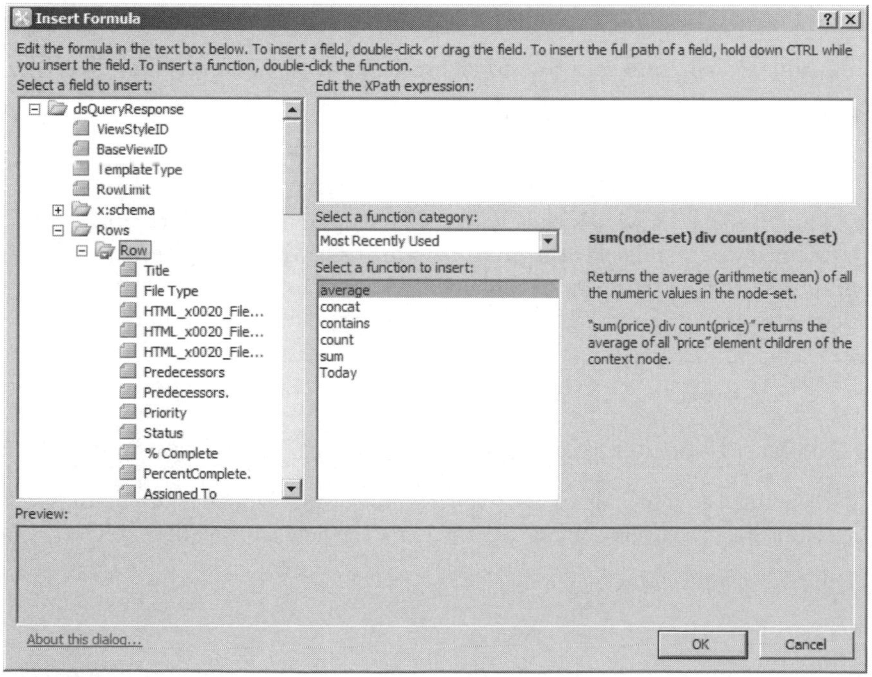

FIGURE 6-20

TRY IT OUT   **Add Grouping and Aggregations Using the Browser**

In this exercise, you add grouping and subtotals to a view using the browser.

1. Navigate your browser to your SharePoint site.

2. Click Site Actions ⇨ More Options to create a new list for this exercise using the dialog in Figure 6-13.

3. Choose the Custom List type and enter **Expenses** in the Name textbox.

4. Click the Create button to create the list.

5. After the browser navigates to the new list, create these columns in the list using what you have learned so far:

NAME	TYPE	REQUIRED	NOTES
Amount	Currency	Yes	Set min value to .01
Project	Lookup	Yes	Choose the Projects list

6. Click the Modify View button in the ribbon.

7. In the Group By section of the View Settings page, choose Project for the first drop-down list and Created By for the second drop-down list.

8. Choose the option to show the grouping Expanded.

9. In the Totals section, choose Sum from the drop-down list next to the Amount column.

10. Click the OK button at the bottom of the screen to save the view.

How It Works

After you click OK, SharePoint updates the view's page with the new grouping and aggregation. Navigating to the view in the browser will display the projects in the list and the expenses for each project just after the project's name. Additionally, the Amount column will contain the sum total of the values for that column aggregated at the project level and a grand total for all of the items visible in the view.

TRY IT OUT   **Add Grouping and Aggregations Using SharePoint Designer**

In this exercise, you add grouping and subtotals to a view using SharePoint Designer. If you did not follow the steps in the previous exercise, follow steps 1–5 to create the new list for this exercise.

1. Open SharePoint Designer from your Start menu.

2. Click the Open Site button.

3. When the Open Site dialog appears, enter the URL to your site in the Site name textbox and click the OK button.

4. If a Windows Security dialog appears, enter your username and password for the SharePoint site and click the OK button.

5. After the site opens, click Lists and Libraries in the Navigation bar on the left.

6. Double-click the Expenses list in the Lists and Libraries tab.

7. If you do not see the Expenses list, press F5 to refresh the list.

8. Click the New button in the Views section.

9. In the Create New List View dialog, enter **My Expenses** in the Name textbox and click the OK button.

10. Click the name of the newly created view.

11. After the new view's aspx page loads, click the Filter button in the ribbon.

12. In the Filter Criteria dialog, enter a filter for only items created by the current user and click the OK button.

13. Click the Sort & Group button in the ribbon.

14. In the Sort and Group dialog, add Project to the Sort order list box.

15. Select the checkbox next to Show Group Header and click the OK button.

16. Click the Save button in the Quick Access Toolbar at the top of the screen.

How It Works

Clicking the New button creates a new web page for the view in the list's root folder. After the web page loads in the editor, you can modify the sorting, grouping and aggregations of the view. Once you have saved your changes, you can preview the web page by selecting Preview in Browser from the Home tab on the ribbon.

Additional Settings

There are a few more settings you should know since they can greatly increase the usability of your view. The first is the Inline Editing. When Inline Editing is enabled for a view, hovering over a list item will display an edit icon as shown in Figure 6-21. Clicking the icon will place the row in edit mode and allow you to edit the list item's values in the row itself instead of in a dialog. There is also a green plus icon at the bottom left of the list that will add a new row in edit mode for adding new items to the list. To enable Inline Editing, select Inline Editing from the ribbon and save your view.

Views can also display their data asynchronously. This means the view can refresh its contents on the page without reloading the browser. To enable this option, select the Asynchronous Update checkbox from the ribbon. Afterwards, the refresh options below the checkbox become available. If you select the checkbox for Refresh Button, the view will display a refresh icon in the page when viewed in the browser. Clicking the icon will cause the view to update the page without reloading the browser. You can also cause the page to refresh periodically by selecting Refresh Interval from the ribbon and choosing the time period in which the view should refresh its data.

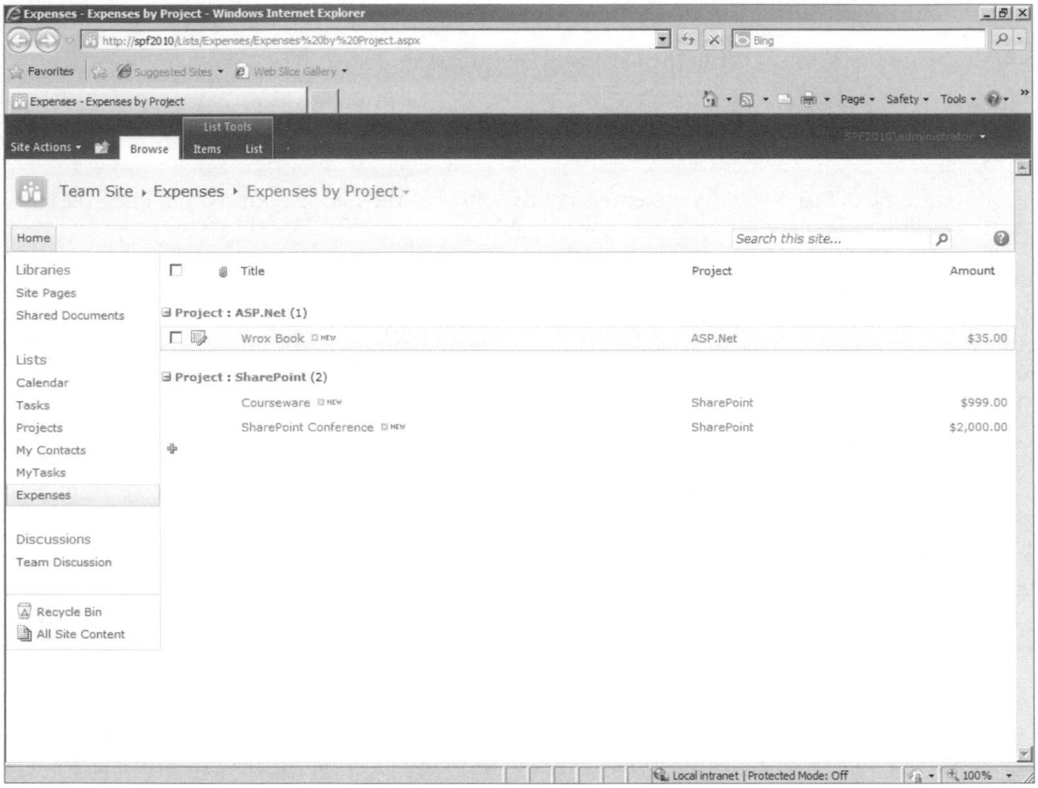

FIGURE 6-21

STRUCTURING YOUR DATA WITH CONTENT TYPES

Content types allow you to apply an entire set of columns to your list and libraries at once. When you add a content type to a list or library, the columns from the content type are automatically added to the list. The content types available in your site is dependent on the site template used to create the site and the activated features. Figure 6-22 shows the content types created from the Team Site template. In addition to predefined columns, content types can have their own entry forms and workflows associated with them.

Content types are particularly important in Publishing Portal sites. In a publishing site, your pages are stored in a single library, and you associate different layout pages with particular content types, such as press releases, executive biographies, and so on.

To view the list of content types for the site, select Content Types from the Navigation bar on left as shown in Figure 6-22. Content types are arranged in groups, and you can filter the list to show only the content types in a select group by using the Show Group drop-down list.

To view the content types for a list, scroll down to the bottom of the list's settings page as displayed in Figure 6-23. Figure 6-23 shows the settings page for the announcements list which has two content types: announcement and folder. The list must be configured to allow management of content types before the content types can be displayed or managed for the list using the browser, but SharePoint Designer can always manage these content types regardless of that setting.

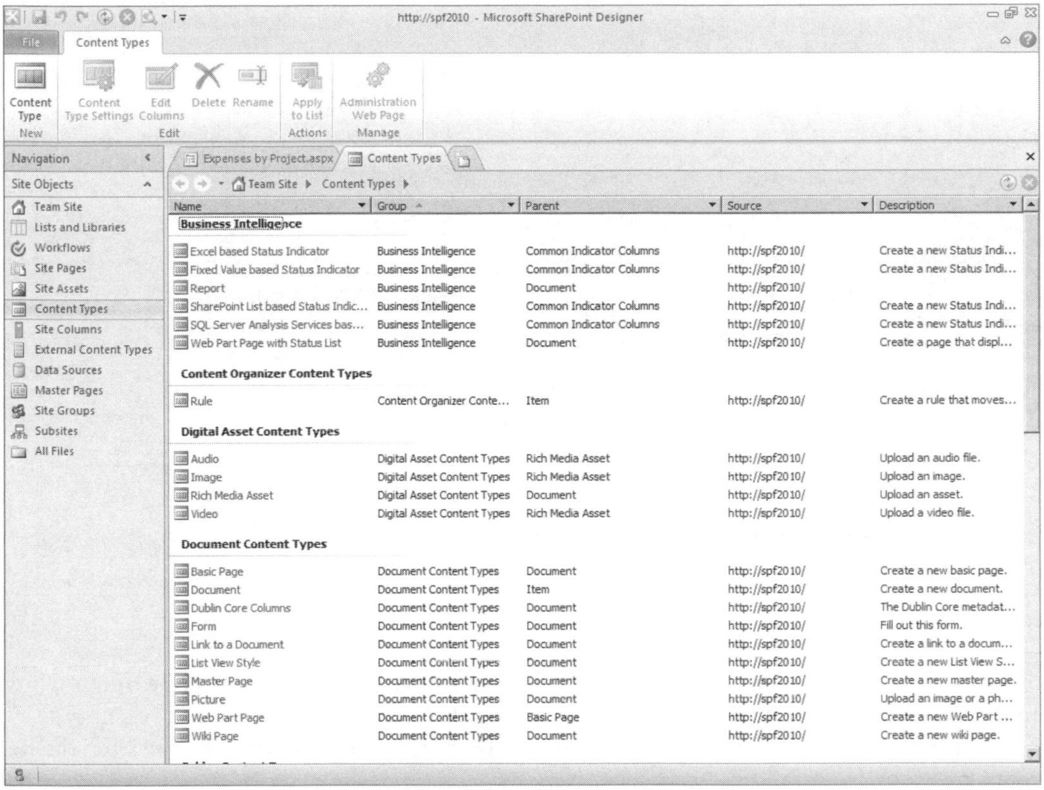

FIGURE 6-22

Making Structure and Order Portable

To create a new content type, select Content Type from the ribbon in Figure 6-22 and the dialog in Figure 6-24 will appear. The dialog allows you to specify a name and description for your content type. You can also select the parent for the new content type. The parent you select for the new content type is important because it determines whether the content type is for lists versus libraries. Additionally, the new content type will "inherit" columns from its parent, which can save time. Any changes to the parent content type will also be applied automatically by default to all the content types inheriting from it. Finally, you can select a group for the content type to keep it organized. It is recommended that you create at least one group to keep your content types separate from the built-in ones.

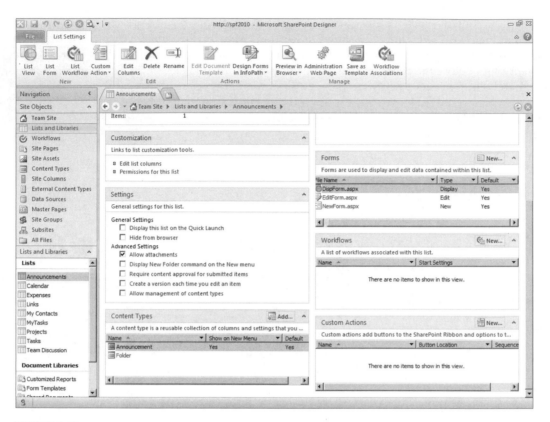

FIGURE 6-23

At the most basic level, all content types meant for lists inherit directly or indirectly from the Item content type and all content types meant for libraries inherit from the Document content type. Because a library is a special list for documents, the Document content type inherits from the Item content type, too.

The Item content type has only one column named Title, which is required. The Document content type has the Title column it inherited from Item and has the additional column Name to store the name of the document.

Once you click OK in the dialog in Figure 6-24, the content type will be created and the list in Figure 6-22 will be updated. To manage the columns in your content type, select it from the list and choose Edit Columns from the ribbon. Figure 6-25 shows the screen for editing the columns of a content type. You can add a column to the content type by selecting Add Existing Site Column from the ribbon. Afterwards, the dialog in Figure 6-26 will display a list of the available columns in the site.

You can only add site columns to a content type. Site columns are preconfigured columns that can be added to any list, library or content type. To see the site columns in your site, select Site Columns from the Navigation bar. Figure 6-27 shows the site columns created from the Team Site template. Site columns are grouped together just like content types. You can add your own site column by choosing New Column from the ribbon and selecting a data type. You must add custom site columns if you want to add custom columns to a content type.

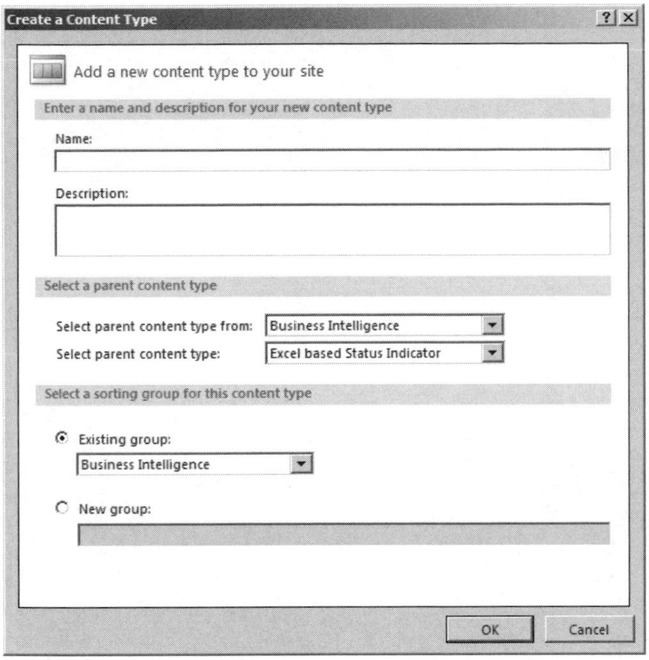

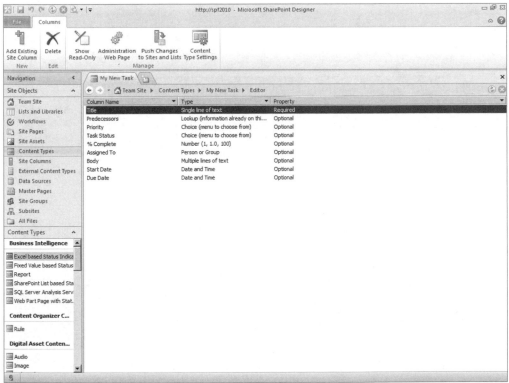

FIGURE 6-24

FIGURE 6-25

FIGURE 6-26

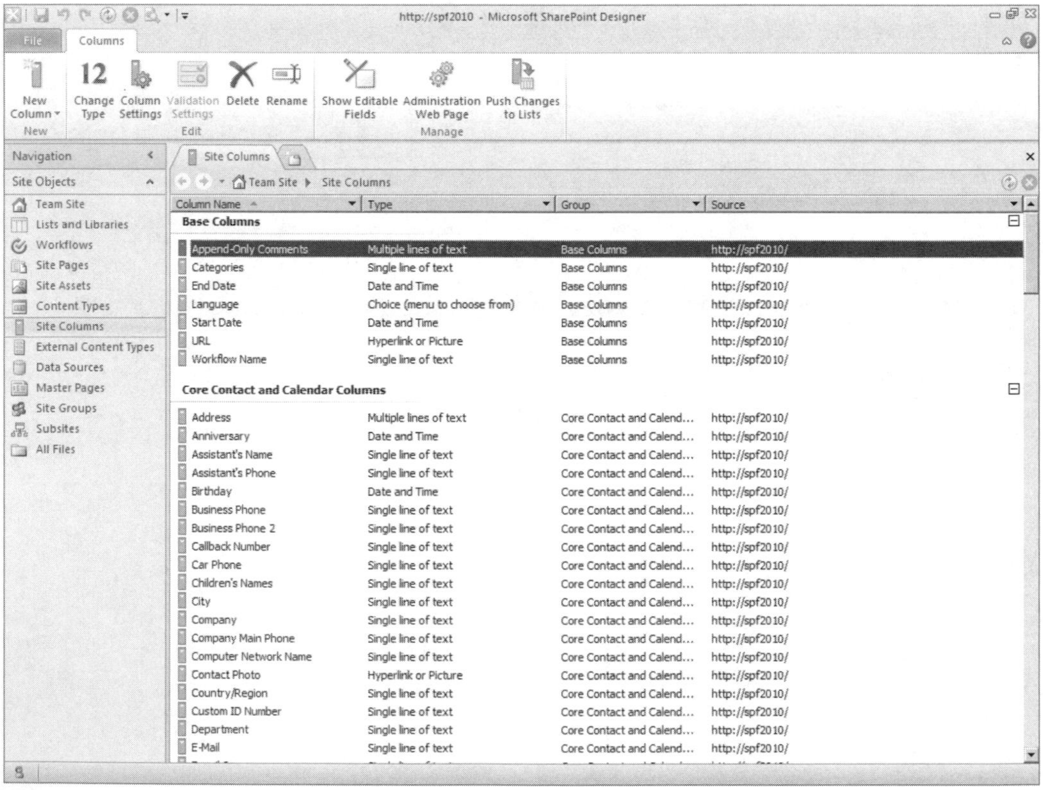

![SharePoint Designer Site Columns screen]

FIGURE 6-27

After you select a data type for the column, the dialog in Figure 6-28 appears. This dialog allows you to specify the site column's name and description. You can also select the group in which it should appear in the list of site columns. Again, it is recommended that you create at least one group for your site columns to keep them separate from the built-in groups.

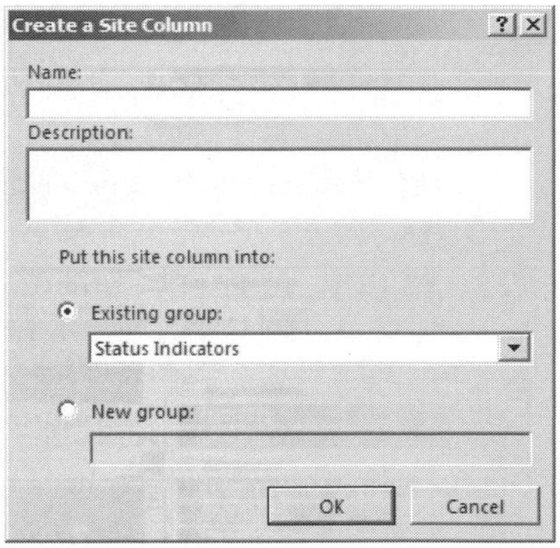

Once you complete the dialog in Figure 6-28, the list of site columns will be refreshed with your new site column. To change the settings of the site column, choose one of the options in the Edit section of the ribbon. If you change a site column, you can propagate the change to all lists and libraries using that site column by selecting Push Changes to Lists from the ribbon.

FIGURE 6-28

To edit the settings of your content type, select the content type from the list in Figure 6-22 and the screen in Figure 6-29 will appear. On this page, you can change the name and description of the view, the view's forms, and make the content read-only. You can also see the workflows associated with the content type. Content types can be associated with workflows, which will execute whenever an item or document with that content type is added or updated. Chapters 11, Workflow Basics, and 12, Advanced Workflows, cover more about workflows.

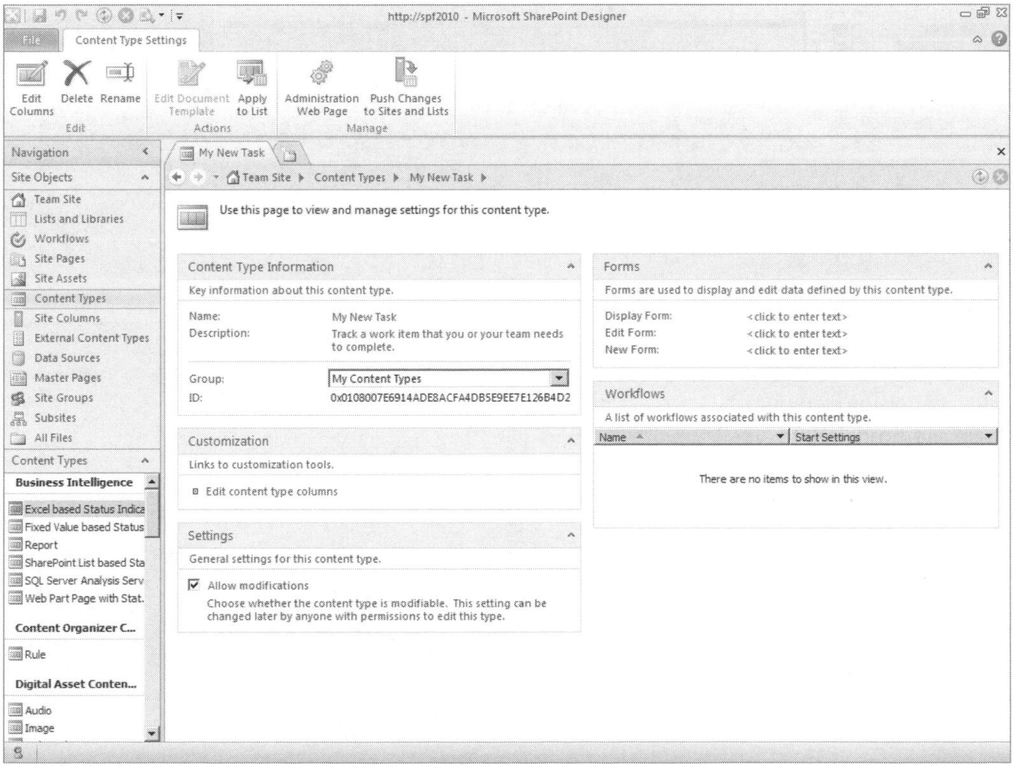

FIGURE 6-29

Not everything about a content type can be configured from SharePoint Designer. If you select Administration Web Page from the ribbon, the browser will open and show the page in Figure 6-30. Clicking the Workflow settings hyperlink will allow you to associate a workflow with the content type. Finally, the Information management policy settings link allows you to enable item and document tracking features as described in the following tables:

TRACKING INSIDE SHAREPOINT

Retention	Expired items and documents can be destroyed, recycled, moved, or sent to a workflow
Auditing	Any actions to an item or document are tracked including viewing, editing, check-in/check-out, moving, copying, and delete operations

TRACKING OUTSIDE SHAREPOINT

Barcodes	Can assign a barcode to the item or document before it is saved or printed
Labels	Can have information be inserted whenever the item or document is saved or printed

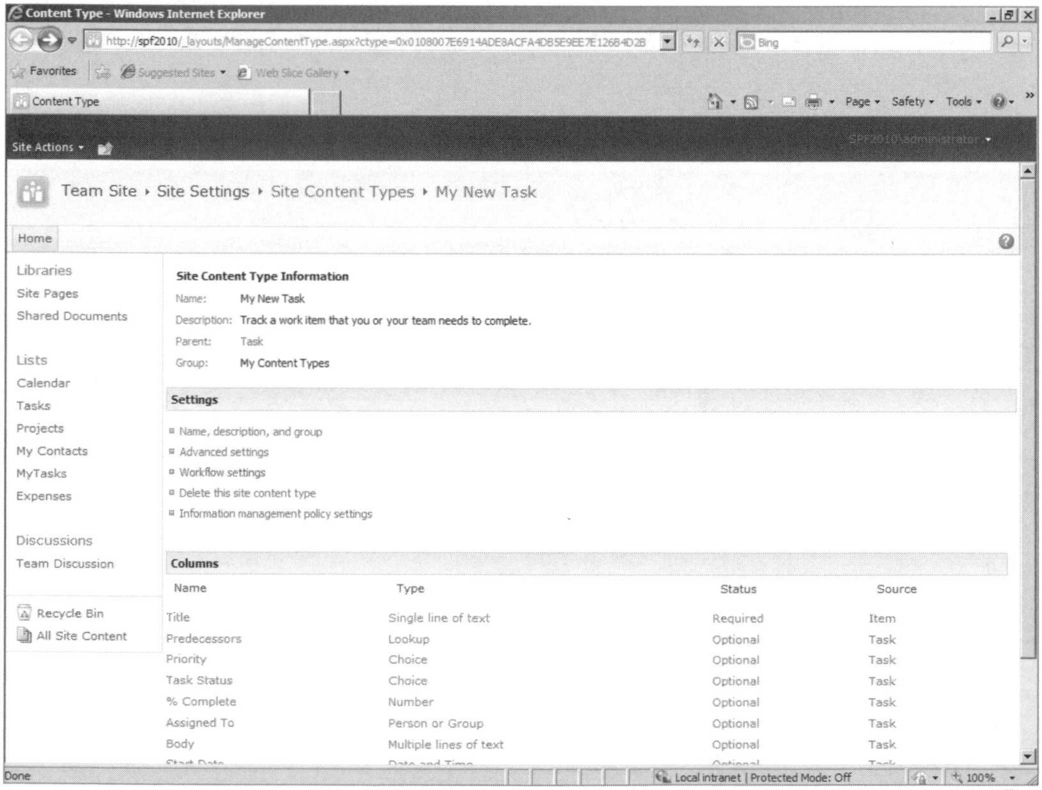

FIGURE 6-30

Hiding and Requiring Fields

Depending on your requirements, you may want to make some columns hidden or required. Though SharePoint Designer can show whether the columns in your content type are required, optionally or hidden as shown in Figure 6-25. You must use the browser to change those settings.

Figure 6-30 also shows the list of fields in the content type. If you click the name of a column, the Change Content Type Column screen in Figure 6-31 appears. On this screen, you can make a column required, optional, or hidden. The following list describes these columns settings:

➤ **Required** — The user must enter data in the column before the item or document can be saved.

➤ **Optional** — The user can optionally enter data in the column.

➤ **Hidden** — The column will not appear on item new, edit, and display forms but can be updated via workflows and custom code. Use this option to store data that is necessary but would not make sense to the user.

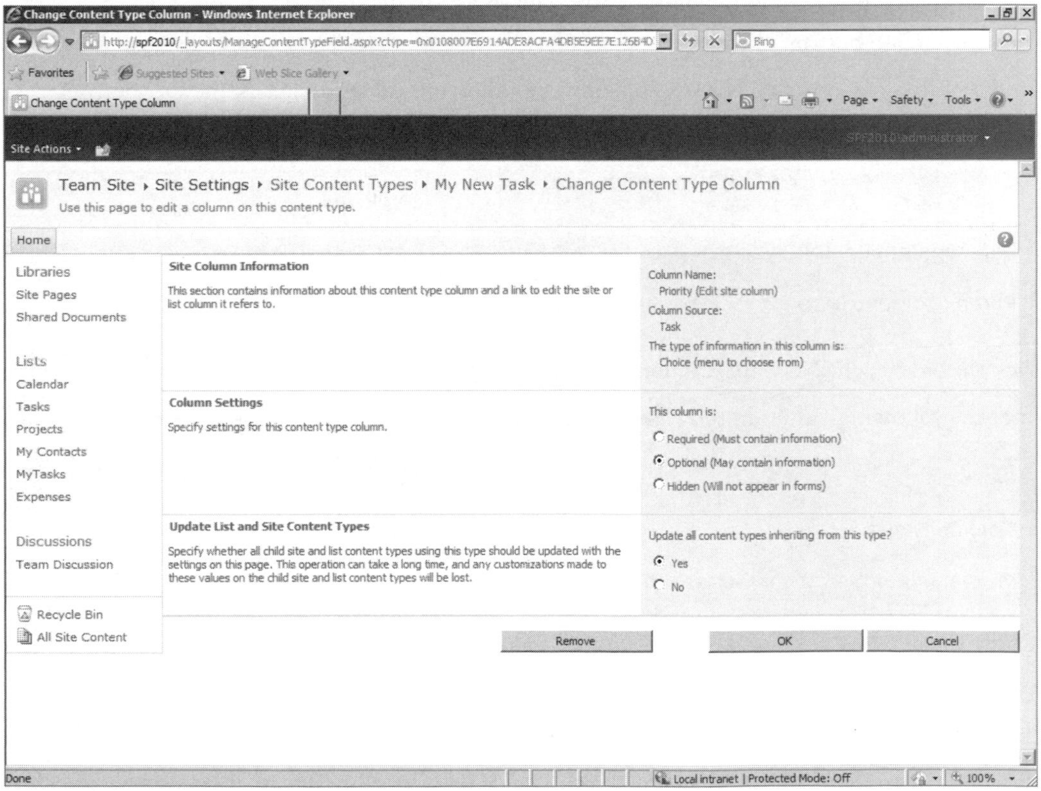

FIGURE 6-31

After you make your changes, you can apply the change to all content types that inherit from this content type by selecting Yes in the Update List and Site Content Types section.

> **NOTE** *Whenever a content type is added to a list or library, SharePoint creates a copy of the content type and adds it to the list or library. That allows the list to function correctly even if the content type is removed from the site. If you update a content type directly in the list or library, your changes will* not *be applied to the original content type. Only update content types from the Site Content Types screen and choose the option to update child types, or your SharePoint site could become unmanageable.*

TRY IT OUT   Create and Use Content Types Using the Browser

In this exercise, you create a custom content type with custom site columns using the browser.

1. Navigate your browser to your SharePoint site.

2. Click Site Actions ⇨ Site Settings to navigate to the Site Settings page.

3. Click the Site Content Types link under the Galleries section.

4. Click the Create button.

5. On the New Site Content Type screen, enter the following values and click the OK button

NAME	VALUE
Name	Employee
Select parent content type from	List Content Types
Parent Content Type	Contact

6. Click the Add From New Site Column link at the bottom of the page.

7. Enter the following values in the New Site Column screen and click the OK button:

NAME	VALUE
Column Name	SSN
Maximum number of characters	9

8. Create a Contacts list by clicking Site Actions ⇨ More Options and using the Create dialog in Figure 6-13.

9. Choose the Contacts type and enter **Department Roster** in the Name textbox.

10. Click the Create button.

11. When the list loads in the browser, in the ribbon click the List tab and choose List Settings.

12. Click the Advanced Settings link in the General Settings section of the list settings page.

13. Choose Yes for Allow management of content types in the Content Types section and click the OK button.

14. Click the Contact content type in the Content Types section.

15. Click the Delete This Content Type link in the Settings section.

16. Click the OK button to confirm the deletion.

17. Click the Add From Existing Content Types link.

18. Add the Employee content type to the Content types to add list box and click the OK button.

19. Click Department Roster in the breadcrumb trail at the top of the screen to return to the list.

20. Click the Add New Item link to show the New Item dialog.

21. Notice the columns are the same as the Contact content type except the new SSN column at the bottom of the dialog.

22. Click the Cancel button to close the dialog.

How It Works

Creating the site column allows you to add a custom column to your content type. You can also reuse the site column in other lists and content types. When you create the content type, SharePoint saves whether each of the columns are required, optional or hidden. When the content type is added to the list, the columns of the content type and the columns of its ancestors are added to the list. Remember that the list effectively saves a copy of the content type and any modifications to the list's copy will not appear in the site content type.

TRY IT OUT   **Create and Use Content Types Using SharePoint Designer**

In this exercise, you create a custom content type with custom site columns using SharePoint Designer. Be sure to complete the "Create and Use Content Types Using the Browser" Try It Out exercise before proceeding further.

1. Open SharePoint Designer from your Start menu.

2. Click the Open Site button.

3. When the Open Site dialog appears, enter the URL to your site in the Site name textbox and click the OK button.

4. If a Windows Security dialog appears, enter your username and password for the SharePoint site and click the OK button.

5. After the site opens, click Content Types in the Navigation bar on the left.

6. Click the New Content Type button in the ribbon.

7. In the Create a Content Type dialog, enter the following values and click the OK button.

NAME	VALUE
Name	Contractor
Select parent content type from	List Content Types
Parent Content Type	Contact

8. Right-click the newly created content type and choose Content Type Settings.

9. Click the Edit Content Type Columns link in the Customization section.

10. Click the Add Existing Site Column button in the ribbon.

11. Choose SSN and click OK in the Site Columns Picker dialog.

12. Click the Save button in the Quick Access Toolbar at the top of the screen.

13. Click Lists and Libraries in the Navigation bar on the left.

14. Click the Department Roster list.

15. Click the Add button in the Content Types section.

16. Select the Contractor content type and click the OK button.

17. Click the Preview in Browser button in the ribbon.

18. In the ribbon, click the Items tab.

19. In the ribbon, click the down arrow under the New Item button.

20. Notice the user now has the option to create an Employee or a Contractor.

How It Works

In SharePoint Designer, you can create a same content type and configure the same settings as you did in the browser in the previous Try It Out. Once you save the content type, SharePoint Designer contacts the SharePoint server to save the content type to the site. Afterwards, you can add the content type to the lists and libraries of the site.

SUMMARY

This chapter explained how SharePoint stores and organizes your data and documents. Using a combination of lists and libraries, you can quickly create an application that includes the raw power of a database engine with the flexibility of a document management system. The next chapter further explains SharePoint's capabilities to access your data outside of SharePoint and across your enterprise.

7

Data Sources and External Content Types

WHAT YOU WILL LEARN IN THIS CHAPTER

➤ The different types of data that SharePoint can access

➤ How to display data from your SharePoint list and libraries

➤ The methods SharePoint supports to access remote data

➤ How to make external data sources appear as lists in your SharePoint site

In the previous chapter, you saw how SharePoint can store your data and documents. This chapter covers reusing your lists and libraries and integrating the rest of your data into SharePoint.

GETTING AT YOUR DATA

SharePoint supports several types of data sources, including lists and libraries in SharePoint itself and databases and data from web pages and web services. When you have a site open in SharePoint Designer, click Data Sources in the navigation bar to list the data sources available for your use. In Figure 7-1, you can see how the data sources are automatically grouped by type.

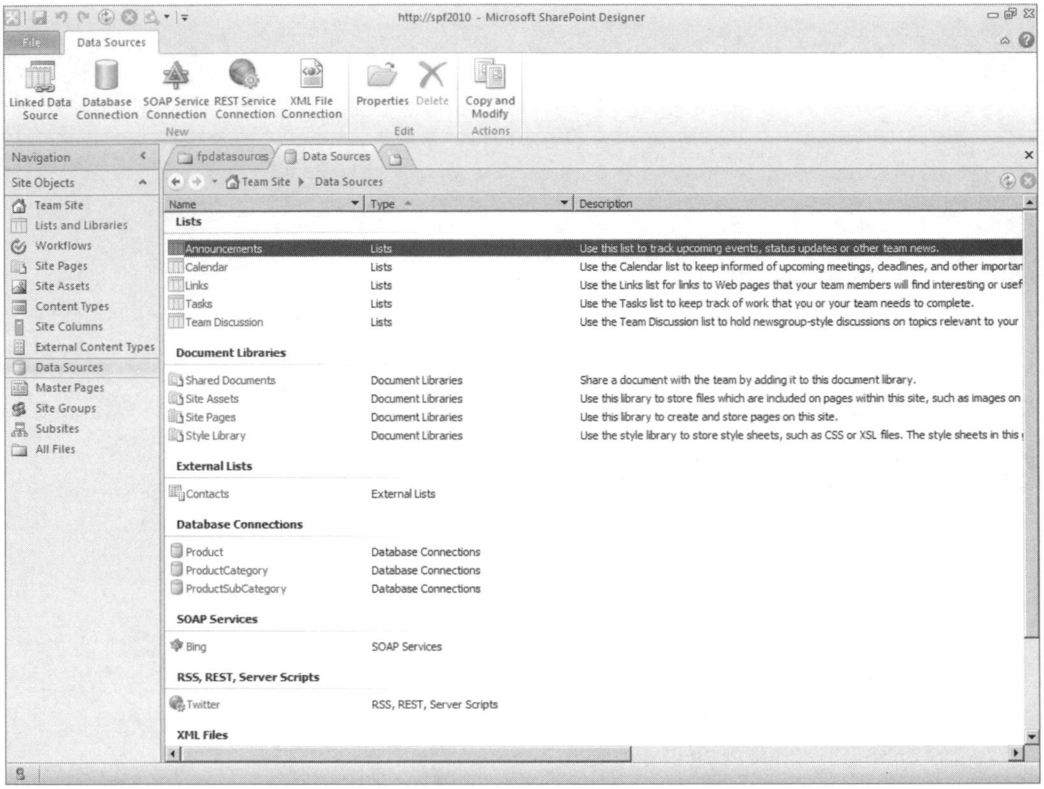

FIGURE 7-1

The following table lists the various types of data sources and their characteristics.

SECTION	DESCRIPTION
Lists and Document Libraries	Lists and libraries are intrinsic data sources in SharePoint. Whenever you create a list or library, whether through the web interface or SharePoint Designer, it automatically becomes available in the appropriate section.
External Lists	External lists represent data sources outside SharePoint, including databases and WCF Services, but look and feel like lists in your SharePoint site. When you modify the contents of an external list, those modifications are sent to the data source by SharePoint.
Database Connections	Database connections enable you to define a source to connect to an arbitrary database on your network. SharePoint Designer supports creating data sources for SQL Server and Oracle, as well as virtually any database for which an OLE DB or ODBC connection is available, such as MySQL.
SOAP Service Connections	Also known as XML Web Services, SOAP Service Connections follow a standardized set of rules called Simple Object Access Protocol (SOAP). This protocol allows a client process to learn about the functions available, query the parameter formats required, and learn result formats provided by the service.

SECTION	DESCRIPTION
REST Service Connections	REST Service connections allow you to connect to data that is returned as the result of calling a web page rather than a web service. The data returned is usually in an XML format called Really Simple Syndication (RSS), which is most commonly used for reading blogs. The data returned can also be in a format called JavaScript Object Notation (JSON), which is used for updating the contents of a web page in the browser without reloading the entire page.
XML Files	All data sources are converted to XML before a Data View Web Part can render them. It's no surprise, then, that you can provide XML directly to the part as a file. SharePoint Designer automatically detects any `.xml` files that may be stored in your site and lists them in the XML Files section. In addition, you can define connections to XML files that reside in other locations on your network.
Linked Sources	Linked sources are made up of combinations of other sources in the Data Source library.

In Figure 7-1, you can also see the different types of data sources that you can create by clicking the buttons in the ribbon. After filling in the definition forms (except for lists and libraries), an XML file defining the data source will be saved in the `/_catalogs/fpdatasources` library.

> **NOTE** *XML definition files are not grouped within the* `fpdatasources` *library folder to match the grouping in the Data Source Library task pane. They are all simply stored at the root level.*

Each type of data source has slightly different configuration requirements and therefore different forms for filling in the details. Nevertheless, certain information is similar for any data source, and you enter that information on the General tab of the Data Source Properties dialog box, as shown in Figure 7-2.

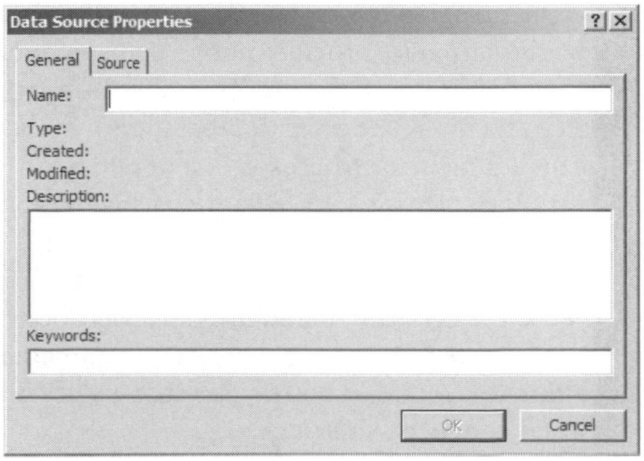

To enter or edit any of this information, switch to the General tab (when you create a new data source by clicking on the buttons in the New section of the ribbon in Figure 7-1, or edit an existing data source, the Source tab is displayed first when the dialog opens). You are not

FIGURE 7-2

required to enter any information on the General tab; however, if you do not enter a friendly name, an arbitrary generic name such as NewDataSource1 is created when you save the data source for the first time.

LISTS AND LIBRARIES

SharePoint lists and libraries are automatically added to the Data Sources tab when they are created. You do not need to create entries for them. In addition, unlike most data source definitions, these automatic entries have direct links to the underlying list or library, and therefore are not normally listed in the `fpdatasources` folder.

Right-clicking any data source and choosing the Properties window normally opens the Data Source Properties dialog shown in Figure 7-2, but for lists and libraries, SharePoint Designer opens a new tab for the list's properties. This is the same tab that opens if you open the list from Lists and Libraries in the navigation bar on the left.

DATABASES

To create a database connection, click the Database Connection button on the ribbon. In Figure 7-3, you can see the Source tab and the Configure Database Connection button. Clicking this button displays the Configure Database Connection wizard shown in Figure 7-4.

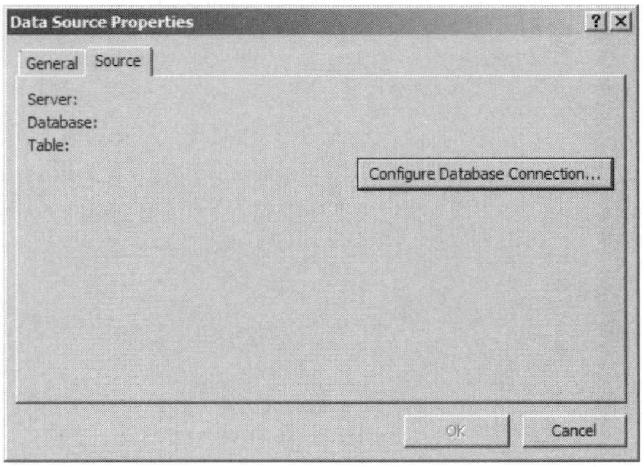

FIGURE 7-3

> **NOTE** *If you are using SharePoint Foundation instead of SharePoint Server, you will not see the option for Single Sign-On authentication in the dialog in Figure 7-4.*

In the first step of the wizard, you must specify the server name, provider name, and credentials for accessing the database. If you are not connecting to a SQL Server database, change the provider name to Microsoft .Net Framework Data Provider for OLE DB. Alternatively, you can select the Use custom connection string checkbox and click the Edit button to specify a connection string manually. This method is helpful when you are connecting to an uncommon data source or when you must specify additional connection settings.

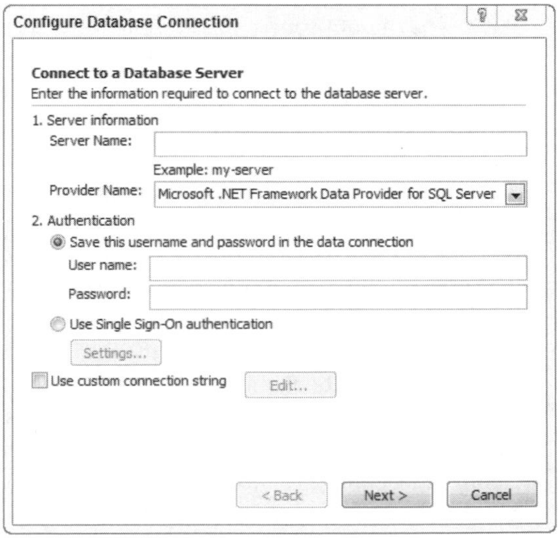

FIGURE 7-4

WARNING *Your credentials and connection string will be stored unencrypted in the database connection XML file. Other authors of this SharePoint site will have the ability to read this password. Be sure to use an account with the least amount of privileges required to access your data.*

After you have configured the first step of the wizard, click the Next button to display the second step shown in Figure 7-5. Before the second step displays, a warning message appears to remind you that the username and password you enter will not be encrypted. Click the OK button to continue.

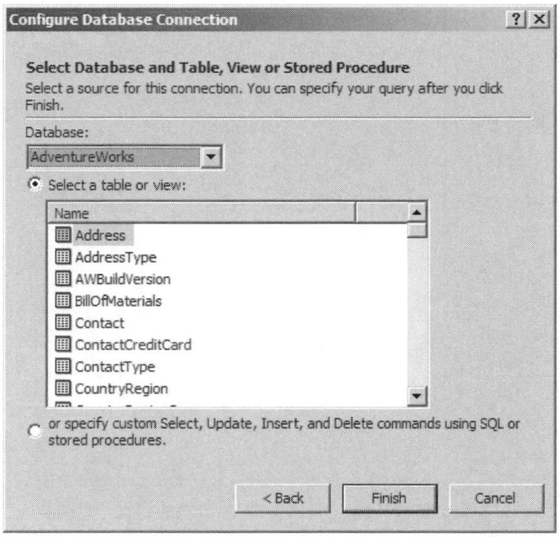

FIGURE 7-5

NOTE *Accessing the data source may take up to a minute and SharePoint Designer may appear to be idle. You can check the right side of the status bar at the bottom of the screen to see whether SharePoint Designer is still talking to the server.*

> **NOTE** *Ensuring that both the SharePoint server(s) and the client running SharePoint Designer have access to the database server is important for this process to succeed. This includes both network access and appropriate client drivers. Visitors to the site will not need client drivers. They may require appropriate credentials if common credentials or anonymous access to the database is not provided. In the second and final step of the wizard, you can select your database and a table or view from the list box. At this point, clicking the Finish button closes the wizard and saves your settings. If you want to filter the data returned or call a stored procedure, select the second radio button instead. Afterward, click the Finish button to display the dialog in Figure 7-6.*

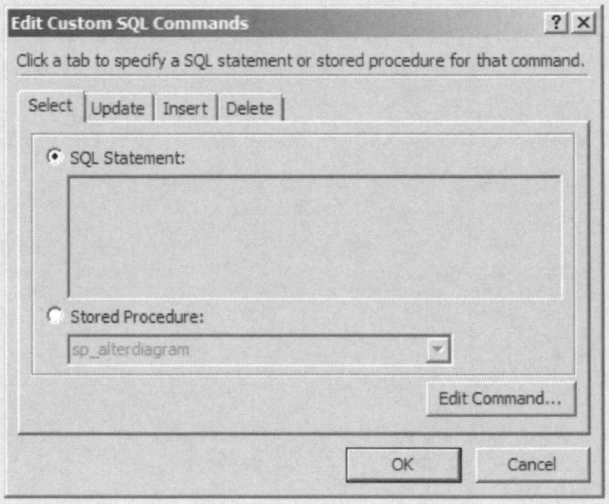

FIGURE 7-6

After you close the Configure Database Connection wizard, you return to the Source tab of the Data Source Properties dialog. The empty bottom half of the tab is now populated with options to control which fields are returned by the connection. You can also add filters and sort orders for the returned data. Specifying options here can save you valuable time later when using this data source on a web page because you will not have to configure as many options every time you use this connection. When you are satisfied with your settings, click the OK button to save the database connection to SharePoint.

TRY IT OUT   Set Up Databases

In this activity, you download and install the AdventureWorks sample SQL Server databases that will be used in later activities.

1. While logged in to your database server, navigate the browser to `http://msftdbprodsamples` `.codeplex.com`.

2. Click the Download button to download the setup file.

3. Save the setup file to your desktop, and run it.

4. Select the box to accept the license terms, and click the Next button.

5. Change the values for Installation Instance and Script Install Directory, if necessary.

6. Click the Install button.

7. When the installation is complete, click the Finish button.

How It Works

The installer extracts various SQL and CSV files which it uses to create the structure of the AdventureWorks databases and load the tables with data. By creating these databases, you have the beginnings of a sandbox where you can try out different things safely before you try your hand in production.

TRY IT OUT   Create a Data Source for a Database Table

In this activity, you create a data source for the Address table in the AdventureWorks database.

1. Open SharePoint Designer from your Start menu.

2. Click the Open Site button.

3. When the Open Site dialog appears, enter the URL to your site in the Site name textbox and click the OK button.

4. If a Windows Security dialog appears, enter your username and password for the SharePoint site and click the OK button.

5. After the site opens, choose Data Sources from the navigation bar on the left.

6. Click the Database Connection button on the ribbon.

7. When the Data Source Properties dialog appears, click the General tab and enter **Address** in the Name textbox.

8. Click the Source tab, and click the Configure Database Connection button.

9. When the Configure Database Connection dialog appears, enter the following information and click the Next button:

➤ Server Name

➤ User Name

➤ Password

10. A message box appears indicating that the credentials you enter will be viewable by other authors of the site. Click the OK button to continue.

11. Select the Address table from the list box in Figure 7-5, and click the Finish button.

12. Click the OK button to save the data source.

How It Works

Using the credentials you enter in the first step of the wizard, SharePoint Designer will query the database for a list of tables and views, including their columns and data types. After you choose a table or view or use the custom option, a SQL query is dynamically generated and stored in the database connection. If you modify the query using the Fields, Filter, or Sort buttons, the SQL query is modified with those additional options.

XML FILES

Creating a new XML reference is very straightforward. You can either import an XML file into your SharePoint site, or, if the XML file is stored online, simply create a link to it. An online XML file does not need to be within a SharePoint site, but it does need to be accessible via either `http` or `https`. To create a new XML reference, select XML File Connection from the ribbon in Figure 7-1.

If the server containing the file does not allow anonymous access, you can provide login information on the Login tab of the data source definition, shown in Figure 7-7.

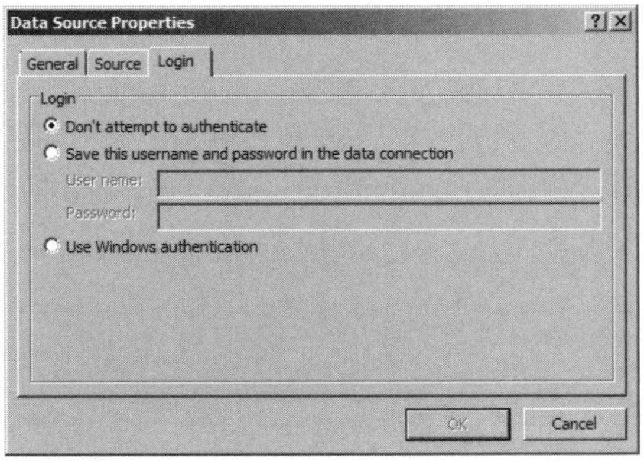

FIGURE 7-7

> **NOTE** *The XML file does not have to be static and the URL does not have to end with XML. Any URL that returns XML, even if the XML changes over time, will work.*

TRY IT OUT   **Create a Data Source for an XML File**

In this activity, you create an external content type from a special XML file called an RSS feed.

1.   Open SharePoint Designer from your Start menu.

2.   Click the Open Site button.

3.   When the Open Site dialog appears, enter the URL to your site in the Site name textbox and click the OK button.

4.   If a Windows Security dialog appears, enter your username and password for the SharePoint site and click the OK button.

5.   After the site opens, choose Data Sources from the navigation bar on the left.

6.   Click the XML File Connection button on the ribbon.

7. When the Data Source Properties dialog appears, click the General tab and enter **RSS Feed** in the Name textbox.

8. Click the Source tab and enter **http://www.endusersharepoint.com/feed/rss/** in the Location textbox.

9. Click the OK button.

How It Works

SharePoint downloads the XML file using the URL and credentials you specify. In this case, the XML file is an *RSS* feed, which is dynamically generated by the website based on the articles that have been uploaded to the site. By examining the content and structure of the XML file, SharePoint can transform it into a tabular or hierarchical structure that you can use when you add the connection to a web page.

REST-BASED WEB SERVICES

Most web pages, such as traditional .asp, .php, and Cold Fusion (.cfm), are designed to accept parameters from the URL used to access the web page or from the user's filling out another web page and clicking a submit button. If the web page can return results in XML format, you can create a connection to that web page that provides the input parameters it expects and then returns the XML to SharePoint.

To create a connection based on a REST web service, click the REST Service Connection button on the ribbon; the Data Source Properties dialog shown in Figure 7-8 appears.

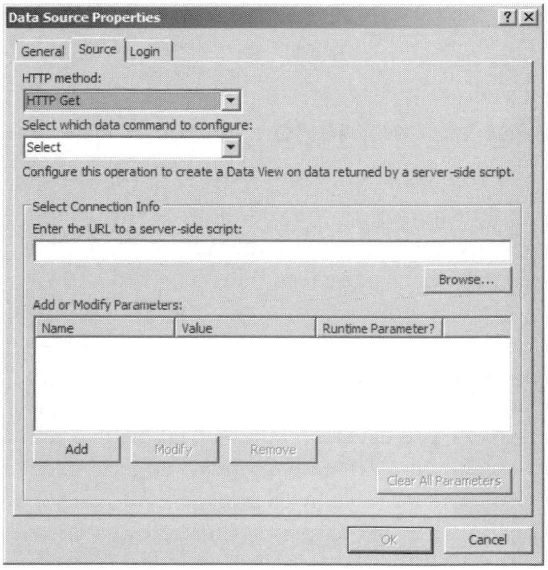

FIGURE 7-8

HTTP Method

Two methods exist for sending parameters to a REST-based web services: GET and POST. The HTTP GET method supplies the parameters at the end of the web service's URL. For instance, given a URL of `http://www.demo.com/MyWebService.php`, a parameter named *CustomerID* with a value of **123**, and a parameter named *Region* with a value of **SouthWest**, the resulting URL for an HTTP GET would be `http://www.demo.com/MyWebService.php?CustomerID=123&Region=SouthWest`.

> **NOTE** *One drawback of the* `HTTP GET` *method is that the total length of the URL cannot exceed 260 characters. That limits the number and size of the parameters you can supply with this method.*

The `HTTP POST` method differs from the `HTTP GET` method in that the URL is never modified. Parameters are posted (sent) to the URL directly, which allows any number of parameters. The small drawback of this method is that you must know the parameters ahead of time by talking to the web developer who created the web service or searching the website for documentation on how to use it. Most websites that allow their web services to be used by the public have abundant documentation including example usage. Some websites also have online forums where users can help each other in using the web service. An example of such a site is Twitter (`http://www.twitter.com`), which you will use in a later activity.

> **NOTE** *A few, very rare scripts depend on certain parameters to be submitted with each method. SharePoint Designer cannot configure connections for scripts that require parameters from both methods simultaneously.*

Data Command

Most of the time, you only want to read and display (that is, Select) information from your external data source, so you simply leave the default Select option chosen (refer to Figure 7-8). In addition to querying, however, some web services allow you to insert, update, or delete the underlying data. To implement those functions in your Data view or forms, select the appropriate command from the data command dropdown. Each of the functions has its own set of parameters defined.

Parameters

After you determine the HTTP method and data command, you can add any required parameters to the parameter table by clicking the Add button in Figure 7-8. In the Parameter dialog that appears, you can specify both the name and a default value for each parameter. In addition, you can designate a parameter at run time by selecting the following box: The value of this parameter can be set via a Web Part connection. Figure 7-9 shows the dialog to add or modify a parameter.

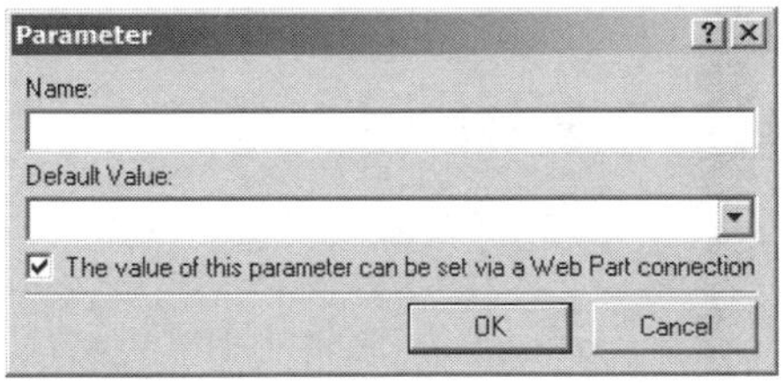

FIGURE 7-9

> **NOTE** *If you choose the HTTP GET method and paste an example URL into the server-side script textbox, SharePoint Designer will automatically parse the URL and populate the list box with any parameters that it finds.*

TRY IT OUT Create a Data Source for a REST-Based Web Service

In this activity, you create a data source from a web service.

1. Open SharePoint Designer from your Start menu.

2. Click the Open Site button.

3. When the Open Site dialog appears, enter the URL to your site in the Site name textbox and click the OK button.

4. If a Windows Security dialog appears, enter your username and password for the SharePoint site and click the OK button.

5. After the site opens, choose Data Sources from the navigation bar on the left.

6. Click the REST Service Connection button on the ribbon.

7. When the Data Source Properties dialog appears, click the General tab and enter **Twitter** in the Name textbox.

8. Click the Source tab and enter **http://search.twitter.com/search.json?q=sharepoint** in the Enter the URL to a server-side script textbox.

9. Press the Tab key to leave the textbox and notice that the query string parameters from the URL were added to the Add or Modify Parameters list.

10. Click the OK button.

How It Works

When you selected the HTTP GET method and pasted a URL into the server-side script textbox, SharePoint Designer parsed the URL and added the q parameter to the list box. The q parameter is used to supply a search query to Twitter's search web service. When you add this data connection to a web page, the Twitter search web service is sent the parameter, and Twitter returns the results of the search query in XML format. That XML can then be displayed on your web page.

SOAP-BASED WEB SERVICES

SOAP-based web services are like an enhancement of REST-based web services, with a major exception — most REST-based web services are meant to be called from other pages within the same application. Web services, on the other hand, are designed specifically to be called by other applications, so some key differences exist between setting up a REST-based web service data source and setting up a SOAP-based web service data source. Select SOAP Service Connection from the ribbon in Figure 7-1 to show the Source configuration screen for a SOAP-based web service in Figure 7-10.

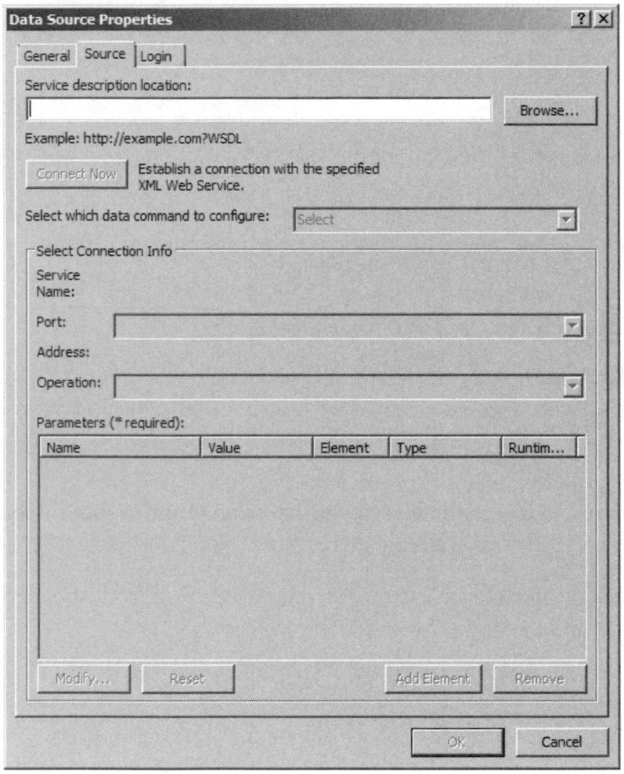

FIGURE 7-10

Service Description Location

As you did for the REST-based web service, you must provide a URL to access a web service. For a SOAP-based web service, however, the URL you enter here typically will include the specific parameter ?WSDL, which means Web Services Description Language, or Web Service Definition Language. This parameter instructs the web service to return information about how it is used in a standardized XML form. SharePoint Designer then uses that information to provide the options for the remainder of the configuration.

> **NOTE** *You can see the WSDL yourself by pasting the URL into a browser. The result will look like XML.*

Data Command

As with the REST-based web service, you configure Select, Insert, Update, and Delete commands independently. Most of the time, you only configure a Select command. If the SOAP-based web service provides operations for the other commands, simply configure the remaining sections appropriately for each command.

Port

If a SOAP-based web service supports multiple interfaces, the Port option allows you to specify which interface to use. You typically use the first option provided, unless the web service provider gives specific instruction to the contrary.

Operation

When you click the Connect Now button, SharePoint Designer downloads the WSDL file and populates the Operation dropdown menu with the supported functions of the web service. Select the operation you want to perform to implement the current command.

Parameters

After you select an operation, SharePoint Designer populates the Parameters table. This is much simpler than discovering the parameters for a REST-based web service because you do not have to guess or dig through possibly unobtainable documentation to determine what the functions expect.

Parameters to a SOAP-based web service may be optional or required. Required parameters are indicated by an asterisk (*). As with REST-based web service parameters, you may predefine a default value for a parameter and also make it configurable at runtime (through a Web Part connection, for instance). Unlike REST-based web service parameters, these values can be complex entities that contain many elements, such as arrays, and have data types that can be enforced. For complex data types, each element can have a default value or runtime source specified.

You cannot add parameters to or remove parameters from a web service data source, because they are predefined in the WSDL. For optional parameters, just leave the configuration elements blank if you are not going to use them.

TRY IT OUT   Setup for Calling the Bing Search Engine API

In this activity, you request an AppID for querying the Bing search engine.

1.   Navigate your browser to `http://www.bing.com/developers`.

2.   Sign in with a Windows Live ID.

3.   Navigate your browser to `http://www.bing.com/developers/appids.aspx`.

4.   Click the Get started by applying for an AppID now hyperlink.

5.   In the screen that appears, enter the required information, agree to the terms and conditions, and click the Agree button.

6.   When your AppID appears on the screen, make a note of it for the next activity. The AppID is a long string of characters and numbers.

How It Works

To query the Bing Search Engine API, you must submit an AppID in addition to the query you send to the SOAP service. Getting an AppID is free, but you should safeguard your AppID so that you are not banned from the API if someone were to break the Bing Terms and Conditions using your AppID.

TRY IT OUT   Create a Data Source for a SOAP-based Web Service

In this activity, you create a data source that queries the Bing search engine using SOAP.

1.   Open SharePoint Designer from your Start menu.

2.   Click the Open Site button.

3.   When the Open Site dialog appears, enter the URL to your site in the Site name textbox and click the OK button.

4.   If a Windows Security dialog appears, enter your username and password for the SharePoint site and click the OK button.

5.   After the site opens, choose Data Sources from the navigation bar on the left.

6.   Click the SOAP Service Connection button on the ribbon.

7. When the Data Source Properties dialog appears, click the General tab and enter **Bing** in the Name textbox.

8. Click the Source table and enter **http://api.search.live.net/search.wsdl** in the Service description location textbox.

9. Click the Connect Now button.

10. After SharePoint Designer connects to the web service, the Parameters list box becomes populated. Select the Query parameter and click the Modify button.

11. In the Parameter dialog, enter **SharePoint** in the Default value textbox, select The value of this parameter can be set via a Web Part connection checkbox, and click the OK button.

12. Select the AppID parameter and click the Modify button.

13. In the Parameter dialog, enter your AppID in the Default Value textbox, select the The value of this parameter can be set via a Web Part connection checkbox, and click the OK button.

14. Select the Sources parameter and click the Details button.

15. In the Parameter Details dialog, select SourceType and click the Modify button.

16. Select Web from the Value dropdown list and click the OK button.

17. Click the OK button to close the Parameter Details dialog.

18. Click the OK button to save the data source.

How It Works

When you specified the URL of the WSDL file and clicked the Connect Now button, SharePoint Designer downloaded the WSDL file and populated the Port and Operations dropdown lists. Additionally, the Parameters list box was populated for the Search operation. Most WSDL files have multiple operations, but this WSDL file only had one. To use Bing's Search web service, you had to sign up for an AppID, which was specified as the default value for the AppID parameter. You also specified Web as the SourceType so that only web pages would be returned. Specifying SharePoint as the default value for Query allows you to have example results to display when you use this data source on a web page, but you can change that value when you add the data source to a web page or through web part connections.

BUSINESS CONNECTIVITY SERVICES

Business Connectivity Services (BCS) provides read and write access to your back-end line of business systems. These systems can be databases, web services, or completely custom integrations. In a custom integration, a .NET developer can write code that will expose the external system in a format that BCS can use.

One of the most powerful features of BCS is the ability to make an external data source look like a list. This type of list is called an *external list* and is based on an *external content type*. To see the list of external content types in your site, click External Content Types in the navigation bar in SharePoint Designer. Figure 7-11 shows the External Content Types list.

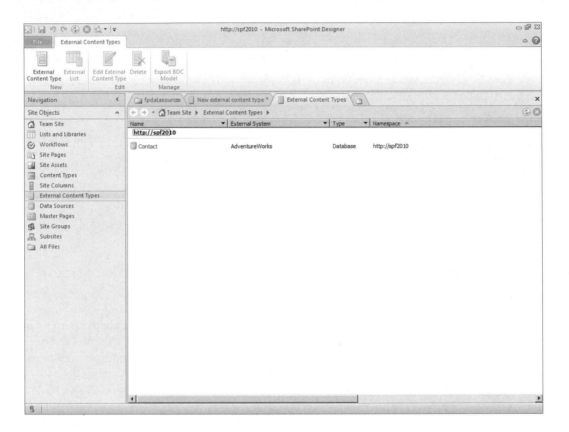

FIGURE 7-11

To create an external content type, click the External Content Type button on the ribbon; a new tab appears. In Figure 7-12, you can see the various settings that you must configure before the external content type can be used. To specify the name of the external content type, click the hyperlink next to Name. Display Name will be filled in automatically, but you can change it.

Because all content types, including external content types, must inherit from a parent content type, you must choose a parent content type from the Office Item Type dropdown list. Generic List is chosen by default, but a best practice is to choose the parent content type that matches your external content type the closest.

The next step is to configure an external data source for the external content type. Choose the Operations Designer View button from the ribbon; the tab changes to show the screen shown in Figure 7-13. The Data Source Explorer tab contains the list of data sources you have used so far. You can choose one of these data sources or click the Add Connection button to create a new one. In Figure 7-14, you can see the first dialog for adding a new connection.

You will likely choose SQL Server or WCF Service because .Net Type is meant for developers. If you choose SQL Server, the dialog in Figure 7-15 appears. In this dialog, you must specify the server and database names. If you do not specify a name for the connection, it will use the database name value for display purposes.

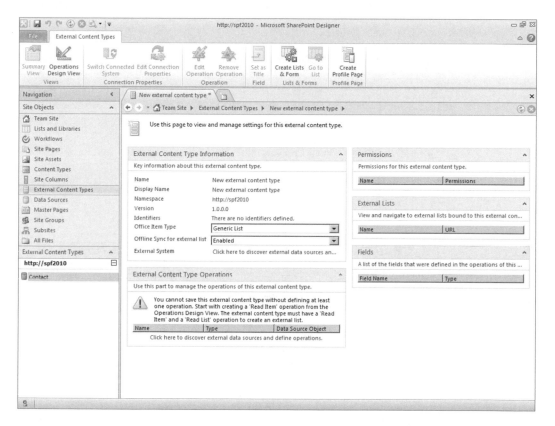

FIGURE 7-12

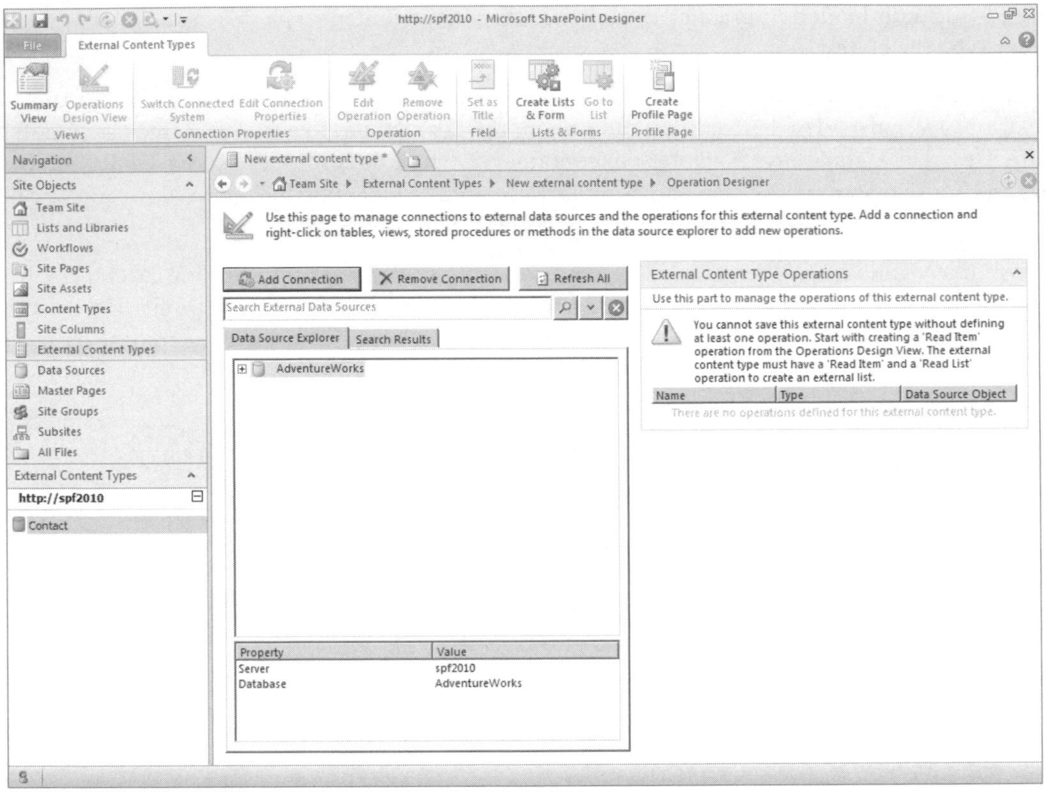

FIGURE 7-13

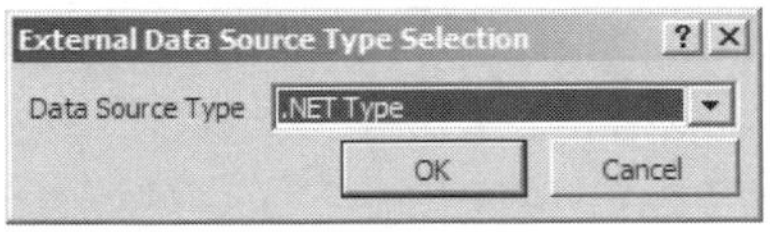

FIGURE 7-14

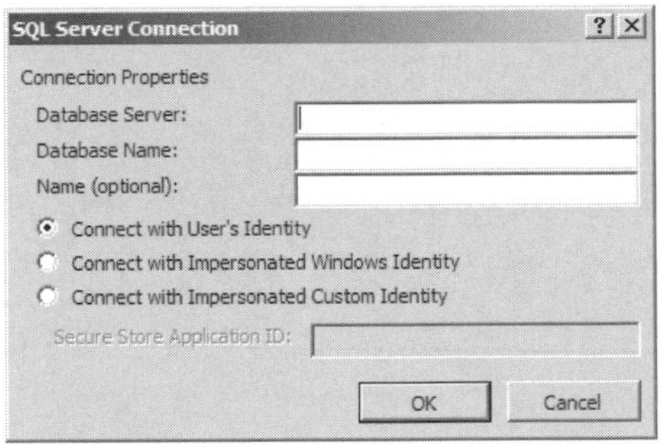

FIGURE 7-15

For configuring security, you can either pass the user's credentials to the database server or use credentials from the Secure Store in SharePoint Central Administration. The Secure Store is a central location to store usernames and passwords for accessing external systems through SharePoint. To manage the Secure Store, open SharePoint Central Administration from the Start menu. Then, click Manage service applications ➤ Secure Store Service.

If you choose WCF Service, the dialog in Figure 7-16 appears. In this dialog, you must specify a URL for getting metadata about the service and the connection mode to get the metadata. In practice, using WSDL as the connection mode is much more common than using Metadata Exchange. You must also specify the service endpoint URL. This is the actual URL that SharePoint must use when communicating with the service. Many times this URL is very similar to the URL for metadata.

If you must use a proxy to access the service, you can specify that information here, too. Unless you have an uncommon proxy configuration, you will likely not have to provide this information here. For security, you have the same options as those for SQL Server, but you can specify different options for accessing the service versus getting the metadata. Usually, you will use the same security settings for both. After you click OK to save the connection, SharePoint Designer validates your settings and, if it's successful, adds the connection to the Data Source Explorer tab as shown in Figure 7-17.

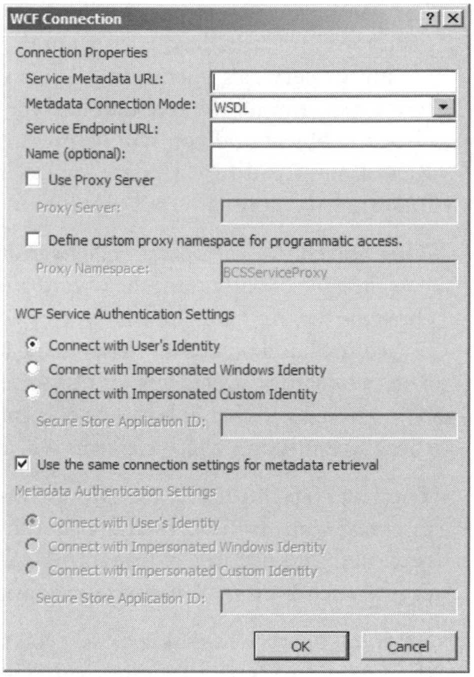

FIGURE 7-16

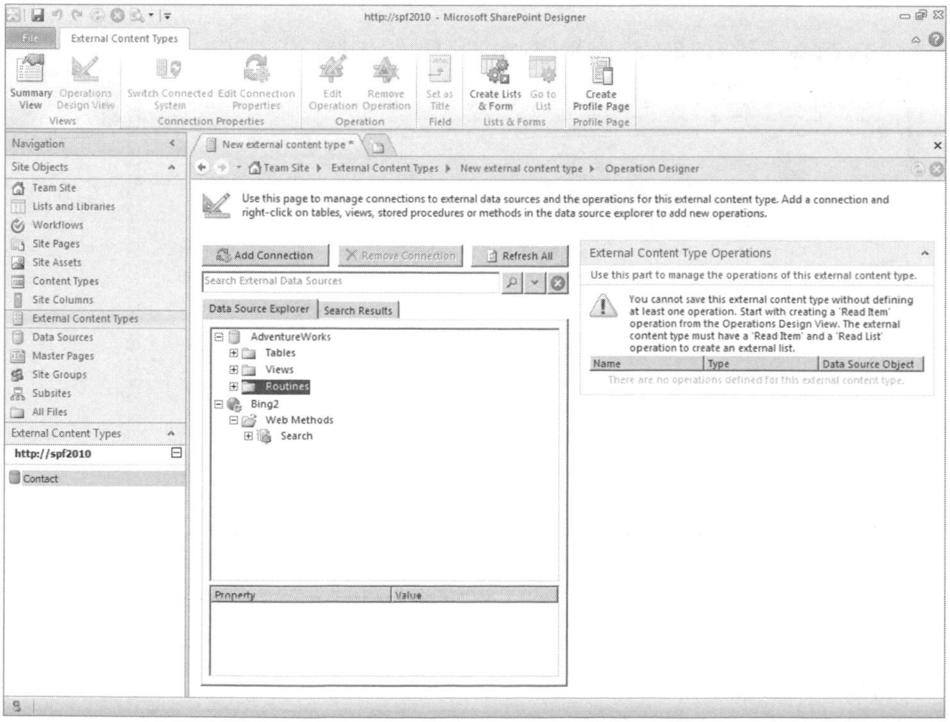

FIGURE 7-17

For database connections, folders exist for tables, views, and routines. Routines are the user-defined functions and stored procedures in the database. For WCF service connections, a single folder exists for all the service's operations. When you are ready to define the operations for your external content type, expand the tree and find the object upon which you want to create the operation(s). Right-click the object and you will be presented options for creating all operations or single operations like Read Item, Read List, Update, or Delete. You can also create a new association, which allows you to link external content types together in a similar manner as foreign key relationships in a database.

After you choose the operation(s) to create, the All operations dialog shown in Figure 7-18 appears. When you click the Next button, the wizard allows you to map the external object to the parent content type you chose earlier. Any unmapped elements will be created as custom SharePoint fields if their data type is supported in SharePoint. Otherwise, that data will not be shown nor will it be updateable through SharePoint. The two main requirements for this screen are making sure one element has the Map to Identifier checkbox selected and that at least one element has the Show In Picker checkbox selected. The Show In Picker checkbox indicates which elements will appear in the external item picker shown in Figure 7-19.

The last step of the wizard allows you to configure filters for the data connection. Though you may not want to filter the data, adding a Limit filter to prevent large amounts of data from being returned and negatively impacting performance is a good idea. The next Try It Out shows how to create such a filter. When you are satisfied, click the Finish button to create your operation(s).

After the operations dialog closes, you still must click the Save button in the Quick Access Toolbar at the top of the screen to commit your changes. Now that you have created an external content type, you must create an external list to allow users to access the content type in SharePoint. To create an external list, click the Create Lists & Forms button in the ribbon; the dialog shown in Figure 7-20 appears.

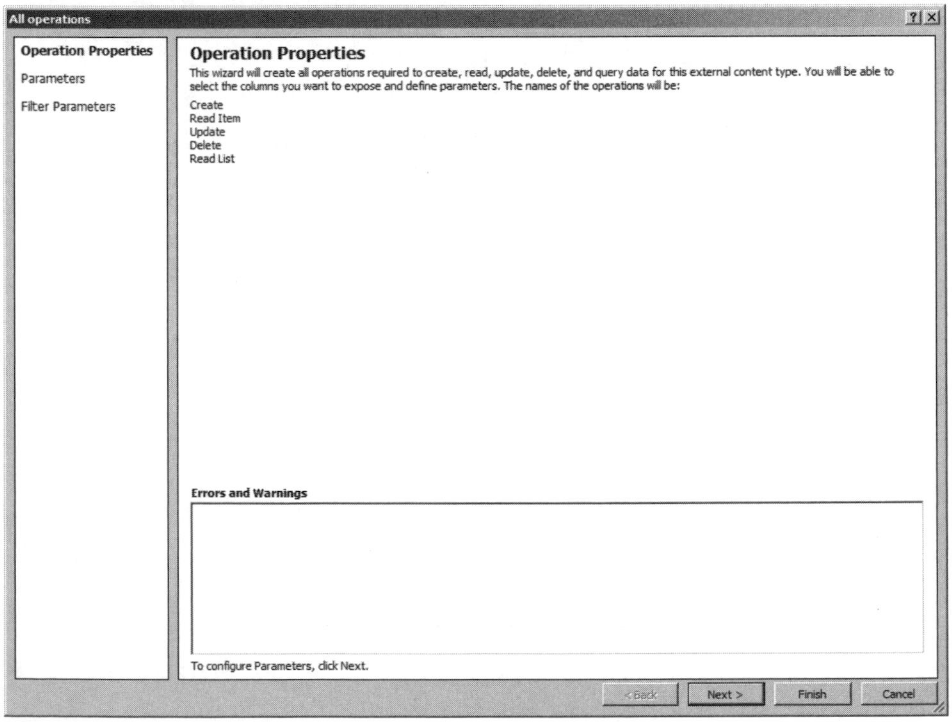

FIGURE 7-18

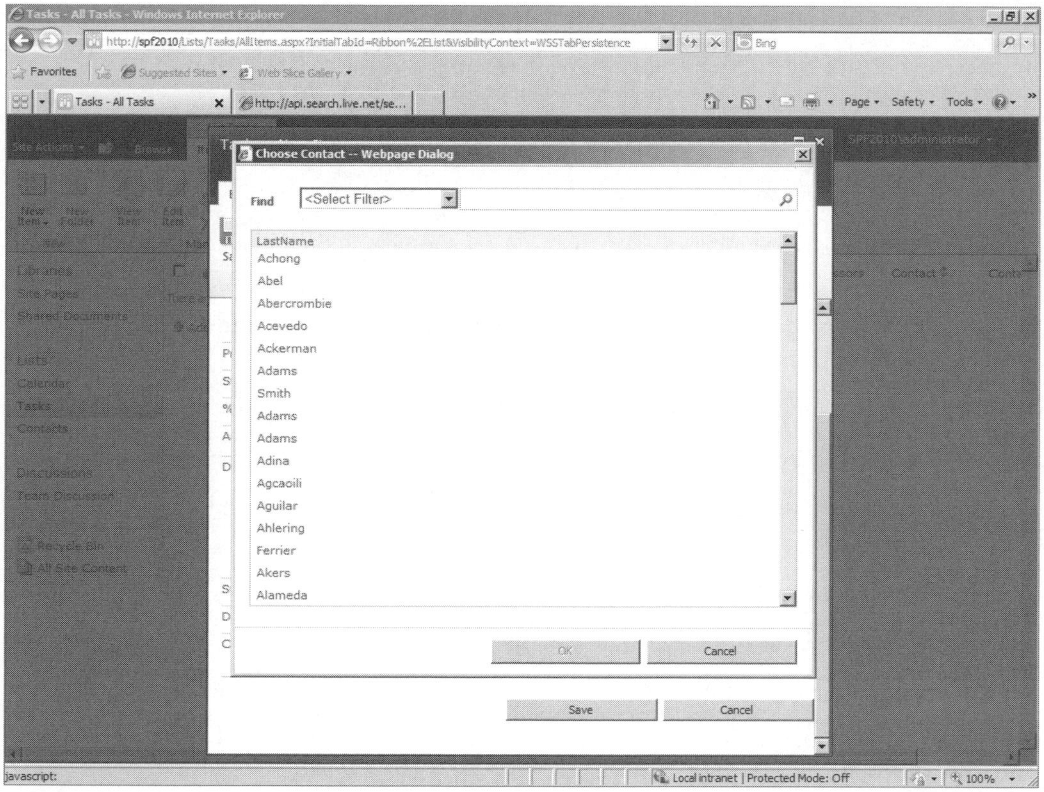

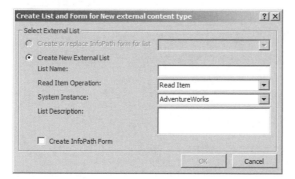

FIGURE 7-19

FIGURE 7-20

To finish creating your external list, enter a unique name for List Name and click the OK button. After the list is created, you can click Lists and Libraries in the navigation bar and see your list in the External Lists section. If you select the list, you can click the Preview in Browser button on the ribbon to see your list in action.

TRY IT OUT   Create an External Content Type for a Database Table

In this activity, you create an external content type that represents the Contact table in the AdventureWorks database.

1.   Open SharePoint Designer from your Start menu.

2.   Click the Open Site button.

3.   When the Open Site dialog appears, enter the URL to your site in the Site name textbox and click the OK button.

4.   If a Windows Security dialog appears, enter your username and password for the SharePoint site and click the OK button.

5.   After the site opens, choose External Content Types from the navigation bar on the left.

6.   Click the External Content Type button from the ribbon.

7.   Enter **Contact** as the value for the Name and Display Name fields. Click the hyperlink beside the field to edit it.

8.   Choose Contact from the Office Item Type dropdown list.

9.   Click the Operations Design View button from the ribbon.

10.   Click the Add Connection button.

11.   In the External Data Source Type Selection dialog (Figure 7-14), choose SQL Server from the Data Source Type dropdown list and click OK.

12.   In the SQL Server Connection dialog (Figure 7-15), enter the name of the server you used to install the AdventureWorks databases in the Set Up Databases activity (previous in the chapter) in the Database Server textbox.

13.   Enter **AdventureWorks** for Database Name and Name, and click OK.

14.   In the Data Source Explorer tab, expand the AdventureWorks tree node and the Tables tree node.

15.   Right-click the Contact table, and choose Create All Operations.

16.   In the All operations dialog (Figure 7-21), click the Next button.

17.   Notice the messages in the Errors and Warnings textbox (Figure 7-22). The next few steps will resolve these messages.

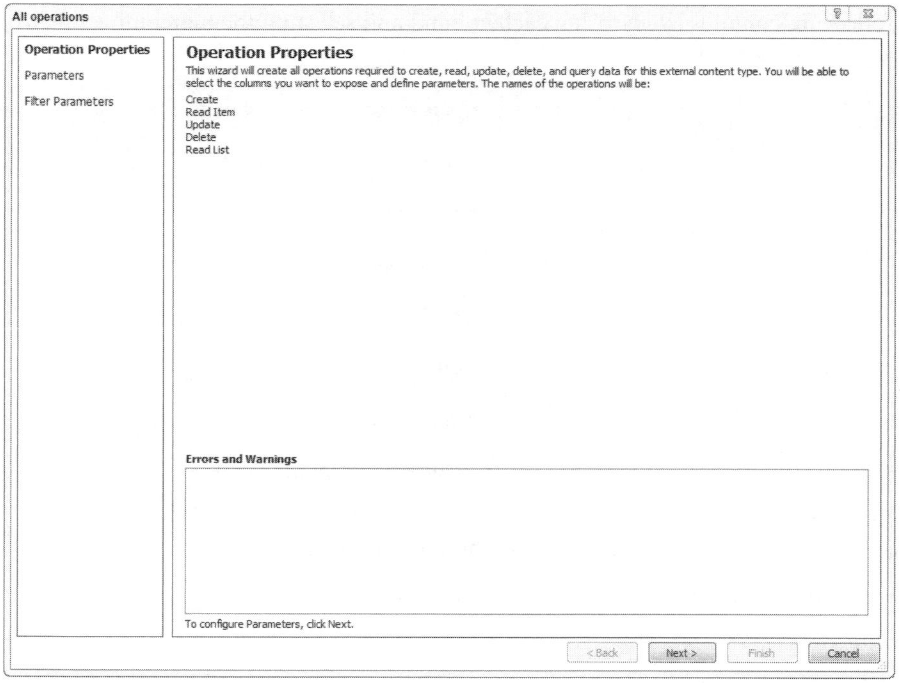

FIGURE 7-21

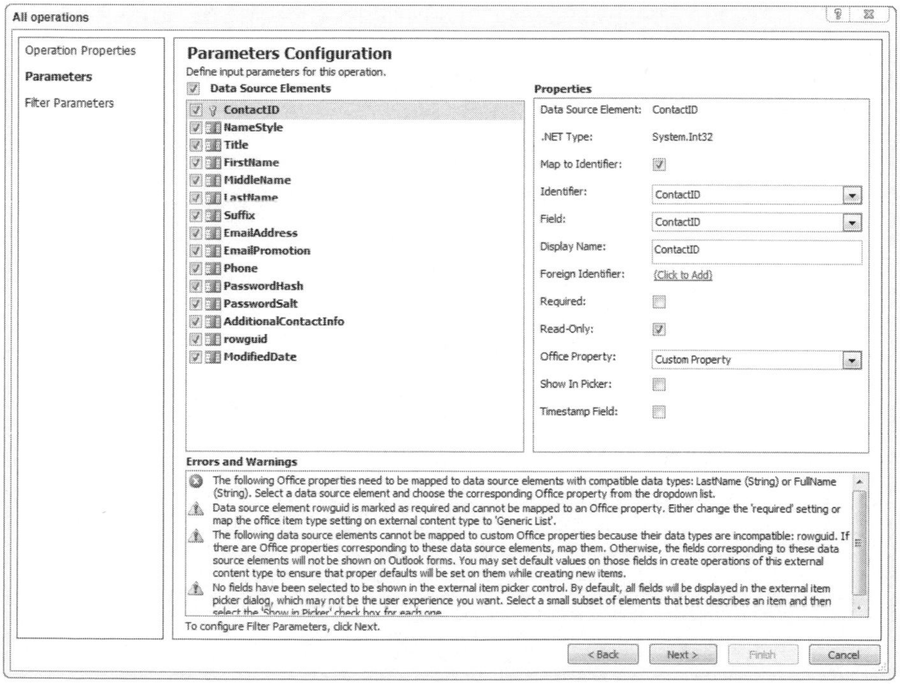

FIGURE 7-22

18. Configure the following columns by choosing each column and selecting the matching value from the Office Property drop down list:

COLUMN	OFFICE PROPERTY
Title	Job Title
FirstName	First Name
MiddleName	Middle Name
LastName	Last Name
Suffix	Suffix
EmailAddress	Email 1 Address
Phone	Business Telephone Number

19. Choose the LastName column, and select the check box for Show in Picker.

20. Choose the rowguid column, and unselect the check box for Required.

21. Click the Next button.

22. Click the Add Filter Parameter button (Figure 7-23).

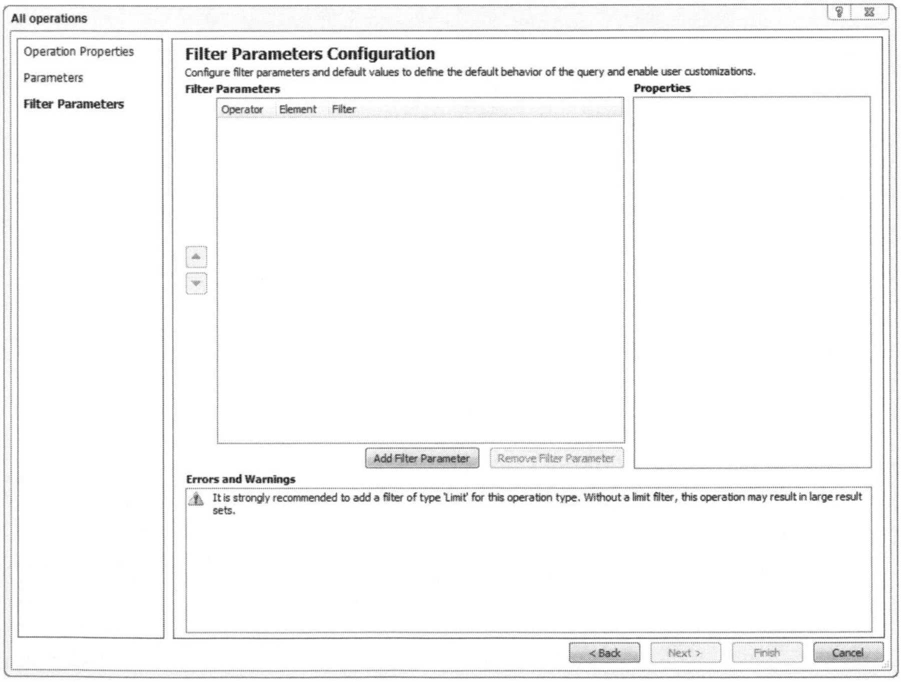

FIGURE 7-23

23. Click the "Click to Add" hyperlink next to the Filter property.

24. Select Limit from the Filter Type dropdown list and click the OK button.

25. Enter **100** in the Default Value drop-down list.

26. Click the Finish button.

27. Click the Save button in the Quick Access Toolbar.

How It Works

Choosing Contact as the parent content type allows you to map its SharePoint fields to the Contact table from the AdventureWorks database. Creating all operations on that table will allow it to function fully as a list in SharePoint with the ability to create, read, update, and delete items using the built-in forms or your custom forms. Selecting the LastName column as one of the fields to show in the picker dialog will have that column displayed when a user creates or edits an item in an external list with this content type.

TRY IT OUT **Create a List Based on an External Content Type**

In this activity, you create a list that uses the Contacts external content type you created in the previous exercise.

1. Open SharePoint Designer from your Start menu.

2. Click the Open Site button.

3. When the Open Site dialog appears, enter the URL to your site in the Site name textbox and click the OK button.

4. If a Windows Security dialog appears, enter your username and password for the SharePoint site and click the OK button.

5. After the site opens, choose External Content Types from the navigation bar on the left.

6. Click the Contact external content type to open it.

7. Click the Create Lists & Forms button on the ribbon.

8. In the Create List and Form for Contact dialog, enter **Contacts** in the List Name textbox and click the OK button.

9. After the list has been created, it appears under the External Lists section of the external content type page. Click the Contacts list and click the Go to List button on the ribbon.

10. When the Contacts list opens, click the Preview in Browser button to see the list in action.

11. After the browser navigates to the list, you may get the following error: "Access denied by Business Data Connectivity." You can resolve this error by following the steps in the next Try It Out.

12. Leave the browser open while you complete the next activity.

How It Works

The external list that you created acts just like a normal list, except that it reads and stores its data in the external AdventureWorks database rather than in the site's content database. You can treat external lists just like normal lists, including the ability to take the data offline to a laptop, update it, and synchronize it when you reconnect the laptop to the network.

TRY IT OUT   Set Permissions on an External Content Type

In this activity, you change the permissions on an external content type.

1. From the Start menu of your SharePoint server, choose All Programs ➤ Microsoft SharePoint 2010 Products ➤ SharePoint 2010 Central Administration.

2. Under the Application Management section, click the Manage service applications hyperlink.

3. When the page loads, click the Business Data Connectivity Service hyperlink that appears next to the Business Data Connectivity Service Application Proxy type.

4. After the View External Content Types page loads, right-click the Contact external content type and choose Set Permissions.

5. Click the Address Book icon and choose All Users from the dialog.

6. Choose All Authenticated Users and click the Add button.

7. Click the OK button to confirm your selection and close the dialog.

8. Click the Add button in the Set Object Permissions dialog.

9. Select the Edit, Execute, Selectable In Clients and Set Permissions checkboxes and click the OK button.

10. Close SharePoint Central Administration and return to the browser you left open in step 12 of the preceding Try It Out.

11. Press F5 to refresh the page; the rows from the database table appear.

How It Works

By default, users will not have access to your external content type. By granting the All Authentication Users group access, all users who are authenticated using *Windows Authentication* or *Forms-Based Authentication* will be able to use the external content type when it is added to an external list.

JOINING YOUR DISPARATE DATA

Previously in the chapter, you saw how you can configure SharePoint to access your lists, libraries, databases, and web services. One powerful way to use these data sources is to join them using a *linked data source*. A linked data source enables you to define a relationship between two or more existing data sources and present them as a single unit.

To create a linked data source, click the Linked Data Source button on the ribbon. When the Data Source Properties dialog appears (see Figure 7-24), click the Configure Linked Source button to display the Linked Data Sources Wizard dialog shown in Figure 7-25.

FIGURE 7-24

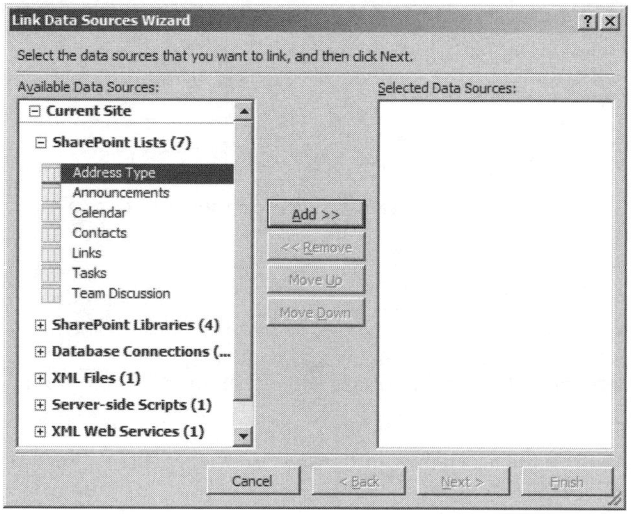

FIGURE 7-25

In the Linked Data Sources Wizard dialog, the list of data sources in your site appears in the Available Data Sources list box on the left. Select the data sources you want to join, and click the Add button to add them to the Selected Data Sources on the right. After you have selected your data sources, you can use the Move Up and Move Down buttons to order them appropriately. The order of the data sources is important when you want to display the linked data source in a hierarchical fashion. When you are finished, click the Next button to continue to the next step in the wizard.

Figure 7-26 displays the two options for relating the data sources you chose in the previous step. If you want to merge the data sources, choose the first option. Merging the data sources is similar to using the UNION clause in a SQL statement. If you want to join the data sources, choose the second option. Joining the data sources is useful for displaying the data in a hierarchical fashion. After you make your selection, click the Finish button to return to the Data Source Properties dialog.

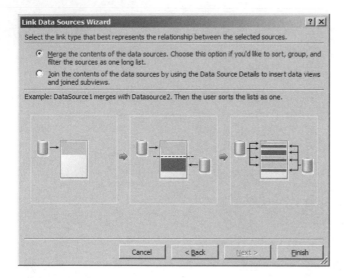

FIGURE 7-26

TRY IT OUT Create a Linked Data Source

In this activity, you create a linked data source by joining the database connections and external content types created in previous Try It Outs.

1. Open SharePoint Designer from your Start menu.

2. Click the Open Site button.

3. When the Open Site dialog appears, enter the URL to your site in the Site name textbox and click the OK button.

4. If a Windows Security dialog appears, enter your username and password for the SharePoint site and click the OK button.

5. After the site opens, choose Data Sources from the navigation bar on the left.

6. Using the Create a Data Source for a Database Table activity previous in the chapter, create Create Database Connection data sources for the Product, ProductSubCategory and ProductCategory tables in the AdventureWorks database.

7. Click the Linked Data Source button from the ribbon.

8. When the Data Source Properties dialog appears, click the General tab and enter **All Products** in the Name textbox.

9. Click the Source tab and click the Configure Linked Source button (Figure 7-24).

10. In Figure 7-25, choose each of the following data sources from the Available Data Sources list box and click the Add button:

TYPE	NAME
Database Connection	Product
Database Connection	ProductSubCategory
Database Connection	ProductCategory

11. Click the Next button.

12. In Figure 7-26, choose the Join the contents radio button and click the Finish button.

13. Click the OK button to save the data source.

How It Works

When you save the linked data source, SharePoint Designer stores the definitions of the component data sources inside it. When you add the linked data source to a web page, the data sources and their columns appear in the Data Source Details pane. You can add these data sources in a hierarchical fashion to display the grandparent, parent, and child relationships among the data sources.

SUMMARY

This chapter explored the many methods you can use to access data outside SharePoint, including:

➤ How to connect to data sources including databases and web services

➤ How to create external content types and external lists that represent external data sources

➤ How to grant permissions on external content types

➤ How to join data sources into a linked data source

The next chapter shows how to add these data sources to your web pages and format the way the data is displayed.

8

XSLT Data Views and Forms

WHAT YOU WILL LEARN IN THIS CHAPTER

➤ How to best utilize the XSLT web parts

➤ Creating powerful data views using the XSLT web parts

➤ Creating custom forms using the XSLT form web parts

➤ Making use of custom actions to execute list forms

SharePoint 2010 is fast becoming the preferred front-end application for many companies. The need for representation of all sorts of data — from both inside and outside of SharePoint — is paramount. The main method that SharePoint uses to expose data is with the use of web parts. The two main categories of web parts are:

➤ Those that are created programmatically (either those with which SharePoint ships or those that developers create)

➤ Those that use XSLT to display data

This chapter focuses on the XSLT web parts, discussing and demonstrating how these web parts have been considered the Swiss army knife of all web parts because of the variety of possibilities they offer to expose and style data from disparate sources.

TWO TYPES OF WEB PARTS TO WORK WITH DATA

One of the most common things that site administrators want to do is display data on SharePoint pages. The data can be from a variety of sources, including SharePoint lists and libraries, XML files, databases, web services, or more. The two main web parts that you can deploy to show data are

➤   XSLT List View Web Part

➤   XSLT Data Form Web Part

Both can be deployed using SharePoint Designer 2010 (SPD 2010). After they are deployed, you can configure them further using SPD 2010 or the browser.

XSLT List View Web Part

The list view web parts are used by SharePoint inherently to show list and library data. When a new list is created, the web part for the list is also created automatically and made available for use on the site. List view web parts can show one view at a time from the list or library to which it is pointing. If you want to change how the information is displayed to the end users, you make those changes at the view level of the list or library. Then, you deploy that view encapsulated in the list view web part on the site. If you want to show more than one view of a list or library on the same page, just deploy a new list view web part pointing to the same list, then configure it to show a different view of the list. For example, you can add two instances of the Shared Documents library to the page and apply a view to the first that shows only documents created by Tim, and another view to the second that displays only those documents created by Irene. It's that easy!

After you insert them on the page, these web parts are easily customizable using the browser and contain properties similar to all other web parts that ship with SharePoint. Customizations such as changing the title, description, width and height, border around the web part, and a whole lot more can be made quickly and easily using the browser.

A Little Bit of History

List view web parts (LVWP) have been around since Windows SharePoint Services v2 (released in 2003). They are written in a language called Collaborative Application Markup Language (CAML). CAML is an XML-based markup language that's used prevalently throughout SharePoint products and technologies to define and display data on web pages. It is a very powerful language yet very difficult to work with directly. You can find more information about CAML at `http://en.wikipedia.org/wiki/Collaborative_Application_Markup_Language`.

The use of this language in this web part has limited its extensibility opportunity through SharePoint Designer 2007 to a minimum. The main restrictions it imposes are the following:

➤   **Changing the data points at a granular level** — When your data is displayed in this web part, you can only change its formatting at the entire web part level and not at the column level. For example, you are unable to change a column that displays a Date to another format (February 21, 1977 instead of 2/21/1977).

➤   **Styling the web part** — This is very difficult because the web part uses the Microsoft proprietary CAML language, which is difficult to work with and does not rely on industry standards.

SharePoint Designer 2007 offers a way to convert these web parts to an XSLT Data View web part (covered later in the chapter), which provides a much more robust set of options for customizations. However, after you have converted this web part to a data view, you lose the option to further customize this web part through the browser (unless you want to get your hands dirty directly coding in XSL — not a good proposition for most people). Essentially you find yourself stuck between a rock and a hard place when trying to customize the display of your data.

What's New in SharePoint 2010

The list view web part has now been retired. A brand-new web part, called XSLT List View Web Part (XLV), takes its place in SharePoint 2010.

You deploy the XLV web part on any SharePoint page by using either the browser or SPD 2010. Adding it using the browser is as simple as using the ribbon on the page to point to and insert the web part on the page, as shown in Figure 8-1.

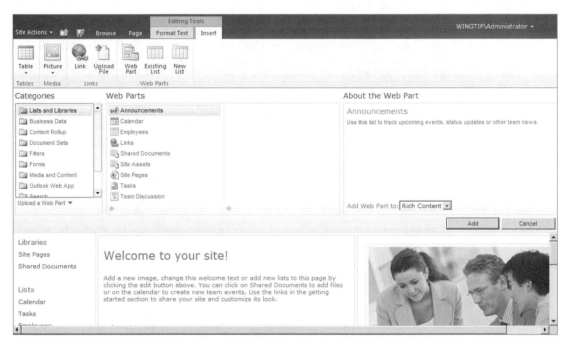

FIGURE 8-1

This web part works very much like the XSLT Data View web part. It first queries the list or library data and retrieves it as XML. Then it uses industry-standard eXtensible Stylesheet Language Transformation (XSLT), which is a style sheet language for XML documents, to convert the XML data into HTML that the browser can understand and display to the end user. The best part of this whole process is that you don't have to dive in and edit raw XML or XSL. Instead, SharePoint Designer 2010 provides you a great WYSIWYG (What You See Is What You Get) experience for editing the XSLT views. Furthermore, it gives you live data preview so you know exactly how your data will look to the end user viewing it in the browser.

XLV uses shared XSLT style sheets that reside in the `_layouts` directory on the server. Every standard list view on the entire server uses the same set of shared XSLT templates. An XLV uses one template to format each field (or column), one template to format the row, and one template to format the table. When you customize the appearance of an XLV, you generate overriding XSL templates only for the specific templates that you modify. For example, if you highlight a field, you generate XSLT that overrides just the shared template for that specific field.

Although working with this web part in the browser is good, working with it through SPD 2010 takes it to another level. Because SPD 2010 is an application that's running on your client computer, you can perform actions on SharePoint a lot faster and don't have to live with inherent browser limitations or server postback delays. SPD 2010 gives you the power you need to customize the data and the look and feel of this web part. Later in this chapter, you use the XSLT List View web part when customizing SharePoint list views.

XSLT Data Form Web Part

The XSLT Data Form Web Part (DFWP) came into existence with SharePoint Designer 2007 (SPD 2007). This web part is not available through the Web Part Gallery and thus cannot be added using the browser. The birth of this web part's true parent predates SPD 2007. The true beginning of this magnificent web part was with FrontPage 2003 when it was called the XSLT Data View Web Part (DVWP). Granted, FrontPage was not very popular with many developers in those days, but one good thing that came out of that product was the ability to get to data from disparate sources using the XSLT Data View Web Part, the parent of both XSLT Data Form Web Part and the XSLT List View Web Part. This web part was way ahead of its time, providing developers and non-developers alike a quick and easy way to pull their data from a variety of sources such as databases, XML files, server-side scripts, web services, and SharePoint lists and libraries. After the data was retrieved, you could style that data, conditionally format it, manage groupings of metadata, and a whole lot more to present it in the best way possible to your users.

When the XSLT Data Form Web Part was introduced in SharePoint Designer 2007, it had kept all the functionality of the XSLT Data View Web Part in addition to now having the facility to write back to the data source, leading to the introduction of the word *Form* in the name instead of *View*. That said, the words *Data View* are still used in a few places within SharePoint to refer to *Data Form*. You will see evidence of this usage later in this chapter.

In SharePoint 2010, the DFWP appears in a variety of places. Whenever SPD 2010 is used to display data on a page from anywhere outside of SharePoint (XML files, databases, web services), the DFWP is the one that displays that data. Figure 8-2 shows a couple of DFWPs deployed on the page. The top web part shows data from a database table while the bottom one shows data retrieved from a query to a web service.

As you may recall from the previous section, the XLV is the web part that is primarily used to display list or library data. However, this web part is unable to allow form functionality, which would let the user manipulate the list data. This is where the DFWP comes into the picture. The DFWP is utilized when a form capability is required for a SharePoint list or library. For example, if you insert an edit item form for the Announcements list on a site page by clicking on the Insert tab and then clicking the Edit Item Form button (see Figure 8-3) on the ribbon and selecting Announcements, SPD 2010 automatically displays the form in a DFWP as shown in Figure 8-4.

WebPartPages:DataFormWebPart				
Contact on AdventureWorks				
ContactID	NameStyle	FirstName	Title	MiddleName
1	No	Gustavo	Mr.	
2	No	Catherine	Ms.	R.
3	No	Kim	Ms.	td.ms-vb
4	No	Humberto	Sr.	
5	No	Pilar	Sra.	
6	No	Frances	Ms.	B.
7	No	Margaret	Ms.	J.
8	No	Carla	Ms.	J.
9	No	Jay	Mr.	
10	No	Ronald	Mr.	L.

1 - 10 ▶

Lists on intranet.spel.com	
Title	Description
Announcements	Use this list to track upcoming events, status updates or other team news.
Calendar	Use the Calendar list to keep informed of upcoming meetings, deadlines, and other important events.
Content type publishing error log	This list stores content type publishing error information for this site.
Converted Forms	List of user browser-enabled form templates on this site collection.
Customized Reports	This Document library has the templates to create Web Analytics custom reports for this site collection
Form Templates	This library contains administrator-approved form templates that were activated to

FIGURE 8-2

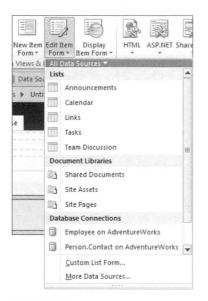

FIGURE 8-3

The DFWP showing the announcement list is now "live" and ready to accept any changes you want to make to the announcement list items. Later in the chapter, you will get a chance to try out this functionality by inserting the edit form for a list on a site page.

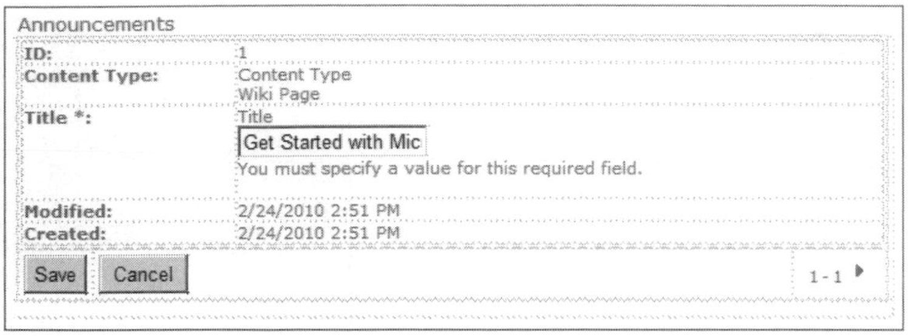

FIGURE 8-4

The DFWP is a great solution for several situations, but it does come with a cost. Unlike XLV, after you deploy the DFWP to the SharePoint page, you can visually enhance it further only using SPD 2010. If you try to edit this web part in the browser, you are presented with the option to dive into the XSL editor and make your changes manually as shown in Figure 8-5.

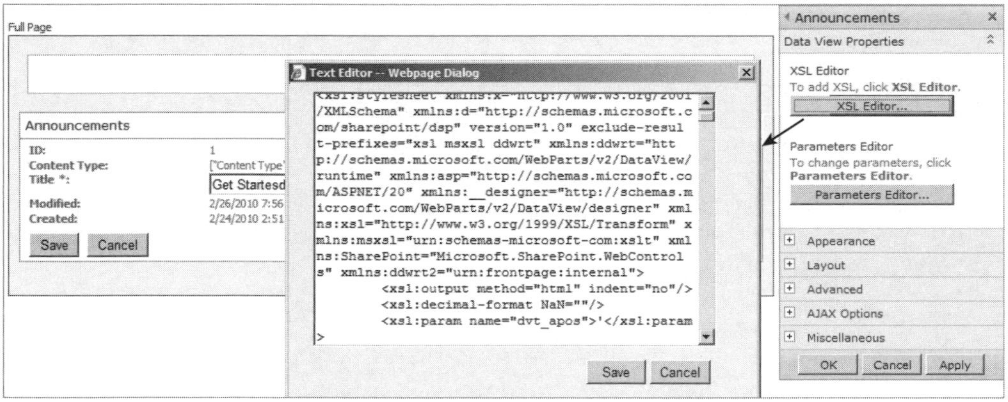

FIGURE 8-5

The following table shows a comparison of features between DFWP and XLV web parts.

FEATURE	XSLT DATA FORM	XSLT LIST VIEW
Render lists	X	X
Render items	X	X
Aggregate data	X	X
Render external data	X	X*
Browser editing		X
SPD editing	X	X
Conditional formatting, high customizability	X	X

* Through a connection to Business Connectivity Services (covered in Chapter 7)

MANAGING VIEWS OF DATA

This section is dedicated to showing how you can manage the information that's displayed for any type of data on a SharePoint page, whether the information is coming from inside or outside of SharePoint.

When you place a view of data on a page, SPD 2010 automatically determines which web part is needed to display that data and takes care of it for you. For views of SharePoint lists and libraries, the XLV is deployed. When you put this web part in context by clicking on it, the contextually sensitive ribbon shows the List View Tools, as shown in Figure 8-6.

FIGURE 8-6

When you place data from external sources, such as databases or web services, on a page, it is displayed with a DFWP. The customization options for DFWP appear in the Data View Tools section of the ribbon (see Figure 8-7) when that web part is in context.

FIGURE 8-7

Both List View Tools and Data View Tools are very similar in nature. Both menus have four tabs: Options, Design, Web Part, and Table. Each of these tabs contains a variety of functionality that you can choose from. They surface up the options that are available to be executed on the type of data that currently is in focus. The remainder of this section explores many of these features to show you the possibilities available for displaying your data.

Custom Views of Lists and Libraries

Creating a new view for a list is as simple as navigating to that list's summary page in SPD 2010 and then clicking on the New button in the Views section. You can then define the name for the view and designate it as a default view if you want. Chapter 6 discusses and demonstrates this procedure. Building on that knowledge, you will now see the options available for customizing the XLV within this view further.

TRY IT OUT Work with List Metadata

In this exercise, you work on an XLV for a view. You first adjust the columns of data as necessary. Then you configure sorting and grouping options on the data. For this exercise and the next, you need the sample data in the Employee.xlsx file (provided as a resource for this book on Wiley's site) The first few steps guide you to setup a list called Employees using that data.

1. Using the browser, go to Site Actions ➪ More Options ➪ Import Spreadsheet. Click the Create button in the task pane on the right.

2. Another screen, titled New, should appear. Enter **Employees** in the Name field. Use the Browse button to browse to and select the Employees.xlsx file on your computer. Then click the Import button on the page.

3. The Excel icon should appear in your taskbar. Click on it. You should see the Excel application and a dialog box titled Import to Windows SharePoint Services list. Click the drop-down list for Select Range and select the only choice that should be present (Employee!Table1). Then click the Import button in the dialog. The Employees list should now appear in the browser.

4. Open up SharePoint Designer 2010. Open the site with the Employees list in SPD. Click on Lists and Libraries in the navigation pane and then click the Employees list to bring up the summary page for the Employees list.

5. Create a new view page for the Employees list by clicking on the New button in the Views section. Name the new view Employees. You should now see that view open up in SPD as shown in Figure 8-8.

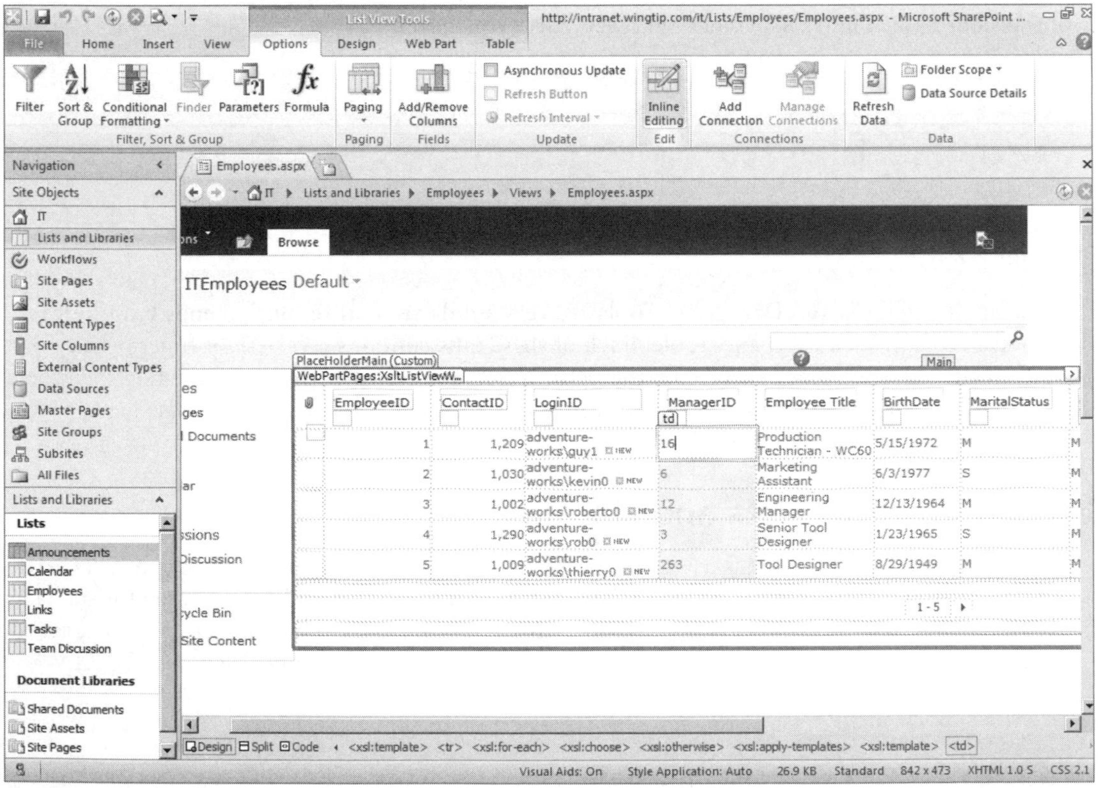

FIGURE 8-8

6. Click anywhere within the Employees list of data in the view. Doing that shows up the List View Tools menu in the ribbon. From the Options tab of List View Tools, click on Add/Remove Columns. Then from the Displayed Fields dialog that appears, remove the following columns: Attachments, SalariedFlag, VacationHours, and SickLeaveHours, then click OK.

7. Change the pagination of the records: Click the Paging button on the same tab and click on the option to Display Sets of 10 Items.

8. To group and sort the data, click on the Sort & Group button. In the Sort and Group dialog that appears, add the following fields to the Sort order pane: ManagerID, MaritalStatus, and HireDate.

9. Select the ManagerID field in the Sort order pane and choose to Show group header. Also, select the Collapse group by default option. Repeat the same procedure for the MaritalStatus field, and click OK.

10. Save all your changes to the view page and navigate to it in the browser. It should look similar to the one in Figure 8-9.

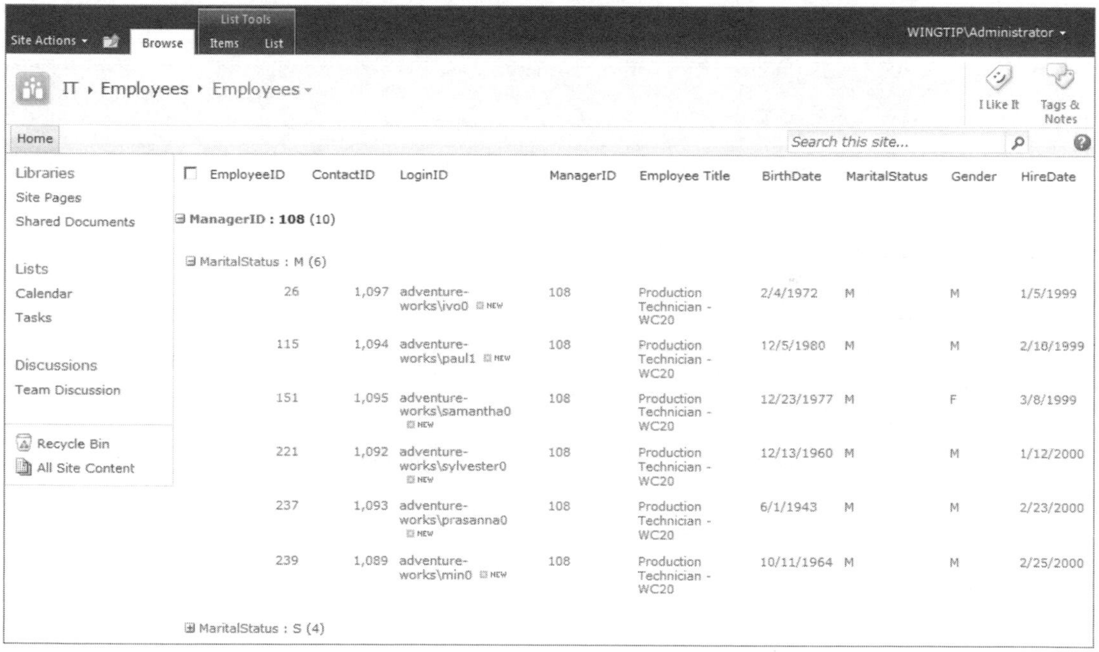

FIGURE 8-9

How It Works

The options on the List View Tools menu let you change the presentation of the underlying data. In the exercise above, you cleaned up the list view by removing the unnecessary fields, changing the amount of records that should be shown at one time and configuring the sort and order options as needed.

When you are looking at a list view in the browser, the ribbon provides access to all the actions that you would need to act upon the list or its list items. SharePoint 2007 had a toolbar that appeared on top of the list that provided these options. This toolbar is still available and can be turned on for a list using SPD 2010. The Design tab of List View Tools has a button labeled Options. Clicking on it presents a drop-down with two choices: Full Toolbar and Summary Toolbar. Turning on the full toolbar here makes it available on top of the list right below the ribbon.

Aside from the ribbon and the toolbar, another option for letting users access an item for editing is a new feature called *inline editing*. In SPD 2010, you can turn on this functionality for a list view by toggling the Inline Editing button on the Options tab. Using the browser, users can then click on the edit icon that appears when they hover the cursor over the item in the list and edit the list item data directly inline. Figure 8-10 shows the before and after pictures of the effects of turning on both inline editing and the toolbar.

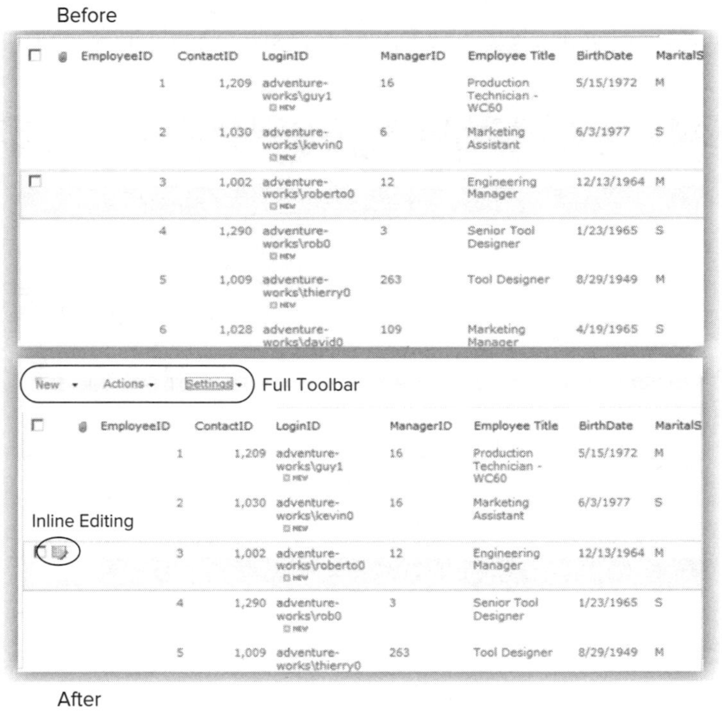

FIGURE 8-10

Another feature to discuss is formatting your data based on predefined criteria. If you have not had the need to do this already, chances are that you will in the future. Consider this example: You are showing company revenue on a list. Some regions in the company are doing poorly whereas others have exceeded their goals. How do you visually draw attention to both types of results? You might want to pinpoint the regions of the company that are doing poorly by showing them in red and the regions that are doing great financially in green. You can make this type of visual enhancement of data fairly easily using the conditional formatting options in SPD 2010. The following exercise demonstrates this functionality.

TRY IT OUT Configure Conditional Formatting on a List

This exercise uses conditional formatting techniques to highlight data matching certain criteria. In addition, it also shows how you can hide data based on predefined conditions. The data used in the list in this example, Employees, is the same list that was utilized in the first exercise.

1. Using SharePoint Designer 2010, create a new view page for the Employee list.

2. To format the whole row based on a criteria, click anywhere within the web part and from the Options tab, click Conditional Formatting ⇨ Format Row.

3. In the Condition Criteria dialog that appears, set the following condition and then click on Set Style.

FIELD NAME	COMPARISON	VALUE	AND/OR
MaritalStatus	Equals	M	And

Note: For the Value field, you have to type in the value *M* directly within the field.

4. In the Modify Style dialog that appears, click on the Background category and select any light color in the Background-color field. After you click OK on this dialog, you will see that all the rows with MaritalStatus M now have a background color applied to them.

5. Now, conditionally hide data based on the BirthDate column. Highlight one of the rows (any row is fine) in the web part, and then click on Conditional Formatting ⇨ Hide Content.

6. In the Condition Criteria dialog that appears, set the following conditions and then click on OK.

FIELD NAME	COMPARISON	VALUE	AND/OR
BirthDate	Greater Than	1/1/1960	And
BirthDate	Less Than	1/1/1970	And

Note: For the Value field, click on the Choose a date option from the drop down menu and then type in the specific dates listed in the preceding table.

7. Save all your changes to the view page and navigate to it in the browser. It should look similar to the one in Figure 8-11. You should not see any records with the BirthDate between 1/1/1960 and 1/1/1970.

FIGURE 8-11

How It Works

Conditional formatting is implemented in XSL using conditional logic, just as a programmer would define it in code. When a condition criterion is defined by a user, the underlying XSL code reacts by creating a new "test" condition. If the condition resolves true then it performs the styling defined by the user. For example, the test for determining whether the MaritalStatus field is equal to M is the following:

```
<xsl:if test=normalize-space($thisNode/@MaritalStatus) = 'M'"
```

Another feature to mention here that deals with the look and feel of your data is the availability of several predefined styles in the Design tab. All the available styles are prepackaged XSL transformations that can be applied to the data with the click of a button, transforming it to display in a variety of ways. Aside from the traditional tabular views of the list data, it can also be represented in a Boxed view, as shown in Figure 8-12 for the Employee list data.

You can manipulate the views of data in libraries exactly like the lists as shown in the preceding exercises. A feature in the library that is used quite often is the arrangement of files in folders. Many people starting out with SharePoint libraries prefer the use of folders to organize their documents just like they have done in the past within their file shares. On the other hand, some people (and also many SharePoint experts) frown upon the use of folders. They argue that the proper use of metadata (columns) in the lists should eliminate the need for using folders for file organization. Also, folders create a nested hierarchy that becomes painful to traverse when looking for documents.

To the rescue comes the Folder Scope feature available in the List View Tools. This feature allows designing a variety of views of files with or without folders. Figure 8-13 shows the four options available for folder scopes.

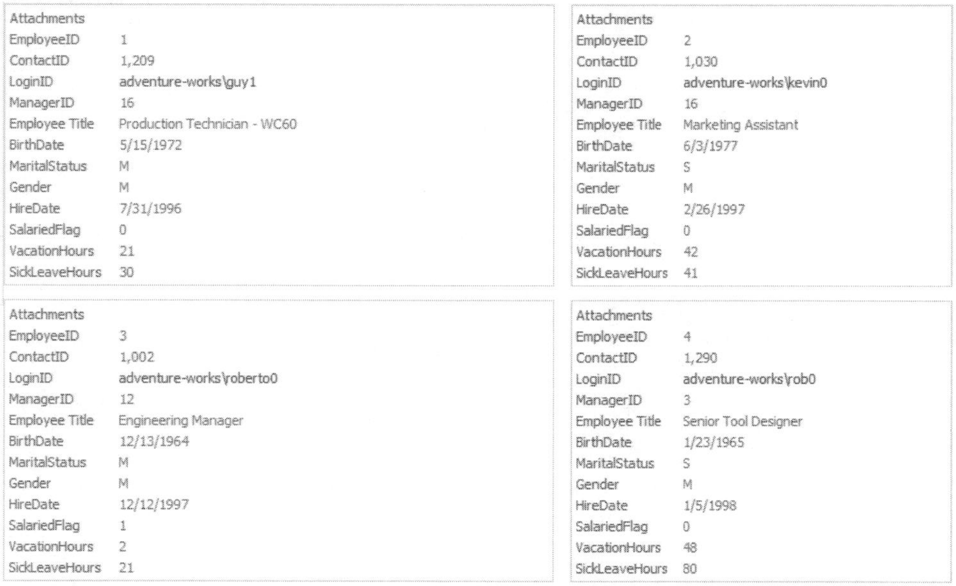
Attachments
EmployeeID 1
ContactID 1,209
LoginID adventure-works\guy1
ManagerID 16
Employee Title Production Technician - WC60
BirthDate 5/15/1972
MaritalStatus M
Gender M
HireDate 7/31/1996
SalariedFlag 0
VacationHours 21
SickLeaveHours 30
Attachments
EmployeeID 2
ContactID 1,030
LoginID adventure-works\kevin0
ManagerID 16
Employee Title Marketing Assistant
BirthDate 6/3/1977
MaritalStatus S
Gender M
HireDate 2/26/1997
SalariedFlag 0
VacationHours 42
SickLeaveHours 41
Attachments
EmployeeID 3
ContactID 1,002
LoginID adventure-works\roberto0
ManagerID 12
Employee Title Engineering Manager
BirthDate 12/13/1964
MaritalStatus M
Gender M
HireDate 12/12/1997
SalariedFlag 1
VacationHours 2
SickLeaveHours 21
Attachments
EmployeeID 4
ContactID 1,290
LoginID adventure-works\rob0
ManagerID 3
Employee Title Senior Tool Designer
BirthDate 1/23/1965
MaritalStatus S
Gender M
HireDate 1/5/1998
SalariedFlag 0
VacationHours 48
SickLeaveHours 80

FIGURE 8-12

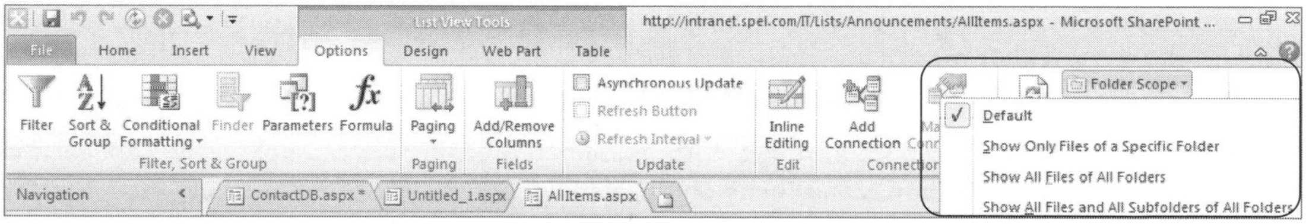
List View Tools
http://intranet.spel.com/IT/Lists/Announcements/AllItems.aspx - Microsoft SharePoint ...
File
Home
Insert
View
Options
Design
Web Part
Table
Filter
Sort & Group
Conditional Formatting
Finder
Parameters
Formula
Paging
Add/Remove Columns
Asynchronous Update
Refresh Button
Refresh Interval
Inline Editing
Add Connection
Filter, Sort & Group
Paging
Fields
Update
Edit
Folder Scope
Default
Show Only Files of a Specific Folder
Show All Files of All Folders
Show All Files and All Subfolders of All Folders
Navigation
ContactDB.aspx
Untitled_1.aspx
AllItems.aspx

FIGURE 8-13

Consider the following file structure in a library:

Shared Documents Library

Files in root — Project Specifications.docx, Training Request Form.xsn

Folder — Sales Docs

File in folder — AW Revenue.xlsx

Subfolder — Large Clients

File in subfolder — Pricing List.xlsx

Each of the folder scope settings, when applied to the view of this library, will produce different results. Figure 8-14 shows how the view of this library looks when each of the folder scopes is applied.

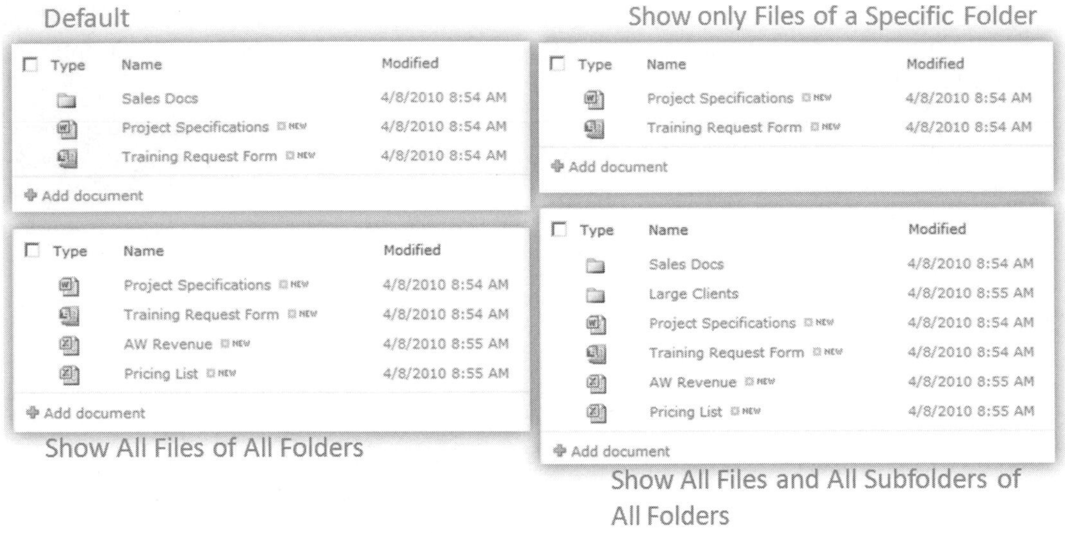

Default

	Type	Name		Modified
□	Type	Name		Modified
	📁	Sales Docs		4/8/2010 8:54 AM
	📄	Project Specifications ☐ NEW		4/8/2010 8:54 AM
	📄	Training Request Form ☐ NEW		4/8/2010 8:54 AM
✛ Add document				

Show only Files of a Specific Folder

	Type	Name		Modified
□	Type	Name		Modified
	📄	Project Specifications ☐ NEW		4/8/2010 8:54 AM
	📄	Training Request Form ☐ NEW		4/8/2010 8:54 AM
✛ Add document				

	Type	Name		Modified
□	Type	Name		Modified
	📄	Project Specifications ☐ NEW		4/8/2010 8:54 AM
	📄	Training Request Form ☐ NEW		4/8/2010 8:54 AM
	📄	AW Revenue ☐ NEW		4/8/2010 8:55 AM
	📄	Pricing List ☐ NEW		4/8/2010 8:55 AM
✛ Add document				

Show All Files of All Folders

	Type	Name		Modified
□	Type	Name		Modified
	📁	Sales Docs		4/8/2010 8:54 AM
	📁	Large Clients		4/8/2010 8:55 AM
	📄	Project Specifications ☐ NEW		4/8/2010 8:54 AM
	📄	Training Request Form ☐ NEW		4/8/2010 8:54 AM
	📄	AW Revenue ☐ NEW		4/8/2010 8:55 AM
	📄	Pricing List ☐ NEW		4/8/2010 8:55 AM
✛ Add document				

Show All Files and All Subfolders of
All Folders

FIGURE 8-14

Now that you have seen a variety of ways that list and library data can be modified, the next section discusses the manipulation of external data on SharePoint pages.

Custom Views to External Sources of Data

SPD 2010 can tap into many sources of data. Databases, XML files, RSS feeds, web services, and more are all possible content sources. Chapter 7 covers connecting to these data sources so there is no need to repeat that information here. The focus of this section is to explore the different possibilities of the display of that external data.

External data can be shown on any page within a SharePoint site; for example, a Wiki page, a web part page, or even list view pages. When you decide to deploy the data on the page, the XSLT Data Form Web Part gets deployed automatically to display the data.

TRY IT OUT   Display Database Data on SharePoint Pages and Customize It to Your Needs

In this exercise, you display and then customize data from a database table using various available options. The prerequisite for this exercise is to make a connection to the Employee table in the sample AdventureWorks database through the Data Source in the navigation pane (refer to Chapter 7 for making connections to databases). The connection is automatically named Employee on AW.

1.   In SharePoint Designer 2010, create a new web part page in the Site Pages library. You can do this by clicking on the Web Part Page button and selecting the desired web part page layout from the choices in the drop-down list. For this example, name this new page **EmployeeDB.aspx**.

2. Click on the `EmployeeDB.aspx` file to get to its summary page. Then click on Edit File under the Customization section to start editing the page.

3. Click inside one of the web part zones on the page and then from the Insert tab in the ribbon, click on Data View ➪ Employee on AW (You may need to scroll down the list of Data View selections to find this). You should now see the Employee data from the database and the Data View Tools appear in the ribbon.

4. Click on the Add/Remove Columns button in the Options tab and then using the Add and Remove buttons as needed, move the following fields to the Displayed Columns pane: EmployeeID, ContactID, BirthDate, SickLeaveHours, and VacationHours. Click OK and you should see only these fields appear now.

5. To make the headings of the table in the web part more readable, add spaces as necessary. For example, change EmployeeID to Employee ID.

6. Drag your mouse over to select the whole header row. From the Home tab in the ribbon, change the font to bold. Also, use the text highlight color button (right next to the font color button) to change the text highlight to a shade of gray color.

7. The ContactID currently has a comma (,) in the number. To get rid of it, click any one of the contact ID numbers and click on the small arrow that appears to the right (officially called a chevron). A pop-up should appear showing you that the Data Field is ContactID and the Format is Number.

8. Click on the Number formatting options link and deselect the checkbox for Use 1000 separator. Click OK and you should see that the comma is now gone.

9. The BirthDate field currently shows time as well as date. However, the time for every record is set to 12:00 AM because the time value is not stored in the database. To change the formatting, click on any one of the birth dates and then click the chevron.

10. In the pop-up that appears, click the DateTime formatting options link. Deselect the checkbox for Show Time. *Optional*: You can also pick a different formatting option for the date from the drop-down list box.

11. To configure conditional formatting on a field, select any one of the numbers in the Sick Leave Hours column. In the Options tab, click Conditional Formatting ➪ Format Selection.

12. In the Condition Criteria dialog that appears, set the following:

FIELD NAME	COMPARISON	AND/OR
SickLeaveHours	Less Than	And

For the Value field, select More Fields from the drop-down list. A More Fields dialog appears, showing all fields in the data source. Select VacationHours, click OK, and then click the Set Style button.

13. In the Modify Style dialog that appears, change the font weight to bold, font style to italic, and color to red. After you click OK on this dialog, you will see all the changes you have made to this web part, as shown in Figure 8-15

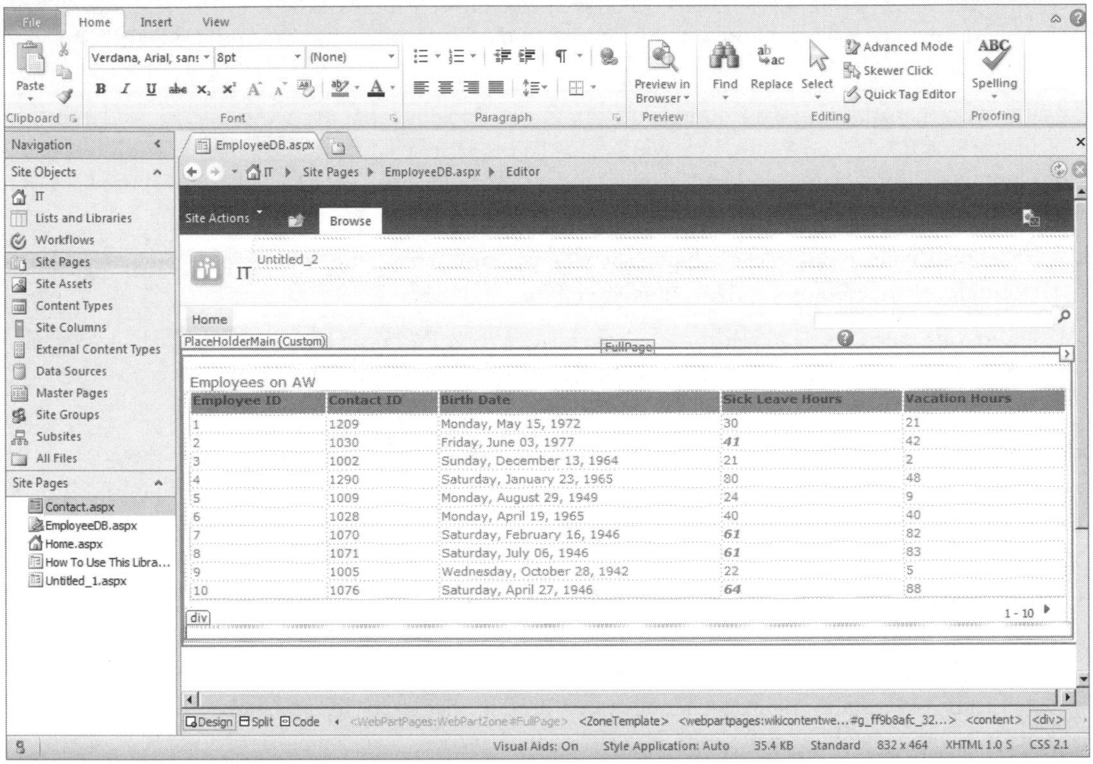

FIGURE 8-15

Because SharePoint Designer 2010 is a WYSIWYG environment, you will see the same data if you navigate to this page in the browser.

How It Works

Just like any other data source, database data can be fetched by a connection on a SharePoint site. The return data set is all XML, which you then manipulate using the Data View Tools menu.

During the XSLT transformation process, the DFWP uses an XSLT extension object that provides access to several functions. These functions help you transform your data at a very granular level. For example, one of the functions available is called FormatDate. You can use this function to change a date field to be represented in a variety of different formats (for example, July 27, 2004, 7/27/2004, and so on). These functions are accessible through the XPath editor window, which you can access by clicking on the Formula button in the ribbon.

> **NOTE** *The XSLT extension object referenced earlier provides the functions from the DDWRT namespace. This namespace is defined within SharePoint's main assembly (*`Microsoft.SharePoint.dll`*). When implemented within a DFWP, a function will look something like this:*
>
> ```
> <xsl:value-of select="ddwrt:FormatDate(string(@HireDate), 1033, 1)" />
> ```
>
> *The second parameter defines the language (1033 means U.S. English) and the last parameter in the function defines the format of the date. For example, 1 is equal to 2/16/2007 whereas 3 is equal to Friday, February 16, 2007.*

TRY IT OUT   Work with XPath Expressions

In this exercise, you work with the XPath expression builder to manipulate the presentation of external data in the DFWP. The prerequisite for this exercise is to first make a connection to the Contact table in the sample AdventureWorks database through the Data Source in the navigation pane (refer to Chapter 7 for making connections to databases). The connection is automatically named Contact on AW.

1. In SharePoint Designer 2010, create a new web part page in the Site Pages library. You can do this by clicking on the Web Part Page button and selecting the desired web part page layout from the choices in the drop-down list. For this example, name this new page **ContactDB.aspx**.

2. Click on the `ContactDB.aspx` file to get to its summary page. Then click on Edit File under the Customization section to start editing the page.

3. Click inside one of the web part zones on the page and then from the Insert tab in the ribbon, click on Data View ➪ Contact on AW. You should now see the Contact data from the database and the Data View Tools appear in the ribbon.

4. Click on the Add/Remove Columns button in the Options tab and using the Add and Remove buttons, move the following fields in the Displayed Columns pane: ContactID, FirstName, and EmailAddress. Click OK and you should see only these fields appear now.

5. Now click and select any of the values in the FirstName field. Then click the *fx* Formula button in the Options tab of the ribbon.

6. Within the Insert Formula dialog that appears, delete the @ FirstName value from the XPath expression area.

7. Using the drop-down menu for the function category, select Text/String, then double-click the `concat` function to have it appear in the XPath expression area.

8. When the `concat` function appears, it presents you with all the fields available in a drop-down menu. Double-click to select the @ Title field. Fill out the rest of the `concat` function to look as follows:

```
Concat(@Title,' ',@FirstName,' ',@MiddleName,' ',@LastName)
```

Figure 8-16 shows the completed XPath expression. The Preview pane in the figure shows how the expression will render.

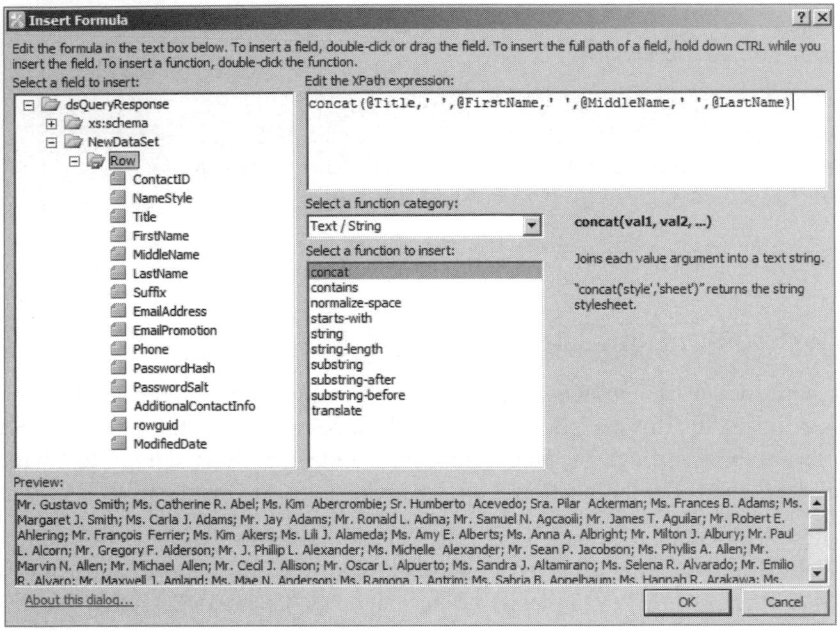

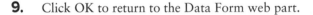

FIGURE 8-16

9. Click OK to return to the Data Form web part.

10. Change the FirstName heading to just **Name** because it now lists the whole name of the individual. To make other headings of the table in the web part more readable, add spaces as necessary. For example, change ContactID to Contact ID. Figure 8-17 shows the finished product.

Because SharePoint Designer 2010 is a WYSIWYG environment, you will see the same data if you navigate to this page in the browser.

How It Works

The xPath expression window used in the exercise above makes it very easy to work with and manipulate XML as needed without having to really get into code. The `concat` function used above works the same way as it would in the Microsoft Excel application. Data Form web parts inherently are synchronized with the data they display. If the data that it is displaying changes in the backend, the data in the web part will also change the next time you come back to that page. However, you can do even better than that. In SPD, the Update section within the Options tab provides the facility to set up asynchronous updates to the web part. This means that the Data Form web part can dynamically refresh its contents without requiring the browser to refresh the entire page. Simply clicking on the Asynchronous Update checkbox enables this functionality. After it is enabled, you need some sort of a way to execute the refresh to the web part. There are a couple of ways to make this happen. One options is that you can select the checkbox for Refresh Button, and it will render a button right above the web part that an end user can click to refresh the web part. Another option is to set an automatic refresh of the data by clicking on Refresh Interval and picking the appropriate option from the drop-down menu, as shown in Figure 8-18.

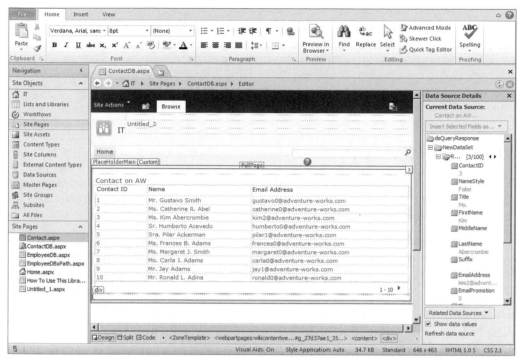

FIGURE 8-17

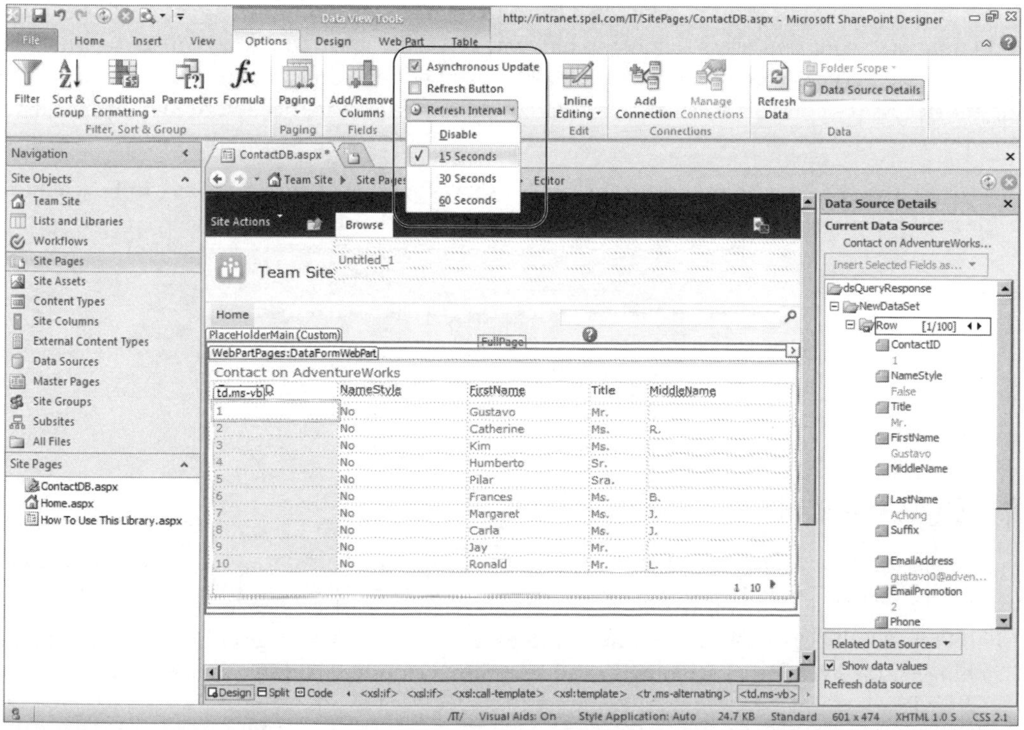

FIGURE 8-18

> **NOTE** *If you do choose to go with setting the refresh interval, your web part will automatically make a call to your backend data source at the specified interval. If you are retrieving a lot of data and have multiple connections set up in this manner, this option could potentially have a detrimental effect in your environment. Consider using this functionality sparingly.*

CREATING CUSTOM FORMS

A form is simply a way to present a customized display of data to users who can then write back to the data source. SharePoint Designer 2010 can create two types of forms: list forms and data forms. Both of them use the Data Form Web Part.

List forms are associated directly with a list. The basic forms that ship out of the box for most lists are used to display data, add new data, and edit existing data. Data forms serve the same purpose as list forms by providing forms to view, add, and edit data. However, these types of forms are hosted within a site page.

The subsequent sections discuss and show the process for creating data and list forms using SPD 2010.

Creating Data Forms

Data management in SharePoint lists can be done directly through the forms attached to the lists. However, at times you will want to provide a form to manage list data on a site page. For example, if you do not want your end users to have to navigate to the list page to manage its data, you can provide them a list form directly on a site page. The form will have a direct link to the list and can provide the necessary controls (such as textbox, checkbox, or button) needed to manage the list data.

The Insert tab lists the New Item, Edit Item, and Display Item Form buttons that can be used to create the desired form. Figure 8-19 shows the three buttons on the ribbon.

FIGURE 8-19

TRY IT OUT Create a Data Form

In this exercise, you create a data form for the Announcements list. This data form can then be used to add new announcements.

1. In SharePoint Designer 2010, create a new web part page in the Site Pages library. You can do this by clicking on the Web Part Page button and selecting the desired web part page layout from the

choices in the drop-down menu. For this example, name this new page **AddNewAnnouncements
.aspx**.

2. Click on the `AddNewAnnouncements.aspx` file to get to its summary page. Then click on Edit File
under the Customization section to start editing the page.

3. Click inside one of the web part zones on the page and then from the Insert tab in the ribbon, click
on New Item Form ⇨ Announcements. You should now see a new form appear, showing some of
the fields from the Announcements list. The Data View Tools menu also appears in the ribbon.

4. From the Options tab of Data View Tools, click on Add/Remove Columns. In the Edit Columns
dialog that appears, remove the following from Displayed Columns: Modified By and Modified.
Then add the Body column to the Displayed Columns pane. Click OK.

5. Click on the Body form field and then click on the arrow (chevron) that appears to the right to display the pop-up for Common FormField Tasks. Change the Format as field to Multiline Text Box,
as shown in Figure 8-20.

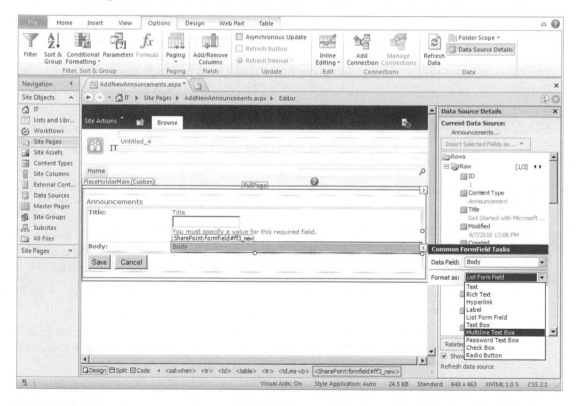

FIGURE 8-20

6. Save the page and navigate to it in the browser.

7. To test out the functionality, add some text in the Title and Body fields and then click the Save button. Now navigate to the Announcements list to look for the new announcement.

How It Works

You can use the DFWP to create a form for any list on the site. After the form is created, the rendering for each of the data points on the form can be changed as needed, as in the preceding exercise (where you changed the Body field from a label to a multiline text box). The Save and Cancel buttons are automatically created on the form to execute the commit and cancel form actions, respectively.

Creating List Forms

Every list and library in a site provides built-in forms to manage its metadata. You can discover these forms by going to the list/library summary page in SharePoint Designer. The forms appear in the Forms section of the page. These built-in forms use List Form Web Parts (LFWP) to display list data. LFWPs are built using CAML/ASP.NET rendering technology. The limitations for this web part are similar to the List View Web Part, which is discussed earlier in this chapter.

You can create new forms by clicking on the New button in the Forms section. When a new form is created, it does not use LFWP. Instead, it uses the DFWP to render list or library data. This is definitely good news because, as discussed earlier in this chapter, DFWP is a far more powerful web part that facilitates deep customization of data displayed within it. The following exercise walks you through creating a new item form that utilizes this web part.

> **TRY IT OUT**   Create a New Item Form

In this exercise, you create a new item form for the Tasks list. You also add a picture to the top of the form.

1. In SharePoint Designer 2010, click on Lists and Libraries and then click the Tasks list to get to its summary page.

2. To create a new form, click on the New button in the Forms section of the page.

3. In the Create New List Form that appears, provide the filename **NewTask**. Leave the type of form as New Item Form. Select the checkbox for making this a default form and click on OK.

4. Click on the `NewTask.aspx` form page to open it up. You should see the DFWP on this page showing the form to create new Tasks.

5. When the form opens, the cursor should be blinking at the top of the form. Click on the Insert tab and then click the Picture button. Navigate to select any picture from your computer to insert on this page.

   Note: When you insert the image, the Accessibility Properties dialog appears; provide any alternative text here that you want to appear in place of the picture if it doesn't successfully load in the browser.

6. When the picture appears at the top of the page, click the Save button to save the page. A dialog box appears to notify you that the picture on your page will be saved in the Site Assets library. Click on OK to accept.

7. Navigate to the Tasks list in the browser. Click on the Add new item link. You should see the new list form, as shown in Figure 8-21.

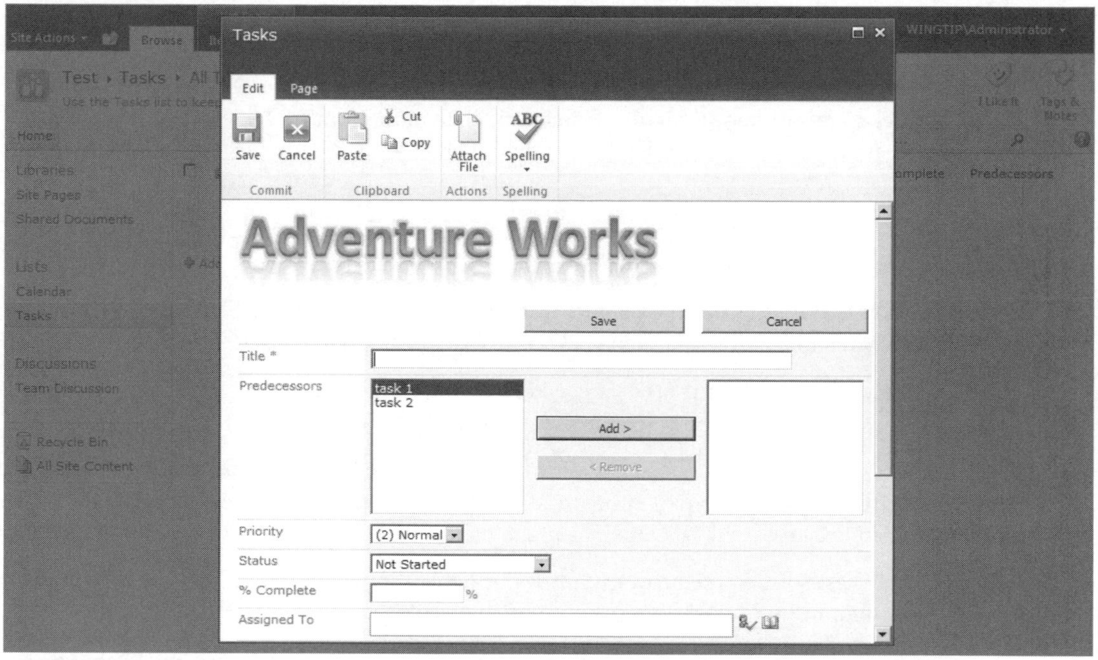

FIGURE 8-21

How It Works

In this exercise, a new item form is created using SPD. This is a new ASP.NET page that serves as the form to create new task items. When this form is created, the DFWP automatically shows up on the page with the capability to add new task items. You can customize the form created in the preceding exercise significantly. Because all the data that's being shown in the form is XML in the backend, you can use XSLT to transform that data as needed. The Data View Tools menu provides a variety of options to perform this transformation.

TRY IT OUT Customize the List Form

In this exercise, you customize the new list form for the Tasks list by changing font properties of labels then adding and removing some fields from the form. The starting point for this exercise is where the previous exercise left off.

1. In SharePoint Designer 2010, click on Lists and Libraries and then the Tasks list to get to its summary page.

2. Click on the NewTask.aspx form page to open it. You should see the DFWP on this page, showing the form to create new Tasks.

3. Put your cursor on the very last field, which is Attachments. Click on the Table tab then click Delete ⇨ Delete Rows to delete that row.

4. Now select the first column containing the labels (such as Title, Predecessors, Priority, and so on). After all the cells are selected, using the Home tab, change the font to Times New Roman and make the font Bold. Then click on the Table tab and change the Shading of the cells to a light shade of gray.

5. Next, click on the form field Start Date (not the label, but the actual field control on the form). Click the Table tab and then click Delete ⇨ Delete Cells to delete the field.

6. While the cursor is blinking where the Start Date used to be, click on the Start Date field in the Data Source Details task pane and then click on Insert Selected Fields as ⇨ Formatted ⇨ DateTime.

Note: If the Data Source Details task pane is not already open, click the Options tab and then click the Data Source Details button to make it appear.

7. In the Format Date and Time dialog that appears, deselect the Show Time checkbox, then use the Date Format drop-down list to pick the second formatting option available. Click OK. The date should appear in the table cell as a label. Save the page.

8. Navigate to the Tasks list in the browser. Click on the Add new item link. You should see the new list form, as shown in Figure 8-22.

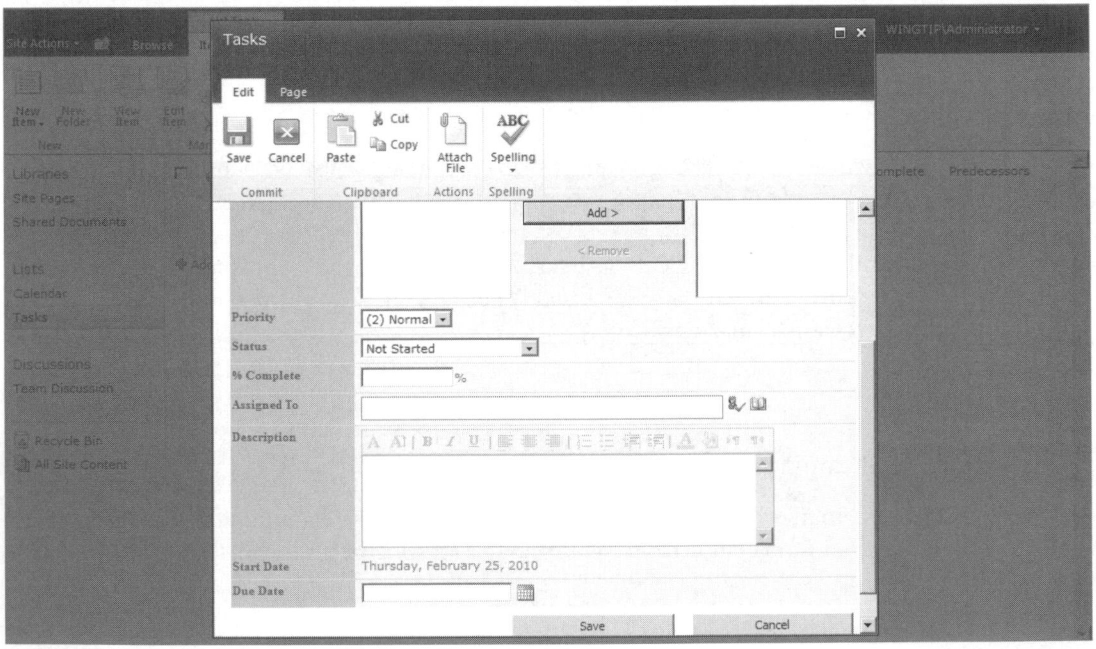

FIGURE 8-22

Note in the preceding figure that the Start Date field is now a label and is no longer editable.

How It Works

You customized the preceding list item form in the same manner you customized a data form earlier in this section. Just like the data form, XSLT is used to transform the XML data that is being fetched from the list and being displayed in the DFWP within the list form.

> **NOTE** *Although SharePoint Designer 2010 supports implementing web forms, many circumstances exist where common types of forms need to be completed, both on the web and off. Microsoft's tool for working with such forms is called InfoPath. InfoPath maintains its own mechanisms for supporting workflow, data validation, conditional formatting, and more.*
>
> *All editions of SharePoint support a Forms Library, which is designed specifically to hold the XML results of InfoPath forms created using the InfoPath client. In addition, SharePoint Server 2010 Enterprise Edition supports web-based forms created using InfoPath. Chapter 9 covers InfoPath 2010 thoroughly.*

Using Custom Actions to Execute List Forms

Enabling end users to easily discover the actions they can take on an item in a list or library is important. The two obvious places that a user will look at are the ribbon and the context menu (also referred to as Edit Control Block (ECB)) of the item. SharePoint Designer 2010 offers an easy way to add customized actions to appear in both of these places. The functionality is called *Custom Actions* and it appears in the summary page of every list and library. You can create Custom Actions to do the following things:

➤ Navigate to an existing list/library form

➤ Start a workflow on an item

➤ Navigate to a URL

Custom Actions basically make solutions easier for people to use by providing the right actions in the correct context.

TRY IT OUT Create a Custom Action to Show a List Form

In this exercise, you create a new custom action on the Tasks list. This custom action will show an existing list form of the Tasks list.

1. In SharePoint Designer 2010, click on Lists and Libraries and then click the Tasks list to get to its summary page.

2. Click on the New button in the Custom Actions section.

3. In the Create Custom Action dialog that appears, enter the name **Edit Task**. Use the Navigate to Form drop-down menu and select the entry pointing to the EditForm.aspx form. Click OK.

4. Navigate to the Tasks list in the browser. If no tasks are present in the list, create a task first. Then hover over the task and click the downward arrow to show the context menu for the item. You should see the Edit Task link in the menu, as displayed in Figure 8-23.

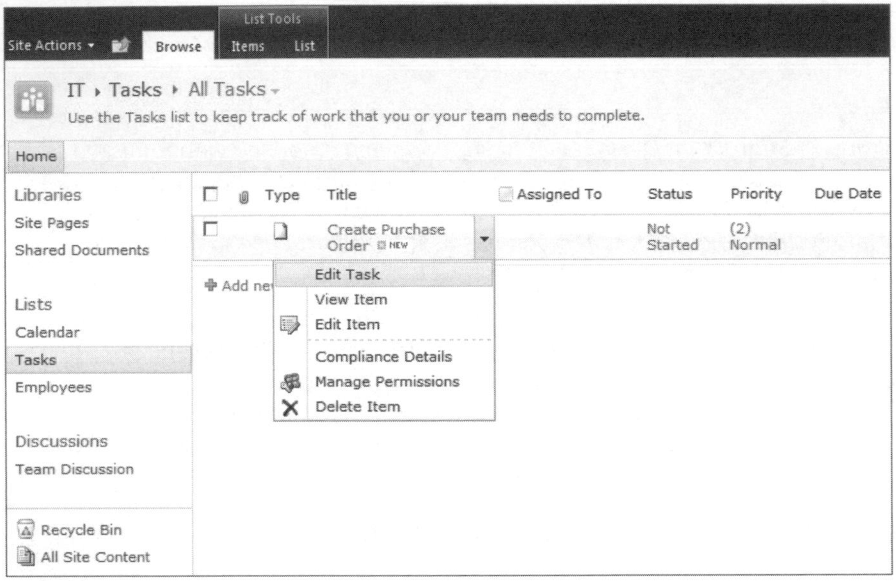

FIGURE 8-23

5. Clicking on the Edit Task link makes the task appear in the edit form.

How It Works

The custom action is created to access functionality. In the case above, the Edit Task action is created to provide quick access to the EditForm.aspx.

SUMMARY

Although other possibilities exist for data presentation on SharePoint pages, the data manipulation possibilities built into SharePoint Designer 2010 make it a very appealing solution for site administrators and power users. Especially now with the availability of XSLT web parts on every page within SharePoint, turning to this application to build robust data-driven solutions is an easy decision for those with little or no programming background.

9

InfoPath Integration

This chapter switches gears a bit to talk about an application called Microsoft Office InfoPath 2010. InfoPath, which is a form generation tool that has been part of the Office suite since 2003, has become an integral part of the SharePoint products and technologies. In this chapter, you discover how you can use InfoPath easily and efficiently to manage SharePoint list and library forms. You also learn about the InfoPath Form web part that ships with SharePoint Server 2010 Enterprise and lets you expose InfoPath forms alongside your other SharePoint components.

THE PATH TO GATHERING INFO

When InfoPath 2003 was released as part of Office 2003, it was ahead of its time, because it was the only product within the Office suite that utilized the power of XML in its inner workings. An InfoPath form is based completely on an XML schema and offers structural editing of the XML data. It is the most appropriate platform for gathering data in the Microsoft Office suite of applications, and the user interface provided is very much like Microsoft Word, so the ramp-up time for a new form designer is minimized. You can build dynamic data-driven forms without needing a programming background.

The latest revision of the product is Microsoft InfoPath 2010. The fluent interface (ribbon) has been introduced in the product, which now provides it a consistent look and feel with the other Office products. Two InfoPath applications are available — Microsoft InfoPath Designer 2010 and Microsoft InfoPath Filler 2010. Designer is used by the form designers to design the form, whereas the Filler is used by the end users to fill out a form and save it. In addition to filling out the form in the Filler, you can also allow end users to fill out forms using the browser, provided that you have the enterprise license of SharePoint Server 2010, which ships with the needed component, Forms Server, to serve up the forms. InfoPath 2010 web browser forms are compliant with Web Content Accessibility Guidelines 2.0 (WCAG 2.0) and are fully XHTML 1.0 compliant. To find more information on the enterprise licensing of SharePoint Server go to http://sharepoint2010.microsoft.com.

A form designer uses InfoPath to create form templates for end users to fill out. After opening the InfoPath Designer application, the first decision that a form designer must make is to choose the type of form template. The Backstage screen of Designer helps with this process. As is apparent in Figure 9-1, you can choose from many form templates.

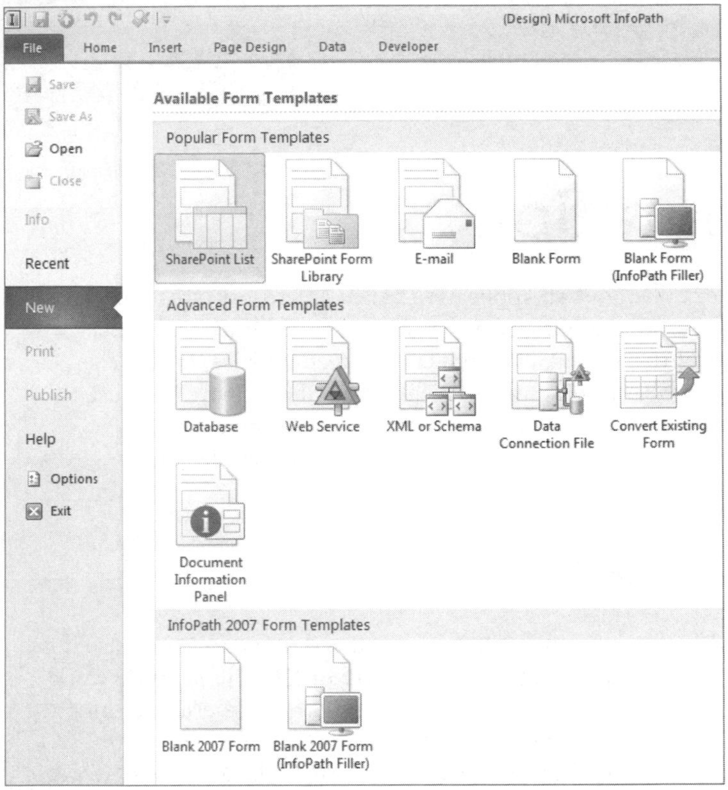

FIGURE 9-1

You can utilize InfoPath Designer to edit SharePoint list or library forms. This chapter provides an example of this functionality later. You can utilize InfoPath completely independent of SharePoint by creating template forms that can be used on their own. You can place form templates on a network share or on an intranet from where users can obtain and fill out the forms. In addition, you can send forms directly to people's inboxes, where they can fill out the form within the Microsoft Outlook 2010 environment and submit it back to the person who sent them the form.

The Designer environment provides a quick and easy interface to get started building your forms. Assuming you start by using the Blank Form template, which starts you out by providing just an empty table, you can quickly decide on a page layout for your form by selecting the Page Design tab and picking a Page Layout template. Then pick a theme for your form by selecting from the provided theme choices. Figure 9-2 shows the page layout templates and a brief view of the available themes.

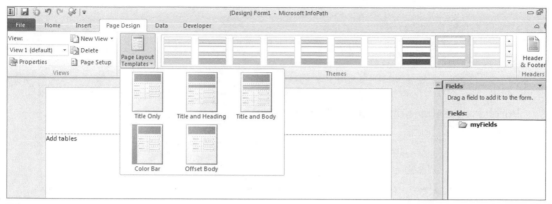

FIGURE 9-2

Form templates generally consist of labels and controls through which you want to accept user input. These elements are best arranged in a table. By clicking on the Insert tab, you see a number of choices for table styles, as shown in Figure 9-3. Pick the style(s) that best suits your need.

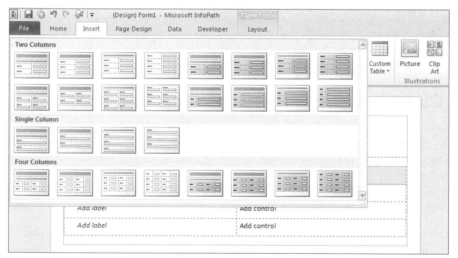

FIGURE 9-3

The next step in creating the form is to populate it with descriptive text and the controls needed for the form. You insert the text and labels simply by typing them directly onto the appropriate places in the form. The controls for the form are available through the Home tab. This is where the true design power of InfoPath forms are realized, because you can use a variety of controls as the designer. As Figure 9-4 shows, controls such as text box, drop-down list, date picker, button, repeating table, and more are all available in the Home tab, ready to be placed on the form. Just place your cursor at the place you want the control to appear and click on the control to insert it in the form template.

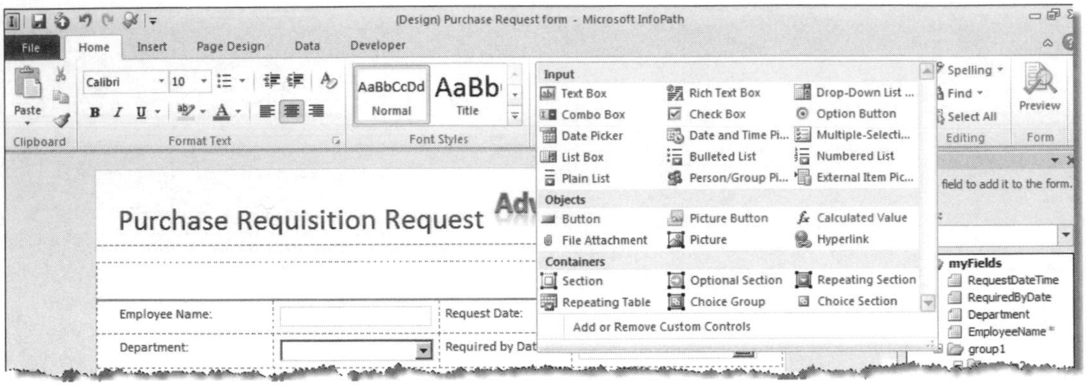

FIGURE 9-4

The form template is aware of the controls placed on it and their associated properties. The form designer can access controls by their name and use them as needed, so a best practice to follow is immediately to name all the controls on the form. You access a control's name and other properties by first clicking on a control and then using the Control Tools tab that appears in the ribbon. The Fields task pane on the right side of the screen reflects that change.

After a form template design meets a designer's required specifications for what the form is intended to accomplish, the next step is to manage the dynamic aspects of the form by using proper validation and formatting rules. This aspect of the form is discussed in the next section.

Using Rules for Conditional Formatting and Data Validation

The InfoPath Designer environment allows you the use of a rules engine with which you can decide how your form and the controls on the form should behave in response to the data that the end user provides. Three types of rules can be created using the rules management interface:

➤ **Validation** — Validate the entered data in controls.

➤ **Formatting** — Change formatting of a control based upon defined condition criteria.

➤ **Action** — Perform an action (such as setting a field's value or submitting data) based upon defined condition criteria.

You can quickly start incorporating rules in your form by using *quick rules*. These are a set of pre-built rules that help validate your data and make forms more dynamic. Simply click on the control that you want to set a rule upon, click the Add Rule button in the ribbon, and then select the condition and subsequent action from the list of options that appear. Figure 9-5 shows a snapshot of these rules in Figure 9-5.

Think of quick rules as a wizard to get you started. You can start instead from scratch by clicking on the Manage Rules button on the ribbon, which displays the Rules task pane on the right, to manage rules. The same task pane also appears after you have picked a quick rule, and lets you manage the properties of that rule further (such as changing its name) as needed. You can configure as many rules as needed for the control. The control's rules appear on this task pane when you place the control in context by clicking on it. You created a new rule by clicking on the New button in the Rules task pane and selecting the appropriate type of rule. A rule is set up much like a mini-workflow in which you define a condition and then a subsequent action for which the condition becomes true. For example, designate a field as required to contain content, so that, if the field is blank and the user tries to submit the form, it shows a validation error. An example of a formatting rule would be to check a field's value with the value of another field to determine whether they are the same, and to change the background color of one or both fields to red to signify when they are not. Figure 9-6 shows a couple of configured rules for a control.

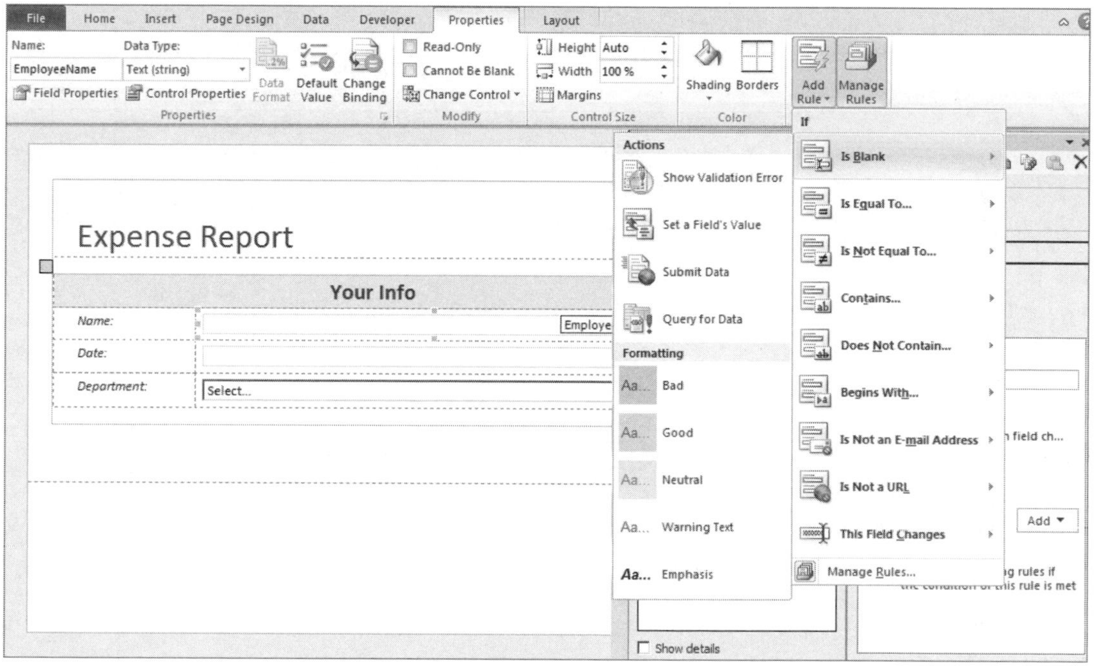

FIGURE 9-5

In a typical form created for business use, you might need to create numerous rules for the controls. A very useful functionality available is the ability to copy and paste rules from one control to another. To copy single or multiple rules, simply select them and click on the copy icon that appears within the Rules task pane. Then select the control to which you want to paste the rule(s), and click on the paste icon in the Rules task pane. All of your rules along with their defined logic are copied to the new control saving you lots of time and effort.

The end goal is for you to publish the form template to a location where users can access it and fill it out with their data. Publishing is covered later in this chapter. Before publishing your form, using the Preview button on the Home tab of the ribbon to preview your form and run through its logic is always a good idea. Figure 9-7 shows how the preview screen looks.

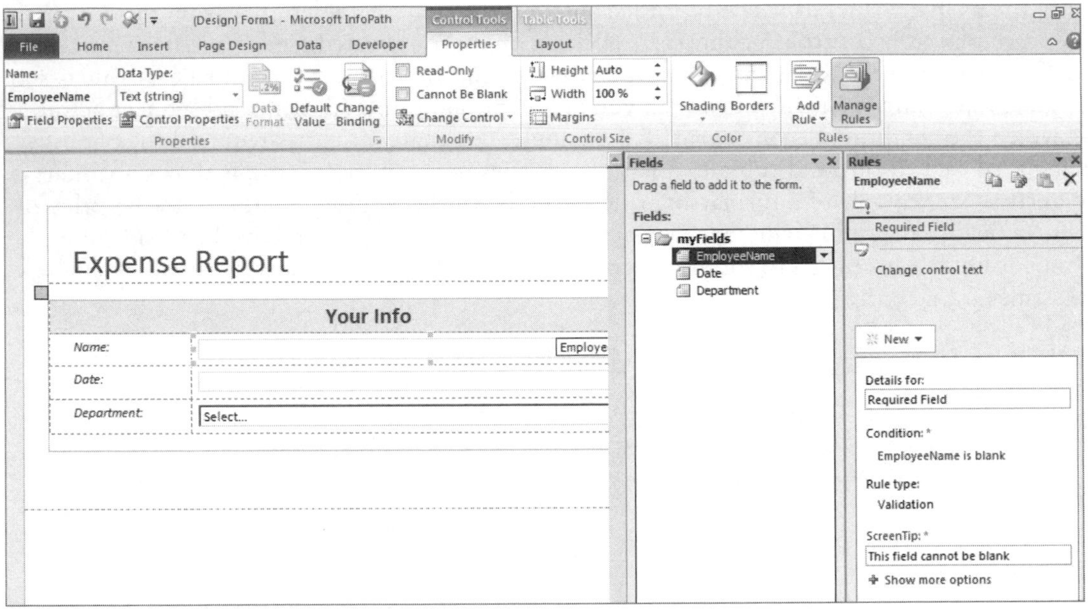

FIGURE 9-6

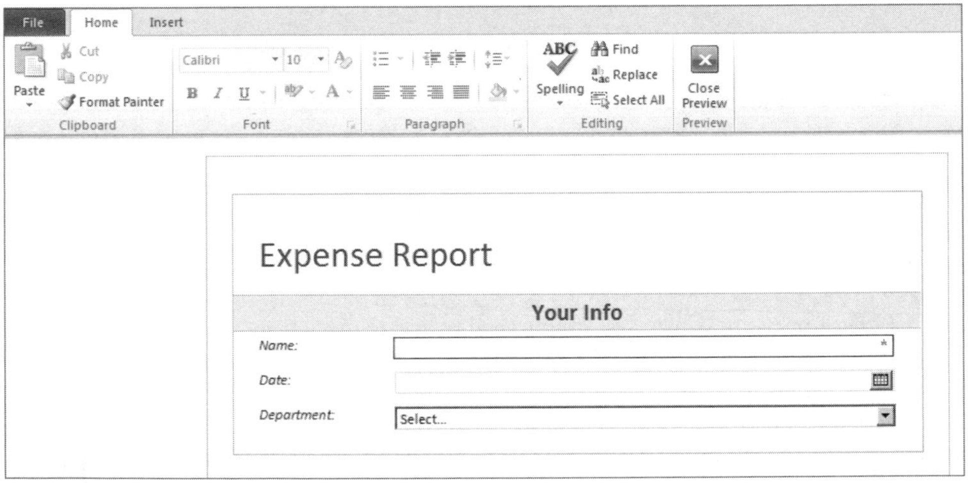

FIGURE 9-7

Fetching Data from Multiple Repositories

InfoPath can make data connections to various data repositories. Depending on what you want the form to do, you can set up data connections for either retrieving data or submitting it to a data source. This section focuses on the receiving part of the equation. The Data tab (see Figure 9-8) within the InfoPath client displays the various repositories of external data you can use.

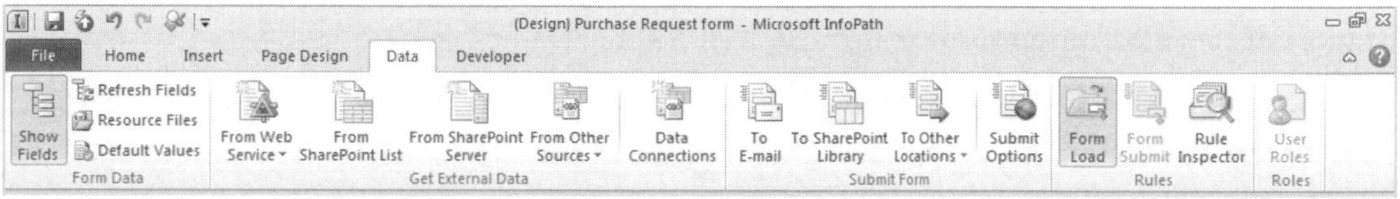

FIGURE 9-8

Following is a list of external data connections you can create:

➤ SOAP web service (Simple Object Access Protocol web service)

➤ REST web service (Representational State Transfer web service)

➤ SharePoint library or list

➤ Database (Microsoft SQL Server only)

➤ XML Document (any URL you can connect to that would return an XML document — for instance, an RSS feed)

You can create each of these connections very simply by following the wizard that appears after you select your data source type. Just because an option to connect to non-SQL databases does not exist in the user interface does not mean that it is not possible. You can use web services to connect to any non-SQL databases (provided that those databases expose web services to consume).

A query data connection gets data from the external data source, which you can then bind to any fields within the form. You see an example of making a connection to a SharePoint list and binding that information to a combo box later in this chapter.

Publishing Forms to a Variety of Locations

An InfoPath form template is saved as an .xsn file. When you publish the form, this file becomes accessible to the end users and works very much like a Microsoft Word document template (.dotx file). The user opens the file and fills out the required information on the form. When the user decides to save or submit the form, it gets saved as an .xml file containing all the user-provided data and a pointer to the original .xsn file used to create this instance.

Publishing and sharing the InfoPath form using SharePoint is recommended. SharePoint framework provides a multitude of built-in options to support the form processes. If your SharePoint instance is running with enterprise client access licenses then the only thing that the users need is the browser to fill out the forms. If SharePoint Server standard licensing or just SharePoint Foundation is deployed, then the end user needs the InfoPath Filler application to fill out the forms. When the form template is published to the form library in SharePoint, the users can take advantage of all the base features available within every library, such as versioning, check-in/check-out, and the ability to attach workflows to the library. The form library provides a superset of features available in a document library. In addition to all the base features of a typical library, a form library is recognized inherently by InfoPath, which can publish forms directly to it. You see an example demonstrating this process later in this chapter. An added benefit of hosting the forms in a form library is that it contains a special built-in view called Merge View that lets you merge the information of multiple instances of the filled-out forms that are hosted in the library.

The publishing options are available through the Publish option on the File tab in the ribbon as shown in Figure 9-9.

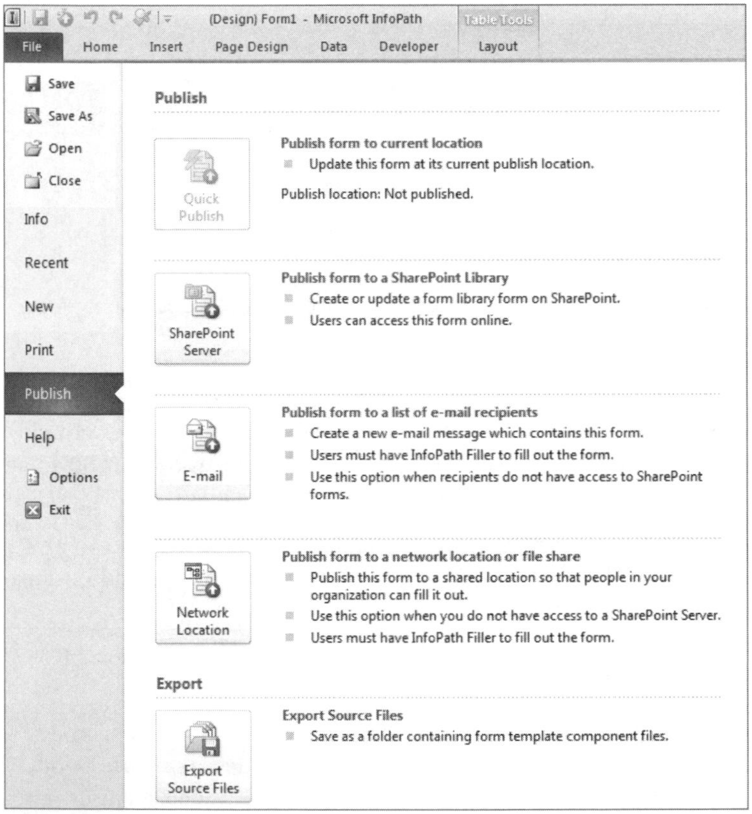

FIGURE 9-9

In addition to publishing to the SharePoint Server, you can also publish the InfoPath form template directly via e-mail to user's inboxes or place it on a network location that's accessible to the intended audience. Both of these options require that users filling out the form have the InfoPath Filler application available to them on their computer. The process to publish the form to a network share is the simplest available within the Designer environment. It entails just pointing to the location where the .xsn file needs to be saved. After the file is published to that location, you can notify your users (via e-mail or otherwise) to fill out the forms using this template. Figure 9-10 shows the wizard screen that you use to define the location and name of the form.

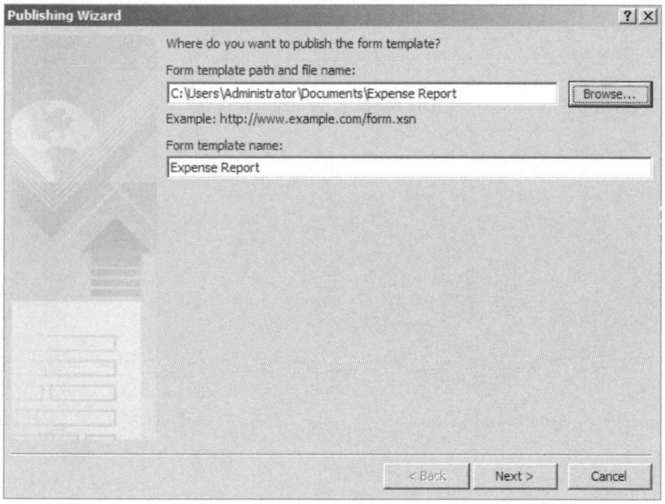

FIGURE 9-10

In a scenario where, for example, you want to collect some information from your users quickly, you can send them an e-mail with the form prominently displayed in the body of the e-mail. As long as the user has InfoPath on his computer, he will see the form ready to be filled out. The E-mail button in the Publish screen starts up the e-mail client and guides the form designer through the process of sending the form. When the end user receives the e-mail, all he will then need to do is to fill out the form directly in the e-mail client application and submit it. The form designer must configure the submission process of InfoPath beforehand for this process to work. It can be configured automatically to submit the form to a variety of places, including sending the form back through e-mail, sending it to a library or to a predefined connection in SharePoint, and submitting to a web service. The submission options are available through the Info selection under the File tab as Figure 9-11 shows.

The information in the preceding sections provide enough guidance to get you started with Microsoft InfoPath 2010. However, by no measure is it an exhaustive list of features available within InfoPath 2010. Learning this product further by picking up a good book that's dedicated to this subject is definitely advisable. Because no books are published on InfoPath 2010 just yet, I advise going through a good InfoPath 2007 book, such as *Designing Forms for Microsoft Office InfoPath and Forms Services* by Scott Roberts and Hagen Green (Addison-Wesley, 2007). This book provides you a good basis for the internals of this product and opens your mind to the possibilities of what is achievable with this platform.

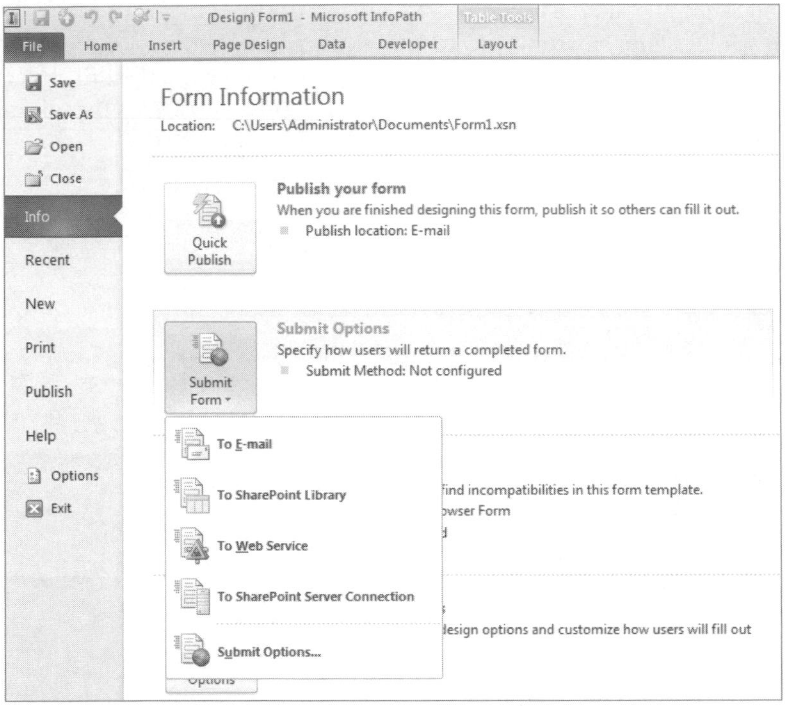

FIGURE 9-11

CUSTOMIZING SHAREPOINT LIST FORMS

When you use a list template in SharePoint to create a new list, it automatically deploys a number of forms for viewing, editing, and creating items in that list. You are not limited to these forms and are allowed to create new forms for users to interact with list data. Chapter 8 discusses and demonstrates the way to create new list forms using SharePoint Designer 2010. You can use those methods with any version of SharePoint. However, if you have the SharePoint Server enterprise license, you have an additional option to customize your list forms using InfoPath 2010.

The earlier sections in this chapter explained the power of InfoPath and declared it as a preferred tool for form generation and manipulation in SharePoint. This section demonstrates how you can use this tool to create robust SharePoint list forms.

Building List Forms Using InfoPath

Building list forms is a new functionality in InfoPath 2010. Earlier versions of InfoPath did not let you create SharePoint list forms. Because InfoPath is the preferred Microsoft tool for form generation, letting this powerful tool generate forms for SharePoint lists and libraries as well just makes sense. In the previous versions of InfoPath, you could use it to create SharePoint library forms (discussed later in this chapter). Now the additional functionality for creating SharePoint list forms has been integrated into the platform. The list form creation process can be instantiated from within InfoPath by choosing the SharePoint List form template, or you can start directly from a SharePoint list as demonstrated in the next exercise.

TRY IT OUT | **Create a SharePoint List Form Using InfoPath**

In this exercise, you will create a new form for the Tasks list using InfoPath.

1. Open a team site in SharePoint Designer 2010. Click on Lists and Libraries in the navigation pane and then click on Tasks list to get to its summary page.

2. Look for and click on the Design Forms in InfoPath button in the ribbon. Select the Task choice from the drop-down list. InfoPath opens, showing you the list form, as displayed in Figure 9-12.

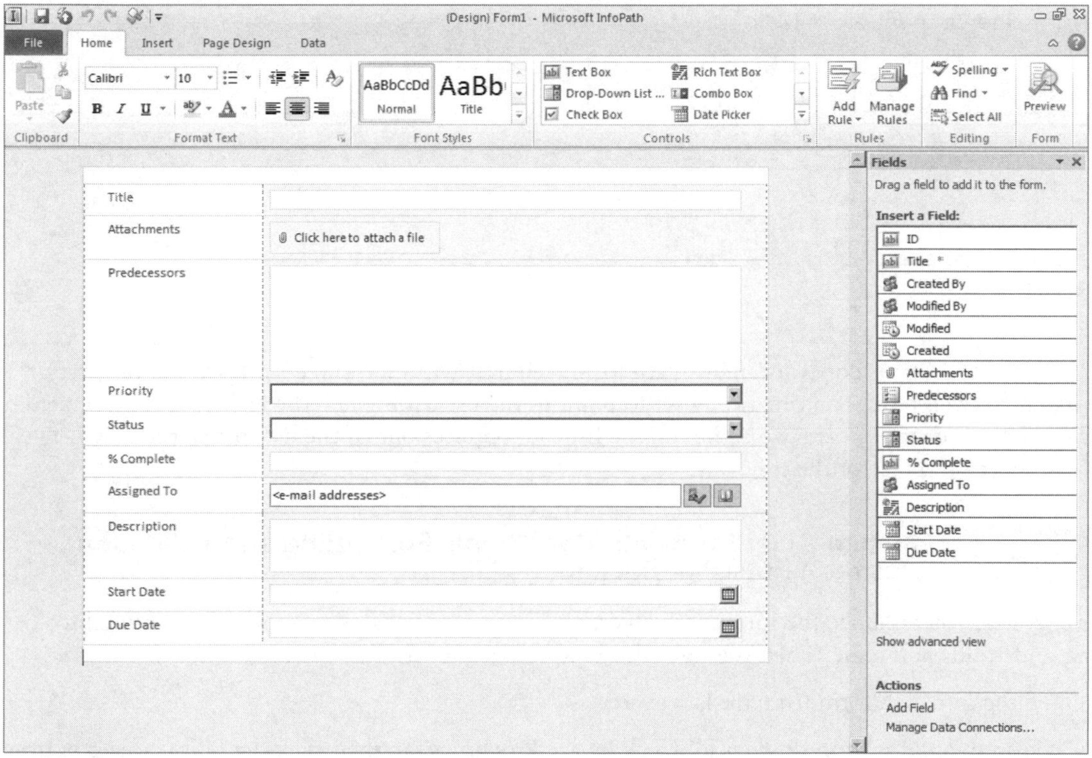

FIGURE 9-12

3. Place your cursor in the first line of the form, click on the Insert tab in the ribbon, and click the Picture button.

4. Select and browse to a picture on your computer that you want to insert at the top of the form (for example, a company or department logo). After the picture is on the form, you can resize it as you need.

5. Drag the Title text box to right after the picture. It should automatically settle underneath the picture. Now while having this text box selected, click on the Home tab and change the font properties to Arial Black font, size 14 and Bold.

6. Click on the Title label that's now below the text box. Because you don't need this row anymore, click the Layout tab in the Table Tools menu and then click Delete ⇨ Rows. The row gets deleted.

7. Click and drag to highlight all the labels in the first column of the form table (that is, Attachments, Predecessors, and so on). Using the Home tab, set the font to Bold. Then click on the Layout tab and use the Shading button to set the shading to a light gray.

How It Works

When you modify a list form using InfoPath, a new set of forms are created and placed side by side with the original forms for the list. You can easily identify these new forms because they all have the suffix *ifs* as shown in Figure 9-13.

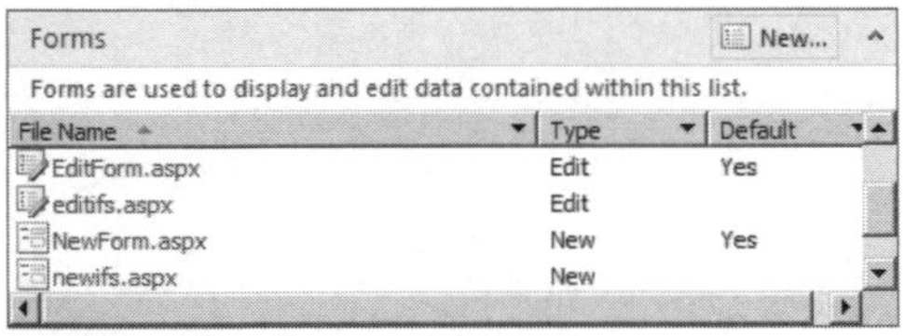

FIGURE 9-13

This new set of forms contains an InfoPath form web part within it; the FormLocation property of this form web part is automatically set to point to the list with which the web part is associated. When the end user performs an action on the list that requires one of the list forms, the new list forms appear in place of the originals.

TRY IT OUT   **Enhance a List Form with Conditional Formatting and Validation Rules then Publish It Back to the Library**

In this exercise, you enhance the form that you created in the previous exercise with conditional formatting and validation logic. Then you publish the form back to the Tasks list.

1. Open the InfoPath form from the last exercise.

2. Click on the Status drop-down field. Click on the Properties tab then click the Edit Choices button to display the drop-down list choices. Make note of the available choices (that is, Not Started, In Progress, Completed, and so on). Click Cancel to dismiss the dialog.

3. While the Status field is still selected, click on Add Rule in the ribbon and then select Is Equal To ⇨ Bad, as shown in Figure 9-14.

4. In the Rule Details dialog that appears, type in **Not Started** in the text box (it might be already filled in when the dialog appears) and then click OK. Your first conditional formatting rule for this field is complete. Verify it in the Rules task pane that appears.

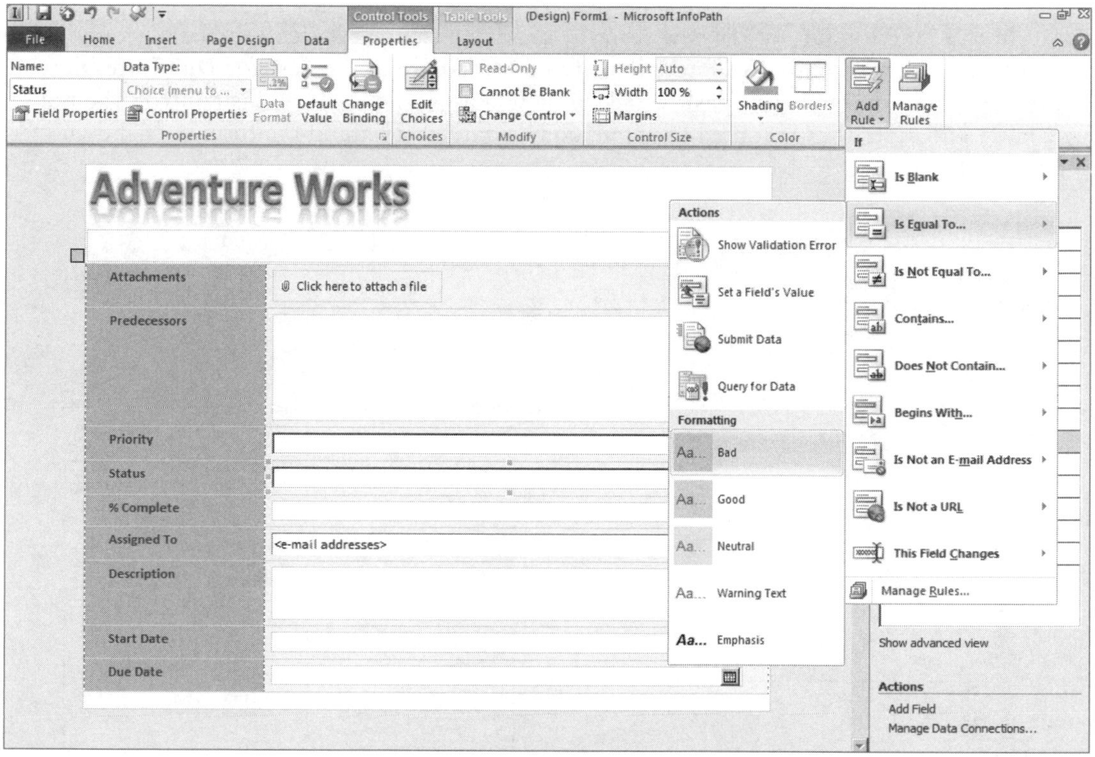

FIGURE 9-14

5. Using the same method in steps 3 and 4, create two new rules. For the first rule click Add Rule in the ribbon and select Is Equal To ⇨ Neutral; in the Rule Details dialog choose In Progress. For the second rule, click Add Rule in the ribbon and select Is Equal To ⇨ Good; in the Rule Details dialog, choose Completed.

6. Click on the Description text field on the form. Click on the Properties tab and then select the Cannot Be Blank checkbox.

7. Click on the Due Date calendar control in the form. Click Add Rule ⇨ Is in the Past ⇨ Show Validation Error. This sets a validation rule for the Due Date field so the date cannot be in the past. The final form now looks like the one shown in Figure 9-15.

8. Click on the File tab and then the Quick Publish button to publish the form back to the list. A Publish dialog appears with confirmation of successful publishing of the form. Click OK to acknowledge it.

9. Navigate to the Tasks list in your site using the browser. Click on the Add New Item link. The newly created form appears.

10. Test out the functionality of the new form by changing the Status field; the background color should change accordingly. Also note that if you put a date in the past for Due Date, the control will be surrounded by dashed red lines. When you hover over this control, the pop-up dialog will state that you need to enter today's date or a date in the future, as shown in Figure 9-16.

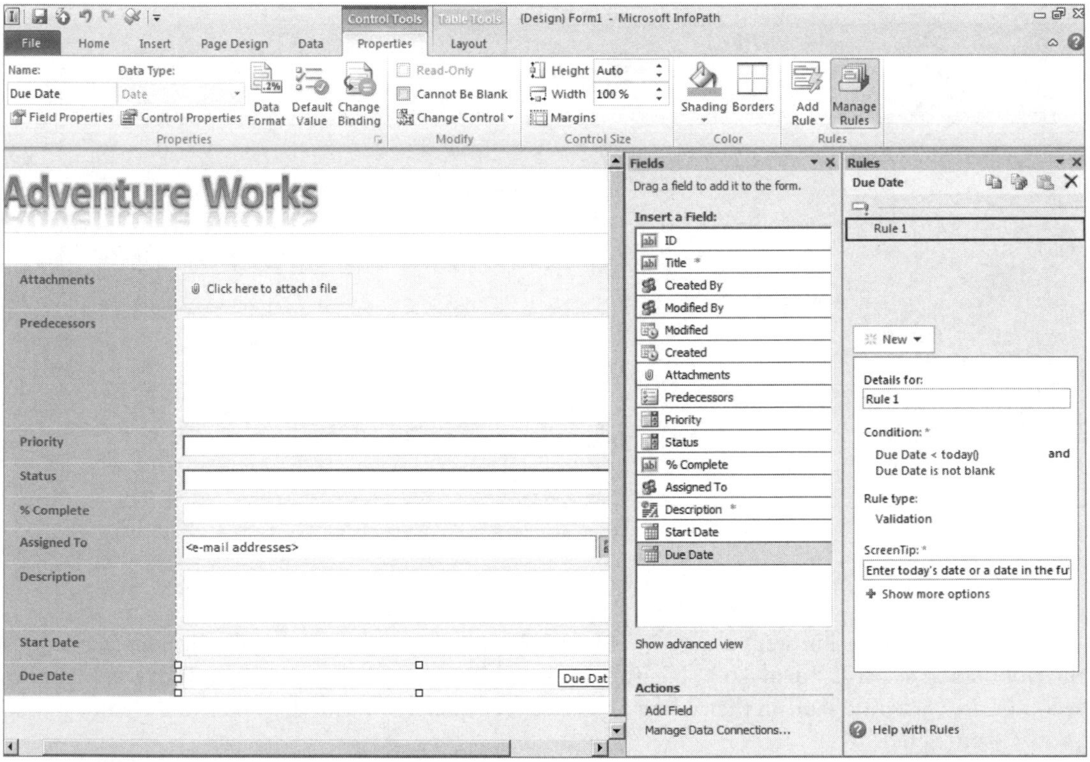

FIGURE 9-15

How It Works

The built-in Rules engine in InfoPath is used to make the form truly dynamic and robust. Once configured, each rule becomes a part of the form itself. These rules will apply to the form logic no matter where the form is eventually used.

The Quick Publish functionality facilitates a quick deployment to wherever the form was published previously.

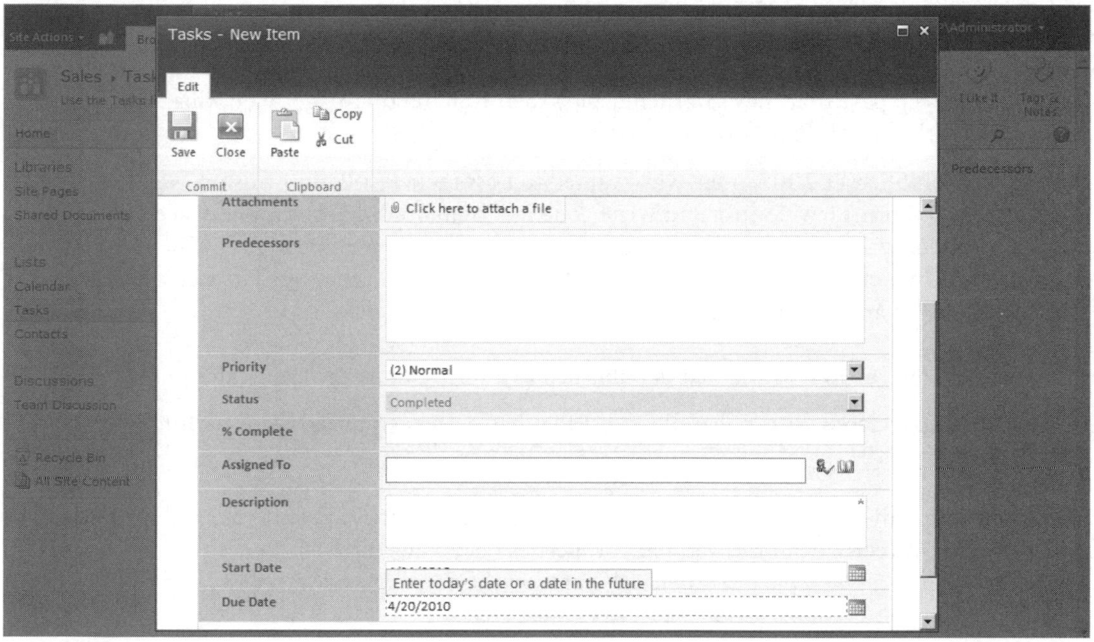

FIGURE 9-16

> *NOTE* *You can use both SharePoint Designer 2010 and InfoPath 2010 for creating SharePoint list forms. Chapter 8 details how to do this using SharePoint Designer, and the preceding section in this chapter lays out the options that are available in InfoPath. Which one should you use? Well, if you don't have the SharePoint Server Enterprise license then the only choice you have is SharePoint Designer for this functionality. On the other hand, if you do have access to the InfoPath application and you have SharePoint Server Enterprise deployed in your environment, then Microsoft recommends that you utilize the inherent power of InfoPath to create your SharePoint list forms.*
>
> *As proof that InfoPath is a more robust platform for this functionality, you create a new form for the same Tasks list using SharePoint Designer in Chapter 8 and using InfoPath in Chapter 9. As you may have noticed, both platforms provide powerful interfaces for list form manipulation. However, InfoPath has a leg up in this process because it provides an easy-to-use Microsoft Word–like interface that form designers can use to create their forms. In addition, using InfoPath form designers can easily implement rules logic to validate and conditionally format data. Also, you can surface your forms on any SharePoint page using the provided InfoPath form web part, as shown in the next section.*

Displaying Forms Using InfoPath Form Web Part

The InfoPath form web part has been introduced as a new web part in SharePoint Server 2010. You need the SharePoint Server Enterprise license to have access to this web part in the web part gallery. InfoPath forms have been capable of being displayed in the browser for many years now using InfoPath Forms Services. Nevertheless, many users have wished that they could encapsulate their forms within a web part that they can then deploy to any SharePoint page. Well, this capability is now possible with the InfoPath form web part!

Back in SharePoint Server 2007, users who wanted to host their InfoPath forms on Web pages had to utilize the XmlFormView control and write code in Visual Studio. You can now accomplish the same goal without writing a single line of code using the InfoPath form web part. The InfoPath form web part works by hosting any already-published InfoPath form on the site. The two types of forms that it can consume are the following:

➤ An InfoPath browser form that is published to a form library (covered later in the chapter).

➤ A form associated with a SharePoint list that has been customized by using InfoPath Designer 2010.

You can configure all common web part properties, such as the title, appearance, and behavior of the web part, directly from the web part properties task pane in the browser. You can also connect the InfoPath form web part to other web parts on the page to send or receive data.

The following exercise shows an example of how to use this web part to show a SharePoint list form.

TRY IT OUT   Consume a SharePoint List Form within an InfoPath Form Web Part

In this exercise, you use the Tasks list view form you created in the preceding exercise with the InfoPath form web part. You use SharePoint Designer 2010 to deploy and configure the web part.

1. In SharePoint Designer 2010, navigate to Lists and Libraries in the navigation pane and then click on the Tasks list to get to its summary page.

2. Click on the All Tasks view to open it. An XSLT List View web part showing the Tasks list appears.

3. Click to place the cursor at the absolute bottom row of the Main web part zone (a `div` tag appears when you click there).

4. Click the Insert tab. Click Web Part ➪ InfoPath Form Web Part to place this web part on the page.

5. While the InfoPath Form web part is still selected, click on the Format tab then click the Add Connection button.

6. In the Web Part Connections wizard that appears, click the drop-down arrow and select Get Form From. Click Next.

7. Choose to connect to a web part on this page and click Next.

8. Select Tasks as the Target Web Part, click Next, and then click Finish. Click the Save icon to save the view page.

9. Navigate to the Tasks list in the browser. If you don't already have any items in the Tasks list, add a couple of items there.

10. Click on one of the double-pointed arrows that appear under the Select column in the list. It shows you the corresponding form, as shown in Figure 9-17.

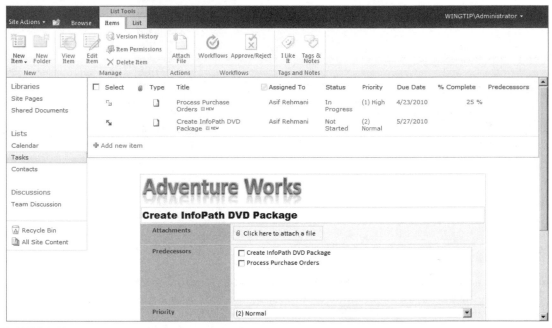

FIGURE 9-17

How It Works

An InfoPath form web part is automatically aware of the InfoPath forms that exist on the site in which the web part is deployed. The preceding example shows how to use this web part using SharePoint Designer 2010. When you configure this web part in the browser, it displays all the lists and libraries that have at least one InfoPath form attached to them. When you choose the list or library of interest, the drop-down below it displays all the available forms on that list. Upon your picking the desired form, the web part encapsulates the form within it.

CUSTOMIZING SHAREPOINT LIBRARY FORMS

All SharePoint libraries require at least one document template to be associated with them. For example, when you create a document library, you have the option of choosing Word, PowerPoint, Excel, or other applications to be the default document template for the library. When a user clicks on the New Document button in the library, he is then presented with the appropriate document template.

InfoPath can also serve as the default document template for a library. The special type of a library that is created to host InfoPath form templates is a *form library*. Figure 9-18 shows the form library in the Create dialog.

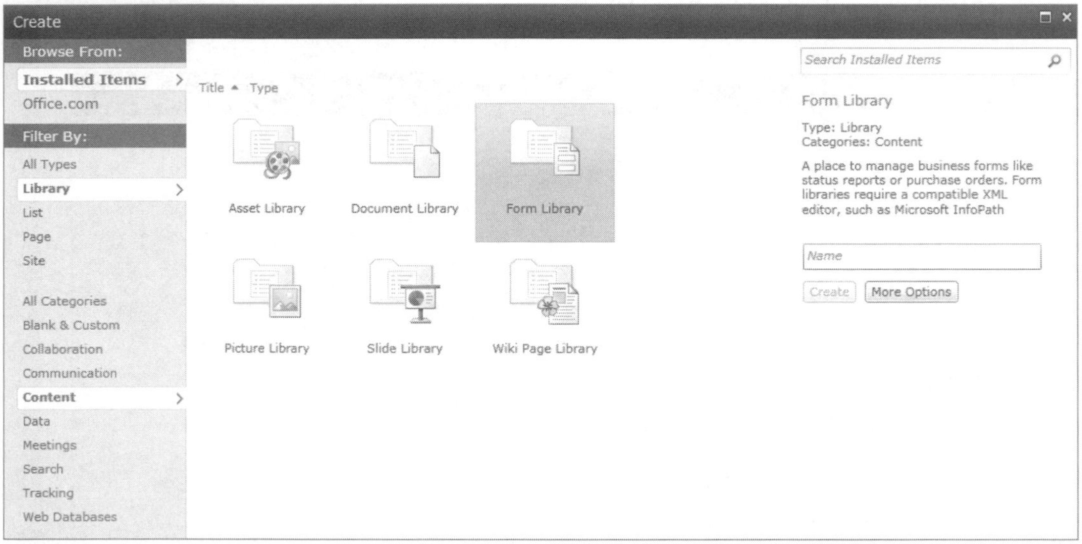

FIGURE 9-18

Form libraries have been around since SharePoint 2003 and have served as a place to hold and manage forms. The InfoPath environment inherently understands form libraries in SharePoint. The form publishing process in InfoPath can either create a new form library or publish a form to an existing form library. The following sections detail the process of creating an InfoPath form and publishing it to a new form library.

Creating the InfoPath Form Template

The first decision you have to make when creating a new InfoPath form template for a library is to choose the appropriate template with which to start. You can start from scratch, if you like, using the Blank Form template, and then choose the design layout for the form, add controls, create rules, and apply formatting. Or you can start with the built-in SharePoint Form Library template that starts you off with a built-in layout that you can then customize to your needs. The following exercise uses the Form Library template as the starting point.

TRY IT OUT   Create an InfoPath Form Using the SharePoint Form Library Template

In this exercise, you create an InfoPath form that you will later publish to a form library.

1. Start Microsoft InfoPath Designer 2010. When the Backstage appears, pick the SharePoint Form Library template and click the Design Form button.

2. Enter the title of form as **Purchase Requisition Request**.

3. Click the Insert tab and then click the Picture button. Browse to any picture you want on your computer, and select it to insert it into the form. Change the alignment of the picture so that it appears to the right of the title of form.

4. You can type labels directly on the form, and controls are available on the Home tab. Enter the following labels and controls on the form (delete any extra rows and tables on the form):

| Employee Name: | Text Box | Request Date: | Date and Time picker |
| Department: | Combo Box | Required by Date: | Date picker |

5. Place a Repeating Table control (four columns) below the table with all the controls. Name the column headers **Item, Quantity, Unit Price**, and **Total**.

6. Below the repeating table, enter a **Final Total** label followed by a text box. The form should now look something like the one shown in Figure 9-19.

7. Optional: If you want, you can use the Page Design tab and pick a different theme for your form.

How It Works

The built in form library template is used in the exercise above to get a quick start in designing the form template. The blank form template can also be used to start from scratch and build your form structure as needed. As the controls are placed on the form, the form's schema is automatically being built and is visible in the Fields task pane.

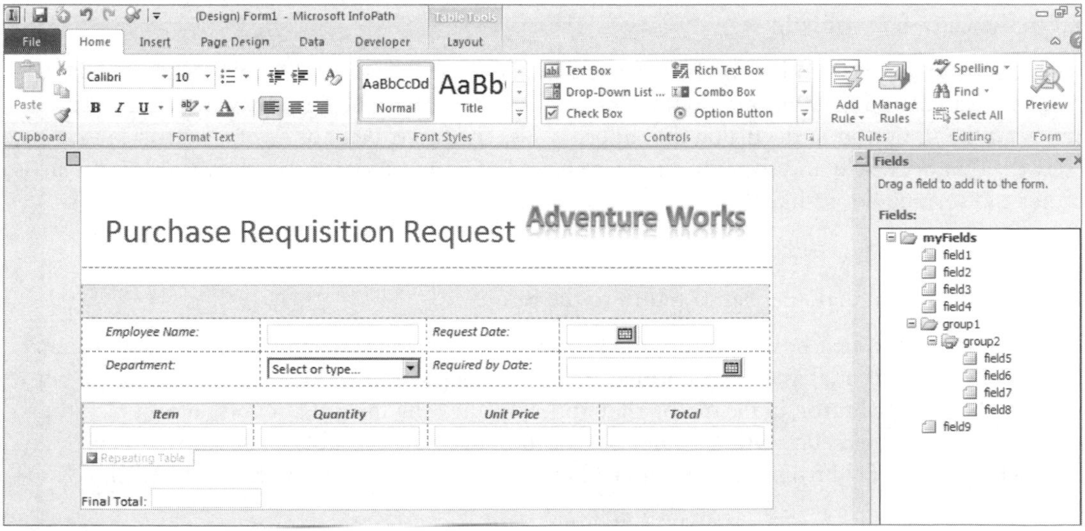

FIGURE 9-19

Now that you've created the shell for the InfoPath form template, the next step is to enhance it using validation and conditional formatting techniques.

TRY IT OUT **Enhance the InfoPath Form with Validation and Conditional Formatting**

In this exercise, you start with the Purchase Requisition Request form you created in the preceding exercise and enhance it with conditional formatting and validation rules.

1. Open the Purchase Requisition Request form.

2. Click in the Employee Name text box. Click on the Properties tab and change the name of the field to **EmployeeName**. Select the Cannot Be Blank checkbox to ensure this becomes a required field.

3. Click on the Request Date's date and time picker control and using the Properties tab, change the control's name to **RequestDateTime**. Click on the Default Value button and then click the *fx* button in the dialog that appears. Now in the Insert Formula dialog, click Insert Function and select the now function (now function is also available under the Date and Time category). Click OK in the dialog boxes that have opened to return to the form.

4. Click in the Required by Date field and using the Properties tab, change its name to **RequiredByDate**. Now from the Home tab, click the Add Rule button and select Is Before ➪ Show Validation Error. In the Rule Details dialog that appears, click the *fx* button. Then click on Insert Field or Group and select the RequestDateTime field. Click OK in all open dialog boxes to return to the form. You should see the new rule in the task pane.

5. Now modify the fields in the Repeating Table (that's the table with four columns that you added in a previous exercise). Select and change the Item text box name to **Item**.

6. Click the Quantity text box in the Repeating Table and using the Properties tab, change its name to **Quantity**. Change the Data Type to Whole Number.

7. Click the Unit Price text box in the Repeating Table and using the Properties tab, change its name to **UnitPrice**. Change the Data Type to Decimal. Click the Data Format button and change the format to the Currency symbol.

8. Click the Total text box and using the Properties tab, change its name to **Total**. Change the Data Type to Decimal and Data Format to the Currency symbol. Click the Default Value button and then click the *fx* button in the dialog that appears. Use the Insert Field or Group button to first insert the Quantity field and then the UnitPrice field. Enter an asterisk (*) in between the two fields so the final formula looks like this:

```
Quantity * UnitPrice
```

9. Click OK in all open dialog boxes to return to the form.

10. Click the Final Total text box and using the Properties tab, change its name to **FinalTotal**. Change the Data Type to Decimal and Data Format to the Currency symbol. Click the Default Value button then click the *fx* button in the dialog that appears. Click the Insert Function button, pick the sum function, and then click OK. Double-click the link that says "double click to insert field" and then pick the Total field from the Select a Field or Group dialog that shows all fields. Click OK to return to the form.

11. While the FinalTotal text box is still selected, click the Add Rule button and choose Is Greater Than ➪ Bad. In the Rule Details dialog, enter **1000** and then click OK.

Your form should look like the one shown in Figure 9-20.

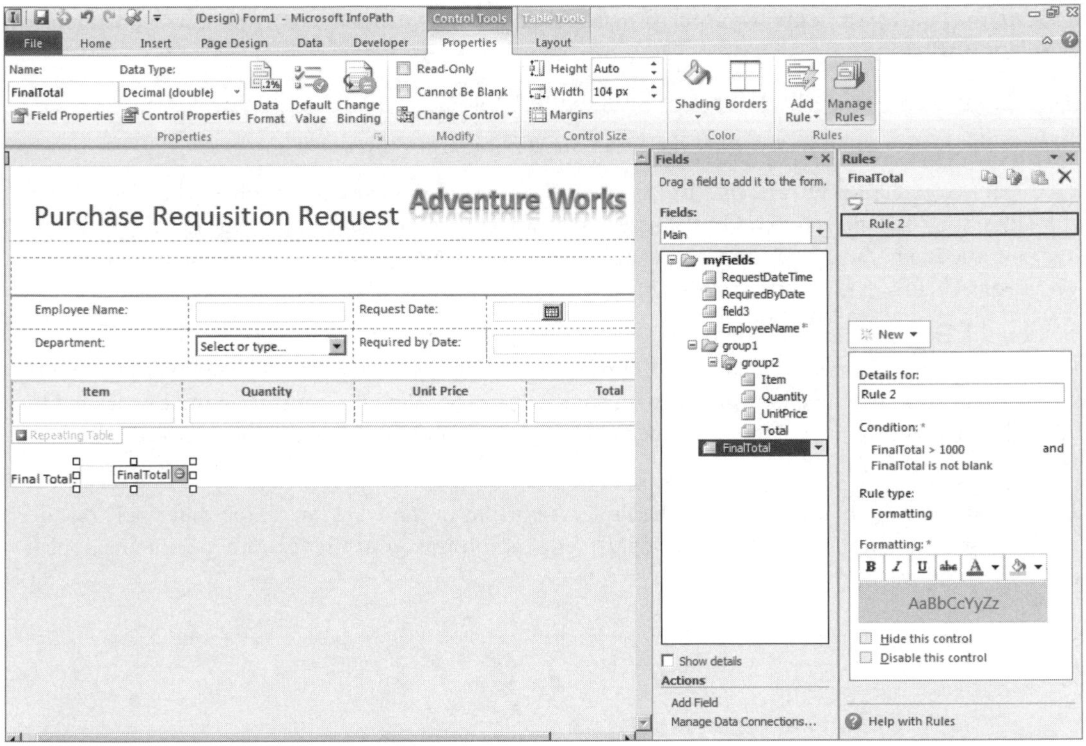

FIGURE 9-20

How It Works

Each InfoPath control supports multiple ways to validate data input. This exercise demonstrated that you can use pre-defined data types, data validation and also conditional formatting rules to guide data input by the user.

The last thing to do before publishing the preceding form is to populate it with external data. As discussed earlier in the chapter, you can fetch the data from many places. The next exercise shows how you can obtain data from a SharePoint list to populate in your form.

TRY IT OUT Fetch SharePoint List Data into the InfoPath Form

In this exercise, you first create a SharePoint list and then you use the Purchase Requisition Request InfoPath form to pull data from that list.

1. Using SharePoint Designer 2010, open a team site.

2. Click on Lists and Libraries, and then using the ribbon, click SharePoint List ➪ Custom List. In the Create list or document library dialog that appears, name the new list **Departments**.

3. Click on the Departments link that shows up to go to the list's summary page. Click the Edit List Columns link there. When you see the Title field, right-click it and rename it **Department Name**. Save the list changes.

4. Navigate to the Departments list in the browser. Add the following list items as new departments: **IT, Sales, Marketing**.

5. Open the Purchase Requisition Request form in InfoPath.

6. Click on the Data tab and then click the From SharePoint List button.

7. In the Data Connection wizard that opens, enter the URL of your team site where the Departments list resides and then click Next. On the screen that appears, choose Departments and then click Next. On the next screen that appears, choose Department Name and then click Next. On the next two screens click Next, and then click Finish.

8. Click on the Department combo box and name it **Department**. Click on the Edit Choices button. In the Combo Box Properties dialog that appears, click the option button to Get choices from an external data source. The Departments data source appears. Click the button by the Entries field and find and select the Department Name field. Click OK in the open dialog boxes to return to the form.

9. Click on the Home tab and then click the Preview button. In the warning dialog that appears, click Yes. The form now appears. Click the Department combo box, and the list of departments appear as shown in Figure 9-21.

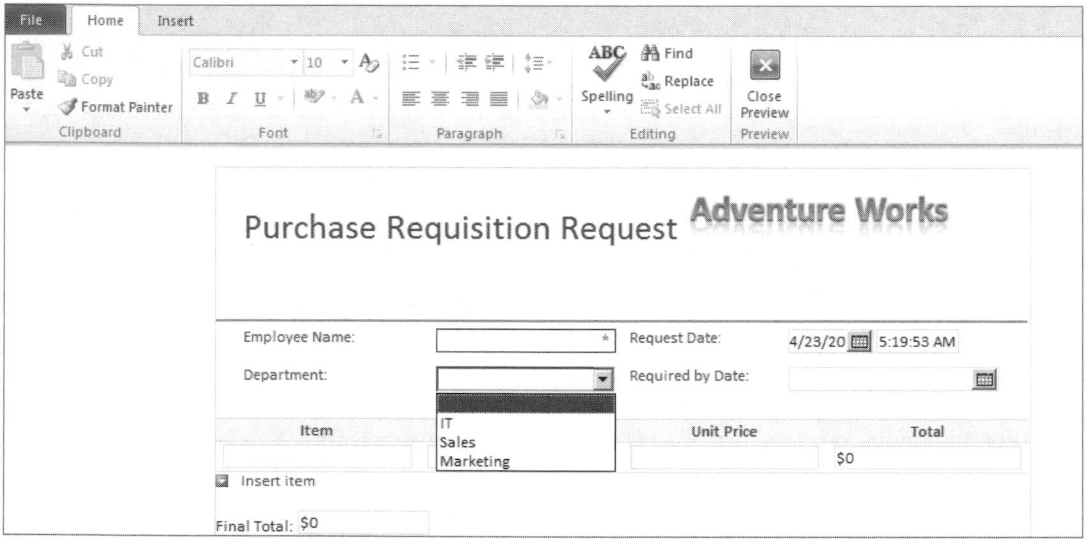

FIGURE 9-21

10. Save the form to any location on your hard drive.

How It Works

Connections that are created in InfoPath 2010 get stored with the InfoPath form template as secondary connections. You can create as many secondary connections as you need in the form. The data from these connections is available to be used anywhere within the form. The preceding exercise demonstrated how to make the connection to the Departments SharePoint list and then use the data from that list in the Department combo box control within the InfoPath form. Because the data received is all in XML form, XPath is utilized to traverse that data and point to the node of interest that contains the data needed to populate the combo box.

Publishing to the Form Library

Publishing InfoPath forms to form libraries is the recommended way to share these forms with users. Because a form library is just an enhanced version of the document library, it takes advantage of all the library features, as well. For example, security at the library, folder, and item levels is available to be set as needed. Check-in/check-out and versioning functionality is available for all forms that would be hosted in the form library, and because all content in SharePoint is stored in the content databases, the forms would be securely stored there as well.

TRY IT OUT   **Publishing an InfoPath Form to a Form Library**

In this exercise, you publish the Purchase Requisition Request form, created in an earlier exercise, to a form library.

1. Open the Purchase Requisition Request form in InfoPath.

2. Click on the File tab and then click Publish. Click on the SharePoint Server button on the Publish screen.

3. In the Publishing wizard that appears, enter the URL of any team site where you want to publish this form and click Next.

4. On the screen that appears, select the option to publish to a form library and click Next.

5. On the screen that appears, select the option to create a new library and click Next.

6. On the next screen that you see, name your form library **Purchase Requests** and click Next.

7. On the next screen that appears, you choose fields to be promoted as columns in the library. Use the Add button to choose and add the following fields: RequestDateTime, Department, EmployeeName, and FinalTotal. Your screen should like Figure 9-22.

8. Click Next and then click Publish.

9. When the publish process is complete, select the Open this form library checkbox that appears and click Close.

10. You should now see the Purchase Requests form library. Click on Add document and the Purchase Requisition Request form appears in the browser.

11. Fill out the form with some sample values and check for the following things:

> ➤ Employee Name should be required.

> ➤ The Department combo box should have all the choices from the Departments list. In addition, you can type in a Department directly.

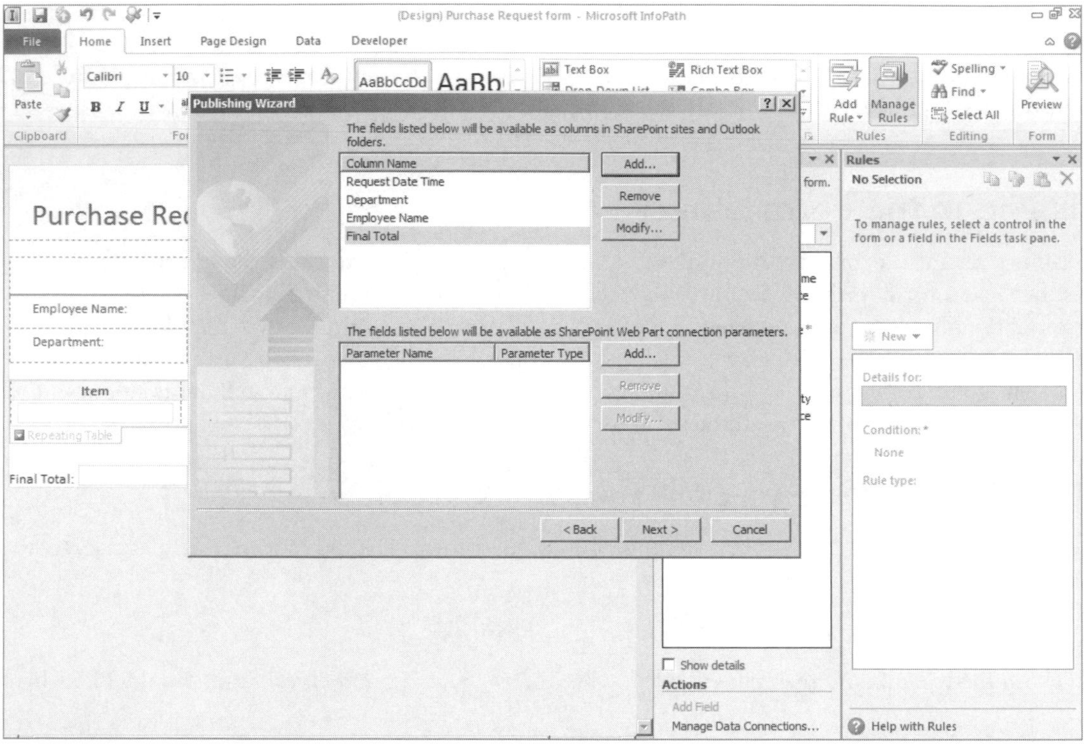

FIGURE 9-22

- ➤ Request Date should automatically be filled with the current date and time.

- ➤ Required by Date has to be in the future, otherwise the field's borders appear in red dots.

- ➤ The Total field in the Repeating Table should automatically provide the total purchase value for each item in the table.

- ➤ The Final Total field should provide the sum of values in the Total field. Also, if this value surpasses $1,000, the font and background should appear in shades of red.

Figure 9-23 shows the form filled out with some test values.

12. Correct any errors that appear in the form data and click on the Save button. Provide a name for the file in the Save As dialog that appears and then click on Save.

13. When back at the form, click on the Close button. The form should now appear as a new item in the library and all the fields that you promoted as columns should show the form values as metadata on the list, as shown in Figure 9-24.

How It Works

The default functionality of a form library is to try to open the InfoPath form in the browser. If it is unable to render the form in the browser, then it will automatically try to open the form in the InfoPath application on the computer, and if InfoPath is not installed on the computer, it will show an error to the user.

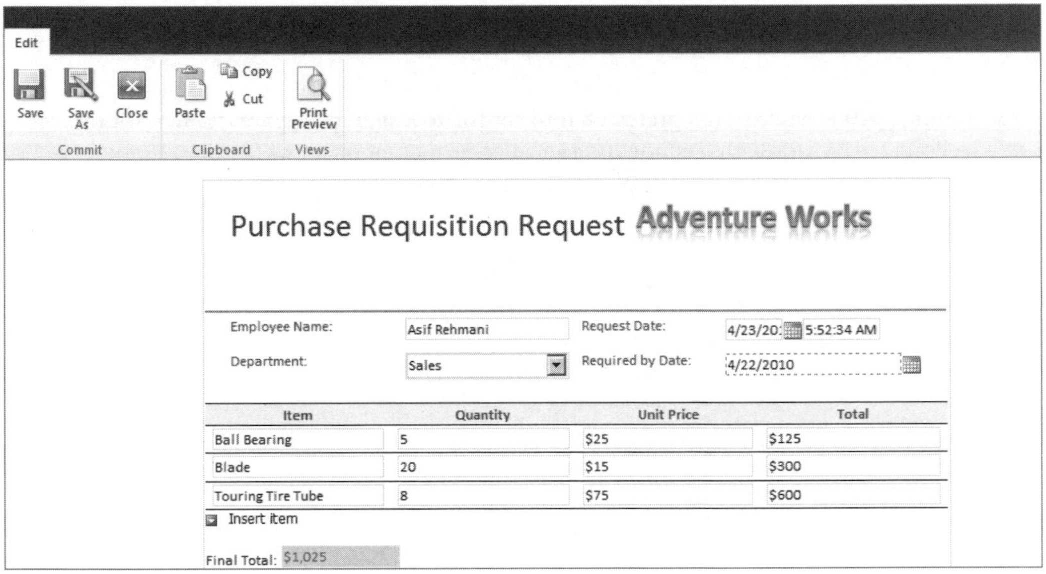

FIGURE 9-23

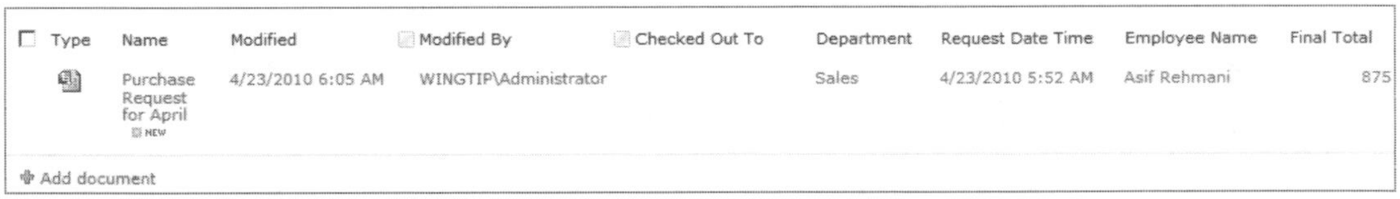

FIGURE 9-24

In addition to merely storing the forms in the form library, you can use them to participate in workflows. Form libraries, just like all other libraries in SharePoint, can have workflows associated with them. One of the ways workflows can be initiated is when a new form is created in the library. Workflows attached to the library can then take advantage of all column information in the library, including the columns that are displaying InfoPath form data. In effect, you can use the form data within your workflows, which makes for an extremely powerful solution. You can use SharePoint Designer 2010 to create workflows and attach them to a library. Chapters 11 and 12 cover these workflows.

In addition to the functionality of "saving" the form to your library, you also have the option to set up the "submit" functionality on your form. You can utilize the submit settings to submit the form to one or more locations, such as a web service and a form library. The submit function is the recommended option to have available for end users. Setting up the submit function requires quite a few more steps and is out of the scope of this chapter; however, you can see the submit functionality in action if you want in a demo presented at www.sharepoint-videos.com.

SUMMARY

Microsoft InfoPath 2010 is Microsoft's preferred tool for form design and generation. With the release of SharePoint 2010, InfoPath has now become a critical component of the SharePoint products and technologies family. It is a robust platform that can be used to create dynamic forms for SharePoint lists and libraries.

PART IV
Taking Action

10

Web Part Connections

WHAT YOU WILL LEARN IN THIS CHAPTER

➤ The function of web parts and web part pages

➤ How to add web parts to pages and configure them

➤ How to use personalized web part configurations

➤ How to export web parts and reuse them in other sites

➤ Creating composite user interfaces by connecting web parts together

TYPES OF WEB PARTS

Web parts are one of the primary means by which content is displayed in SharePoint. A *web part* may display static content, a view of a list or library, the interface for a business application, or virtually anything else. This chapter explains which web parts are available in SharePoint, how to arrange them on your pages, and how to connect them together to create rich, composite user interfaces.

Web Part Gallery

The Web Part Gallery is a special, hidden document library that contains the list of allowable web parts for the site collection. In Figure 10-1, you can see the Web Part Gallery contents as they appear in the browser. To display the Web Part Gallery in the browser, choose Site Actions ➪ Site Settings ➪ Galleries ➪ Web Parts.

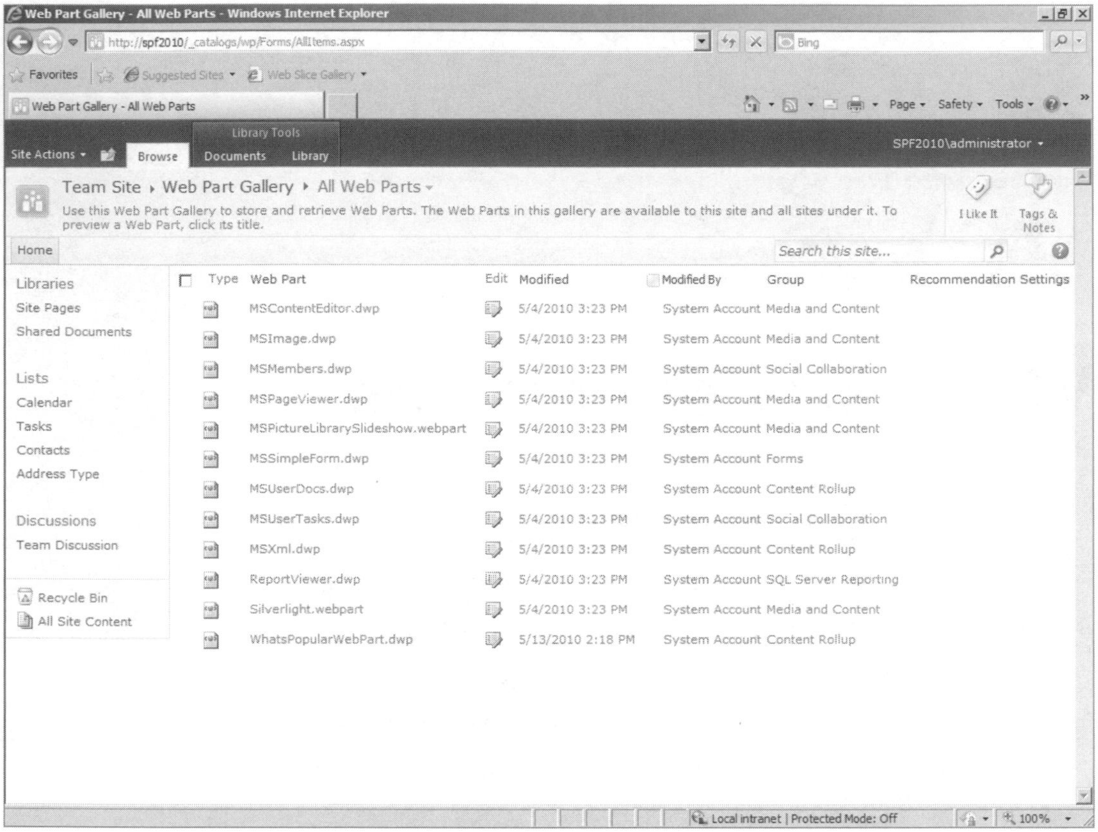

FIGURE 10-1

The available web parts are different depending on the edition of SharePoint and the SharePoint features that have been activated. You can also export web parts from your SharePoint sites and upload them into the Web Part Gallery. That technique will be covered later in the chapter.

You can also add additional web parts by choosing the Documents tab from the ribbon and clicking New Document. SharePoint then checks its `web.config` file to see which web parts have been authorized to run in the web application and displays the dialog shown in Figure 10-2. To add one or more of the web parts to the Web Part Gallery, select the appropriate checkboxes and click the Populate Gallery button.

Some of the key web parts are:

➤ **List View Web Part** — One of the most common SharePoint web parts, it is almost never shown by this name. That's because when a new list or library is created, a List View Web Part with the same name is created to go with it. Most standard list types include a hidden summary view that the automatic web part uses by default. You can edit the properties of the current view, or you can replace it with any existing view of the list or library. More about this web part was covered in Chapter 8, "XSLT Data Views and Forms."

➤ **Image Web Part** — Enables you to display a picture on a page.

➤ **Page Viewer Web Part** — Enables you to add content from another location to a page. This content can be another web page (or web application), a file share, or even an individual document and is typically displayed in an IFRAME on the current page.

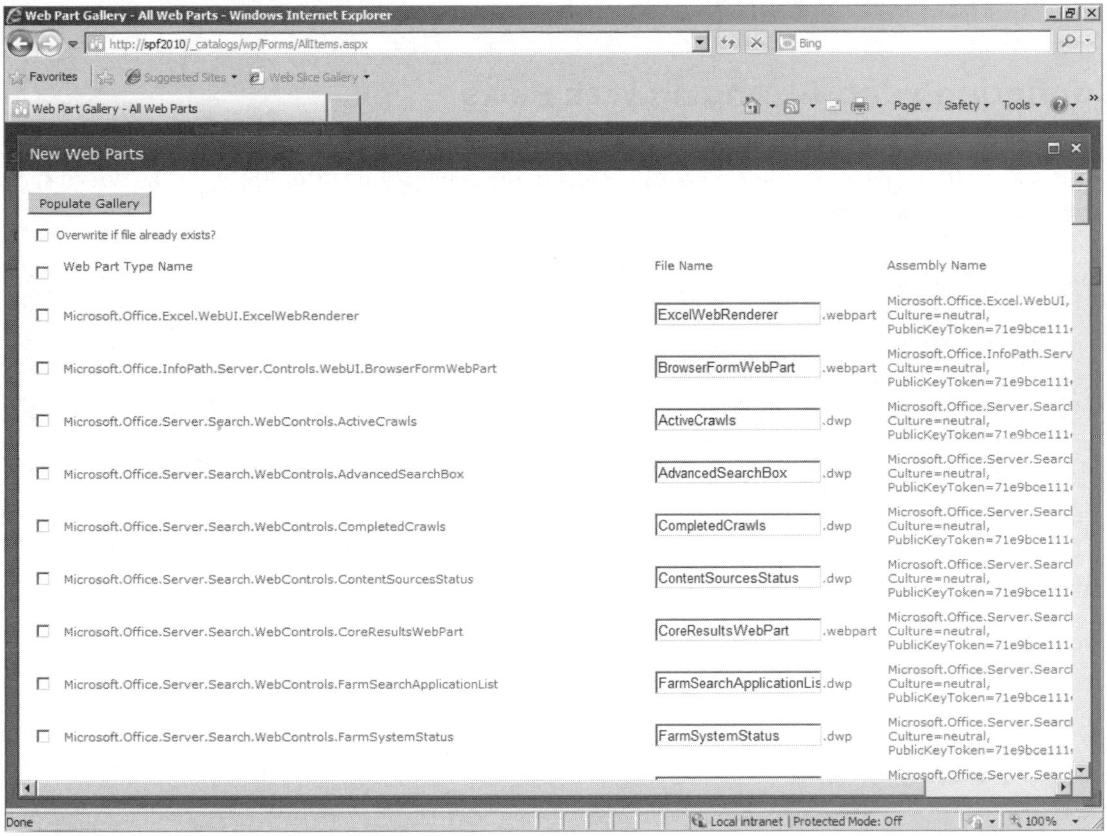

FIGURE 10-2

> **NOTE** *If the content cannot be rendered in an* IFRAME *in the user's browser, a popup window may be opened automatically to display it.*

➤ **Form Web Part** — Enables you to add HTML form field elements and other content to a page.

➤ **Content Editor Web Part** — Enables you to insert virtually any valid HTML into a page. Although it is often used for static rich text, this web part also allows client-side scripts.

➤ **XML Web Part** — Enables you to display and style XML data. Both the XML data and the XSL styling can be statically entered in the web part, or read from an external source. This allows for flexible presentation of many kinds of information.

➤ **Data View/Form Web Part** — Not available for insertion directly from the web interface. It can be added only through SharePoint Designer and is one of the most powerful tools in your arsenal. Several chapters later in the book are dedicated to showing you how to use the amazing Data View Web Part. More about this web part was covered in Chapter 8, "XSLT Data Views and Forms."

Configuring and Arranging Web Parts

To add a web part to a page, you must first create or open a web part page in SharePoint Designer. To see the list of pages in a site, click Site Pages in the Navigation bar on the left. The screen shown in Figure 10-3 appears.

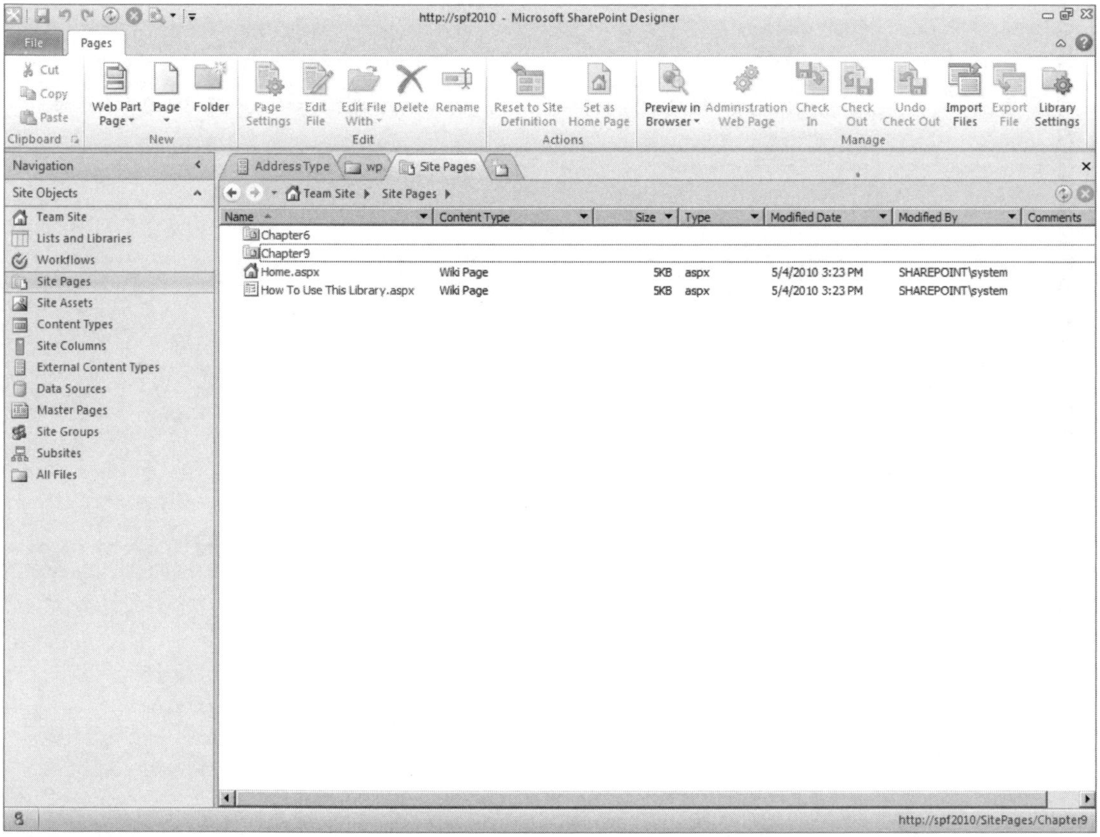

FIGURE 10-3

Site Pages is actually a document library that is automatically added when the site is first created. You can also create pages in document libraries and in the folders of the site directly. To create pages directly in the site's folders, click All Files in the Navigation bar on the left.

NOTE *The advantage of storing your pages in document libraries is that they are treated like any other document in SharePoint. That means you can use versions, content approval, custom permissions, and workflows to manage them. This functionality is the basis of all content management websites.*

To create a web part page, click the Web Part Page button in the ribbon. The layout choices shown in Figure 10-4 appear. Hover over any of the choices to display a tooltip describing the arrangement of the web part zones.

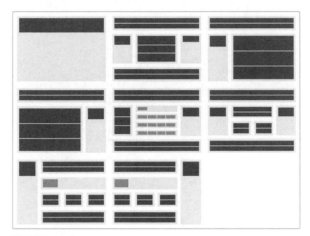

FIGURE 10-4

After you choose the best layout option, SharePoint Designer adds a web part page with that layout to your library. The page will first be named `Untitled1.aspx`, so be sure to rename it before editing it. To edit the page, choose the file and click the Edit Page button in the ribbon. The two modes for editing pages are normal and advanced. Choose normal editing when you simply want to manage the web parts on a page. Choose advanced editing when you want to alter the layout of the page drastically. You need to choose advanced editing mode when you want to add or remove the web part zones on the page.

WARNING *Editing pages in advanced mode causes the pages to become customized, which negatively impacts performance. Avoid using that option if the site will have a high volume of web traffic. The reason performance is affected is that your page will originally be read from the web server's file system, and after customization, it is detached from the site definition and stored in the content database. From that point forward, the page is read from the content database, which is much slower than reading it from the file system.*

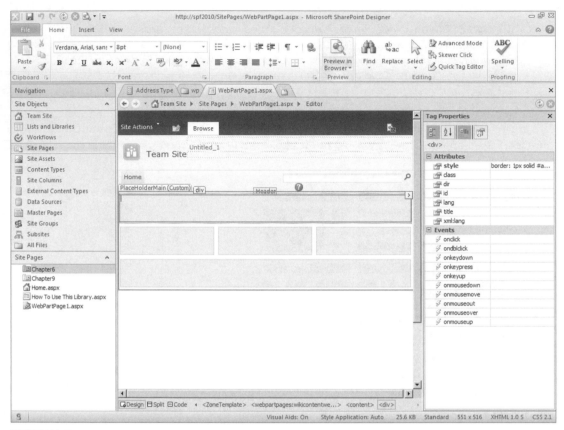

FIGURE 10-5

Figure 10-5 shows the page in normal edit mode. Notice the gray areas of the page. These gray areas are *web part zones*. Web part zones are the only places where you can position web parts. To add a web part to a zone, position the cursor inside the destination zone, and from the ribbon, choose the Insert tab and select Web Part. SharePoint Designer displays a list of web parts that you can choose. If you have many web parts in your site's Web Part Gallery, you can choose More Web Parts at the bottom of the list to display the dialog in Figure 10-6.

You can also insert web parts to display and manipulate data in lists and libraries by clicking one of the buttons in the Insert tab ⇨ Data Views & Forms section of the ribbon. One neat use of adding a list to a web part zone is that you can filter it using connections to other web parts (covered later in the chapter).

After you add a web part to the zone, a new tab named Format appears in the ribbon. The Format tab allows you to change the appearance and custom properties of the web part. You can see the Format tab in Figure 10-7. The web part in the figure is the Page Viewer Web Part, which you can use to display a web page from another website.

FIGURE 10-6

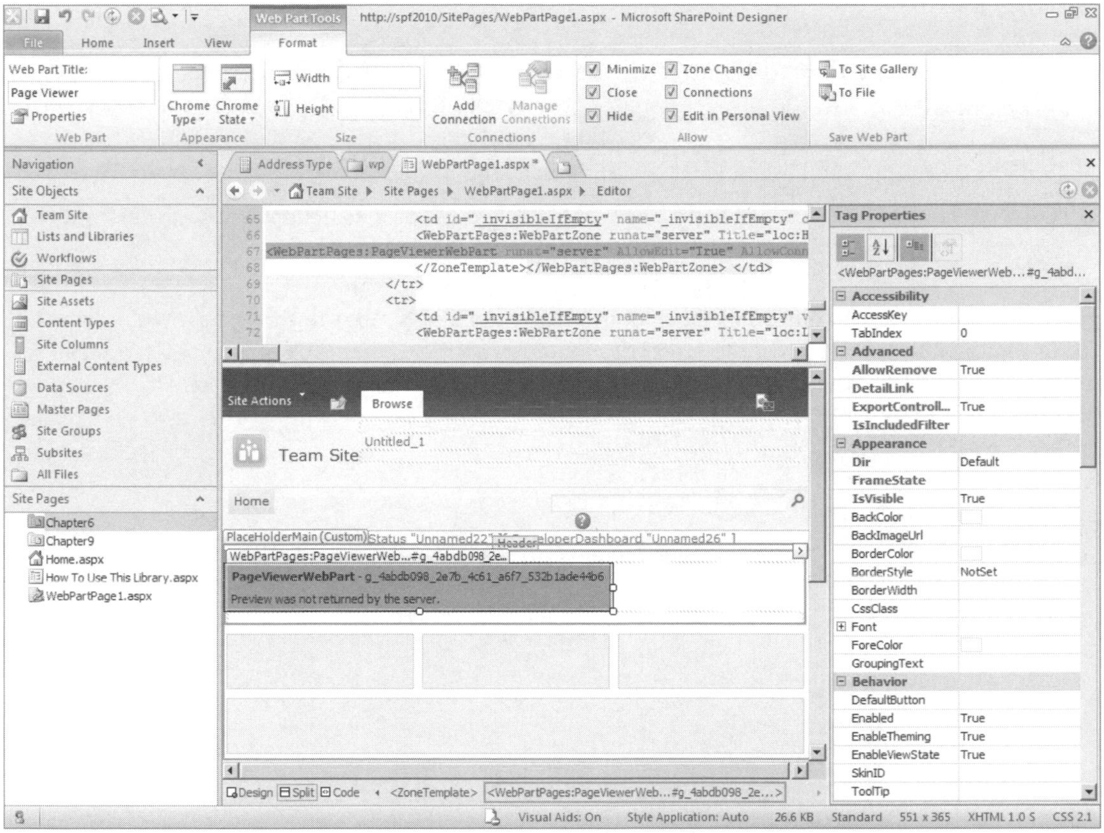

FIGURE 10-7

The following table explains the different settings you can change via the Format tab in the ribbon:

NAME	DESCRIPTION
Web Part Title	This is the text displayed at the top of the web part.
Chrome Type	A web part's chrome is the combination of its surrounding border and title bar. This setting allows you to change which part, if any, of the chrome is displayed.
Chrome State	This option controls whether the web part is expanded or collapsed.
Width/Height	Controls the size of the web part. If you leave it blank, the web part will be sized automatically.
Minimize	The web part can be minimized by the user.
Close	The web part can be closed by the user.
Hide	The web part can be made invisible by the user. This means that the web part is invisible unless the page is being edited.

continues

(continued)

NAME	DESCRIPTION
Zone Change	The web part can be moved between web part zones by the user.
Connections	The user can add or remove web part connections.
Edit in Personal View	The user can edit the web part's properties if he edits the page in personal mode. This is covered later in the chapter.

Clicking the Properties button in the ribbon displays a dialog similar to the one shown in Figure 10-8. This dialog allows you to edit the properties that are specific to that type of web part. You can see the different options for the URL to display and the type of link that the URL represents.

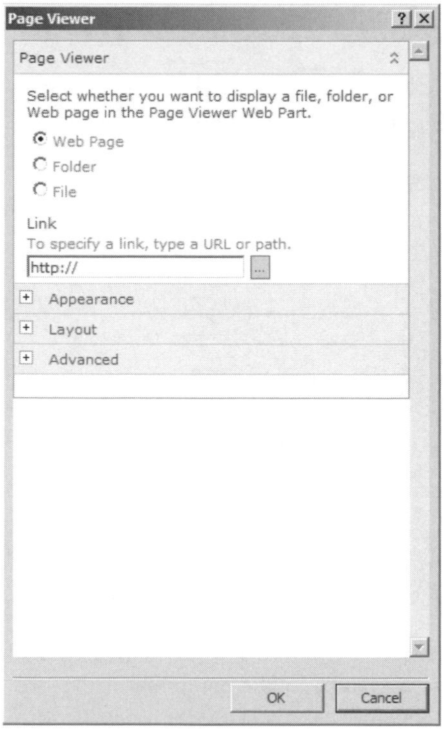

FIGURE 10-8

The Save Web Part section in the ribbon has two options for exporting the configuration of the web part's properties. You can choose to save the configuration to the Web Part Gallery or to a file. If you export to a file, you can upload it to any other site's Web Part Gallery, provided that the destination site has that web part installed and has been configured to allow it to be used.

TRY IT OUT   **Add a Web Part to a Web Part Page Using the Browser**

In this activity, you use the browser to add a web part to a page in a SharePoint site.

1.   Navigate your browser to your SharePoint site.

2.   Click More Options from the Site Actions menu.

3. When the Create dialog appears, select Web Part Page from the list and click the Create button.

4. Enter **MyWebPartPage** in the Name textbox and keep the default layout selected in the Layout listbox.

5. Select Site Pages from the Document Library drop-down list.

6. Click the Create button.

7. When the newly created web part page loads, click the Add a Web Part link in the Header web part zone.

8. When the list of web parts appears, choose Media and Content from the Categories list.

9. Select Content Editor from the Web Parts list and click the Add button.

10. Add the following web parts using the following information and repeating Steps 7–9:

ZONE	CATEGORY	WEB PART
Left Column	Media and Content	Page Viewer
Middle Column	Social Collaboration	Site Users

11. Click the "Click here to add new content" hyperlink in the Content Editor web part.

12. Type the text **Hello World!**

13. Highlight the text from Step 12 and click Bold from the Format Text tab in the ribbon.

14. Change the font size to 48pt and click the color button to change the color to green.

15. Hover the mouse over the title of the Page Viewer Web Part, and click the black down arrow to display the web part menu.

16. Select Edit Web Part from the web part menu.

17. Enter **http://www.wrox.com** in the link textbox and click the OK button.

18. Commit your changes to the page by clicking the Page tab on the ribbon and clicking the Stop Editing button.

How It Works

A new web part page with the layout you chose was added to the Site Pages document library. When you added the web parts to the web part zones on the new page, they were added using their default properties as configured in their dwp and webpart files in the Web Part Gallery. The Web Part Gallery is actually a document library that contains these special XML files containing the default properties for the web parts available in the site. Some web parts support changing their configuration by using the web part directly. The Content Editor Web Part can be directly edited in place without using the Web Part Properties pane. The Page Viewer Web Part does not support direct configuration, and you must choose Edit Web Part from the web part menu to change its configuration. Some web parts, such as the Site Users Web Part, do not need to be configured before they can be used. Until you click the Stop Editing button, your changes will not be saved and other users will not be able to see them.

TRY IT OUT **Add a Web Part to a Web Part Page Using SharePoint Designer**

In this activity, you will use SharePoint Designer to add a web part to a page in a SharePoint site.

1. Open SharePoint Designer from your Start menu.

2. Click the Open Site button.

3. When the Open Site dialog appears, enter the URL to your site in the Site name textbox and click the OK button.

4. If a Windows Security dialog appears, enter your username and password for the SharePoint site and click the OK button.

5. After the site opens, select Site Pages from the Navigation bar on the left.

6. Click the Web Part Page button from the ribbon and choose the middle image in the first row.

7. After the new page appears in the Site Pages library, change its name to **MyWebPartPage2.aspx**. Be sure to end the filename with the .aspx file extension or the page will not work properly.

8. After SharePoint Designer renames the page, click the Edit File button from the ribbon.

9. When the page editor loads, click inside the top gray box. The word *Header* should appear on top of the box.

10. From the ribbon, choose the Insert tab and click the Web Part button.

11. Select HTML Form Web Part from the web part list.

12. Position the cursor just after the Go button and type **Hello World!**

13. Click inside the left gray box in the second row.

14. From the ribbon, choose the Insert tab and click the Web Part button.

15. Select Image Viewer from the web part list.

16. From the ribbon, choose the Format tab and click the Properties button to display the web part properties dialog.

17. Enter the URL to an image in the Image Link textbox.

18. Enter some descriptive text in the Alternative Text textbox.

19. Click the OK button.

20. Click inside the middle gray box in the second row.

21. From the ribbon, choose the Insert tab and click the Web Part button.

22. Select XML Viewer from the web part list.

23. Double-click the web part to display the web part properties dialog.

24. Enter **http://blogs.msdn.com/sharepoint/rss.xml** in the XML Link textbox.

25. Enter **http://blogs.msdn.com/utility/FeedStylesheets/rss.xsl** in the XSL Link textbox.

26. Click the OK button to save your changes.

27. Click the Save button in the Quick Launch bar at the top of the screen.

28. From the ribbon, click the Home tab and click the Preview in Browser button to display your page in the browser.

How It Works

Using SharePoint Designer, you can create web part pages and add web parts much faster than using the browser. After adding the web part page to the Site Pages library, clicking the Edit File button opens the page in normal edit mode, which allows you to add and configure web parts just as you did using the browser in the previous activity. Editing the page in normal edit mode also has the benefit of keeping the page in its default, uncustomized status, which helps with performance.

> **NOTE** If a page is giving you a web part error or someone has accidently closed a web part, you can use Web Part Page Maintenance to remove the offending web part or restore the closed web part. To use Web Part Page Maintenance, navigate your browser to your ShaerPoint site and choose Page tab ⇨ Edit Properties button from the ribbon. Then, click the Open Web Part Page in maintenance view hyperlink. If you are unable to follow the previous steps due to a server error, you can try appending `?Contents=1` to the end of the URL; for example, `http://local.demo.com/SitePages/Home.aspx?Contents=1`.

Personalization

Personalization is a functionality in SharePoint that allows users to customize the configuration of web parts for their own use. Normally, users will see the *shared view* of a page. When a page is in shared view, any modifications are seen by everyone. To modify the shared view of a page, the user must have Design permission for the site.

When a page is in *personal view*, users can modify the page, but those modifications are only seen by the individual user. SharePoint stores personalized web part configurations separately for each user. To place a web part page into personal view, choose Personalize this Page from the personal menu as shown in Figure 10-9. To revert to shared view, choose Show Shared View from the same menu. You can also remove your personalizations by choosing Reset Page Content.

One reason you may want to use the personal view is to accommodate web part configurations that would only have value for yourself. Examples include web parts that would display your own stock portfolio or a rollup of blogs that are of interest to you.

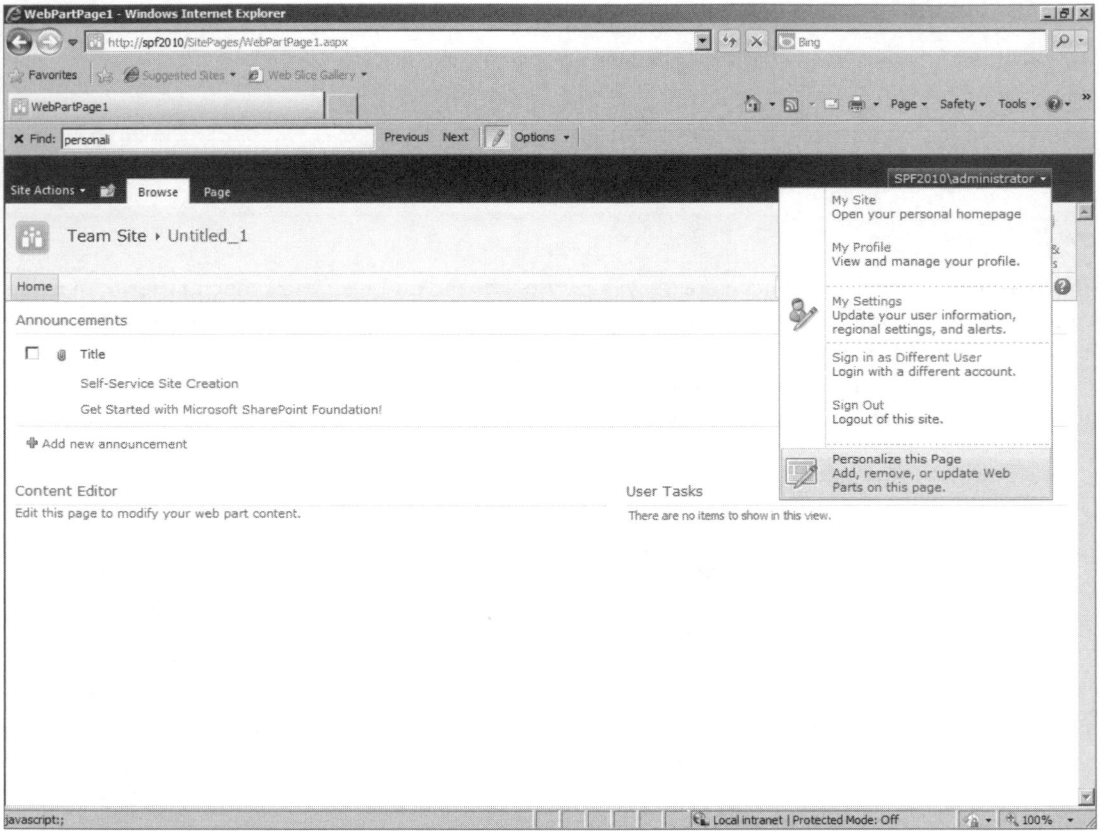

FIGURE 10-9

TRY IT OUT   Personalize a Web Part Page

In this activity, you personalize a web part page and compare the differences between the shared and personal view of the page.

1.   Navigate your browser to your SharePoint site.

2.   Click Site Pages on the Navigation bar on the left.

3.   Click `MyWebPartPage2.aspx` that you created in a previous activity.

4.   Click your name in the upper-right corner of the screen.

5.   Select Personalize this Page from the menu.

6.   Hover your mouse over the title of the HTML Form Web Part, and click the black down arrow to display the web part menu.

7.   Choose Edit My Web Part from the menu.

8.   Notice the following message at the top of the web part properties pane to the right: "The custom properties of the Form Web Part are not available in personal view."

9. Click the Add a Web Part hyperlink in the Middle Column web part zone.

10. Choose Media and Content ⇨ Page Viewer and click the Add button.

11. Click the open the tool pane hyperlink in the Page Viewer web part.

12. Enter **http://www.microsoft.com** in the Link textbox in the Page Viewer properties pane on the right.

13. Click the OK button.

14. Drag each web part to a different web part zone.

15. Save your changes by clicking the Page tab in the ribbon and clicking Stop Editing.

16. Switch to the shared view of the page by clicking your name in the upper-right corner of the screen and selecting Show Shared View from the menu.

17. Notice that the Page Viewer Web Part is not on the page and the web parts have returned to their original positions.

18. Return to the home page of your site by clicking the Browse tab and then the Home tab from the ribbon.

19. Click Site Pages on the Navigation bar on the left.

20. Click `MyWebPartPage2.aspx` that you created in a previous activity.

21. Notice that the personal view appears automatically.

22. From the ribbon, click the Page tab and select Edit Properties.

23. Click the "Open Web Part Page in maintenance view" hyperlink.

24. Notice that the list contains the web parts that are on the web part page.

25. Notice the new column, Personalized, added at the end of the list.

26. Click the Switch to shared view hyperlink.

27. Click the Go Back to Web Part Page hyperlink.

28. Remove all personalizations by clicking your name in the upper-right corner of the screen and selecting Reset Page Content from the menu.

29. Click OK in the confirmation dialog box.

How It Works

When you personalize a web part page, SharePoint stores your changes in the content database separately from the shared view of the page and loads your personal view whenever you access the page. When you were in personal view, you saw that some web parts, including the HTML Form Web Part, only allowed the Appearance and Layout settings to be changed. The developer of the web part decides which properties can be changed in the web part properties pane and which properties can be personalized. Though you may be restricted from modifying the custom settings of some web parts, you can still minimize, close, and move them around the page. Additionally, you can add your own web parts and configure them to suit your needs.

Exporting Web Part Configurations

As previously mentioned, you can export the configuration of your web parts. This feature is very useful when you need to add the same web part to multiple pages with the same configuration. To export a web part, open a web part page in SharePoint Designer. Then, select a web part and from the Format tab, click the To Site Gallery button. As shown in the dialog in Figure 10-10, you can enter a

FIGURE 10-10

name and description for the web part. You should always give a unique name for the web part to avoid confusion for other users. Also, you can click the Set Properties button to modify the new web part's properties before saving it to the Web Part Gallery.

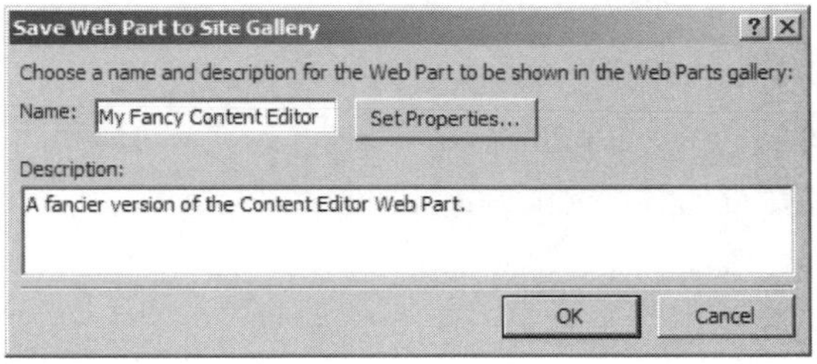

When you click the OK button, the web part is saved to the Web Part Gallery. You can see the exported web part in the menu shown in Figure 10-11. When that web part is added to a page using the browser or SharePoint Designer, it will be automatically configured.

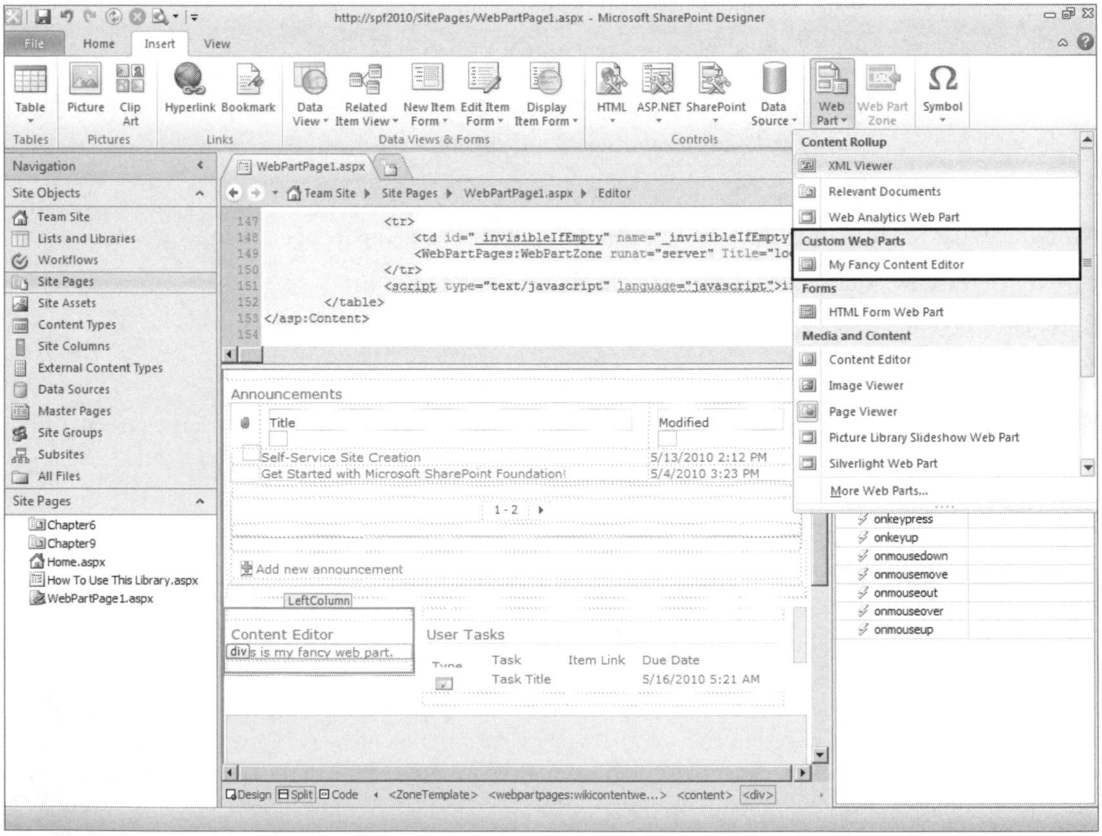

FIGURE 10-11

You can also export the web part to a file by choosing the Format tab and clicking the To File button. A File Save dialog appears, allowing you to choose the location and name to save the web part configuration. Configuration files can have either the `.webpart` or `.dwp` file extension. If you open the web part file, you will see XML like the file shown in Figure 10-12.

```
FancyContentEditor.dwp - Notepad
File  Edit  Format  View  Help
<?xml version="1.0" encoding="utf-8" ?>

<webPart xmlns:xsi="http://www.w3.org/2001/XMLSchema-instance" xmlns:xsd="http://www.w3.org/2001/XMLSchema"
        xmlns="http://schemas.microsoft.com/WebPart/v2">
    <Assembly>Microsoft.SharePoint, Version=14.0.0.0, Culture=neutral, PublicKeyToken=71e9bce111e9429c</Assembly>
    <TypeName>Microsoft.SharePoint.WebPartPages.ContentEditorWebPart</TypeName>
    <Title>Content Editor</Title>
    <FrameType>Default</FrameType>
    <Description>Allows authors to enter rich text content.</Description>
    <IsIncluded>true</IsIncluded>
    <PartOrder>2</PartOrder>
    <FrameState>Normal</FrameState>
    <Height />
    <Width />
    <AllowRemove>true</AllowRemove>
    <AllowZoneChange>true</AllowZoneChange>
    <AllowMinimize>true</AllowMinimize>
    <AllowConnect>true</AllowConnect>
    <AllowEdit>true</AllowEdit>
    <AllowHide>true</AllowHide>
    <IsVisible>true</IsVisible>
    <DetailLink />
    <HelpLink />
    <HelpMode>Modeless</HelpMode>
    <Dir>Default</Dir>
    <PartImageSmall />
    <MissingAssembly>Cannot import this Web Part.</MissingAssembly>
    <PartImageLarge>/_layouts/images/mscontl.gif</PartImageLarge>
    <IsIncludedFilter />
    <ExportControlledProperties>true</ExportControlledProperties>
    <ID>g_e3442bcf_2568_40a8_abd7_cdd4370848f7</ID>
    <ContentLink xmlns="http://schemas.microsoft.com/WebPart/v2/ContentEditor" />
    <Content xmlns="http://schemas.microsoft.com/WebPart/v2/ContentEditor"><![CDATA[<p>This is my fancy web part.</p>]]><
    <PartStorage xmlns="http://schemas.microsoft.com/WebPart/v2/ContentEditor" />
</webPart>
```

FIGURE 10-12

If you are careful, you can modify this file, thereby changing the properties of the web part before you upload it to the Web Part Gallery. If you are planning to edit these files routinely, purchasing XML editing software that will validate your file, rather than using Notepad, would be a good idea.

> **NOTE** If you rename the web part file to have an `.XML` file extension, you can open it in Internet Explorer as a quick check to see if your XML is properly formatted. If the file is valid XML, Internet Explorer will show you the contents of the file. Otherwise, Internet Explorer will display an error and indicate which part of the file is causing the problem.

To upload the web part file, you must navigate your browser to the Web Part Gallery by choosing Site Actions ➪ Site Settings ➪ Galleries ➪ Web Parts. When the list of web parts appears, from the ribbon, choose the Documents tab and click Upload Document. In the dialog shown in Figure 10-13, click the Browse button to locate the web part file and click OK to upload it to the Web Part Gallery.

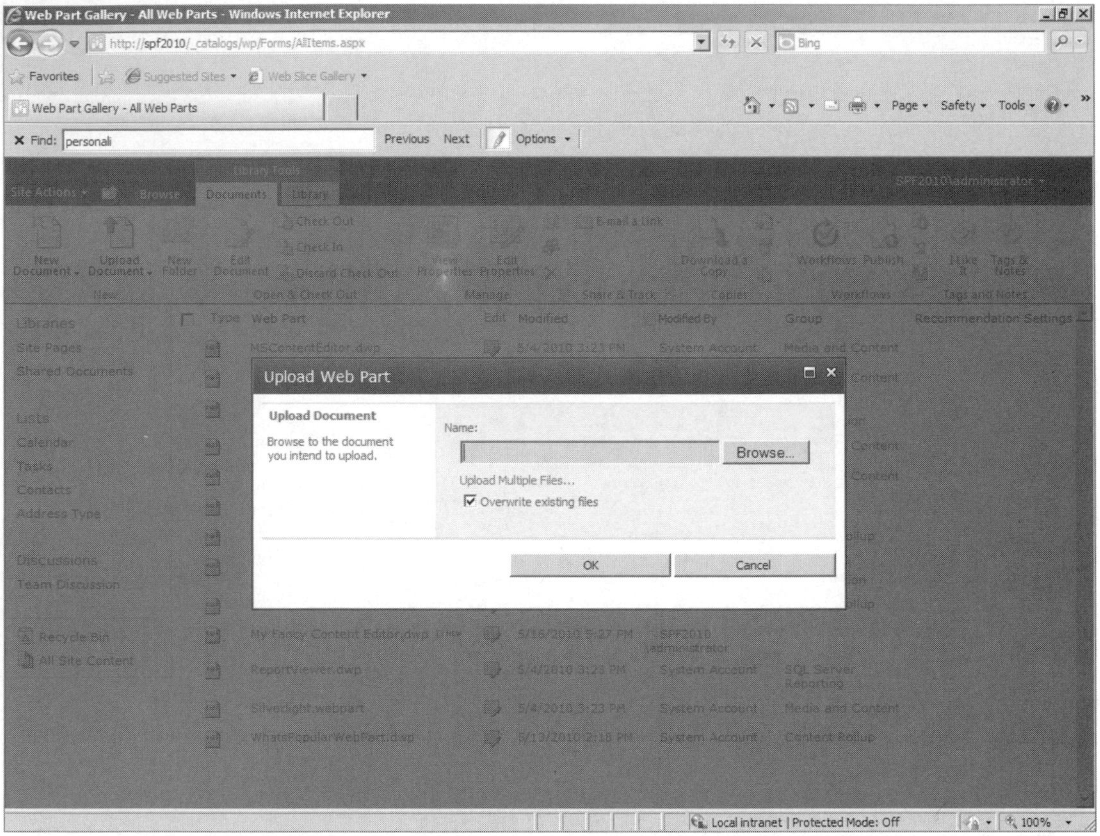

FIGURE 10-13

> **WARNING** *Be sure to change the filename of the web part file so it is different from the other web parts in the Web Part Gallery or you may overwrite an out-of-the-box web part.*

After the web part uploads, the dialog shown in Figure 10-14 appears. In this dialog, you can change the name, title, and description of your web part. You can also add the web part to a group to make it easy to find. If you don't choose a group, the web part will be added to the Custom Web Parts group. After you click the Save button, the web part becomes available for use in the browser and SharePoint Designer.

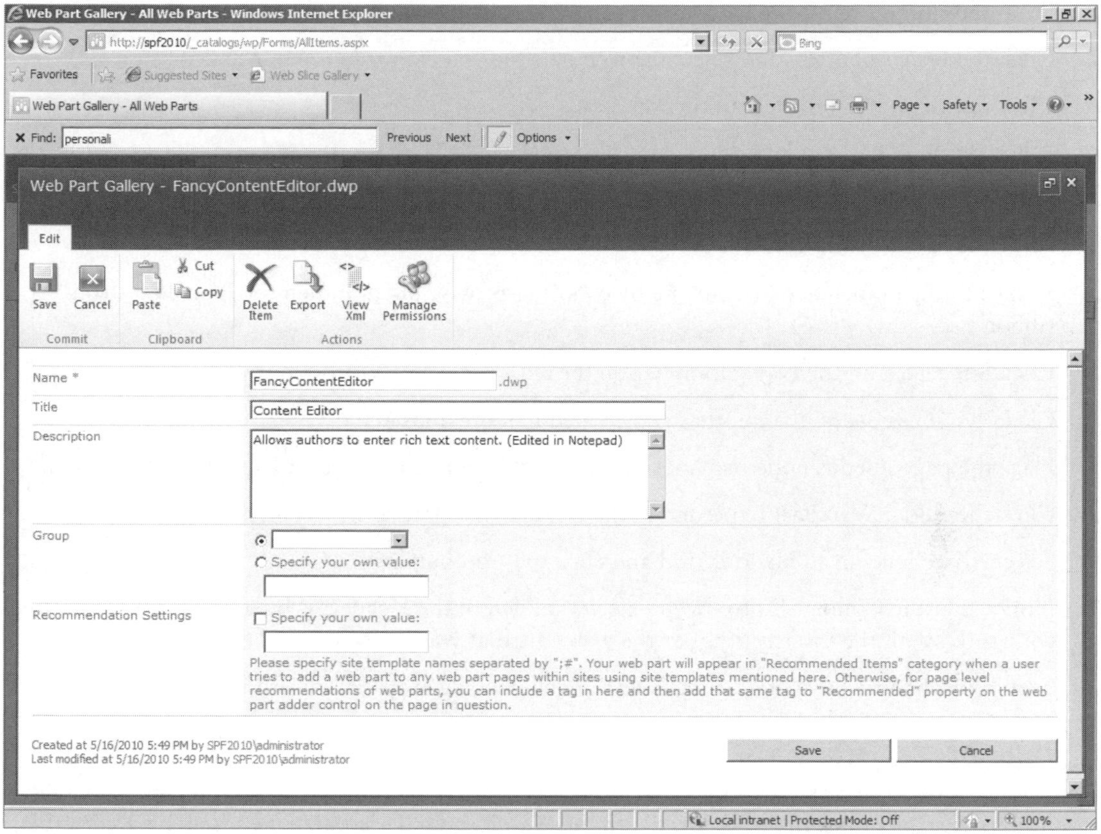

FIGURE 10-14

TRY IT OUT Export a Web Part Using the Browser

In this activity, you export a web part and reuse it in the same site.

1. Navigate your browser to your SharePoint site.

2. Click Site Pages on the Navigation bar on the left.

3. Click `MyWebPartPage.aspx` that you created in a previous activity.

4. Hover your mouse over the title of the Content Editor Web Part and click the black down arrow to display the web part menu.

5. Choose Export from the menu.

6. When the File Download dialog appears, save the file to your desktop.

7. Select Site Settings from the Site Actions menu.

8. Click the Web Parts hyperlink under the Galleries section.

9. From the ribbon, select the Documents tab and click Upload Document.

10. Click the Browse button and select the web part file you exported to your desktop.

11. Click the OK button to upload the web part.

12. When the Web Part Gallery dialog appears, enter **Hello World** in the Name and Title textboxes.

13. Delete the text from the Description textbox.

14. Click the Save button from the ribbon.

15. Return to the home page of your site by choosing Browse tab and then the Home tab from the ribbon.

16. Click Site Pages on the Navigation bar on the left.

17. Click `MyWebPartPage2.aspx` that you created in a previous activity.

18. Place the page in edit mode by choosing the Page tab and clicking Edit Page from the ribbon.

19. Click the Add a Web Part hyperlink in the Header web part zone.

20. Select Miscellaneous ➪ Hello World and click the Add button.

21. Notice that the Content Editor Web Part was added to the Header web part zone and was already configured with the same settings as the web part that was exported.

22. Save your changes by choosing the Page tab and clicking Stop Editing from the ribbon.

How It Works

When you exported the web part, an XML file was generated that contained all the exportable settings of the web part. Uploading the web part file to the Web Part Gallery adds a new web part with the preconfigured settings. Adding the new web part to a page automatically configures it with those settings. You can even upload the file to a Web Part Gallery in another site as long as the web part has been installed and has been configured to allow the web part to be used.

TRY IT OUT **Export a Web Part Using SharePoint Designer**

In this activity, you export a web part and reuse it in the same site.

1. Open SharePoint Designer from your Start menu.

2. Click the Open Site button.

3. When the Open Site dialog appears, enter the URL to your site in the Site name textbox and click the OK button.

4. If a Windows Security dialog appears, enter your username and password for the SharePoint site and click the OK button.

5. After the site opens, select Site Pages from the Navigation bar on the left.

6. Click `MyWebPartPage2.aspx` that you created in a previous activity.

7. Click the Image Viewer Web Part located in the Left Column web part zone.

8. Export the web part to the Web Part Gallery by choosing the Format tab and clicking the To Site Gallery button.

9. When the Save Web Part to Site Gallery dialog appears, enter the following values:

FIELD	NAME	DESCRIPTION
Value	My Image	A preconfigured Image Viewer Web Part

10. Click the Set Properties button.

11. Notice that the Image Viewer properties dialog is the same as the dialog shown when you click the Properties button on the Format tab in the ribbon.

12. Click Cancel to close the Image Viewer properties dialog.

13. Click OK to save the web part to the Web Part Gallery.

14. Click Site Pages in the Navigation bar on the left.

15. Click `MyWebPartPage.aspx` that you created in a previous activity.

16. Click the space under the Site Users Web Part located in the Middle Column web part zone.

17. Insert the new My Image Web Part by clicking the Insert tab from the ribbon and choosing Web Part ➪ Custom Web Parts ➪ My Image.

18. Click the Save button in the Quick Launch bar at the top of the screen.

19. Preview the page by selecting the Home tab from the ribbon and clicking Preview in Browser.

20. Notice that the new web part is present on the screen, already configured with the image.

How It Works

The web part export functionality in SharePoint works in a way similar to the functionality in the browser. Both allow you to export a web part with its configuration settings. However, the SharePoint Designer experience is much simpler and allows you to change the exported web part's settings without affecting the existing web part on the page. You can still export the web part to a file as the browser does, but you would only need to do that when you want to reuse the web part in a different site collection.

CREATING A COMPOSITE USER INTERFACE

SharePoint is quickly becoming the "glue" that ties together the disparate back-end systems of any enterprise. With web parts, you can expose those back-end systems through a simple, consistent user interface. Additionally, you can tie these web parts together, thereby tying the back-end systems themselves together, as will be shown in the next section.

Web Part Connections

One of the most powerful features of web parts is their ability to exchange data with each other via *web part connections*. A web part connection is a link between two web parts on the same page. Web parts can exchange a single value or multiple values. For multiple values, the data is exchanged via a row-like structure or a table-like structure. Exchanging a single value is the most common scenario, though.

To create a web part connection, open a web page in SharePoint Designer and ensure it has two or more web parts. Select the web part that will provide the data to the other web part, and from the ribbon, choose the Format tab and click the Add Connection button. The Web Part Connections Wizard shown in Figure 10-15 launches.

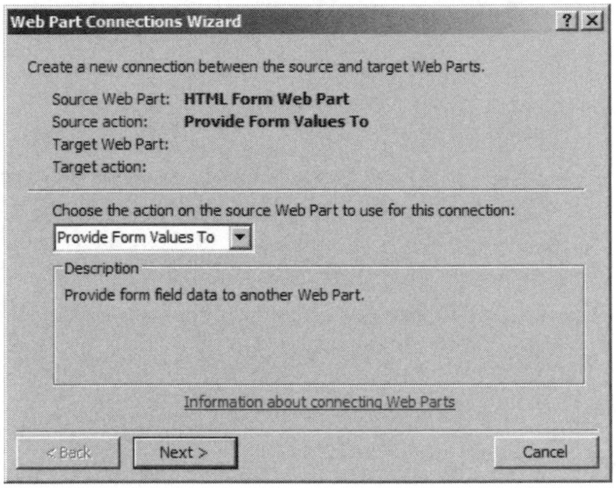

In the first step of the wizard, you can choose whether the web part will provide data or receive data from the other web part. Because the web part chosen in Figure 10-15 is an HTML Form Web Part, which only provides data, only the option to provide form values appears in the drop-down list. When you click the Next button, the dialog in Figure 10-16 appears.

FIGURE 10-15

In the second step of the wizard, you can either connect to a web part on this current page or another page in the site. When you choose the second option, you can click the Browse button to find the page you want. After you have selected an option, click the Next button to display the next step in the wizard, shown in Figure 10-17.

In this step, you select the target web part from the first drop-down list and the target property from the second drop-down list. In this example, the target web part and property are the Image Viewer and Image URL. That means that the first web part will provide the Image Viewer web part the value it needs to display its image. Click the Next button to display the step shown in Figure 10-18.

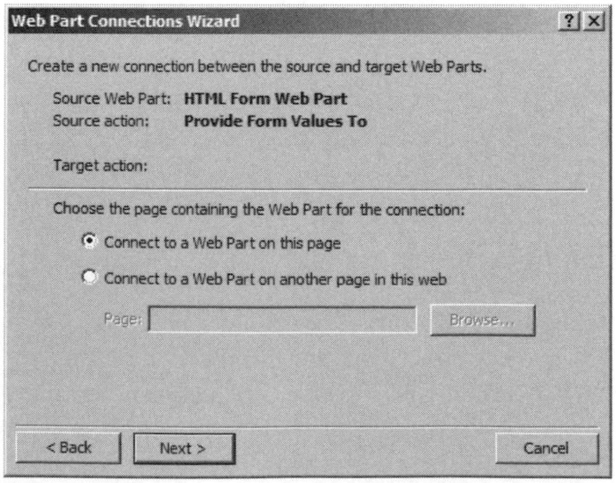

FIGURE 10-16

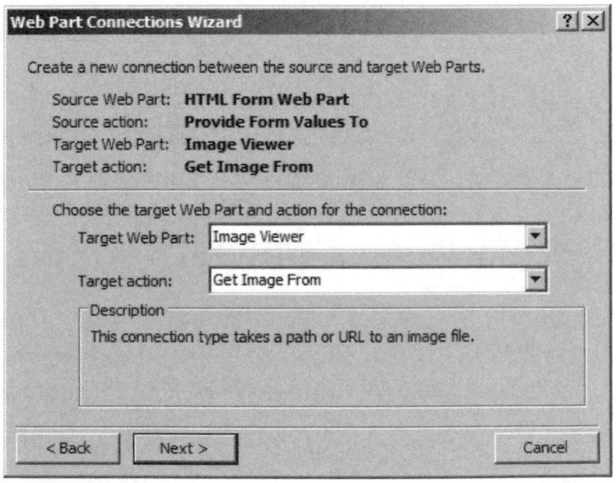

FIGURE 10-17

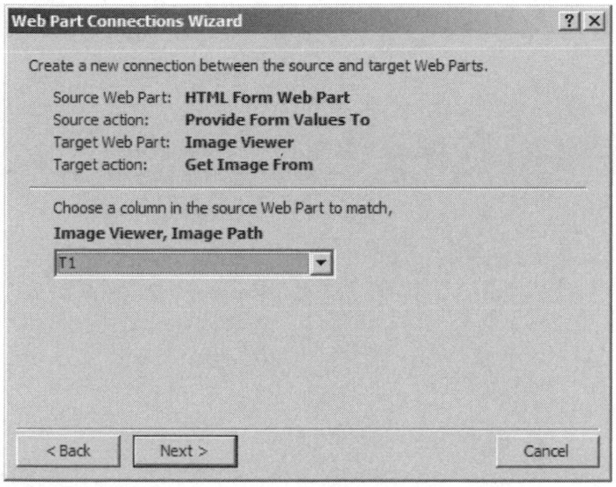

FIGURE 10-18

In this step, you must select the property from the source web part that will provide the value for the property on the destination web part. The first web part is the HTML Form Web Part, which allows you to add HTML and JavaScript to a web page without using a tool such as SharePoint Designer. By default, it contains the following HTML:

```
<div onkeydown="javascript:if (event.keyCode == 13) _SFSUBMIT_">
<input type="text" name="T1"/>
<input type="button" value="Go" onclick="javascript:_SFSUBMIT_"/>
</div>
```

Any input elements in the code snippet will appear in the drop-down list shown in Figure 10-18. In this case, only the input element named T1 appears, which is selected in Figure 10-18. Click Next to display the final confirmation step, and, finally, click Finish to create the web part connection.

> **NOTE** *In the browser, clicking the OK or Apply button on any arbitrary screen will save your changes. In SharePoint Designer, you will almost always have to click the Save button in the Quick Launch bar at the top of the screen to save your changes.*

After you save your page, from the ribbon, click the Home tab and click Preview in Browser to test your web part connection. In Figure 10-19, you can see the web page with the two web parts. If you enter any valid URL for an image in the textbox and click the Go button, the Image Viewer will display the image you entered. In Figure 10-20, you can see the Wrox logo after its location was entered in the textbox.

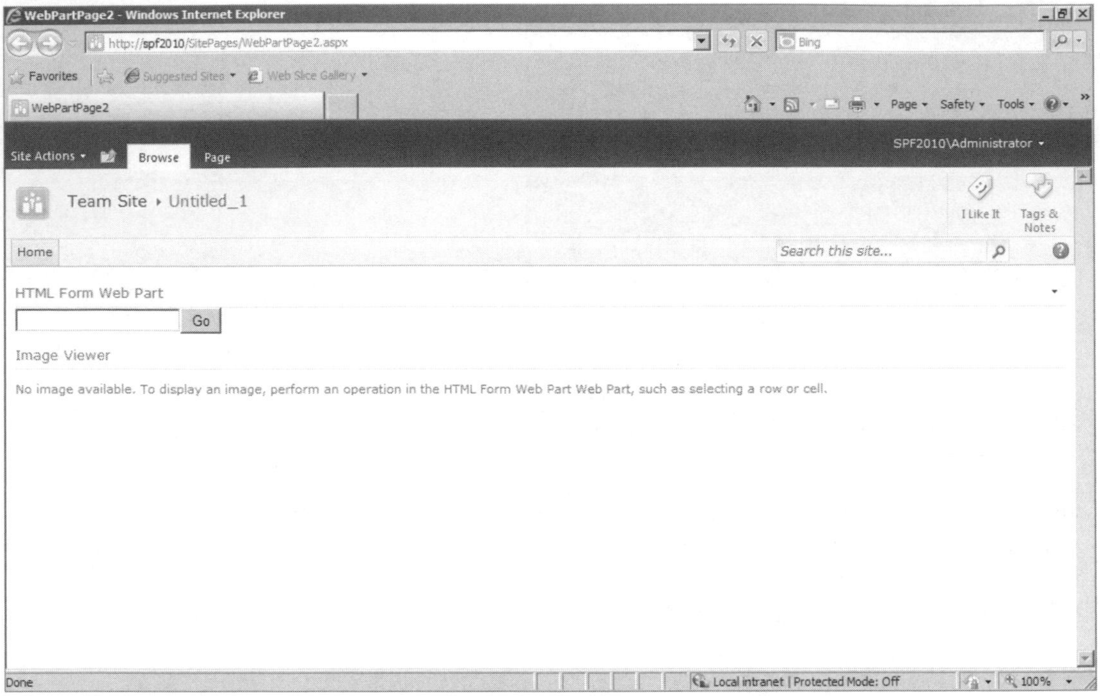

FIGURE 10-19

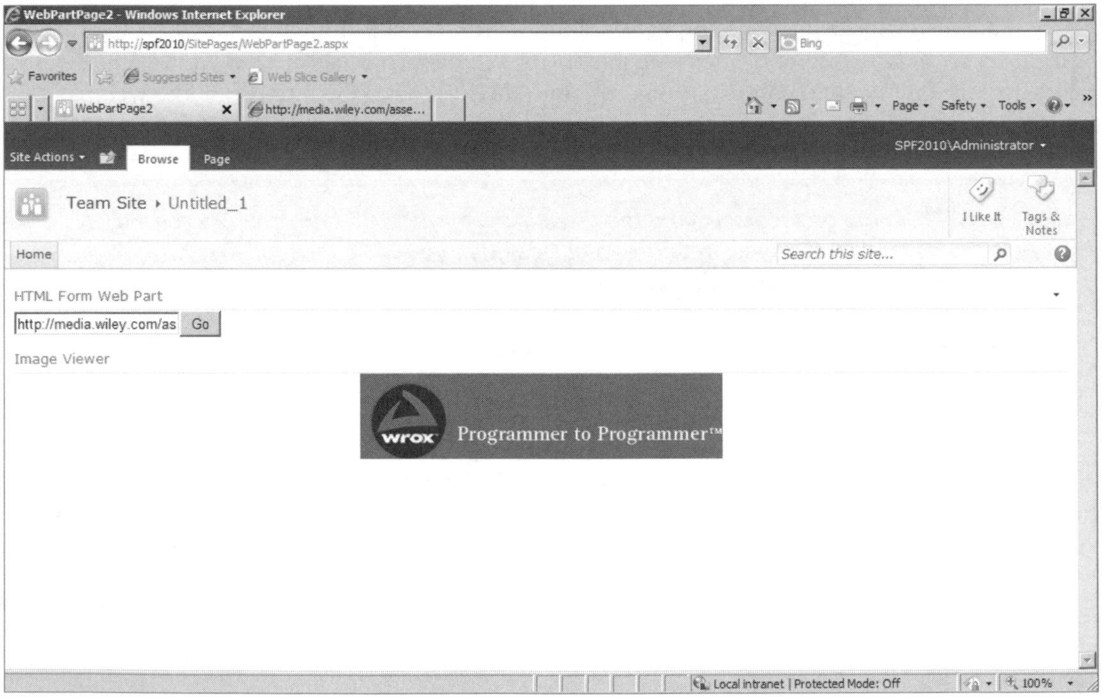

FIGURE 10-20

TRY IT OUT **Create a Web Part Connection Using the Browser**

In this activity, you connect three web parts using the browser.

1. Navigate your browser to your SharePoint site.

2. Click More Options from the Site Actions menu.

3. When the Create dialog appears, select Custom List from the list.

4. Enter **Departments** in the Name textbox, and click the Create button.

5. Add a new item by selecting the Items tab from the ribbon and clicking New Item.

6. Enter **Information Technology** in the Title textbox and click the Save button.

7. Repeat Steps 5 and 6 using the following data to create more items:

TITLE
Human Resources
Operations
Sales
Marketing

8. Click More Options from the Site Actions menu.

9. When the Create dialog appears, select Tasks from the list.

10. Enter **Departmental Tasks** in the Name textbox, and click the Create button.

11. After the list is created, select the List tab from the ribbon and click Create Column.

12. Enter the following information and click the OK button at the bottom of the screen:

FIELD	VALUE
Column name	Department
Type	Lookup
Get information from	Departments
In this column	Title

13. Repeat Steps 5 and 6 using the following data to create new items:

TITLE	STATUS	DEPARTMENT
Upgrade to Exchange 2010	Not Started	Information Technology
Send out employee satisfaction surveys	Completed	Information Technology

continues

(continued)

TITLE	STATUS	DEPARTMENT
Put together sales kits	Not Started	Marketing
Attend industry conference	In Progress	Sales
Calculate commissions	Not Started	Sales

14. Click More Options from the Site Actions menu.

15. When the Create dialog appears, select Web Part Page from the list, and click the Create button.

16. Enter **MyWebPartConnectionsPage** in the Name textbox and keep the default layout selected in the Layout listbox.

17. Select Site Pages from the Document Library drop-down list.

18. Click the Create button.

19. When the newly created web part page loads, click the Add a Web Part link in the Left Column web part zone.

20. Select Lists and Libraries ⇨ Departments from the Web Part Selection pane and click the Add button.

21. Click the Add a Web Part link in the Middle Column web part zone.

22. Select Lists and Libraries ⇨ Departmental Tasks from the Web Part Selection pane and click the Add button.

23. Hover the mouse over the title of the Departmental Tasks web part, and select Edit Web Part from the web part menu.

24. Click the Edit the current view hyperlink in the web part properties pane to the right.

25. Select the Department checkbox, and click the OK button.

26. Place the page into edit mode by selecting the Page tab from the ribbon and clicking Edit Page.

27. Click the Add a Web Part link in the Header web part zone.

28. Select Forms ⇨ HTML Form Web Part from the Web Part Selection pane and click the Add button.

29. Hover the mouse over the title of the HTML Form Web Part, click the black down arrow, and select Edit Web Part from the web part menu.

30. Click the Source Editor button in the web part properties pane.

31. When the Text Editor dialog appears, replace the existing code with the following snippet of HTML:

```
<div onkeydown="javascript:if (event.keyCode == 13) _SFSUBMIT_">
<select name="T1">
<option value="Not Started">Not Started</option>
<option value="In Progress">In Progress</option>
<option value="Completed">Completed</option>
```

```
<option value="Deferred">Deferred</option>
<option value="Waiting on someone else">Waiting on someone else</option>
</select>
<input type="button" value="Go" onclick="javascript:_SFSUBMIT_"/>
</div>
```

32. Hover the mouse over the title of the Departments web part, click the black down arrow, and select Connections ➪ Send Row of Data To ➪ Departmental Tasks from the web part menu.

33. When the Choose Connection dialog appears, ensure Get Filter Values From is selected in the Connection Type drop-down list, and click the Configure button.

34. Enter the following values and click the Finish button:

FIELD	VALUE
Provider Field Name	ID
Consumer Field Name	Department

35. Hover the mouse over the title of the HTML Form web part, click the black down arrow, and select Connections ➪ Provide Form Values To ➪ Departmental Tasks from the web part menu.

36. When the Choose Connection dialog appears, ensure Get Filter Values From is selected in the Connection Type drop-down list, and click the Configure button.

37. Enter the following values and click the Finish button:

FIELD	VALUE
Provider Field Name	T1
Consumer Field Name	Status

38. Save your changes by selecting the Page tab from the ribbon and clicking Stop Editing.

39. Click the select arrows in the Departments web part. Notice how the Departmental Tasks Web Part changes based on the department selected.

40. Click the select arrow next to the Information Technology department.

41. Select each value from the drop-down list and click the Go button in the HTML Form Web Part. Notice that the Departmental Tasks Web Part is filtered even further.

42. Select Not Started from the drop-down list in the HTML Form Web Part, and click the Go button.

43. Click the select arrows in the Departments Web Part. Notice how the Departmental Tasks Web Part changes based on the department selected.

How It Works

This activity is a one of the most common examples of web part connections: you get data from source A and filter it using data from source B or from user input. When you added the lists to the web part page, a web part was created for each list using the list's default view. Afterward, the two web parts could be connected with the Departments Web Part filtering the Departmental Tasks Web Part on the Department column. The lookup column from the Departmental Tasks list to the Departments list is not actually required to make the web part connection. A text column could have been used, but using a lookup column to a list or a choice column instead to enforce the domain integrity of that column is a best practice.

The HTML Form Web Part was added to the page to supply an additional filter on the Status column. This showed that a web part can have more than one web part connection and that a List View Web Part can have more than one filter supplied to it. At the end of the activity, you use the HTML Form and Departments Web Parts alternately to show that the web parts and the filter values they supplied operated independently. Though the two data web parts in this activity were both lists, the next activity will show that any data web part can both provide and consume filters via web part connections.

TRY IT OUT **Create a Web Part Connection Using SharePoint Designer**

In this activity, you connect three web parts using SharePoint Designer.

Before you start this activity, you must finish the Setup databases activity from Chapter 7, "Data Sources and External Content Types."

1. Open SharePoint Designer from your Start menu.

2. Click the Open Site button.

3. When the Open Site dialog appears, enter the URL to your site in the Site name textbox, and click the OK button.

4. If a Windows Security dialog appears, enter your username and password for the SharePoint site, and click the OK button.

5. After the site opens, select Data Sources from the Navigation bar on the left.

6. Click the Database Connection button on the ribbon.

7. Click the General tab and enter Categories in the Name textbox.

8. Click the Source tab and click the Configure Database Connection button.

9. When the Configure Database Connection dialog appears, specify the following values specific to your environment and click Next:

   ➤ **Server Name**

   ➤ **User name**

   ➤ **Password**

10. Click OK when the warning dialog appears.

11. Select AdventureWorks from the Database drop-down list.

12. Select ProductCategory from the table list box.

13. Click the Finish button to close the Configure Database Connection dialog.

14. Click the Sort button.

15. When the Sort dialog appears, select Name from the Available fields list box, and click the Add button.

16. Click the OK button to close the Sort dialog.

17. Click the OK button to close the Data Source Properties dialog.

18. Repeat Steps 6–17 using the following values:

DATA SOURCE NAME	TABLE NAME
Subcategories	ProductSubcategory
Products	Product

19. Select Site Pages from the Navigation bar on the left.

20. Click the Web Part Page button from the ribbon and choose the middle image in the first row.

21. After the new page appears in the Site Pages library, change its name to **MyWebPartConnectionsPage2.aspx**. Be sure to end the filename with the `.aspx` file extension or the page will not work properly.

22. After SharePoint Designer renames the page, click the Edit File button from the ribbon.

23. When the page loads, click inside the top gray box.

24. From the ribbon, click the Insert tab and choose Data View ➪ Database Connections ➪ Categories.

25. Click inside the middle gray box in the second row.

26. Select the Insert tab from the ribbon and choose Data View ➪ Database Connections ➪ Subcategories.

27. Click inside the bottom gray box.

28. Select the Insert tab from the ribbon and choose Data View ➪ Database Connections ➪ Products.

29. Click the Categories Web Part, select the Web Part tab, and click Add Connection.

30. When the Web Part Connections Wizard loads, ensure Send Row of Data To is selected in the drop-down list and click Next.

31. Ensure the Connect to a Web Part on this page is selected, and click Next.

32. Enter the following values and click Next:

FIELD	VALUE
Target Web Part	Subcategories
Target action	Get Filter Values From

33. Assign ProductCategoryID in the Categories column to ProductCategoryID in the Subcategories column, and click Next.

34. Select Name from the drop-down list and select the Indicate current selection using checkbox.

35. Select the ProductCategoryID checkbox and click OK.

36. Click Next.

37. Click Finish to close the Web Part Connections Wizard.

38. Click the Subcategories Web Part, select Web Part tab from the ribbon, and click Add Connection.

39. When the Web Part Connections Wizard loads, ensure Send Row of Data To is selected in the drop-down list and click Next.

40. Ensure the Connect to a Web Part on this page is selected, and click Next.

41. Enter the following values and click Next:

FIELD	VALUE
Target Web Part	Products
Target action	Get Filter Values From

42. Assign ProductSubcategoryID in the Categories column to ProductSubcategoryID in the Subcategories column and click Next.

43. Select Name from the drop-down list and select the Indicate current selection using checkbox.

44. Select the ProductSubcategoryID checkbox and click OK.

45. Click Next.

46. Click Finish to close the Web Part Connections Wizard.

47. Click the Save button in the Quick Launch bar at the top of the screen.

48. Test your page by selecting the Home tab from the ribbon and clicking Preview in Browser.

49. Click Clothing inside the Categories Web Part.

50. Click Gloves inside the Subcategories Web Part.

51. Notice that the contents of the Subcategories and Products Web Parts change depending on the filters selected.

How It Works

In this activity, you saw how three web parts can be connected in a chain where each web part filters the next. The ProductCategory, ProductSubcategory, and Product tables from the AdventureWorks database were good candidates for this exercise because they already had columns in common due to the foreign key relationships between the tables. When you inserted the data connections for the tables into the web part zones, data view web parts were added to the page. Those web parts can both provide and consume data from web part connections. To reflect the database relationships between the tables, the web parts were connected in a daisy chain where the Categories Web Part filtered the Subcategories Web Part, which, in turn, filtered the Products Web Part.

When you previewed the page in the browser, you may have noticed that the web parts were already filtered. The first row in the Categories and Subcategories Web Parts was automatically selected. Though all of these web parts were of the same type, you can connect any number and type of web parts.

Example Scenarios

This section of the chapter gives you some ideas for applying what you have learned so far. Two of the more common uses for web parts beyond simple web portals are *dashboards* for reporting and *workspaces* that revolve around a single task or job function.

Dashboards

In Figure 10-21, you can see an example of a dashboard. The Item Name and Ship Province Web Parts filter the data used to create the bar and pie charts at the bottom of the screen. In this type of dashboard, the user can manipulate the filters to examine the data from different perspectives. You can create dashboards from any number or type of web parts, but the key is to display charts and graphs rather than tables or lengthy paragraphs. The end result should allow the user to take the "pulse" of the company or department at a glance.

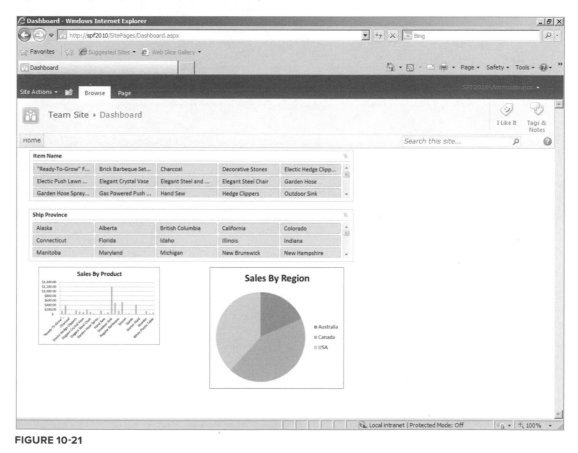

FIGURE 10-21

Task-centric Workspaces

Task-centric workspaces are websites that revolve around a particular job function or repetitive task. If you were to create such a site for a user who worked in a call center, the web pages would be populated with web parts that tied the various back-end systems together in one place. Call center users likely need to use a ticketing system for tracking calls, a customer relationship management system for recording ongoing customer interactions, and a searchable knowledge base of information to help the customer. SharePoint gives you the power to bring those systems together so users have one place to go for their information needs. No longer will users have to open several applications on their desktop and constantly switch between them to get their jobs done.

SUMMARY

This chapter explains how you can customize the user interface of SharePoint using web parts. SharePoint provides many web parts out of the box and a massive community exists providing free and for-sale web parts for your use. With web parts, you can quickly create workspaces for knowledge workers and dashboards for managers and executives. In the next chapter, you learn the basics of workflows and how they can extend SharePoint with powerful capabilities.

11

Workflow Basics

WHAT YOU WILL LEARN IN THIS CHAPTER

➤ The different types of workflows that can be created in SharePoint

➤ SharePoint Designer workflow fundamentals

➤ Creating List/Library workflows

➤ Building Reusable workflows

➤ Utilizing the Site based workflows

➤ Limitations and considerations when using SharePoint Designer workflows

The ability to create powerful and robust workflows is one of the most promising features of SharePoint Designer 2010. If you are familiar with the workflow story in SharePoint Designer 2007, much has changed since those days. This chapter explores all the workflow fundamentals as they exist in SharePoint Designer 2010 such as the ability to create list, reusable, and site based workflows. The story continues in Chapter 12 where you will dive even deeper into workflows with more advanced functionality and integration with other Microsoft Office applications.

WAYS TO CREATE WORKFLOWS IN SHAREPOINT

Workflow components come bundled with the .NET 3.5 framework. When the .NET framework (a prerequisite for installing SharePoint) gets installed on top of Windows Server 2008, the building blocks of workflow get baked into the platform. Because SharePoint sits on top of Windows, it is able to utilize these building blocks to create the workflows.

There are two types of workflows: sequential and state machine. Sequential workflows are those that follow a prescribed path with a definite beginning and end. State machine workflows, on the other hand, are typically much more complex. They are based on the concept of conditions and transitions. A condition is a set of circumstances that indicate the current status or situation of the process being modeled. Events occur and cause a transition from one condition to another. There is no prescribed path for the workflow. The path taken by the workflow is determined by the events that occur as the workflow is processing.

SharePoint workflows can be created in a variety of ways. The tool of choice depends on the person creating the workflow and the complexity required for the steps in the workflow. The following sections briefly describe the three ways in which workflows can be built on SharePoint.

Built-in Workflow Templates

SharePoint foundation ships with one workflow template (Three-state workflow). If you have the SharePoint Server Standard or Enterprise license, you get four more templates to work with. You can start taking advantage of these workflow templates right away by using the browser and building your workflows, as shown in Figure 11-1. No special software is required to build these workflows. All of these workflows are sequential workflows.

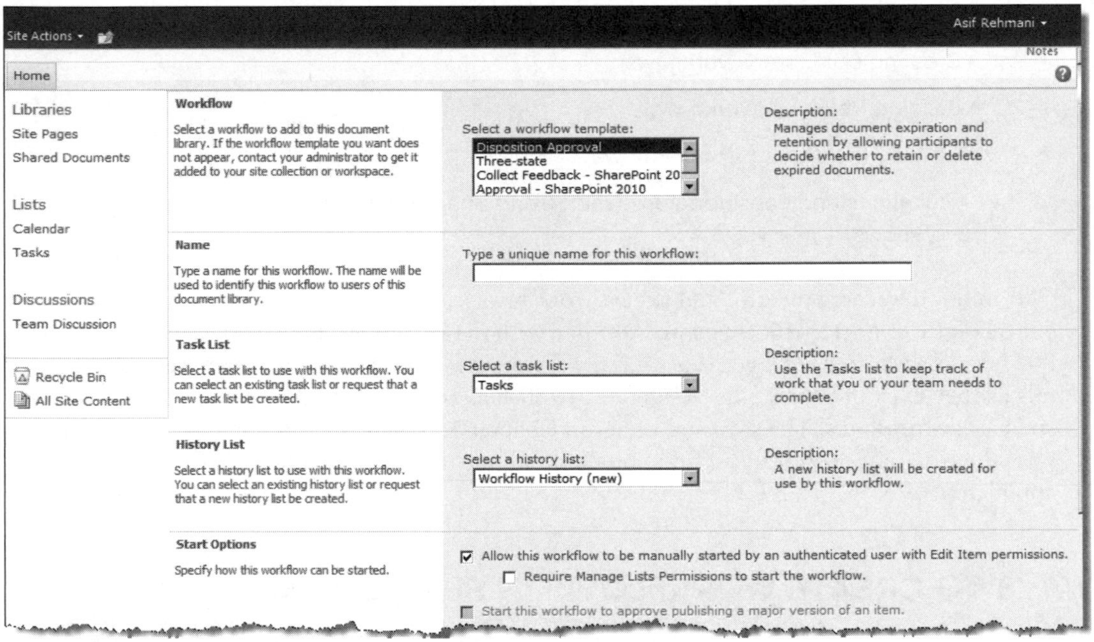

FIGURE 11-1

Most of these workflows are geared toward typical document or list management tasks. These will not serve all your workflow needs, but they still are a good start toward satisfying many of the existing processes in the organization. In addition, because they are created directly using the browser, creating them quickly without any prior training on creating workflows is easy for any site administrator.

SharePoint Designer 2010 Workflows

At times, you might want to perform a task based on a value entered by your user, such as creating a new item in a different list, or escalating an issue after a certain amount of time has passed and an action has not been taken. Although SharePoint's workflow engine is capable of such things, no web interface exists for creating these more sophisticated functions.

That's where the SharePoint Designer 2010 Workflow Designer comes in. The Workflow Designer is a tool that enables you to create a sequence of actions (executed serially or in parallel) that must be taken when certain conditions are met for a document or list item. It provides pre-built building blocks in forms of conditions and actions that you can use to create your flexible yet powerful workflow scenarios. The tool resembles an e-mail inbox rules wizard, making it easy for people without a procedural programming background to produce sophisticated workflow applications. Site administrators and power users can use SharePoint Designer 2010 to create powerful workflows. Having said that, keep in mind that only sequential workflows (as discussed in the last section) are created using SharePoint Designer 2010. This workflow designer environment does not support creating state machine workflows.

You find many examples later in this chapter on how to create the various types of workflows available within SharePoint Designer 2010. The following example gives you a taste of how to create a simple list workflow.

TRY IT OUT   Create a List Workflow Using SharePoint Designer 2010

In this exercise, you will create a simple workflow using the Workflow Designer interface in SharePoint Designer 2010. This workflow will look at the Title field of a document being uploaded to a library, and, if it's not already populated, it will populate it with the information in the Name field of the document.

1. Open any Team Site in SharePoint Designer 2010, and click on Workflows in the navigation pane.

2. Click the List Workflow button in the ribbon and from the drop-down select Shared Documents.

3. In the Create List Workflow dialog that appears, name the workflow **Populate Title** and click OK. The Workflow Designer interface appears.

4. Click the Condition button in the ribbon and from the drop-down select "If current item field equals value." This inserts the condition on the Workflow Designer as shown in Figure 11-2.

5. Click the `field` link and from the drop-down, select Title. Click the `equals` link and then select "is empty" from the drop-down.

6. Click right below the condition to place the cursor (the orange blinking line) there and then (in the ribbon) click Action ⇨ Set Field in Current Item.

7. Click the `field` link and select Title. Click value, and then click the *fx* button. From the dialog box that appears, click the drop-down for Field from source, select the Name field, and then click OK.

8. Put the cursor right underneath this action and click Action ⇨ Log to History List.

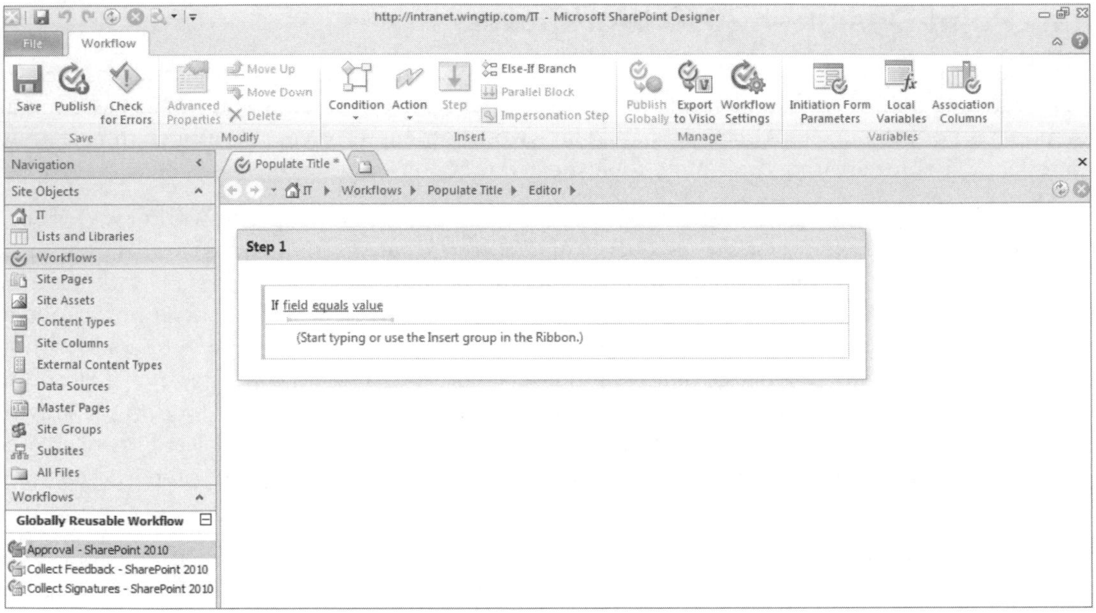

FIGURE 11-2

9. Click the `this message` link and type in **Title changed to file name**.

10. Put the cursor right underneath and click the Else-If Branch button in the ribbon.

11. Click right under the text "Start typing or use the Insert group in the Ribbon." Type in **log**. Press Enter on your keyboard to see the "Log this message" action appear.

12. Click the `this message` link and type in **Title is already filled in**. Your workflow should now look like the one in Figure 11-3.

13. Click the Check for Errors button on the ribbon. If any errors are in the workflow, you will see a warning icon next to the condition or action where the problem exists. Otherwise, a dialog box will notify you that no errors exist in the workflow.

14. Click the Workflow Settings button on the ribbon and from the settings page, select the checkbox for Start workflow automatically when an item is created.

15. Click Save button to save this workflow and then click the Publish button to publish it to the Shared Documents library.

How It Works

The workflow designed in this exercise is a fairly simple workflow that solves a very common need. All files have a name because that's a requirement for them to exist; however, often the titles for the files are not populated by the end users. This workflow executes every time a new file is uploaded to the Shared Documents library. If the Title field is empty, it automatically fills it in with the name of the file. In either case, it logs a statement of what it did in the history list.

You can verify that this workflow actually works by going to the Shared Documents library and uploading a document that does not have the `Title` property filled in. After the document is uploaded, the workflow should run automatically and set the title for this document. The name of the workflow is displayed as a new column in the library, and when the workflow finishes, the status `Completed` appears under the column. When you click the `Completed` link, it takes you to a workflow status page that looks like the one in Figure 11-4.

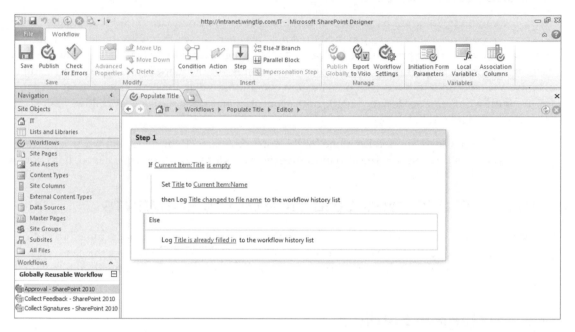

FIGURE 11-3

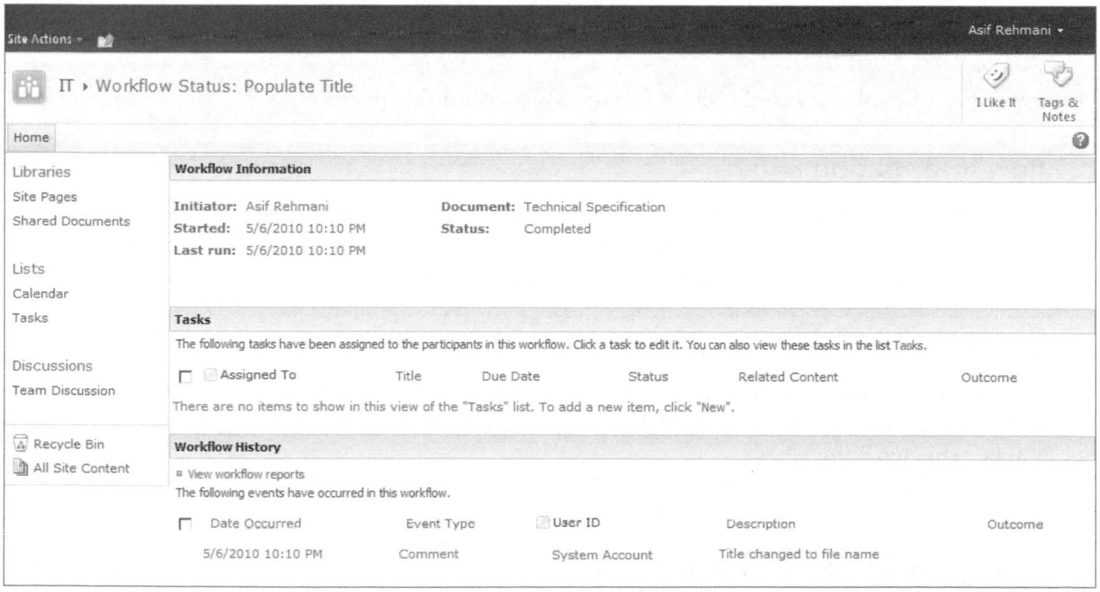

FIGURE 11-4

A bit later in this chapter, all the components of the Workflow Designer interface are dissected and explained.

Visual Studio Workflows

Workflows in SharePoint are based on the Windows Workflow Foundation (WF). Although many powerful actions are available to you in SharePoint Designer, these are but a sample of the kinds of functions the WF can be programmed to perform. By using Microsoft Visual Studio, you can create custom workflows programmatically to take full advantage of the workflow objects in WF. You can also use Visual Studio to build your own custom conditions and actions, and make them available for use within SharePoint Designer 2010. Both sequential and state machine workflows can be created using Visual Studio.

Visual Studio workflows are best left alone for developers to create. Remember that when you create your workflows in this manner, you also must manage the code (at least, someone has to, if it's not you).

SHAREPOINT DESIGNER 2010 WORKFLOW ELEMENTS

The Workflow Designer has a lot of moving parts. It will benefit you to get accustomed to these parts before venturing on to making your own workflows. This section explores the elements available in the Workflow Designer interface. Use this section as a reference when building your workflows.

Workflow General Settings

The summary page of the workflow is the Workflow Settings page. You get to this page by clicking on any of the existing workflows or clicking on the Workflow Settings button on the ribbon when you are editing a workflow. Figure 11-5 shows the Workflow Settings page.

Following is an explanation of each of the sections within this page.

Workflow Information

This section shows the name and description of the workflow. Both can be changed from this interface (just don't forget to click on the Save button to save your changes). In addition, you can also see what type of workflow it is and whether it is associated with a list or a library.

Customization

Clicking on Edit Workflow in this section takes you to the Workflow Designer interface. You can also see several other links here. These links provide you an easy way to navigate to the related components of this workflow.

Settings

The Task List and History List drop-downs in this section show the lists that will contain the tasks and the history logs (respectively) that this workflow might generate. You can use the drop-downs to select lists other than the default ones selected already.

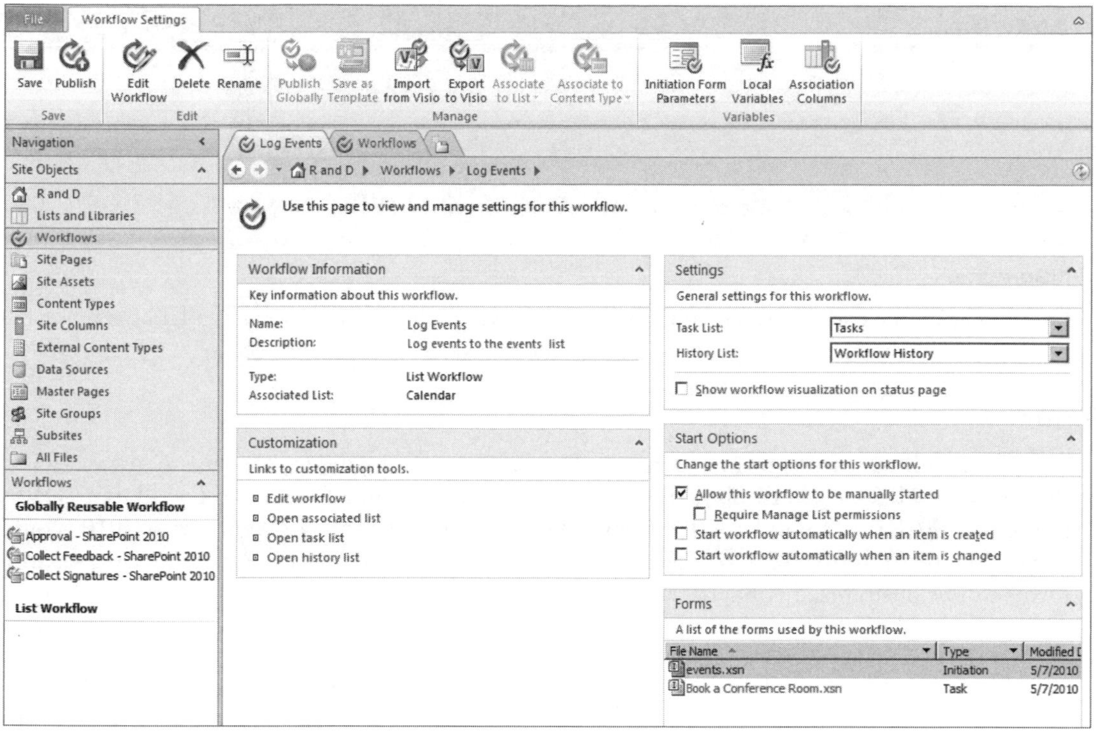

FIGURE 11-5

You use the checkbox below the drop-down lists that states "Show workflow visualization on status page" to turn on visualization of the workflow using Visio services. This visualization is then presented on the workflow history page. Chapter 12 covers the Visio integration with workflows.

Workflow Start Options

You start running a SharePoint Designer workflow in one of three ways:

➤ Allow your user to start the workflow manually (selected by default).

➤ Start the workflow automatically when a new item is created.

➤ Start the workflow automatically when an item is edited.

When the workflow is automatically started, no workflow form is presented — execution simply proceeds to the first step in the workflow. However, when starting a workflow manually, the initiation form for the workflow is presented to the user. Initiation forms are discussed a bit later in this section.

By default, a user has two ways to invoke a workflow through the browser:

➤ A Workflows command on the item's Action menu

➤ The Workflows command button on the ribbon, as shown in Figure 11-6

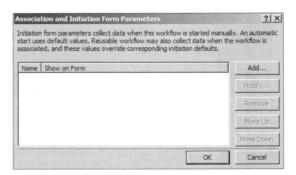

FIGURE 11-6

In either case, the user is presented with a page showing a list of workflows available to items in the list or library, and the status of any workflows currently associated with the item.

Forms

Workflows utilize various forms, such as initiation, association, and task forms, to interact with the end user. This section displays those forms. If you are running SharePoint Foundation 2010 on the server, these forms will be ASPX forms. On the other hand, if SharePoint Server 2010 is on the server then these forms are XSN (the extension for Microsoft InfoPath) forms. In both cases, these forms can be customized. Chapter 12 shows how to customize the workflow forms.

Initiation Parameters

Occasionally, you may want to start your workflow with information that isn't already in SharePoint. Workflow initiation parameters enable you to provide (or request) that information from the user. When you define a parameter, you give it a name and a data type. Initiation parameters are accessed in the Workflow Designer by clicking the Initiation button on the ribbon.

When you click the Initiation button, the Workflow Association and Initiation Parameters dialog appears, as shown in Figure 11-7.

You can click the Add button here to open the Add Field wizard where you can add or remove parameters, or change the order in which they will appear on the initiation form.

The Add Field wizard first asks for the name of the field, and provides a dropdown for the type of data. Click Next, and a form appropriate for selecting a default value for your field appears. This is provided because the initiation form is not displayed if the workflow is started automatically and the default value (if provided) is automatically used. Figure 11-8 shows the Default value entry form for a Date and Time field.

FIGURE 11-7

FIGURE 11-8

Initiation parameters can each be any of the following types:

➤ Single line of text

➤ Multiple lines of text

➤ Number

➤ Date and time

➤ Choice (a list of preset values to choose from)

➤ Yes/No (a Boolean/checkbox)

➤ Person or Group

➤ Hyperlink or Picture

➤ Assignment Stages (used in the Task Process Designer)

Initiation Form

An initiation form is created automatically by the Workflow Designer when you save your workflow. It is used to allow the user to enter the initiation parameters you have defined (if any), as well as to verify that the user actually wants to start processing a workflow that was initiated manually. An example initiation form is shown in Figure 11-9.

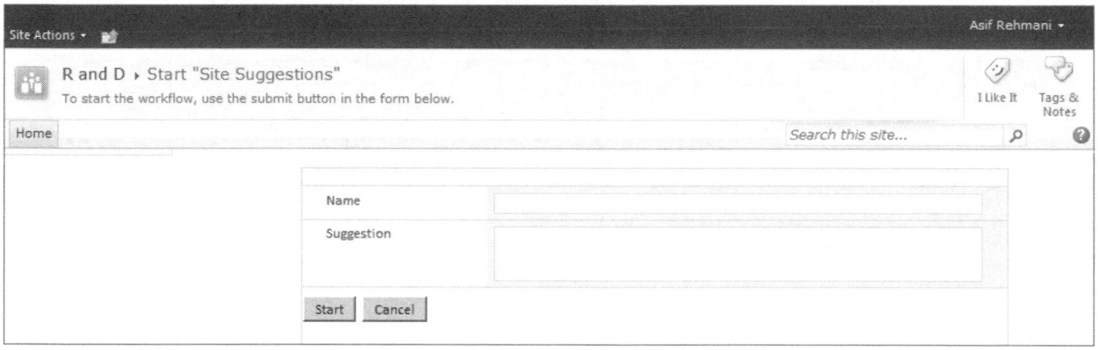

FIGURE 11-9

If your server is running SharePoint Server 2010, then all the forms that are generated automatically by workflows will be InfoPath forms (Chapter 9 covers InfoPath thoroughly). You can easily use InfoPath 2010 to change the appearance and layout of the form. You can also add validation and formatting rules to an InfoPath form. You can simply click on the form in the Workflow Designer and it opens it up in InfoPath 2010 (provided that InfoPath is installed on your computer). This point of integration is discussed in much more depth in Chapter 12.

The initiation form in a server running SharePoint Foundation 2010 is a SharePoint ASPX page. It contains a static Data Form Web Part (not a Web Part Zone) to support the entry of the initiation information. This form is customizable, as well. Chapter 8 describes in detail the customization of Data Form Web Parts.

Association Columns

Columns (or fields) called *association columns* can be declared within reusable workflows. The benefit of doing this is that when the workflow is deployed to a list or library, the association columns get added to that list or library, as well.

Variables

Variables in a workflow give you a place to store values, such as for storing information between steps, holding interim calculation results, or just about anything else. In the workflow, information held in variables and initiation parameters is accessed in the same way. The key difference is that users have the opportunity to interact directly with initiation parameters, whereas variables are used only within your workflow.

You can create variables by clicking the Local Variables button on the ribbon in Workflow Designer interface, or when configuring an action that can use a variable as an information target. Although similarities exist between variables and initiation parameters, some significant differences also exist.

Like an initiation parameter, a variable has a name (otherwise you couldn't refer to it) and a data type. Your workflow can read variables' current values in conditions, and set their values as actions. Unlike initiation parameters, variables do not have a default value, nor is a data entry form automatically generated for them.

Slight differences also exist in the data types available. The variable data types are:

➤ Boolean

➤ Date/Time

➤ Integer

➤ List Item ID

➤ Number

➤ String

Because users do not enter variables directly, and no form is generated to represent them, there is a single String data type instead of the Choice, Single line of text, and Multiple lines of text types seen in initiation parameters.

Steps

Steps are the major blocks of instructions for a workflow. They contain the conditions and actions that are executed to perform the workflow's functions. Each step is executed in sequence, unless a Stop Workflow action is executed.

A workflow always has at least one step. For simple workflows, that may be all that is needed. For more complex workflows, however, they provide an intuitive separation of logic. You should give steps descriptive names, so that when you or someone else comes back to manage the items within the step, the purpose of the step is readily apparent.

Steps can be nested within other steps as well and act as substeps, as shown in Figure 11-10.

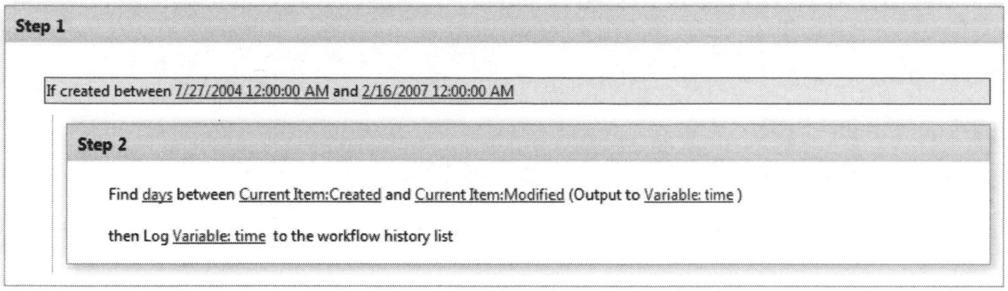

FIGURE 11-10

Impersonation Steps

Just like with regular steps, you can place impersonation steps on the Workflow Designer environment with conditions and actions encapsulated within. These also execute sequentially. However, a major difference exists between the impersonation step and a regular step.

At times, the workflow might need to perform certain actions that are above the permission level of the person who initiated the workflow. For these times, you use the impersonation step when designing your workflow to ensure that any conditions and actions that get inserted within the impersonation step will automatically run under the identity of the user who authored the workflow. Having said that, recognize that this can be an extremely dangerous proposition, because the workflow now has a higher permission level than the person who kicked it off. This functionality, therefore, should be used with extreme care. In fact, when you're trying to save a workflow with an impersonation step, SharePoint Designer 2010 will warn you, as is shown in Figure 11-11, and ask you to confirm that you understand the ramifications of using an impersonation step.

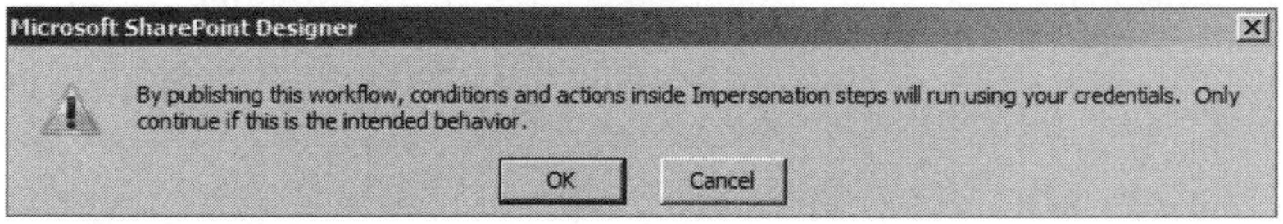

FIGURE 11-11

Conditions

Encapsulating your actions within a condition allows you to control the execution of the actions in your workflow. They provide the `if-else` construct that developers have been using for decades now. Conditions can be nested within other conditions, as well. You will see an example of nesting an `If` statement within another in one of the later examples in the chapter.

The types of conditions you can set in a workflow include:

➤ Comparisons to fields in the current list or library

➤ Comparisons between any two data sources internal to the site (including lists, libraries, workflow variables, or initiation parameters, but not external data sources like XML files and web services)

➤ Checking the title field for specific keywords

➤ Checking whether the file was created or modified, either by a specific person or within a specific date range

➤ Checking whether a person is a valid SharePoint user

➤ Checking the file type*

➤ Checking the size of the file*

➤ Checking list item permission or permission levels**

*Only available when the workflow is being created on a library or scoped to the Document content type
**Only available within the impersonation step

Notice that several of these conditions could be interpreted as subsets of others. In those cases, the selection user interface is streamlined and tailored specifically to the comparison at hand. For example, comparisons among "any" data sources require you to choose not only the data sources, but the values for each side of the comparison.

Actions

Actions are the key elements of a workflow. Although every workflow has at least one step, and conditions are optional, nothing happens unless an action is defined.

The default actions provided with SharePoint fall into six categories:

➤ **Core actions** — These revolve around manipulating a particular piece of information (a variable or list field, for instance), or control overall workflow execution.

➤ **List actions** — These work on an entire list item at one time.

➤ **Task actions** — These manipulate the Tasks list and pause the workflow until completed.

➤ **Document Set actions** — These work on an entire document set once. A document set has to be defined ahead of time before you can use these actions on the set.

➤ **Utility actions** — These actions lets you perform utility types of functions such as working with string values.

➤ **Relational actions** — Only one action is available in this group. It deals with finding relational data for a user.

In many conditions and actions, you have the capability to look up or update information in other lists or libraries on the site. To access an item in another list or library, you must provide some query information to determine the particular item you want to read or modify. Such a lookup is shown in Figure 11-12.

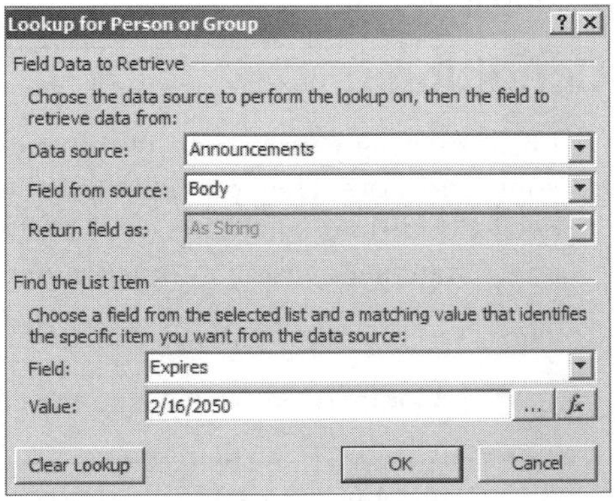

FIGURE 11-12

If you have ever used a `Select` statement to query a database, consider the following example to understand the dialog box in Figure 11-12:

```
SELECT Body FROM Announcements
WHERE Expires = '2/16/2050'
```

Note that if the query you entered results in more than one list or library item being returned, only the first result is used for the action.

Core Actions

Core actions let you set values, send e-mails, pause, or even prematurely end the workflow. They are described in the following table.

CORE ACTION	DESCRIPTION
Add a Comment	This is analogous to commenting your code in a programming environment. It's for reference within the workflow design and does not actually perform an action.
Add Time to Date	Enables you to perform date arithmetic. You can add a specified amount of time to an existing date/time element, and store the results in a workflow variable. Adding a negative unit of time results in subtracting time. You can add Minutes, Hours, Days, Months, and Years.
Do Calculation	Performs a simple arithmetic operation (add, subtract, multiply, divide, or mod/remainder) on two values, and stores the result in a workflow variable.
Log to History List	Enables you to write an item to the hidden list (History list) that stores workflow history information.
Pause For Duration	One of the timer actions. It causes the workflow to wait a specified amount of time before proceeding to the next action in the workflow.
Pause Until Date	Causes the workflow to wait until a specified date and time before continuing to the next action. The date may be hard-coded into the workflow, or it may be a lookup value.
Send an Email	Enables you to send an e-mail to a user or a set of users. The body of the e-mail is sent as HTML.
Send Document to Repository	Send the document to another repository (for example, another document library in a different site collection).
Set Time Portion of Date/ Time Field	Overrides the current time in a date/time lookup value, leaving the date intact. It then stores the new date/time value into a date/time variable.

continues

(continued)

CORE ACTION	DESCRIPTION
Set Workflow Variable	Although several other actions set the values of workflow variables with their results, this one enables you to directly set the value of a variable or Initiation Form field. You can set it to either a static value or a lookup.
Set Workflow Status	Use this action to set the status of the workflow. The built-in choices are Canceled, Approved, and Rejected. You could also type in a custom status if you wanted.
Stop Workflow	Stops the execution of the workflow immediately and logs a specified message into the Workflow History list. No further steps or actions are performed.

List Actions

The List actions let you perform such tasks as checking items in or out; creating new items; and copying, editing, or deleting items. Many of these actions default to acting on the current item (the one for which the workflow was initiated), although in most cases you can specify a different item — even one in a different list. If you want to act on an item other than the current item, you are presented with the Choose List Item dialog shown in Figure 11-13.

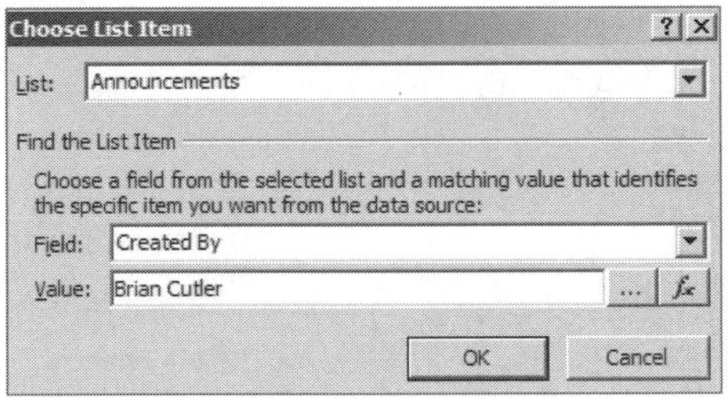

FIGURE 11-13

The Value field will be compared to the field selected. You can use a lookup, or enter a specific value to compare. If multiple items match your query, the action will take place on the first matching item, so try to ensure that your queries will return a single item. Otherwise, you could end up deleting the wrong document, for instance.

The following table shows the descriptions of all List actions.

LIST ACTION	DESCRIPTION
Add List Item Permissions*	Specify users/groups and give them a specified level of permissions on any item on the site.
Check In Item	Checks in the specified item and sets the check-in comment appropriately.
Check Out Item	Locks an item so that only the person who has it checked out can make changes. There is no comment on a check out.
Copy List Item	Copies items between almost any two lists on the site. The lists must be of compatible types (both must be document libraries, for instance) or allow mixed content types. The default source is the current list item.

LIST ACTION	DESCRIPTION
Create List Item	Enables you to create a new item in any list. Each field in the list may be populated from a different source. The ID code of the item created is returned to create a new workflow variable.
Declare Record	Declare the current item as a record. Depending on record declaration settings set at the site collection or list/library level, the record can then be protected from being edited or deleted.
Delete Drafts	Delete all drafts (or minor versions) of the current item.
Delete Item	Removes the specified item from the list.
Delete Previous Versions	Delete all previous versions of the item.
Discard Check Out Item	Undoes any changes made since the item was checked out and removes the change lock.
Inherit List Item Parent Permissions*	Inherit the permission of the immediate parent object.
Remove List Item Permissions*	Specify users/groups and remove specified level of permissions for them on any item on the site.
Replace List Item Permissions*	Replace the permission level of the specified item on the site.
Set Content Approval Status	When content approval is turned on for the list, this action enables you to change the status of the current item directly and set the approval comment. The comment may be static text or a lookup value.
Set Field in Current Item	Sets the specified field to either a static or lookup value.
Undeclare Record	Undeclare the current item as a record and make it behave like all other items in the list/library.
Update List Item	Enables you to change the fields of an existing item. The interface for setting the field values is the same as that used in the Create List Item action.
Wait for Change in Document Check Out Status	Wait for the document to be in a certain checkout status (Checked Out, Checked In, Unlocked by document editor, or Discarded)
Wait for Field Change in Current Item	Pauses the workflow until a field matches a particular condition.

*These actions are only available within an impersonation step.

Task Actions

Task actions enable you to pause a workflow for more user input. The kind of input, and who must provide it, varies from action to action.

Because these tasks pause your workflow, you cannot use the current workflow to set the task fields dynamically on initiation. You can, however, create a separate workflow on the Tasks list, which is invoked by the creation of the task item by this action. This is called a secondary workflow. The ramifications of secondary workflows are discussed later in the "SharePoint Designer 2010 Workflow Considerations" section.

Task actions are described in the following table:

TASK ACTION	DESCRIPTION
Assign a Form to a Group	Enables you to create a survey that everyone in a group needs to complete in order for the workflow to continue to the next action. The results are stored as items in the Task list.
Assign a To-do Item	Creates a standard task that must be marked as Complete before the workflow will continue. The Custom Task wizard shows the same initiation form as for the Group form, but does not call for the addition of any fields.
Collect Data from a User	Similar to the Assign a Form to a Group action. The primary differences are that the survey form is targeted to a single user, rather than a group, and that because only one instance of the form is created, its ID is available to be assigned to a workflow variable.
Start Approval Process	This one action is actually an entire task process and is based on the built-in Approval workflow template. When deployed, it lets you define various pieces of the process using the Task Process Designer. Chapter 12 provides more information on this process.
Start Custom Task Process	This action provides a Task Process Designer environment much like the Approval process. However, this action lets you build the process from scratch. Chapter 12 provides more information on this topic.
Start Feedback Process	This one action is actually an entire task process and is based on the built-in Collect Feedback workflow template. When deployed, it lets you define various pieces of the process using the Task Process Designer. Chapter 12 provides more information on this process.

Users who are assigned a task receive an e-mail. They need to click the Edit this Task link in the e-mail to see any instructions or fill in any requested information. This takes them to the edit form defined for the task. In the case of Assign a To-do Item, it is simply the standard edit form for the Tasks list. For the Assign a Form to a Group or Collect Data from a User actions, you create a custom form for the user to fill in.

If you click the A Custom Form link (for the Group action) or the Data link (for the User action) in the action definition window, the Custom Task Wizard launches. That's where you define your form. The first page of the wizard describes how the form you are about to create is used. Click Next to begin entering information.

The first real step of the Custom Task Wizard (see Figure 11-14) enables you to provide some descriptive information about the form for your users.

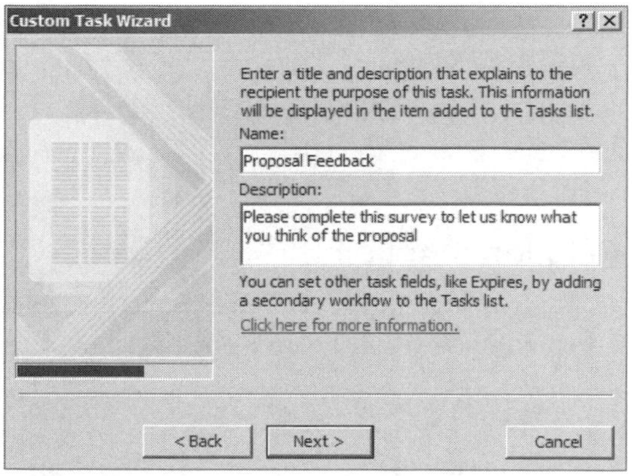

After clicking Next, you add the fields/questions to which you want your users to respond. This operates just like selecting Initiation form fields, except that you can provide additional descriptive text for each field. The following field types are available:

➤ Single line of text

➤ Multiple lines of text

➤ Number

➤ Currency

➤ Date and Time

➤ Choice

➤ Yes/No

➤ Person or Group

➤ Hyperlink or Picture

FIGURE 11-14

The field types available are the same for the actions Assign a Form to a Group and Collect Data from a User.

Utility Actions

Utility actions are available to work with any workflow or site data. They are there to support data manipulation (mainly strings) and feed the result back into the workflow as a variable to be used by some other condition or action.

TASK ACTION	DESCRIPTION
Extract Substring from End of String	Copy specified number of characters from the end of a string and save the resulting string in a variable.
Extract Substring from Index of String	Copy a part of the string starting after a specified number of characters. Save the resulting string in a variable.
Extract Substring from Start of String	Copy a specified number of characters from the start of a string and save the resulting string in a variable.
Extract Substring of String from Index with Length	Copy a part of the string starting after a specified number of characters and ending after a specified number of characters. Save the resulting string in a variable.

continues

(continued)

TASK ACTION	DESCRIPTION
Find Interval Between Dates	Determine an interval (in minutes, hours, or days) between two specified dates. Save the result in a variable.

Relational Actions

Only one action is available in the Relational actions group. The action deals with retrieving relational data from the user profile database.

TASK ACTION	DESCRIPTION
Look Up Manager of a User	Retrieves the manager of the specified user from the user profile database.

Document Set Actions

Document sets pull multiple items together to create a single work product. For example, think of document set as a package of related documents (like a loan application). This set of documents then can be managed, edited, and worked on as a single entity. You can find more information on document sets at `http://msdn.microsoft.com/en-us/library/ee559339(v=office.14).aspx`.

TASK ACTION	DESCRIPTION
Capture a Version of the Document Set	Create a new version for the document set. You can specify to take either the last major or the last minor version of each document in the set to create your version.
Send Document Set to Repository	Send the document set to another repository (for example, another document library in a different site collection)
Set Content Approval Status for the Document Set	When content approval is turned on for the list, this action enables you to directly change the status of the document set and also create a comment. The comment may be static text or a lookup value.
Start Document Set Approval Process	This one action is an entire task process and is based on the built-in Approval workflow template. However, this processes actions on a document set instead of a single document. When deployed, it lets you define various pieces of the process using the Task Process Designer. Chapter 12 provides more information on this process.

Parallel Block

By default, when you place conditions and actions on the Workflow Designer, they are set to execute in serial — one after another. However, you can configure conditions/actions to execute in parallel by first clicking on the Parallel Block button on the ribbon and then creating your conditions/actions within it. Alternatively, you can place a parallel block on the design surface and then move within it the conditions/actions that you want to execute in parallel.

This functionality can be useful for scenarios where you don't want the workflow execution to be paused waiting for a certain task to finish. For example, when you use the Collect Data From User action, it creates a sort of survey form that the user has to fill out. Until the user fills out the form and submits it, the execution will not proceed to the next action unless these actions have been put into a parallel block, as shown in Figure 11-15.

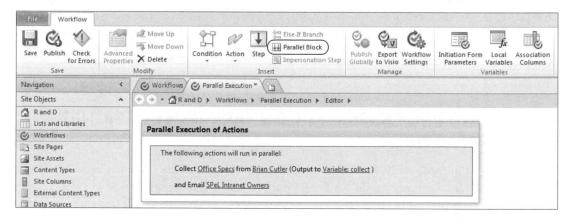

FIGURE 11-15

Advanced Properties

The Advanced Properties button in the ribbon simply shows the properties of the selected action or condition. These properties can then be managed in this screen much like you would manage it in the Workflow Designer surface itself. Figure 11-16 shows the Advanced Properties dialog box.

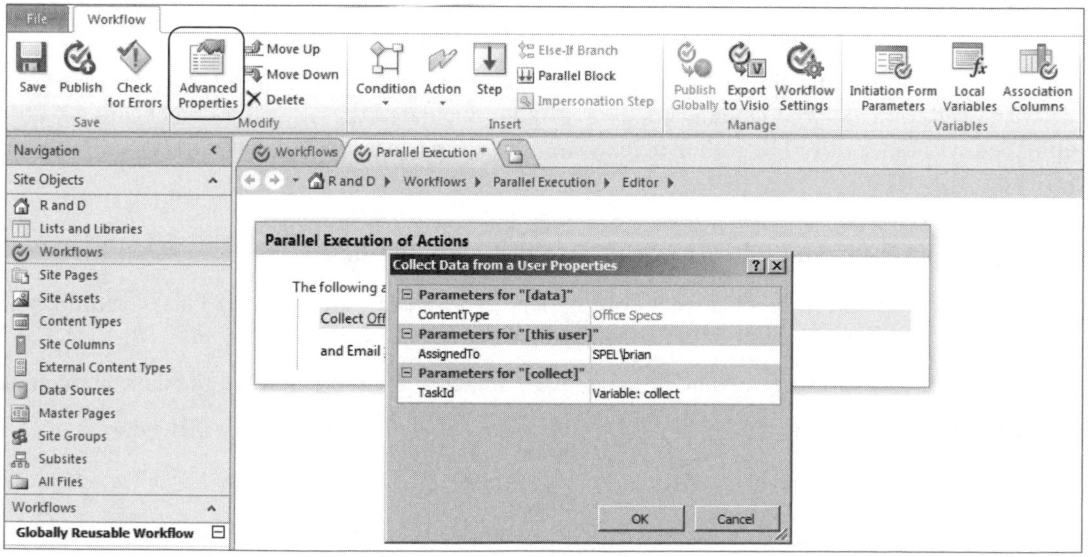

FIGURE 11-16

Saving and Publishing the Workflow

FIGURE 11-17

When you are done designing a workflow, it needs to be published somewhere (a list, library, or the site). You can simply click on the Publish button (see Figure 11-17) to publish the workflow and make it "Live on the current site." The publishing process will check the workflow for errors, save the workflow, create any necessary forms needed for the workflow, and then finally publish it to the site. If you are not ready to publish the workflow yet, you can click the Check For Errors button to check whether you must attend to any errors. Also, you can use a Save button to save the workflow in a draft state to which you can later come back.

AUTOMATING PROCESSES USING SHAREPOINT DESIGNER 2010 WORKFLOWS

In the SharePoint Designer 2010 environment, you can create three types of workflows: List, Reusable, and Site. Each one serves a different purpose and is important in its own right. The following sections provide an explanation and an example of each of these workflows.

List Workflows

A list workflow is associated with a list or library directly when it is created in SharePoint Designer 2010. It then becomes tightly coupled with that list and cannot be moved to any other list. You should create these workflows only when you are sure that they will not need to be relocated later.

The benefit of making a list workflow is that you have access to all the specific metadata (columns) of that list. In other words, the list workflow has an inherent understanding of the schema of that specific list and any custom columns that have been created on that list.

You saw an example of a simple list workflow at the beginning of this chapter. The workflow was attached to the Shared Documents library and it populated the title of documents that were uploaded without a title. The following exercise is another example. This one is associated with the Calendar list.

> **TRY IT OUT**   Create a List Workflow on the Calendar List
>
> In this exercise, you will create a list workflow associated with the Calendar list. This workflow will make use of the parallel branch and nested conditional statement.
>
> **1.**   Open any team site in SharePoint Designer 2010 and click on Workflows in the navigation pane.
>
> **2.**   Click the List Workflow button in the ribbon and from the dropdown select Calendar.

3. In the Create List Workflow dialog that appears, name the workflow **Event Announcements** and click OK. The Workflow Designer interface appears.

4. Click Step 1 and change the name of the step to **Announce the Event**.

5. Place the cursor within the workflow design environment, click the Condition button in the ribbon, and from the dropdown select "If current item field equals value." This inserts the condition on the Workflow Designer.

6. Click the `field` link and from the drop-down, select Category. Click the `value` link and then select Business from the drop-down.

7. Click and place the cursor below where it says "(Start typing or use…)." Click Condition ⇨ Created by a specific person. Click "specific person" and from the dialog that appears, pick any person who is a member of this team site.

8. Place the cursor right below this condition and click the Parallel Block button on the ribbon.

9. Click to place the cursor underneath where it says "The following actions will run in parallel." Click Action ⇨ Assign a To-do Item. Click `a to-do item` link, and from the Task Wizard that appears, create the task Book a Conference Room. Click `these users` and assign this task to any member of the site.

10. Click below this action and then click Action ⇨ Create List Item. Click `this list`.

11. In the Create New List Item dialog, choose the Announcements list from the dropdown. Click the Title (*) field and then click Modify. In the dialog that pops up, click *fx*. In the lookup dialog, click the Field from source dropdown and select Title. Click OK on the opened dialog boxes to get back to the Create New List Item dialog. Click the Add button, and from the dialog that appears, select Body field in the first drop-down. Click *fx* and in the lookup dialog, click Field from source drop-down and select Description. Click OK on all opened dialog boxes to get back to the Workflow Designer interface.

12. Click and highlight the condition If Current Item: Category equals Business. Then, click on the Else-If Branch button on the ribbon to create the `else-if` branch for this conditional logic.

13. Click Condition ⇨ If current item field equals value. Click the `field` link and from the dropdown, select Category. Click the `value` link and then select Holiday from the drop-down.

14. Click below this condition and then click Action ⇨ Create List Item. Click `this list`.

15. In the Create New List Item dialog, choose the Announcements list from the drop-down. Click the Title (*) field and then click Modify. In the dialog that pops up, click *fx*. In the lookup dialog, click the Field from source drop-down and select Title. Click OK on the opened dialog boxes to get back to the Create New List Item dialog. Click the Add button and from the dialog that appears, and select Body field in the first dropdown. Click *fx* and in the lookup dialog, click the Field from source drop-down and select Description. Click OK on all opened dialog boxes to get back to the Workflow Designer interface.

16. Place the cursor below the Announce the Event step and then click on the Step button on the ribbon to insert another step below it. Name this step **Set Workflow Status**.

17. Click inside the step and then click Action ⇨ Set Workflow Status. Click on Canceled. This is a combo box with which you can choose one of the available workflow status choices (Canceled, Approved, Rejected) or type in a new workflow status altogether. Type **Done** here.

18. Save the workflow by clicking on the Save icon. Your workflow should now look similar to the one shown in Figure 11-18.

19. Click the Workflow Settings button on the ribbon and from the Settings page, select the checkbox for Start workflow automatically when an item is created, and then click the Publish button to publish the workflow to the Calendar list.

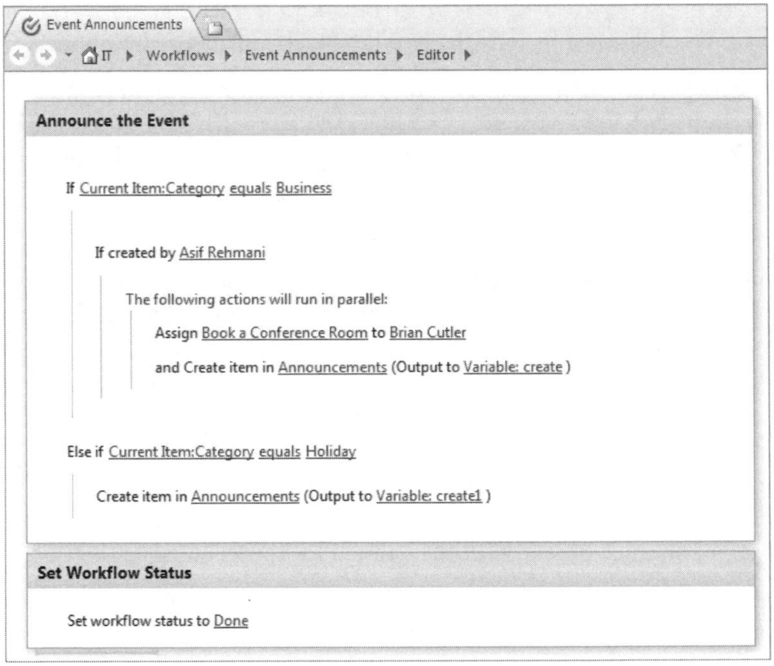

FIGURE 11-18

How It Works

The workflow designed in this exercise is attached to the Calendar list. It is activated and executed automatically when a new item is created in the Calendar list. The field that this workflow monitors is the Category field in the calendar item.

If the category is Business then the nested conditional logic kicks in and it looks to see who created the event (in the preceding workflow, for example, it's looking to see whether Asif Rehmani created the workflow). If the conditional logic here returns true then it executes a couple of actions in parallel — assign a person (Brian Cutler in the preceding example) to book a conference room and create an announcement in the Announcements list with the information from the calendar item. The reason these actions execute in parallel using the parallel block is so that the workflow doesn't wait for Brian to complete the task before announcing the new event in the announcements list.

If the category for the new calendar item is Holiday, then an announcement is created directly with the information from the calendar item. If the category is neither Business nor Holiday then the execution of the workflow goes directly to the next step. The next step (Set Workflow Status) is a logical separation of the execution of the workflow. This step has only one action, which sets the status of the workflow to Done.

The list workflow created in the preceding Try It Out is designed specifically for this Calendar list and is not meant to be portable. However, in many instances, you will want a workflow that can be moved around and be made reusable. That is the focus of the next section.

Reusable Workflows

Reusable workflows are exactly what they sound like — reusable. You can create these workflows once and reuse them by attaching them to a list, library, or a content type. If you update the workflow, it gets updated everywhere the workflow is being used.

Creating a reusable workflow is a very similar process to creating a list workflow with the exception that you don't pick a list or library at the onset to attach to. What you do have to decide, though, is a base content type scope of this workflow. Content types in SharePoint can be simply described as a reusable collection of settings and columns. You can define a content type once and use it several times in lists and libraries throughout your site collection. You can find more information on content types in SharePoint at `http://msdn.microsoft.com/en-us/library/ms472236.aspx`.

When creating a reusable workflow, you scope it to be used by a specific content type and all of its child content types (see Figure 11-19). Later when ready, you can associate the workflow with that specific content type or with any content type that inherits from that content type. The benefit of attaching reusable workflows to content types is that the workflow will then travel with that content type wherever it goes, which means that this workflow will be available in all lists and libraries where this content type is being used. Later, if you need to change the workflow, your modifications need to be made only in one place, the original workflow, and all lists/libraries using this workflow will automatically be updated.

Reusable workflows can be made at any site within the site collection. If you create a reusable workflow at the top site of the site collection, it becomes globally available and reusable to be attached to lists, libraries, and content types within the site collection. If you make the reusable workflow at a subsite in a site collection, then the scope of that workflow is that particular subsite. It cannot be used in any other site unless it's packaged and exported to that site. The packaging and portability of reusable workflows is covered as an advanced workflow subject in Chapter 12.

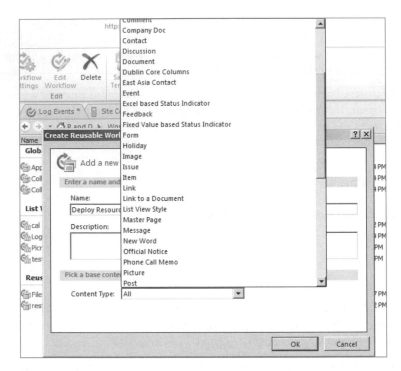

FIGURE 11-19

TRY IT OUT   Create a Reusable Workflow and Attach It to a Content Type

In this exercise, you create a reusable workflow and associate it with a content type. This workflow will utilize the impersonation step to move documents from one library to another with the authority of the author of the workflow. You also make use of the association column in this workflow.

1. Make sure you are logged in to your machine as an owner of a SharePoint site and then open that team site in SharePoint Designer 2010. Click on Lists and Libraries in the navigation pane.

2. Click the Document Library button on the ribbon and then click Document Library selection from the dropdown. Name the new library **Marketing Docs** and click OK.

3. Click on Marketing Docs to go to the summary page of this library and then click Permissions for this list, which opens the browser and navigates you to the permissions page of the library. Click on the Stop Inheriting Permissions button and then click OK on the dialog that appears.

4. Select the checkboxes for all groups except the Owners group and click Remove User Permissions button to revoke their permissions, as shown in Figure 11-20. Click OK to the dialog that opens to confirm your action.

5. Perform Steps 1–4 to create and configure another document library named **Sales Docs**.

6. Click on Site Columns in the navigation pane. Click New Column ➪ Choice. Name the column **Division** and click OK. Add the choices Marketing and Sales to this new column. Erase any value in the Default value field and click OK. Click on the Save icon to save the change to the Site Column Gallery.

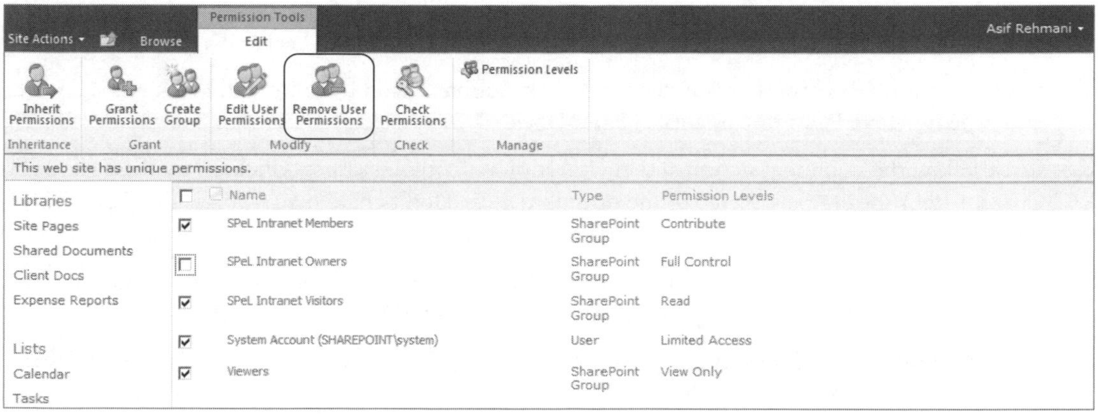

FIGURE 11-20

7. Click on Content Types in the navigation pane. Click new Content Type button. Name the content type **AW Document**. Choose the Parent content type from the Document Content Types and then choose the Document content type. Click OK.

8. Click on the AW Document content type then click the Edit content type columns link. Use the Add Existing Site Column button to add the Division site column and click the Save icon to save the changes to the content type.

9. To start creating the workflow, click on Workflows in the navigation pane and then click the Reusable Workflow button on the ribbon.

10. Name the workflow **File Document** and choose the content type AW Document, from the dropdown as the base content type. Click OK, and the Workflow Designer interface should open.

11. Click underneath Step 1 and then click on the Impersonation Step button on the ribbon. Click on Step 1 and click Delete in the ribbon to delete it.

12. Click the Association Columns button on the ribbon. Click the Select Site Column button and select the Division site column. Click OK in this dialog and the next to return to the Workflow Designer environment.

13. Click within the impersonation step and click Condition ⇨ If current item field equals value. Click field and select Division. Click value and select Marketing.

14. Put the cursor below the If statement and type in **Comment**. Then press Enter on the keyboard to have the Add a Comment action autocompleted. Click comment text and type in **Move Marketing documents to Marketing Docs**.

15. Click below the comment action and click Action ⇨ Copy List Item. Click on the first this list link. Current Item should be selected in the pop-up dialog. Don't change anything; click OK. Now click on the second this list link and select Marketing Docs from the drop-down that appears.

16. Click below the action and then choose Action ⇨ Delete Item. Click on `this list`. Current Item should be selected in the pop-up dialog. Don't change anything, and click OK.

17. Click below the action and then click the Else-If Branch button. Click Condition ⇨ If current item field equals value. Click `field` and select Division. Click `value` and select Sales.

18. Put the cursor below the `If` statement and click Action ⇨ Add a Comment. Click `comment text` and type in **Move Sales documents to Sales Docs**.

19. Click below the comment action and click Action ⇨ Copy List Item. Click on the first `this list`. Current Item should be selected in the pop-up dialog. Don't change anything, and click OK. Click on the second `this list` and select Sales Docs from the dropdown that appears.

20. Click below the action and then click Action ⇨ Delete Item. Click on `this list`. Current Item should be selected in the pop-up dialog. Don't change anything, and click OK.

Your workflow should look like the one shown in Figure 11-21.

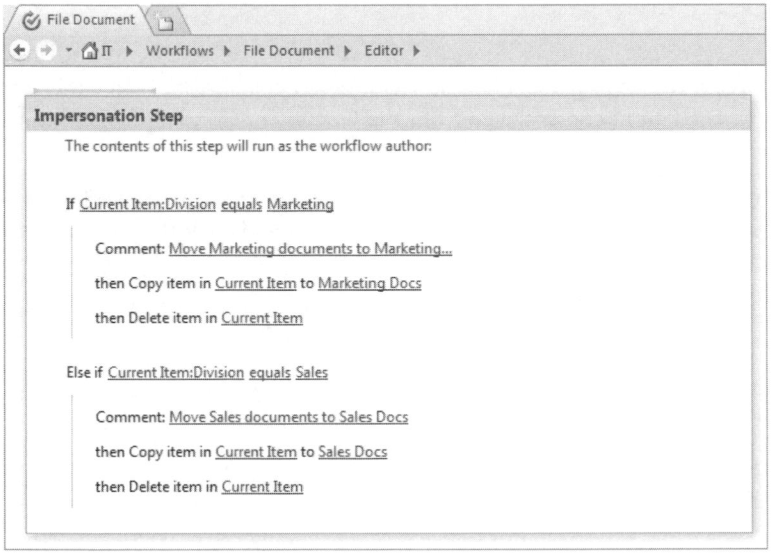

FIGURE 11-21

21. Click the Publish button to publish the workflow and make it available at the site level. You will see a warning dialog appear to warn you about the use of the impersonation step. Click OK on it to acknowledge it, and the workflow will be published.

22. Click the Workflow Settings button. Then click Associate to Content Type ⇨ AW Document. Your Internet browser should open and show the Add a Workflow page. Click OK at the bottom of the page to complete the workflow association.

23. Close the browser to return to SharePoint Designer 2010. Click on Lists and Libraries in the navigation pane. Click on Document Library ⇨ Document Library and name the new library **Drop Off Library**. Click OK.

24. Click Drop Off Library to go to its summary page. In the Settings section, click the checkbox for Allow management of content types. Then click on the Add button in the Content Types section. Choose the AW Document content type and click OK.

25. Click to highlight the AW Document row (don't click on the AW Document link itself). Click the Set as Default button. Then click the save icon to save your changes.

26. Click on the All Documents view in the Views section. The XSLT List View Web Part (covered in Chapter 8) should be highlighted. Click the Add/Remove Columns button in the ribbon, add the Division column in the Displayed fields section, and then click OK. Save this list view page by clicking the save icon.

How It Works

The workflow created in the preceding example will allow end users to start this workflow on any item in the Drop Off Library. The end user will select the document and click the Workflows button in the ribbon, as shown in Figure 11-22, and then choose the File Document workflow and click the Start button on the next screen to start the workflow.

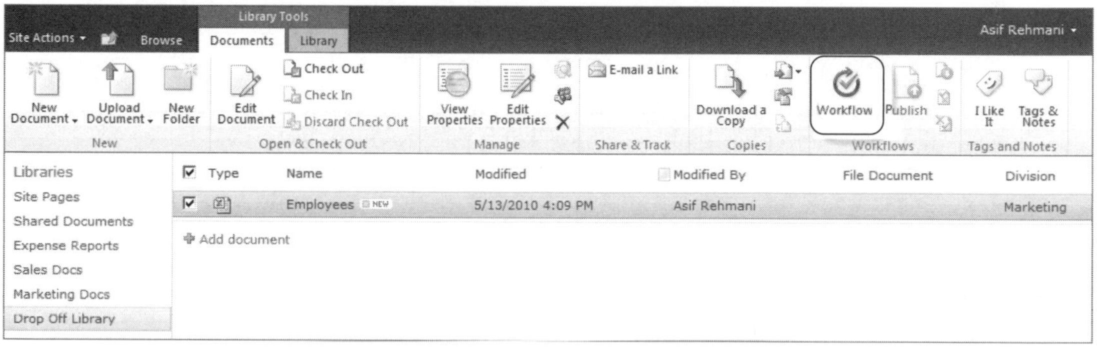

FIGURE 11-22

When the workflow is run on a document, depending on the selected choice in the Division column of the document, it will get routed to either the Sales Docs or Marketing Docs library. Subsequently, the original document will be deleted from the Drop Off Library.

Because the workflow is associated with the content type, this same functionality can now be reused throughout the site by associating the AW Document content type to any library within the site. Also, in the next chapter you will see how easy it is to even package up this functionality and deploy it to another site collection.

Site Workflows

All workflows talked about this far need a list, library, or content type to host them. Site workflows on the other hand are general site-wide processes that do not need a list, library, or content type attachment. They are simply published and attached to the site itself and can work upon any object within the site. A user manually executes this workflow by going to the All Site Content page. The following exercise provides an example of how this type of workflow can be utilized.

TRY IT OUT   Create a Site Workflow

In this exercise, you create a site workflow that will serve as a survey for the SharePoint site.

1.   Open a team site in SharePoint Designer 2010. Click on Workflows in the navigation pane.

2.   Click the Site Workflow button. Name the workflow **Site Suggestions** and click OK. The Workflow Designer interface appears.

3.   Click the Initiation Form Parameters button. In the dialog that appears, click the Add button. Set the Field name to **Name**, click Next, and then click Finish on the next screen.

4.   Click the Add button to add a second parameter named **Suggestion**. Change the Information type dropdown to say Multiple lines of text. Click Next and then click Finish on the next screen. Click OK on the Form Parameters dialog to return to the Workflow Designer.

5.   Click inside the step; then click Action ⇨ Send an Email. Click `these users` to open the e-mail composition window.

6.   Click the address book icon for the To field, select the owners group as Selected Users, and then click OK. For the Subject, click on the ellipsis button (...) to open the String Builder window. Type in **Suggestion from**, then click on Add or Change Lookup. Select Data source as Workflow Context (this is a new functionality in SPD 2010). Click the Field from source dropdown and select Initiator. Click the Return field as dropdown and select Display Name. Click OK and then click OK once more to get back to the e-mail window. Click in the body of the e-mail and type in **Suggestion Info: and** then press Enter to go to the next line. Click on the Add or Change Lookup button. Select Data source as Workflow Variables and Parameters, and Field from source as Parameter: Suggestion. Leave the last dropdown as it is and click OK. Your e-mail window should look like that shown in Figure 11-23.

7.   Click OK in the e-mail window to return to the Workflow Designer interface and then click the Publish button to publish the workflow.

How It Works

The site workflow designed in the exercise makes use of initiation form parameters. These parameters appear to the user when the workflow starts. Because a site workflow is always going to be started manually by a user, you can take this opportunity to ask the user some questions through these parameters.

To execute this workflow, navigate to this team site in the browser. Then click on the All Site Content link in the Quick Launch bar. Click on the Site Workflows link here to go to the page where all site workflows are listed. The Site Suggestion workflow should be listed. When the workflow is clicked, it presents the Initiation Form that looks like the one in Figure 11-24.

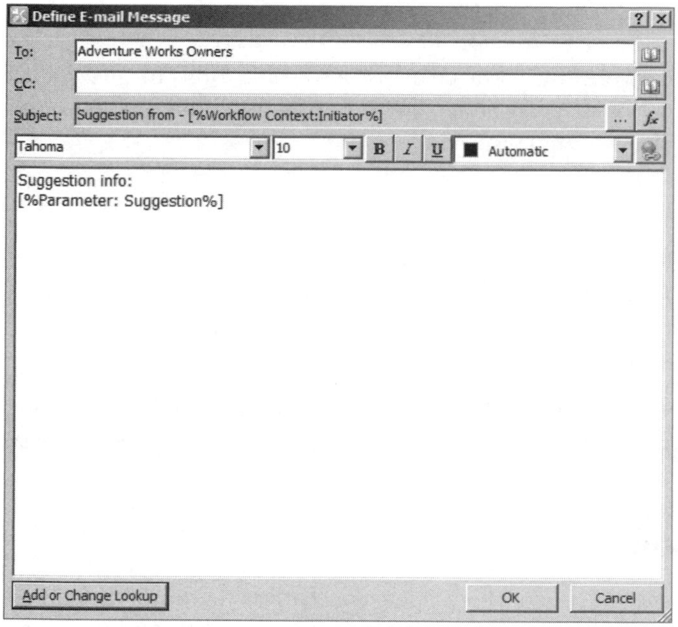

FIGURE 11-23

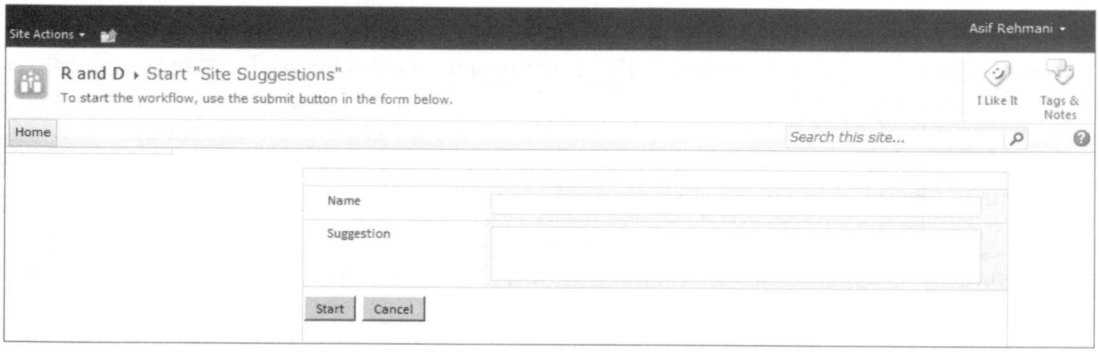

FIGURE 11-24

When you fill out the Name and Suggestion parameters and then click the Start button, the workflow starts and sends the e-mail with the site suggestion to all the owners of the site.

Although this chapter covers a lot of workflow fundamentals, looking for supplemental sources to enhance your knowledge further on this topic is still advisable. The SharePoint Designer team blog is a great resource for this sort of information and you should visit it often to see how the SharePoint Designer team recommends using various features. Also, to see many of the exercises covered in this chapter in action, you can watch the workflow-related screencasts (videos) at www.sharepoint-videos.com.

SHAREPOINT DESIGNER 2010 WORKFLOW CONSIDERATIONS

As you have seen, SharePoint Designer workflows provide many powerful actions for manipulating the information in your site. This functionality has limits, however, as well as some areas where you should be cautious of the ramifications of your choices.

Limitations

SharePoint Designer creates workflows that can execute actions either in sequence or in parallel. Although SharePoint's built-in workflows offer a state-based execution flow, SharePoint Designer workflows do not. There is no built-in looping or iteration mechanism. For example, you cannot create a SharePoint Designer workflow that automatically performs an action on every item in a list.

If you have multiple workflows defined on a list or library, and you invoke a workflow on an item in that list (whether manually or automatically), you cannot invoke a second workflow on the same item until the first completes.

Ramifications and Cautions

As you have seen, a SharePoint Designer 2010 workflow can make changes to information anywhere on a site. Some of the items a workflow can change may themselves start another workflow associated with that item. If a SharePoint Designer 2010 workflow makes a change to such a list, the workflow that is triggered is considered a secondary workflow to the workflow that triggered it.

Secondary workflows can be a powerful tool. For example, although the Task actions described earlier in this chapter will stop executing until their associated tasks have been completed, you can place a workflow on the Tasks list that will pick up where the primary workflow leaves off. Such a workflow might set an expiration date on the task, thus allowing the original workflow to continue if the task is never acted upon by the user.

This brings up an important point about workflows: Your users may not always behave in the way you expect. Whenever you implement a workflow that requires user input, test it thoroughly to see how it behaves if the user inserts incorrect or invalid data, or if the user completely ignores it. Otherwise, you may find your system littered with partially executed workflows. On a busy site, and a list with frequent additions and changes, this could potentially cause performance issues, as the lists used to control workflows grow to thousands of active and unresolved items.

Another potential issue is the circular reference, which can lead to an infinite loop. A circular reference occurs when an item refers to another, which in turn refers back to the original item. It may be a direct reference, as just described, or the reference may pass through several other items, but it always gets back to the item that originally started the chain, which then starts the chain all over again. If these references trigger actions and no mechanisms are set up to stop them (a passage of time, for instance, or a comparison to some maximum or minimum value that is incremented or decremented by the chain itself), the result is never-ending activity — the infinite loop.

Consider the case where a workflow makes a change to a list that triggers an automatic workflow. That secondary workflow makes a change to the original list, triggering the workflow that changes the secondary list again. If you do not detect this condition and stop the workflows, it can quickly result in thousands of workflow instances, absorbing system resources and ultimately leading to a system crash — and a nightmare to clean up.

One way to build in some control over runaway workflows is to create a list with a known item in it for your workflow. The item should contain a number field to use as a counter. When you create a workflow that you believe has the potential to "run away," the first action should test the list item for the current value of the counter. If it is not over some reasonable value (which only you can determine, based upon your environment), the next action increments the counter, and you then proceed with the workflow. The last action of any step that terminates the workflow should decrement that counter. If the initial comparison is greater than your threshold, end the workflow immediately. (You may opt to send an e-mail notice of the termination to the site owner, but that may be problematic if the runaway process is not controlled by your workflow.)

You learned earlier that SharePoint Designer 2010 workflows do not have a built-in mechanism for loops or state-based control flow. If you build appropriate logic into your workflows, and are careful to avoid infinite loops, circular references and secondary workflows can be used to work around this limit. You can deliberately create loops to execute a certain number of times, or until other desired conditions are met.

SUMMARY

This chapter discussed many aspects of the foundation of workflow design using SharePoint Designer 2010. You were exposed to the various elements in the Workflow Designer environment and also the different types of workflows you can create using this product. The next chapter picks up where this chapter leaves off and discusses advanced workflow methods as well as the packaging of workflows and the integration of the SharePoint Designer 2010 workflows with Microsoft Visio 2010 and InfoPath 2010.

Advanced Workflows

WHAT YOU WILL LEARN IN THIS CHAPTER

➤ Generating workflow designs using Visio Premium 2010

➤ Visualize a running workflow using Visio Graphics Services

➤ Modifying Workflow Forms using InfoPath 2010

➤ Working with Globally Reusable Workflows

➤ Exporting Reusable Workflows

Chapter 11 laid out the fundamentals of SharePoint Designer 2010 workflows. Building on that knowledge, this chapter shows how SharePoint Designer 2010 integrates with Visio 2010 and InfoPath 2010 to provide a complete solution to model the workflows and design dynamic user interfaces.

The last part of this chapter dives into strategies of packaging and deploying reusable workflows and shows how you can scale out your workflows to be used throughout your company.

MODELING WORKFLOWS USING VISIO 2010

The Microsoft Visio application has served a great role in the past, helping to visualize complex information such as network diagrams, maps, and floor plans. Now, the same functionality comes to SharePoint 2010. The designer surface for Visio 2010 can be used to model and visualize your workflows

A business or process analyst who understands business processes would be the ideal candidate for using this functionality. The analyst might prefer to use this method to sketch out the model of the workflow and then hand it to an IT professional or an owner of a SharePoint site to automate the processes in SharePoint. On the flip side, when an IT professional or site owner receives a workflow created in Visio, the visual nature of the workflow makes its intent self-evident and becomes a sort of contract of what is agreed to be the scope of the processes being implemented.

The following sections explain how the built-in functionality in Visio 2010 facilitates the workflow modeling in SharePoint 2010.

Exploring the Visio 2010 SharePoint Workflow Stencils

In SharePoint Designer 2007 days, there was no way to visualize workflows created in the workflow designer environment. When the workflows became complicated, getting a bird's-eye view of how all the workflow pieces fit together was very difficult. To solve this problem, SharePoint Designer and Visio teams joined forces. Microsoft Visio Premium 2010 ships with the SharePoint workflow stencils, containing the shapes for all standard workflow activities — conditions and actions (the Standard and Professional versions of Visio do not have this functionality) — that you can use to design a workflow. Then, you can export this workflow in a format that's understood by and imported in SharePoint Designer 2010.

When you start the Visio Premium 2010 application, you can find the Microsoft SharePoint Workflow template under the Flowchart template category. Upon selecting this template, the stencils showing the workflow shapes appear as shown in Figure 12-1.

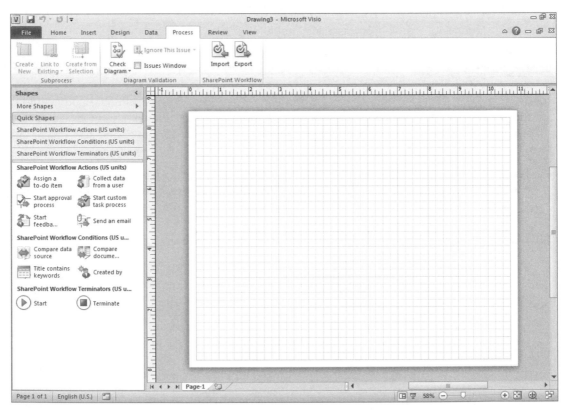

FIGURE 12-1

Building the Visio Workflow

Three stencils contain the workflow shapes:

➤ SharePoint Workflow Actions

➤ SharePoint Workflow Conditions

➤ SharePoint Workflow Terminators

You must place the Start and Terminate objects in the SharePoint Workflow Terminators stencil on the design surface to designate the starting and ending points of the workflow design. Then, you can place conditions and actions in the middle of these terminators as needed to design the workflow logic. The design interface in Visio 2010 expands automatically to another page if more space is needed for the design. Visio 2010's features, such as themes and auto alignment, can be utilized for enhancing the look and feel of the workflow diagram as needed.

No support exists in Visio 2010 for creating logical workflow steps or configuring the rules of each condition and action placed in the designer environment. These things are taken care of after you import the workflow in SharePoint Designer 2010. Also, when building a SharePoint workflow, you can only utilize the shapes in the stencils mentioned earlier. Non-SharePoint shapes from other stencils in Visio 2010 are not supported and produce an error when you try to export the final workflow.

After you finish building the workflow, you must validate it. The Process tab (see Figure 12-2) in Visio 2010 provides the option to check your diagram for any logical errors.

FIGURE 12-2

The Check Diagram button works with built-in rules for SharePoint workflow functionality that check the validity of the diagram. This allows the diagram designer to check for any common errors, such as loose connectors in the workflow.

The following exercise walks you through building a workflow in Visio 2010, then validating it and exporting it.

TRY IT OUT Create a Workflow in Visio 2010

In this exercise, you create a workflow using Visio Premium 2010 and export it. This workflow is a slight variation of a workflow you created in Chapter 11 using SharePoint Designer 2010.

1. Start Microsoft Visio Premium 2010.

2. From the Backstage of Visio, click the Flowchart template category.

3. Choose the Microsoft SharePoint Workflow template and click the Create button.

4. The Quick Shapes stencil should be visible. Drag the Start terminator onto the far left side of the Visio drawing. Now drag the Terminate terminator onto the far right side of the Visio drawing. The workflow components will go between these two terminators.

5. Click on the SharePoint Workflow Conditions stencil.

6. Drag the Compare document field shape on the Visio drawing surface right after the Start terminator.

7. Click on the SharePoint Workflow Actions stencil.

8. Drag the Assign a to-do item action in front of, but a little higher than, the compare condition.

9. Drag a Create list item action in front of the Assign a to-do item action.

10. Drag another Create list item action right below the other Create List Item action.

11. Drag the Set workflow status action right behind the Terminate terminator.

12. Now, to start drawing connections between the activities, click the Connector button on the toolbar.

13. Hover the mouse over the Start terminator until a small red square appears at one of the corners of the object. Then left-click on the square and, while holding down the mouse button, hover over the Compare document field until a small red square appears at one of the corners of that condition. When it does, let the mouse button go to create the connection between the two objects.

14. Use the same connecting technique to create one connection between the Compare document condition to the Assign a to-do item action at the top and another connection between the Compare document condition to the Create list item action at the bottom.

15. Connect the Assign a to-do item action to the Create list item action in front of it.

16. Create a connection from one of the Create list item actions to the Set workflow status action. Create a connection from the other Create list item action to the Set workflow status action.

17. Create a connection between the Set workflow status action and the Terminate terminator.

18. The connections coming out of the condition, Compare document field, need to be labeled. Right-click on the top connection, and select Yes from the pop-up menu. Now right-click on the bottom connection and select No.

Your workflow should look similar to the one shown in Figure 12-3.

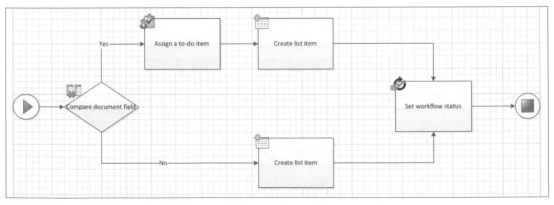

FIGURE 12-3

19. Click on the Process tab in the ribbon. To check the diagram and make sure no errors exist, click on the Check Diagram button. If the workflow is valid, you will see a pop-up dialog telling you that no issues were found. If issues are found, you will see an Issues task pane displayed below the design surface. You must read and fix these errors before moving on to the next step.

20. Click on the Export button. Using the Export Workflow window that appears, save the workflow anywhere on your hard drive. To follow along this example, name the file **Process Events.vwi**. You use this file in the next exercise.

How It Works

In the preceding exercise, you built a workflow diagram using Visio's workflow shapes. The connector tool lets you connect these shapes to define how the execution will proceed in the workflow. Then, the workflow is checked for any common errors such as loose connections or unlabeled conditional objects. Lastly, you package the workflow and export it as a VWI file.

The VWI extension stands for Visio Workflow Interchange. This type of file is understood both by Visio Premium 2010 and SharePoint Designer 2010. Within, it contains the workflow rules and the Visio diagram. This file is actually a packaged ZIP file. In fact, if you temporarily changed the extension of the file to .zip, you could double-click on it to open it and see its contents, as shown in Figure 12-4.

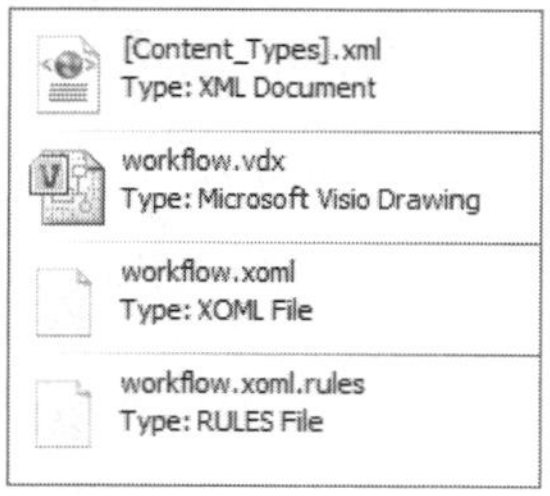

Make sure to change the file extension back to .vwi if you plan to import this file into SharePoint Designer 2010 as discussed in the next section.

FIGURE 12-4

WORKING WITH VISIO 2010 WORKFLOWS IN SHAREPOINT DESIGNER 2010

Both Visio Premium 2010 and SharePoint Designer 2010 applications can import and export the VWI file. This section discusses how the workflow in the VWI file is handled within SharePoint Designer 2010.

Importing Workflows in SharePoint Designer 2010

To start the workflow import process in SharePoint Designer 2010, go to Workflows in the navigation pane and click the Import from Visio button in the ribbon. This starts up the Import Wizard that asks you to browse to the VWI file that you would like to import. After selecting the file, choose the type of workflow to import it as. The choices you have are *List* or *Reusable Workflows*, so you can choose either to attach this workflow to any list or library on this site directly or import it as a reusable workflow and choose a base content type for it.

The following Try It Out shows the import process in SharePoint Designer 2010.

Import the Visio 2010–Built Workflow into SharePoint Designer 2010

In this exercise, you import the workflow that you exported from Visio 2010 in the last exercise into SharePoint Designer 2010 and attach it to a list.

1.   Open a typical Team Site in SharePoint Designer 2010, and click on the Workflow section in the navigation pane.

2.   Click on the Import from Visio button on the ribbon.

3.   In the Import Workflow from Visio Drawing dialog that appears, click on Browse and browse to the location of the `Process Events.vwi` file. Select the file and click on the Open button.

4.   Click the Next button, and you'll be asked to choose the type of workflow to import, as shown in Figure 12-5. Choose the Calendar list from the List Workflow drop-down as shown in Figure 12-5 and click Finish. You should now see your workflow in the work-flow design environment.

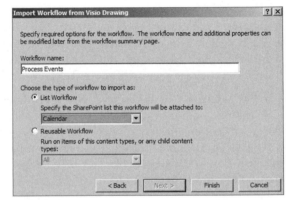

How It Works

The Visio Workflow Interchange file contains the information required by the SharePoint Designer 2010 workflow engine to import it and show it in the workflow designer environment.

FIGURE 12-5

The workflow actions can then be configured further in SharePoint Designer 2010 as the next section shows.

Configuring and Publishing the Workflow

You must configure the actions and conditions in a workflow in SharePoint Designer 2010. The exercise in the last section showed how to import a workflow into SharePoint Designer 2010. After importing the workflow, you can use the workflow elements in the workflow designer environment (discussed in Chapter 11) to further enhance the workflow. The following exercise provides an example of configuring the imported workflow.

Configure the Workflow with Rules and Publish It

In this exercise, you configure the workflow with logic that you imported in the last exercise. Then, you publish it to the Calendar list. The intent of this workflow is to monitor the Calendar list, and, if a Birthday or Anniversary type of event is created, assign an appropriate task and start a discussion thread on that topic.

You start out with the imported workflow that looks like the one in Figure 12-6.

FIGURE 12-6

1. Click the current step name (it should start with letters *ID* and then a number), and change it to **Process the Calendar Item**.

2. Click Field link and from the drop-down, select Category. Click Value link and then select Get-together from the drop-down.

3. Click a To-do item link and from the Task Wizard that appears, create the task Arrange for Catering. Click the These users link and assign this task to any member of the site.

4. Click this List link on the next action item. In the Create New List Item dialog that appears, choose the Team Discussion list from the drop-down. Click the Subject (*) field and then click Modify. In the dialog that appears, click *fx*. In the lookup dialog, click Field from the source drop-down and select Title. Click OK on the opened dialog boxes to get back to the Create New List Item dialog. Click the Add button and, in the dialog that appears, select the Body field in the first drop-down. Click *fx*, and in the lookup dialog, click Field from the source drop-down, select Description, and then click OK. The dialog should now look like the one in Figure 12-7.

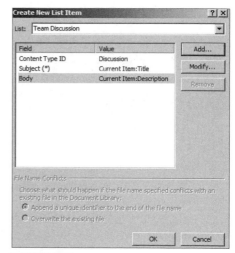

FIGURE 12-7

5. Click OK in the Create List Item dialog to get back to the workflow designer interface.

6. Click on create and from the drop-down that appears, click Create a new variable. The Edit Variable dialog appears. Name the variable **DiscussionID** and click OK.

7. Click right below the Create Item action to place the cursor there and then click the Parallel Block button on the ribbon. Now select the Create Item action and click the Move Down button on the

ribbon to move this action in the parallel block. Do the same with Assign a to-do item action to move it down inside the parallel block.

8. In the Create Item action below the Else condition, click this list link. In the Create New List Item dialog, choose the Announcements list from the drop-down. Click the Title (*) field and then click Modify. In the dialog that appears, click *fx*. In the lookup dialog, click Field from the source drop-down and select Title. Click OK on the opened dialog boxes to get back to the Create New List Item dialog. Click the Add button and, in the dialog that appears, select the Body field in the first drop-down. Click *fx* and, in the lookup dialog, click Field from the source drop-down and select Description. Click OK on all opened dialog boxes to get back to the workflow designer interface.

9. Click on create and, from the drop-down that appears, click Create a new variable. The Edit Variable dialog appears. Name the variable **AnnouncementID** and click OK.

10. In the Set workflow status action, click the Canceled status and type in **Done**.

11. Click below the step on the workflow design surface and then click the Step button on the ribbon to create a new step. Name the step **Finishing Up**.

12. Select the Set workflow status action and click Move Down to move it within the Finishing Up step. Your workflow should now look similar to the one shown in Figure 12-8.

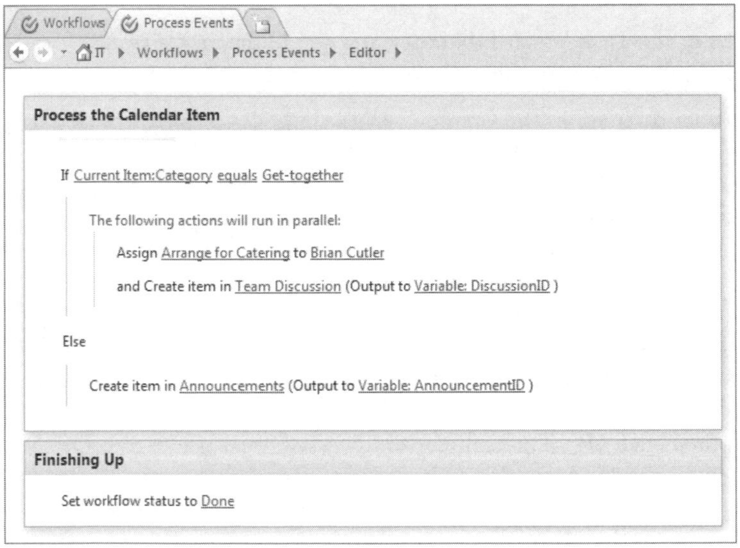

FIGURE 12-8

13. Check the workflow for any errors by clicking on the Check for Errors button. If errors exist, fix them before proceeding.

14. Click the Workflow Settings button on the ribbon and, on the Settings page, select the checkbox for Start workflow automatically when an item is created. Save the workflow by clicking on the Save button.

15. Click the Publish button to publish the workflow to the Calendar list.

How It Works

The exercise starts out with an imported workflow. You configure the rules just as in any other work-flow. Then, you create the additional step and use a parallel block to run a couple of actions in parallel. When this workflow is published, SharePoint treats it just like a workflow that would have originated in SharePoint Designer 2010.

Visualizing a Workflow Using Visio Visualization

Visio Services, a new feature of SharePoint 2010, provides Visio functionality at the server level. Visio Services lets you view Visio diagrams in the browser without the need for the Visio application on your client machine.

Visio Services is integrated into the SharePoint workflow functionality. Users can view the visual status of any running workflow that has the Visio visualization turned on. A Visio 2010 diagram of your workflow is automatically created and displayed in a Visio 2010 web part on the workflow status page. This visualization shows the exact status of the current stage of the workflow. For this functionality to work, SharePoint server must be running Visio graphics services (controlled through SharePoint Central Administration). An image of a sample Visio visualization is shown in Figure 12-9.

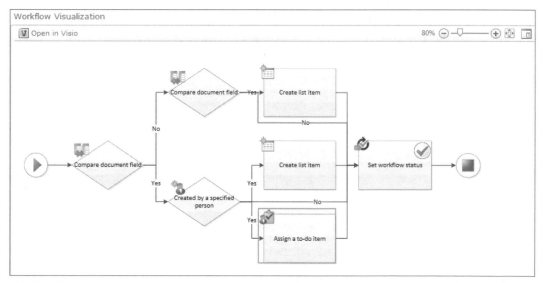

FIGURE 12-9

The Visio diagram renders in full fidelity in the browser if the machine being used has Microsoft Silverlight installed. If it does not, then the diagram renders in PNG format.

The visualization of a workflow has to be turned on individually for each workflow that you want Visio Services to process. In the workflow settings page of a workflow is a checkbox labeled "Show workflow visualization on status page." This checkbox must be selected before the workflow is pub-lished for the visualization to be generated as part of the workflow history page.

The next exercise shows how to configure the visualization of SharePoint Designer 2010 workflows.

TRY IT OUT   **Visualize SharePoint Designer 2010 Workflows**

In this exercise, you turn on the Visio workflow visualization of the workflow you created in the last exercise. Then, you execute the workflow and observe the status in Visio.

1.   In SharePoint Designer 2010, click on Workflows in the navigation pane. Open the Process Events workflow you created in the last exercise.

2.   While at the summary page of the workflow, click on the checkbox for Show workflow visualization on status page.

3.   Click the Publish button to republish the workflow to the Calendar list.

4.   Now, to see the visualization, you must run the workflow. Navigate to the Calendar list in the browser.

5.   Click the Events tab and then click the New Event button to start creating a new event.

6.   Set the Title to "Celebrating Jim's Birthday." Set the Description to "Let's get together in the Wrigley conference room to celebrate Jim's Birthday." Set the Category to Get-together. Click Save to save the event.

7.   Now, click the event you just created on the calendar. Click the Workflows button. You should see that the Process Events workflow is In Progress. Click the In Progress link and you should see the workflow visualization come up on the workflow history page, as displayed in Figure 12-10. You can also open this diagram in Visio by clicking on the Open in Visio link.

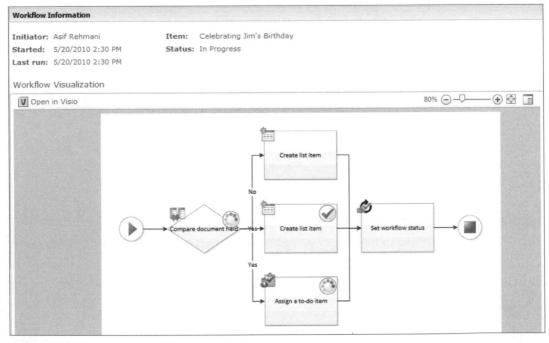

FIGURE 12-10

8. According to the diagram, a list item has been created and a task has been assigned waiting to be acted on. Navigate to the Team Discussions list; you should see a new discussion thread (see Figure 12-11) with the same information as the calendar item.

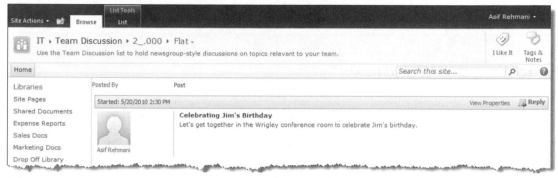

FIGURE 12-11

9. Now, click on the Tasks list and you should see a task assignment titled Arrange for Catering. Click on the task and you should see the workflow task form. Click on the Complete Task button.

10. Return to the Calendar list and, as before, navigate to the workflow page of the event. This time, the workflow should have the status of Done. Click on it to get to the workflow history page. You should see the workflow visualization, as shown in Figure 12-12.

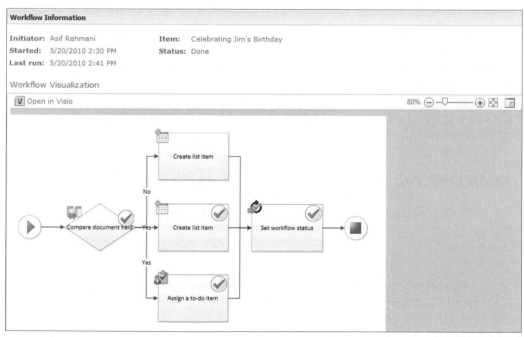

FIGURE 12-12

All the activities in the workflow have been completed as depicted in the visualization.

How It Works

Visio Graphics Services (part of SharePoint Server Enterprise) provides the visualization for the running workflow directly in the workflow history page. The visualization shows up with Silverlight (if installed). Otherwise, it will render as HTML.

Exporting the Workflow

The workflow settings page for every list and reusable workflow has an Export to Visio button on the ribbon. This means that you can export the design of any list or reusable workflow (site workflows are not supported by this functionality) to visualize in Visio Premium 2010. When importing a workflow in Visio 2010, if the workflow file is already open in Visio 2010, the diagram will be updated to show any changes made in SharePoint Designer 2010. If the diagram file is not open, it will make a new diagram based on the workflow.

One of the advantages of taking the workflow to Visio 2010 is to visualize the processes better. You might want to store the workflow as a Visio diagram so that the visual depiction of the workflow processes is communicated to all stakeholders and so that everyone is clear on what is being implemented.

You can make as many roundtrips as you want between SharePoint Designer 2010 and Visio Premium 2010 with no loss of data or functionality. In other words, none of the rules, steps, variables, and all other, configured workflow elements are lost going back and forth between the two applications.

The SharePoint object model provides the ability to create new workflow activities using Visual Studio. You can also buy activities from third-party vendors and plug them into SharePoint. The question then becomes: if new activities are designed and installed in SharePoint, and then used in a workflow that's imported in Visio Premium 2010, how will these activities surface? The answer is that Visio 2010 will show these custom activities as generic box shapes, because it will not know how else to present them. However, the good news is that you will not lose any configurations made to them in SharePoint Designer 2010.

CUSTOMIZING WORKFLOW FORMS WITH INFOPATH 2010

Microsoft InfoPath 2010 provides a robust and powerful environment in which to create electronic forms. Chapter 9 is devoted to discussing how InfoPath 2010 works and the integration points of InfoPath in SharePoint. This section discusses InfoPath form integration within SharePoint Designer 2010 workflows.

SharePoint Designer 2010 workflows make ample use of forms to interact and gather data from users. These forms are created automatically by a workflow at the time it is published. SharePoint Designer 2010 generates three types of workflows automatically:

➤ **Initiation form** — This form is presented to the user when the workflow is started manually on a list or library item. If any initiation form parameters are declared for the workflow, then they show up on this form. The user must then provide input. If no initiation form parameters are declared, then the form only contains a Start and a Cancel button.

➤ **Task form** — Workflows often contain actions that create tasks in the Tasks list on the site. When users interact with these tasks, they are presented with this form. If custom form fields are defined for the task in the workflow, then these fields appear on the task form.

➤ **Association form** — A reusable workflow makes use of association columns (fields). These columns (or fields) are added to the list when the workflow is added to that list. An association form enables you to associate fields with a reusable workflow so that the fields will be available when you design and run the workflow.

> **NOTE** *Initiation forms, form parameters, and association columns are all topics covered in Chapter 11.*

When you publish a workflow in SharePoint Designer 2010, the appropriate forms automatically get generated. You can modify workflow forms after they already exist as part of the workflow. These forms cannot be generated from scratch starting from InfoPath. These forms are visible in the Forms section of the workflow settings page, as shown in Figure 12-13. The XSN extension on these forms clearly indicates that these are InfoPath forms.

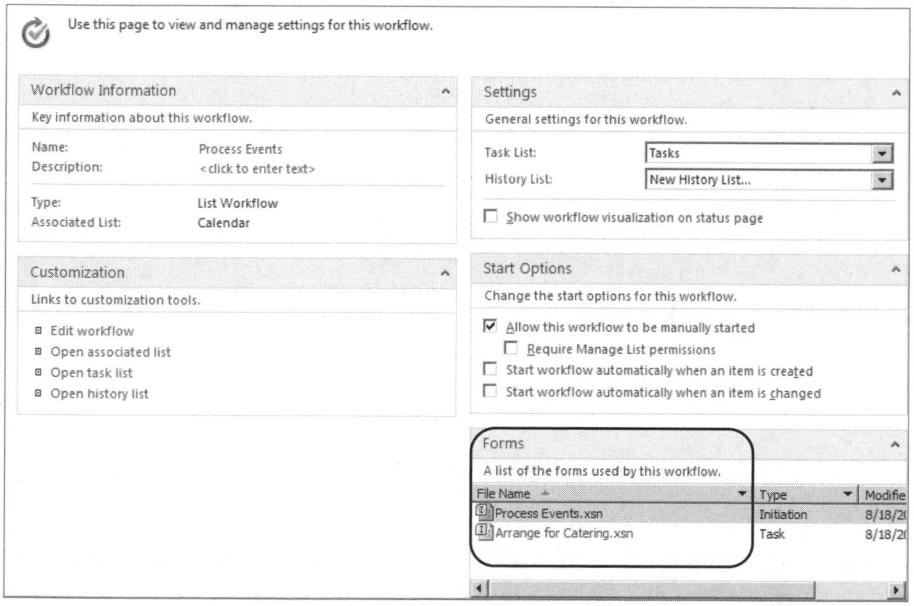

FIGURE 12-13

To modify these forms, click on the appropriate form to open it in InfoPath 2010. You can take advantage of all the features of InfoPath 2010 (for example, page layout design, data validation, conditional formatting, and more) to enhance this form further. When you are done with your enhancements, simply click the File button and then the Quick Publish button to publish the form back to the workflow from which it came.

The next exercise walks you through customizing a workflow form in InfoPath 2010.

TRY IT OUT | **Customize a SharePoint Designer 2010 Workflow Form in InfoPath 2010**

In this exercise, you modify the initiation form of the workflow created in the last exercise.

1. In SharePoint Designer 2010, click on Workflows in the navigation pane. Open the Process Events workflow you created in an earlier exercise.

2. While at the summary page of the workflow, if the checkbox for starting the workflow automatically is selected, deselect it and click the Publish button to republish the workflow.

3. Click the `Process Events.xsn` file in the Forms section. InfoPath should open the form.

4. Click on the Start button, and using the Properties tab in the ribbon, change the Label of the control to Process.

5. Place your cursor in the table cell above the buttons. Click the Insert tab and then click the Picture button on the ribbon. Look for and select a picture (something that can work as a logo) on your hard drive. Click the Insert button to insert it on the form.

6. After the picture is inserted on the form, press Enter on your keyboard to put your cursor right under it. Type in **Click the Process button below to start processing the event**. Using the Home tab on the ribbon, enhance the font (bold, italicize) as you want to enhance this message.

    Your form should now look something like the one shown in Figure 12-14.

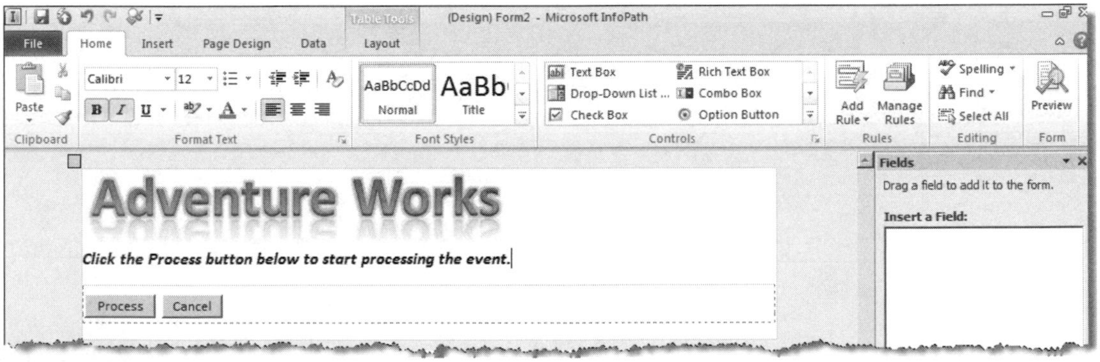

FIGURE 12-14

7. Click the File button on the ribbon. Then click on the Quick Publish button. You should get a message to save the form before it is published. Click OK and save it somewhere on your hard drive. A message appears that your form template was published successfully.

8. Open the Internet browser and navigate to your site. Click on the Calendar list and enter a new event titled **Board Meeting**.

9. After the event is created, click on it to open it, and then click the Workflows button. When you see the Process Events workflow, go ahead and click on it. Now, you should see the form that you just modified in InfoPath (see Figure 12-15).

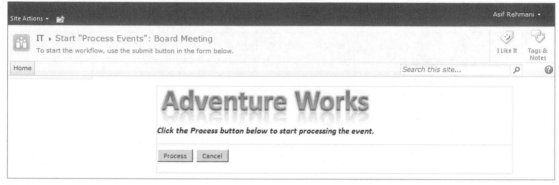

FIGURE 12-15

10. Click the Process button and the workflow should start.

How It Works

InfoPath 2010 has a direct tie in to the workflow packages created by SharePoint Designer 2010. Once the form is modified in InfoPath 2010, it can be easily published back to the workflow where it originated from.

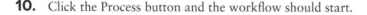

For all of this functionality to work as described in the preceding exercise, you need the InfoPath 2010 application on the client machine to modify your forms. Also, at the server level, you must be running SharePoint Server (Standard or Enterprise). If you are running SharePoint Foundation 2010, the workflow forms that get generated in SharePoint Designer 2010 are ASPX forms, which means these are ASP.NET forms that can be modified within SharePoint Designer 2010, but not in InfoPath 2010. To see the differences between customizing a form using InfoPath 2010 and SharePoint Designer 2010, you can watch the videos at www.sharepoint-videos.com.

BUILT-IN GLOBAL WORKFLOWS

SharePoint Server ships with five built-in workflow templates: Approval, Collect Feedback, Collect Signatures, Disposition Approval, and Three-State. You can start using these directly in your Internet browser by accessing them through any list or library's workflow settings page.

Three of the most popular built-in workflows (Approval, Collect Feedback, Collect Signatures) are built as declarative globally reusable workflows in team sites. An additional workflow called Publishing Approval, similar to Approval workflow, is available when you are working in publishing sites to approve publishing pages. These workflows are available to be fully customized, using SharePoint Designer 2010, by the owner of the top-level site of the site collection.

> **NOTE** *If you make changes directly to a built-in workflow, you are modifying that workflow for everyone in the site collection. That means that your built-in workflows in this site collection would work differently from the ones in other site collections, thus potentially confusing your end users running the same name workflows, but getting different results in two different site collections.*
>
> *To avoid this situation, you can make a copy of the workflow instead and give it a unique name before modifying it and publishing it to be used globally throughout the site collection.*

You can also copy any of these workflows and create a new one with your own custom modifications. You can do this within any site of the site collection. In SharePoint Designer 2010, select the workflow you want to copy and click the Copy and Modify button on the ribbon. This creates a reusable workflow local to that site. After you have made the modifications, then publish the workflow to the site.

Creating New Globally Reusable Workflows

The three globally reusable workflow templates mentioned earlier are available throughout the site collection. You can also create new globally reusable workflows. However, you must have Full Control permission at the top-level site to make this happen.

You can publish any reusable workflow at the top-level site as a globally reusable workflow by going to the workflow settings page and clicking on the Publish Globally button on the ribbon. Publishing a workflow globally places it in the Global workflows catalog, making it reusable on every site within the site collection and visible to all users.

The following exercise shows how you can create a globally reusable workflow.

TRY IT OUT **Create a Globally Reusable Workflow**

In this exercise, you take a reusable workflow and convert it into a globally reusable workflow.

1. Start SharePoint Designer 2010 and open the top-level site of the site collection.

2. Use the skills you learned in Chapter 11 to create a simple, reusable workflow with the base content type of All. A sample workflow, named Log Keyword, is depicted in Figure 12-16.

3. Click the Save button to save the workflow, and then click the Publish Globally button on the ribbon. An information dialog appears, stating that publishing the workflow globally will make it available all throughout the site collection. Acknowledge the message by clicking on the OK button.

4. After the workflow finishes publishing, verify it by clicking Workflows in the navigation pane. You should see that your reusable workflow now shows up in the Globally Reusable Workflow section as well (see Figure 12-17).

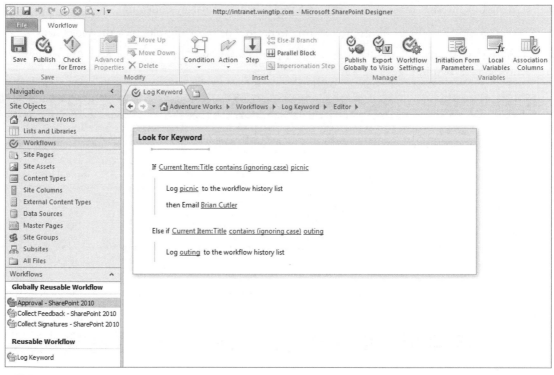

FIGURE 12-16

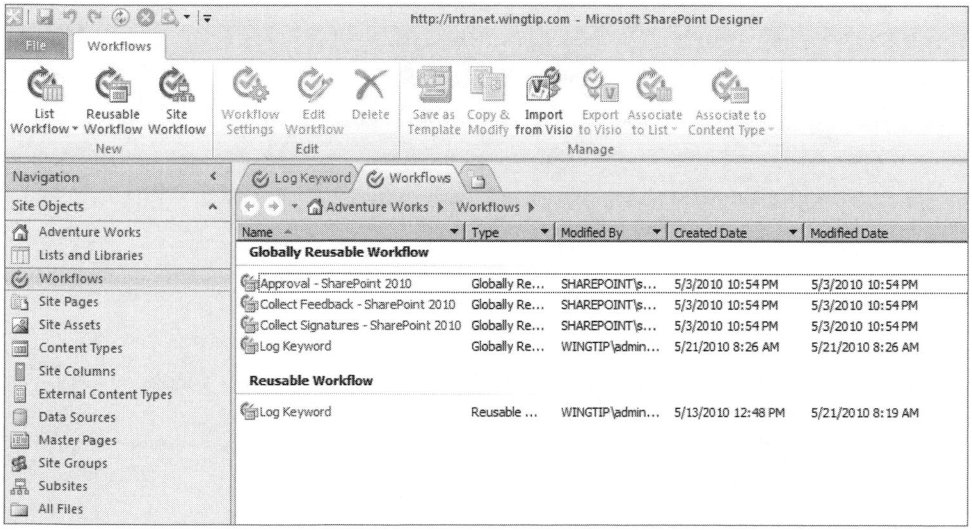

FIGURE 12-17

5. Open your Internet browser and navigate to a subsite in this site collection.

6. You can pick any list or library to test this scenario. For this example, pick the Links list.

7. Click the List tab, click the drop-down for workflow settings, and click the Add a Workflow choice, as shown in Figure 12-18.

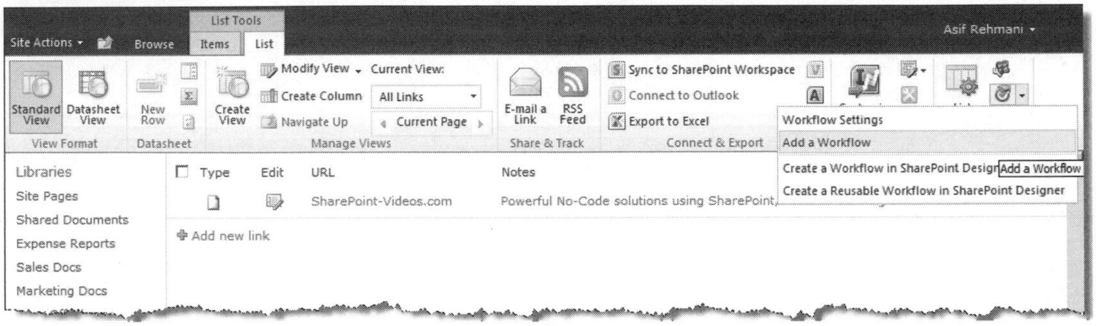

FIGURE 12-18

8. The Add a Workflow screen should show your workflow template in the Select a Workflow template text area (see Figure 12-19).

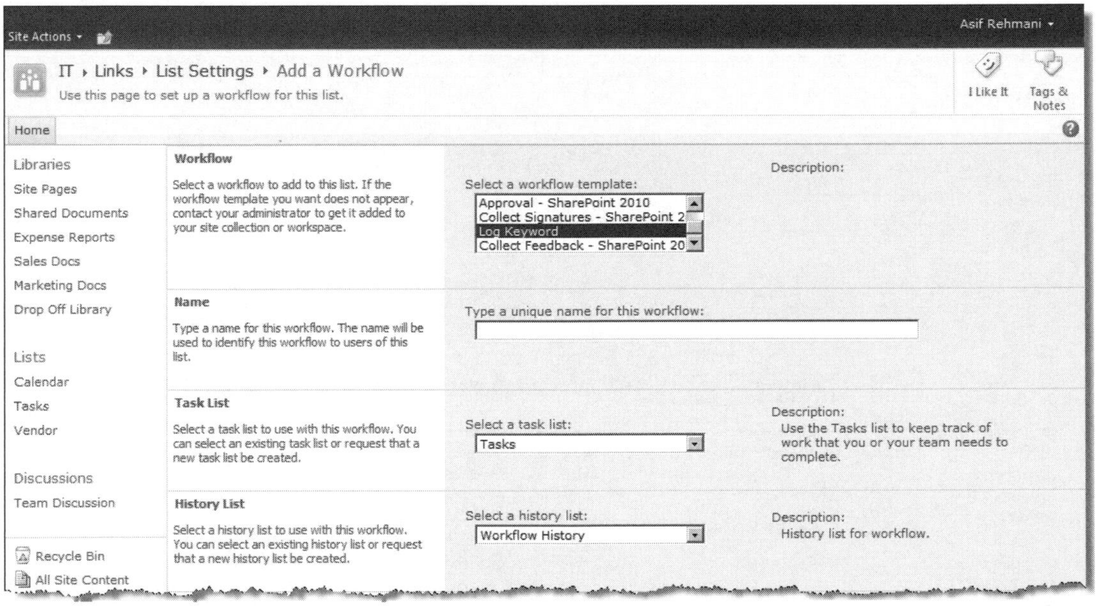

FIGURE 12-19

You can now use this global workflow template like all other built-in templates.

How It Works

When you publish a reusable workflow globally, a copy of the workflow is made. The original workflow still remains at the site level and can be used independently of the newly created globally reusable workflow.

Using the Task Process Designer

Two of the three built-in global workflows that you can customize are built with actions available under the Actions button, as shown in the following table:

ACTION	BUILT-IN WORKFLOW
Start Approval Process	Approval
Start Feedback Process	Collect Feedback

The third workflow, Collect Signatures, uses a slight variation of the Start Feedback Process action. Also, another action, Start Document Set Approval Process, has the process design that's based on the Start Approval Process action, with the exception that this action works on whole document sets instead of a single document.

These workflows are all completely event-driven, and all the important events in the workflows are available to be customized within the Workflow Editor using the Task Process Designer. Think of the Task Process Designer as a workflow designer within a workflow designer. Each task in the process or the process as a whole can be customized using the Task Process Designer. Figure 12-20 shows the Workflow Editor interface of the Approval workflow. It also shows the Task Process Designer environment that you can enter by clicking on the Approval link in Start Approval Process action.

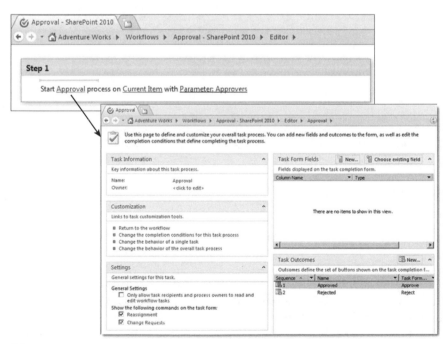

FIGURE 12-20

The next exercise walks you through copying the Approval workflow and customizing it and deploying it onto a site.

TRY IT OUT Copy and Change the Approval Workflow at a Subsite

In this exercise, you copy the built-in Approval workflow to a subsite and then modify the activities to your needs.

1. Open or create a team site anywhere under the top-level site of the site collection. Open this subsite in SharePoint Designer 2010, and click on the Workflow section in the navigation pane.

2. Click on the Approval - SharePoint 2010 workflow. A dialog appears, informing you that it is read-only and to ask whether you want to make a copy of the workflow. Click Yes.

3. Name the workflow **AW Approval**, and leave the base content type selection to All.

4. When the workflow designer surface appears, click on Approval Workflow Task to enter the Task Process Designer environment that's shown in Figure 12-21.

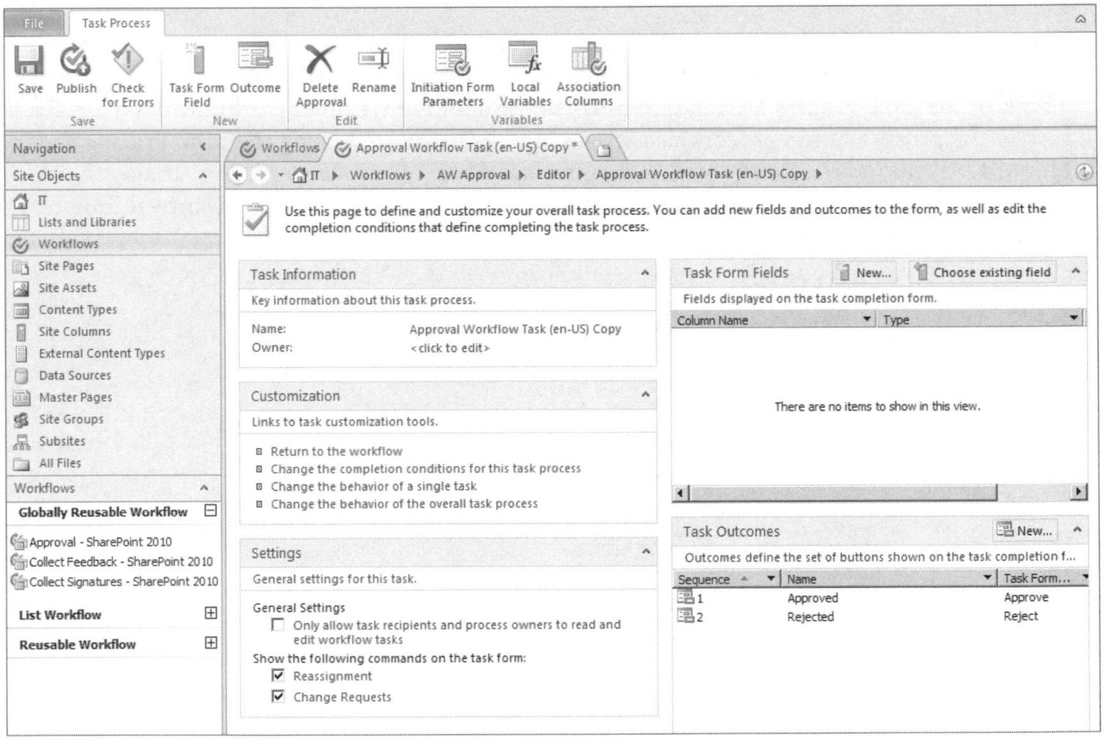

FIGURE 12-21

5. Click on the link "Change the behavior of the overall task process."

6. Find the When the Task Process is Running step and then find the "When the Item is Changed" substep. Under the wording "Wait for change in item that the task process is running on," click on the [%Task Process:Process Name%]... link; a dialog box appears as shown in Figure 12-22.

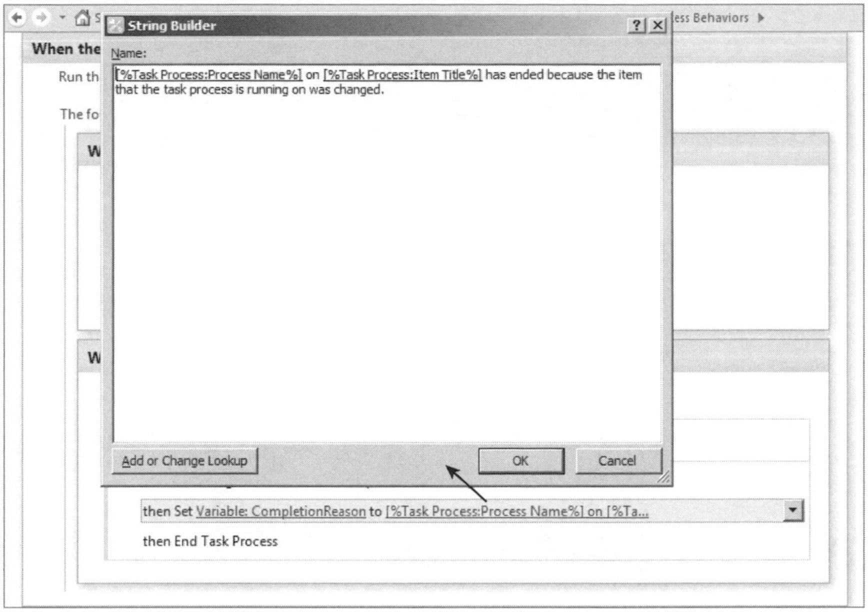

FIGURE 12-22

7. Append the following wording at the end of the message in the dialog: **The process needs to be restarted so all approvers can see the change and approve it.** Click OK.

8. Now look for the When the Task Process Completes step. Under the step, look for and click on the link in the Log action to change the message.

9. In the String Builder dialog that appears, append the following text: **Check out the workflow status field to see whether the process completed successfully.** Click OK.

10. Find and click the link in the Email action under the Else branch to modify the e-mail message that gets sent out to the initiator of the workflow.

11. Change the wording of the e-mail as desired. A sample change is shown in Figure 12-23. Click OK.

12. Check the workflow for errors (click the Check for Errors button on the ribbon) and if no errors are found, click the Publish button to publish the workflow.

13. Click Workflows in the navigation pane and you should now see the AW Approval workflow in the Reusable Workflow section.

How It Works

The AW Approval workflow created in the preceding exercise now acts just like any other reusable workflow on the site. To use it, an administrator of the site would go to the Add a Workflow screen for any list or library on the site. The AW Approval should be readily available at this location as a workflow template to be used (see Figure 12-24). This workflow will behave just like the original built-in Approval workflow. The only changes are the textual ones made in the preceding exercise.

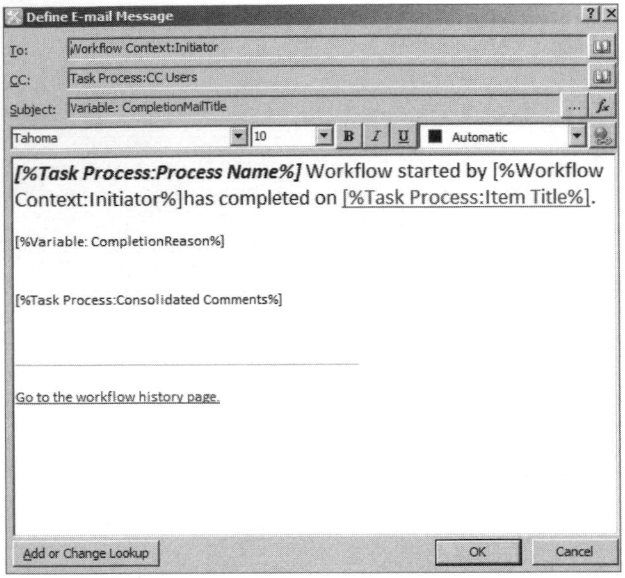

FIGURE 12-23

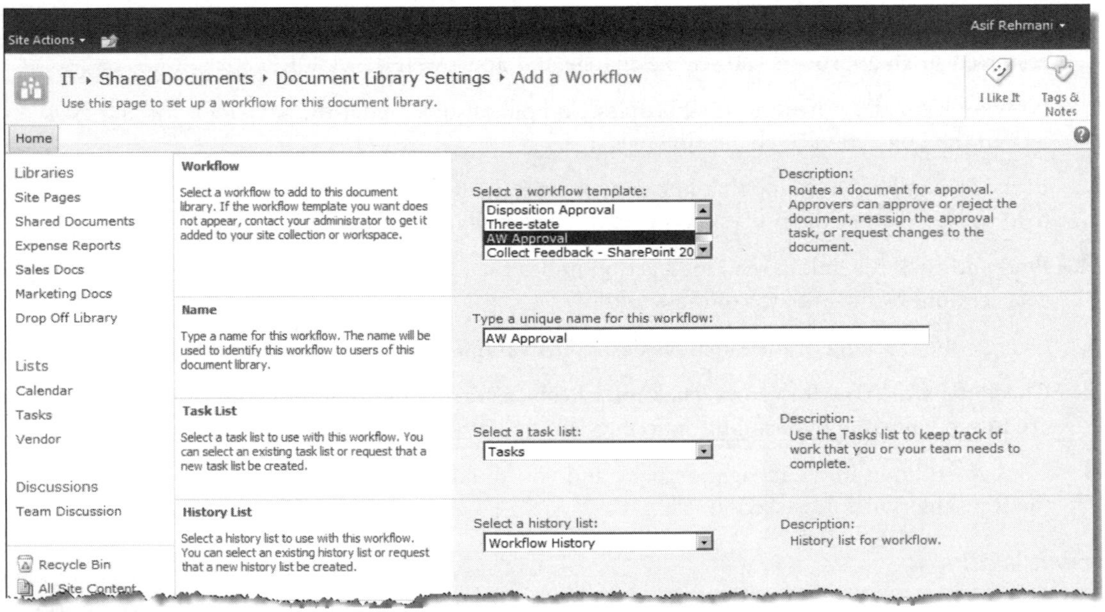

FIGURE 12-24

EXPORTING WORKFLOWS AS A PACKAGE

In the preceding sections, you learned how to create reusable workflows that you can use within a site or even publish globally so they can be used throughout the site collection. SharePoint Designer 2010 also supports exporting a reusable workflow as a package so that it can be deployed to another site collection or further extended using Visual Studio.

Packaging up a reusable workflow is a simple one-step process executed from the workflow settings page of the reusable workflow. At this page, clicking on the Save as Template button on the ribbon packages up the reusable workflow in a WSP file (SharePoint solution package) and automatically stores it in the Site Assets library of the site, as shown in Figure 12-25.

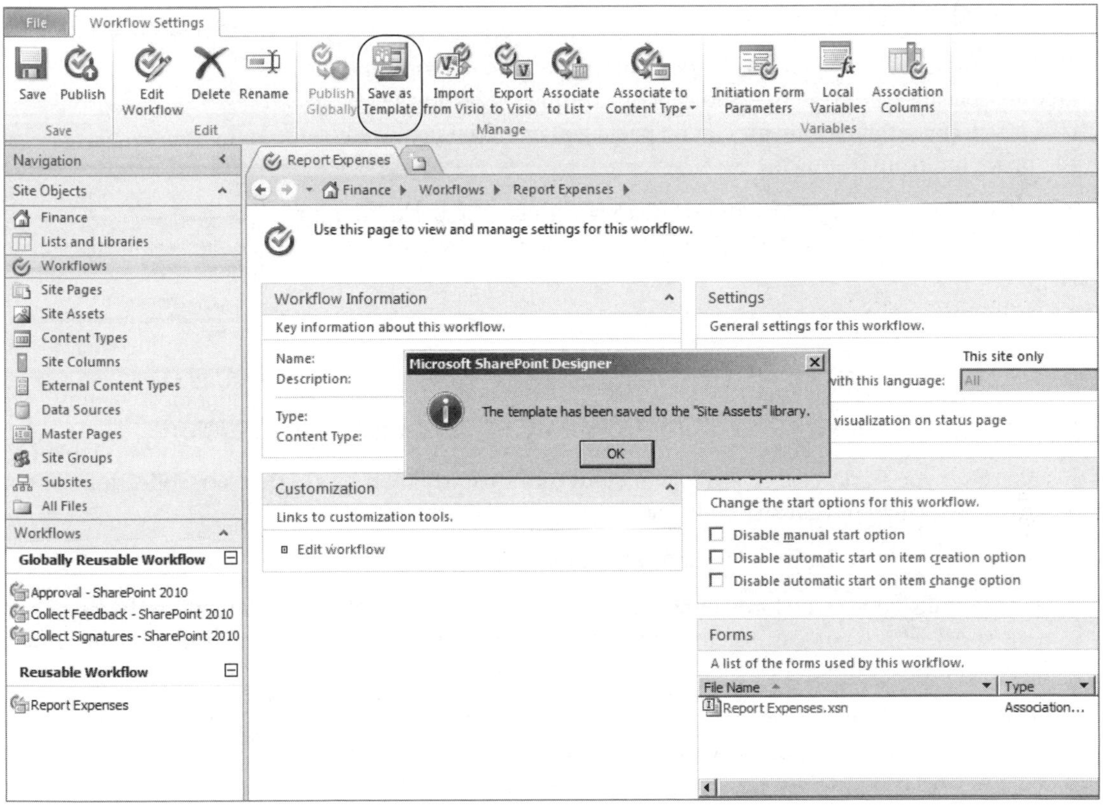

FIGURE 12-25

After you have the file in the Site Assets library, you can export it to your hard drive or file share to transport it as necessary. In SharePoint Designer 2010, click Site Assets in the navigation pane. You can select the WSP file (if the WSP file is not there, refresh the page) and click the Export File button on the ribbon to start the export process.

The following sections explain what you can do with this WSP file after you export it.

Deploying a Workflow Package to a Site Collection

A file with a .wsp extension is referred to as a SharePoint solution file in SharePoint. This file is usually generated by developers and bundles within it components such as features, site definitions, and more.

SharePoint Designer 2010 also has the capability to produce a SharePoint solution file containing a reusable workflow, as shown in the previous section. This file has a .cab-based format but a .wsp file extension. In fact, if you change the file extension of a WSP file (containing a workflow) to CAB temporarily and then double-click on it to open it, you will see the contents of this package are similar to what's shown in Figure 12-26.

You can use the WSP solution file to transfer reusable workflows created in one site collection to another. For example, workflows created in a development environment can be packaged and then deployed to the production environment.

The following exercise walks you through the process of packaging up a reusable workflow as a WSP file and then deploying it to another site collection.

2FileDocuments.xoml.wfconfig.xml
XML Document
2.51 KB

4FileDocuments.xoml.rules
RULES File
9.33 KB

5FileDocuments.xoml
XOML File
4.90 KB

6FileDocuments.xsn
Microsoft InfoPath Form Template
6.99 KB

Elements.xml
XML Document
21.4 KB

Feature.xml
XML Document
1.00 KB

manifest.xml
XML Document
286 bytes

resources.en-US.resx
.NET Managed Resources File
0 bytes

Schema.xml
XML Document
65.4 KB

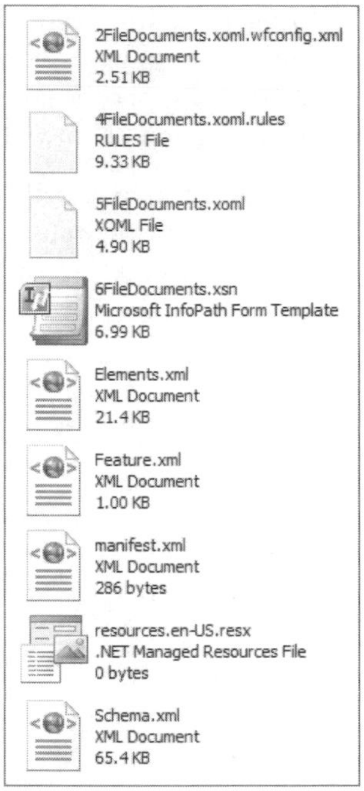

FIGURE 12-26

TRY IT OUT   Deploy a Reusable Workflow to Another Site Collection

In this exercise, you package a reusable workflow and then deploy it to another site collection. Then, you use that workflow in that site collection.

1. Start SharePoint Designer 2010 and open a team site.

2. Use the skills you learned in Chapter 11 to create a simple reusable workflow with the base content type of All. Hint: You can use the simple Log Keyword workflow created and used in an earlier exercise in this chapter.

3. While the workflow is selected (either in the main Workflows page or at the Workflow Settings page of the workflow), click the Save as Template button on the ribbon. You should see a dialog box informing you that the workflow template has been saved to the Site Assets library.

4. Click on Site Assets in the navigation pane. You should see your workflow template (if you don't, refresh the screen).

5. Highlight the workflow and click the Export File button on the ribbon. Save this solution file somewhere on your computer.

6. Using your Internet browser, open the top-level site of another site collection that you have access to as a site collection administrator.

7. Go to the Site Settings page and click on Solutions under the Galleries section.

8. Now at the Solution Gallery, click the Solutions tab and then click the Upload Solution button.

9. Browse to the location of the solution file you exported earlier to your computer and select it to be uploaded. Click the OK button in the Upload Document dialog.

You should now see the Activate Solution dialog, as shown in Figure 12-27.

FIGURE 12-27

10. Click the Activate button in the dialog. Your workflow is now activated and available within this site collection.

11. Navigate to the Site Settings page of any site within the site collection. Click the Manage site features link under the Site Action section.

12. You should see your workflow template as a feature on this page, as shown in Figure 12-28. Click the Activate button to activate it. This workflow is now available on the site as a reusable workflow.

FIGURE 12-28

How It Works

The Solution Gallery of a site collection holds the WSP solution files. In the preceding exercise, the workflow solution package is deployed to this gallery. Then, the package is activated to make it available as a site feature in the site collection. Each individual site owner can then choose to activate the feature in the site to enable the reusable workflow. If the feature is activated, the workflow will behave much as any other reusable workflow on the site.

Importing a Workflow Package in Visual Studio

Visual Studio 2010 provides a project template named Import Reusable Workflow. This project understands the structure of the packaged WSP file containing the reusable workflow and lets you point to and import the solution file into the Visual Studio environment, as shown in Figure 12-29.

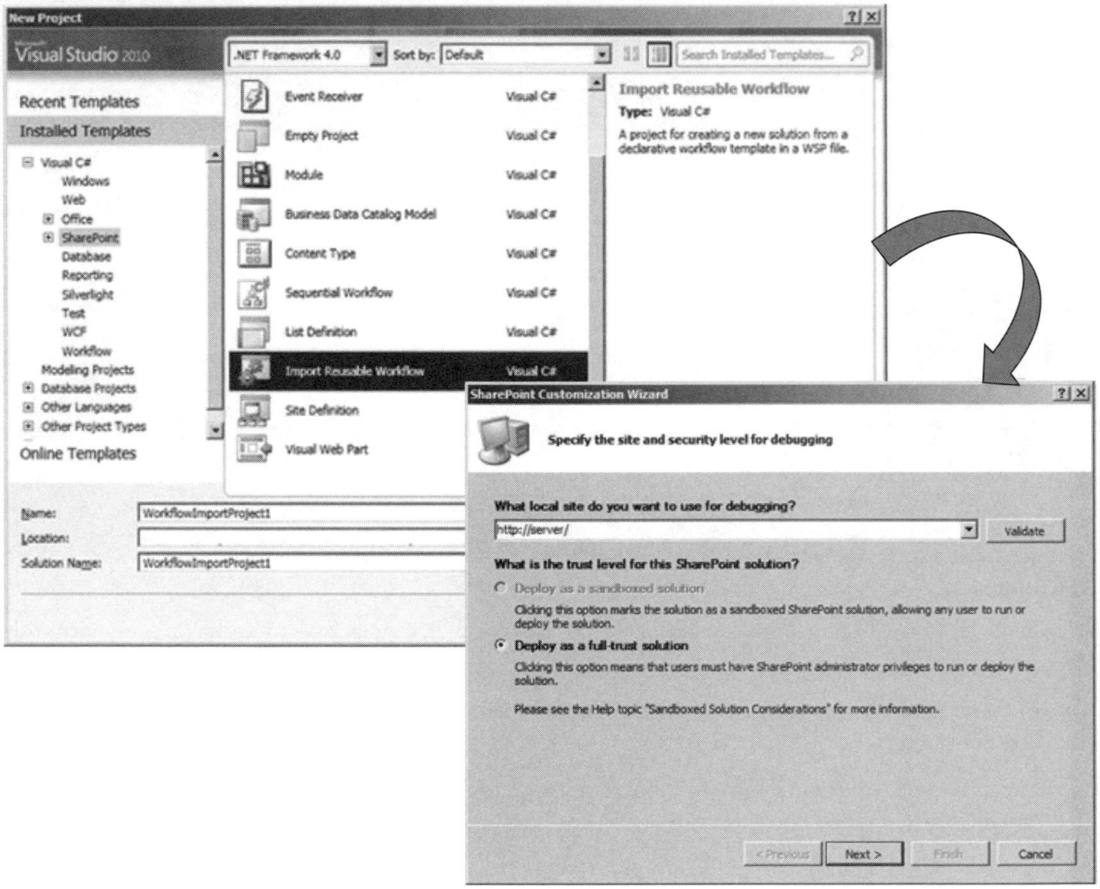

FIGURE 12-29

The story here is that a site administrator or a designer would create the reusable workflow initially in SharePoint Designer 2010, package it up into a solution file, and then pass it on to a developer, who can import it into Visual Studio and extend it as necessary with code. This process is also detailed in an MSDN article located at `http://msdn.microsoft.com/en-us/library/ee231580.aspx`.

In concept, this is a great idea and provides hope for a rapid development solution that involves the business owner and the developer working side by side. However, before moving forward with this idea, consider the following facts:

➤ A single action in SharePoint Designer 2010 may render as dozens of activities in Visual Studio 2010.

➤ Workflows with large numbers of activities in Visual Studio 2010 are not easily manageable. The design surface just isn't designed to manage workflows of 100 activities or more, so it seems a bit unwieldy.

➤ Workflows transitioned to Visual Studio 2010 cannot be run as declarative workflows any longer and, therefore, must be deployed as farm solutions.

A much larger discussion can be had here from a developer's perspective as to the pros and cons of using this method. Because this is not a book focused on SharePoint development, the discussion of this methodology stops here. You are encouraged to experiment within this area to determine whether this functionality could be useful for your needs.

SUMMARY

This chapter exposed you to the advanced workflow features in SharePoint Designer 2010. You learned how Microsoft Visio, InfoPath, and SharePoint Designer teams have joined forces together to enable these systems to build workflows and interactive forms, and to visualize running processes.

Business analysts can use Visio Premium 2010 to model the processes in a workflow then pass it on to developers or power users, who can import these processes into SharePoint Designer 2010 and configure the workflow further. Also, Visio Services plays a major part in being able to visualize the path and history of a workflow. Furthermore, InfoPath is used by form designers to extend the functionality provided in the default forms that the workflows in SharePoint Designer 2010 create automatically.

The second part of the chapter discussed the opportunities to package up and deploy reusable workflows in a variety of ways — global to a site collection, exported to another site collection, and imported in Visual Studio. This is a major step in making your workflows truly scale throughout your enterprise systems.

Quite a bit of knowledge was presented in the last two chapters on workflows. Nevertheless, the author advises you to continue the journey and keep learning and discovering new ways that you can take advantage of the workflow systems available in SharePoint 2010.

13

Client-side Programming in JavaScript

WHAT YOU WILL LEARN IN THIS CHAPTER

- ➤ Setting up a page to use the Client Object Model
- ➤ Reading data from SharePoint using CAML
- ➤ Creating, updating, and deleting list items
- ➤ Adding commands to the ribbon

THE CLIENT OBJECT MODEL

In the past, the primary way to integrate with SharePoint externally was to use one of the many ASMX web services it provides. Using these web services, you could read and update items and documents, manage sites, lists and libraries, and configure permissions from any external application. Unfortunately, these web services were not easy to use and only supported Windows Authentication. Additionally, any knowledge you had in extending SharePoint by writing server code using the built-in object model did not help much in trying to use the web services.

Over time, adding additional functionality to these web services has become more and more expensive in terms of complexity and effort. To resolve the problems of using the non-intuitive web services and yet extend the available functionality, SharePoint has introduced the Client Object Model.

The Client Object Model is a set of technology-specific libraries that function similarly to the way the built-in object model does. These libraries support accessing SharePoint using JavaScript, Silverlight, or .NET. Using the Client Object Model, you can automate many of the tasks that you would otherwise have to perform manually using the browser or SharePoint Designer.

Some of these capabilities include creating and manipulating lists, accessing data and documents, and managing workflows. One of the more impressive features of the Client Object Model is the similarities among the classes inside the libraries, although the technologies they support are very different. Because SharePoint Designer only supports code written in JavaScript and Silverlight, the .NET version of the Client Object Model will not be covered.

> **NOTE** If you search the Internet regarding the Client Object Model, you find many references to ECMAScript, including the documentation on Microsoft's website. ECMAScript is essentially the standard upon which JavaScript and JScript are based. JScript is Microsoft's implementation of the standard within Internet Explorer. The JavaScript code in this chapter works with Microsoft Internet Explorer, Mozilla Firefox, and possibly other browsers. The use of the word "JavaScript" in this chapter is meant to refer to JavaScript, JScript, and ECMAScript.

> **NOTE** You can use the activities in this chapter with either JavaScript or Silverlight.

GETTING STARTED

The JavaScript Client Object Model is the easiest of the three object models to begin using because it requires the least amount of software and is already familiar to most web designers and developers. You only need SharePoint Designer to add JavaScript to web pages and web parts. Though you could add a web part, such as the HTML Form Web Part, to a web part page using the browser, you would not get any of the design-time support offered by SharePoint Designer, and writing code in this manner would be much more difficult.

The easiest way to start using the JavaScript Client Object Model is to open SharePoint Designer, open your site, and select Site Pages from the Navigation bar, as shown in Figure 13-1. After the list of pages appears, create a new page by selecting Page ⇨ ASPX from the ribbon and name the page appropriately. Afterwards, click the newly created page from the list and select Edit File ⇨ Edit File in Advanced Mode from the ribbon to open the page for editing.

> **NOTE** You must edit your files in Advanced Mode rather than Normal Mode in order to add JavaScript code directly to them. The side effect of this is your file will be customized. Customized files run slower since they must be read from the content database rather than the file system.

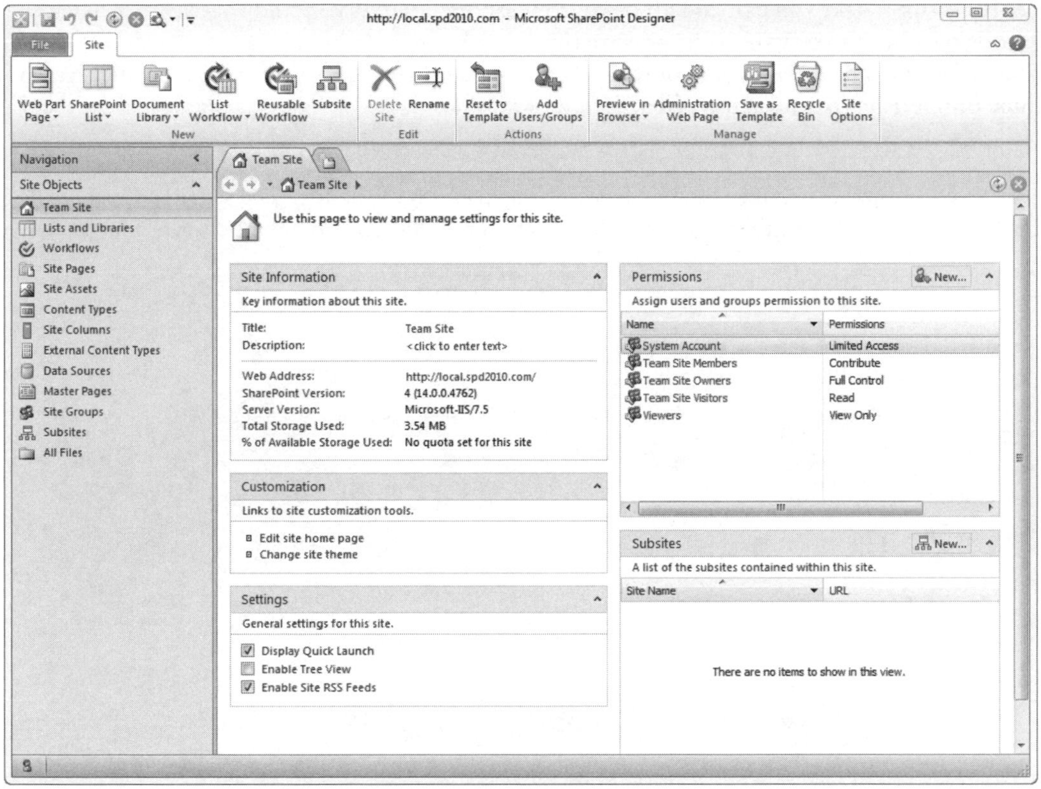

FIGURE 13-1

After the page is open for editing, attach the site's master page by selecting Attach from the Style tab of the ribbon and selecting the default master page of the site. Then, click the Split button at the bottom of the screen. This changes the editor to display both the Design view and Code view at the same time. You will see a screen similar to the one shown in Figure 13-2.

The markup of the new page looks like the following:

```
<%@ Page Language="C#" masterpagefile="~masterurl/default.master"
    title="Untitled 1"
    inherits="Microsoft.SharePoint.WebPartPages.WebPartPage, Microsoft.SharePoint,
    Version=14.0.0.0, Culture=neutral, PublicKeyToken=71e9bce111e9429c"
    meta:webpartpageexpansion="full"
    meta:progid="SharePoint.WebPartPage.Document" %>

<asp:Content id="Content1" runat="Server" contentplaceholderid="PlaceHolderMain">
</asp:Content>
```

Essentially, this markup is just a shell that will contain the controls and JavaScript code you will add later. To add code to the page, add a script block inside the `asp:Content` tag. The following snippet shows the script block you need to add:

```
<script type="text/javascript">
</script>
```

Inside this script block, you can add all of your JavaScript code. If you find that you are using the same code over and over again, you can save those JavaScript functions in a text file and store it in a document library. Then, you would only need to add a script tag that refers to your file. Here is an example of referring to a JavaScript file:

```
<script type="text/javascript" src="../SiteAssets/MyFunctions.js"></script>
```

Notice the additional attribute src that specifies the location of the file. The snippet also has an ending script tag. This ending tag is required, but do not add code inside the script block.

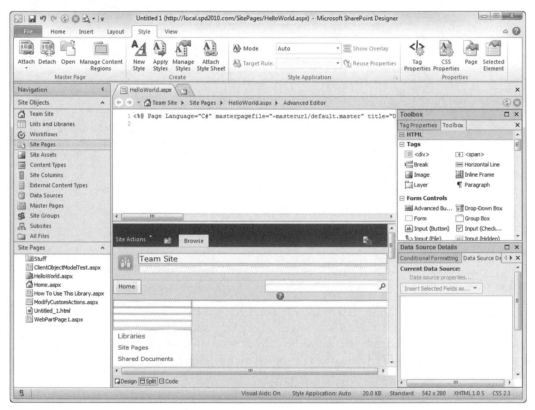

FIGURE 13-2

After you have added a script block, you need to create three functions to use the JavaScript Client Object Model. The first function will contain the code you write to request information from SharePoint. The second function will contain the code you write to process that information if the first function is successful. The third function will contain the code you write to handle any errors from communicating with SharePoint. Ensure you add the JavaScript functions inside the script tags. The following snippet shows an example of these functions:

```
function callSharePoint() {
    var context = new SP.ClientContext.get_current();

    this.site = context.get_web();
```

```
        context.load(this.site);
        context.executeQueryAsync(Function.createDelegate(this, this.onSuccess),
            Function.createDelegate(this, this.onFailure));
    }

    function onSuccess(sender, args) {
        var output = "Site Properties:\n";

        output += "Title : " + this.site.get_title();
        output += "\n"
        output += "URL : " + this.site.get_serverRelativeUrl();
        output += "\n"
        output += "Created : " + this.site.get_created();
        output += "\n"

        alert(output);
    }

    function onFailure(sender, args) {
        var output = "Call to SharePoint failed:\n";

        output += "Error Code: " + args.get_errorCode() + "\n";
        output += "Error Details: " + args.get_errorDetails() + "\n";
        output += "Error Type: " + args.get_errorTypeName() + "\n";
        output += "Error Value: " + args.get_errorValue() + "\n";
        output += "Error Message: " + args.get_message() + "\n";
        output += "Stack Trace: " + args.get_stackTrace() + "\n";

        alert(output);
    }
```

> **NOTE** *The names of these functions are not important but you should follow a standard convention when naming them. This best practice will reduce any confusion between yourself and others who may be customizing your site.*

The next few paragraphs will dissect and explain the previous code snippet. In the `callShare-Point` function, the first line gets an instance of the `ClientContext` class. The `ClientContext` class contains methods to get an instance of the objects that represent a site and its site collection in SharePoint. Two ways exist to get an instance of the `ClientContext` class. The first way is to use the following snippet:

```
var context = new SP.ClientContext.get_current();
```

Calling the `get_current` method will return an instance of the `ClientContext` class for the current site and site collection. To get an instance for a different site and site collection, use the following code snippet:

```
var context = new SP.ClientContext("relativeurl");
```

In the code snippet, you would replace *relativeurl* with the server relative URL of a site. The site must be in the same web application as the site containing the page with your JavaScript code. After you have an instance of the `ClientContext` class, you can use these methods to get the site and site collection:

NAME	DESCRIPTION
get_site()	Gets a Site object representing the current SharePoint site collection
get_web()	Gets a Web object representing the current SharePoint site

> **NOTE** *You may be confused with the object model using the Site class for site collections and the Web class for sites. This is due to maintaining backward compatibility with previous versions of SharePoint. Though the JavaScript Client Object Model is new, it really does represent the true SharePoint object model running behind the pages in a SharePoint site.*

Before you can read any properties of the Site or Web objects returned by the ClientContext class, you must call the load method on the ClientContext class passing a variable that refers to the Site or Web object. This following snippet shows this in action:

```
this.site = context.get_web();
context.load(this.site);
```

In the code snippet, this represents the window object in the browser. Because JavaScript is a dynamic language, setting this.site to the value of the Web object from the ClientContext object will automatically create a new property on the window object. Afterwards, you can refer to this .site in any script block on the page. After you set this.site to the value of the SharePoint site, you pass it to the load method of the ClientContext object.

> **NOTE** *If any of the properties and methods of the classes in the JavaScript Client Object Model return objects instead of primitive types like integer or string, you will have to call the load method on your ClientContext object for those objects, too. If you wanted to access the lists in a site, you would have to call load on the Site object and its lists method, too, as shown in the following snippet:*
>
> ```
> this.site = context.get_web();
> this.lists = this.site.get_lists();
> context.load(this.site);
> context.load(this.lists);
> ```

After you have called the load method on the ClientContext object for each of the objects that you want to retrieve from SharePoint, you must call the executeQueryAsync method on the ClientContext object. The executeQueryAsync method takes two parameters. The first parameter is the JavaScript function to execute when the call to SharePoint succeeds. The second parameter is the JavaScript function to execute when the call to SharePoint fails. Both of the JavaScript functions need to have two parameters, sender and args, which are supplied by the JavaScript Client Object Model when the JavaScript functions are executed after the call to SharePoint is made. More about these parameters is covered later in the chapter.

The following code snippet shows how to call the executeQueryAsync method:

```
context.executeQueryAsync(Function.createDelegate(this, this.onSuccess),
    Function.createDelegate(this, this.onFailure));
```

In the snippet, the JavaScript functions passed to the executeQueryAsync method are this.onSuccess and this.onFailure. They are passed to the executeQueryAsync method by creating a delegate using the Function.createDelegate method. If your JavaScript functions are a part of a class, you would pass in parameters in this manner:

```
context.executeQueryAsync(Function.createDelegate(myobject, myobject.onSuccess),
    Function.createDelegate(myobject, myobject.onFailure));
```

In the snippet, **myobject** is an instance of your class. After this method executes, the JavaScript Client Object Model calls SharePoint and retrieves the objects you passed to the load method of the ClientContext class. If the call to SharePoint is successful, the first JavaScript function is called as shown in the following code snippet:

```
function onSuccess(sender, args) {
    var output = "Site Properties:\n";

    output += "Title : " + this.site.get_title();
    output += "\n"
    output += "URL : " + this.site.get_serverRelativeUrl();
    output += "\n"
    output += "Created : " + this.site.get_created();
    output += "\n"

    alert(output);
}
```

In the snippet, the sender and args parameters are supplied by the JavaScript Client Object Model. The sender parameter is an instance of the ClientRequest class. You can use the get_webRequest method of the ClientRequest class to get the object used to call SharePoint. The object has a property named _body that returns the XML sent to SharePoint during the request. This XML may be helpful for troubleshooting if you encounter problems with the request. The args parameter is an instance of the ClientRequestEventArgs class. The ClientRequestEventArgs class has a get_request method that returns the same object returned by the get_webRequest method of the ClientRequest class.

The code in the snippet reads the site's title, server-relative URL, and creation date and displays that information in a dialog box using the JavaScript alert function. Notice that the code using the this.site property, which at this point has been populated with data from SharePoint. If the call to SharePoint fails, the second function you passed to the executeQueryAsync method of the ClientContext class executes:

```
function onFailure(sender, args) {
    var output = "Call to SharePoint failed:\n";
```

```
        output += "Error Code: " + args.get_errorCode() + "\n";
        output += "Error Details: " + args.get_errorDetails() + "\n";
        output += "Error Type: " + args.get_errorTypeName() + "\n";
        output += "Error Value: " + args.get_errorValue() + "\n";
        output += "Error Message: " + args.get_message() + "\n";
        output += "Stack Trace: " + args.get_stackTrace() + "\n";

        alert(output);
    }
```

This function has the same parameters as the first function, but its $args$ parameter is an instance of the `ClientRequestFailedEventArgs` class. The `ClientRequestFailedEventArgs` class has the following methods you can use to troubleshoot the failed request:

NAME	DESCRIPTION
get_errorCode()	The code for the error
get_errorDetails()	Additional information about the error
get_errorTypeName()	The type of error
get_errorValue()	The value indicating the error
get_message()	The actual error message
get_stackTrace()	The stack trace of the code executed before the error occurred

The final step in using the JavaScript Client Object Model is to add controls to the page to execute your JavaScript functions. Normally, you add a control similar to the one in the following code snippet:

```
<input name="Button1" type="button" value="Go" onclick="callSharePoint();" />
```

In the snippet, a button is added to the page that calls a JavaScript function named `callSharePoint` when the button is clicked. The problem is that the code in the JavaScript function may fail if the user clicks the button to run your code before the browser is finished downloading the JavaScript files for the Client Object Model. If that occurs, you get an error message similar to this one:

"Message: 'SP.ClientContext.get_current' is null or not an object"

To avoid this problem, you can use a special function in the Client Object Model to ensure the appropriate script files have been download before it executes your JavaScript function. The special function is the `executeOrDelayUntilScriptLoaded` function on the SP.SOD class. To call this function, use the following code snippet:

```
SP.SOD.executeOrDelayUntilScriptLoaded(functionToExecute, 'sp.js');
```

In the snippet, **functionToExecute** is the function you want to execute. The second parameter is the JavaScript file that must be downloaded before your code is executed. Usually, you need only download the sp.js file which contains the JavaScript version of the Client Object Model. The SOD class will download any dependencies for the JavaScript file automatically. To call this function when a button is clicked, you use this modified code:

```
<input name="Button1" type="button" value="Go"
    onclick="SP.SOD.executeOrDelayUntilScriptLoaded(callSharePoint, 'sp.js');" />
```

TRY IT OUT   Display the Properties for the Current Site and Site Collection

In this activity, you create a page that will display information about the current site and site collection.

1. Open SharePoint Designer from your Start menu.

2. Click the Open Site button.

3. When the Open Site dialog appears, enter the URL to your site in the Site name textbox and click the OK button.

4. If a Windows Security dialog appears, enter your username and password for the SharePoint site and click the OK button.

5. After the site opens, select Site Pages from the Navigation bar on the left.

6. Select Page ⇨ ASPX from the ribbon and modify the name of the page appropriately.

7. You can double-click the icon to open the file, but clicking the filename will open the properties of the page, at which point you can click the Edit button in the Ribbon or on the properties page.

8. If you are prompted to open the page in Advanced mode, choose Yes.

9. After the page is open, select Attach from the Style tab of the ribbon. Select a master page from the drop-down list under the Attach button.

10. Click the Split tab at the bottom of the page.

11. In the code window, type the following code at the bottom of the page:

```
<asp:Content id="Content1" runat="server"
    contentplaceholderid="PlaceHolderMain">
</asp:Content>
```

12. Select SharePoint ⇨ Show Toolbox from the Insert tab on the ribbon.

13. Position the mouse cursor inside the `asp:Content` tag.

14. Double-click Input (Button) in the HTML/Form Controls section of the Toolbox.

15. In the Code view, modify the new button and configure the following properties (you must add the onclick property yourself):

PROPERTY	VALUE
value	Show Site Properties
onclick	SP.SOD.executeOrDelayUntilScriptLoaded(c allSharePoint, 'sp.js');

16. Place the cursor below the newly created button and double-click div in the HTML/Tags section of the Toolbox.

17. Add the ID attribute to the `div` tag and set its value to **divResults**.

18. Insert the following code snippet just above the closing `asp:Content` tag:

```
<script type="text/javascript">
</script>
```

19. Insert the following code snippet inside the `script` tag:

```
function callSharePoint() {

}

function onSuccess(sender, args) {

}

function onFailure(sender, args) {

}
```

20. In the `callSharePoint` function, insert the following code between the {} braces:

```
var context = new SP.ClientContext.get_current();

this.site = context.get_web();

context.load(this.site);

context.executeQueryAsync(Function.createDelegate(this, this.onSuccess),
    Function.createDelegate(this, this.onFailure));
```

21. In the `onSuccess` function, insert the following code between the {} braces:

```
var output = "Site Properties:<br/>";

output += "Title : " + this.site.get_title();
output += "<br/>"
output += "URL : " + this.site.get_serverRelativeUrl();
output += "<br/>"
output += "Created : " + this.site.get_created();
output += "<br/>"

document.getElementById("divResults").innerHTML = output;
```

22. In the `onFailure` function, insert the following code between the {} braces:

```
var output = "Call to SharePoint failed:<br/>";

output += "Error Code: " + args.get_errorCode() + "<br/>";
output += "Error Details: " + args.get_errorDetails() + "<br/>";
output += "Error Type: " + args.get_errorTypeName() + "<br/>";
output += "Error Value: " + args.get_errorValue() + "<br/>";
output += "Error Message: " + args.get_message() + "<br/>";
output += "Stack Trace: " + args.get_stackTrace() + "<br/>";

document.getElementById("divResults").innerHTML = output;
```

23. Save the page by clicking the Save button in the Quick Access Toolbar at the top of the screen.

24. Select Preview in Browser from the Home tab on the ribbon.

25. After the page loads in the browser, click the Show Site Properties button to test your code. You should see the site's title, URL, and creation date appear on the page, as shown in Figure 13-3.

Note that the URL is relative to the server name. Don't be surprised if URL is a single slash if your code is running in the root site collection of your SharePoint web application.

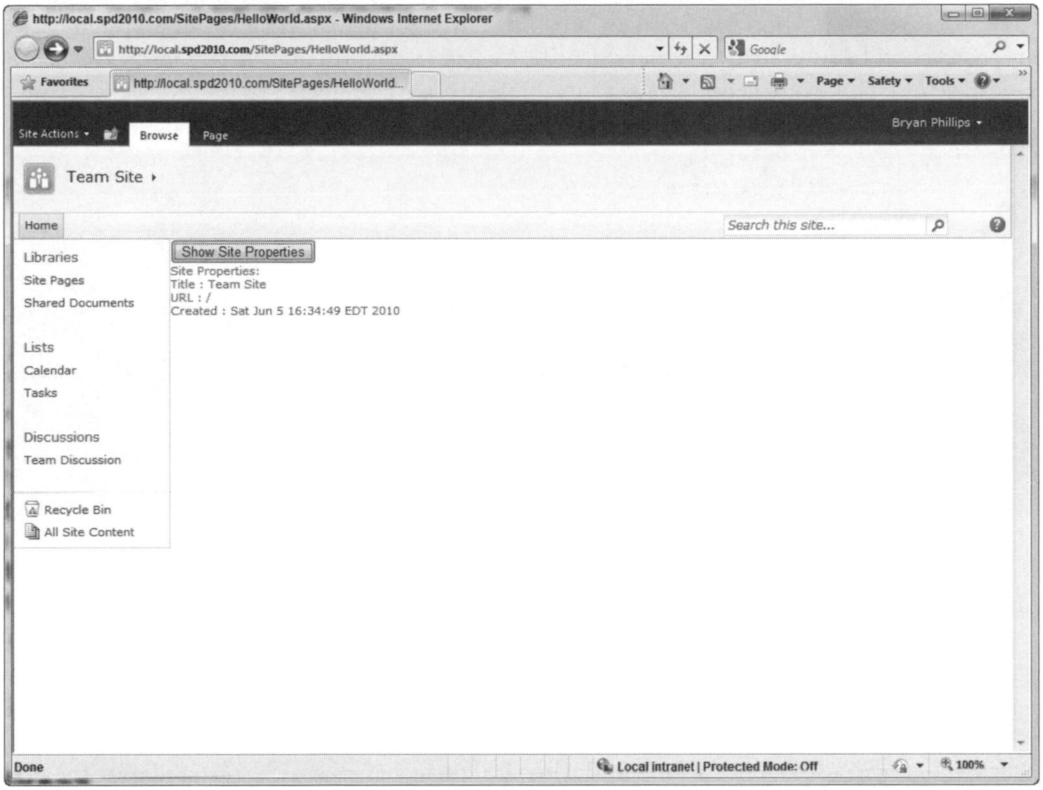

FIGURE 13-3

How It Works

When you click the Show Site Properties button, the executeOrDelayUntilScriptLoaded function executes. If the sp.js file or any of its dependencies have not been downloaded, execution of the callSharePoint function is delayed until the JavaScript has been downloaded.

When the callSharePoint function executes, the current ClientContext object is retrieved and stored in the context variable. The get_web function on the context variable is called to get the current site, which is stored in the site property on the browser's window object. Because the site property is not defined on the window object, it is dynamically created by the JavaScript engine.

Next, this.web is passed to the load function on the context variable so that the properties for the site are retrieved. Then, the executeQueryAsync function is called to retrieve the objects passed to the load function from SharePoint.

After the data is returned from SharePoint, the onSuccess function executes. Finally, the output variable is populated with a string representing a few properties of the site, and its contents are displayed in the divResults div tag.

RETRIEVING DATA USING CAML

You can retrieve data from lists and libraries by using a query language called *CAML*, which stands for Collaborative Application Markup Language. It is used for many things inside SharePoint, but in this case, it can be used to filter data returned by a list. In a word, it is XML that looks like the Where clause of a SQL statement. Here is an example of a CAML query:

```
<View>
    <ViewFields>
        <FieldRef Name='Title'/>
    </ViewFields>
    <Query>
        <Where>
            <And>
                <Neq>
                    <FieldRef Name='Status' />
                    <Value Type='Choice'>Completed</Value>
                </Neq>
                <Eq>
                    <FieldRef Name='AssignedTo' />
                    <Value Type='User'>John Public</Value>
                </Eq>
            </And>
        </Where>
        <OrderBy>
            <FieldRef Name='Title' Ascending='True' />
        </OrderBy>
    </Query>
    <RowLimit>2</RowLimit>
</View>
```

The CAML query in the snippet is for a Tasks list. It returns only the Title field and only the first two items matching the Where clause. The Where clause only returns the items where Status is not Completed and the item is assigned to John Public. Additionally, it sorts the results by the Title field in ascending order.

> ![X] **WARNING** *CAML is case-sensitive and SharePoint will not throw any errors if you build your CAML query incorrectly. In fact, it may not filter the results at all. For those reasons, you should use a tool to build your CAML. You can download a tool at* www.u2u.net/res/Tools/CamlQueryBuilder.aspx. *Download the 2007 version of the tool. It will work on SharePoint 2007 and 2010.*

The following table lists the components of a CAML query and their usage:

NAME	DESCRIPTION
View	The outermost element in the query.
ViewFields	Contains the fields to return in the results.

NAME	DESCRIPTION
FieldRef	A reference to a field in the list. The Name attribute should be set to the internal name of the field. The internal name is the name of the field when it was originally created.
Query	Contains the Where and OrderBy clauses.
Where	Contains the filter for the query.
And	Represents the And operator when two or more fields are used in the Where clause.
Or	Represents the Or operator when two or more fields are used in the Where clause.
Eq	Represents the Equals operator.
Neq	Represents the Not Equals operator.
Gt	Represents the Greater Than operator.
Geq	Represents the Greater Than or Equal To operator.
Lt	Represents the Less Than operator.
Leq	Represents the Less Than or Equal To operator.
IsNull	Filters on a field not having a value.
IsNotNull	Filters on a field having a value.
BeginsWith	Filters where the field value begins with the specified string.
Contains	Filters where the field value contains the specified string.
DateRangesOverlap	Used to filter recurring items, such as recurring events in a Calendar list.
Value	Used in combination with FieldRef. Contains the value to filter. The Type attribute must match the field type of the FieldRef.
OrderBy	Contains the fields to order by. The FieldRefs in this element have an Ascending attribute set to True or False to indicate the direction in which to sort the field.
RowLimit	Specifies the maximum number of items to return that match the Where clause.

Now that you have been introduced to the CAML query syntax, you can start using the JavaScript Client Object Model to get data from your SharePoint site. You use the `CamlQuery` class to specify the query to use against a `List` object. To use the `CamlQuery` class, you need to write code similar to the following snippet:

```
var caml = "<View>" +
    "    <ViewFields>" +
    "        <FieldRef Name='Title'/>" +
    "    </ViewFields>" +
    "    <Query>" +
    "        <Where>" +
    "            <Eq>" +
    "                <FieldRef Name='AssignedTo'/>" +
    "                <Value Type='User'>John Public</Value>" +
    "            </Eq>" +
    "        </Where>" +
    "    </Query>" +
    "    <RowLimit>2</RowLimit>" +
    "</View>";

var query = new SP.CamlQuery();
query.set_viewXml(caml);
```

In the snippet, the `query` variable is set to a new instance of the `CamlQuery` class. Afterwards, you specify the CAML query by passing a string containing the query to the `set_viewXml` method on the `query` object. After you have the `CamlQuery` object configured, you need to get an instance of the list to query against. To get the list instance, you can call the `getByTitle` method on the `Site` object's `get_lists` method as shown in the following snippet:

```
var tasks = context.get_web().get_lists().getByTitle("Tasks");
this.results = tasks.getItems(query);

context.load(this.results);

context.executeQueryAsync(Function.createDelegate(this, this.onSuccess),
    Function.createDelegate(this, this.onFail));
```

In the snippet, the `get_lists` method returns a `ListCollection` object containing the lists and libraries in the site. The `ListCollection` object has a `getByTitle` method, which you use to get an instance of your list by passing in the display name of the list. The `List` class has a `getItems` method that you pass the `CamlQuery` object in order to get an instance of a `ListItemCollection` class. Like all other SharePoint objects returned in the JavaScript Client Object Model, you must store it in a property or variable and pass the property or variable to the `load` method of the `ClientContext` object. Finally, you call the `executeQueryAsync` method of the `ClientContext` object to call SharePoint and return the results of your query.

After the query executes, your code can call the `getEnumerator` method on the `ListItemCollection` class to get an object to use in a `while` loop to read each `ListItem` object in the `ListItemCollection`. The enumerator object has a `moveNext` method, which returns `False` when all the `ListItem` objects have been read from the `ListItemCollection`. Inside the loop, you can call the `get_current` method on the enumerator to get the current `ListItem` in the `ListItemCollection`. The following snippet shows these objects and methods in action:

```
var output = "Results:<br/>";

var enumerator = this.results.getEnumerator();

while (enumerator.moveNext()) {
    var item = enumerator.get_current();

    output += "ID : " + item.get_id();
    output += "<br/>"
    output += "Title : " + item.get_item("Title");
    output += "<br/>"
    output += "Status : " + item.get_item("Status");
    output += "<br/>"
    output += "Assigned To : " + item.get_item("AssignedTo").get_lookupValue();
    output += "<br/>"
}

document.getElementById("divResults").innerHTML = output;
```

In the snippet, an enumerator for the results of the CAML query is assigned to the `enumerator` variable. The enumerator and its `moveNext` method are used in the condition for the `while` statement. Every time the `while` loop runs, the `ListItem` returned from the `get_current` method is changed to the next `ListItem` in the result set. When the last `ListItem` in the result set is reached, the `moveNext` method returns `False`, which causes the `while` loop to exit. Inside the `while` loop, the current `ListItem` is retrieved from the `get_current` method and stored in the item variable. Using the item variable, you call the `get_id` method to get the ID of the `ListItem` and the `get_item` method to get the values of other fields in the `ListItem`. In the `get_item` method, you need to pass in the original name of the field. That means if you renamed the Title column of a list, you must still pass in "Title" instead of your new name for the column.

Some values for the fields in a list might be more complex than numbers, strings, or dates. In the code snippet, the `AssignedTo` field is actually a Person column in the list, which is a special lookup column that refers to the hidden UserInformationList list that contains the users in the site. The following table lists the column types that are more complex and the methods you can use to display their data:

TYPE	METHOD	DESCRIPTION
Date and Time	`format(format)`	Formats the date using the invariant culture. Valid values for `format` are listed in the following table.
	`localeFormat(format)`	Formats the date using the user's current culture. Valid values for `format` are listed in the following table.
Choice (Allow Multiple Values)		Returns a string array of selected values.

continues

(continued)

TYPE	METHOD	DESCRIPTION
Hyperlink or Picture	`get_description()`	Returns the description of the hyperlink or picture.
	`get_url()`	Returns the URL of the hyperlink or picture.
Lookup	`get_lookupId()`	Returns the ID value of the selected `ListItem` in the lookup list.
	`get_lookupValue()`	Returns the display value of the selected `ListItem` in the lookup list.
Lookup (Allow Multiple Values)		Returns an array of Lookup values.
Person or Group	`get_lookupId()`	Returns the ID of the selected user or group from the UserInformationList list.
	`get_lookupValue()`	Returns the display name of the selected user or group from the UserInformationList list.

The following table contains the valid formats you can pass to the `format` and `localeFormat` functions of Date and Time values returned from SharePoint.

FORMAT	DESCRIPTION	EXAMPLES
`"d"`	Short date format	6/1/2010
`"D"`	Long date format	Tuesday, June 1, 2010
`"F"`	Long date time format	Tuesday, June 1, 2010 11:00:00 AM
`"M"` or `"m"`	Month day format	June 1
`"s"`	Sortable date time format	2010-06-01T11:00:00
`"t"`	Short time format	11:00 AM
`"T"`	Long time format	11:00:00 AM
`"Y"` or `"y"`,	Year month	June, 2010

TRY IT OUT   Prep Work for Querying a SharePoint List

In this activity, you create a Task list and populate it with data in preparation for the next activity.

1. Open SharePoint Designer from your Start menu.

2. Click the Open Site button.

3. When the Open Site dialog appears, enter the URL to your site in the Site name textbox and click the OK button.

4. If a Windows Security dialog appears, enter your username and password for the SharePoint site and click the OK button.

5. When the site opens, select Lists and Libraries from the Navigation bar on the left.

6. Select SharePoint List ⇨ Tasks from the ribbon. The Create list or document library dialog appears.

7. Enter **MyTasks** in the Name textbox and click the OK button. After the list is created, a new tab with the name of the newly created list appears.

8. If the new tab in Step 7 does not appear, click your list and select List Settings from the ribbon.

9. Select Preview in Browser from the ribbon.

10. After the browser opens and navigates to the new list, add the following items to the list

TITLE	PRIORITY	STATUS
Upgrade to Exchange 2010	(1) High	In Progress
Migrate intranet to SharePoint 2010	(2) Normal	Not Started
Create marketing presentation	(2) Normal	Completed

How It Works

Since this is preparation for the next Try It Out, please read the How It Works at the conclusion of the next activity for the full explanation.

TRY IT OUT   Query a SharePoint List

In this activity, you query the items in a Task list and display them on a page.

1. Open SharePoint Designer from your Start menu.

2. Click the Open Site button.

3. When the Open Site dialog appears, enter the URL to your site in the Site name textbox and click the OK button.

4. If a Windows Security dialog appears, enter your username and password for the SharePoint site and click the OK button.

5. After the site opens, select Site Pages from the Navigation bar on the left.

6. Select Page ⇨ ASPX from the ribbon and modify the name of the page appropriately.

7. You can double-click the icon to open the file, but clicking the filename will open the properties of the page, at which point you can click the Edit button in the Ribbon or on the properties page.

8. If you are prompted to open the page in Advanced mode, choose Yes.

9. After the page is open, select Attach from the Style tab of the ribbon. Select a master page from the drop-down list under the Attach button.

10. Click the Split tab at the bottom of the page.

11. In the code window, type the following code at the bottom of the page:

```
<asp:Content id="Content1" runat="server"
    contentplaceholderid="PlaceHolderMain">
</asp:Content>
```

12. Select SharePoint ⇨ Show Toolbox from the Insert tab on the ribbon.

13. Position the mouse cursor inside the asp:Content tag.

14. Double-click Input (Button) in the HTML/Form Controls section of the Toolbox.

15. In the Code view, modify the new button and configure the following properties (you must add the onclick property yourself):

PROPERTY	VALUE
value	Show Tasks
onclick	SP.SOD.executeOrDelayUntilScriptLoaded(call SharePoint, 'sp.js');

16. Place the cursor below the newly created button and double-click div in the HTML/Tags section of the Toolbox.

17. Add the ID attribute to the div tag and set its value to **divResults**.

18. Insert the following code snippet just above the closing asp:Content tag:

```
<script type="text/javascript">
</script>
```

19. Insert the following code snippet inside the script tag:

```
function callSharePoint() {

}

function onSuccess(sender, args) {

}

function onFailure(sender, args) {

}
```

20. In the `callSharePoint` function, insert the following code between the {} braces:

```
var context = new SP.ClientContext.get_current();

var tasks = context.get_web().get_lists().getByTitle("MyTasks");

var caml = "<View>" +
    "   <Query>" +
    "       <Where>" +
    "           <Neq>" +
    "               <FieldRef Name='Status'/>" +
    "               <Value Type='Choice'>Completed</Value>" +
    "           </Neq>" +
    "       </Where>" +
    "       <OrderBy>" +
    "           <FieldRef Name='Title' Ascending='True'/>" +
    "       </OrderBy>" +
    "   </Query>" +
    "</View>";

var query = new SP.CamlQuery();
query.set_viewXml(caml);

this.results = tasks.getItems(query);

context.load(this.results);

context.executeQueryAsync(Function.createDelegate(this, this.onSuccess),
    Function.createDelegate(this, this.onFailure));
```

21. In the `onSuccess` function, insert the following code between the {} braces:

```
var output = "Results:<br/>";

output += "<table>"

var enumerator = this.results.getEnumerator();

output += "<tr>";
output += "<th>ID</th>";
output += "<th>Title</th>";
output += "<th>Priority</th>";
output += "<th>Status</th>";
output += "</tr>";

while (enumerator.moveNext()) {
    var item = enumerator.get_current();

    output += "<tr>"

    output += "<td>" + item.get_id() + "</td>";
    output += "<td>" + item.get_item("Title") + "</td>";
    output += "<td>" + item.get_item("Priority") + "</td>";
    output += "<td>" + item.get_item("Status") + "</td>";

    output += "</tr>"
}
```

```
output += "</table>"

document.getElementById("divResults").innerHTML = output;
```

22. In the `onFailure` function, insert the following code between the {} braces:

```
var output = "Call to SharePoint failed:<br/>";

output += "Error Code: " + args.get_errorCode() + "<br/>";
output += "Error Details: " + args.get_errorDetails() + "<br/>";
output += "Error Type: " + args.get_errorTypeName() + "<br/>";
output += "Error Value: " + args.get_errorValue() + "<br/>";
output += "Error Message: " + args.get_message() + "<br/>";
output += "Stack Trace: " + args.get_stackTrace() + "<br/>";

document.getElementById("divResults").innerHTML = output;
```

23. Save the page by clicking the Save button in the Quick Access Toolbar at the top of the screen.

24. Select Preview in Browser from the Home tab on the ribbon.

25. After the page loads in the browser, click the Show Tasks button to test your code. You should see the site's title, URL, and creation date appear on the page, as shown in Figure 13-4.

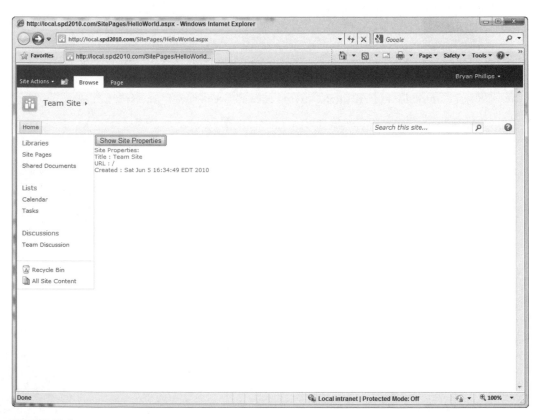

FIGURE 13-4

How It Works

Using the `context` variable, you can get a reference to the current site and its collection of lists. Calling the `getByTitle` method of the `ListCollection` returns the `List` object representing the MyTasks list in SharePoint. Afterwards, you create a `CamlQuery` object specifying a CAML query that returns only the tasks from the list that are not complete and sorts the results by the Title column in ascending order.

Using the `getItems` method on the `List` object, you pass in the `CamlQuery` object and call the `load` method on the `ClientContext` object to request the results of the query from SharePoint. Finally, the `executeQueryAsync` method is called to initiate the call to SharePoint.

After the call to SharePoint succeeds, it populates the `this.results` property you used to store the return value of the `getItems` method, and the `onSuccess` method executes. Inside the `onSuccess` method, you obtain an enumerator from the `getEnumerator` method on the `ListItemCollection` class and use it to loop through the items returned by the CAML query. Looping through the items, you build an HTML table to display the results using the `get_id` and `get_item` methods on the `ListItem` class to retrieve the values of the fields in each item.

QUERYING DOCUMENT LIBRARIES

You can use the same techniques on document libraries as for lists. The list items for the documents in a document library have additional fields that you can use. Here is a list of these fields:

NAME	DESCRIPTION
FileLeafRef	The name of the file
FileRef	The server-relative URL of the file
File_x0020_Type	The file extension of the file
File_x0020Size	The size of the file in bytes

TRY IT OUT Prep Work for Querying a Document Library

In this activity, you create a document library and upload documents to it in preparation for the next activity.

1. Open SharePoint Designer from your Start menu.

2. Click the Open Site button.

3. When the Open Site dialog appears, enter the URL to your site in the Site name textbox and click the OK button.

4. If a Windows Security dialog appears, enter your username and password for the SharePoint site and click the OK button.

5. When the site opens, select Lists and Libraries from the Navigation bar on the left.

6. Select Document Library ➪ Document Library from the ribbon. The Create list or document library dialog appears.

7. Enter **MyDocuments** in the Name textbox and click the OK button. After the list is created, a new tab with the name of the newly created list appears.

8. If the new tab in Step 7 does not appear, click your list and select List Settings from the ribbon.

9. Select Edit Columns from the ribbon.

10. Select Add New Column ➪ Choice from the ribbon.

11. Type in the following choices in the Choices textbox:

➤ Project 1

➤ Project 2

➤ Project 3

12. Type in **Project 1** in the Default value textbox and click the OK button.

13. Right-click the new column and select Rename.

14. Type in **Project** as the name of the new column and press the Enter key.

15. Save the list by clicking the Save button in the Quick Access Toolbar at the top of the screen.

16. Select List Settings from the ribbon.

17. Select Preview in Browser from the ribbon.

18. After the browser opens and navigates to the new library, upload a few documents and choose a value for the Project column.

How It Works

Since this is preparation for the next Try It Out, please read the How It Works at the conclusion of the next activity for the full explanation.

TRY IT OUT   **Query a SharePoint Document Library**

In this activity, you query the documents in a document library and display them on a page.

1. Open SharePoint Designer from your Start menu.

2. Click the Open Site button.

3. When the Open Site dialog appears, enter the URL to your site in the Site name textbox and click the OK button.

4. If a Windows Security dialog appears, enter your username and password for the SharePoint site and click the OK button.

5. When the site opens, select Site Pages from the Navigation bar on the left.

6. Select Page ➪ ASPX from the ribbon and modify the name of the page appropriately.

7. You can double-click the icon to open the file, but clicking the filename will open the properties of the page, at which point you can click the Edit button in the Ribbon or on the properties page.

8. If you are prompted to open the page in Advanced mode, choose Yes.

9. After the page is open, select Attach from the Style tab of the ribbon. Select a master page from the drop-down list under the Attach button.

10. Click the Split tab at the bottom of the page.

11. In the code window, type the following code at the bottom of the page:

```
<asp:Content id="Content1" runat="server"
    contentplaceholderid="PlaceHolderMain">
</asp:Content>
```

12. Select SharePoint ⇨ Show Toolbox from the Insert tab on the ribbon.

13. Position the mouse cursor inside the asp:Content tag.

14. Double-click Input (Button) in the HTML/Form Controls section of the Toolbox.

15. In the Code view, modify the new button and configure the following properties (you must add the onclick property yourself):

PROPERTY	VALUE
value	Show Documents
onclick	SP.SOD.executeOrDelayUntilScriptLoaded(callSharePoint, 'sp.js');

16. Place the cursor below the newly created button and double-click div in the HTML/Tags section of the Toolbox.

17. Add the ID attribute to the div tag and set its value to **divResults**.

18. Insert the following code snippet just above the closing asp:Content tag:

```
<script type="text/javascript">
</script>
```

19. Insert the following code snippet inside the script tag:

```
function callSharePoint() {

}

function onSuccess(sender, args) {

}

function onFailure(sender, args) {

}
```

20. In the callSharePoint function, insert the following code between the {} braces:

```
var context = new SP.ClientContext.get_current();
```

```
var docs = context.get_web().get_lists().getByTitle("MyDocuments");

var caml = "<View>" +
    "    <Query>" +
    "        <Where>" +
    "            <Eq>" +
    "                <FieldRef Name='Project'/>" +
    "                <Value Type='Choice'>Project 1</Value>" +
    "            </Eq>" +
    "        </Where>" +
    "    </Query>" +
    "</View>";

var query = new SP.CamlQuery();
query.set_viewXml(caml);

this.results = docs.getItems(query);

context.load(this.results);

context.executeQueryAsync(Function.createDelegate(this, this.onSuccess),
    Function.createDelegate(this, this.onFailure));
```

21. In the `onSuccess` function, insert the following code between the {} braces:

```
var output = "Results:<br/>";

output += "<table>"

var enumerator = this.results.getEnumerator();

output += "<tr>";
output += "<th>ID</th>";
output += "<th>File Name</th>";
output += "<th>File Type</th>";
output += "<th>File Size</th>";
output += "</tr>";

while (enumerator.moveNext()) {
    var item = enumerator.get_current();

    output += "<tr>"

    var id = item.get_id();

    output += "<td>" + id + "</td>";
    output += "<td><a target='_blank' href='" + item.get_item("FileRef") + "'>"
        + item.get_item("FileLeafRef") + "</a></td>";
    output += "<td>" + item.get_item("File_x0020_Type") + "</td>";
    output += "<td>" + item.get_item("File_x0020_Size") + "</td>";

    output += "</tr>" }

output += "</table>"

document.getElementById("divResults").innerHTML = output;
```

22. In the `onFailure` function, insert the following code between the {} braces:

```
var output = "Call to SharePoint failed:<br/>";

output += "Error Code: " + args.get_errorCode() + "<br/>";
output += "Error Details: " + args.get_errorDetails() + "<br/>";
output += "Error Type: " + args.get_errorTypeName() + "<br/>";
output += "Error Value: " + args.get_errorValue() + "<br/>";
output += "Error Message: " + args.get_message() + "<br/>";
output += "Stack Trace: " + args.get_stackTrace() + "<br/>";

document.getElementById("divResults").innerHTML = output;
```

23. Save the page by clicking the Save button in the Quick Access Toolbar at the top of the screen.

24. Select Preview in Browser from the Home tab on the ribbon.

25. After the page loads in the browser, click the Query Doc Lib button to test your code. You should see the documents appear on the page, as shown in Figure 13-5.

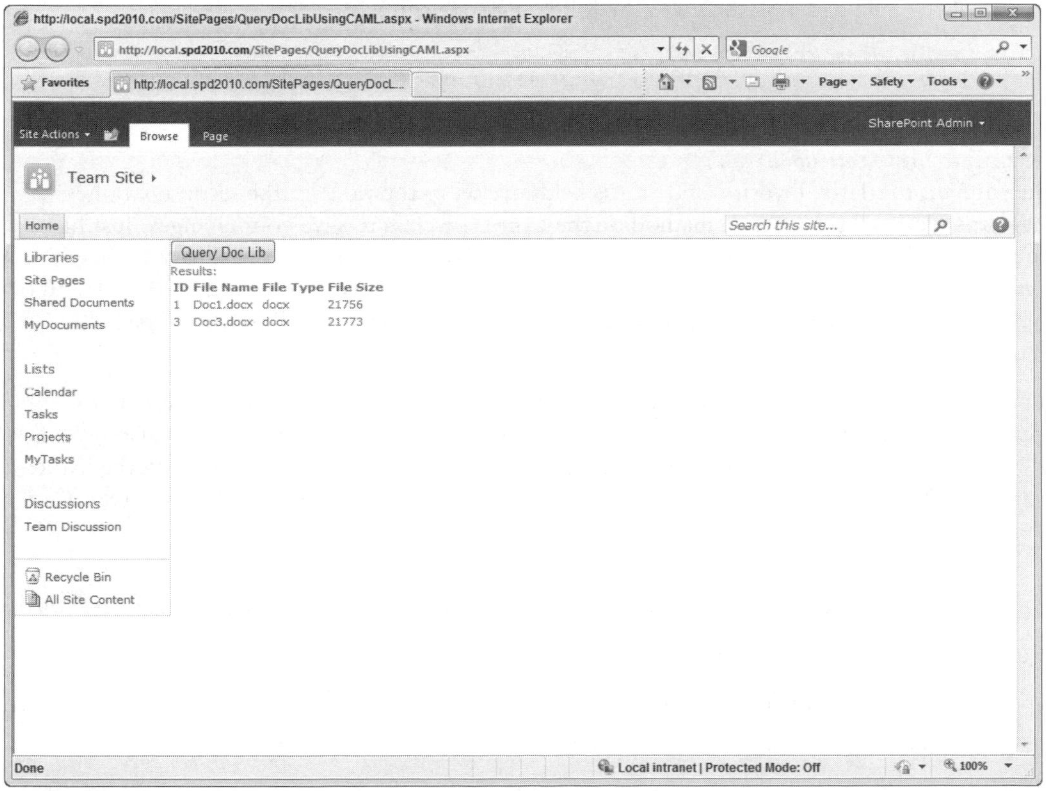

FIGURE 13-5

How It Works

Although document libraries store documents, they are still lists and documents are still list items. You can use the same code to query and manipulate a document library that you would use for a list. The difference is that the list item that represents the document has additional file-specific fields for the file's name, path, type, and size. In the activity, you used the values of these fields to build a table on the page that included hyperlinks linking to the documents themselves.

MANAGING LIST ITEMS

Previously in the chapter, you learned how to query lists and libraries. Next, you will learn how to create, update, and delete list items. To create a list item, you need to create an instance of the `ListItemCreationInformation` class and use it to call the `addItem` method on the `List` object. The following code snippet shows this in action:

```
var itemInfo = new SP.ListItemCreationInformation();
this.newListItem = tasks.addItem(itemInfo);
```

In the snippet, the `addItem` method returns an instance of the `ListItem` class, which is stored in the `newListItem` variable. Using the `set_item` method of the `ListItem` class, you pass in the name and the value of the field to set as shown in the following code snippet:

```
this.newListItem.set_item("Title", "My New Task");
this.newListItem.set_item("Priority", "(3) Low");
this.newListItem.set_item("Status", "In Progress");

this.newListItem.update();
```

In the snippet, the Title, Priority, and Status fields are set to the value of the second parameter. Afterwards, you call the `update` method on the `ListItem` class to save your changes. Just like before, you still must call the `executeQueryAsync` method to submit your new item to SharePoint. If you want to get the value of the new item's ID field, you would need to call the `load` method of the `ClientContext` class passing in the `newListItem` variable before the call to the `executeQueryAsync` method.

To update an existing list item, you use perform the same steps as for creating a list item except that you call `getItemById` on the `List` class to get an instance of the list item. You can also use a CAML query to get the list item. To delete an existing item, you call the `recycle` method on the list item, which sends the item to the Recycle Bin. To delete the item permanently, call the `deleteObject` method instead.

TRY IT OUT   **Prep Work for Inserting, Updating, and Deleting Items in a SharePoint List**

In this activity, you create and populate a generic list for the next activity.

1.   Open SharePoint Designer from your Start menu.

2.   Click the Open Site button.

3.   When the Open Site dialog appears, enter the URL to your site in the Site name textbox and click the OK button.

4.   If a Windows Security dialog appears, enter your username and password for the SharePoint site and click the OK button.

5.   When the site opens, select Lists and Libraries from the Navigation bar on the left.

6.   Select Custom List from the ribbon. The Create list or document library dialog appears.

7.   Enter MyGroceryList in the Name textbox and click the OK button. After the list is created, a new tab with the name of the newly created list appears.

8.   If the new tab in Step 7 does not appear, click your list and select List Settings from the ribbon.

9.   Select Preview in Browser from the ribbon.

10.   After the browser opens and navigates to the new list, add the following items to the list:

➤   **Eggs**

➤   **Milk**

➤   **Bread**

11.   Leave the browser window open so you can compare the results of the next activity with the contents of the list.

How It Works

Since this is preparation for the next Try It Out, please read the How It Works at the conclusion of the next activity for the full explanation.

TRY IT OUT   Insert, Update, and Delete Items in a SharePoint List

In this activity, you insert, update, and delete tasks from a SharePoint list.

1.   Open SharePoint Designer from your Start menu.

2.   Click the Open Site button.

3.   When the Open Site dialog appears, enter the URL to your site in the Site name textbox and click the OK button.

4.   If a Windows Security dialog appears, enter your username and password for the SharePoint site and click the OK button.

5.   After the site opens, select Site Pages from the Navigation bar on the left.

6.   Select Page ➪ ASPX from the ribbon and modify the name of the page appropriately.

7.   You can double-click the icon to open the file, but clicking the filename will open the properties of the page, at which point you can click the Edit button in the Ribbon or on the properties page.

8.   If you are prompted to open the page in Advanced mode, choose Yes.

9.   After the page is open, select Attach from the Style tab of the ribbon. Select a master page from the drop-down list under the Attach button.

10.   Click the Split tab at the bottom of the page.

11. In the code window, type the following code at the bottom of the page:

```
<asp:Content id="Content1" runat="server"
    contentplaceholderid="PlaceHolderMain">
</asp:Content>
```

12. Select SharePoint ➪ Show Toolbox from the Insert tab on the ribbon.

13. Position the mouse cursor inside the `asp:Content` tag.

14. Double-click Input (Button) in the HTML/Form Controls section of the Toolbox.

15. In the Code view, modify the new button and configure the following properties (you must add the onclick property yourself):

PROPERTY	VALUE
value	`Show Grocery List`
onclick	`SP.SOD.executeOrDelayUntilScriptLo aded(populateItems, 'sp.js');`

16. Double-click Input (Button) in the HTML/Form Controls section of the Toolbox.

17. Click the new button and configure the following properties:

PROPERTY	VALUE
value	`Add Item`
onclick	`SP.SOD.executeOrDelayUntilScript Loaded(showAddItem, 'sp.js');`

18. Place the cursor below the newly created button and double-click `div` in the HTML/Tags section of the Toolbox.

19. Add the `ID` attribute to the `div` tag and set its value to **divItem**.

20. Add the `style` attribute to the `div` tag and set its value to **display:none**.

21. Position the mouse cursor inside the `div` tag.

22. Double-click `span` in the HTML/Tags section of the Toolbox.

23. Add text to the span so that it looks like this:

```
<span>Item:</span>
```

24. Double-click Input (Text) in the HTML/Form Controls section of the Toolbox.

25. Add the `ID` attribute to the `input` tag and set its value to **titleText**.

26. Double-click Input (Button) in the HTML/Form Controls section of the Toolbox.

27. Click the new button and configure the following properties:

PROPERTY	VALUE
value	Save
onclick	SP.SOD.executeOrDelayUntilScriptLoaded(addItem, 'sp.js');

28. Place the cursor below the newly created button and double-click `div` in the HTML/Tags section of the Toolbox.

29. Add the `ID` attribute to the `div` tag and set its value to **divResults**.

30. Insert the following code snippet just above the closing `asp:Content` tag:

```
<script type="text/javascript">
</script>
```

31. Insert the following code snippet inside the `script` tag:

```
function populateItems() {

}

function onSuccess(sender, args) {

}

function onFailure(sender, args) {

}

function showAddItem() {

}

function addItem() {

}

function updateItem(id){

}

function deleteItem(id){

}
```

32. In the `populateItems` function, insert the following code between the {} braces:

```
document.getElementById("divItem").style.display = "none";
document.getElementById("divResults").innerHTML = "Loading...";

var context = new SP.ClientContext.get_current();

var items = context.get_web().get_lists().getByTitle("MyGroceryList");
```

```
var caml = "<View><RowLimit>100</RowLimit></View>";

var query = new SP.CamlQuery();
query.set_viewXml(caml);

this.results = items.getItems(query);

context.load(this.results);

context.executeQueryAsync(Function.createDelegate(this, this.onSuccess),
    Function.createDelegate(this, this.onFailure));
```

33. In the `onSuccess` function, insert the following code between the {} braces:

```
var output = "Results:<br/>";

output += "<table>";

var enumerator = this.results.getEnumerator();

output += "<tr>";
output += "<th>ID</th>";
output += "<th>Title</th>";
output += "<th></th>"
output += "<th></th>"
output += "</tr>";

while (enumerator.moveNext()) {
    var item = enumerator.get_current();
    var id = item.get_id();

    output += "<tr id='row" + id + "'>";

    output += "<td>" + id + "</td>";
    output += "<td>";
    output += "<input id='titleText" + id + "' type='text' value='" +
        item.get_item("Title") + "'/>";
    output += "</td>";
    output += "<td>";
    output += "<input type='button' value='Update' onclick='updateItem(" +
        id + ");' />";
    output += "</td>";
    output += "<td>";
    output += "<input type='button' value='Delete' onclick='deleteItem(" +
        id + ");' />";
    output += "</td>";

    output += "</tr>"
}

output += "</table>"

document.getElementById("divResults").innerHTML = output;
```

34. In the `onFailure` function, insert the following code between the {} braces:

```
var output = "Call to SharePoint failed:<br/>";

output += "Error Code: " + args.get_errorCode() + "<br/>";
output += "Error Details: " + args.get_errorDetails() + "<br/>";
output += "Error Type: " + args.get_errorTypeName() + "<br/>";
output += "Error Value: " + args.get_errorValue() + "<br/>";
output += "Error Message: " + args.get_message() + "<br/>";
output += "Stack Trace: " + args.get_stackTrace() + "<br/>";

document.getElementById("divResults").innerHTML = output;
```

35. In the `showAddItem` function, insert the following code between the {} braces:

```
document.getElementById("divItem").style.display = "";
```

36. In the `addItem` function, insert the following code between the {} braces:

```
var context = new SP.ClientContext.get_current();

var items = context.get_web().get_lists().getByTitle("MyGroceryList");

var itemInfo = new SP.ListItemCreationInformation();
var item = items.addItem(itemInfo);

item.set_item("Title", document.getElementById("titleText").value);
item.update();

context.executeQueryAsync(Function.createDelegate(this, this.populateItems),
    Function.createDelegate(this, this.onFailure));
```

37. In the `updateItem` function, insert the following code between the {} braces:

```
var context = new SP.ClientContext.get_current();

var items = context.get_web().get_lists().getByTitle("MyGroceryList");

var item = items.getItemById(id);

item.set_item("Title", document.getElementById("titleText" + id).value);
item.update();

context.executeQueryAsync(Function.createDelegate(this, this.populateItems),
    Function.createDelegate(this, this.onFailure));
```

38. In the `deleteItem` function, insert the following code between the {} braces:

```
var context = new SP.ClientContext.get_current();

var items = context.get_web().get_lists().getByTitle("MyGroceryList");

items.getItemById(id).recycle();

context.executeQueryAsync(Function.createDelegate(this, this.populateItems),
    Function.createDelegate(this, this.onFailure));
```

39. Save the page by clicking the Save button in the Quick Access Toolbar at the top of the screen.

40. Select Preview in Browser from the Home tab on the ribbon.

41. After the page loads in the browser, click the Show Grocery List button to test your code. You should see a screen similar to the one shown in Figure 13-6.

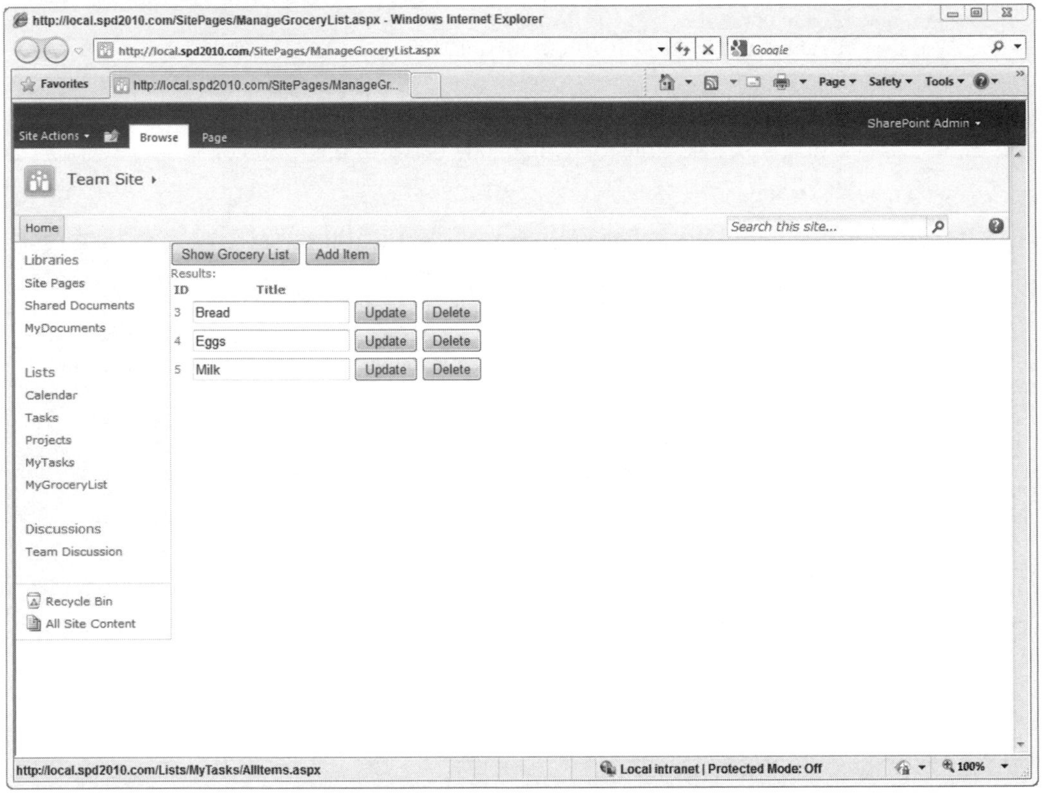

FIGURE 13-6

42. Click the Add Item button.

43. Enter **Cereal** in the textbox and click the Save button.

44. Repeat Steps 42–43 for the following items:

➤ **Bacon**

➤ **Bagels**

➤ **Ham**

45. Switch to the browser window you used in step 11 of the previous activity "Prep Work for Inserting, Updating, and Deleting Items in a SharePoint List" to add items to the MyGroceryList list.

46. Refresh the page and you should see the new items, as shown in Figure 13-7.

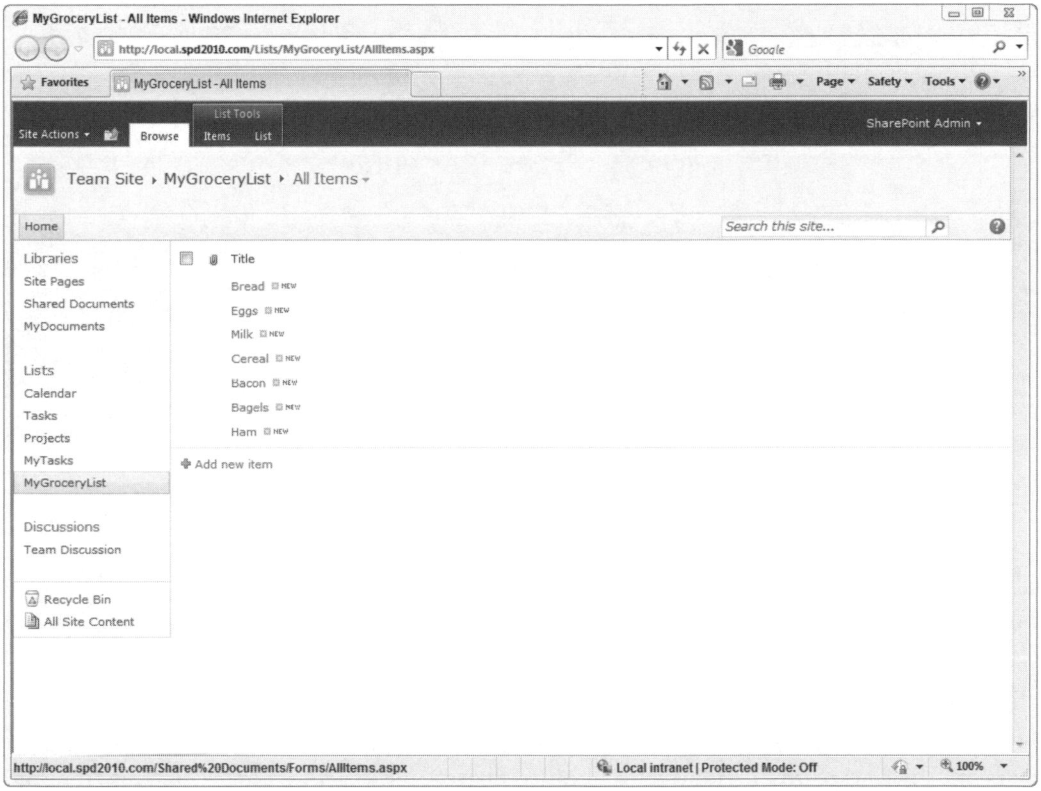

FIGURE 13-7

47. Switch back to the browser window you were using to test your page.

48. Click the Delete button beside Bacon and Ham.

49. Change Milk to read **Soy Milk** and click the Update button.

50. Switch to the browser you used in the previous activity to add items to the MyGroceryList list.

51. Refresh the page and you should see the new items, as shown in Figure 13-8.

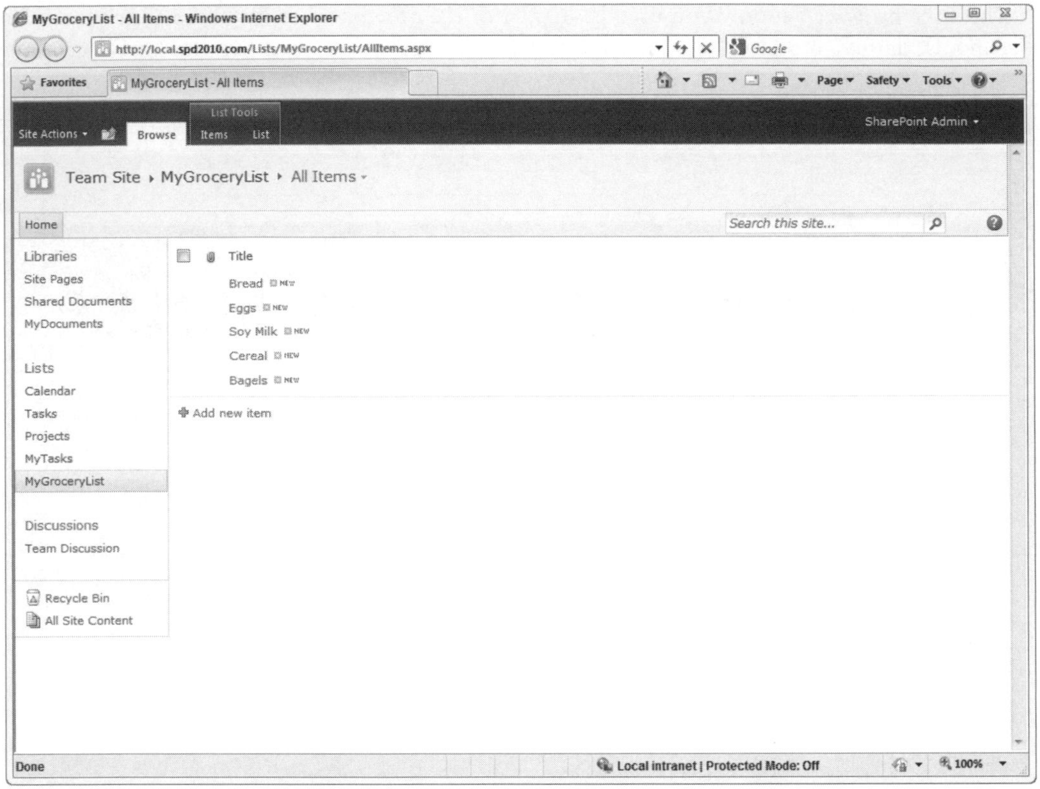

FIGURE 13-8

How It Works

When you clicked the Show Grocery List button, the `populateItems` function executed, which set the contents of `divResults` to "Loading…" and called SharePoint to get the first 100 items from the MyGroceryList list. After the data was returned from the server, the `onSuccess` function was called to build a table out of the data and place it inside `divResults`.

The table was constructed with columns for the items' ID and Title fields and buttons for updating and deleting the items. When you clicked the Add Item button, the `showAddItem` function was called and `divItem` was made visible by setting its CSS display value to `blank`. After you entered a new item in the textbox and clicked the Save button, the `addItem` function was called.

In the `addItem` function, a new `ListItem` object was created and subsequently populated with data using the `set_item` function. Afterwards, calling the update function on the `ListItem` object queued the new item for insertion when the `executeQueryAsync` method was called.

You also changed one of the items and clicked its Update button. This, in turn, called the `updateItem` function, passing in the ID of the item. Using the item's ID, you were able to get a reference to the item by calling the `getItemById` function of the `List` class. Just like the `addItem` function, you used the `set_item` and `update` functions on the `ListItem` class to save and queue the change to be sent to SharePoint.

Deleting an item works the same way as updating the item when you use the `getItemById` function of the `List` class to get a reference to the item. Calling the `recycle` function on the `ListItem` class sends the item to the Recycle Bin.

Finally, whether you insert, update, or delete an item, the `onSuccess` function refreshes `divResults` with the current contents of the MyGroceryList list.

MANAGING USER CUSTOM ACTIONS

Custom actions are the links that appear on menus, toolbars, the ribbon, the edit control block for items and documents, and practically everywhere else in SharePoint. You can use the Client Object Model to modify these custom actions or create your own.

To get a list of the user custom actions in a site, you call the `get_userCustomActions` function on the Web class, which returns a collection that you populate using the `load` function on the `ClientContext` class. By default, there are no user custom actions.

To create a new user custom action, you call the `get_userCustomActions` function on the Web class to get the collection of existing user custom actions and then call the `add` function on the `UserCustomActionCollection` to get a reference to a new `UserCustomAction` object. You must call several functions on the `UserCustomAction` class before you can add it to SharePoint:

NAME	DESCRIPTION
set_location	The place where the custom action should appear. See the following table for a list of common locations.
set_group	Some locations subdivide their custom actions into groups. Depending on the location you choose, you may need to specify this value, too. For example, adding a custom action to the Site Actions menu requires this. See the following table for a list of common locations and groups.
set_sequence	The order in which the custom action should appear. Actions in the same location are sorted in ascending order based on their value for sequence.
set_title	The actual text to display in the custom action.
set_url	The URL for navigating the browser when the custom action is clicked. You can use a URL token as a part of the URL automatically to replace it with an actual value when the page is rendered. A table later in the chapter provides a list of tokens.

continues

(continued)

NAME	DESCRIPTION
set_imageUrl	The icon to display next to the custom action. This is not required but adds a lot toward a good user experience.
set_description	The description to display with the custom action. This is not required but adds a lot toward a good user experience.

The following table contains the valid locations you can pass to the set_location function of the UserCustomAction class:

LOCATION	GROUP	DESCRIPTION
EditControlBlock	N/A	The drop-down list when hovering the mouse over a list item or document
Microsoft.SharePoint.StandardMenu	SiteActions	The Site Actions menu
Microsoft.SharePoint.StandardMenu	ActionsMenu	The ribbon on a list view page

The following table contains the valid tokens you can use in the URLs you pass to the set_url function of the UserCustomAction class:

NAME	DESCRIPTION
~site	The relative URL to the current site. Use at the beginning of the URL.
~sitecollection	The relative URL to the current site collection. Use at the beginning of the URL.
{ItemId}	The ID of the list item or document. Useful for actions in an edit control block.
{ItemUrl}	The URL of the list item or document. Useful for actions in an edit control block.
{ListId}	The ID of the current list.
{SiteUrl}	The URL of the current site.
{RecurrenceId}	The ID of an instance of a recurring item. Given a recurring meeting in a calendar list, the recurrence ID would be for one of the meetings on the calendar.

> **NOTE** *You can use the* `set_url` *method of the* `UserCustomAction` *class to specify a snippet of JavaScript to run instead of an actual URL. Clicking the custom action executes the JavaScript. Here is an example:*
>
> ```
> customAction.set_url("javascript:alert('Hello world!');");
> ```
>
> *Clicking the custom action calls the JavaScript alert function, which displays a message box with the text "Hello world!".*

Adding custom actions to the ribbon and edit control block requires two more functions to be called: `set_registrationType` and `set_registrationId`. Combined, these two functions determine which types of lists, content types, or even file types should display the custom action. For example, you could have a custom action appear in the edit control block for only `.docx` files. The following code snippet shows this in action:

```
customAction.set_registrationType(SP.UserCustomActionRegistrationType.fileType);
customAction.set_registrationId("docx");
```

In the snippet, you specify `SP.UserCustomActionRegistrationType.fileType` for the registration type, and pass in the file extension to the `set_registrationId` function. The following table lists the most common values for the `set_registrationType` function:

NAME	DESCRIPTION
`list`	Use this to apply the custom action to items and lists of a certain type. You must call `set_registrationId` with the list template type. A list of commonly used list template types is in the following table.
`contentType`	Use this to apply the custom action to certain content types. You must call `set_registrationId` with the content type ID. You can get the ID of a content type by clicking on a content type in the Site Content Types gallery and looking at the value after `ctype` in the browser's address bar. A following table lists the most common content type IDs for your convenience.
`fileType`	Use this to apply the custom action to files with a certain file extension. You must call `set_registrationId` with the file extension.

The following table contains the valid list template types you can pass to the `set_registrationId` function of the `UserCustomAction` class when you set the `set_registrationType` function to `SP.UserCustomActionRegistrationType.list`:

NAME	DESCRIPTION
genericList	Custom lists
documentLibrary	Normal document libraries
survey	Surveys
links	Link lists
announcements	Announcement lists
contacts	Contact lists
events	Calendar lists
tasks	Task lists
discussionBoard	Discussion lists
pictureLibrary	Picture libraries
xmlForm	Form libraries
ganttTasks	Project task lists
externalList	External lists

The following table contains the valid list template types you can pass to the set_registrationId function of the UserCustomAction class when you set the set_registrationType function to SP.UserCustomActionRegistrationType.contentType:

NAME	ID
Item	0x01
Document	0x0101
Form	0x010101
Picture	0x010102
Announcement	0x0104
Contact	0x0106
Event	0x0102

NAME	ID
Issue	0x0103
Link	0x0105
Task	0x0108

After you have configured your `UserCustomAction` object, you must call its `update` method to queue it for the next call to the `executeQueryAsync` method of the `ClientContext` class. After your code runs, you won't immediately see your new custom action if your code is on the same page on which the custom action should appear. Simply reload the page and your new custom action will appear in the right place.

If you want to remove a custom action, get a reference to its `UserCustomAction` object and call its `deleteObject` method. You can also remove all of your custom actions at once by calling the `clear` method on the `UserCustomActionCollection` class. As always, you must call the `executeQueryAsync` method on the `ClientContext` class to submit your changes to SharePoint.

TRY IT OUT Manipulate User Custom Actions

In this activity, you create custom actions that will appear in various places in your site.

1. Open SharePoint Designer from your Start menu.

2. Click the Open Site button.

3. When the Open Site dialog appears, enter the URL to your site in the Site name textbox and click the OK button.

4. If a Windows Security dialog appears, enter your username and password for the SharePoint site and click the OK button.

5. After the site opens, select Site Pages from the Navigation bar on the left.

6. Select Page ➪ ASPX from the ribbon and modify the name of the page appropriately.

7. You can double-click the icon to open the file, but clicking the filename will open the properties of the page, at which point you can click the Edit button in the Ribbon or on the properties page.

8. If you are prompted to open the page in Advanced mode, choose Yes.

9. After the page is open, select Attach from the Style tab of the ribbon. Select a master page from the drop-down list under the Attach button.

10. Click the Split tab at the bottom of the page.

11. In the code window, type the following code at the bottom of the page:

```
<asp:Content id="Content1" runat="server"
    contentplaceholderid="PlaceHolderMain">
</asp:Content>
```

12. Select SharePoint ➪ Show Toolbox from the Insert tab on the ribbon.

13. Position the mouse cursor inside the `asp:Content` tag.

14. Double-click Input (Button) in the HTML/Form Controls section of the Toolbox.

15. In the Code view, modify the new button and configure the following properties (you must add the onclick property yourself):

PROPERTY	VALUE
value	`Show Custom Actions`
onclick	`SP.SOD.executeOrDelayUntilScriptLoaded(showCustomActions, 'sp.js');`

16 Repeat Step 15 using the following information to create six additional buttons:

VALUE	ONCLICK
Clear All	`clearAll();`
Add to Site Actions Menu (URL)	`SP.SOD.executeOrDelayUntilScriptLoaded(addToSiteActionsMenu, 'sp.js');`
Add to Site Actions Menu (JavaScript)	`SP.SOD.executeOrDelayUntilScriptLoaded(addToSiteActionsMenuJavaScript, 'sp.js');`
Add to Edit Control Block (File Extension)	`SP.SOD.executeOrDelayUntilScriptLoaded(addToEditControlBlockFileExtension, 'sp.js');`
Add to Edit Control Block (Content Type)	`SP.SOD.executeOrDelayUntilScriptLoaded(addToEditControlBlockContentType, 'sp.js');`
Add to Ribbon	`SP.SOD.executeOrDelayUntilScriptLoaded(addToRibbon, 'sp.js');`

17 Place the cursor below the newly created buttons and double-click `div` in the HTML/Tags section of the Toolbox.

18. Add the `ID` attribute to the `div` tag and set its value to **divResults**.

19. Insert the following code snippet just above the closing `asp:Content` tag:

```
<script type="text/javascript">

</script>
```

20. Insert the following code snippet inside the `script` tag:

```
function showCustomActions() {
}

function clearAll(){
}
```

```
function onSuccess(sender, args) {
}

function onFailure(sender, args) {
}

function addToSiteActionsMenu() {
}

function addToSiteActionsMenuJavaScript() {
}

function addToEditControlBlockFileExtension() {
}

function addToEditControlBlockContentType() {
}

function addToRibbon() {
}
```

21. Inside the showCustomActions method, type the following code to request the list of user custom actions from SharePoint:

```
var context = new SP.ClientContext.get_current();

this.site = context.get_web();

context.load(this.site, 'UserCustomActions');

context.executeQueryAsync(Function.createDelegate(this, this.onSuccess),
    Function.createDelegate(this, this.onFailure));
```

22. Inside the clearAll method, type the following code to remove all of your user custom actions:

```
document.getElementById("divResults").innerText = "";

var context = new SP.ClientContext.get_current();

this.site = context.get_web();

this.site.get_userCustomActions().clear();

context.load(this.site, 'UserCustomActions');

context.executeQueryAsync(Function.createDelegate(this, this.onSuccess),
    Function.createDelegate(this, this.onFailure));
```

23. Inside the onSuccess method, type the following code to display the list of user custom actions on the screen:

```
var output = "Custom Actions:<br/>";

var enumerator = this.site.get_userCustomActions().getEnumerator();

while (enumerator.moveNext()) {
    var item = enumerator.get_current();
```

```
            output += item.get_title() + " " + item.get_location()  + "<br/>";
        }

        document.getElementById("divResults").innerHTML = output;
```

24. Inside the `onFailure` method, type the following code to display any errors that occur during the calls to SharePoint:

```
        var output = "Call to SharePoint failed:<br/>";

        output += "Error Code: " + args.get_errorCode() + "<br/>";
        output += "Error Details: " + args.get_errorDetails() + "<br/>";
        output += "Error Type: " + args.get_errorTypeName() + "<br/>";
        output += "Error Value: " + args.get_errorValue() + "<br/>";
        output += "Error Message: " + args.get_message() + "<br/>";
        output += "Stack Trace: " + args.get_stackTrace() + "<br/>";

        document.getElementById("divResults").innerHTML = output;
```

25. Inside the `addToSiteActionsMenu` method, type the following code to add a custom action to the Site Actions menu:

```
        var context = new SP.ClientContext.get_current();

        this.site = context.get_web();

        var customAction = this.site.get_userCustomActions().add();
        customAction.set_location("Microsoft.SharePoint.StandardMenu");
        customAction.set_group("SiteActions");
        customAction.set_sequence(100);
        customAction.set_title("End User SharePoint.com");
        customAction.set_description("Navigate to EndUserSharePoint.com.");
        customAction.set_url("http://www.endusersharepoint.com");
        customAction.update();

        context.load(this.site, 'UserCustomActions');

        context.executeQueryAsync(Function.createDelegate(this, this.onSuccess),
            Function.createDelegate(this, this.onFailure));
```

26. Inside the `addToSiteActionsMenuJavaScript` method, type the following code to add a custom action to the Site Actions menu that executes JavaScript:

```
        var context = new SP.ClientContext.get_current();

        this.site = context.get_web();

        var customAction = this.site.get_userCustomActions().add();
        customAction.set_location("Microsoft.SharePoint.StandardMenu");
        customAction.set_group("SiteActions");
        customAction.set_sequence(100);
        customAction.set_title("Hello World");
        customAction.set_description("Runs JavaScript.");
        customAction.set_url("javascript:alert('Hello world!');");
```

```
customAction.update();

context.load(this.site, 'UserCustomActions');

context.executeQueryAsync(Function.createDelegate(this, this.onSuccess),
    Function.createDelegate(this, this.onFailure));
```

27. Inside the `addToEditControlBlockFileExtension` method, type the following code to add a custom action to all Word documents in the site:

```
var context = new SP.ClientContext.get_current();

this.site = context.get_web();

var customAction = this.site.get_userCustomActions().add();
customAction.set_location("EditControlBlock");
customAction.set_sequence(100);
customAction.set_title("Wrox");
customAction.set_description("Navigate to the Wrox Publishing web site.");
customAction.set_url("http://www.wrox.com");
customAction.set_registrationId("docx");
customAction.set_registrationType(
    SP.UserCustomActionRegistrationType.fileType);

customAction.update();

context.load(this.site, 'UserCustomActions');

context.executeQueryAsync(Function.createDelegate(this, this.onSuccess),
    Function.createDelegate(this, this.onFailure));
```

28. Inside the `addToEditControlBlockContentType` method, type the following code to add a custom action to all Task items in the site:

```
var context = new SP.ClientContext.get_current();

this.site = context.get_web();

var customAction = this.site.get_userCustomActions().add();
customAction.set_location("EditControlBlock");
customAction.set_sequence(100);
customAction.set_title("The Sanity Point");
customAction.set_description("Navigate to Woody's blog.");
customAction.set_url("http://www.thesanitypoint.com");
customAction.set_registrationId("0x0108");
customAction.set_registrationType(
    SP.UserCustomActionRegistrationType.contentType);

customAction.update();

context.load(this.site, 'UserCustomActions');

context.executeQueryAsync(Function.createDelegate(this, this.onSuccess),
    Function.createDelegate(this, this.onFailure));
```

29. Inside the `addToRibbon` method, type the following code to add a custom action to the ribbon of a list:

```
var context = new SP.ClientContext.get_current();

this.site = context.get_web();

var customAction = this.site.get_userCustomActions().add();
customAction.set_location("Microsoft.SharePoint.StandardMenu");
customAction.set_group("ActionsMenu");
customAction.set_sequence(100);
customAction.set_title("SharePoint eLearning");
customAction.set_description("Navigate to Asif's blog.");
customAction.set_url("http://blog.sharepointelearning.com/");

customAction.update();

context.load(this.site, 'UserCustomActions');

context.executeQueryAsync(Function.createDelegate(this, this.onSuccess),
    Function.createDelegate(this, this.onFailure));
```

30. Save the page by clicking the Save button on the Quick Access Toolbar at the top of the screen.

31. Select Preview in Browser from the Home tab on the ribbon.

32. When the page loads in the browser, it should be similar to the one shown in Figure 13-9.

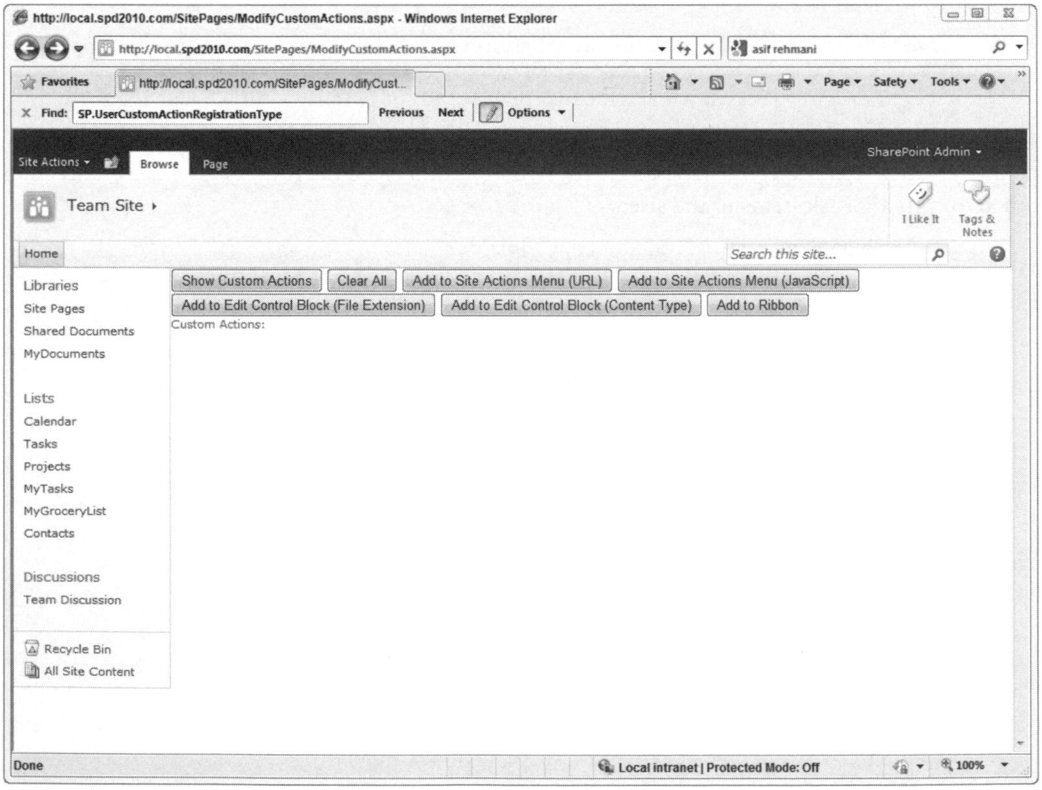

FIGURE 13-9

33. Click the Show Custom Actions button. If you have any user custom actions, they will be listed under the buttons.

34. Click the Add to Site Actions Menu (URL) button. After the custom action is created, it will be listed on the page.

35. Click the Add to Site Actions Menu (JavaScript) button. After the custom action is created, it will be listed on the page.

36. Refresh the page and click the Site Actions menu. Notice the new custom actions as shown in Figure 13-10.

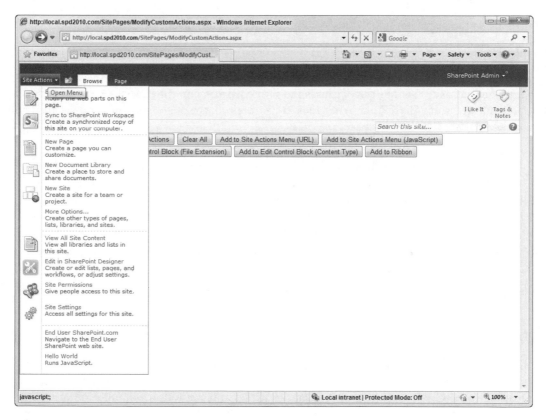

FIGURE 13-10

37. Select Hello World from the Site Actions menu. When the dialog box appears, click OK to close it.

38. Click the Edit Control Block (File Extension) button. Open a new browser window and navigate to a document library that contains Word documents whose file extension is .docx.

39. Display the document's edit control block by click the document's drop down menu and notice the new custom action.

40. Click the Edit Control Block (Content Type) button. Open a new browser window and navigate to a Task list.

41. Display the task's edit control block by click the document's drop down menu and notice the new custom action.

42. Navigate to other lists and libraries and notice that the new custom actions are not visible on their edit control blocks.

43. Click the Add to Ribbon button.

44. Navigate to any list and notice the new Custom Commands tab on the ribbon.

45. Click the Custom Commands tab on the ribbon. Notice the new custom action.

46. Click the Clear All button.

47. Navigate to the pages in the previous steps and notice that all the custom actions are now gone.

How It Works

In the `showCustomActions` method, calling the `load` method of the `ClientContext` class with the string parameter `'UserCustomActions'` causes the site properties and the `UserCustomActions` collections to be requested from SharePoint. After the data is received, the `onSuccess` method is called and the custom actions are listed on the page.

When you click one of the buttons to add a custom action, the `add` method of the `UserCustomActionsCollection` class is called to create a new `UserCustomAction` object. Using the various methods of the `UserCustomAction` object, you configure the custom action to appear on the Site Actions menu, the edit control block, or the ribbon. In the case of the edit control block, setting the registration ID and registration type of the custom action control causes the configured items and documents to display the new custom action on their edit control blocks.

Finally, clicking the Clear All button removes all the user custom actions by calling the `clear` method of the `UserCustomActionsCollection` class.

SUMMARY

In this chapter, you have seen how to extend your SharePoint sites using JavaScript. Using the Client Object Model, you can manipulate lists, libraries, and practically everything else in your sites. The best feature of the Client Object Model is that the classes and methods are similar in both JavaScript and Silverlight. In the next chapter, you will learn more about the capabilities of the Client Object Model and how you can use Silverlight to take advantage of them.

14

Client-side Programming in Silverlight

WHAT YOU WILL LEARN IN THIS CHAPTER

- ➤ Reading data from SharePoint using Silverlight, CAML, and LINQ
- ➤ Progammatically creating, updating, and deleting list items
- ➤ Modifying the configuration of lists and libraries
- ➤ Managing the files and folders in your site
- ➤ Modifying the Quick Launch and Top Navigation bars

> **NOTE** *You can do the activities in this chapter with either JavaScript or Silverlight, with the exception of querying the SharePoint Client Object Model using LINQ to Objects. LINQ is only supported in Silverlight via LINQ to Objects. LINQ to SharePoint is only supported with the Server Object Model.*

WHY SILVERLIGHT?

Silverlight gives you the ability to build applications rich with functionality and usability far beyond what is possible in JavaScript alone. With Silverlight, you can create C# and VB.Net applications that run in the browser as part of your SharePoint site. Like JavaScript, Silverlight has its own libraries for accessing SharePoint via the Client Object Model. Whether you are using JavaScript or Silverlight, they both communicate with SharePoint via the client.svc web service. The URL for this web service is located at `http://yoursiteurl/_vti_bin/client .svc` where *yoursiteurl* is the URL of your SharePoint site.

One of the advantages of the Client Object Model is that you can supplement the functionality of the sandbox solutions in SharePoint. In some environments, developers do not need or are restricted from using certain, possibly-unsafe functionality in their SharePoint code. SharePoint addresses these problems by providing a "sandbox" inside which a developer's code can run. This sandbox runs outside of the main SharePoint web application and protects the web site from being unavailable if the developer's code crashes or uses too many server resources. To safely circumvent some of the restrictions of sandbox solutions, you could include JavaScript or Silverlight code that uses the Client Object Model.

Another reason to use Silverlight is its ability to process and display large amounts of data on the screen, and generally, it performs faster than JavaScript. The real trade-off is your ramp-up time to become proficient in Silverlight versus using the JavaScript experience you already have. Now that you have a good understanding of some of the issues and opportunities around using Silverlight inside SharePoint, continue to the next section to get started.

GETTING STARTED

Before you jump in and get busy with Silverlight, you must install a few things:

➤   Microsoft Visual Studio 2010

➤   Microsoft Silverlight 4 Tools for Visual Studio 2010
    `http://www.microsoft.com/downloads/details.aspx?FamilyID=40ef0f31-cb95-426d-9ce0-00dcfabf3df5`

➤   Silverlight Toolkit `http://silverlight.codeplex.com` — contains many useful, free controls for your Silverlight projects.

➤   Microsoft Expression Blend 4 (optional, but recommended)

If you are new to Silverlight development, visit `www.silverlight.net/getstarted/` for videos, tutorials, and other resources to get you up and running quickly.

> *TIP* *The Silverlight.net website has many free samples, examples, and tutorials available for your use. If you do not have much experience with Silverlight, doing the tutorials on the website before continuing further in the chapter would be a good idea.*

Creating a New Silverlight Application

After you have installed the requisite software, the last thing you need is the Silverlight Client Object Model, which is contained in these two files:

➤   `Microsoft.SharePoint.Client.Silverlight.dll`

➤   `Microsoft.SharePoint.Client.Silverlight.Runtime.dll`

These files are located on your SharePoint server at `C:\Program Files\Common Files\Microsoft Shared\Web Server Extensions\14\TEMPLATE\LAYOUTS\ClientBin`. Copy these files to your local machine because you will need to use them in your Silverlight projects.

To create a new Silverlight application, follow these steps:

1. Open Visual Studio 2010 from your Start menu, and select File ⇨ New ⇨ Project from the menu bar. The New Project dialog appears (see Figure 14-1).

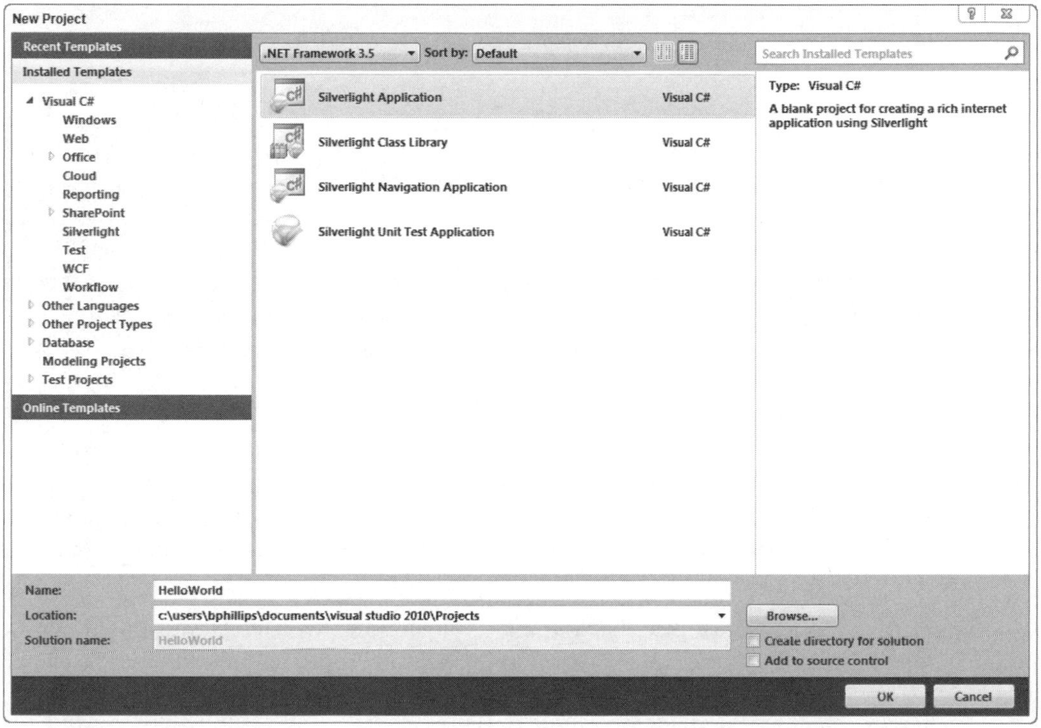

FIGURE 14-1

> **NOTE** *Depending on which settings you chose when you first opened Visual Studio, your New Project dialog may look different from the one shown in Figure 14-1.*

2. Select Silverlight from the templates on the left, and select Silverlight Application from the list of projects.

3. Enter a name for your project and click the OK button. The New Silverlight Application dialog shown in Figure 14-2 appears.

4. Uncheck the "Host the Silverlight application in a new Web Site" checkbox and ensure Silverlight 4 is selected in the Silverlight Version drop-down list. Click the OK button.

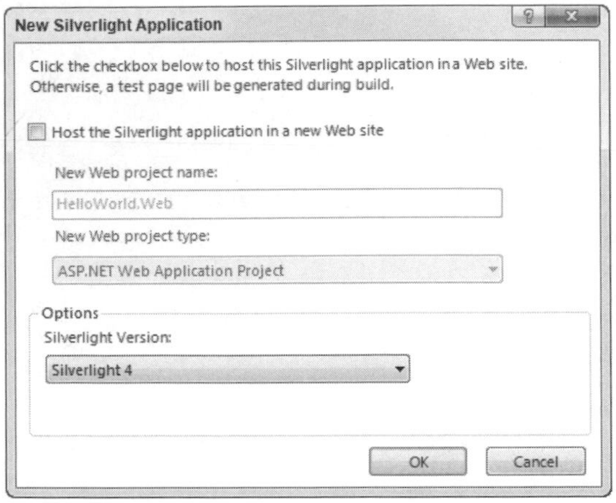

FIGURE 14-2

> **NOTE** *If you get the message "An update to Microsoft Visual Studio is required to target Silverlight 4" when the project opens, make sure you have installed Microsoft Silverlight 4 Tools for Visual Studio 2010.*

After the project is created, the screen shown in Figure 14-3 appears. Notice the Toolbox pane containing the available Silverlight controls on the left side of the screen. Depending on whether you installed the Silverlight Toolkit or controls from a third-party vendor, you may have more or fewer controls.

On the right side of the screen, you see the Solution Explorer pane, which contains the files in the Silverlight project. Underneath the Solution Explorer pane, the Properties pane shows you the properties of the object you have selected in the IDE. When designing controls in Silverlight, you use the Properties pane to configure the controls you use in the project.

The center of the screen contains the Error List pane at the bottom and the design area at the top. The Error List pane displays any errors, warnings, or messages from Visual Studio while you write code and whenever you compile the project. The design area displays the documents you have open. When you open an XAML file, the design area is split into two sections: the WYSIWYG (What You See Is What You Get) designer and the text editor containing the corresponding XML. In the WYSIWYG designer, the Silverlight screens you design in Visual Studio will look the same as when they run in the browser.

Whenever you want to test your code, you must compile it and deploy it to a SharePoint document library. To compile your project, select Build ➪ Build Solution from the menu bar. If your code compiles successfully, you see the message "Build Succeeded" in the status bar in the lower-left side of the screen. Otherwise, a list of errors will be displayed in the Error List pane. Once you fix the errors, you can try compiling again.

When you compile a Silverlight application project, it creates an XAP file, which contains the code and resources of your project. Any zip file–compatible application can open this XAP file.

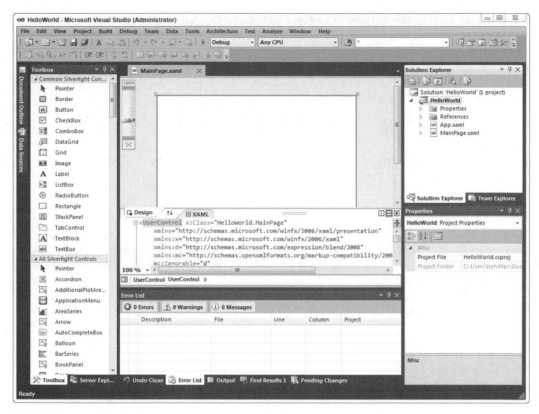

FIGURE 14-3

The location of the XAP file is located in the `Bin\Debug` or `Bin\Release` folder under the folder where your project is located. If you chose to compile your code in Debug mode, your XAP file will be in the `Bin\Debug` folder. Otherwise, it will be in the `Bin\Release` folder.

> **NOTE** If you compile the project in Debug mode, you can attach Visual Studio to your project and debug the project. The drawback of Debug mode is that the XAP file will be much larger and the code will run slower due to the inclusion of the information Visual Studio needs to allow you to debug your code. When you are satisfied with your project, compile the project in Release mode before you deploy it to production.

> **NOTE** You can easily get the location of the XAP file by clicking the Show All Files button in the toolbar of the Solution Explorer pane. The `Bin` folder will appear, and you can navigate to the XAP file. When you select the XAP file, the Properties pane displays the full path to the file. Copy this path to paste into the upload file dialog in SharePoint.

Adding a Silverlight Web Part to a Web Page

After you have uploaded the XAP file to a document library in your site, you must add your Silverlight control to a web page. SharePoint has a convenient way to display Silverlight controls: the Silverlight Web Part. The Silverlight Web Part allows you to add your Silverlight control to any web part page. To add the Silverlight Web Part to a page, follow these steps:

1. Navigate to a web part page in your site and select Edit Page from the Site Actions menu to put the page in Edit mode.

2. Select Web Part from the Insert tab on the ribbon. The web part catalog appears, as shown in Figure 14-4.

FIGURE 14-4

3. Choose Media and Content from the Categories list and select Silverlight Web Part from the Web Parts list.

4. Select the appropriate location from the Add Web Part To drop-down list and click the Add button. The Silverlight Web Part dialog shown in Figure 14-5 appears.

5. Enter the URL to the XAP file you uploaded earlier and click the OK button. After the web part is added, a page similar to the one shown in Figure 14-6 appears. By default, the web part has a height of 300 pixels and a width of 400 pixels. If your web part is larger than these dimensions, edit the web part's properties and adjust accordingly.

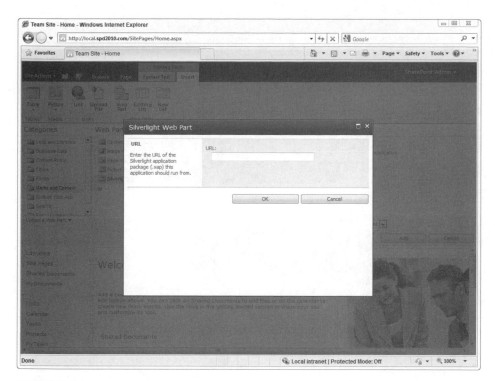

FIGURE 14-5

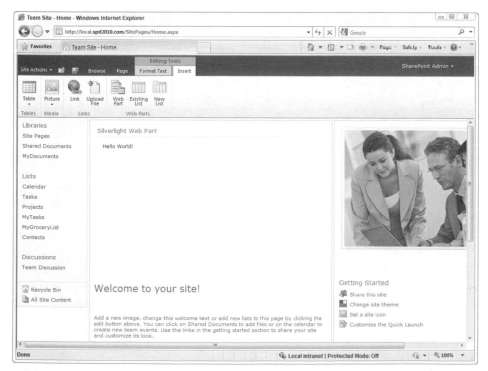

FIGURE 14-6

> **NOTE** *If your Silverlight application needs initialization parameters configured, you can scroll to the bottom of the web part properties window and put them in the Custom Initialization Parameters textbox, shown in Figure 14-7.*

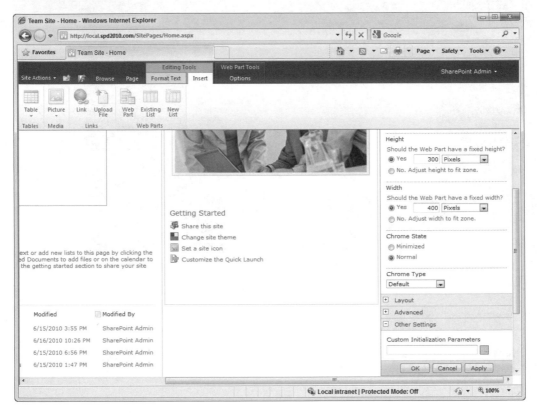

FIGURE 14-7

Debugging a Silverlight Project

Every now and then, you may need to debug your Silverlight code. You cannot just run your Silverlight project by choosing Debug ➪ Start Debugging from the menu bar, as you may be accustomed. To debug a Silverlight project, follow these steps:

1. Deploy your XAP file to a document library and add it to a web part page as shown previously in the chapter.

2. Select Debug ➪ Attach to Process from the menu bar. When the Attach to Process dialog appears (see Figure 14-8), click the Select button to show the Select Code Type dialog shown in Figure 14-9.

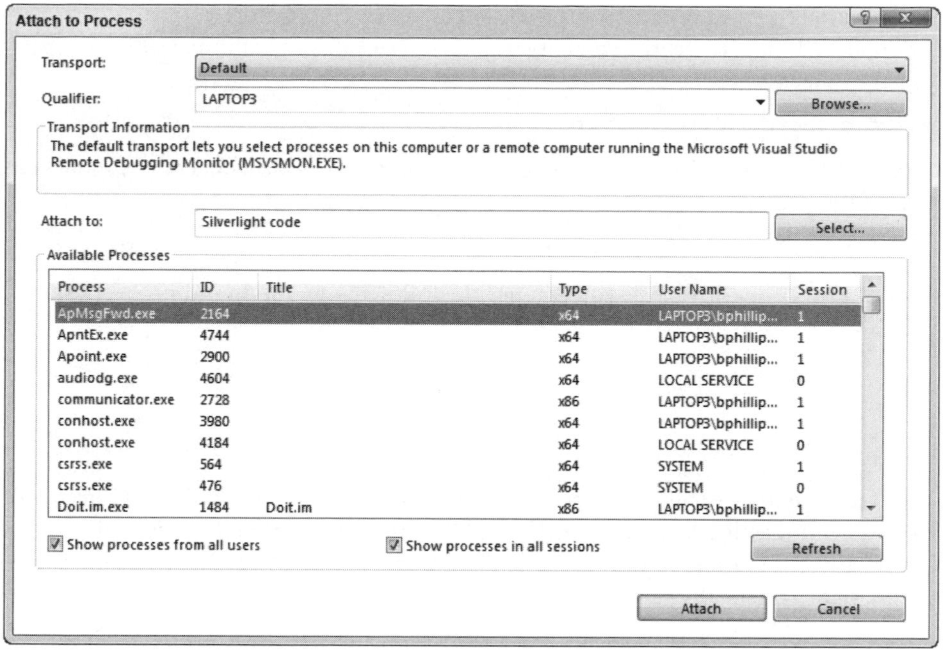

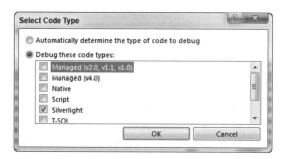

FIGURE 14-8

3. Choose the "Debug these code types" radio button and ensure that only Silverlight is selected in the list box. This makes Visual Studio load fewer debug symbol files after you attach to your browser.

4. Click OK to return to the Attach to Process dialog shown in Figure 14-8. In the Available Processes list box, select all the processes for your browser where Silverlight is listed in the Type column. If you are using Internet Explorer, look for processes named iexplore.exe. If you are using Firefox, look for processes named firefox.exe.

FIGURE 14-9

5. Click the Attach button. You are ready to debug.

RETRIEVING DATA USING SILVERLIGHT

The code you write to retrieve data in Silverlight is almost the same as the code you write in JavaScript. The main difference is that in JavaScript, you must access the properties of an object by calling `set_propertyname` and `get_propertyname` styled methods. In Silverlight, you only need to use the name of the property itself.

As in JavaScript, you must get an instance of the `ClientContext` class before you can do anything with the Client Object Model. To get the current `ClientContext` object, call the `Current` property of the `ClientContext` class:

```
ClientContext context = ClientContext.Current;
```

If you want to get a different `ClientContext` object, you can use the following code snippet, supplying the full URL of the site:

```
ClientContext context = new ClientContext(fullsiteurl);
```

After you get the `ClientContext` object, you can use the following methods and properties:

➤ `Site`

➤ `Web`

➤ `ExecuteQueryAsync`

You may notice that the names of all properties and methods in the Silverlight Client Object Model are proper cased. One interesting feature of the Client Object Model in Silverlight is that you can use LINQ in a very limited manner to query lists and libraries. Without LINQ, you would write the following code snippet to query the Tasks list:

```
ClientContext context = ClientContext.Current;
Web site = context.Web;

List tasks = site.Lists.GetByTitle("MyTasks");
this.items = tasks.GetItems(new CamlQuery());

context.Load(this.items);

context.ExecuteQueryAsync(OnSuccess, OnFailure);
```

You get the list and call the `GetItems` method, passing in an instance of the `CamlQuery` class. Notice that a blank `CamlQuery` class was passed into the method. That just means that SharePoint will return all items from the list. With LINQ, you could write the following code snippet instead:

```
ClientContext context = ClientContext.Current;
Web site = context.Web;

this.tasks = site.Lists.GetByTitle("MyTasks");
ListItemCollection items = tasks.GetItems(new CamlQuery());

var query = from t in items
        select t;

this.results = context.LoadQuery(query);

context.ExecuteQueryAsync(OnSuccess, OnFailure);
```

In the code snippet, the LINQ query is highlighted. Essentially, it creates a query that returns all the items in the list. You could add a filter to the query based on one of the built-in properties of the `ListItem` class. You cannot add a filter on one of the columns in the list, though. Here is an example of using LINQ to return the item whose ID equals 5:

```
var query = from t in items
      where t.Id == 5
      select t;
```

After you get your results back from SharePoint, you may be tempted to bind the list of `ListItem` objects directly to a control like the DataGrid control. That will not work because the list item's field values are actually stored in the `ListItem`'s default property, which is actually a `Dictionary` object. You cannot bind to a `Dictionary` object, but you can convert it to something else using LINQ.

To bind to your list items, create a class with similar properties and data types as their parent list. Here is an example for a few columns from a Task list:

```
public class Task {
  public int Id { get; set; }
  public string Title { get; set; }
  public string Status { get; set; }
  public string Priority { get; set; }
}
```

With the `Task` class, you can use LINQ to convert the `ListItem` objects to Task objects, which you can bind to a control such as the DataGrid control. The following code snippet shows this in action:

```
var data = from t in this.results
      select new Task {
        Id = t.Id,
        Title = (string)t.FieldValues["Title"],
        Status = (string)t.FieldValues["Status"],
        Priority = (string)t.FieldValues["Priority"]
      };

dataGrid1.ItemsSource = data;
```

One additional caveat is that Silverlight is multi-threaded, which is great for performance, but it requires you to add some additional code before you can bind your data. All controls in the UI run on the main thread, which is the first thread created when the application starts. When you call SharePoint, the Client Object Model creates a background thread to send the request to SharePoint and wait for a response. After the call succeeds or fails, the corresponding method you passed to the `ExecuteQueryAsync` method of the `ClientContext` class executes. The execution occurs on the background thread instead of the main UI thread, and you cannot update the UI from a background thread.

To resolve this problem, you can use a control's `Dispatcher` property to execute your code and update the UI. The `Dispatcher` will run the code you give it on the main UI thread. The `Dispatcher` class has the `BeginInvoke` method you use to supply the code to execute. You only need to give it the name of a method in your class or an anonymous method. Delivering your code via an anonymous method is faster because you can add your code on the spot instead of creating a new method and passing the method to the `BeginInvoke` method. The following code snippet shows using an anonymous method with the `Dispatcher` property:

```
dataGrid1.Dispatcher.BeginInvoke(delegate() {
  var data = from t in this.results
        select new Task {
          Id = t.Id,
          Title = (string)t.FieldValues["Title"],
```

```
            Status = (string)t.FieldValues["Status"],
            Priority = (string)t.FieldValues["Priority"]
        };

    dataGrid1.ItemsSource = data;
});
```

In the code snippet, `delegate() {}` creates an anonymous method that is passed to the `BeginInvoke` method of the `Dispatcher` class. You need only place your UI-updating code between the two curly braces. One neat feature of anonymous methods is that you can still access the local variables and parameters of the method containing this code. In the following activity, you use these classes to query a SharePoint list.

TRY IT OUT   Query a List using Silverlight

In this activity, you query a list and bind it to a Silverlight control. You must complete the "Prep Work for Querying a SharePoint List" activity in Chapter 13, "Client-side Programming in JavaScript," before proceeding.

1. Open Visual Studio 2010 from your Start menu.

2. Select File ➪ New ➪ Project from the menu bar to display the New Project dialog in Figure 14-1.

3. Choose Silverlight from the list of templates and select Silverlight Application from the list of applications.

4. Enter a name for your project and click the OK button.

5. In the New Silverlight Application dialog (Figure 14-2), uncheck the "Host the Silverlight application in a new Web site" checkbox, ensure that Silverlight 4 is selected in the drop-down list, and click the OK button.

6. After the project loads, the `MainPage.xaml` file should automatically open. If it does not open, double-click the file in the Solution Explorer pane (Figure 14-3).

7. Right-click the References folder in the Solution Explorer pane and choose Add Reference.

8. Click the Browse button and navigate to the location of the `Microsoft.SharePoint.Client .Silverlight.dll` and `Microsoft.SharePoint.Client.Silverlight.Runtime.dll` files. (These files are located on your SharePoint server at C:\Program Files\Common Files\Microsoft Shared\Web Server Extensions\14\TEMPLATE\LAYOUTS\ClientBin.)

9. Click the Open button to return to the Add Reference dialog.

10. Click the Add button to add the references to the project.

11. Drag the DataGrid control from the Toolbox pane and drop it on the white area of the `MainPage.xaml` designer surface. This adds the control to the page.

12. In the text editor, remove all attributes on the `DataGrid` tag except for the `Name` attribute. If you do not see the text editor, click the XAML tab as shown in Figure 14-3.

13. In the text editor, click the `UserControl` tag and, in the Properties pane, click the Events button.

14. Locate the `Loaded` event and double-click it to create an event handler in the `MainPage.xaml.cs` file. The `MainPage.xaml.cs` file should automatically open.

15. In the `MainPage.xaml.cs` file, add the following `using` statements to the top of the screen:

```
using Microsoft.SharePoint.Client;
using System.Collections;
```

16. Add the following private fields to the `MainPage` class just before the `public MainPage() {` line:

```
private List tasks;
private IEnumerable<ListItem> results;
```

17. In the `UserControl_Loaded` method, type the following code to request the MyTasks list from SharePoint:

```
ClientContext context = ClientContext.Current;
Web site = context.Web;

this.tasks = site.Lists.GetByTitle("MyTasks");
ListItemCollection items = tasks.GetItems(new CamlQuery());

var query = from t in items
  select t;

this.results = context.LoadQuery(query);

context.ExecuteQueryAsync(OnSuccess, OnFailure);
```

> **NOTE** The MyTasks list is simply a Tasks list named MyTasks. Create that list in your site in order to use this activity's code without changing it.

18. Add the following two methods before the `UserControl_Loaded` method:

```
void OnSuccess(object sender,
  ClientRequestSucceededEventArgs e) {
}

void OnFailure(object sender,
  ClientRequestFailedEventArgs e) {
}
```

19. In the `OnSuccess` method, type the following code to convert the list items to Task objects and bind it to the DataGrid control:

```
dataGrid1.Dispatcher.BeginInvoke(delegate() {
  var data = from t in this.results
        select new Task {
          Id = t.Id,
          Title = (string)t.FieldValues["Title"],
          Status = (string)t.FieldValues["Status"],
          Priority =
            (string)t.FieldValues["Priority"]
        };
```

```
dataGrid1.ItemsSource = data;
});
```

20. In the `OnFailure` method, type the following code to display any errors that occur during the call to SharePoint:

```
this.Dispatcher.BeginInvoke(delegate() {
  TextBlock textBlock = new TextBlock();
  textBlock.Text = e.Exception.ToString();
  this.Content = textBlock;
});
```

21. Add a new class to the project by right-clicking the project in Solution Explorer and choosing Add ⇨ Class from the context menu.

22. Enter Task.cs as the name of the class file.

23. When the Task.cs file opens, update the Task class to include the properties as shown here:

```
public class Task {
  public int Id { get; set; }
  public string Title { get; set; }
  public string Status { get; set; }
  public string Priority { get; set; }
}
```

24. Compile the project by selecting Build ⇨ Build Solution from the menu bar.

25. Check the Error List pane for any errors and fix them before continuing.

26. Click the Show All Files button in the Solution Explorer pane.

27. In the Solution Explorer pane, expand the `Bin` and `Debug` folders and select the XAP file.

28. Double-click the value of the Full Path property in the Properties pane to select it and press Ctrl+C to copy the path to the clipboard.

29. Navigate your browser to a document library in your SharePoint site.

30. Select Upload Document from the Documents tab on the ribbon.

31. In the Upload Document dialog that appears, click the Browse button.

32. Paste the file path from Step 28 and click Open.

33. Click the OK button to close the Upload Document dialog and upload the XAP file to SharePoint.

34. When the document library is updated with your file, right-click its name and choose Copy Hyperlink to copy the URL of your XAP file.

35. Navigate your browser to a web part page in your site.

36. Select Edit Page from the Site Actions menu.

37. Select Web Part from the Insert tab on the ribbon.

38. Choose Media and Content from the Categories list and select Silverlight Web Part from the Web Parts list (Figure 14-4).

39. Select the location to put the web part from the "Add Web Part to" drop-down list and click the Add button.

40. In the Silverlight Web Part dialog, paste the URL from step 34 and click the OK button (Figure 14-5).

41. Select Save & Close from the Page tab on the ribbon.

42. Verify that your Silverlight control displays data, as shown in Figure 14-10.

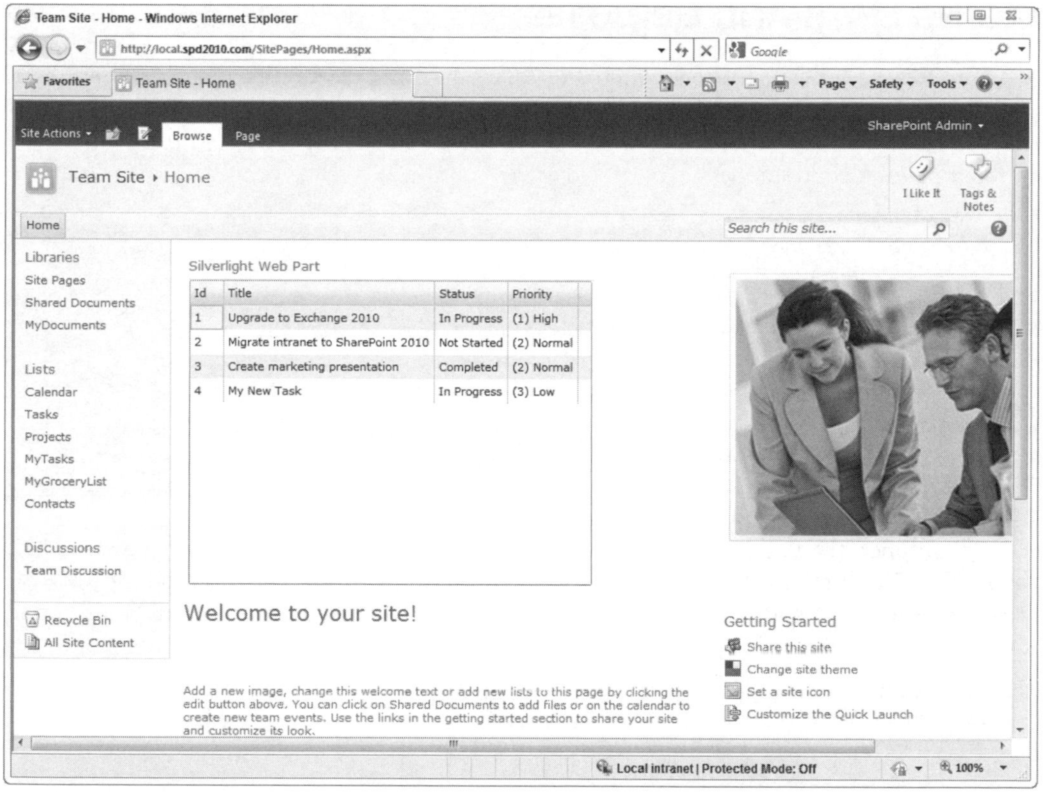

FIGURE 14-10

How It Works

When the Silverlight control loads on the web page, the `UserControl_Loaded` method is called. Inside the method, the current `ClientContext` object is used to get the current site and, in turn, the MyTasks list. With the MyTasks list, the `GetItems` method is called with a blank `CamlQuery` object to get all the items in the list.

Afterwards, the list items are processed by the LINQ query and queued for retrieval from SharePoint by passing the LINQ query to the `LoadQuery` method of the `ClientContext` object. The `LoadQuery` method returns an `IEnumerable` object of `ListItems`, which is stored in a private class field.

After the `ExecuteQueryAsync` method is called, the Client Object Model requests the data from SharePoint, populates the private class field, and calls the `OnSuccess` method.

Inside the `OnSuccess` method, LINQ transforms the non-bindable `ListItem` objects into new `Task` objects. Finally, the `Task` objects are bound to the DataGrid control, which displays the information you see in Figure 14-10.

MANAGING LISTS AND LIBRARIES

The Client Object Model also allows you to create, modify, and delete lists and document libraries in your SharePoint site. To get a list of the lists and libraries in a site, you use the Lists property of the Web class. You can also use LINQ to filter the lists and libraries returned from the site by using the following code snippet:

```
var query = from l in site.Lists
       where !l.Hidden
       select l;

this.listResults = context.LoadQuery(query);
```

> ⊗ **WARNING** *In general, avoid displaying hidden lists and libraries to the user because modifying them could irreparably break functionality in your site.*

In the code snippet, the `Lists` property is filtered for only the lists and libraries that are not hidden in the browser UI. Afterwards, the LINQ query is passed to the `LoadQuery` method for retrieval from SharePoint. In the following code snippet, the result of the query from SharePoint is bound directly to a DataGrid control:

```
listsDataGrid.Dispatcher.BeginInvoke(delegate() {
  listsDataGrid.ItemsSource = listResults;
});
```

Note that you must still use the `Dispatcher` property of a control to update it from the background thread that called your `OnSuccess` method. Unlike the `ListItem` class, the `List` class has many useful properties that you can directly bind to. In the following table, you can see some of the most common properties and methods that you will use when dealing with lists and libraries.

The following table displays commonly used List properties:

NAME	DESCRIPTION
`AllowContentTypes`	If true, the content types associated with the list or library can be managed via the browser.
`BaseTemplate`	Indicates which list template was used to create the list. A list of common list template types appears later in the chapter.
`ContentTypes`	The collection of `ContentType` objects associated with the list.

NAME	DESCRIPTION
Created	When the list or library was created.
Description	The description for the list or library.
EnableAttachments	If true, the list supports attaching files to list items. Only applies to lists, not document libraries.
EnableFolderCreation	If true, users can create folders inside the list or library.
Fields	The collection of Field objects in the list.
HasExternalDataSource	If true, the list is an external list.
Hidden	If true, the list does not appear in the browser.
Id	The GUID identifier of the list.
ItemCount	The number of items or documents in the list or library.
LastItemDeletedDate	Specifies the last time a list or document was deleted from the list. This is useful for checking if you need to refresh your data from SharePoint.
LastItemModifiedDate	Specifies the last time the list or its contents was modified. This is useful for checking if you need to refresh your data from SharePoint.
OnQuickLaunch	If true, the list will appear in the Quick Launch bar on the left side of the screen.
RootFolder	The root folder of the list. Use this to get the files and folders in a document library.
Title	The display name of the list.

The following table displays commonly used List methods:

NAME	DESCRIPTION
AddItem	Adds an item to the list.
DeleteObject	Deletes the list *permanently*.
GetItemById	Gets an item from the list using the item's ID.
GetItems	Gets a collection of items based on the supplied CamlQuery object.
Recycle	Sends the list to the Recycle Bin. This is what happens when you delete a list via the browser.
Update	Saves your changes to the list, which are applied the next time ExecuteQueryAsync is called.

To create a new list or library, you use the `ListCreationInformation` class. The `ListCreationInformation` class has various properties you must populate before passing it to the `Add` method on the `Lists` collection of the site. At a minimum, you must populate the `Title` and `TemplateType` properties as shown in the following code snippet:

```
ListCreationInformation info = new ListCreationInformation();
info.Title = "My New List";
info.TemplateType = (int)ListTemplateType.Tasks;

site.Lists.Add(info);

context.ExecuteQueryAsync(OnListCreated, OnFailure);
```

In the code snippet, the new list is named "My New List" and the template type is Tasks. After the `ListCreationInformation` object is configured, pass it to the `Add` method on the site's `Lists` property. After the `ExecuteQueryAsync` method is called, SharePoint will create the list. Notice that the `TemplateType` property is set to the `ListTemplateType.Tasks` enumeration value. You must cast the `ListTemplateType` enumeration value to the `int` (integer) data type when setting the value of the `TemplateType` property. The following table lists the values of the `ListTemplateType` enumeration and their descriptions:

NAME	`ListTemplateType` VALUE
Announcements	Announcements
Calendar	Events
Contacts	Contacts
Custom List	GenericList
Discussion Board	DiscussionBoard
Document Library	DocumentLibrary
Form Library	XMLForm
Issue Tracking	IssueTracking
Links	Links
Picture Library	PictureLibrary
Project Tasks	GanttTasks
Survey	Survey
Tasks	Tasks
Wiki Page Library	WebPageLibrary

To modify a list or library, you must call the `GetByTitle` method of the Lists collection to get the `List` object. Afterwards, you can modify the list's properties and call the list's `Update` method to save your changes. To delete a list, call the `Recycle` method of the list, which sends the list to the Recycle Bin. To permanently delete the list, call the `DeleteObject` method instead.

Other than managing the items or documents in a list or library, managing the fields in a list or library will be your most common list-related task. The `Fields` property on the `List` class returns a collection of field properties that you can use to add new fields, remove fields, or access the properties of the fields themselves. All `Field` objects have the following properties and methods:

PROPERTY	DESCRIPTION
CanBeDeleted	If true, the field can be removed from the list.
DefaultValue	The default value, if any, for the field.
Description	The description for the field.
FieldTypeKind	The type of field. There is a list of field types later in the chapter.
Filterable	If true, the field can be used to filter the list. Some fields, including "Multiple lines of text" fields, cannot be used as filters.
Hidden	If true, the field does not appear in the browser UI.
Id	The GUID identifier for the field.
InternalName	The original name of the field. The internal name can never be changed after the field is created.
ReadOnlyField	If true, the field is read-only.
Sealed	If true, the field cannot be deleted or modified in any way.
Sortable	If true, the field can be used to sort the list. Some fields, including "Multiple lines of text" fields, cannot be used to sort the list.
Title	The display name of the field.
TypeDisplayName	The display name for the field's type.

METHOD	DESCRIPTION
DeleteObject	Deletes the field *permanently* from the list.
Update	Saves your changes to the field, which are applied the next time `ExecuteQueryAsync` is called.

You may have noticed that the previous tables of field properties and methods did not include any of the settings you have used to add a field via the browser. This is because the `Field` class is the parent or base class of the various classes used to create fields. When you want to add or modify a field in a list, you use one of the following classes that matches the type of your field:

FIELD TYPE	CLASS	INTERNAL TYPE
Single line of text	`FieldText`	Text
Multiple lines of text	`FieldMultiLineText`	Note
Choice (menu to choose from)	`FieldChoice` (multiple choices not allowed) `FieldMultiChoice` (multiple choices allowed)	Choice
Number (1, 1.0, 100)	`FieldNumber`	Number
Currency ($, ¥, €)	`FieldCurrency`	Currency
Date and Time	`FieldDateTime`	DateTime
Lookup (information already on this site)	`FieldLookup`	Lookup
Yes/No (checkbox)	`Field`	Boolean
Person or Group	`FieldUser`	User
Hyperlink or Picture	`FieldUrl`	URL
Calculated (calculation based on other columns)	`FieldCalculated`	Calculated
External Data	Can be any of the `Field` classes because you choose which field(s) to display in the list.	BusinessData
Managed Metadata	`FieldLookup`	TaxonomyFieldType

To add a field to a list, you must call the `AddFieldAsXml` method on the list's `Fields` collection. The `AddFieldAsXml` method takes primarily a string parameter with the XML of the field definition and returns a `Field` object that you can cast to one of the classes in the previous table to configure extra settings. The `AddFieldAsXml` method also takes a Boolean parameter for adding the field to the list's default view and an `AddFieldOptions` value to specify additional options for the field. Consider the following code snippet:

```
Field field = list.Fields.AddFieldAsXml(@"<Field DisplayName='My New Field'
  Type='Note' />", true, AddFieldOptions.DefaultValue);

FieldMultiLineText textField = context.CastTo<FieldMultiLineText>(field);
textField.NumberOfLines = 6;
textField.RichText = true;
textField.Update();

context.ExecuteQueryAsync(OnFieldCreated, OnFailure);
```

The `AddFieldAsXml` method is called to create a rich text field using the field XML string with the default options. The field is added to the list and its default view. The `AddFieldAsXml` method returns a `Field` object, which is subsequently cast to a `FieldMultiLineText` object by calling the

`CastTo<>` method on the `ClientContext` class. The previous table contains a list of the valid values you use for the `Type` attribute in your field XML.

Using the `FieldMultiLineText` object, the number of lines and rich text support is configured for the field as in the browser UI. Finally, the `Update` method is called on the field to save your changes. After the `ExecuteQueryAsync` method is called, SharePoint adds the field to the list.

To modify a field, you call either the `GetByInternalNameOrTitle` or `GetByTitle` method on the `Fields` property of the list. Afterwards, you can cast it to the appropriate field class as shown in the previous code snippet. When you are finished with your changes, call the `Update` method on the field and the `ExecuteQueryAsync` method on the `ClientContext` class. To delete a field, you call the `DeleteObject` method on the field. In the next activity, you will use these `List` and `Field` classes to display, modify, and create lists in your site.

> ⊗ **WARNING** *There is no* `Recycle` *method on the* `Field` *class so when you delete the field, it is permanent. When you delete a field, the values for the deleted field in the existing items and documents are permanently deleted, too.*

TRY IT OUT   **Manage Lists and Libraries**

In this activity, you create a simple Silverlight control to display your site's lists and libraries and their fields. You will also create a list and a field using the Client Object Model.

1. Open Visual Studio 2010 from your Start menu.

2. Select File ➪ New ➪ Project from the menu bar to display the New Project dialog in Figure 14-1.

3. Choose Silverlight from the list of templates and select Silverlight Application from the list of applications.

4. Enter a name for your project and click the OK button.

5. In the New Silverlight Application dialog, uncheck the "Host the Silverlight application in a new Web site" checkbox, ensure that Silverlight 4 is selected in the drop-down list, and click the OK button.

6. When the project is loaded, the `MainPage.xaml` file should automatically open. If it does not open, double-click the file in the Solution Explorer pane.

7. Right-click the `References` folder in the Solution Explorer pane and choose Add Reference. The Add Reference dialog appears.

8. Click the Browse button and navigate to the location of the `Microsoft.SharePoint.Client .Silverlight.dll` and `Microsoft.SharePoint.Client.Silverlight.Runtime.dll` files.

9. Click the Open button to return to the Add Reference dialog.

10. Click the Add button to add the references to the project.

11. In `MainPage.xaml`, set the following property values on the `UserControl` tag:

PROPERTY	VALUE
d:DesignHeight	400
d:DesignWidth	600

12. With the `UserControl` selected, click the Events button in the Properties window and double-click the `Loaded` event.

13. In `MainPage.xaml`, set the following property values on the `Grid` tag:

PROPERTY	VALUE
Width	600
Height	400

14. In `MainPage.xaml`, add a DataGrid from the toolbox and configure the following properties:

PROPERTY	VALUE
HorizontalAlignment	Stretch
Name	listsDataGrid
VerticalAlignment	Top
Height	164
AutoGenerateColumns	False

15. With the DataGrid selected, click the Events button in the Properties window and double-click the `SelectionChanged` event.

16. In `MainPage.xaml`, add a Button from the toolbox and configure the following properties:

PROPERTY	VALUE
Content	Add List
Height	23
HorizontalAlignment	Left
Margin	12,170,0,0
Name	addListButton
VerticalAlignment	Top
Width	75

17. In `MainPage.xaml`, add a Button from the toolbox and configure the following properties:

PROPERTY	VALUE
Content	Delete List
Height	23
HorizontalAlignment	Left
Margin	93,170,0,0
Name	deleteListButton
VerticalAlignment	Top
Width	75

18. In `MainPage.xaml`, add a Button from the toolbox and configure the following properties:

PROPERTY	VALUE
Content	Add Field
Height	23
HorizontalAlignment	Left
Margin	12,369,0,0
Name	addFieldButton
VerticalAlignment	Top
Width	75

19. In `MainPage.xaml`, add a Button from the toolbox and configure the following properties:

PROPERTY	VALUE
Content	Delete Field
Height	23
HorizontalAlignment	Left
Margin	93,369,0,0
Name	deleteFieldButton
VerticalAlignment	Top
Width	75

20. Add event handlers for each of the buttons created in Steps 16–19 by selecting the button, clicking the Events button in the Properties pane, and double-clicking the `Click` event.

21. In `MainPage.xaml`, add a DataGrid from the toolbox and configure the following properties:

PROPERTY	VALUE
AutoGenerateColumns	False
Height	164
HorizontalAlignment	Stretch
Margin	0,199,0,0
Name	fieldsDataGrid
VerticalAlignment	Top

22. Inside the `listsDataGrid` tag, insert the following code:

```
<sdk:DataGrid.Columns>
  <sdk:DataGridTextColumn Binding="{Binding Title}" Header="Title" />
  <sdk:DataGridTextColumn Binding="{Binding BaseType}" Header="Base Type" />
  <sdk:DataGridTextColumn Binding="{Binding Description}"
    Header="Description" />
</sdk:DataGrid.Columns>
```

23. Inside the `fieldsDataGrid` tag, insert the following code:

```
<sdk:DataGrid.Columns>
  <sdk:DataGridTextColumn Binding="{Binding Title}" Header="Title" />
  <sdk:DataGridTextColumn Binding="{Binding Description}"
    Header="Description" />
  <sdk:DataGridTextColumn Binding="{Binding TypeDisplayName}"
    Header="TypeDisplayName" />
  <sdk:DataGridTextColumn Binding="{Binding TypeAsString}"
    Header="TypeAsString" />
</sdk:DataGrid.Columns>
```

24. Compare the layout of your `MainPage.xaml` file with the one shown in Figure 14-11 and make any necessary changes.

25. In `MainPage.xaml.cs`, add the following `using` statement at the top of the page:

```
using Microsoft.SharePoint.Client;
```

26. Add the following `private` fields inside the `MainPage` class:

```
private IEnumerable<List> listResults;
private IEnumerable<Field> fieldResults;
```

27. Add the following methods inside the `MainPage` class:

```
private void OnFailure(object sender, ClientRequestFailedEventArgs e) {
}

private void RefreshLists() {
}
```

```
private void OnListsSuccess(object sender, ClientRequestSucceededEventArgs e) {
}

private void OnListCreated(object sender, ClientRequestSucceededEventArgs e) {
}

private void OnListDeleted(object sender, ClientRequestSucceededEventArgs e) {
}

private void RefreshFields() {
}

private void OnFieldsSuccess(object sender,
  ClientRequestSucceededEventArgs e) {
}

private void OnFieldCreated(object sender, ClientRequestSucceededEventArgs e) {
}

private void OnFieldDeleted(object sender, ClientRequestSucceededEventArgs e) {
}
```

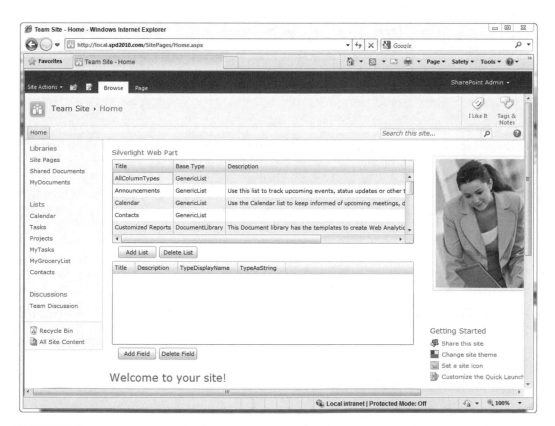

FIGURE 14-11

28. In the `addFieldButton_Click` method, insert the following code to add a field to the selected list in the listsDataGrid control:

```
ClientContext context = ClientContext.Current;

if (listsDataGrid.SelectedItem is List) {
  List list = (List)listsDataGrid.SelectedItem;

  Field field = list.Fields.AddFieldAsXml(@"<Field DisplayName='My New Field'
    Type='Note' />", true, AddFieldOptions.DefaultValue);

  FieldMultiLineText textField = context.CastTo<FieldMultiLineText>(field);
  textField.NumberOfLines = 6;
  textField.RichText = true;
  textField.Update();

  context.ExecuteQueryAsync(OnFieldCreated, OnFailure);
}
```

29. In the `addListButton_Click` method, insert the following code to add a new list to the site:

```
ClientContext context = ClientContext.Current;
Web site = context.Web;

ListCreationInformation info = new ListCreationInformation();
info.Title = "My New List";
info.Description = "List created using the Silverlight Client Object Model.";
info.TemplateType = (int)ListTemplateType.Tasks;

site.Lists.Add(info);

context.ExecuteQueryAsync(OnListCreated, OnFailure);
```

30. In the `deleteFieldButton_Click` method, insert the following code to delete the selected field in the fieldsDataGrid control:

```
ClientContext context = ClientContext.Current;

if (fieldsDataGrid.SelectedItem is Field) {
  Field field = (Field)fieldsDataGrid.SelectedItem;

  field.DeleteObject();

  context.ExecuteQueryAsync(OnFieldDeleted, OnFailure);
}
```

31. In the `deleteListButton_Click` method, insert the following code to delete the selected list in the listsDataGrid control:

```
ClientContext context = ClientContext.Current;

if (listsDataGrid.SelectedItem is List) {
  List list = (List)listsDataGrid.SelectedItem;
  list.DeleteObject();

  context.ExecuteQueryAsync(OnListDeleted, OnFailure);
}
```

32. In the `listsDataGrid_SelectionChanged` method, insert the following code to call the `RefreshFields` method when a list is selected in the listsDataGrid control:

```
RefreshFields();
```

33. In the `OnFailure` method, insert the following code to display any errors from the call to SharePoint:

```
this.Dispatcher.BeginInvoke(delegate() {
  MessageBox.Show(e.Message);
});
```

34. In the `OnFieldCreated` method, insert the following code to call the `RefreshFields` method:

```
fieldsDataGrid.Dispatcher.BeginInvoke(delegate() {
  RefreshFields();
});
```

35. In the `OnFieldDeleted` method, insert the following code to call the `RefreshFields` method:

```
fieldsDataGrid.Dispatcher.BeginInvoke(delegate() {
  RefreshFields();
});
```

36. In the `OnFieldsSuccess` method, insert the following code to bind the fields from SharePoint to the fieldsDataGrid control:

```
fieldsDataGrid.Dispatcher.BeginInvoke(delegate() {
  fieldsDataGrid.ItemsSource = fieldResults;
});
```

37. In the `OnListCreated` method, insert the following code to call the `RefreshLists` method:

```
listsDataGrid.Dispatcher.BeginInvoke(delegate() {
  RefreshLists();
});
```

38. In the `OnListDeleted` method, insert the following code to call the `RefreshLists` method:

```
listsDataGrid.Dispatcher.BeginInvoke(delegate() {
  RefreshLists();
});
```

39. In the `OnListsSuccess` method, insert the following code to bind the lists from SharePoint to the listsDataGrid control:

```
listsDataGrid.Dispatcher.BeginInvoke(delegate() {
  listsDataGrid.ItemsSource = listResults;
});
```

40. In the `RefreshFields` method, insert the following code to request the fields for the selected list in the listsDataGrid control:

```
fieldsDataGrid.ItemsSource = null;

if (listsDataGrid.SelectedItem is List) {
  List list = (List)listsDataGrid.SelectedItem;

  ClientContext context = ClientContext.Current;
```

```
    var query = from f in list.Fields
        where !f.Hidden
        select f;

    this.fieldResults = context.LoadQuery(query);

    context.ExecuteQueryAsync(OnFieldsSuccess, OnFailure);
}
```

41. In the `RefreshLists` method, insert the following code to request the lists for the current site:

```
ClientContext context = ClientContext.Current;
Web site = context.Web;

var query = from l in site.Lists
    where !l.Hidden
    select l;

this.listResults = context.LoadQuery(query);

context.ExecuteQueryAsync(OnListsSuccess, OnFailure);
```

42. In the `UserControl_Loaded` method, insert the following code to call the `RefreshLists` method:

```
RefreshLists();
```

43. Compile the project by selecting Build ➪ Build Solution from the menu bar.

44. Check the Error List pane for any errors and fix them before continuing.

45. Click the Show All Files button in the Solution Explorer pane.

46. In the Solution Explorer pane, expand the `Bin` and `Debug` folders and select the XAP file.

47. Double-click the value of the Full Path property in the Properties pane to select it and press Ctrl+C to copy the path to the clipboard.

48. Navigate your browser to a document library in your SharePoint site.

49. Select Upload Document from the Documents tab on the ribbon.

50. In the Upload Document dialog, click the Browse button.

51. Paste the file path from Step 47 and click Open.

52. Click the OK button to close the Upload Document dialog and upload the XAP file to SharePoint.

53. When the document library is updated with your file, right-click its name and choose Copy Hyperlink to copy the URL of your XAP file.

54. Navigate your browser to a web part page in your site.

55. Select Edit Page from the Site Actions menu to place the page in Edit mode.

56. Select Web Part from the Insert tab on the ribbon.

57. Choose Media and Content from the Categories list and select Silverlight Web Part from the Web Parts list.

58. Select the location to put the web part from the "Add Web Part to" drop-down list and click the Add button.

59. In the Silverlight Web Part dialog, paste the URL from Step 53 and click the OK button.

60. Configure the web part properties as follows:

Height	400
Width	600

61. Select Save & Close from the Page tab on the ribbon.

62. Refresh the page in your browser.

63. Wait until the upper DataGrid control is populated with the non-hidden lists in the site.

64. Select various lists from the upper DataGrid control and watch the non-hidden fields in the list populate the bottom DataGrid control.

65. Click the Add List button, and the new list "My New List" appears in the upper DataGrid control.

66. Select the "My New List" list in the upper DataGrid control and click the Add Field button.

67. Notice the new field "My New Field" in the bottom DataGrid control.

68. Select the "My New Field" field in the bottom DataGrid control and click the Delete Field button.

69. Notice the "My New Field" field disappear from the list.

70. Select the "My New List" list in the upper DataGrid control and click the Delete List button.

71. Notice the "My New List" list disappear from the site.

How It Works

When the Silverlight control loads, it calls SharePoint to get the non-hidden lists and libraries in the site. The list is bound to the upper DataGrid control. When you select a list in the upper DataGrid control, the control calls SharePoint to get the non-hidden fields for the selected list and bind them to the bottom DataGrid control. When you click the Add List button, a Tasks list is added to the site. When you click the Add Field button, a rich text field is added to the selected list. The Delete List and Delete Field buttons delete the selected list and field, respectively.

MANAGING FILES AND FOLDERS

In Figure 14-12, you see the virtual file system of SharePoint that appears when you pin the All Files window in SharePoint Designer. Many files and folders do not appear in the UI. At times, you may need to manipulate files and folders using the Client Object Model, especially if you want to upload documents or create folders inside a document library.

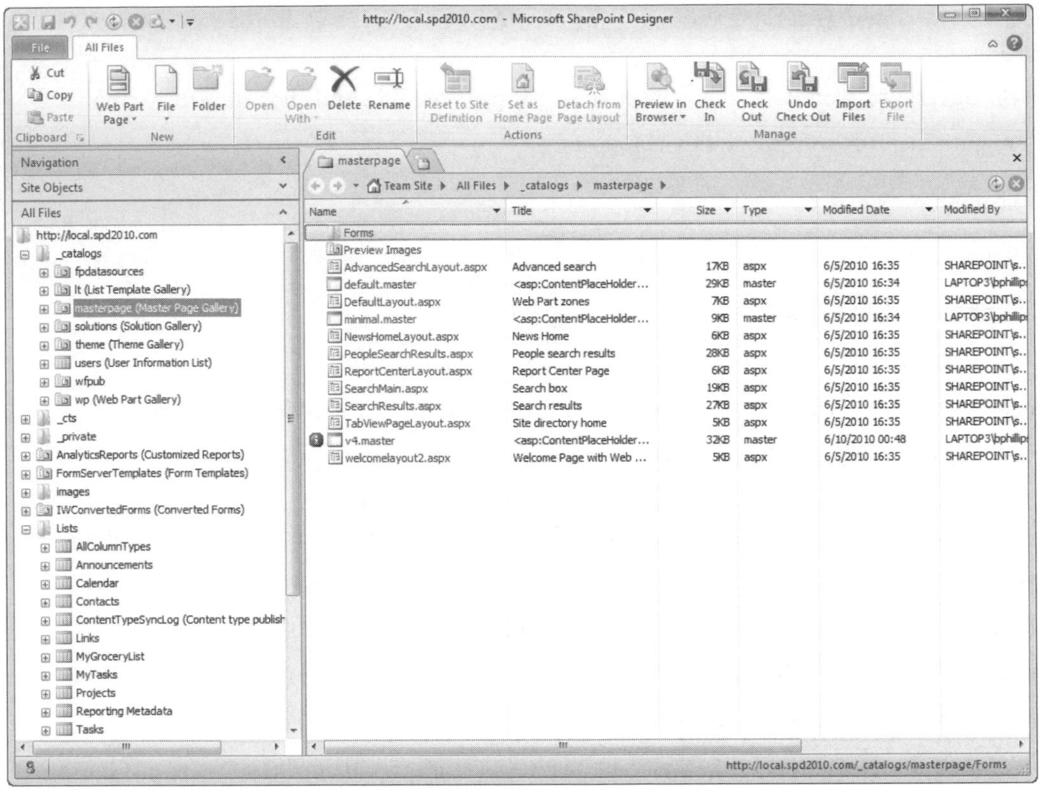

FIGURE 14-12

In the Client Object Model, folders are represented by the `Folder` class and files are represented by the `File` class. Not all files and folders are in a document library but you can still access them using the Client Object Model. You can get a `Folder` object by using one of the following:

➤ Calling the `Web` class's `RootFolder` property, which returns the folder at the root of the SharePoint site.

➤ Calling the `List` class's `RootFolder` property, which returns the folder at the root of the SharePoint list.

➤ Calling the `Web` class's `GetFolderByServerRelativeUrl` method, passing in the server-relative URL of the folder.

If you already have a `Folder` object, you can get its parent folder using the `ParentFolder` property or its subfolders using the `Folders` property. The `Folder` class also has a `Files` property that returns a list of `File` objects for the files in the folder.

You create a folder by calling the `Add` method on the `Folders` property on an existing `Folder` object, passing in the name of the new folder. The `Add` method returns a `Folder` object, which you can use to create subfolders or add files.

To rename a folder, you get the `Folder` object representing the folder and modify its `Name` property. Afterwards, you call the `Folder` object's `Update` method. To delete a folder, you call the

`Folder` object's `Recycle` method, which sends the folder to the Recycle Bin. To permanently delete a folder, call the `DeleteObject` method instead, which also permanently deletes the folder's contents.

The `File` object represents a file in the virtual file system whether the file is located in a document library or not. The `File` object is interesting because you can modify its properties, including its name, and you can modify its contents. The `File` class has the following properties and methods:

PROPERTY	DESCRIPTION
Author	The user who created the file
CheckedOutByUser	The user who has the file checked out
CustomizedPageStatus	Whether the page has been customized or not
Level	Whether the file is checked out, draft, or published
MajorVersion	The major version of the file
MinorVersion	The minor version of the file
ModifiedBy	The user who last modified the file
Name	The name of the file
ServerRelativeUrl	The URL of the file relative to the server name
Title	The display name of the file
Versions	The previous versions of the file

METHOD	DESCRIPTION
CheckIn	Checks in the file.
CheckOut	Checks out the file so nobody else can modify it.
CopyTo	Copies the file to another location.
DeleteObject	Deletes the file *permanently*.
GetLimitedWebPartManager	Returns a `LimitedWebPartManager` object that you use to manipulate the web parts on a web part page.
MoveTo	Moves a file.
OpenBinaryDirect	Gets the contents of the file itself.
Publish	Publishes the file for approval.
Recycle	Sends the file to the Recycle Bin.

continues

(continued)

METHOD	DESCRIPTION
SaveBinary	Updates the contents of an existing file.
UndoCheckOut	Reverses a checkout and any pending file changes.
UnPublish	If the file is submitted for approval, this method un-submits the file. Otherwise, this method rolls back to the previous major version of the file.

To add a file to a folder, you create a `FileCreationInformation` object and configure its properties. Afterwards, you call the `Add` method on the `Files` property for a `Folder` object passing in the `FileCreationInformation` object. The following code snippet shows this in action:

```
foreach (System.IO.FileInfo file in files) {
  using (System.IO.FileStream fs = file.OpenRead()) {
    byte[] b = new byte[fs.Length];
    fs.Read(b, 0, (int)fs.Length);
    fs.Close();

    FileCreationInformation info = new FileCreationInformation();
    info.Content = b;
    info.Overwrite = false;
    info.Url = file.Name;

    folder.Files.Add(info);
  }
}

context.ExecuteQueryAsync(OnUploadedSuccess, OnFailure);
```

In the snippet, a `foreach` loop is used to iterate a list of `FileInfo` objects that represent files on a workstation. Inside the loop, the `OpenRead` method is called on the `FileInfo` object to get a `FileStream` object and load the file's contents into a byte array. Next, the `FileCreationInformation` object is created and populated with the file's name and contents. The `FileCreationInformation` object is also configured to not override an existing file. Finally, the `FileCreationInformation` object is added to the `Folder` object's `Files` property via the `Add` method. Like everything else in this chapter, you still must call the `ExecuteQueryAsync` method for SharePoint to process any of these operations.

To modify a file, you loop through the `Files` property on a folder or, more commonly, call the `GetFileByServerRelativeUrl` method on the `Web` class, passing in the server relative URL of the file. With the `File` object, you can rename it using the `Name` property, read its contents using the `OpenBinaryDirect` method, or update its contents using the `SaveBinary` method. Afterwards, call the `Update` method to save your changes. With the `File` and `Folder` classes, you can create a tree displaying the content and structure of your site as shown in the following activity.

> **WARNING** *Calling the* Update *method on a* File *object is the same as clicking the Save button in SharePoint Designer when a file is opened in Advanced mode. This causes the file to become customized. For updating files in a document library, this is normal behavior. But using this method to update ASPX or master pages can negatively impact performance, especially on sites with heavy usage.*

TRY IT OUT **Manage Files and Folders**

In this activity, you create a Silverlight control that you can use to display the virtual file system of the SharePoint site and drag and drop files into any folder in the site.

1. Open Visual Studio 2010 from your Start menu.

2. Select File ➪ New ➪ Project from the menu bar.

3. Choose Silverlight from the list of templates and select Silverlight Application from the list of applications.

4. Enter a name for your project and click the OK button.

5. In the New Silverlight Application dialog, uncheck the "Host the Silverlight application in a new Web site" checkbox, ensure that Silverlight 4 is selected in the drop-down list, and click the OK button.

6. When the project is loaded, the MainPage.xaml file should automatically open. If it does not open, double-click the file in the Solution Explorer pane.

7. Right-click the References folder in the Solution Explorer pane and choose Add Reference. The Add Reference dialog appears.

8. Click the Browse button and navigate to the location of the Microsoft.SharePoint.Client .Silverlight.dll and Microsoft.SharePoint.Client.Silverlight.Runtime.dll files.

9. Click the Open button to return to the Add Reference dialog.

10. Click the Add button to add the references to the project.

11. In MainPage.xaml, select the UserControl tag and set its width to 700, then click the Events button in the Properties window, and double-click the Loaded event.

12. Select the Grid control and click the Ellipsis button next to ColumnDefinitions in the Properties pane.

13. When the Collection Editor dialog appears, add three column definitions with the following widths:

➤ 35*

➤ 10

➤ 65*

14. Click the OK button to save the column definitions.

15. Add a StackPanel to the Grid control. In the text editor, remove any attributes on the newly added `StackPanel` tag.

16. Add a TreeView to the StackPanel control and set its Height to 270. In the text editor, remove any other attributes on the newly added `TreeView` tag.

17. Insert the following code just after the TreeView control:

```
<StackPanel Orientation="Horizontal" Margin="0,4,0,0">
  <TextBox Height="23" Name="nameTextBox" Width="160" />
  <Button Content="Add Folder" Height="23" Name="addFolderButton" Width="75"
    Margin="4,0,0,0" />
</StackPanel>
```

18. With the addFolderButton selected, click the Events button in the Properties window and double-click the `Click` event.

19. Add a GridSplitter to the Grid control and configure the following properties and remove any other properties:

PROPERTY	VALUE
Width	10
Grid.Column	1

20. Add a StackPanel to the Grid control and set its `Grid.Column` property to 2 and remove any other properties.

21. Inside the recently added StackPanel control, insert the following code:

```
<sdk:DataGrid Name="dataGrid1" AutoGenerateColumns="False" AllowDrop="True"
  Drop="dataGrid1_Drop" Height="270">
  <sdk:DataGrid.Columns>
    <sdk:DataGridTextColumn Header="Title" Binding="{Binding Title}" />
    <sdk:DataGridTextColumn Header="Name" Binding="{Binding Name}" />
  </sdk:DataGrid.Columns>
</sdk:DataGrid>
<StackPanel Orientation="Horizontal" Margin="0,4,0,0">
  <Button Content="Delete Folder" Height="23" Name="deleteFolderButton"
    Width="75" />
  <Button Content="Delete File" Height="23" Name="deleteFileButton"
    Width="75" Margin="4,0,0,0" />
</StackPanel>
```

22. Double-click each of the deleteFolderButton and deleteFileButton controls to add event handlers for their `Click` events.

23. Compare your MainPage control with Figure 14-13 and make any adjustments.

24. In the `MainPage.xaml.cs` file, add the following `using` statement at the top of the file:

```
using Microsoft.SharePoint.Client;
```

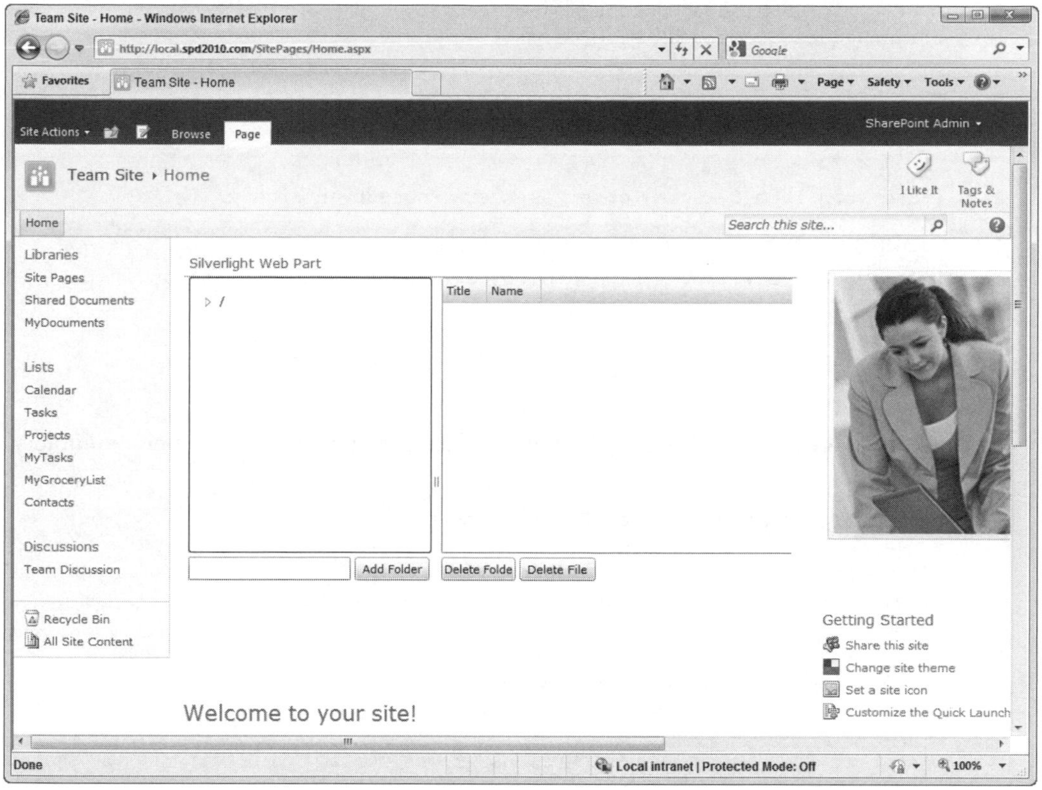

FIGURE 14-13

25. Add the following fields inside the `MainPage` class:

```
private TreeViewItem lastExpanded;
private TreeViewItem lastSelected;
```

26. Add the following methods inside the `MainPage` class:

```
private void AddFolderToTree(Folder folder, ItemCollection parentCollection) {
}

private void AddLoadingNode(TreeViewItem parent) {
}

private void OnFailure(object sender, ClientRequestFailedEventArgs e) {
}

private void OnFileSuccess(object sender, ClientRequestSucceededEventArgs e) {
}

private void OnFolderSuccess(object sender,
  ClientRequestSucceededEventArgs e) {
}
```

```
        private void OnUploadedSuccess(object sender,
          ClientRequestSucceededEventArgs e) {
        }

        private void RefreshFiles(TreeViewItem item) {
        }

        private void item_Selected(object sender, RoutedEventArgs e) {
        }

        private void treeViewItem_Expanded(object sender, RoutedEventArgs e) {
        }

        private void dataGrid1_Drop(object sender, DragEventArgs e) {
        }
```

27. Inside the `addFolderButton_Click` method, insert the following code to add a new subfolder to the selected folder:

```
        ClientContext context = ClientContext.Current;

        if (treeView1.SelectedItem != null) {
          TreeViewItem item = (TreeViewItem)treeView1.SelectedItem;
          Folder folder = (Folder)item.Tag;

          if (!string.IsNullOrEmpty(nameTextBox.Text)) {
            folder.Folders.Add(nameTextBox.Text);

            context.ExecuteQueryAsync(OnFolderSuccess, OnFailure);
          }
        }
```

28. Inside the `AddFolderToTree` method, insert the following code to add folders to the TreeView control:

```
        TreeViewItem item = new TreeViewItem();
        item.Header = folder.Name;
        item.Tag = folder;
        item.Expanded += new RoutedEventHandler(treeViewItem_Expanded);
        item.Selected += new RoutedEventHandler(item_Selected);

        item.Dispatcher.BeginInvoke(delegate() {
          AddLoadingNode(item);

          lastExpanded.Items.Add(item);
        });
```

29. In the `AddLoadingNode` method, insert the following code to add a dummy node to unexpanded folders so that the expand icon appears in case the folder has subfolders:

```
        TreeViewItem loading = new TreeViewItem();
        loading.Header = "Loading...";
        parent.Items.Add(loading);
```

30. In the `dataGrid1_Drop` method, insert the following code to upload any files that are dropped on the DataGrid control to the selected folder:

```
ClientContext context = ClientContext.Current;

if (treeView1.SelectedItem != null) {
  TreeViewItem item = (TreeViewItem)treeView1.SelectedItem;
  Folder folder = (Folder)item.Tag;

  if (e.Data != null && e.Data.GetDataPresent(DataFormats.FileDrop)) {
    System.IO.FileInfo[] files = e.Data.GetData(DataFormats.FileDrop) as
System.IO.FileInfo[];

    if (files != null) {
      foreach (System.IO.FileInfo file in files) {
        using (System.IO.FileStream fs = file.OpenRead()) {
          byte[] b = new byte[fs.Length];
          fs.Read(b, 0, (int)fs.Length);
          fs.Close();

          FileCreationInformation info =
            new FileCreationInformation();
          info.Content = b;
          info.Overwrite = false;
          info.Url = file.Name;

          folder.Files.Add(info);
        }
      }

      context.ExecuteQueryAsync(OnUploadedSuccess, OnFailure);
    }
  }
}
```

31. In the `deleteFileButton_Click` method, insert the following code to delete the selected file in the DataGrid control:

```
ClientContext context = ClientContext.Current;

if (dataGrid1.SelectedItem is File) {
  File file = (File)dataGrid1.SelectedItem;

  file.DeleteObject();
  context.ExecuteQueryAsync(OnFolderSuccess, OnFailure);
}
```

32. In the `deleteFolderButton_Click` method, insert the following code to delete the selected folder in the TreeView control:

```
ClientContext context = ClientContext.Current;

if (treeView1.SelectedItem != null) {
  TreeViewItem item = (TreeViewItem)treeView1.SelectedItem;
  Folder folder = (Folder)item.Tag;

  folder.DeleteObject();
  context.ExecuteQueryAsync(OnFolderSuccess, OnFailure);
}
```

33. In the `item_Selected` method, insert the following code to call the `RefreshFiles` method when a folder is selected in the TreeView control:

```
TreeViewItem item = (TreeViewItem)sender;

RefreshFiles(item);
```

34. In the `OnFailure` method, insert the following code to display any error messages from the call to SharePoint:

```
this.Dispatcher.BeginInvoke(delegate() {
  MessageBox.Show(e.Message);
});
```

35. In the `OnFileSuccess` method, insert the following code to bind the list of files for the selected folder to the DataGrid control:

```
lastSelected.Dispatcher.BeginInvoke(delegate() {
  Folder folder = (Folder)lastSelected.Tag;

  dataGrid1.ItemsSource = folder.Files;
});
```

36. In the `OnFolderSuccess` method, insert the following code to add the subfolders for the expanded folder to the TreeView control:

```
lastExpanded.Dispatcher.BeginInvoke(delegate() {
  Folder folder = (Folder)lastExpanded.Tag;

  lastExpanded.Items.Clear();

  var results = from f in folder.Folders.ToArray()
        orderby f.Name
        select f;

  foreach (Folder child in results) {
    AddFolderToTree(child, lastExpanded.Items);
  }
});
```

37. In the `OnUploadedSuccess` method, insert the following code to refresh the files in the DataGrid control after a file has been uploaded to the folder:

```
treeView1.Dispatcher.BeginInvoke(delegate() {
  if (treeView1.SelectedItem != null) {
    RefreshFiles((TreeViewItem)treeView1.SelectedItem);
  }
});
```

38. In the `RefreshFiles` method, insert the following code to request the files in the selected folder from SharePoint:

```
ClientContext context = ClientContext.Current;

Folder folder = (Folder)item.Tag;

lastSelected = item;

dataGrid1.ItemsSource = null;
```

```
context.Load(folder.Files);
context.ExecuteQueryAsync(OnFileSuccess, OnFailure);
```

39. In the `treeViewItem_Expanded` method, insert the following code to request the subfolders for the expanded folder in the TreeView control:

```
TreeViewItem item = (TreeViewItem)sender;

if (item.Items.Count > 0 && (item.Items[0] as TreeViewItem).Tag == null) {
  ClientContext context = ClientContext.Current;

  Folder folder = (Folder)item.Tag;

  lastExpanded = item;

  context.Load(folder.Folders);
  context.ExecuteQueryAsync(OnFolderSuccess, OnFailure);
}
```

40. In the `UserControl_Loaded` method, insert the following code to add the root node to the TreeView control and request the subfolders of the site's root folder from SharePoint:

```
ClientContext context = ClientContext.Current;

TreeViewItem root = new TreeViewItem();
root.Header = "/";
root.Tag = context.Web.RootFolder;
root.Expanded += new RoutedEventHandler(treeViewItem_Expanded);
root.Selected += new RoutedEventHandler(item_Selected);

AddLoadingNode(root);

treeView1.Items.Add(root);
```

41. Compile the project by selecting Build ➪ Build Solution from the menu bar.

42. Check the Error List pane for any errors and fix them before continuing.

43. Click the Show All Files button in the Solution Explorer pane.

44. In the Solution Explorer pane, expand the `Bin` and `Debug` folders and select the XAP file.

45. Double-click the value of the Full Path property in the Properties pane to select it and press Ctrl+C to copy the path to the clipboard.

46. Navigate your browser to a document library in your SharePoint site.

47. Select Upload Document from the Documents tab on the ribbon.

48. In the Upload Document dialog, click the Browse button.

49. Paste the file path from Step 45 and click Open.

50. Click the OK button to close the Upload Document dialog and upload the XAP file to SharePoint.

51. When the document library is updated with your file, right-click its name and choose Copy Hyperlink to copy the URL of your XAP file.

52. Navigate your browser to a web part page in your site.

53. Select Edit Page from the Site Actions menu.

54. Select Web Part from the Insert tab on the ribbon.

55. Choose Forms from the Categories list and select HTML Form Web Part from the Web Parts list.

56. Edit the web part's properties and click the Source Editor button.

57. In the Text Editor dialog, insert the following code, replacing **XAPFileUrl** with the URL from Step 51 and **SiteUrl** with the absolute URL to the site:

```
<div id="SilverlightObjectDiv" style="display:block">
<object id="SilverlightObjectTag" data="data:application/x-silverlight-2,"
type="application/x-silverlight-2" style="display:block" height="400px"
width="600px" class="ms-dlgDisable">
<param name="source" value="XAPFileUrl"/>
<param name="background" value="white" />
<param name="initParams" value="MS.SP.url=SiteUrl" />
<param name="windowless" value="false" />

<a href="http://go.microsoft.com/fwlink/?LinkID=149156&v=3.0.40624.0"
  style="text-decoration: none;">
<img src="http://go.microsoft.com/fwlink/?LinkId=108181"
  alt="Get Microsoft Silverlight" style="border-style: none"/>
</a>

</object>
<iframe id="_sl_historyFrame"
  style='visibility:hidden;height:0;width:0;border:0px;display:block'>
</iframe>
</div>
```

58. Select the location to put the web part from the "Add Web Part to" drop-down list and click the Add button.

59. In the Silverlight Web Part dialog, paste the URL from Step 51 and click the OK button.

60. Configure the web part properties as follows:

Height	400
Width	600

61. Select Save & Close from the Page tab on the ribbon.

62. Refresh the page in your browser.

63. Expand the folders in the TreeView control to show the subfolders loading dynamically.

64. Select some of the folders in the TreeView control and watch the files appear in the DataGrid control.

65. Select one of the folders in the TreeView control, enter the name for a folder in the textbox under the TreeView control, and click the Add Folder button.

66. Select the newly created folder.

67. Drag some files from your workstation and drop them on top of the DataGrid control.

68. Watch the DataGrid refresh with the addition of your files.

69. Select the root folder for a document library and repeat Step 67.

70. Open a new browser window and navigate to the document library from Step 69.

71. Notice that the files are in the document library.

72. Select each of the files you uploaded in the DataGrid control and click the Delete File button.

73. Watch the files disappear from the DataGrid control and from the document library.

74. Select the folder you created in Step 65 and click the Delete Folder button.

How It Works

When the Silverlight control loads, the subfolders of the root folder of the website are requested from SharePoint and added to the TreeView control. When you expand a folder in the TreeView control, its subfolders are requested from SharePoint if they have not already been loaded. When you select a folder in the TreeView control, its files are requested from SharePoint and bound to the DataGrid control. Clicking the Add Folder button adds a new folder to the selected folder in the TreeView control using the value entered into the textbox and the name of the folder. Dragging and dropping files on the DataGrid control causes Silverlight to read the contents of those files and add them to the selected folder in the TreeView control. Finally, the Delete Folder and Delete File buttons delete the selected folder and file, respectively.

> **NOTE** If you are wondering why you used the HTML Form Web Part instead of the Silverlight Web Part, here is the reason: the Silverlight Web Part configures the Silverlight object tag to run in windowless mode. This allows the web part menu to appear on top of the Silverlight control when the menu is displayed. If the Silverlight object tag were not running in windowless mode, the web part menu would appear behind the Silverlight control the same way an HTML element does when it overlaps space with a listbox or drop-down list. One of the disadvantages of running in windowless mode is that drag-and-drop events are not supported. You still can use the Silverlight Web Part to host the control from this activity, and all the functionality will still work except for dragging and dropping files.

MANAGING NAVIGATION

You can also use the object model to modify the Quick Launch and Top Navigation bars in your site. You access the Quick Launch and Top Navigation bars via the following code snippet:

```
ClientContext context = ClientContext.Current;
Web site = context.Web;
```

```
context.Load(site.Navigation.QuickLaunch);
context.Load(site.Navigation.TopNavigationBar);

context.ExecuteQueryAsync(OnSuccess, OnFailure);
```

When the OnSuccess method is called, the site.Navigation.QuickLaunch and site.Navigation .TopNavigationBar properties are populated with the NavigationNode objects that correspond to the clickable items on both bars. The NavigationNode object has the following properties and methods:

PROPERTY	DESCRIPTION
Title	The text displayed for the navigation node
Url	The URL for the navigation node's hyperlink
Children	The list of child navigation nodes

METHOD	DESCRIPTION
DeleteObject	Deletes the navigation node and its children
Update	Saves your changes to the navigation node

When you start using the Client Object Model to modify these bars, determining where to put the nodes to make them appear where you want on the screen may be a little difficult. Take a look at Figure 14-14.

In the figure, the Quick Launch bar is organized with Libraries, Lists, and Discussions at the top levels and the individual lists and libraries underneath the appropriate top level. If you look at the tree control for the Quick Launch, you will notice that it matches the structure of the Quick Launch bar except that it does not display any nodes lower than two levels deep. The node named Level3 does not appear at all under Site Pages in the Quick Launch bar.

If you look at the Top Navigation bar, you see these four tabs:

➤   Home

➤   Level2(Home)

➤   Level1

➤   Level2

But in the tree control for the Top Navigation bar, you see only the Home and Level1 nodes at the top level. This means that all nodes at levels 1 and 2 will appear as tabs on the Top Navigation bar. Nodes at level 3 will appear as menu items under their parent node's tab. Nodes at levels 4 and below will not appear at all.

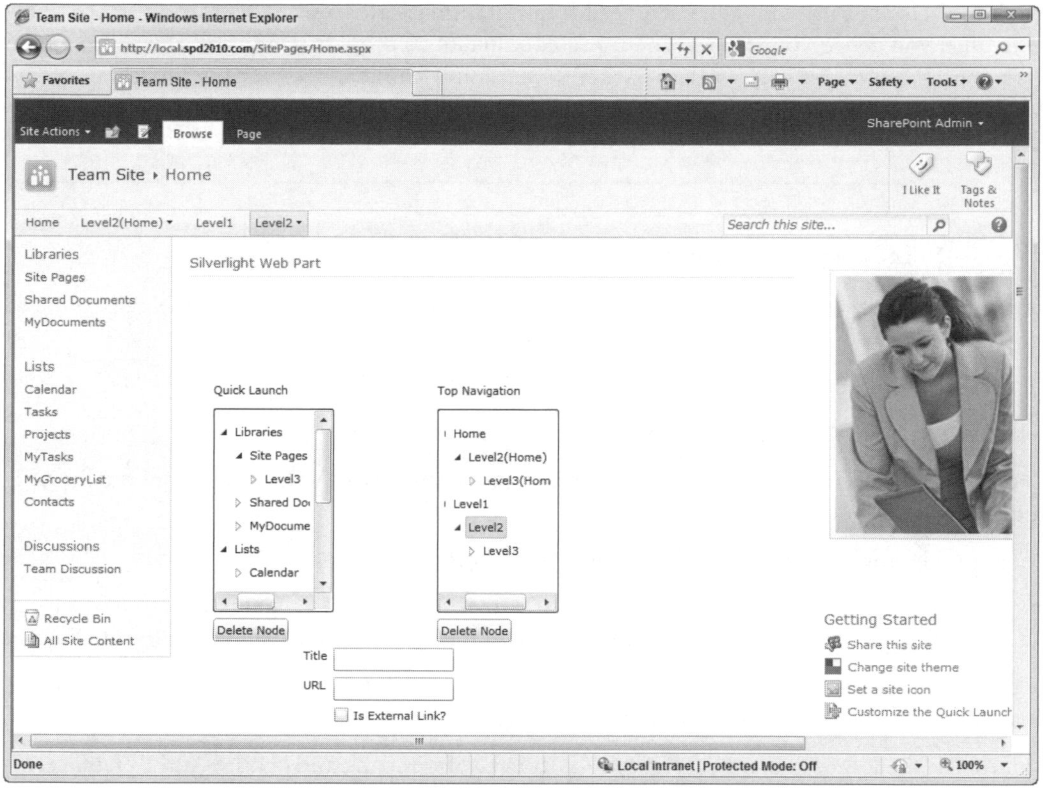

FIGURE 14-14

To create a navigation node, you must create a NavigationNodeCreationInformation object. The NavigationNodeCreationInformation class has the same properties as the NavigationNode, including the following additional properties:

NAME	DESCRIPTION
IsExternal	If true, the Url property points to a file outside the site. If false, the Url is internal to the site. If the file does not exist and IsExternal is set to false, SharePoint will return an error message.
PreviousNode	Specifies the node after which the new node should be inserted.
AsLastNode	If you set this to true, the node is added at the end of the list. Otherwise, it is added at the beginning of the list if PreviousNode is not specified.

After you have configured the NavigationNodeCreationInformation object, you call the Add method on the Children property of a NavigationNode object or the Add method on the Navigation.QuickLaunch or Navigation.TopNavigation properties of the Web object.

To update a `NavigationNode`, you will need to programmatically traverse the `NavigationNode` objects until you get to your target. Then, you can update its properties and call the `Update` method to save your changes. To delete a `NavigationNode`, simply call its `DeleteObject` method. Now that you have been introduced to the `Navigation` and `NavigationNode` classes, you can modify your site's navigation by following the steps in the next activity.

TRY IT OUT   **Manage Navigation**

In this activity, you create a Silverlight control to modify the Quick Launch and Top Navigation bars of your SharePoint site.

1. Open Visual Studio 2010 from your Start menu.

2. Select File ➪ New ➪ Project from the menu bar.

3. Choose Silverlight from the list of templates and select Silverlight Application from the list of applications.

4. Enter a name for your project and click the OK button.

5. In the New Silverlight Application dialog, uncheck the "Host the Silverlight application in a new Web site" checkbox, ensure that Silverlight 4 is selected in the drop-down list, and click the OK button.

6. When the project is loaded, the `MainPage.xaml` file should automatically open. If it does not open, double-click the file in the Solution Explorer pane.

7. Right-click the `References` folder in the Solution Explorer pane and choose Add Reference. The Add Reference dialog appears.

8. Click the Browse button and navigate to the location of the `Microsoft.SharePoint.Client .Silverlight.dll` and `Microsoft.SharePoint.Client.Silverlight.Runtime.dll` files.

9. Click the Open button to return to the Add Reference dialog.

10. Click the Add button to add the references to the project.

11. In `MainPage.xaml`, set the following property values on the `UserControl` tag:

PROPERTY	VALUE
d:DesignHeight	450
d:DesignWidth	400

12. With the UserControl selected, click the Events button in the Properties window and double-click the `Loaded` event.

13. In `MainPage.xaml`, set the following property values on the `Grid` tag:

PROPERTY	VALUE
Width	400
Height	450

14. Add a TreeView control to the Grid control and set the following properties:

PROPERTY	VALUE
Height	200
HorizontalAlignment	Left
Margin	23,54,0,0
Name	quickLaunchTreeView
VerticalAlignment	Top
Width	120

15. Add another TreeView control to the Grid control and set the following properties:

PROPERTY	VALUE
Height	200
HorizontalAlignment	Left
Margin	246,54,0,0
Name	topNavTreeView
VerticalAlignment	Top
Width	120

16. Add a Label to the Grid control and set the following properties:

PROPERTY	VALUE
Height	28
HorizontalAlignment	Left
Margin	23,28,0,0
VerticalAlignment	Top
Width	120
Content	Quick Launch

17. Add another Label to the Grid control and set the following properties:

PROPERTY	VALUE
Height	28
HorizontalAlignment	Left

continues

(continued)

PROPERTY	VALUE
Margin	246,28,0,0
Name	label2
VerticalAlignment	Top
Width	120
Content	Top Navigation

18. Add a Button to the Grid control and set the following properties:

PROPERTY	VALUE
Content	Delete Node
Height	23
HorizontalAlignment	Left
Margin	23,260,0,0
Name	deleteQuickLaunchButton
VerticalAlignment	Top
Width	75

19. Add another Button to the Grid control and set the following properties:

PROPERTY	VALUE
Content	Delete Node
Height	23
HorizontalAlignment	Left
Margin	246,260,0,0
Name	deleteTopNavButton
VerticalAlignment	Top
Width	75

20. Add another Button to the Grid control and set the following properties:

PROPERTY	VALUE
Content	Add Quick Launch
Height	23

PROPERTY	VALUE
HorizontalAlignment	Left
Margin	23,390,0,0
Name	addQuickLaunchButton
VerticalAlignment	Top
Width	120

21. Add another Button to the Grid control and set the following properties:

PROPERTY	VALUE
Content	Add Top Nav
Height	23
HorizontalAlignment	Left
Margin	246,390,0,0
Name	addTopNavButton
VerticalAlignment	Top
Width	120

22. Add another Label to the Grid control and set the following properties:

PROPERTY	VALUE
Height	28
HorizontalAlignment	Left
Margin	113,289,0,0
Name	label3
VerticalAlignment	Top
Content	Title

23. Add another Label to the Grid control and set the following properties:

PROPERTY	VALUE
Content	URL
Height	28
HorizontalAlignment	Left

continues

(continued)

PROPERTY	VALUE
Margin	113,318,0,0
Name	label4
VerticalAlignment	Top

24. Add a TextBox to the Grid control and set the following properties:

PROPERTY	VALUE
Height	23
HorizontalAlignment	Left
Margin	143,289,0,0
Name	titleTextBox
VerticalAlignment	Top
Width	120

25. Add another TextBox to the Grid control and set the following properties:

PROPERTY	VALUE
Height	23
HorizontalAlignment	Left
Margin	143,318,0,0
Name	urlTextBox
VerticalAlignment	Top
Width	120

26. Add a checkbox to the Grid control and set the following properties:

PROPERTY	VALUE
Content	Is External Link?
Height	16
HorizontalAlignment	Left
Margin	143,347,0,0
Name	isExternalLinkCheckBox
VerticalAlignment	Top

27. Double-click each of the buttons to generate event handlers for their `Click` events.

28. Compare your MainPage control with Figure 14-15 and make any necessary modifications.

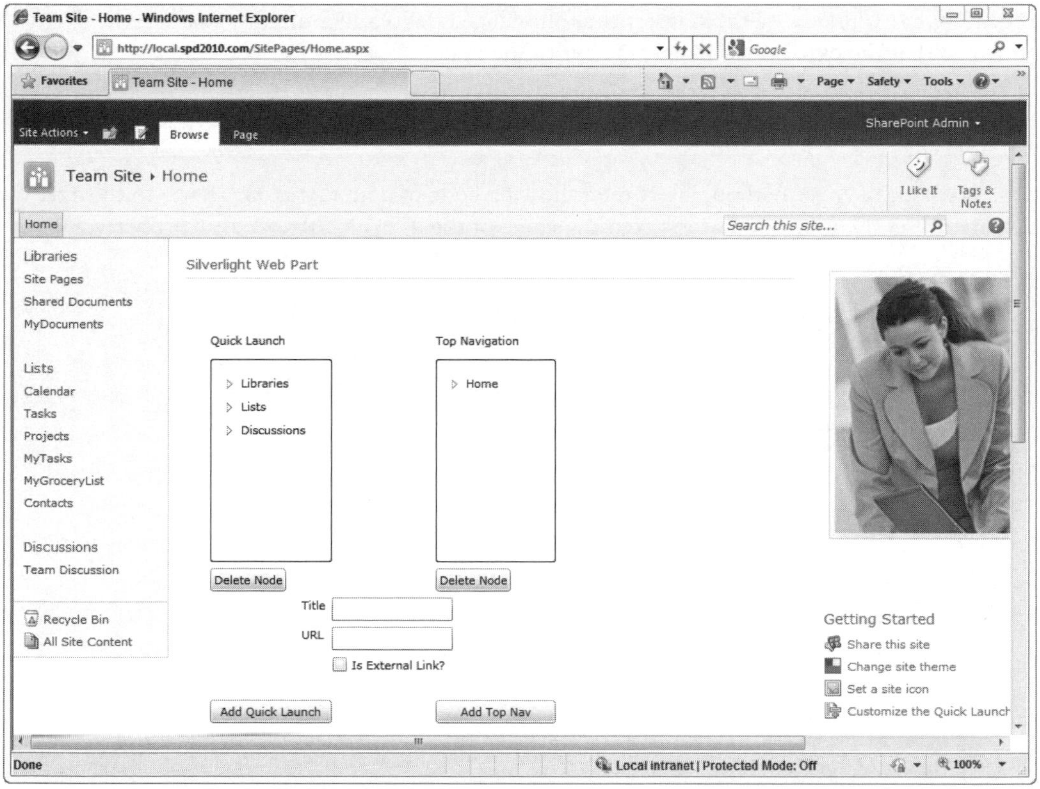

FIGURE 14-15

29. In the `MainPage.xaml.cs` file, add the following `using` statement to the top of the page:

```
using Microsoft.SharePoint.Client;
```

30. Add the following field to the `MainPage` class:

```
private TreeViewItem lastExpanded;
```

31. Insert the following methods inside the `MainPage` class:

```
void AddLoadingNode(TreeViewItem parent) {
}

void AddNodeToTree(NavigationNode node, ItemCollection parentCollection) {
}

void OnFailure(object sender, ClientRequestFailedEventArgs e) {
}

void OnNodeSuccess(object sender, ClientRequestSucceededEventArgs e) {
}
```

```
void OnSuccess(object sender, ClientRequestSucceededEventArgs e) {
}

void treeViewItem_Expanded(object sender, RoutedEventArgs e) {
}
```

32. In the `AddLoadingNode` method, insert the following code to add a dummy node to the TreeView control so that the expand icon appears next to the node:

```
TreeViewItem loading = new TreeViewItem();
loading.Header = "Loading...";
parent.Items.Add(loading);
```

33. In the `AddNodeToTree` method, insert the following code to add a `NavigateNode` to the TreeView control and set the new node's tooltip to the value of the `NavigateNode`'s `Url` property:

```
TreeViewItem item = new TreeViewItem();
item.Header = node.Title;
item.Tag = node;
ToolTipService.SetToolTip(item, "Url = " + node.Url);
item.Expanded += new RoutedEventHandler(treeViewItem_Expanded);

item.Dispatcher.BeginInvoke(delegate() {
  AddLoadingNode(item);

  parentCollection.Add(item);
});
```

34. In the `addQuickLaunchButton_Click` method, insert the following code to add a `NavigationNode` to the selected node in the TreeView control:

```
ClientContext context = ClientContext.Current;
Web site = context.Web;

if (!string.IsNullOrEmpty(titleTextBox.Text)) {
  NavigationNodeCollection nodes;

  if (quickLaunchTreeView.SelectedItem == null) {
    nodes = site.Navigation.QuickLaunch;
  } else {
    TreeViewItem item = (TreeViewItem)quickLaunchTreeView.SelectedItem;
    NavigationNode parentNode = (NavigationNode)item.Tag;
    nodes = parentNode.Children;
  }

  NavigationNodeCreationInformation info =
    new NavigationNodeCreationInformation();
  info.Title = titleTextBox.Text;
  info.Url = urlTextBox.Text;
  info.AsLastNode = true;
  if (isExternalLinkCheckBox.IsChecked.HasValue
&& isExternalLinkCheckBox.IsChecked.Value) {
    info.IsExternal = true;
  } else {
    info.IsExternal = false;
  }

  nodes.Add(info);
```

```
context.ExecuteQueryAsync(OnSuccess, OnFailure);
}
```

35. In the `addTopNavButton_Click` method, insert the following code to add a `NavigationNode` to the selected node in the TreeView control:

```
ClientContext context = ClientContext.Current;
Web site = context.Web;

if (!string.IsNullOrEmpty(titleTextBox.Text)) {
  NavigationNodeCollection nodes;

  if (topNavTreeView.SelectedItem == null) {
    nodes = site.Navigation.TopNavigationBar;
  } else {
    TreeViewItem item = (TreeViewItem)topNavTreeView.SelectedItem;
    NavigationNode parentNode = (NavigationNode)item.Tag;
    nodes = parentNode.Children;
  }

  NavigationNodeCreationInformation info =
    new NavigationNodeCreationInformation();
  info.Title = titleTextBox.Text;
  info.Url = urlTextBox.Text;
  info.AsLastNode = true;
  if (isExternalLinkCheckBox.IsChecked.HasValue
&& isExternalLinkCheckBox.IsChecked.Value) {
    info.IsExternal = true;
  } else {
    info.IsExternal = false;
  }

  nodes.Add(info);

  context.ExecuteQueryAsync(OnSuccess, OnFailure);
}
```

36. In the `deleteQuickLaunchButton_Click` method, insert the following code to delete the selected node and its children from the Quick Launch bar:

```
ClientContext context = ClientContext.Current;

if (quickLaunchTreeView.SelectedItem != null) {
  TreeViewItem item = (TreeViewItem)quickLaunchTreeView.SelectedItem;
  NavigationNode node = (NavigationNode)item.Tag;

  node.DeleteObject();

  context.ExecuteQueryAsync(OnSuccess, OnFailure);
}
```

37. In the `deleteTopNavButton_Click` method, insert the following code to delete the selected node and its children from the Top Navigation bar:

```
ClientContext context = ClientContext.Current;

if (topNavTreeView.SelectedItem != null) {
  TreeViewItem item = (TreeViewItem)topNavTreeView.SelectedItem;
```

```
    NavigationNode node = (NavigationNode)item.Tag;

    node.DeleteObject();

    context.ExecuteQueryAsync(OnSuccess, OnFailure);
}
```

38. In the `OnFailure` method, insert the following code to display any error messages from the call to SharePoint:

```
this.Dispatcher.BeginInvoke(delegate() {
  MessageBox.Show(e.Message);
});
```

39. In the `OnNodeSuccess` method, insert the following code to populate the expanded node with its children:

```
lastExpanded.Dispatcher.BeginInvoke(delegate() {
  NavigationNode node = (NavigationNode)lastExpanded.Tag;

  lastExpanded.Items.Clear();

  foreach (NavigationNode child in node.Children) {
    AddNodeToTree(child, lastExpanded.Items);
  }
});
```

40. In the `OnSuccess` method, insert the following code to populate the TreeViews with the Quick Launch bar and Top Navigation bar `NavigationNode` objects:

```
ClientContext context = ClientContext.Current;
Web site = context.Web;

quickLaunchTreeView.Dispatcher.BeginInvoke(delegate() {
  quickLaunchTreeView.Items.Clear();

  foreach (NavigationNode node in site.Navigation.QuickLaunch) {
    AddNodeToTree(node, quickLaunchTreeView.Items);
  }
});

topNavTreeView.Dispatcher.BeginInvoke(delegate() {
  topNavTreeView.Items.Clear();

  foreach (NavigationNode node in site.Navigation.TopNavigationBar) {
    AddNodeToTree(node, topNavTreeView.Items);
  }
});
```

41. In the `treeViewItem_Expanded` method, insert the following code to request the children of the node that is expanded:

```
TreeViewItem item = (TreeViewItem)sender;

if (item.Items.Count > 0 && (item.Items[0] as TreeViewItem).Tag == null) {
  ClientContext context = ClientContext.Current;

  NavigationNode node = (NavigationNode)item.Tag;
```

```
            lastExpanded = item;

            context.Load(node.Children);
            context.ExecuteQueryAsync(OnNodeSuccess, OnFailure);
        }
```

42. In the `UserControl_Loaded` method, insert the following code to request the Quick Launch and Top Navigation bars from SharePoint:

```
            ClientContext context = ClientContext.Current;
            Web site = context.Web;

            context.Load(site.Navigation.QuickLaunch);
            context.Load(site.Navigation.TopNavigationBar);

            context.ExecuteQueryAsync(OnSuccess, OnFailure);
```

43. Compile the project by selecting Build ⇨ Build Solution from the menu bar.

44. Check the Error List pane for any errors and fix them before continuing.

45. Click the Show All Files button in the Solution Explorer pane.

46. In the Solution Explorer pane, expand the `Bin` and `Debug` folders and select the XAP file.

47. Double-click the value of the Full Path property in the Properties pane to select it and press Ctrl+C to copy the path to the clipboard.

48. Navigate your browser to a document library in your SharePoint site.

49. Select Upload Document from the Documents tab on the ribbon.

50. In the Upload Document dialog, click the Browse button.

51. Paste the file path from Step 47 and click Open.

52. Click the OK button to close the Upload Document dialog and upload the XAP file to SharePoint.

53. When the document library is updated with your file, right-click its name and choose Copy Hyperlink to copy the URL of your XAP file.

54. Navigate your browser to a web part page in your site.

55. Select Edit Page from the Site Actions menu to place the page in Edit mode.

56. Select Web Part from the Insert tab on the ribbon.

57. Choose Media and Content from the Categories list and select Silverlight Web Part from the Web Parts list.

58. Select the location to put the web part from the "Add Web Part to" drop-down list and click the Add button.

59. In the Silverlight Web Part dialog, paste the URL from Step 53 and click the OK button.

60. Configure the web part properties as follows:

Height	500
Width	400

61. Select Save & Close from the Page tab on the ribbon.

62. Refresh the page in your browser.

63. Enter the following values in the Silverlight control and click the Add Quick Launch button:

Title	Level 1
URL	`http://www.microsoft.com`
Is External Link?	Checked

64. Select the newly created node, enter the following values in the Silverlight control, and click the Add Quick Launch button:

Title	Level 2
URL	`http://www.wrox.com`
Is External Link?	Checked

65. Refresh the page to see the Quick Launch bar updated with your changes.

66. Select the Level 1 node and click the Delete Node button.

67. Refresh the page to see the Quick Launch bar updated with your changes.

68. Select the Home node, enter the following values in the Silverlight control, and click the Add Top Nav button. (Note that URL should be left blank.):

Title	Useful Sites
URL	
Is External Link?	Unchecked

69. Select the newly created node, enter the following values in the Silverlight control, and click the Add Top Nav button:

Title	End User SharePoint
URL	`http://www.endusersharepoint.com`
Is External Link?	Checked

70. Select the newly created node, enter the following values in the Silverlight control, and click the Add Top Nav button:

Title	Woody's Blog
URL	`http://www.thesanitypoint.com`
Is External Link?	Checked

71. Select the newly created node, enter the following values in the Silverlight control, and click the Add Top Nav button:

Title	Asif's Blog
URL	`http://blog.sharepointelearning.com`
Is External Link?	Checked

72. Refresh the page to see the Top Navigation bar updated with your changes.

73. Select the Useful Sites node and click the Delete Node button.

74. Refresh the page to see the Top Navigation bar updated with your changes.

How It Works

The QuickLaunch and TopNavigation properties are actually `NavigationNodeCollection` objects. That is why you can call the `Add` method on them to add top-level nodes to the Quick Launch and Top Navigation bars. Clicking one of the Add buttons creates a new `NavigationNode` and adds it as a child of the selected node. Clicking one of the Delete Node buttons deletes the selected node. As described earlier, the Quick Launch bar only looks at the first two levels of nodes. The Top Navigation bar creates tabs for the first two levels of nodes and adds menu items for the third level of nodes.

LIMITATIONS

No discussion about any functionality this powerful would be complete without covering its limitations. Whether you are using JavaScript or Silverlight, these are some of the limitations you will face:

➤ Your code can access any site collection as long as it is in the same SharePoint web application as the one where the code is running.

➤ Only Windows, Forms Based, and Anonymous authentication are supported.

➤ If you are using Silverlight and the site uses Forms Based Authentication, you must manually change the authentication mode of the ClientContext class and specify a username and password as shown in the following code snippet:

```
ClientContext context = ClientContext.Current;
context.AuthenticationMode = ClientAuthenticationMode.FormsAuthentication;
clientContext.FormsAuthenticationLoginInfo =
  new FormsAuthenticationLoginInfo("yourusername", "yourpassword");
```

> **NOTE** The username and password are sent in "clear text" and can be viewed by anybody monitoring your server or network traffic. If you must use Silverlight in conjunction with Forms Based Authentication, make sure you secure the site with an SSL certificate to encrypt the traffic between the web server and the user's browser.

➤ If you query an external list using the Client Object Model, you must specify the columns to return in your CAML query and the call to the `Load` method of the `ClientContext` class. Otherwise, you will get the error message "The given key was not present in the dictionary."

➤ If you are using JavaScript with the Client Object Model, you must include the FormDigest control in the master page. By default, this control is already in the site's master pages, but it could be accidently removed or you could create a page that does not use the site's master page.

➤ If you intend to update list items or documents in the site, you may need to re-query the list or library before performing your update. Another user may have updated your list item or document after you queried the list or library but before your code tried to execute an update. If that is the case, you will get an error message stating the item or document has been updated since you last retrieved it.

SUMMARY

In this chapter, you have seen how to use Silverlight to greatly extend the functionality of your SharePoint sites. Practically nothing has been taken off the table in terms of what you are able to do in the Client Object Model versus the Server Object Model. With the Client Object Model, your SharePoint sites no longer have to be used out-of-the-box, even if they are hosted by a third party that does not allow the traditional methods of customization used by SharePoint developers. With the techniques you learned in this chapter, you should be able to increase the ROI value of your SharePoint investment by several orders of magnitude.

A Brief History of SharePoint and SharePoint Designer

This book has thoroughly introduced you to Microsoft SharePoint Designer 2010. Many readers will be satisfied understanding the present state of the product. Others, however, may find a history of this latest in a long line of web design tools from Microsoft useful. In particular, it may help in understanding those "What were they thinking?" moments. This appendix discusses the evolution of SharePoint Designer and Microsoft SharePoint Products and Technologies, and how they influenced each other.

FROM FRONTPAGE TO SHAREPOINT DESIGNER

The year was 1995. Although the Internet had been around for many years, only recently had its Hypertext Transfer Protocol (HTTP) and the associated Hypertext Markup Language (HTML) caught the public eye in the form of the World Wide Web. While the general public was falling in love with the Web through web browsers such as Mosaic, Netscape, and Internet Explorer, many companies were struggling to come up with ways to produce the content this new market was demanding.

One such company was Vermeer Technologies. Vermeer came up with a unique, modular approach to web design that it called FrontPage. It included prebuilt functionality for the server — the FrontPage Server Extensions (FPSE) — and modules for the design client (which it called WebBots). Unlike most web design tools, FrontPage included not only a WYSIWYG (what-you-see-is-what-you-get) editor (the FrontPage Editor), but full site management features for the client as well (the FrontPage Explorer). FrontPage 1.0 had only been on the market for a few months when the announcement came that Vermeer had been purchased by Microsoft, and that the FrontPage system was going to form the basis of Microsoft's web design strategy.

As advanced as it was, FrontPage was not immune to problems. In particular, the FrontPage editing client had a tendency to rewrite a page's code to meet its own specifications, which often resulted in nonfunctional scripts — a trait that most developers did not find endearing. Although each subsequent release of FrontPage was better behaved than its predecessor, the damage to its reputation was done. Ultimately, the name FrontPage had to be retired.

The product that was originally to become FrontPage 2007 lived on, however. In fact, it was reformed (and re-formed) into not one, but two, distinct products — SharePoint Designer 2007 and Expression Web 1.0.

Expression Web was designed primarily to satisfy the web designers who not only had no interest in working with SharePoint, but were among the most vocal critics of FrontPage's flaws. Virtually all support for SharePoint and the legacy FrontPage functionality was removed. In their place, Expression Web was given deep support for designing to web standards, including standards-based ways of doing many of the things FrontPage did with its WebBots.

SharePoint Designer 2007 was effectively a superset of Expression Web 1.0. It gained all the new standards support, as well as retained the ability to work with SharePoint sites and the various FrontPage components.

In the years between the release of SharePoint Designer 2007 and 2010, Expression Web has been updated twice, adding ever more design tools, support for other standards, such as PHP, as well as having deeper integration with the rest of the Expression family. SharePoint Designer's feature set, on the other hand, remained static until the release of SharePoint 2010 (which is thoroughly covered in the rest of this book).

The following table shows the timeline of major milestones from the first release of FrontPage to SharePoint Designer 2010.

DATE	EVENT	DESCRIPTION
Oct-95	Vermeer introduces FrontPage 1.0	First version
Jan-96	Microsoft announces purchase of Vermeer	
Jan-96	Microsoft introduces FrontPage 1.1	Microsoft branding
Dec-96	Microsoft introduces FrontPage 97	Improved features, first MS Office integration
Jun-98	Microsoft introduces FrontPage 98	New features — Navigation, Shared Borders, Themes
Jan-99	Microsoft introduces FrontPage 2000	Unified Explorer and Editor into a single interface
May-01	Microsoft introduces FrontPage 2002 (XP)	Support for SharePoint Team Services
Nov-03	Microsoft introduces FrontPage 2003	Support for Windows SharePoint Services 2.0 and SharePoint Portal Server 2003, improved support for web standards

DATE	EVENT	DESCRIPTION
Nov-06	Microsoft replaces FrontPage with two products — Expression Web 1.0 and SharePoint Designer 2007	Expression Web: Supports web standards, but has no support for SharePoint-based sites

SharePoint Designer: Supports all previous FrontPage features and provides support for Windows SharePoint Services 3.0 and Microsoft Office SharePoint Server 2007 |
| Apr-09 | SharePoint Designer is now free | Microsoft makes SharePoint Designer 2007 available for download at no cost to all comers. |
| May-10 | SharePoint Designer 2010 | Breaking from the past, SharePoint Designer 2010 is dedicated strictly to customizing sites based on SharePoint 2010. It is still free, but all ability to edit non-SharePoint 2010 sites has been removed. |

THE SHAREPOINT FAMILY TREE

Meanwhile, back on the server, the FrontPage Server Extensions (FPSE) were being enhanced until, in the Microsoft Office 2000 releases, a new layer was created over the FPSE called the Office Server Extensions (OSE). The OSE added services for managing discussions and sending email alerts. In addition, file management protocols — including the then-new WebDAV — were added, allowing the Office client applications such as Microsoft Word and Microsoft Excel both to read from and write to websites directly for the first time.

> **NOTE** *Office 97 applications supported reading and writing via the FTP protocol.*

The Years BSP (Before SharePoint)

Many other web server initiatives were taking place at Microsoft during this time frame. Two of them — Microsoft Site Server 3.0 and the Digital Dashboard Resource Kit (DDRK) — warrant special notice as ancestors of SharePoint, as shown in the family tree in Figure A-1.

Microsoft Site Server 3.0 was a massive product with many parts that were not directly related to one another beyond being installed and accessed through a common user interface. Several of these components, however, form conceptual (if not direct code) predecessors to components of Microsoft

Office SharePoint Server 2007. Site Server included content management and deployment functionality, allowing the staging and incremental updating of websites. Also, Site Server contained a Knowledge Management framework, which let administrators define property sets that could be applied to items of content. Finally, Site Server introduced Microsoft's first Enterprise-class search engine (Site Server Search).

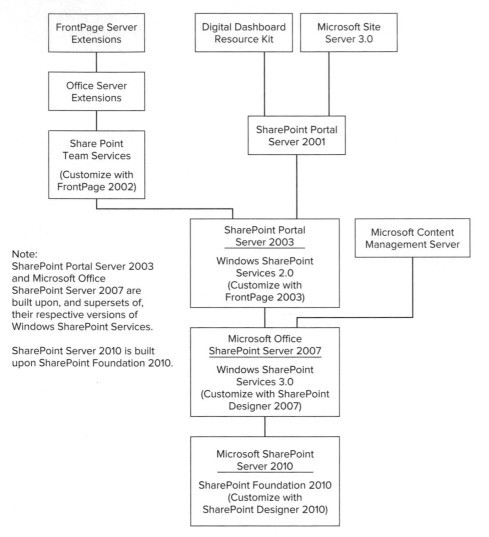

FIGURE A-1

The Digital Dashboard Resource Kit (DDRK) was a set of tools to present pieces of content on a special web page called a dashboard. The pieces were called Web Parts and could be sourced a number of ways, from static content to JavaScript to ASP code. The dashboards and Web Parts were stored server-side — either in the file system, a SQL Server database, or an Exchange message store — accessed via standard HTTP and managed through the WebDAV protocol.

Fraternal Twins — It's All in the Name

The first products actually to bear the name *SharePoint* were released at about the same time as Microsoft Office XP (whose individual components were known as the 2002 Office Products). Two distinct products were named SharePoint: SharePoint Portal Server 2001 (SPS) and SharePoint Team Services (STS). Although some functional overlap existed, they were architecturally very different.

SharePoint Team Services (1.0)

SharePoint Team Services was an enhancement to the Office Server Extensions and was shipped with Microsoft Office XP Professional. Unlike the OSE and the FrontPage Extensions, however, SharePoint Team Services (STS) functioned as a full web-based application in its own right. STS included predesigned web pages, and introduced several key concepts — particularly lists, document libraries, and views. Although still conceptually present in current versions of SharePoint, these objects are very dissimilar in implementation from the way they were in STS. For example, STS used the web server's file system to store all pages and the physical documents for libraries, but kept configuration info, lists, and document metadata in a database. Although some elements are mentioned briefly in this appendix, Appendix B covers the present architecture of SharePoint in detail.

One of the key ways of manipulating these objects in code is called the *Collaborative Application Markup Language (CAML)*. CAML was introduced in STS, has evolved considerably (like the objects it is designed to manipulate), and is still a key part of programming for SharePoint. For example, the query used by the modern Data View (a concept that did not exist in STS) of a SharePoint list or library is generated in CAML, not SQL.

Figure A-2 shows a typical SharePoint Team Services site. FrontPage 2002 was "aware" of all SharePoint Team Services features and could be used to customize and configure STS pages, lists, and libraries.

SharePoint Portal Server 2001

SharePoint Portal Server 2001 made use of the Digital Dashboard technology from the DDRK, and backed it up with many powerful server-side capabilities. Unlike the multiple back-end options provided for the DDRK, SPS exclusively used an updated version of the Exchange message store, which was renamed the *Web Storage System*. The Web Storage System held dashboard pages and Web Parts, as it did with the DDRK, but in SPS it also stored documents and other content.

SPS also included document library functionality, although it was very different from that provided in STS. SPS document libraries offered workflow and granular control over permissions. SPS also included an updated version of the enterprise search engine from Site Server, allowing SPS to crawl and index information from a wide variety of corporate data sources. Figure A-3 shows a typical SharePoint Portal dashboard.

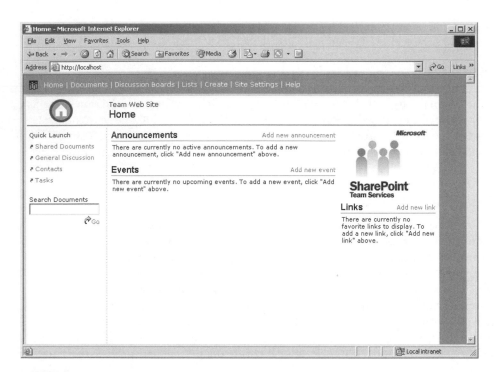

FIGURE A-2

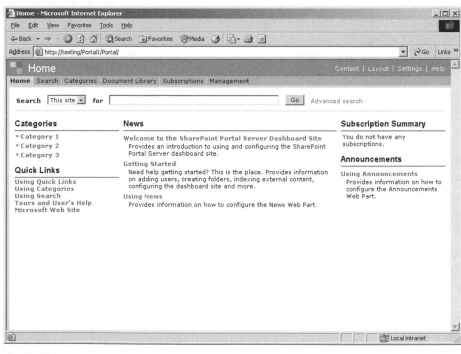

FIGURE A-3

Let's Get Together — Casting the (dot) Net

By the year 2003, SharePoint Team Services and SharePoint Portal Server had each secured a following, but a great deal of confusion existed because of the combination of similar names and superficially similar functionality with vast differences in architecture, programming models, and user interface between the two products. There had also been many changes to web programming. Microsoft had introduced the .NET Framework and with it ASP.NET. Web services and the SOAP protocol were starting to make inroads, and XML was becoming the *lingua franca* of data interchange.

Windows SharePoint Services — A Platform Is Born

For the next wave of SharePoint products, Microsoft attempted to resolve some of the confusion by moving both SharePoint Team Services and SharePoint Portal Server onto the .NET platform. This required a significant amount of rework to both the STS and SPS platforms, as well as going beyond the standard ASP.NET 1.1 ways of doing things. When the dust had settled, a new SharePoint foundation had been created.

This new child contained elements of both parents, as well as several characteristics of its own. In the process, SharePoint Team Services had earned a new name, *Windows SharePoint Services* (*WSS*), and a new place in the family tree. WSS would now be considered part of Windows Server, rather than Microsoft Office. As acknowledgment of its STS predecessor, WSS was deemed a 2.0 (version 2) product.

From SharePoint Portal Server 2001, Windows SharePoint Services inherited the concept (but not the implementation) of Web Parts as easily configurable modules to display content of various types on pages (now called *Web Part Pages* rather than dashboards). From SharePoint Team Services, WSS gained easily customizable lists, libraries, and views. Most of these elements, as well as library documents and other site-specific files, were now served from a re-architected content database.

Web Part Pages were a special case. Templates for Web Part Pages, and site definitions for the core website types, were housed on the file system. When one of these elements was instantiated, a placeholder, or ghosted item, was placed in the content database. The ghosted item contained a pointer to the original file and the instance information needed to make the item unique. These pages could be customized, however, by an editing tool such as FrontPage 2003, and in the process, a full instance of the customized file was stored in the database. That was called *unghosting* the file, and it could result in performance degradation, as well as complications when broader-scale changes needed to be made to all pages in a site.

Finally, the new platform introduced the capability to spread its functions across multiple servers and to serve the same content from multiple web front ends. This farm system was critical to improving SharePoint's scalability and resilience.

Opening a New Portal

SharePoint Portal Server 2003 was built upon the WSS foundation, and therefore contained all the WSS functionality. However, many features that were carried forward from SPS 2001 but not included in WSS were implemented through custom code in SPS 2003. In particular, portal sites and areas used a different page model and site hierarchy than standard WSS sites. Also, because the WSS document storage framework did not implement certain features that were present in SPS 2001 document libraries (such as item-level permissions and workflows), an option was provided to use a special backward-compatible document library, which continued using the Web Storage System instead of the new content database structure. Figure A-4 shows a typical page from a WSS or SPS 2003 site.

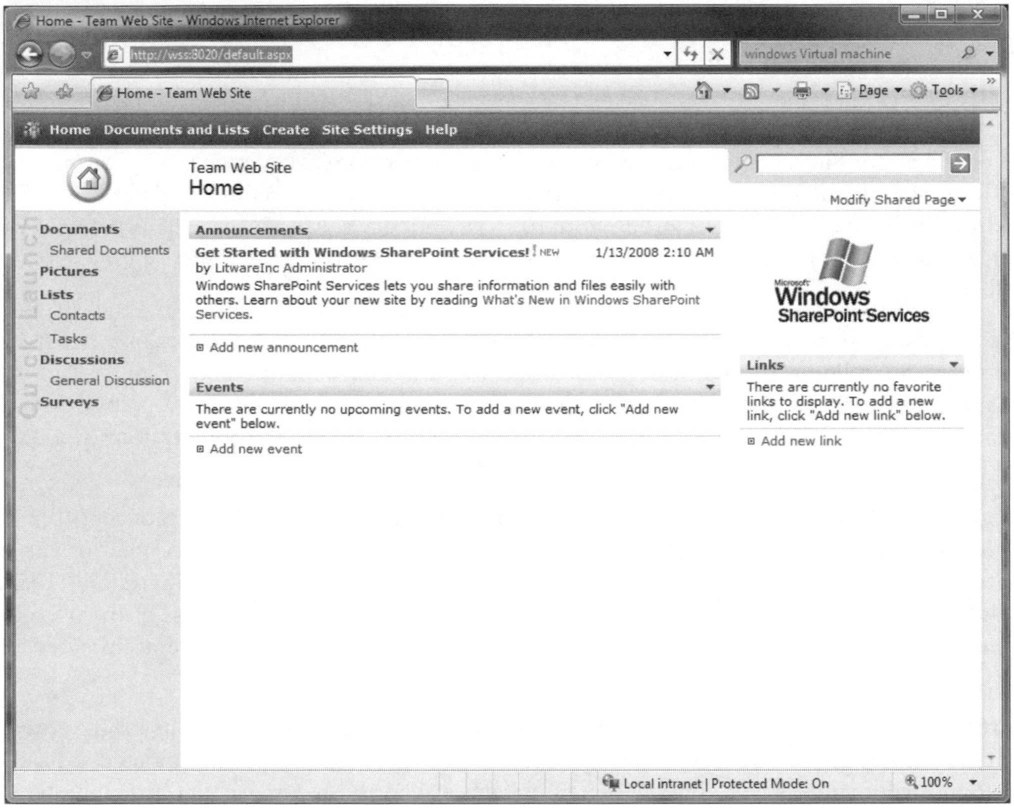

FIGURE A-4

GATHERING MOSS — WINDOWS SHAREPOINT SERVICES 3.0 AND MICROSOFT OFFICE SHAREPOINT SERVER 2007

For the 2007 Microsoft Office System, Windows SharePoint Services was again significantly enhanced over its predecessor. WSS 3.0 was built on the ASP.NET 2.0 framework, which itself was enhanced with several concepts taken from SharePoint — specifically, ASP.NET 2.0 includes support for a Web Part framework. WSS 3.0 also made use of the Windows Workflow Foundation and ASP.NET 2.0 authentication models. In addition, many weaknesses of WSS 2.0 are addressed in WSS 3.0, including the following:

➤ Item-level security was now allowed in lists and libraries.

➤ Security trimming was implemented to hide items and functions a user does not have permission to use.

➤ An extensibility framework was created to make it easier to create and deploy new functionality on the Windows SharePoint Services platform.

➤ New site types, including basic blogs and wikis, were added.

SharePoint Portal Server 2003 was replaced with Microsoft Office SharePoint Server 2007 (MOSS). As the name implies, MOSS was far more than a portal product. Enterprise Content and Records Management, enhanced social networking through My Sites, and the latest version of Microsoft's Enterprise Search technology were just the starting point.

A new level of MOSS functionality became available through the Enterprise Features. Although these Features were installed on all MOSS servers, they needed to be enabled with a special code, and could only be "legally" accessed by users who have an Enterprise Client Access License (CAL). Enterprise CALs are an extra-cost option. They permit access to server-side Excel Services, an InfoPath Forms engine, business reporting functions such as KPIs, and easy integration with third-party systems through the Business Data Catalog (BDC). Figure A-5 shows a default MOSS home page.

FIGURE A-5

CONTINUING EVOLUTION — SHAREPOINT FOUNDATION 2010 AND SHAREPOINT SERVER 2010

For the 2010 edition of SharePoint Products and Technologies, Microsoft has taken a more evolutionary approach. It again changed the product names, with SharePoint Foundation 2010 replacing WSS while once again becoming independent of Windows, and MOSS evolving simply into SharePoint Server 2010.

Much of the underlying structure is very similar to that of WSS 3.0 and MOSS (and is described in detail in Appendix B). Nevertheless, many new features have been added and a fairly significant change has been made to the underlying design elements of SharePoint master pages themselves. Although these elements are quite different under the skin, Figure A-6 shows that the core functionality of SharePoint remains.

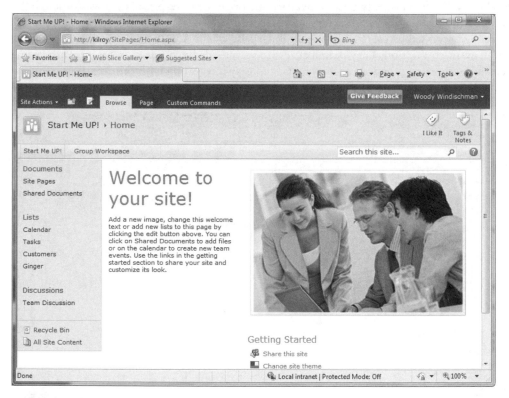

FIGURE A-6

Notice the distinct family resemblance in all the screenshots shown in this appendix. The number one request of people implementing SharePoint has historically been, "Can you make it look less like SharePoint?" As you have learned throughout this book, with your mastery of Microsoft SharePoint Designer 2010, the answer is a resounding "Yes!" However, you should also have learned how not to make these changes blindly, so as to retain all the goodness the SharePoint Foundation provides.

B

Just What Is SharePoint Anyway?

SharePoint Designer includes a broad array of features and functions that make it a powerful tool, not only to "make it look less like SharePoint," but also to leverage and build upon a number of SharePoint's features. What does that mean? What is SharePoint? Remember that you (or your clients) are implementing SharePoint for a reason. In your efforts to customize its look, you must be sure you retain its feel — its core capabilities.

Many SharePoint elements can be configured to some extent through the web interface. Although you will have a much greater capability to customize them in SharePoint Designer, understanding this built-in functionality gives you a better foundation for your construction. Some of the useful building blocks you will find in SharePoint include its

- ➤ Basic structure
- ➤ Lists and libraries
- ➤ Web parts
- ➤ Navigation
- ➤ Site management
- ➤ Server architecture

A DEFAULT SHAREPOINT HOME PAGE

On the surface, SharePoint is a fully functional web application. Out of the box, you get pages you can browse, places you can put information, and many ways to get that information back out again. Figure B-1 shows a basic SharePoint site.

Scratch that surface, and you find a whole lot more, including the capability to define new forms of information, to pick and choose what gets displayed on a page, and to create new pages. You can do it all without programming or even leaving the friendly confines of your web browser.

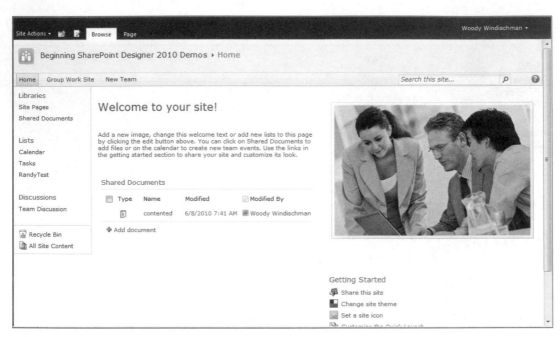

FIGURE B-1

The first instinct of many web designers new to SharePoint is to create a site the way they always have, and then try to graft on bits and pieces of SharePoint functionality. Although that approach *can* create sites that are functional, it often presents challenges for maintainability, future expansion, and consistency.

SharePoint provides a number of functions for you (refer to Figure B-1):

➤ Global navigation

➤ Site-level navigation

➤ Breadcrumbs

➤ Personalization and social functions

➤ Site and page titles

➤ Logos and other branding

➤ Administrative functions

➤ Search

➤ Site content

These are all features needed by virtually every website in one form or another. The default cosmetic aspects of these features may not be to your liking, but that doesn't mean you have to scrap them. This book shows you how to change those cosmetics without discarding and rebuilding the features themselves.

SHAREPOINT CONTENT: LISTS, LIBRARIES, AND MORE

At its basic level, virtually everything that is displayed in a SharePoint site comes out of a list. A list is much like a database table, in that it is made up of rows of data, which in turn are composed of fields of different types. Many types of lists are predefined in SharePoint, but they fall into two main categories. One is simply called the *list*. The rows of a list are called items. The other category is the *library*. The fundamental difference is that a library's principal row element is a file, or document.

Almost any list can have a file as an attachment, but in those cases, the individual fields of the list are primary, and the attachment is just another piece of data in the list. In the case of the library, however, the file is considered the core element, and the fields are considered properties or metadata for that document.

> **NOTE** *Although thinking of lists and libraries as tables is convenient for management and display purposes, their architectures are very different, as described in more detail in Chapter 6.*

Depending on the template or site definition used to create a SharePoint site, certain lists are automatically created. The home page displayed in Figure B-1 shows several lists and libraries in the left navigation bar (also called the Quick Launch bar). You can access these lists through Quick Launch, or place views of these lists (or any others that might be defined on the site) in the content zones of a page.

You are not stuck with the lists and libraries created by default in a site. You can create new lists and libraries and delete existing ones at any time. When creating a new list or library, you can choose from several standard and custom types, and elect whether to display a link to it on the Quick Launch. In addition, you can display information from diverse sources both inside and outside of your enterprise with external lists based on the SharePoint Business Connectivity Services (see Chapter 7 for more about these).

List and Library Types

SharePoint provides a number of standard list types. Anyone with sufficient rights can add new lists to a site at any time. The particular list types available depend on a number of factors, including the edition of SharePoint installed, the features activated, and the template used for the site. Figure B-2 shows some typical list types available in SharePoint 2010.

The page in Figure B-2 was accessed from Site Actions ➪ More Options. In addition to providing existing list and library templates, the Create page may allow you to make custom lists, site pages, or even child sites, depending upon the site template.

Although they share many common elements, each list and library type has some unique characteristics — such as predefined fields, views, and custom actions that can be performed automatically on its items. For example, one of the most commonly used library types is the document library, which is primarily designed to contain documents such as those produced by word-processing, spreadsheet, and presentation applications, or final-form files such as Adobe PDF. It includes features suitable for that task, such as versioning, check-in, and check-out. The Shared Documents library in the default site shown earlier is a document library. Other list and library types may be available in your particular installation of SharePoint.

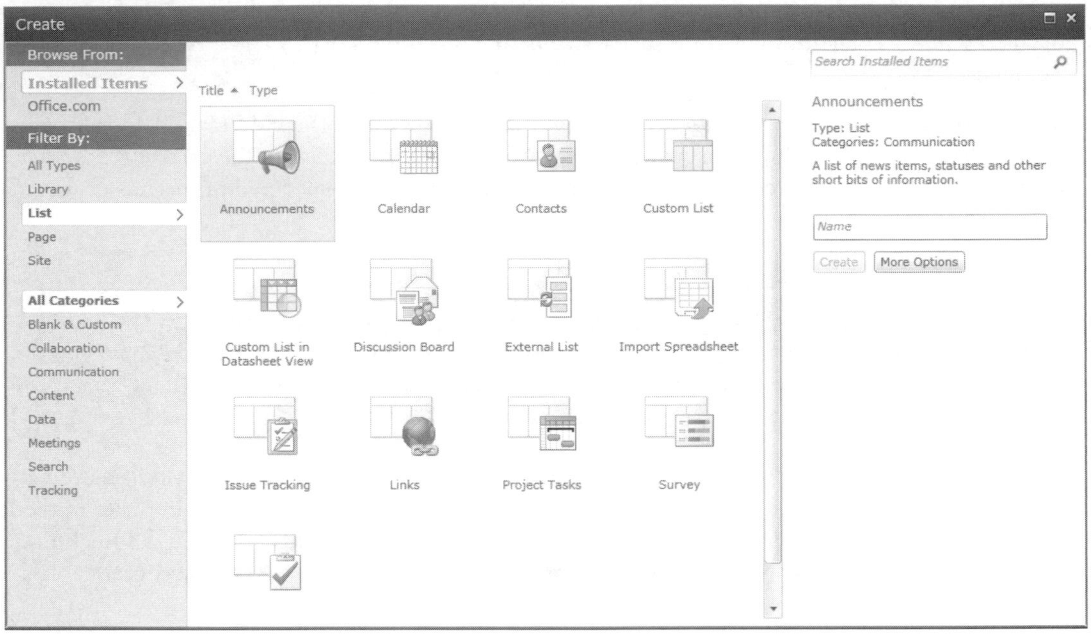

FIGURE B-2

Customizing Lists and Libraries

After a list or library has been created, it contains a number of characteristics that you can customize. You may alter some of the ones you need on a "day-to-day" basis via the ribbon. Figure B-3 shows the Library ribbon tab. In addition to the settings, the Library (or List, as appropriate) tab gives you quick access to many connection and sharing options.

FIGURE B-3

Other settings don't need to be changed as often and are available through the List or Library Settings icon on the ribbon. Clicking this icon summons a page upon which these settings are arrayed, as shown for a document library in Figure B-4. Other lists and libraries may have other options available.

General Settings	Permissions and Management	Communications
Title, description and navigation	Delete this document library	RSS settings
Versioning settings	Save document library as template	
Advanced settings	Permissions for this document library	
Validation settings	Manage files which have no checked in version	
	Workflow Settings	

Columns

A column stores information about each document in the document library. The following columns are currently available in this document library:

Column (click to edit)	Type	Required
Title	Single line of text	
Created By	Person or Group	
Modified By	Person or Group	
Checked Out To	Person or Group	

Create column
Add from existing site columns
Column ordering
Indexed columns

Views

A view of a document library allows you to see a particular selection of items or to see the items sorted in a particular order. Views currently configured for this document library:

View (click to edit)	Default View	Mobile View	Default Mobile View
All Documents	✔	✔	✔

FIGURE B-4

Although you can do a lot of customization through the web interface, certain settings, including hiding particular lists or libraries, can be set only through SharePoint Designer. They are discussed throughout the main part of the book. Some settings can only be changed in the web interface, and some settings can be changed in either place, though not all options may be equally available.

Columns (Fields)

Each list or library contains certain default columns. You are not limited to using them as is. Just as you can add and remove lists or libraries from a site, you can also easily add and remove most columns.

> **NOTE** *You cannot remove key identity columns, such as ID and Title (Name in some lists), and administrative columns, such as Modified By, from a list or library.*

You can add or remove columns via the web interface, as well as through SharePoint Designer. Figure B-5 shows some of the column types available out of the box. The available types may vary based upon the list or library template. You also can create and deploy custom column types via SharePoint features.

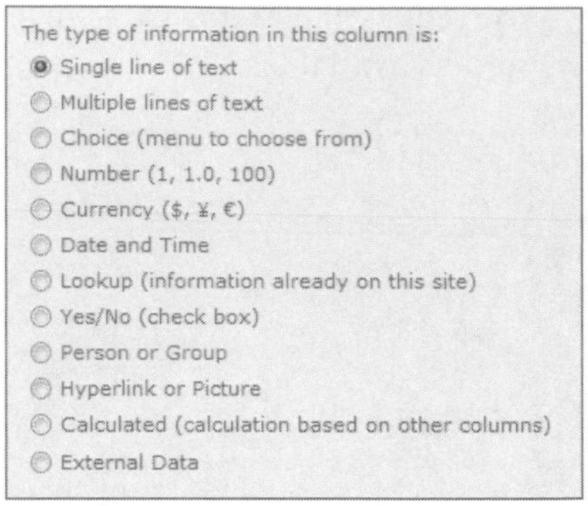

Content Types

In a database, each table is defined with a particular schema, or set of columns. If you want to store a different kind of information, you use a different table. In SharePoint, you can store information with more than one schema in a single list or library, through a mechanism called *content types*.

The type of information in this column is:
- ◉ Single line of text
- ○ Multiple lines of text
- ○ Choice (menu to choose from)
- ○ Number (1, 1.0, 100)
- ○ Currency ($, ¥, €)
- ○ Date and Time
- ○ Lookup (information already on this site)
- ○ Yes/No (check box)
- ○ Person or Group
- ○ Hyperlink or Picture
- ○ Calculated (calculation based on other columns)
- ○ External Data

FIGURE B-5

SharePoint content types enable you to define a schema for a particular type of object, such as a news article or a contact, and use it wherever it makes sense in your site. Consider an inventory application for a hardware store. You can create a single list for your stock that includes a content type for paint, which includes columns for latex and oil base, color, and interior or exterior application, whereas a content type for lumber might include the type of wood, dimensions, and so on.

Each content type can have its own entry forms and workflow associated with it. When you create or edit items with different content types, the appropriate form — with the fields defined for that type — is shown. You can also create custom forms for individual content types.

Understanding Views

Information from lists and libraries is typically presented in a *view*. A view consists of selected information from a list or library, presented in a particular way. You can choose a subset of columns, filter and group data, or even change the format of the information. Figures B-6 and B-7 show two very different views of the same data. You can apply several predefined view styles to various lists. You can present almost any list with a date column, for example, as a calendar.

One of the powerful features of SharePoint is the capability to personalize the user experience. To that end, a user can create views to be either public or private. A sales manager, for example, might want to see information grouped by region and ordered by total sales, whereas an individual sales rep would need a view showing the details of her closings for the month and would not be allowed to see the details for the other representatives.

WEB PARTS

Web parts are one of the primary means by which content is displayed in SharePoint. Publishing pages use a slightly different model, called layout pages. A web part may display static content, a view of a list or library, the interface for a business application, or virtually anything else.

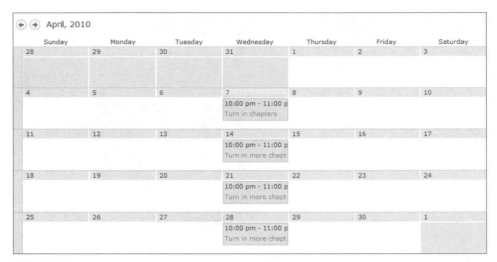

FIGURE B-6

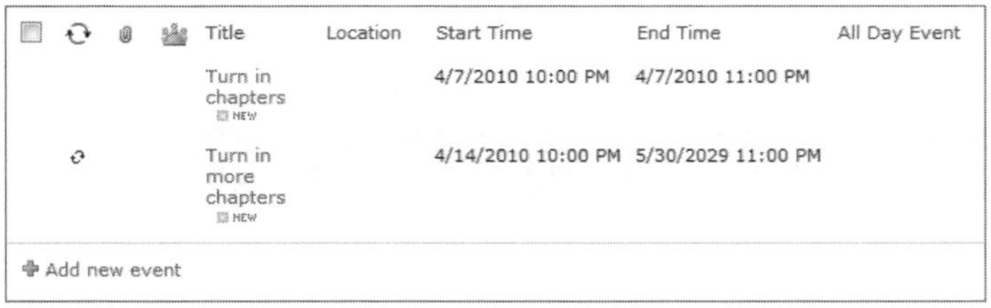

FIGURE B-7

In the Zone

A typical page in SharePoint consists of *content zones* into which a user may enter text, images, or place any of the web parts available on the site. Several page templates are provided with SharePoint, with varying sizes and positions of zones.

Figure B-8 shows a page in edit mode.

Like list views, most SharePoint pages can have a public and a personal view. You edit the public view by selecting Site Actions ⇨ Edit Page. You edit the personal view by selecting Welcome ⇨ Personalize this Page.

Adding a web part to a content zone is as simple as clicking the Editing Tools Insert tab, then clicking the Web Part icon. You may then select from the many parts that may be available on your site, as shown in Figure B-9.

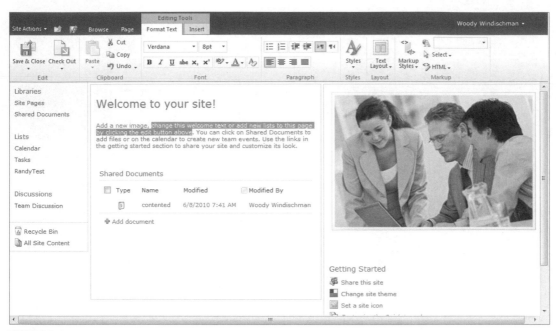

FIGURE B-8

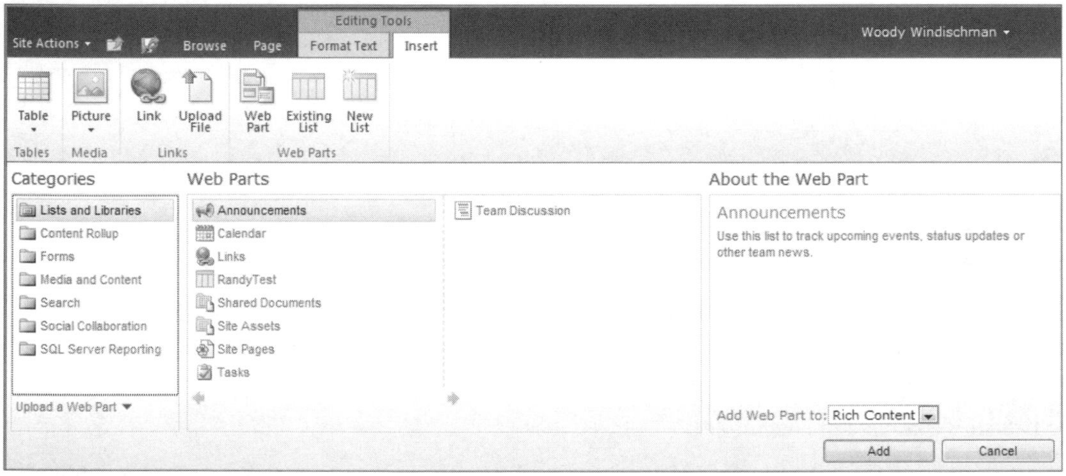

FIGURE B-9

NOTE *You can have multiple instances of the same web part on a page.*

After you add a web part to a zone, you can change its properties by selecting the web part contextual tab. Figure B-10 shows many of the contextual tabs available when editing a web part within a content zone.

FIGURE B-10

Depending upon the web part, some properties can be set only through the web interface, and others may only be available, or offer significantly easier control, when using SharePoint Designer.

> **NOTE** *Web parts are one of the principal expansion points in SharePoint. Many third-party web parts are available, and you can create your completely custom web parts in Visual Studio.*

Making the Connection

Web parts are more than just static display containers. Many web parts support an interpart communications mechanism called *web part connections*. Web part connections allow you to use the contents of one web part to affect the data displayed in another.

For example, selecting a client's name from a drop-down menu can filter lists of orders, contacts, and service calls. As long as all the parts support connections, it does not matter what the source of the data is — SharePoint, XML, or your corporate Customer Relationship Management (CRM) system. This allows heterogeneous applications to be developed with little or no code. Some people refer to this kind of application development as a *mashup*.

When combined with the Data View Web Part and SharePoint Designer, web part connections provide an easy yet powerful way to provide rich functionality to your users. Chapter 10 describes web part connections in detail.

MANAGING A SHAREPOINT SITE

In addition to editing pages and web parts, the designated owner can manage many elements of a site without the assistance of a server administrator or web designer. Figure B-11 shows the main settings page of a SharePoint site. You access the page with these functions through Site Actions ⇨ Site Settings.

This book is not about SharePoint administration, so you don't need to worry about all the items on the list. Clearly, though, the user can manage many aspects of his site, from permissions to creating reports to determining the hierarchy of the sites in the collection. This section looks at how some of these administrative elements can (and should) play a crucial role in how you approach the design and customization of a SharePoint site. In particular, you'll see how you can simplify ongoing site maintenance by leveraging SharePoint's user management, navigation, and resource galleries.

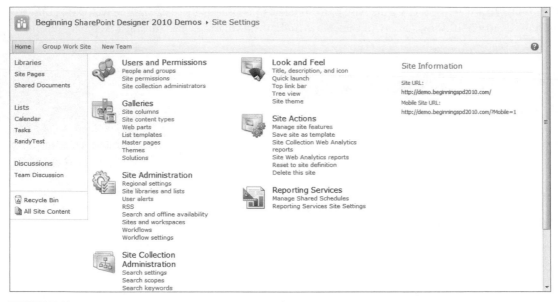

FIGURE B-11

Users and Permissions

One of the most important functions that you can delegate to site owners is the management of permissions for their sites. Most functions in SharePoint feature *security trimming*. This means that user interface elements are hidden for users who do not have permission to access the underlying data or function. For example, a site owner can typically see everything on the site, including administration and control functions. An average user, on the other hand, might see a subset of the content, and no administration features. Figure B-12 shows the site owner's view, while Figure B-13 shows the same site as viewed by a visitor. Note that in Figure B-13, the user has no access to the PermitRevenueYTD workbook or the Executive Summit site.

By making use of the standard SharePoint controls in your designs, you inherit this trimming, which makes site maintenance much easier in the long run, because you will not have to create separate pages for each user or role. Chapter 4 shows you how to incorporate security trimming controls into your site designs.

Managing Users

SharePoint can use any of the authentication methods supported by ASP.NET, including Windows-integrated, forms, LDAP, and even claims-based authentication.

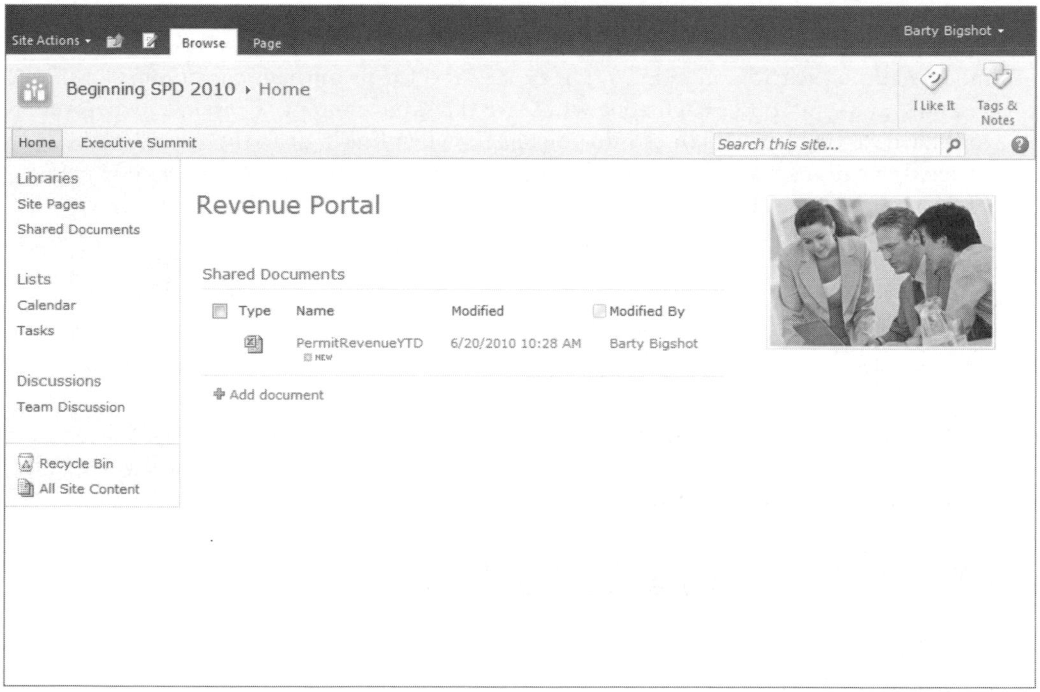

FIGURE B-12

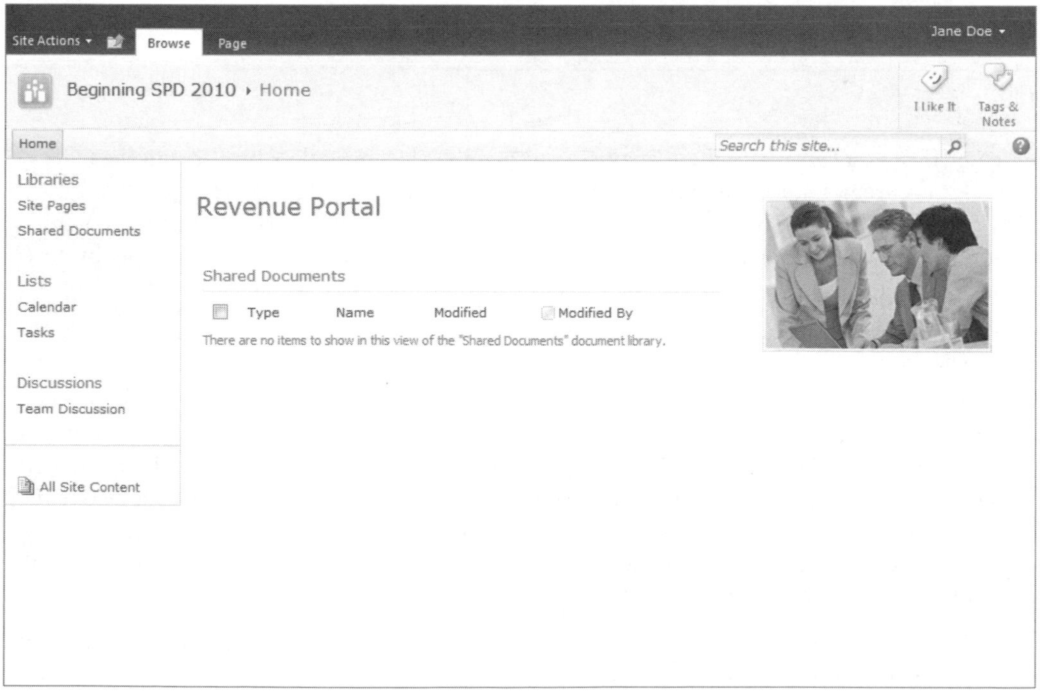

FIGURE B-13

Although configuration of authentication mechanisms is beyond the scope of this book, be aware that each membership provider requires its own web application zone to be configured (that is, Windows authentication on `http://intranet`, and forms authentication on `http://intranet.pro-spd.com`). Each zone will serve the same content. Therefore, wherever possible, avoid hard-coding server names into your pages when linking to other pages in the same namespace. Instead, use *root relative* references (that is, use "`/sites/finance/default.aspx`" rather than "`http://intranet/sites/finance/default.aspx`") in your links.

> **NOTE** *When using claims-based authentication, you can serve multiple zones without "extending" the web application.*

Regardless of the authentication method, you assign permissions to users the same way. When assigning permissions to a resource, whether it is a list item or an entire site, you typically manually enter users' IDs into a web dialog, as shown in Figure B-14.

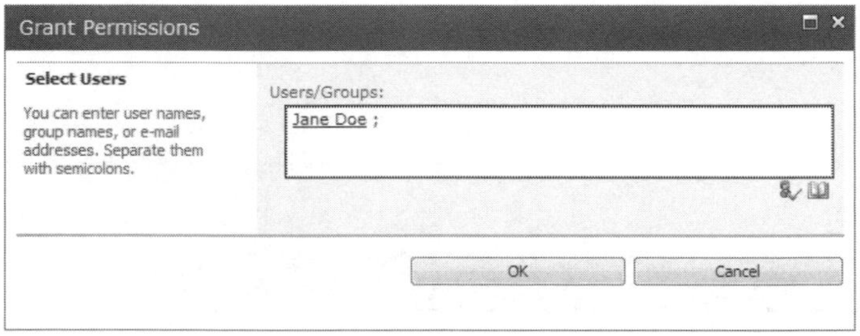

Grant Permissions

Select Users

You can enter user names, group names, or e-mail addresses. Separate them with semicolons.

Users/Groups:

Jane Doe ;

OK   Cancel

FIGURE B-14

After you enter IDs, you can verify them against your membership providers by clicking the Check Names icon. If you are not sure of a user's ID, SharePoint provides a standard user browser, accessed by the Browse icon. Clicking that icon summons the People and Groups selector, which enables you to select users from whatever authentication providers may be installed, simply by entering a portion of the user's name. Figure B-15 shows the People and Groups selector window.

Managing Groups

The most convenient way to manage permissions on a SharePoint site is by assigning users to groups. These may be groups created in your role provider. You can also use the dialogs described in the previous section to assign users or role provider groups to SharePoint groups, which are created within a SharePoint site and used to grant access to particular resources. For example, someone in a Site Members group might have permissions to modify the content of lists and libraries, but not to make any changes to their structure. The Site Visitors group might have read-only access to most of the site, but added permission to post to discussion boards.

Groups are each assigned *permission levels* — a set of default permissions constructed from a broad spectrum of rights that apply across the entire site, except where explicitly overridden.

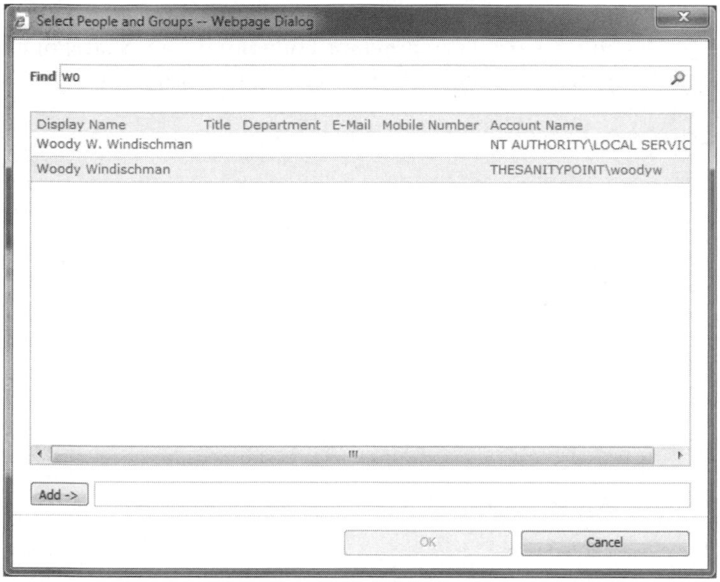

FIGURE B-15

> **NOTE** *SharePoint groups are distinct from any groups that may be defined in your ASP.NET membership or role providers (for example, Windows domain groups), but may contain such groups as members.*

When you create a SharePoint site, you also have the option to create certain groups and permission levels by default. The exact items created will depend upon the version of SharePoint and the type of site being provisioned. You can then add to, remove from, or edit the items in these lists. Figure B-16 shows a selection of groups created by SharePoint Server 2010 for a typical publishing site.

The default description shows the permission level associated with the group. You can see the groups available on your own site by starting from the Site Settings page, clicking the People and Groups link, and then clicking the Groups section header in the Quick Launch bar.

> **NOTE** *The permission levels Full Control and Limited Access are defined by SharePoint and you cannot edit them.*

Look and Feel — Navigational Elements and More

Almost all sites require navigation, and SharePoint provides two primary navigation hierarchies: a global navigation bar, represented by default as a tab strip below the site title, and local navigation, represented by the groups of related elements in the Quick Launch bar, on the left of the page.

SharePoint provides a built-in capability for site owners to modify the items and their order. Figure B-17 shows the editor for the Quick Launch bar on a SharePoint Foundation site. SharePoint Server publishing sites have a more extensive editing capability. In particular, publishing sites support the easy editing of two-level navigation.

Group	Edit	About me
Approvers		Members of this group can edit and approve pages, list items, and documents.
Designers		Members of this group can edit lists, document libraries, and pages in the site. Designers can create Master Pages and Page Layouts in the Master Page Gallery and can change the behavior and appearance of each site in the site collection by using master pages and CSS files.
Hierarchy Managers		Members of this group can create sites, lists, list items, and documents.
NT AUTHORITY\authenticated users		
Quick Deploy Users		Members of this group can schedule Quick Deploy jobs.
Restricted Readers		Members of this group can view pages and documents, but cannot view historical versions or review user rights information.
Start Me Up! Members		Use this group to grant people contribute permissions to the SharePoint site: Start Me Up!
Start Me Up! Owners		Use this group to grant people full control permissions to the SharePoint site: Start Me Up!
Start Me Up! Visitors		Use this group to grant people read permissions to the SharePoint site: Start Me Up!
Style Resource Readers		Members of this group are given read permission to the master page gallery and the Restricted read permission to the Style Library. By default, all authenticated users are a member of this group. To further secure this site, you can remove all authenticated users from this group or add users to this group.
Viewers		Members of this group can view pages, list items, and documents. If the document has a server rendering available, they can only view the document using the server rendering.

FIGURE B-16

By retaining and styling the elements provided by SharePoint to match your vision, you can save yourself a lot of work when your customer comes back to you in six months saying, "I need to change 'Widget Construction' to 'Gizmo Assembly.'" In the case of navigation, this can simply be changed by the user in the navigation screens just described. On publishing sites, you can also create reusable content, which, when edited, will propagate to all pages in which that content is used. Chapter 5 shows you how to customize the look of these standard menus.

New Navigation Link   New Heading   Change Order

- Libraries
  - Site Pages
  - Shared Documents
- Lists
  - Calendar
  - Tasks
- Discussions
  - Team Discussion

FIGURE B-17

There are a few other "branding" related elements your users can control from the Look and Feel section of the Site Settings page.

The Site icon is the picture that (by default) appears to the left of the site title in the page header. Changing the image used is as simple as entering the URL of the preferred image in the Title,

Description, and Icon form, accessed through the Title, Description, and Icon link. Of course, the text of the site title is edited on the same form.

The other key item to notice in this section is the Site Theme option. A SharePoint theme is a collection of images and Cascading Style Sheets (CSS) files that can be applied to a site at any time. Users can import theme definitions from Microsoft PowerPoint, and apply them to your site. Making your own styling elements compatible with this theming system is also possible.

You can easily make both subtle and drastic changes to virtually any element on a page. As long as those changes can be implemented via CSS, all of SharePoint's functions will operate correctly. CSS also offers powerful layout capability, which you can leverage in SharePoint Designer. Chapters 3 and 5 show you how to create and deploy custom CSS, themes, and master pages to brand a site thoroughly while letting your users manage them with all of SharePoint's power.

Using Galleries

SharePoint galleries are lists or libraries of elements that are used throughout a site. Some galleries apply to an entire site collection, whereas others apply only to the current site and its children.

As a web designer, the galleries list most relevant to you is the Master Pages gallery. This gallery is essentially a specialized document library designed to hold — surprise! — master pages. Site owners can upload any number of customized master pages, which can then be applied to the content of the site. Other galleries relevant to users of SharePoint Designer are those for content types, site and list templates, and web parts.

After you make changes to a list or a site, whether through the web interface or in SharePoint Designer, you can save your changes as a template, either with or without data (content). These templates automatically go into the site collection's list or site template gallery, as appropriate. Site templates and exported workflows are stored as SharePoint Solution (.WSP) files, which you can transport to other sites directly, or even import into Visual Studio 2010 for further development.

> **NOTE** *Site and list templates are keyed to site definitions and features. A site template can only be instantiated on a server that has the site definition upon which it is based installed. In addition, any additional features used by the template must be installed and activated. A list template can only be installed on a site that has the features the list depends upon activated.*

ARCHITECTURAL BACKGROUND ON THE SERVER

As you have seen, SharePoint presents a consistent, unified face to its users and site owners. That all changes when you get to the server; it is here that the long and varied history, described in Appendix A, surfaces in the many different methods used to perform individual tasks. Although most common administration can be performed through the Central Administration web interface, other tasks can best be performed by editing configuration files manually, or using the SharePoint command-line tool STSADM.EXE. Still other tasks require some combination of these methods.

Also, SharePoint now fully supports the PowerShell command line management console. A vast library of commandlets is provided out of the box, making virtually the entire SharePoint API available to administrative scripting.

Again, the purpose of this book is not to explain all the nuances of SharePoint administration; however, you need to know certain things to make appropriate customization choices. This section presents an overview of a SharePoint Server farm. Details of particular configuration tasks are provided as needed throughout the rest of the book.

Central Administration

SharePoint Central Administration is the primary control panel for a SharePoint Server farm. Figure B-18 shows the Central Administration home page. If you think it looks a lot like a SharePoint site, you're right!

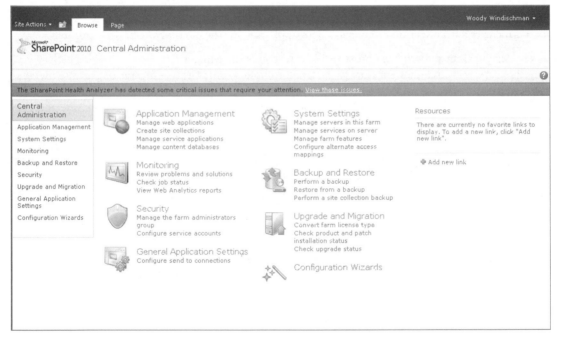

FIGURE B-18

The Central Administration site is a custom SharePoint *web application*, created automatically with a random TCP port on the first server configured in your farm. It is called a farm because SharePoint's functions can be spread across multiple servers for performance and resilience.

> **NOTE** *Even if SharePoint is configured on a single server, that one system is still referred to as a farm.*

Although the exact functions available in Central Administration depend on which edition of SharePoint you have installed, these functions will be logically arranged in groups similar to those in the screen shot.

Many elements of SharePoint, such as search and Office web applications are managed through service applications. Service applications are functions that can be shared across multiple web applications, or even multiple SharePoint farms.

The Application Management section of Central Administration contains many functions relevant to SharePoint site customization. In particular, it enables you to create and manage the web applications and site collections that make up your SharePoint site. A web application is the logical top-level container for SharePoint content. A SharePoint farm hosts one or more web applications. Each web application contains one or more site collections.

Site collections are the primary units of granularity in the overall scheme of SharePoint administration. A site collection has its own permission groups, template galleries, and navigation hierarchy. Site collections cannot be split across content databases. In addition, the site collection is the smallest unit that can be backed up or restored with full fidelity. Most important, from the standpoint of this book, a site collection is the scope that can be browsed easily in SharePoint Designer.

Each site collection contains one or more sites or webs. The site is the working unit of SharePoint, containing the pages, lists, and libraries used to present content to your users. The first site created in a site collection is called the *root*. This root web has certain unique properties. For example, the root web of a site collection is where the site and list template galleries are stored. The root web may contain zero or more child webs, which in turn may be nested to an arbitrary level. Figure B-19 illustrates the logical hierarchy of content in a SharePoint farm.

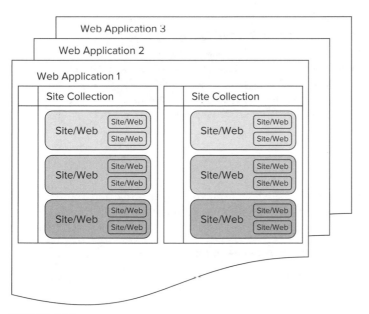

FIGURE B-19

The File Structure

The physical layout of files on a SharePoint server bears no resemblance at all to the logical content hierarchy described in the previous section. In fact, files critical to the operation of SharePoint are stored in up to four locations on the server, and that doesn't even count the databases! These four areas, in increasing order of relevance to the web designer, are:

➤ **The SharePoint installation directory** — This is selected at install time for some editions of SharePoint Server.

➤ **The Windows Global Assembly Cache (GAC)** — Typically this is C:\Windows\Assembly\.

➤ **The SharePoint website root** — By default this is C:\inetpub\wwwroot\wss\VirtualDirectories.

➤ **The SharePoint root** — Typically this is C:\Program Files\Common Files\Microsoft Shared\ web server extensions\14.

> **NOTE** *Ironically, the path containing the files you most likely need to manipulate is the longest path. Even more, the SharePoint root itself contains very complicated folder structure, most of which resides in the .\14\TEMPLATE subtree.*

Chapter 3 describes in detail the hybrid nature of serving SharePoint files, with each page being assembled at service time from a combination of information stored on the file system and in the content database. The TEMPLATE subtree contains the portions that are served from the file system.

> **WARNING** *Never open the files in the TEMPLATE subtree directly from the disk with SharePoint Designer. Many of these files contain tokens that only make sense to SharePoint Designer when opened in the context of a website, as preprocessed by the SharePoint server. When they are opened outside of this context, SharePoint Designer attempts to treat them as if they were on a website, and save them incorrectly, resulting in a corrupt template file.*

The SharePoint Databases

With all the files and locations mentioned in the previous section, you might think that your content has to be in there someplace. Well, it isn't. At its heart, SharePoint is a database application, and it doesn't stop with just your content.

SharePoint uses several types of databases. The primary types you need to recognize are:

➤ **Content databases** — These store all of your lists, documents, user details, and virtually everything else that exists inside your sites.

➤ **Configuration database** — This contains most of the information related to the configuration of the SharePoint environment, as well as detailed information about your sites.

These databases can be stored on virtually any available SQL server in your environment, as long as it is running at least SQL Server 2005 with the latest service pack. The many factors involved in the selection and configuration of a SQL Server environment are beyond the scope of this book.

Alternatively, SharePoint itself ships with a limited version of SQL Server — SQL Server Express — which is used in the case of a Basic or Trial install. If this option is selected, the SQL databases for this edition are stored in a branch of the SharePoint installation directory.

The Configuration Database

The main things to remember about the configuration database are as follow:

➤ Only one configuration database exists per SharePoint Server farm, and it defines the farm.

➤ The configuration database is created when the farm is first installed, and cannot be changed, although it can be moved to a different server in most cases, with some effort.

➤ The configuration database can be backed up, but not restored under normal circumstances.

The Content Databases

All the site-specific information that is presented to your users comes from the content databases. Although one content database per web application is created by default, you can add more at any time. At minimum, each content database in use contains the information for a complete site collection — including its root and any child webs that may be created. If multiple content databases are created for a web application, new site collections are allocated to content databases in an unpredictable order, until the configured maximum number of collections for a particular database is reached.

> **NOTE** *There is one exception to this unpredictability. If one content database has more "availability" (the difference between the existing, and maximum configured, number of site collections) than any other, and is not read-only, it will always be selected to host the next site collection you create.*

Earlier this appendix mentioned how SharePoint lists and libraries, to a large extent, behave like database tables. Back in SharePoint Team Services (described in Appendix A), the metadata for each list and library was actually stored as a distinct table in a database; WSS 2.0 and SPS 2003 changed that, and introduced the content database structure that is still used — in expanded form — by SharePoint today.

In current versions of SharePoint, all fields, from every list and library, in every site, are stored in a single table. This table is preconfigured with every possible column/field, which may be defined in a SharePoint list or library. In WSS 2.0/SPS 2003, this resulted in hard limits to the number of fields of any given type that could be created. In later versions, the schema has been updated to use multiple AllUserData rows for each list or library item if more fields of a particular type than were predefined are required.

Because of this unusual, highly denormalized schema, direct user access to the database is problematic. In fact, direct access to any SharePoint database (except the reporting database) is considered unsupported by Microsoft in most cases, and is highly discouraged in the one case that is supportable (nonexclusive read-only queries).

One result of this architecture is of keen interest to web designers. A performance issue with the rendering (but not the querying) of large result sets can occur. In earlier versions of SharePoint, some people called this "The 2000 Item Limit." SharePoint 2010 includes several mechanisms that both raise this "limit," and make it far less likely for your users to hit it. The key thing to remember is that any large dataset renders more slowly than a smaller one. Use caution when designing pages and web parts that may result in large numbers of items being returned.

INDEX

INDEX